NATIONAL
HEALTH INSURANCE

NATIONAL HEALTH INSURANCE

CONFLICTING GOALS AND POLICY CHOICES

Edited by
Judith Feder
John Holahan
Theodore Marmor

The Urban Institute

HD7102
U4
N27

TABLE OF CONTENTS

LIST OF TABLES

LIST OF FIGURES

FOREWORD

D espite bipartisan support for national health insurance throughout the 1970s, consensus on a legislative proposal has been elusive. This situation reflects the obvious pressures to limit federal expenditures, but also the less obvious change in the nature of national health insurance politics. The chief preoccupation today is the control of costs, not their distribution. And although concerns about access to care remain, plans for national health insurance are as much proposals for reorganizing medical care and controlling costs as for expanding insurance coverage. As a result, there is broad bipartisan expression of the idea that medical care expenditures in the aggregate might represent an insupportable burden for society and that the expansion of medical benefits must be balanced against other desirable programs.

Public and private health expenditures in the United States increased from 7.2 percent of the gross national product in 1970 to 9.1 percent in 1978, a jump from less than $70 billion to more than $190 billion. Some observers believe that enactment of a national health insurance plan is the only way to control medical cost inflation, while others believe an expansion of insurance coverage would just add fuel to the fire.

The validity of either position relates less to the issues on which the antagonists have publicly disagreed—the scope and timing of expanded insurance coverage—than to the government's capacity to negotiate less generous terms of provider payment than currently exist. Congress's failure to enact a hospital cost containment bill suggests its reluctance to address the cost control question directly. Unless policy makers are willing to deal with difficult and controversial questions of expenditure limits and resource allocation, national health insurance would indeed encourage medical cost inflation.

The purpose of this book is to raise and consider the questions policy makers must address if they wish to expand access to care while controlling costs. The policy options discussed and developed here are not limited to particular plans, but could be incorporated into most of those plans already proposed. For examples of approaches to particular issues the authors have drawn on various national health insurance proposals; but they do not specifically endorse any particular plan, in part because they believe that all plans would be changed in the process of actually being enacted into law. The authors assume that major institutional changes are unlikely. For example, in the discussion of physician reimbursement, the author emphasizes fee-for-service not because that system is preferred, but because large-scale displacement of it seems a remote possibility. The authors draw heavily on historical material in this country (how Medicare and Medicaid have exacerbated medical cost inflation since their enactment in 1965), on Canada's experience with national health insurance, and on other foreign experience with government programs.

The main problem is, of course, that the objectives of national health insurance programs are conflicting. As the authors note, each component of a national health insurance program—utilization controls, facility regulation, physician or hospital reimbursement—should contribute to the overall goals of (1) guaranteeing an adequate supply of medical services, particularly to the people whose access to services is now limited, (2) encouraging provision of high-quality services, and (3) restraining the rising costs of health services.

Pursuing these goals simultaneously involves uncomfortable trade-offs. For example, increasing access of the poor to quality care without raising costs may require reductions in access for people who are not poor. Measures to control hospital revenues or physicians' earnings may mean reductions in the quality of care provided. Obviously, policy makers confront hard choices, and any decisions they make are going to be unpopular in some quarters.

This book tries to identify what needs to be done to make a national health insurance plan successful. The analysis presented clarifies the choices that will affect all parties to the health insurance debate—physicians, hospitals, and other health care providers; public and private insurers; federal, state, and local governments; and the general public. Analysis is no substitute for what are, in the end, political decisions.

But this analysis should help participants in the political process understand the implications of particular choices and make decisions that will ultimately achieve the results they intend.

December 1979   William Gorham
                                                President
                                                The Urban Institute

ACKNOWLEDGMENTS

The development of this book involved a diverse set of authors, institutions, and financial supporters. The project was inspired by meetings of the Sun Valley Health Forum, especially the 1975 session on the lessons of Canadian national health insurance for the United States. That inspiration and support from the Robert Wood Johnson Foundation led, in 1976, to the beginning of a research effort to explore issues in the implementation of national health insurance. The project, interdisciplinary from the start, involved collaboration between a group of researchers, directed by Theodore Marmor, then at the University of Chicago's Center for Health Administration Studies, and members of The Urban Institute's Health Policy Research Program, directed by John Holahan. The National Center for Health Services Research and the Administration on Aging of the Department of Health, Education, and Welfare supported the participation of other researchers, who expanded the scope of the project. The first product of this project was an extensive report on implementation issues, produced after considerable review and comment, and submitted to the Johnson Foundation in 1978.

But reports do not make books. The editors of this book, led by John Holahan, turned that original report into this relatively cohesive volume. Judith Feder handled most of the substantive editing and coordination. The revision and preparation of the final product were made possible by the Ford Foundation's financial support to The Urban Institute, and by the commitment of Robert Harris, The Urban Institute's Executive Vice President. Without his encouragement—and periodic harassment—we might never have completed the work.

The authors owe special thanks to those who served as an advisory committee to the Johnson Foundation project— William Fullerton, Arthur Hess, Beverlee Myers, and Jonathan Spivak. The constructive advice of these experienced administrators and journalists helped guide us through the world of health insurance programs, private and public, federal, state, and local. Participants in the long-standing workshop of Chicago's Center for Health Studies made useful criticisms during the early stages of the research, and the center itself, with Odin Anderson's loyal aid, encouraged the development of a team of economists and political scientists.

Authors Conrad, Dunham, and Marmor especially want to acknowledge the assistance of two colleagues in the Chicago group, Amy Bridges and James Morone. Feder and Holahan owe special thanks to their Urban Institute colleagues William Scanlon and Judith Wagner, who helped throughout the project.

The authors also want to acknowledge the help of James Blumstein, Lawrence D. Brown, Peter Budetti, John Bunker, Alain Enthoven, Robert G. Evans, Richard Foster, Polly Keller, Rudolf Klein, Philip R. Lee, Deborah Lewis, Jack Needleman, David Salkever, Frank Sloan, William Sobaski, and Irwin Wolkstein.

We are especially grateful to our editor, Priscilla Taylor, for her skillful professional work. She forced us to make this book clearer and, in many places, more felicitous, a task to which the subject matter did not readily lend itself. And to Martina Pass and Elizabeth Straus of The Urban Institute, our gratitude for their conscientious preparation of the manuscript.

Judith Feder, John Holahan, and Theodore R. Marmor
Washington, D.C., December 1979

AUTHORS

Douglas Conrad
Assistant Professor
Departments of Community
   Dentistry and Health Services
University of Washington

Andrew B. Dunham
Instructor
Department of Political Science
Middlebury College

Judith Feder
Senior Research Associate
The Urban Institute

Jack Hadley
Senior Research Associate
The Urban Institute

John Holahan
Senior Research Associate
The Urban Institute

Robert T. Kudrle
Associate Professor
Hubert H. Humphrey Institute
   of Public Affairs
and
Associate Director
Harold Scott Quigley Center
   of International Studies
University of Minnesota

Karen D. Lennox
Market Research Analyst
Kaiser Foundation Health Plan
Northern California Region

Harold S. Luft
*Associate Professor of Health
   Economics*
Health Policy Program
University of California
San Francisco

Theodore R. Marmor
*Professor of Political Science &
   Public Health*
and
Chairman, Center for Health Studies
   Institution for Social &
   Policy Studies
Yale University

William Pollak
Associate Professor
School of Social Services
   Administration
University of Chicago

Dorothy L. Robyn
Ph.D. Candidate
Graduate School of Public Policy
University of California
Berkeley

Bruce Spitz
Senior Research Associate
The Urban Institute

Bruce Stuart
Associate Professor
Health Administration Program
Division of Public Health
University of Massachusetts

INTRODUCTION

THEODORE R. MARMOR
JUDITH FEDER
JOHN HOLAHAN

THE debate about compulsory national health insurance (NHI) has extended over fully one-third of America's life as a nation. Teddy Roosevelt first made national health insurance an issue in the Bull Moose campaign in 1912. Since then and with varying degrees of intensity, the issue has held a place on the national political agenda. In the 1960s, national health insurance returned squarely to center stage; enactment of Medicare and Medicaid represented the culmination of a decade-long struggle to provide health care to the aged. But Medicaid and Medicare did not resolve the essential political issue. The basic question of universal, government health insurance remained despite national programs for the poor and the old.

Over the years, "national health insurance" has come to mean different things to different people. Conceptions of what national health insurance ought to be affect both the likelihood of a program's enactment and the impact a program would have on the health care system. The purpose of this book is to examine the components the authors believe critical to an effective national health insurance program—one that would improve access to care while restraining total as well as individuals' medical expenses. This introduction first characterizes

---

[1] Daniel S. Hirschfield provides an excellent narrative account of the struggle for a compulsory health insurance program in the United States in his book, *The Lost Reform* (Cambridge, Mass.: Harvard University Press, 1970). Although Hirschfield focuses on the period from 1932 to 1943, he provides a useful account of the work undertaken on behalf of compulsory health insurance in the early decades of the twentieth century. On the relationship of Medicare and Medicaid to this earlier history, see Theodore R. Marmor with Jan S. Marmor, *The Politics of Medicare* (Chicago: Aldine Publishing Co., 1973).

the prevailing views of national health insurance as represented by the variety of legislative proposals that have been
introduced. Different types of proposals serve different political purposes at different times. After tracing the political
roots of various proposals, this chapter characterizes their use
in the current national health insurance debate. This debate,
which focuses on the "affordability" of national health insurance, provides the opportunity—indeed, the necessity—for the
policy analysis this book presents.

Competing National Health Insurance Proposals

A typology of national health insurance proposals can be
developed on several different criteria. One is administrative:
In what people and institutions is administrative control
vested? A second focuses on the definition and scope of benefits provided: Who is eligible to receive what medical services?
A third is fiscal: Who pays and how—through premiums, payroll taxes, user charges?

The differing political perspectives on national health insurance are best understood when proposals are characterized by
their source of financing and scope of benefits. No descriptive
category can be exclusive, and it will be necessary to refer to
administrative and other considerations when discussing both
financing and benefit criteria.

The use of financing and benefit provisions as base criteria
gives us a spectrum of proposals broken into three distinctive
bands:

1. Narrow coverage, minimal federal financial role;
2. Wide coverage, limited federal financial role; and
3. Wide coverage, large federal financial role.

An accurate description of financing provisions is not so easy
as it might appear to be. Three distinct cost figures are involved. The first is the total cost of any national health insurance program; this figure is the sum of the costs to individuals,
employers, subfederal units of government, and the federal
government. The second notion of cost includes costs incurred
by *government* at all levels, and the third is the *federal* cost
alone. (In public discussion, cost figures are sometimes used
in misleading ways as, for example, when the federal cost is

used to mean total program cost. Total program cost figures would, if complete, incorporate private contributions and private payments.)

NARROW COVERAGE, MINIMAL FEDERAL FINANCIAL ROLE

Proposals in this class address an explicitly defined problem or population segment. Catastrophic medical expense is the problem most frequently addressed, and since about 1974, the Long-Ribicoff-Waggonner bill has been the most prominent legislative example. This bill proposes to pay for hospital, physician, and other medical services for all U.S. residents who have incurred what the law defines as "catastrophic expenses." The prerequisite for hospital benefits under this plan is sixty days in the hospital; the prerequisite for physician benefits is family medical bills of $2,000. With the exception of employees whose employers choose approved private insurance plans, benefits for expenses beyond these amounts would be federally financed (through a payroll tax) and administered by the federal government.

The Long-Ribicoff-Waggonner plan is not the only approach to catastrophic protection. Other proposals define catastrophic expenses as a percentage of income rather than a fixed amount. The "major risk" proposal of Professor Martin Feldstein,[2] for example, would pay all medical bills that exceeded 10 percent of annual income. Quite similar, but to be administered by the Internal Revenue Service as a tax credit for large medical bills, is the Brock bill (proposed in 1976).

President Carter's National Health Plan also begins with catastrophic coverage. The plan's first phase proposes to cover hospital and physician expenses after individuals incur $2,500 in medical expenses.

Proposals that emphasize catastrophic protection may provide other coverage as well. Typically, this coverage concentrates on discrete populations—the old, the poor, or the very young. The Long-Ribicoff-Waggonner bill includes Medicaid reform along with catastrophic coverage; and the Carter plan proposes to reform Medicaid and Medicare. The Carter plan

---

[2] Martin Feldstein, "A New Approach to National Health Insurance," *The Public Interest* 23 (Spring 1971).

would also cover the very young, by protecting all citizens against the costs of prenatal care, delivery, and the costs of medical care in a child's first year. Others have proposed that more extensive coverage of children, "Kiddie Care," be combined with catastrophic protection to constitute a national health insurance plan.[3]

The unifying characteristics of proposals within this class are (1) their focus on a particular problem or population group and (2) their limits on federal financial responsibility. Such proposals often leave largely untouched the present organization and prerogatives of the medical care industry. What makes such plans national is their applicability across the country on terms that treat beneficiaries similarly.

WIDE COVERAGE, LIMITED FEDERAL FINANCIAL ROLE

The national health insurance proposals that fall within this second category would provide wider benefit and population coverage than proposals in the category just discussed, but would still call for a limited federal financing role. The limitation would be achieved through distribution of premium costs among employers, employees, and government, and through reliance on private insurance companies to underwrite benefits. Plans of this kind could be voluntary (with participation at the discretion of employers and individuals) or mandatory (with all employers and individuals required to obtain coverage). The Medicredit scheme introduced in the early 1970s by the American Medical Association (AMA) is an example of a voluntary plan that proposed an extensive array of benefits to all U.S. residents. Under this plan, the federal government would encourage coverage by offering to extend to individuals and employers a tax credit for insurance premiums to replace the present tax deduction for medical expenses. Credits to individuals were to vary with income; employers were encouraged to participate by the inclusion of tax deduc-

---

[3] See, for instance, the plan advanced in Theodore R. Marmor, "Rethinking National Health Insurance," *The Public Interest*, Winter 1977. In 1978, Senator Gary Hart introduced a bill combining national comprehensive child health insurance with catastrophic protection for all based on this plan.

tions that would be triggered by the adoption of qualifying health insurance policies.

More recently, Professor Alain Enthoven has employed the tax credit approach to develop the Consumer Choice Health Plan (CCHP). This plan, like the AMA's Medicredit, would provide tax credits (private vouchers, for the poor) for the purchase of private insurance plans. Credits would vary with income (and actuarial risk category); for those who could afford to pay, credits would equal 60 percent of the actuarial cost of a specified basic benefit plan in each geographic area. In addition, the current tax-exempt status of employer contributions to employee insurance premiums would be withdrawn. Finally, in sharp contrast to the AMA's plan, CCHP included several measures to prohibit insurers from competing by denying or limiting coverage to high-risk populations. These measures were intended to allow and encourage all individuals to consider costs as well as benefits in the selection of insurance policies, thereby encouraging competition in the delivery of care as well as in claims administration.

The mandatory approach to employer-based insurance coverage is illustrated by the Nixon-Ford administrations' Comprehensive Health Insurance Plan (CHIP). Because requiring a person to pay something is taxing that person, mandatory plans are, in effect, taxation—but in a form that does not appear in the federal budget. CHIP would require employers who employ more than a certain number of workers to provide medical insurance to them; premium liability would be divided between employers and employees in specific proportions. CHIP also specifies the benefits employers would have to provide their employees. Although benefit packages explicitly require employee cost sharing (deductibles and coinsurance), the benefits would be considerably broader than those in the first category of plans directed at catastrophic expense. Like other plans in the second category, CHIP would not restrict its attention to employment-based coverage. Rather it would combine this coverage with public plans for the poor and the elderly to constitute a universal health insurance plan (or plans) for the entire population by aggregation.

The Kennedy-Waxman plan is another example of national health insurance by aggregation. Like CHIP, this plan relies

on mandated private coverage. Employers would be required
to offer their employees a choice of private insurance plans.
In contrast to CHIP, individuals not covered through employment would have access to the same insurance plans as employees. Premiums would be calculated as a percentage of
income, and, for the poor, government would pay the premium
in full. Medicare, with some modifications, would remain the
public insurance program for the elderly and disabled population.

Plans in this category are national in scope, extending their
reach to specified beneficiaries wherever they are in the United
States. They propose government health insurance in the sense
of coercing participation, although the (compulsory) financing
is formally off the budget. And they constitute schemes of
universal insurance in the sense that, for practical purposes,
all Americans fall into one or another of the subplans. These
are proposals for universalizing health insurance by aggregating different plans, not by creating one plan for all.

WIDE COVERAGE,
LARGE FEDERAL FINANCIAL ROLE

The most far-reaching of the proposals within this third
category is the Kennedy-Corman bill (prominent through most
of the 1970s), which in effect proposes a federal monopoly of
the medical insurance business. Rather than relying on the
private insurance market, this plan proposes to establish a
single national health insurance program for all U.S. residents
—employed or unemployed, old or young, rich or poor. Benefits
would be extremely broad and patients would not share the
costs at time of service use. The plan would be financed jointly
by payroll taxes and general revenues, and administered by
the federal government. Administration in this plan would go
beyond payment of claims to allocation of a predetermined
national health budget, by type of medical service, to regions
and localities.

This plan's universal scope, comprehensive benefits, and
public financing are similar to national health insurance plans
in other Western industrial nations. This similarity, however,
should not obscure considerable diversity in financing and
administration. In the United Kingdom, for example, the na-

tional government not only pays for all services; it also owns the health facilities and employs the providers. In Canada, the national government pays only a portion of total expenses. The rest is paid by the provincial governments, which, within certain nationally uniform conditions, administer their own plans.

The Politics of National Health Insurance

The foregoing classification of legislative proposals highlights the primary source of controversy in political debates on national health insurance—the legitimacy and desirability of government intervention in health care. Government intervention involves such fundamentals as the redistribution of income, status, and influence, and the legitimacy of highly valued political beliefs. Because the stakes are so high, national health insurance generates an ideological intensity matched by few other issues in American politics.

The antagonists in the debate are well defined and well known, and they have remained relatively stable over time. One camp wishes to shift medical care financing from the private to the public sector, in the belief that private financing of medical care has produced intolerable inequities in the distribution of services. The large industrial unions such as the United Automobile Workers have traditionally led this coalition, whose membership also includes a variety of liberal religious, service, charitable, and consumer groups. The members of the coalition are united in their belief that universal, government-financed health insurance is the crucial missing element in the panoply of social welfare programs enacted in the 1930s. They mean to repair that omission through a system like that proposed in Kennedy-Corman—prepaid medical services financed by a national tax system that assures to everyone access to medical care and freedom from catastrophic medical expense.

An equally broad coalition, ranging in membership from medical and hospital groups to the U.S. Chamber of Commerce and the Young Americans for Freedom, has traditionally opposed comprehensive government health insurance. This coalition views government financing as synonymous with government control, and government control as synonymous with impersonal and inadequate medical care. Medical professionals particularly have feared national health insurance as a threat to their professional status and discretion. These groups have favored, at most, limited federal involvement in a national health insurance program.

The arguments and the alignments in the national health insurance debate have remained much the same over time. The nature of the battlefield has changed but the antagonists and the underlying principles at stake have hardly changed at all.[4] The emergence of voluntary private health insurance programs in the 1930s momentarily dampened but did not eliminate the demand for government intervention. The enactment of Medicare and Medicaid in 1965 marked a decisive step in the direction of national health insurance. Although heralded as major innovations, both had been preceded by smaller steps taken to expand the government role in the financing of medical care. Some veterans, for example, have for years enjoyed free government health care.

This building-block approach to national health insurance, which establishes government intervention by increments of discrete population groups, might have been expected to have removed beyond dispute the basic principle of a major government role in medical care. But this has not been the case. As the disagreements narrow, the antagonists nonetheless contend sharply. The stakes are seen still to be very high.

The intensity of the battle has been compounded by the rapid growth of medical expenditures in recent years. In 1950, the United States spent $12 billion on medical care; by 1977 the national medical care bill had exceeded $160 billion. Per capita expenditures grew from $78 to $730 in the same period. Within a quarter-century, the percentage of the gross national product committed to medical care has almost doubled, and now amounts to about 9 percent.[5]

Increases in medical expenses predate enactment of Medicare and Medicaid and are generally attributed to the expansion of insurance coverage. Public insurance programs, after all, are intended to reduce financial barriers to care and can

---

[4] This interpretation is more fully developed in Marmor, *The Politics of Medicare*, Chapter 6 and Epilogue; and idem, "Rethinking National Health Insurance."

[5] U.S., Executive Office of the President, Office of Management and Budget, *Special Analyses, Budget of the United States Government, Fiscal Year 1979*, Special Analysis L, "Health," p. 242.

therefore be expected to increase the volume of services provided. But experience with insurance in general and public insurance in particular reveals that the price as well as the volume of services rises with insurance coverage. Part of the price increase undoubtedly reflects the rising cost of necessary resources and changes in the quality of the service provided. Some proportion, however, represents a transfer of income to providers, the social value of which has been called into question.

Historically, medical prices have risen faster than prices for consumer goods and, as overall prices have risen, medical prices have increased even more rapidly. Before 1966, consumer prices exclusive of medical services rose at 2 percent per year, medical prices at 3.2 percent. Between 1966 when Medicare and Medicaid went into effect and 1971 when price controls were introduced, general prices increased at 5.8 percent per year and medical prices at 7.9 percent.[6] Hospital prices have risen particularly rapidly, with increases in expenses per day often exceeding 14 percent annually since price controls were removed. The appropriateness of this increase has been subject to particular challenge, because hospital occupancy rates have been declining.[7]

Table 1 illustrates the way in which prices relate to other factors in raising health expenditures. Although the figures can be presented in a variety of ways, this tabulation distinguishes among the contributions of price changes, population changes, and changes in the volume and intensity of services per capita ("changes in the health care system"). The measures are imperfect, for intensity of service undoubtedly shows up in price changes as measured by the consumer price index, as well as in "changes in the health care system." Nevertheless, the figures are instructive. With the exception of the price control period (1971–74), price changes have been the largest single factor (over 40 percent) in medical expenditure increases since 1950. Their importance grew after enactment of Medicare and Medicaid and, since the removal of

[6] U.S., Executive Office of the President, Council on Wage and Price Stability, "The Problem of Rising Health Care Costs," Staff Report, April 1976, p. 7.

[7] Expenditure and utilization data are presented in Robert M. Gibson and Charles R. Fisher, "National Health Expenditures, Fiscal Year 1977," *Social Security Bulletin* 41 (July 1978):16, Table 6.

price controls, they have been responsible for 78.3 percent of the rise in expenditures.

Table 1

SOURCES OF INCREASE IN COST OF HEALTH CARE,
1950–76

Source of Increase	1950–65	1965–71	1971–74	1974–76
	Amount of increase (in $ billions)			
Total	$23.1	$33.7	$24.1	$29.1
Price	10.1	16.8	10.4	22.8
Population	4.9	3.0	1.9	1.7
Changes in health care system	8.1	13.9	11.8	4.6
	Percentage distribution			
Total	100.0	100.0	100.0	100.0
Price	43.8	49.9	43.1	78.3
Population	21.0	8.9	7.9	5.7
Changes in health care system	35.2	41.2	49.0	15.9

Source: Robert M. Gibson and Marjorie Smith Mueller, "National Health Expenditures, Fiscal Year 1976," *Social Security Bulletin* 4 (April 1977):14.

Because of the government's sizable commitment to health care, these expenditure increases take their toll on the federal budget. In 1965, before Medicare and Medicaid, the federal government spent 4.8 percent of its budget, $5.2 billion, on health care. By 1969, the share of the budget allocated to health care had doubled.[8] Rising continually, federal health expenditures represented 12.4 percent of the federal budget in 1977.[9]

---

[8] U.S., Executive Office of the President, Office of Management and Budget, *Special Analyses, Budget of the United States Government, Fiscal Year 1975*, Special Analysis J, "Federal Health Programs," p. 136.

[9] U.S., Executive Office of the President, Office of Management and Budget, *Special Analyses, Fiscal Year 1979*, p. 242.

These expenditure increases have significantly affected the debate on national health insurance. Until recently, the issue of cost took a particular and limited form: how to reduce or eliminate the financial barriers between individuals and adequate medical care. Within the space of a few years, cost has become a fundamental political constraint. The cost question is properly framed not by asking, "How can the American citizen secure medical care?" but rather, "How can the American government afford a national health insurance program?" Concern about the organization, quality, and distribution of medical care has somewhat receded in importance. But the question of overall program costs in a national health insurance plan now casts a pervasive and distinctive shadow over all other issues, in a way that it never did before.

Specifically, the cost issue dominates the debate on the desirability of greater government intervention in the health sector. Based on experience to date, many NHI opponents argue that expansion of insurance coverage will serve primarily to exacerbate the recent growth in medical care expenditures. Although some segments of the population would benefit from greater insurance protection, this argument goes, the bulk of the population would suffer from higher taxes, premiums, or rising costs for whatever medical bills national health insurance did not cover. Even the benefits associated with expanded protection have been questioned. Third parties pay 94 percent of expenses on hospital care, but they pay only 61 percent of expenses of physicians' services.[10] Expansion of coverage, therefore, is directed primarily at physicians' services. As insurance lowers prices to consumers, there is reason to believe that physicians will provide and patients will receive services for which costs exceed health benefits derived. Finally, beyond these effects on the health sector, there is opposition to the expansion of the federal budget that national health insurance would entail. Many believe a larger federal budget would divert resources from more productive activities, to the detriment of the nation's economic health.

These considerations have been used to justify the assertion that the nation cannot afford national health insurance. This

---

[10] Gibson and Fisher, "National Health Expenditures, Fiscal Year 1977," p. 10, Chart 1.

argument is espoused by the new breed of conservative Democrats, who join with Republicans in opposition to national health insurance. The counterargument, made by liberal Democrats and their constituencies, is that national health insurance is required to bring the current medical inflation under control—in other words, that the nation cannot afford not to have national health insurance, specifically of the Kennedy-Corman variety.

Senator Kennedy takes the latter position, maintaining that comprehensive coverage and expenditure control can be compatible. Fiscal concerns have led the senator and his organized labor supporters to abandon their insistence on the single, government-run NHI plan of the Kennedy-Corman bill. Instead, they are willing to approach national health insurance plans by aggregating public and private plans. But the benefits the 1979 Kennedy-Waxman plan would offer and the controls it would establish on all health spending remain very much the same as those in the earlier bill.

President Carter has been reluctant to offer such comprehensive coverage or to undertake such extensive government control. The president is caught between the concerns of his economic advisers that a major increase in government spending would be inflationary and the pressure of his social policy and political advisers to improve insurance coverage available to American citizens. The president's compromise position is to offer comprehensive coverage in phases, beginning with more extensive population coverage (and therefore more public spending) than his economic advisers recommend, but less coverage than Senator Kennedy has proposed.

Cost concerns, then, have focused the NHI debate on the scope and timing of coverage expansion. Along with sources of financing, these issues are clearly important to the effect of national health insurance on health expenditures and access to care. But equally important and less carefully studied are the mechanisms used to put any new coverage into effect. Demonstrating this position and identifying the instruments that show promise of bringing about desired results are the tasks of policy analysis.

National Health Insurance:
Policy Analysis and Policy Choices

In an age of skepticism about government efficacy and honesty, the passage of a national health insurance program that actually delivered what it promised would contribute significantly to the health of our political order. Conversely, the passage of a national health insurance program that seriously faltered in its delivery of promised results would exacerbate already widespread feelings of resentment toward public authority. This book focuses on the policy choices necessary to make any national health insurance plan reasonably approximate its objectives.

Policy implementation is less visible, less glamorous, and less dramatic than policy legislation. The procedures involved in implementing complex programs are unwieldy, messy, prolonged, and unmarked by the neatness of roll calls and election results. The *Congressional Record* is wordy but understandable; the *Federal Register* is wordy and, save to those tutored in its language, incomprehensible.

In matters of policy implementation, the public rarely gets a chance to witness hearings in which the stakes of interested parties are clearly in view. Implementation decisions tend to be cast in the form of mundane rules and procedures and to disperse the focus intellectually, temporally, and geographically. This dispersal is compounded by the fragmentation of the American political system and by congressional susceptibility to organized interests. Furthermore, American federal politics tend to highlight questions of whether or not to enact a program; issues of administrative design usually attract less interest.

When policy makers pay little attention to implementation issues, government policies too often have unintended and undesirable consequences. Exacerbation of medical cost inflation by Medicare and Medicaid is a case in point. When these programs were being enacted, methods of paying and regulating providers received little attention. What little concern administrators had for inflation was heavily outweighed by the desire to assure provider participation and the delivery of care to prospective beneficiaries. Administrators accordingly adopted payment mechanisms that gave providers considerable autonomy in the determination of rates and revenues. Partly as a consequence, costs have risen rapidly and benefits have been cut back.[11]

This example is one of many from the 1960s that can be used to illustrate the discrepancies that occur between legislative intent and institutional practice. It highlights the kind of problem that the programs of the 1980s *ought* to address more fully. The authors hope this book will contribute to that effort.

Because much of the analysis here involves prediction of behavior, this study has drawn heavily on relevant historical material. In the United States, a decade and a half of experience with Medicare and Medicaid offer useful, if still limited, records of organizational practice from which inferences can be drawn. Americans also can learn much from foreign experience with national health insurance programs, particularly in Canada, because Canadian society is strikingly similar to that of the United States. Canada began its national program of health insurance with a universal hospital plan in 1958; full-scale comprehensive government health insurance has been operating since 1971.

The inferences to be drawn from both domestic and foreign empirical material must be weighed carefully. Detailed case studies do not always support the generalizations they initially suggest. It is deceptively easy to confuse what is typical and what is idiosyncratic, and, in the case of foreign experiences, to ignore fundamental cultural differences that undercut the validity of comparative lessons. The authors proceed with these caveats in mind.[12]

Throughout the book, the authors draw on the various national health insurance plans that have been proposed in this country for examples of approaches to particular issues. This practice has been followed for two reasons. First, our book

---

[11] These interpretations are more fully developed in Judith M. Feder, *Medicare: The Politics of Federal Hospital Insurance* (Lexington, Mass.: D.C. Heath, Lexington Books, 1977) and John Holahan and William Scanlon, "Medicaid: Current Issues and Potential Reforms," in George Peterson, *Fiscal Choices* (Washington, D.C.: The Urban Institute, forthcoming).

[12] See T.R. Marmor, A. Bridges, and W. Hoffman, "Health Policies and Comparative Politics: Notes on Costs, Benefits, Limits," in D. Ashford, ed., *New Approaches in Comparative Politics* (Los Angeles: Sage Yearbook in Public Policy, 1978).

obviously cannot keep pace with the ongoing NHI debate. Evaluation of bills by the details of their current form would ignore the fact that legislative proposals are beginnings, not finished products; clearly, bills would be revised and refined in the legislative process. Second, and more important, it is our view that most of the policy options developed here are not limited to a particular type of national health insurance plan but, rather, could be incorporated by almost any plan.

Because the achievement of policy objectives may well depend on who is chosen to carry them out, Chapter 1 begins with the question of responsibility for administering national health insurance. Consistent with NHI proposals, the chapter considers three options—administration by the federal government, by state governments, or through the private insurance market. The strengths and weaknesses of each approach are assessed by examining past performance and considering likely responses to the new demands that national health insurance will make. Then the authors identify policy measures that will increase the probability of satisfactory administrative performance, regardless of the administrative arrangement actually chosen. State administration receives particular emphasis, in order to overcome the conventional wisdom that Medicaid demonstrates the undesirability of reliance on the states.

Turning to the policy choices NHI administrators will face, Part II focuses on the treatment of physicians. Chapter 2 analyzes the choices inherent in adopting a physician reimbursement policy, and assesses the consequences of alternative reimbursement strategies for costs, quality, and access. Fee-for-service reimbursement receives the most detailed attention because of its likely predominance under national health insurance. After alternative fee-for-service approaches are described, the chapter examines the potential each has for constraining physician fees, the opportunities available to physicians to evade whatever constraints are imposed, and the options available to policy makers to cope with undesirable responses to reimbursement policy. The chapter concludes with consideration of the feasibility and desirability of salary and capitation arrangements for payment of physicians.

Health maintenance organizations (HMOs) are explored as an alternative delivery system in Chapter 3. This chapter takes a critical look at evidence on HMO performance and tries to explain HMOs' generally lower costs. Drawing on past experience with the Federal Employees Health Benefits Plan and the Medicare program, the authors then analyze the pros and cons of alternative contracting arrangements under national health insurance. Examining this experience highlights the problems the government will face in designing policies to capture the savings that HMOs offer. To illustrate the effect of NHI policies other than contracting arrangements (scope of benefits and eligibility, cost-sharing arrangements, methods of physician payment, and tax subsidies), the chapter concludes with an analysis of the likely consequences of four NHI proposals for HMO development and operations.

Chapters 4 and 5 consider the likely effects of national health insurance on the supply and distribution of health personnel. Chapter 4 concentrates on physicians, beginning with a description of current problems with aggregate supply and with geographic and specialty distribution. This chapter then evaluates three principal corrective strategies: altering physician earnings, directly intervening in the delivery system, and manipulating the financing and organization of physician education. The author evaluates each strategy for its potential effect on physician supply and behavior. A crucial question is how the projected increases in supply will affect efforts to redistribute physicians and constrain expenditures for physicians' services. Canada's experience with national health insurance provides valuable source material for this analysis.

Chapter 5 addresses the issues that national health insurance raises for new health occupations, using nurse practitioners and physicians' assistants as prototypes. The chapter explores the potential of using these health personnel to reduce health costs. Of particular concern is the possible conflict between the growing supply of physicians and the increased use of nurse practitioners and physicians' assistants as substitutes for physicians. The larger the supply of physicians, the authors argue, the more likely it is that nurse practitioners and physicians' assistants will be used to provide additional services rather than to act as less expensive substitutes. Based on available evidence on the deployment and performance of people in these occupations, the authors consider whether (and to what extent) national health insurance should promote their availability and use. They then analyze opportunities and obstacles to expanded use of these persons with respect to payment, training, deployment, and physician attitudes.

Part III examines policies toward hospitals under national health insurance. Chapter 6 deals with hospital payment, beginning with an analysis of the objectives and values that have shaped current hospital payment policies. To contain hospital costs, the authors argue, payment objectives as well as payment methods must be altered. The chapter identifies several specific decisions necessary to contain costs, and reviews the experiences of Canada and the United Kingdom to illustrate the concomitant political conflicts and consequences, intended and unintended.

Government regulation of hospital investment is the subject of Chapter 7. The objectives behind facilities regulation are outlined and evidence on its impact to date reviewed. By delineating the factors limiting this impact, this chapter reveals the obstacles to effective regulation of facilities under national health insurance. The importance of regulation is then explored through an analysis of the implications of other policies for facility growth—including expansion of HMOs, utilization review, payment mechanisms, and capital budgeting. The consequences of these and other NHI policies, acting in combination, are assessed through an examination of the likely operation of facility regulation under four NHI proposals.

Part IV turns to policy options for avoiding inappropriate or excessive use of medical services under national health insurance. There are two distinct approaches to utilization control. The first involves cost sharing. If consumers make direct payments for services, the argument goes, they will consider benefits in relation to costs in using services. In other words, the market will control utilization. Chapter 8 explores the likelihood that cost sharing (as envisaged by its proponents) can actually be put into effect, and examines the administrative problems of cost sharing, particularly those associated with an income-related approach. Then the possibility of supplementation—that is, the purchase of private insurance to cover the cost sharing of a national health insurance plan—is analyzed, for widespread supplementation would, in effect, vitiate cost sharing's impact on service use.

Chapter 9 presents an alternative approach to utilization control—regulation of covered services or utilization review. This chapter specifies the elements necessary to an effective system for oversight and control of service use under national health insurance: surveillance of the system, establishment of standards for appropriate use, assessment of actual use, selection of targets for intervention, choice of an intervention mechanism, and evaluation of results. Each of these tasks entails many specific choices, which are detailed.

To this point, the authors have concentrated on national health insurance policies toward services traditionally covered by insurance—hospital and physician care. The final section of the book addresses issues that arise in extending benefits to long-term care, drugs, and dental services. Coverage of long-term care prompts considerable concern about the costs of increased use of services, particularly if services in the home were covered. Chapter 10 uses available evidence to examine the likely cost implications of a long-term-care benefit package that includes noninstitutional as well as institutional services. The chapter then evaluates alternative approaches to financing, eligibility, service allocation, and cost sharing to limit expenditures while expanding benefits.

For drugs, the critical problem is reaching the population for whom expenditures on drugs are a sizable financial burden, without exacerbating excessive and harmful drug consumption. Chapter 11 outlines some proposed solutions to drug coverage issues, including the creation of an approved drug list or formulary, the design of reimbursement, the use of cost sharing, and the administration of benefits including utilization controls.

Finally, Chapter 12 analyzes the implications of including dental coverage in national health insurance. Demand for dental care—even if offered "free"—is limited, and closely tied to educational level and social class. Expanded benefits, therefore, would have only a limited positive impact on service use by people currently underserved, generally the low-income, poorly educated population. The chapter outlines the unintended and undesirable consequences of a national health insurance dental plan that fails to recognize this problem. Then, using relevant evidence from other countries, the authors explore ways to achieve more satisfactory results.

The book ends with a summary of the main arguments presented in each chapter plus the authors' recommendations for policy design. For readers' convenience, we have included outlines of the main provisions of the major national health insurance proposals in the Appendix.

Conclusion

In sum, this book addresses the choices that administrators of any national health insurance plan would have to confront: questions of reimbursement, regulation, and range of insurance benefits. Under each heading, we have asked, What are the policy options and what forms are these options most likely to take in practice? We have attempted to make our chapter topics general, but the illustrative applications are clearly limited. For each of the crucial policy tasks, we have intensively investigated only a few applications, not all or even most. For example, with respect to reimbursement, we have concentrated on reimbursement of hospitals and physicians, not of nursing homes or nurse practitioners. In regulation, we have emphasized regulation of facilities not the issues of professional licensure. And with regard to benefits that national health insurance might include, we have concentrated on drugs, nursing home services, and dentistry rather than on preventive health or mental health services. In some instances, the explanation for the choice lies with the limitations of our resources and expertise; mental health issues, for example, as well as a number of other topics we considered, were beyond the scholarly expertise of our group.

In addition, the authors have focused not on the points of cleavage in the political debate over national health insurance, but rather on areas in which the most serious gaps between policy promise and performance are likely to occur. Policy analyses typically have avoided the nuts and bolts of administrative action required for execution and compliance. We have tried to identify the manipulable sources of gaps between policy intent and program operation in the past. In other words, we have tried to identify likely operational disappointments that would occasion reconsideration of policy rather than a resolution to implement particular policies more energetically.

The result is a book that skirts some of the most profound normative issues in national health insurance. Instead of examining the merits of fee-for-service reimbursement, for example, we have asked what various fee-for-service policies would become as operational programs. Instead of discussing the merits of patient cost sharing and its relationship to egalitarian ideas of access, we have considered what would happen between the enactment of cost sharing and its adaptation by providers and consumers.

We hope that an informed discussion will make for an informed choice among national health insurance alternatives. Although policy analysis can neither transform political attitudes and alignments nor shape the arguments about the proper aims of national health insurance, we can anticipate disputes and problems and point out instruments for policy execution that show promise of producing more desirable results. Policy analysis has a role in appraising the relationships among policy choice, government implementation, and program impact. We have tried to substitute realistic descriptions of the programs that policies would produce for the descriptions generated in the heat of political debate. This task is especially important with respect to national health insurance at a time of fiscal constraint on public expenditure.

As noted throughout, we believe the most neglected area of policy research to be implementation. The essence of the problem is not the intent of the legislation but the distance between the aims of the programs and their results in practice. For national health insurance, the large fiscal stakes make problems of implementation particularly worrisome. Failure to deliver promised results in an area of such immediate concern to citizens would mean serious, not peripheral, citizen disappointment. In that respect, national health insurance may have profound implications for the health of the political order.

Chapter 1
ADMINISTRATIVE CHOICES

JUDITH FEDER
JOHN HOLAHAN

A NATIONAL health insurance program must encompass policies on eligibility, benefits, provider payment and regulation, quality and utilization control, and claims administration. In theory, these functions can be administered by the national government,[1] state governments, or insurance carriers. In practice, these functions have been and may continue to be distributed among them.

The national health insurance debate reveals the importance that participants attach to the distribution of administrative authority. Some attack national government as too big, too isolated, and too rigid to respond efficiently to its beneficiaries. Some say that state governments are too incompetent, biased toward providers, and unsympathetic to the poor to operate efficiently and equitably. And some say that private insurers are too much concerned with profits or growth to act in the public interest.

These assertions frequently reflect not dispassionate analysis but ideological predispositions toward private versus public administration, dispersed versus concentrated authority, and incremental versus radical change. Seldom are questions asked about what can be learned from actual experience under different administrative arrangements. For example, what kinds of programs does national government generally administer well or poorly? What skills or deficiencies have states demonstrated in their administration of health programs? What strong features of the private health insurance market could be adapted to national health insurance?

---

[1] To avoid confusion of the "federal government" with a "federal system," we use the term "national government" throughout this chapter.

Answers to these questions are unlikely to eliminate the influence of ideology on policy choice. But even proponents of a specific approach may acknowledge the implicit risks in that approach and welcome measures to mitigate them. This chapter analyzes what is likely to happen with three alternative approaches to national health insurance: national, state, and market administration. With the first, or national, approach, which has been most actively promoted by labor leaders, national government would be fully responsible for making and implementing almost all NHI policies. Not all decisions would have to be made and carried out in Washington, but a nationwide network of administrative offices responsible to national government would be established. The Kennedy-Corman Health Security plan proposes such a structure, modeled on the Social Security Administration (SSA).

Authority in a national organization could be centralized, as has been the case with retirement programs in Social Security. Alternatively, administration could be decentralized in several ways: The central office could delegate substantial discretionary authority to its regional or district offices. It could rely on private administrative agents for specific tasks, as with insurance carriers under Medicare. Or it could support the creation of new institutions, like Health Systems Agencies (HSAs) or Professional Standards Review Organizations (PSROs), for specific tasks at the local level. In all these systems, administrative agents are responsible to national government for their performance.

The second administrative strategy involves delegation of authority to state or local governments. Although the national government can set the terms under which authority is delegated, state and local governments are responsible primarily to the constituencies that elect them, not to the national government. State administration, then, is characterized by the independence and importance of geographic constituencies. The Nixon-Ford administrations' Comprehensive Health Insurance Plan (CHIP) proposes to rely most heavily on state administration. Under this plan, states would have the responsibility to operate insurance plans for the poor, to regulate the insurance market for the general population, to license and regulate providers, and to set rates of provider payment.

The third administrative option involves delegation of authority to private insurers. While national government could specify the terms under which insurers operate, this system would rely on the market for administration. Thus insurance carriers, as independent underwriters, would be responsible to insurance purchasers—not to the government—for their performance. The Long-Ribicoff-Waggonner bill proposes this arrangement for basic insurance protection for all persons except the poor and the elderly, and the recently developed Consumer Choice Health Plan proposes to rely on the market for all insurance for almost the entire population.

State administration has received less thoughtful analysis than any other NHI administrative option. Dissatisfaction with state Medicaid programs has led many observers to summarily reject reliance on states under national health insurance. Limits to federal willingness to spend, however, suggest that the states will be asked to play a role in financing any national health insurance enacted. The states' role could range from continued responsibility for health care for the poor to participation in a financing scheme for the general population. States would undoubtedly seek authority to control whatever dollars they spend. The likelihood of the states' involvement in national health insurance makes an assessment of their administrative capacity particularly important. This chapter therefore places considerable emphasis on the strengths and weaknesses of state administration.

The discussion that follows evaluates national, state, and market administrations in terms of their contribution to the following policy goals:

- Equitable treatment of the population served, or equal treatment of people in equal circumstances, regardless of place of residence;
- Reduction of inequality in ability to pay for medical care among people of different economic circumstances or races;
- Responsiveness to differences in beneficiaries' needs and to variations in geographic preferences or circumstances;
- Flexibility to adapt to changing conditions, including rising costs; and
- Public accountability, that is, public control over administrative behavior.

No arrangement is likely to satisfy all these goals simultaneously. Reliance on the federal government to promote equity and equality, for example, might conflict with responsiveness to varied client preferences or geographic circumstances, while reliance on insurers to achieve administrative flexibility might conflict with public accountability. These trade-offs are precisely what this chapter will identify and explore.

National Administration

The advantages of a centralized national administration rest on the potential of the national government to make and enforce policies that apply uniformly to all citizens.[2] Uniform administrative behavior contributes to equity by assuring equal treatment of citizens in equal circumstances, regardless of place of residence. It enhances equality by setting limits to differences in the treatment of people who differ by race, income, or other factors. The belief that a centralized national administration would promote equity and equality had much to do with the enactment of a national Supplemental Security Income (SSI) program to replace state-administered public assistance programs.[3] Similar concerns underlie advocacy of centralized national administration for national health insurance.

To determine whether this confidence in national administration is warranted, we first explore the concerns that prompt its support, and then examine the capacity of a centralized administration to satisfy these concerns. In the process, the risks as well as advantages of a nationally administered program will be clarified.

ADVANTAGES OF
CENTRALIZED NATIONAL ADMINISTRATION

National administration has been the exception rather than the rule in social policy. The national government usually

---

[2] For elaboration of this argument, see Christopher C. Hood, *The Limits of Administration* (New York: John Wiley and Sons, 1976), especially pp. 160–63; and David O. Porter and Eugene A. Olsen, "Some Critical Issues in Government Centralization and Decentralization," *Public Administration Review* 36 (January 2, 1976):72–84.

[3] U.S. Congress, Senate, Committee on Finance, *The Supplemental Security Income Program*, Report of the Staff to the Committee on Finance, 95th Congress, 1st session, April 1977, pp. 23–24.

promulgates objectives (e.g., with respect to health care for the disadvantaged), provides funds to support achievement of those objectives, and delegates responsibility for using those funds to others, primarily state governments. As Michael Reagan has observed, this approach to national policy has allowed national government to exercise considerable influence while reducing objections to national "intrusion" in state and local affairs.[4]

In designing national health insurance, it is important to distinguish circumstances in which this approach is desirable from those in which it is not. Simple promulgation of national goals, especially when supported by national funds, can affect the behavior of state and local governments and private organizations. First, national standards can serve an educational purpose—informing governments and private organizations where they stand with respect to national objectives. Second, for public and private organizations who share these objectives, national involvement reduces the political as well as the economic costs of their pursuit and, as a result, increases the likelihood of their achievement. Medicare's national standards for hospital quality, for example, enhanced the capacity of state public health departments and hospital administrators to promote improvements they favored; and national financing for Medicaid allowed states to expand their expenditures on medical care for the poor.

When states and private organizations do not share national goals, however, statutory objectives may not be achieved. In some cases, the national government's willingness to share program costs is insufficient to produce the desired state action. For example, national government shares the costs of home health services in state Medicaid programs, and regulations encourage states to employ liberal criteria for coverage. But states have not responded to this encouragement, apparently because of fears that their share of expenditures will exceed what they are willing and able to spend.[5] In these circumstances, the national government can offer further encouragement to states by raising its share of expenses. But

---

[4] Michael D. Reagan, *The New Federalism* (New York: Oxford University Press, 1972), p. 58.

[5] U.S. General Accounting Office, "Home Health Benefits Under Medicare and Medicaid," B-146031, July 9, 1974.

this action, too, may have limited effect. Payments higher than the basic Medicaid matching rates have been offered to states for family planning services and management information systems. Although some states have responded, many have not been induced to alter their programs.[6] Finally, even penalties have been less than successful in assuring desired state performance. Statutes frequently specify that national funds will be reduced or terminated when states or private groups fail to comply with program requirements, but because national administrators often consider these penalties too severe and controversial to justify their use,[7] penalties are rarely imposed.

Rewards and penalties in national-state programs are part of a bargaining process between independent and autonomous political entities—the national government on one hand and individual states on the other. Sometimes negotiations between these entities produce desired outcomes, sometimes not.[8] This experience suggests that when states cannot or will not meet national goals and when Congress determines that achievement of those goals is critical, equity and equality dictate that national government should take responsibility for implementation. The Voting Rights Act of 1965 provides perhaps the most dramatic example of these circumstances; distrust of states' commitment to minorities' rights led to reliance on federal marshals to enforce federal law.

LIMITS OF
CENTRALIZED NATIONAL ADMINISTRATION

Reliance on national officials may be preferable to reliance on recalcitrant states for policy implementation, but national

---

[6] Personal communication with an official of the Department of Health, Education, and Welfare (DHEW).

[7] See, for example, the dispute over nursing home utilization review requirements in Medicaid reported in Commerce Clearing House, *Medicare and Medicaid Guide*, paragraphs 27,483, 27,813, and 27,834.

[8] On the negotiation process, see Martha Derthick, *The Influence of Federal Grants: Public Assistance in Massachusetts* (Cambridge, Mass.: Harvard University Press, 1970); Gilbert Y. Steiner, *Social Insecurity: The Politics of Welfare* (Chicago: Rand, McNally and Co., 1966); Jerome T. Murphy, "Title I of ESEA: The Politics of Implementing Federal Education Reform," *Harvard Educational Review* 41 (February 1971): 35–63; and Jerome T. Murphy, "The Education Bureaucracies Implement Novel Policy: The Politics of Title I of ESEA, 1965–72," in Allen P. Sindler, ed., *Policy and Politics in America* (Boston: Little, Brown, 1973), pp. 160–98.

administration does not assure that programs will be implemented effectively or uniformly. The reason is that conflict over goals can exist within as well as between levels of government; moreover, even when decision makers agree, they may be unable to control their subordinates' behavior. Conflict over appropriate strategies for program administration and cost containment, for example, has restricted Medicare's encouragement of health maintenance organizations (HMOs) despite a proclaimed national commitment to HMO promotion. Similarly, dispute about the appropriate locus of Medicare and Medicaid utilization review—independent from or internal to the payment bureaucracy—has produced conflicts and delays in implementation of a review system.

Even when goals are not in dispute, obstacles to managerial control abound, affecting both the equity and the accountability of national government's performance. Limits on acquisition and communication of information pose problems for control in any organization.[9] In national government, the problems are compounded by the relatively brief tenure of political executives; by bureaucrats' access to external sources of political support, notably from Congress and interest groups;[10] and by civil service regulations that inhibit rewards or sanctions for administrative performance.[11]

Finally, and perhaps least surmountable, are the obstacles that complexity poses for managerial control. The more complex the program, the more difficult it is to measure and control its performance by simple, explicit rules. Age-based criteria for Social Security or Medicare eligibility, for example, make determination of eligibility a straightforward assessment of age and calendar quarters of covered employment. Social Security retirement benefits are similarly determined by simple calculations according to specified rules. To ensure uniform application of these rules, the Social Security Administration

---

[9] For a discussion of intended as well as unintended limits to such information, see Herbert Kaufman with the collaboration of Michael Couzens, *Administrative Feedback: Monitoring Subordinates' Behavior* (Washington, D.C.: The Brookings Institution, 1973).

[10] For a discussion of national government's management problems and ways to overcome them, see Hugh Heclo, *A Government of Strangers: Executive Politics in Washington* (Washington, D.C.: The Brookings Institution, 1977).

[11] Committee for Economic Development, "Revitalizing the Federal Personnel System," 1978.

until 1972, reviewed all field office decisions on retirement and disability claims in its regional or central offices. This combination of relatively simple rules and comprehensive, centralized review no doubt contributed to the SSA's longstanding reputation for uniform and equitable administration.

As SSA's responsibilities have expanded, the uniformity of its administration has declined. Charges of unacceptable variation and inequity have replaced earlier encomiums, both with respect to the disability program, which has grown substantially in recent years, and the Supplemental Security Income (SSI) program, which began to operate in 1974. Although SSA's current difficulties have many causes, the problems appear to indicate the obstacles that complexity poses for uniform benefit distribution and control of administrative behavior. Rules have become complicated; discretion is frequently required; and the extensive review system has been abandoned. The Senate Finance Committee staff, which has examined these changes in SSA's administrative behavior, has observed that SSI differs from traditional Social Security programs both in the detailed review of individual incomes and assets required to determine benefits and in the impact of benefit determinations on claimants' basic means of survival. According to the committee staff, humane administration requires that administrators have the freedom to respond to situations that do not fit simple rules—such as delays in eligibility determinations for those who appear to meet the requirements, expenses exceeding monthly entitlements as a result of natural disasters, and lost or stolen benefit checks. If administrators are not free to exercise some discretion, beneficiaries suffer. Congress recognized the problem of emergencies, the staff observed, but legislated only limited measures to deal with it "since it was not possible to make the SSI program highly responsive to individual circumstances without seriously undermining its intended manner of operation. . . ." [12]

Variation in SSI administration may reflect an attempt to balance one administrative goal (equity through uniformity) against another (responsiveness to individual needs). Although there may have been many reasons why SSA abandoned central office review, the incompatibility of total review and timely

---

[12] Senate Finance Committee, *The Supplemental Security Income Program*, pp. 98–100 and 106–07.

response in a complex program was probably an important consideration.

SSA's experience suggests that if centralized national administration were adopted without recognition of its limitations, the results would be disappointing. When rules are relatively simple and variation is neither necessary nor desirable, expectations for uniformity and equity in centralized national administration are appropriate. When these conditions do not exist, uniformity is hard to impose, and if it is successfully imposed, it may lead to a decline in responsiveness.

Trade-offs between uniformity and equity, on one hand, and responsiveness, on the other, raise important questions for national health insurance. First, because health insurance coverage affects access to care that may be essential to survival, public health insurance, like income maintenance programs, requires timely response to beneficiaries' needs. Second, the need for responsiveness in a program like national health insurance goes beyond adaptation to varied individual needs. It applies as well to geographic variations in patterns of medical practice, in patients' needs or preferences for specific services, and in familiarity with particular modes of organization or administration. The importance that communities as well as providers attach to policy responsiveness was apparent in the recent controversy over national health planning guidelines. The decision by the Department of Health, Education, and Welfare (DHEW) to revise the guidelines to emphasize local autonomy was made in response to widespread resistance to nationally uniform standards for adequate medical services. If national health insurance is to be responsive as well as equitable, alternatives to centralized national administration must be considered.

DECENTRALIZED NATIONAL ADMINISTRATION

Decentralization is frequently advocated as a means to make programs responsive to varied circumstances and preferences. Within a national administrative structure, authority can be delegated to field offices, "new" institutions, or private insurers acting as government agents. Each of these arrangements implies differences in the groups or interests to which administrators will respond, in the equity of their operations, and in their accountability to the public.

Delegation of Authority to Field Offices

Administration of the Supplemental Security Income program, characterized by inadequate rules and little review of field office behavior, offers an example of delegation of authority to field offices. In this case, decentralization appears to have been as much a function of circumstances as of choice. According to the Senate Finance Committee staff, not only did the central office consciously eliminate review of field office decisions, but also there were delays in policy development and malfunctions in the computer system that unexpectedly shifted decision-making responsibilities to field personnel. At the same time, field office ability to handle these responsibilities was reportedly curtailed by the limited number, training, and experience of personnel. The resulting variations in the disposition of cases—with 1976 error rates ranging from 8.7 percent in Oklahoma to 33.4 percent in Massachusetts—may have been as much a result of variations in ability to cope as of concern with responding to beneficiary needs.[13]

Haphazard variation is clearly inequitable. When a claimant's treatment varies primarily with field officials' attitudes and abilities rather than with the legitimacy of a claim, equal claimants are likely to be treated unequally. Furthermore, when the central office fails to control field office behavior, field officials are not accountable to the public. In a hierarchical system, only senior bureaucrats are directly accountable to publicly elected representatives, that is, to the president and to Congress. If these bureaucrats fail to control their subordinates, field officials become independent agents, accountable for their action only through the courts. Although the courts can ultimately promote both equity and accountability, the legal process is time consuming and burdensome.

Delegation of authority to field offices does not necessarily produce uncontrolled variation. As the Finance Committee Staff recommends, more personnel can be added to serve the public, and all can be better trained to understand the rules they are administering and the appropriate use of discretion. Transferring personnel among regions and between field offices

---

[13] Ibid., pp. 51–52.

and the central office is a way to promote a common perspective on appropriate responsiveness.

This system may permit responsiveness to individual circumstances while maintaining an acceptable degree of uniformity and equity. Accommodating geographic circumstances or preferences may be more difficult. Because field officers operate amid the communities they affect, they are likely to recognize local concerns and interests. But in a nationally administered program, field officers are responsible to national not local officials for their performance. Their ability to respond to local preferences, then, depends on the degree to which local variation is allowed or encouraged by the national office. Responsiveness to local concerns also would be affected by congressional intervention in executive decision making. But congressional representatives differ in their willingness and ability to intervene, and executive agencies vary in their willingness to respond. Thus, the effectiveness of intervention may vary from place to place and from issue to issue. Whether this interaction is perceived as a desirable tension between national and local values or as an unsystematic approach to local influence—particularly as compared with the delegation of authority to local government—may well depend on the importance attached to local variation in national health insurance policy.

Creation of Local Institutions

The creation of locally selected but nationally sponsored institutions is an alternative form of administrative decentralization. These organizations are legally responsible to national government, which determines their structure and authority. But their tie to local constituencies establishes a more systematic local influence on decision making than that offered by the field office design. Professional Standards Review Organizations and Health Systems Agencies are examples of this type of organization in health policy making. Examples in other fields include the farmer committees that administer national agricultural policies, generally considered the prototype of this approach, and the Community Action Program (CAP) agencies of the poverty program.

To whom have organizations like these tended to be responsive? Have they been held accountable to the public for the policy they make? Experience has shown that boards of this type tend to concentrate power and influence in a small segment of the population. This situation is not surprising when boards are designed to establish the power of a specific group, such as farmers in the agricultural committees or the poor in CAPs. But even within these groups, activity and influence appear to be concentrated. Voter turnouts for board elections tend to be extremely low. In 1961, only 23 percent of the eligible people participated in elections for Agricultural Stabilization and Conservation Community Committees;[14] and minute proportions of eligible voters turned out in CAP elections in the mid-1960s in Philadelphia (3 percent), Cleveland (4 percent), and Kansas City (5 percent).[15] Harold Seidman has commented on the results of low voter turnout for farm committee behavior:

> Voter apathy has made it possible for committee careerists to gain and hold on to committee memberships and to operate the system for the primary benefit of the dominant economic groups within the community.[16]

Thus, farmer committees in the South have been found to discriminate against black or poor farmers in the distribution of federal benefits, and poverty programs have frequently rewarded some segments of the target population at the expense of others.[17]

To achieve broader community involvement, national government sometimes requires that board structures include representatives of varied segments of the local communities. This is the case, for example, with respect to Health Systems Agencies. This program is too new to determine whether these requirements enable representatives of the unorganized and sometimes apathetic "consumer" population to participate in decision making as effectively as do representatives of well-

---

[14] Harold Seidman, *Politics, Position and Power: The Dynamics of Federal Organization* (New York: Oxford University Press, 1970), p. 130.

[15] Theodore J. Lowi, *The End of Liberalism* (New York: W.W. Norton and Co., 1969), p. 243.

[16] Seidman, *Politics, Position and Power*, p. 130.

[17] Ibid., and Lowi, *The End of Liberalism*, pp. 240–49.

organized, highly interested providers. But evidence of self-perpetuating boards and other methods for manipulating membership already reveal the potential for bias.[18]

Finally, in spite of national sponsorship, national influence on local committees appears decidedly limited. As the interest group best organized and most directly affected by outsiders' efforts to influence committee behavior, the committees themselves command substantial influence over legislation that affects them: Efforts to reorganize the agricultural committee system encountered powerful and effective opposition in Congress,[19] and attempts to overcome medical society control of Professional Standards Review Organizations might face similar obstacles. Ultimately, then, nationally sponsored, locally led institutions may become accountable only to themselves.

Whether the biases of nationally sponsored institutions are greater than those of state or local governments is an open question, which is discussed later. Specific exclusion of certain interests from administrative structures (e.g., exclusion of payers or consumers from PSROs), however, seems particularly likely to narrow the range of interests to which policy makers will be responsive.

Insurers as Administrative Agents

Arguments for the use of insurers as administrative agents in public health insurance differ from those used to justify other forms of administrative decentralization. In pre-Medicare deliberations, reliance on private agents was perceived as a means of overcoming provider resistance to public insurance. Thus, to allay hospital fears of government control, Medicare advocates publicly declared that Blue Cross plans—then closely affiliated with the American Hospital Association—would serve as "buffers" between the government and hospitals. Although some people considered this approach an inappropriate conflict of interest, Medicare supporters generally considered it an acceptable price for provider support.[20]

This political justification for use of insurers seems inappropriate in today's environment. Providers have become ac-

---

[18] Wayne Clark, *Placebo or Cure? State and Local Health Planning Agencies in the South,* Southern Governmental Monitoring Project, Southern Regional Council, 1977.

[19] Lowi, *The End of Liberalism,* Chapter 4.

[20] Feder, *Medicare,* pp. 36–41.

customed to dealing with the government; the relationship between the Blues and providers is changing; and, for the Blues as well as for commercial insurance companies, administrative performance under national health insurance is likely to be more closely related to economic incentives than to traditional loyalties. In these circumstances, a second argument for reliance on private agents—that the private sector offers greater flexibility and therefore greater efficiency in management than the public sector can hope to provide—carries more weight.

Current criticism of public management focuses chiefly on the civil service system.[21] The civil service was created to take public administration "out of politics" by replacing political affiliation with merit as the criterion for employment. Over time, however, the civil service has replaced the merit criterion with longevity and mediocrity. As a result, the system has become an impediment to government operations. Among the problems that critics attribute to the civil service system are the following: the system gives priority to employee security over positive personnel management; the system's methods of hiring, particularly written examinations, provide little assurance that candidates can do the job; the system's personnel processing delays discourage the most desirable candidates; and the system fails to emphasize performance evaluations as a condition for advancement or removal. These problems, which are further complicated by the growth of public employee unions, have imposed such rigidity on public management that many observers have expressed skepticism about the government's capacity to implement social goals.

To correct these problems, the federal government and many state and local governments have undertaken personnel reform. Reforms will doubtless make public service more manageable, but the absence of competitive economic pressures

[21] This discussion is based on Neal R. Peirce, "State-Local Report/Civil Service Systems Experience 'Quiet Revolution,'" *National Journal*, November 29, 1975, pp. 1643–48 and "State-Local Report/Proposed Reforms Spark Civil Service Debate," *National Journal*, December 6, 1975, pp. 1673–78; E.S. Savas and Sigmund G. Ginsburg, "The Civil Service: A Meritless System?" *Public Interest* 32 (Summer 1973):70–85; and Randall F. Smith, "Living with Civil Service: The Massachusetts Experience," Harvard Center for Community Health and Medical Care, Report Series R–45–4, Boston, Massachusetts, March 1976.

makes it unlikely that public management will ever match the private sector in flexibility. For this reason, use of the private sector to help administer national health insurance remains an attractive possibility.

Management flexibility, however, is not the sole attribute of private enterprise. Whether flexibility will be used to the government's advantage will depend on the incentives private firms face in their private as well as public operations. Medicare and Medicaid suggest that these incentives may be inconsistent with responsiveness to public over private interests. In Medicare and Medicaid, for example, Blue Cross plans are responsible for simultaneously pursuing their own interests in the private market and assuring the financial integrity of a public program. Under present arrangements, these responsibilities are clearly in conflict. As intermediaries for Medicare and Medicaid, Blue Cross plans oversee the allocation of a hospital's costs among third-party payers. The more hospital overhead costs public payers absorb, the less Blue Cross has to pay for each of its subscribers. The smaller the Blue Cross share, the lower its premiums and the greater its competitive advantage in the private insurance market. Thus Blue Cross plans have an incentive to allow hospitals to shift costs from private to public patients. Although there is no evidence available on Blue Cross plans' response to this incentive, the existence of such an incentive creates an inherent conflict of interest in Blue Cross administrators' determination of public payments.[22]

Because this conflict is related to current hospital reimbursement mechanisms, it could be eliminated if all third parties paid hospitals the same rate. But other conflicts of interest are less tractable. Participation in public programs increases the size of a private firm's operations, allowing administrative costs to be spread over a larger number of units. Ideally, these economies of scale benefit all purchasers equally, but if public clients can be made to pay a disproportionate share of overhead, private firms enhance their position

---

[22] Sylvia Law's review of Blue Cross performance presents evidence on the plans' lax hospital auditing procedures, frequently subcontracted to accounting firms. The consequences of this behavior, however, are unclear. For these and other conflicts of interest in intermediary performance, see Sylvia A. Law, *Blue Cross: What Went Wrong?* (New Haven: Yale University Press, 1974), pp. 93–95 and Chapter 3 in the same book.

in private competition. Some intermediaries have in fact taken advantage of the incentive to shift overhead costs to public programs, offsetting savings from the anticipated efficiency of private enterprise.[23]

Finally, conflicts of interest aside, the efficiency with which private agents respond to the public interest will depend on the way they are paid. Retroactive cost-based reimbursement, Medicare's current approach, not only offers private agents every incentive to shift overhead onto public accounts, but also provides no incentive for efficient administration of claims. The situation is exacerbated by Medicare's apparent reluctance to hold agents accountable by identifying and punishing poor performers. Medicaid uses a variety of payment methods, some of which pose a different problem. Some states have paid private claims processors a proportion of the total dollars processed, a practice that clearly discourages concern with controlling payment.[24]

Experience under present payment arrangements offers two lessons for future policy. First, the likelihood that private agents will have conflicts of interest as public agents will depend on the private market that remains once national health insurance is enacted. For health insurers, this market could be small if Congress were to enact a single plan with universal coverage, but it could be large if Congress were to leave the market intact for those who can afford to pay for care. The pool of administrative agents is not restricted to health insurers. Data processors, for example, would retain an outside market regardless of the national health insurance plan adopted. As long as administrative agents are active in a private market, conflicts of interest remain likely.

The second lesson from current programs is that payment mechanisms should discourage private agents from resolving those conflicts in their own, rather than the public, interest, and should encourage efficient claims administration. One way

---

[23] On intermediaries' charging administrative costs to public programs, see ibid. and Touche Ross and Co., *Study of State Agency Performance Under Medicaid*, June 21, 1973, report to the Department of Health, Education, and Welfare (DHEW).

[24] On inefficiencies in intermediary performance, see Law, *Blue Cross*, Chapter 3, pp. 46–48; Touche Ross and Co., *Study of State Agency Performance Under Medicaid*; and Roger D. Blair and Ronald J. Vogel, "The Cost of Administering Medicare," *Quarterly Review of Economics and Business* 17 (1977):67–77.

to encourage efficiency would be to pay a fixed amount to cover administrative costs per claim. The amount would be arrived at through competitive bidding. To assure qualified participants, the public program would have to specify the tasks private agents would perform, establish standards for satisfactory performance, and then accept the lowest bidder meeting those qualifications. Performance would be reviewed periodically on a sample basis, to verify the appropriate disposition of claims. Agents could be rewarded or penalized according to their performance. To encourage competition, programs should avoid large contracts and instead promote involvement of a large number of firms. This approach should encourage efficient administration and claims control. Its potential disadvantages, however, would be the risk and disruption associated with competition.

In general, if the potential risks of reliance on private agents are considered excessive, it becomes appropriate to explore alternative routes to management flexibility, including explicit statutory exemption of the administrative apparatus from civil service requirements.

ADJUSTING TO RISING COSTS

It is now widely recognized that government involvement in health financing has significant implications for the costs of medical care, inside and outside public programs. As a result, a capacity to cope with rising costs has become as important as equity and responsiveness are in national health insurance design. National government has, in fact, demonstrated less flexibility than have other levels of government in dealing with the cost implications of its policies. In part, this situation has to do with Medicare's location within the social insurance system, which has been insulated from the budget process and administratively oblivious to cost concerns.[25] These problems may have been remedied through the reorganization that established the Health Care Financing Administration. But this inflexibility on the part of the national government also appears related to that government's

[25] Judith M. Feder, *Medicare: The Politics of Federal Hospital Insurance* (Lexington, Mass.: D.C. Heath, Lexington Books, 1977), Chapters 4–7.

relative insulation from rising costs, as a result of rising tax revenues and the freedom to deficit spend.

Until recently, analysts have attributed the national government's avoidance of cost containment to the fact that the government has a limited share of health financing.[26] Only concentration of responsibility for all health expenditures in national government, it was argued, would create adequate motivation for cost control. According to this argument, sharing expenditures among governments and with the private sector allows each payer to shift some costs to other payers, reducing each one's incentive to limit expenses. To assure consideration of total costs relative to total benefits, concentration is therefore required. Concentration, in turn, would eliminate providers' ability to play off one payer against another, thereby increasing the leverage of the payer over providers. Finally, the argument goes, the burden of concentrated spending at the national level and the competition health services would face from other spending priorities would create considerable pressure to control program costs. For these reasons, analysts have advocated closed or fixed national budgeting for health expenditures.

Concentration of responsibility for health expenditures does not appear to be essential to ensure concern over costs. Some states have been sufficiently concerned with their share of expenses that they have undertaken aggressive and innovative cost control measures. Nationally, as liabilities for existing health programs have absorbed an increasing share of the budget, the executive branch has paid considerable attention to cost containment. The Carter administration's first proposed health legislation was to place a ceiling on the rate of increase in hospital expenses. Concern with cost containment appears to rise as the size of even a share of total health expenditure grows, but Congress's handling of the Carter proposal indicates a limit to its concern. In its first legislative session, Congress failed to deal with the bill. In the last days of the 95th Congress, the Senate authorized action by the government to contain costs if hospitals' voluntary efforts failed. The House did not act.

---

[26] See, for example, Theodore R. Marmor, Donald A. Wittman, and Thomas C. Heagy, "The Politics of Medical Inflation," *Journal of Health Politics, Policy and Law* 1 (Spring 1976):69–84.

Some of the differences between the perspectives of Congress and the president on cost containment may reflect differences in their responsibility for balancing expenditures and revenues. The president bears direct political responsibility for the size of the budget. As a politician, the president weighs his desire to avoid charges of fiscal irresponsibility against the risks of antagonizing particular interest groups—notably the health care industry—through pursuit of cost containment. The president's varied constituency gives him the freedom to risk offending the medical care providers. Despite the new congressional budget process, individual members of Congress are in a different position. They are less likely to be held politically responsible for the size of the budget and they have narrower constituencies, but they bear more directly the political consequences of actions opposed by the medical profession and industry. Rising federal revenues and the ability to deficit spend allow representatives to avoid taking a stand against rising costs without voting for unpopular tax increases.[27] As a result, Congress has less incentive than the president to pursue cost containment.

As many analysts have observed, willingness to control costs might, in fact, decline if the national government were the sole payer for medical costs. With no direct stake in program costs, other levels of government, which have already demonstrated cost concerns, could be expected to seek maximum resources for their areas, increasing the pressure on Congress not to limit expenses. Despite problems with fragmented financing, therefore, there may be disadvantages to concentration of responsibility for payment. Financing arrangements that employ national-state sharing to encourage cost containment are discussed later.

LESSONS FOR NATIONAL HEALTH INSURANCE

Inability to control costs is not the only potential weakness in a nationally administered NHI program. Our analysis suggests that national administration is unlikely to live up to

---

[27] Although programs financed through earmarked taxes and a trust fund must balance expenditures with tax revenues, deficit spending allows tax increases for these programs to be cushioned by other tax reductions. This approach can be seen in recent handling of Social Security financing.

expectations for uniformity and equity when program administration is extremely complex. Even if a national program
could achieve uniformity, it would require some sacrifice of
responsiveness to varied individual and geographic preferences. Although administrative decentralization could alleviate
this problem, it is unlikely to eliminate it.

If the design of national health insurance required the
choice of a single administrative arrangement, opting for national administration would imply acceptance of these weaknesses. But a single choice is neither necessary nor desirable.
Instead, national health insurance should draw selectively upon
national government, that is, for certain tasks and under
certain conditions. The promulgation of national policies is
clearly in order with respect to matters in which no geographic
or individual variation is desired. This criterion seems applicable to eligibility and minimum benefits, for which almost all
NHI proposals establish national standards. It might also apply to the commitment of national revenues, that is, to determination of the total amount national government would spend
on health insurance. Beyond these policy areas, it may be
appropriate to leave either state and local governments or the
market considerable autonomy in policy design.

National government should administer the policies it promulgates—it should actually determine eligibility and operate
programs—when and if state and local governments or the
private sector are unwilling or unable to implement national
policies. Whether state and local governments or market forces
are sufficiently willing and able to administer national health
insurance is an empirical question. The remainder of this
chapter explores evidence on past performance in an effort to
provide an answer.

State Administration

State administration emphasizes responsiveness to varied
geographic circumstances and preferences over national uniformity. In evaluating the state administrative approach, the
primary question is, What inequities and inequalities are likely
to result? The answer depends in large part on the interests
to which states are responsive and accountable. Evidence on

this question comes from a general analysis of state performance and from analysis of the particular experience of Medicaid.

ISSUES IN EVALUATING STATE PERFORMANCE

Skepticism about state or local administration frequently reflects the belief that state governments, more than national government, represent and respond to so-called special interests (in this case, health care providers) at the expense of others (notably the poor and racial minorities). Arguments on the relative biases of state versus national jurisdictions frequently focus on the scope of their jurisdictions.[28] Because large jurisdictions comprise numerous and diverse interests, some have argued, majorities are difficult to form and a single oppressive interest is unlikely to take hold. The smaller the jurisdiction, the less numerous the interests, and the more easily a single interest can obtain control at others' expense. These concerns have been reinforced by structural features often present in state and local government. Detailed constitutions, a multitude of administrative departments, and the chief executive's limited appointment authority, for example, frequently have fragmented authority and compounded complexity in state administration.[29] The result, it is feared, is the enhancement of the power of the organized relative to the unorganized—that is, special interests vis-à-vis the interests of the general public.

It is hard to assess these arguments conclusively. It is true that minorities have been oppressed within local communities. It also is true that special interests, particularly business interests, have used state and local governments to further their private interest at the expense of public health and

---

[28] James Madison's arguments are presented in *The Federalist Papers*, Number 10. For expansion of these arguments, see Grant McConnell, *Private Power and American Democracy* (New York: Alfred A. Knopf, 1966) ; and E.E. Schattschneider, *The Semisovereign People: A Realist's View of Democracy in America* (New York: Holt, Rinehart and Winston, Inc., 1960).

[29] See, for example, Richard H. Leach, *American Federalism* (New York: W.W. Norton and Co., 1970), Chapter 5, and McConnell, *Private Power and American Democracy*, Chapter 6.

safety.[30] It is even true that some interests have manipulated constituencies—through gerrymandering—to protect their special position and to minimize the political influence of opposing groups.[31] In many instances, excluded interests—often the blacks, the poor, and labor—have overcome their minority status within the local jurisdictions by combining and mobilizing political support at the national level.[32]

Conversely, not all state or local government is oppressive. The interests to which levels of government are responsive vary over time and from place to place.[33] A decision not to rely on any state government because of poor performance by some ignores this variation. Policy makers acting on such a decision risk losing the contribution of states that are more progressive than national government in order to avoid the risk of reinforcing states that are less progressive. James Sundquist has labeled this approach to administration the "Alabama syndrome."

> Any suggestion within the poverty task force that the states be given a role in the adminstration of the (Economic Opportunity) act was met with the question, "Do you want to give that kind of power to George Wallace?" And so, in the bill submitted by President Johnson to the Congress, not only George Wallace but Nelson Rockefeller and George Romney and Edmund Brown and all the other governors were excluded from any assigned role.[34]

---

[30] State protection of narrow economic interests is discussed in Harmon Ziegler, *Internal Groups in American Society* (Englewood Cliffs, New Jersey: Prentice-Hall, Inc., 1964), Chapter 2; Terry Sanford, *Storm Over the States* (New York: McGraw-Hill Book Co., 1967), pp. 33–38; and McConnell, *Private Power and American Democracy*, pp. 164–65.

[31] McConnell calls the gerrymander "perhaps the most characteristic American contribution to the art of politics. . . ." Ibid., p. 92.

[32] On access to and use of different levels of government, see Schattschneider, *The Semisovereign People*, and Ziegler, *Internal Groups in American Society*, pp. 42–53.

[33] Ziegler, pp. 42–53, and Ira Sharkansky, *The Maligned States: Policy Accomplishments, Problems, and Opportunities* (New York: McGraw-Hill Book Co., 1972).

[34] James L. Sundquist with the collaboration of David W. Davis, *Making Federalism Work* (Washington, D.C.: The Brookings Institution, 1969), p. 271.

A decision to use or to ignore the states has policy implications beyond equity and responsiveness. When different states are free to take different approaches to policy, there is an opportunity for flexibility in administration that is not possible when all policy is made by the national government. This potential advantage that state administration carries, however, must be weighed against the potential risk that state administrative abilities are too limited to handle successfully any administrative innovation. If such were the case, state administration most likely would be unsatisfactory by several if not all of our criteria.

Concern that the states are incompetent has become widespread and has generated a catalogue of states' alleged administrative deficiencies.[35] The list begins with state constitutions, the detailed nature of which, many argue, has inhibited gubernatorial control of administrative machinery. Constitutional limits on the length and number of governors' terms in office and requirements for the election of numerous state officials, for example, leave governors without the political or administrative resources to control their administrations. The resulting fragmentation of authority is reinforced by statutory establishment of boards and commissions, whose members the governor appoints but cannot remove.

State legislatures, too, have been criticized as inadequately organized to perform their functions. Legislatures, it is charged, meet too infrequently and too briefly to effectively oversee the executive. Unlike Congress, legislatures in many states have sometimes met less frequently than annually, and restrictions have been placed on duration of sessions. Inadequate financial and personnel resources have further weakened legislative effectiveness. Finally, it is argued, relatively poor press coverage and reportedly meager popular interest have meant relatively little public attention to and oversight of state performance.

As this criticism has gained prominence, its relevance has, in fact, declined. In the late 1960s and early 1970s, administrative reform gained momentum in the states. As a result,

---

[35] These arguments are developed in Leach, *American Federalism;* Reagan, *The New Federalism;* Sanford, *Storm Over the States;* Sharkansky, *The Maligned States;* and Douglas M. Fox, *The Politics of City and State Bureaucracy* (Pacific Palisades, Calif.: Goodyear Publishing Co., Inc., 1974).

despite continued criticism in the literature, many features
of state government have undergone considerable change. According to the *National Journal* in 1975:

> The dominant thrust of the waves of constitutional
> change has been to strengthen the executive authority
> of the Governor by such steps as limiting the number
> of principal executive departments and providing
> that the heads of most will be gubernatorial appoint-
> ees, by increasing the number of Governors with four
> year terms (from less than half the states in 1950 to
> all but seven at present), by providing for election of
> the Governor and Lieutenant Governor as a single
> team (now the law in 20 states) and by permitting
> Governors to run for election to succeed themselves
> (15 had a one term limit in 1960; only eight do
> now).[36]

As a result of constitutional and executive action, forty
states reorganized their administrations in the late 1960s and
early 1970s. By consolidating functions and reducing the number of departments, states simplified administration and enhanced central control and responsibility. According to the
governors who promoted reorganization, these changes also
enhanced public accountability, as government became less
mysterious and more comprehensible to the average citizen.[37]
Administrative capacity also may have improved as state and
local government salaries have increased relative to those in
the private sector. In 1965, state and local government wages
(other than wages in education) were 95 percent of private
wages; by 1973, they were 104 percent. While these figures
mask geographic variations and do not control for differences
between public and private sectors in the mix of employee
skills, they suggest significant improvements in compensation
of government employees.[38]

Legislative reforms also have contributed to greater public
accountability in state administration. Legislative apportion-

---

[36] Neal R. Peirce, "State-Local Report/Structural Reform of Bureaucracy Grows Rapidly," *National Journal*, April 5, 1975, p. 502.

[37] Ibid., pp. 502–08; and The National Governors' Conference, "The
State of the States 1974: Responsive Government for the Seventies," pp.
20–21.

[38] Neal R. Peirce, "State-Local Report/Public Worker Pay Emerges as
a Growing Issue," *National Journal*, August 23, 1975, pp. 1199–1206.

ment has reduced rural dominance in state legislatures, and legislative oversight has been improved by the replacement of biennial with annual sessions (authorized in four states in 1943, in forty-two states in 1976), expansion of legislative staffing, and increased legislative involvement in program evaluation.[39]

Reform has not, however, removed all obstacles to equitable and accountable administration. Reapportionment has meant disproportionate representation of the suburbs;[40] independently elected officials and special commissions maintain considerable autonomy from chief executives; and reforms in some states have been defeated at the polls.[41] As with political responsiveness, it seems that administrative capacity varies considerably from place to place.

State experience with Medicaid offers an opportunity to explore these variations and their implications for health policy goals. Experience, as anticipated, varies considerably across states. States have moved toward a national norm in coverage and services for the poor—indicating greater equity and equality in Medicaid than had previously been assumed—but some states demonstrate low and probably undesirable rates of coverage. Experience in administration is even more mixed, with persistent problems in claims payment and oversight that raise questions about state performance with respect to all of our criteria. Yet, some states have demonstrated considerable flexibility in adjusting to rising costs, including a willingness to challenge provider interests in the financing and delivery of medical care. A review of state Medicaid administration will identify lessons for national health insurance.

STATE MEDICAID ADMINISTRATION

Despite Medicaid's overall achievements in improving access to services for the poor, state-by-state variations in expenditures have aroused widespread concern. Data on the percentage of the poor covered by Medicaid, on expenditures per recipient

---

[39] National Governors' Conference, "The State of the States 1974," pp. 21–22.

[40] Rochelle Stanfield, "The Suburban Counties Are Flexing Their Muscles," *National Journal*, May 7, 1977, pp. 704–09.

[41] Peirce, "State-Local Report/Structural Reform of Bureaucracy," and National Governors' Conference, "The State of the States 1974."

for both mandatory and optional services, and on per capita expenditures have shown wide variations among states; for example, wealthier states have made very large expenditures while other states have had low levels of spending.[42] In 1970, expenditures per eligible person were eight to ten times as great in the most generous state as in the least.[43] These data have led many observers to conclude that state administration implies inequity and inequality in access to medical care.

Action by the national government and by state governments since 1970, however, has considerably reduced differentials among states in Medicaid coverage. In 1976, states with the lowest incomes per capita still tended to have the lowest total expenditures per capita, but their expenditures were closer to those of other states than they had been in 1970. Differences among states also appear much less dramatic when acute-care expenditure is separated from long-term-care expenditure. That is, geographic differences in long-term-care expenditures are somewhat greater than differences in acute-care spending. Because the need for long-term care varies among regions with differences in age structure, income, rates of out-migration of the population under age sixty-five, and the like,[44] such variations may be justifiable.

When data on changes in per capita acute-care expenditures are examined, it is clear that differentials among states have been significantly reduced in the past seven years. Table 2 shows that, in 1976, states with the lowest per capita incomes no longer had the lowest levels of Medicaid acute-care expenditures. For example, Arkansas and Mississippi, whose 1970 per capita expenditures were close to the lowest, ranked sixteenth and fourteenth in 1976. More broadly, the rank order correlation between per capita income and acute-care expenditures fell from .48 to .28 between 1970 and 1976. At the same time that expenditures grew rapidly in virtually all states, the variation in acute expenditures per capita decreased. Expenditures

---

[42] Karen Davis, *National Health Insurance: Benefits, Costs and Consequences;* and John Holahan, *Financing Health Care for the Poor: The Medicaid Experience* (Lexington, Mass.: D.C. Heath, Lexington Books, 1975).

[43] Holahan, *Financing Health Care for the Poor.*

[44] William Scanlon, "A Theory of the Nursing Home Market," *Inquiry,* forthcoming.

in twelve states—Virginia, South Carolina, Tennessee, Mississippi, Arkansas, Louisiana, New Jersey, Maine, Ohio, Indiana, Illinois, and Michigan—increased more than 20 percent per year in that period. At the same time, many states that had been very generous initially (e.g., Washington and Pennsylvania) had to curtail expenditures during the recession of 1974–75.

Many states significantly expanded their programs during the 1970s, but there were several notable exceptions. First, a number of states with many poor people had quite low ratios of recipients to population: Texas (.058), Florida (.047), and Virginia (.064). Second, expenditures per recipient of acute-care services in the South were only 60 percent to 70 percent of such expenditures in eastern and western states. Some of these differences stem from variations in hospital rates and other prices. For example, hospital per diem rates in the South are approximately 75 percent of those in eastern states and 65 percent of those in western states. There are, nevertheless, important interstate variations in program scope.

Examination of the data suggests that although low-income states, particularly in the South, were slow to adopt Medicaid and reluctant to finance program expansion, their hesitancy has declined over time. To some extent, this program expansion has been induced by higher federal matching rates in the poorer states and thus may not reflect changes in political philosophy. The program expansion does suggest, however, that many low-income states do not rigidly oppose financing health care for the poor and do react to economic incentives coming from the national government. Yet state generosity continues to vary, with some states providing what is generally viewed as inadequate health insurance for the poor. This experience suggests that assurance of adequate and equitable health insurance coverage for the poor requires uniform national standards for eligibility and benefits.

Whether the national government or state governments should implement these standards depends on the states' administrative capacity. State administrative performance under Medicaid suggests cause for concern, for deficiencies in state administration have frequently been identified as the source of Medicaid's problems. For example, New York, Massachusetts, California, Pennsylvania, and North Carolina have been

Table 2

LEVELS AND RATES OF CHANGE IN MEDICAID EXPENDITURES AND PER CAPITA INCOMES, BY STATE, 1970–76

State	Income per Capita 1976	Annual Growth Rates, Income per Capita 1970–76	Total Medicaid Expenditures, per Capita 1976	Medicaid Acute-Care Expenditures, per Capita 1976	Annual Growth Rates, Medicaid Acute-Care Expenditures, per Capita 1970–76	Acute-Care Recipients, per Capita 1976	Acute-Care Expenditures, per Recipient 1976
Illinois	$7,432	8.4%	$70.89	$49.87	19.5%	.130	$383.27
Connecticut	7,373	6.9	62.24	34.33	17.5	—	—
Nevada	7,337	7.8	34.43	24.59	6.8	.042	569.80
Delaware	7,290	8.8	29.21	20.62	13.6	.090	229.51
New Jersey	7,269	8.9	54.93	31.62	23.9	.090	353.58
California	7,164	8.5	74.40	53.07	5.2	—	—
Maryland	7,036	8.7	54.77	41.02	15.7	.099	415.82
Michigan	6,994	9.1	77.55	49.10	21.9	.108	456.61
Hawaii	6,969	7.2	59.76	40.59	15.5	.129	314.55
Washington	6,772	8.8	49.56	27.41	10.0	—	—
Wyoming	6,723	10.7	15.39	5.13	8.3	—	—
Colorado	6,503	8.1	41.43	19.75	10.1	—	—
Rhode Island	6,498	8.5	97.08	56.09	10.1	—	—
Kansas	6,495	8.8	54.11	31.17	13.0	.078	401.19
Pennsylvania	6,466	8.3	66.23	35.38	12.8	—	—
Iowa	6,439	9.3	42.51	18.82	15.5	.054	349.19

State							
Ohio	6,432	8.1	41.73	26.01	20.5	.075	346.01
Oregon	6,331	8.1	40.79	18.03	15.0	.081	221.53
Wisconsin	6,293	8.9	88.74	38.62	17.9	.112	344.39
Virginia	6,276	9.2	37.36	20.67	20.9	.064	324.63
Indiana	6,257	8.4	38.85	19.05	24.5	—	—
Texas	6,243	9.5	45.57	18.02	16.0	.058	311.42
Nebraska	6,240	8.5	38.83	18.06	10.3	.043	422.92
Minnesota	6,153	8.0	80.20	32.03	13.9	.068	471.93
Florida	6,108	8.6	21.01	12.23	17.0	.047	258.68
Missouri	6,005	8.1	26.27	19.05	12.9	.080	238.98
New Hampshire	5,973	8.5	41.37	15.82	11.0	.060	264.60
Idaho	5,726	9.6	37.31	16.85	16.0	.050	335.66
Oklahoma	5,657	9.0	58.21	27.84	10.2	.076	364.94
Montana	5,600	8.5	41.17	21.25	15.9	.055	385.05
Georgia	5,571	8.5	51.31	27.97	12.7	.119	235.18
Utah	5,482	9.0	33.19	16.90	4.5	.049	334.14
Vermont	5,480	7.7	65.13	37.82	11.9	.120	316.36
Tennessee	5,432	9.4	41.53	22.78	22.9	.085	267.67
Kentucky	5,423	9.5	43.76	26.55	11.0	.118	224.74
North Dakota	5,400	9.8	35.77	12.44	3.9	.041	304.32
West Virginia	5,394	9.7	31.86	26.36	16.4	.106	249.06
Louisiana	5,386	9.5	53.37	30.20	23.2	.112	270.49
Maine	5,385	8.4	79.44	51.40	25.2	.118	436.19
New Mexico	5,213	8.5	30.82	22.26	10.6	.070	319.75
South Carolina	5,126	9.3	36.17	21.07	22.7	.103	204.15
Alabama	5,105	9.7	43.66	22.65	15.0	.088	258.09

Table 2
(continued)

State	Income per Capita 1976	Annual Growth Rates, Income per Capita 1970-76	Total Medicaid Expenditures, per Capita 1976	Medicaid Acute-Care Expenditures, per Capita 1976	Annual Growth Rates, Medicaid Acute-Care Expenditures, per Capita 1970-76	Acute-Care Recipients, per Capita 1976	Acute-Care Expenditures, per Recipient 1976
Arkansas	5,073	10.0	55.48	26.08	37.0	.105	248.88
South Dakota	4,796	6.9	34.99	13.12	15.7	.059	222.46
Mississippi	4,575	9.6	47.16	31.44	29.7	.127	246.72

Sources: Medicaid Expenditures, 1976—"Data on the Medicaid Program: Eligibility, Services, Expenditures: Fiscal Years 1966—77 (Washington, D.C.: House Committee on Interstate and Foreign Commerce, 1977).

Medicaid Expenditures, 1970—U.S. Department of Health, Education, and Welfare, Social and Rehabilitation Service, National Center for Social Statistics, *Recipients and Payments Under Medicaid and Other Medicaid Programs Financed from Public Assistance Funds,* Report B–4, 1970.

Population, 1970—U.S. Department of Commerce, Bureau of Census. *Statistical Abstract of the United States* (Washington, D.C.: U.S. Government Printing Office, 1972) Table 12, p. 12.

Population, 1976—U.S. Department of Commerce, Bureau of the Census. *Current Population Reports— Population Estimates Provisional Series* P-26, No. 76 (1–50).

Personal Income, 1970—U.S. Department of Commerce, Bureau of the Census. *Statistical Abstract of the United States* (Washington, D.C.: U.S. Government Printing Office, 1972, Table 519, p. 319.

Personal Income, 1976—U.S. Department of Commerce, *Survey of Current Business 57* (April 1977), Table 1, p. 20.

Note: Data were not available for Alaska, Massachusetts, New York, and North Carolina. Arizona does not participate in the Medicaid program.

unable or unwilling to regularly comply with national data requirements. Virtually all states have had Medicaid eligibility error rates in excess of 3 percent despite the threat of significant penalties. Allegations of provider fraud and abuse are common, and the Medicaid-mill phenomenon has received considerable attention. Severe problems of poor-quality care cited in nursing homes and health maintenance organizations have been traced to inadequate monitoring by the states. The failure of most states to implement the Medicaid Management Information System (MMIS) also has been cited as evidence of weak administrative capacity. Finally, lags of up to four months in processing claims and paying providers have been traced to inefficient administration and cited as a cause of low provider participation in the program.

While many of these charges are deserved, much criticism fails to take into account the complexity of the Medicaid program and the constraints and incentives it has created. Medicaid requires the provision of an extremely comprehensive benefit package to a poor, and often poorly informed, population at zero cost to the users. Determining eligibility for these benefits, as well as monitoring their use and delivery, is a more complicated administrative task than that now performed by Medicare or private insurance. Charges of state ineptitude frequently ignore the problems states face.

Eligibility error rates exceeding 3 percent, for example, attest to the inordinate complexity of the eligibility determination system and to the inherent problems in any income-related program aimed at people whose incomes are low and constantly fluctuating. The failure of virtually all states to keep within the federally targeted maximum 3 percent error rate may indicate that the benefits of avoiding federal penalties and reducing the state share of Medicaid outlays are less than the costs of monitoring and case review. Similarly, allegations of excessive fraud and abuse ignore conflicts in program goals. Provider fraud and abuse constitute, in part, an unfortunate side effect of the effort to contain costs by reducing provider payments. One provider reaction to low fees has been to specialize in Medicaid recipients and to provide a large number of services with each patient contact. State efforts to increase rates of payments might minimize incentives for excessive provision of services, but such efforts also would defeat attempts to contain costs. Furthermore, identifying and proving fraud, that is, willful intent, are difficult and expensive. Despite glaring examples in newspaper accounts, the line between abuse and "defensive medicine" is difficult to establish. It is not surprising that states are somewhat unwilling to devote extraordinary resources to the differentiation. Advocates of increased monitoring efforts often overlook the fact that the costs of limiting overprovision can be quite high once the most glaring problems are eliminated.

Program complexity and limits on state freedom to maneuver also have had important implications for Medicaid cost control efforts. Medicaid expenditures increased from $2.3 billion in 1967 to $17.2 billion in 1977, an annual rate exceeding 23 percent. This increase is a function of expanded eligibility and services—especially long-term care—and general inflation in medical costs.[45] Medicaid's capacity to control this inflation is limited by its share of the medical market. Although Medicaid is a significant purchaser of medical services, it falls far short of monopsonistic power; Medicaid recipients are a small share of all states' populations and Medicaid accounts for only about 10 percent of all medical expenditures. Attempts to restrict Medicaid expenses therefore may mean that providers will deny service to program beneficiaries. Hence states have limited ability to control Medicaid costs.

Despite these problems, many states have been highly resourceful in their cost containment measures. Although some measures such as cutbacks and cost sharing have reduced benefits and may therefore be viewed as undesirable, other measures have been instituted to control what are perceived as excessive payment to providers. Medicaid programs are permitted to reimburse physicians up to ceilings imposed by Medicare. These ceilings are based on a system of customary, prevailing, and reasonable charges, an arrangement now regarded as both generous and inflationary. Most states have attempted to keep reimbursement rates below this level. As of 1975, only fourteen states paid physician fees at the Medicare level and twenty states employed fee schedules that offered physi-

---

[45] John Holahan and William Scanlon, "Medicaid: Current Issues and Potential Reforms," in *Fiscal Choices*, G. T. Peterson, ed. (Washington, D.C.: The Urban Institute, forthcoming).

cians relatively low rates.[46] These limitations on Medicaid reimbursement rates have clearly affected the access of the poor to services of private physicians.[47] Yet should the blame for reduced access be attributed to the states for restricting fees or to the federal government for permitting Medicare "reasonable" charges to increase so rapidly? Recent evidence indicates that increases in Medicare's fees have, in fact, encouraged increases in private fees; and increases in private fees have more directly affected Medicaid patients' access to care than have cutbacks of comparable magnitude in Medicaid fees.[48]

Some states also have limited hospital payment, although federal Medicaid regulations on "reasonableness" and hospitals' capacity to manipulate or challenge the system or to deny patients access have restricted experimentation in this area. Several states (New York, Massachusetts, Colorado, Michigan, Rhode Island, and Wisconsin) have nevertheless requested and received DHEW approval to implement their own reimbursement methods. Payment regulation that limits non-Medicaid as well as Medicaid hospital reimbursement reduces hospitals' desire or ability to discriminate against Medicaid patients. To control costs while maintaining equitable access to care, some states have undertaken regulation of all hospital payment. States in which agencies regulate Medicaid as well as non-Medicaid rates include Massachusetts, New York, Maryland, and Washington. State policy also has contributed to cost control with the initiation of capital expenditures regulation, which applies to all hospitals, regardless of their revenue sources. Congress mandated this regulation for all states in the National Health Planning and Resource Development Act of 1974.

Review and regulation of hospital utilization provide another mechanism for controlling hospital expenditures. Several

[46] John Holahan and Bruce Spitz, "Physician Reimbursement," in John Holahan et al., *Altering Medicaid Provider Reimbursement Methods* (Washington, D.C.: The Urban Institute, June 1977).

[47] Jack Hadley, "An Econometric Analysis of Physician Participation in the Medicaid Program," The Urban Institute, Washington, D.C., April 1978.

[48] Jack Hadley and Robert Lee, "Physicians' Price and Output Decisions: Theory and Evidence," The Urban Institute, Washington, D.C. April 1978. This effect has to do with the greater quantitative importance to physician revenues of private fees vs. Medicaid fees.

state Medicaid programs have aggressively attempted to monitor and control hospital admissions and lengths of stay. California has instituted perhaps the most rigorous controls on hospital admissions and days of care by requiring medical review prior to nonemergency hospital admission and prior authorization of extensions of stay for emergency and nonemergency hospitalization. Prior authorization for hospital services also occurs in Massachusetts, New Hampshire, Florida, Minnesota, Maryland, New Mexico, Connecticut, New York, Washington, Arkansas, Hawaii, Rhode Island, Louisiana, and Kentucky.[49] Some of these states use prior authorization to monitor nonemergency admissions; some use it to monitor extensions of stays; and some, elective surgery. The effect of prior authorization on costs and quality of most of these programs is not known; the California program, however, appears to have reduced admissions and total days of care for Medicaid patients.[50]

Other state efforts in this area have been less impressive. For example, the surveillance and utilization review component of the Medicaid Management Information System is designed to provide a large amount of data, based on claims information, on service delivery, and on utilization patterns. This expensive but potentially very powerful regulatory mechanism permits states to establish uniform standards for payment, to determine when care has exceeded those standards, and to deny payment in such cases.

Since 1974, the national government has reimbursed states for 90 percent of the costs of the design, development, and implementation of new systems (or improvements to old systems) and 75 percent of the operating expenses of a certified system. Despite generous federal financing and the potential for significant program cost savings, only eight states have certified systems in place. Ten more states were developing the MMIS as of mid-1976.[51] With or without MMIS, federal Medicaid regulations require concurrent review of hospital use. That requirement can be met in several ways: (1) internal

[49] Bruce Stuart, "Utilization Controls," in John Holahan and Bruce Stuart, *Controlling Medicaid Utilization Patterns* (Washington, D.C.: The Urban Institute, June 1977).

[50] State of California, Department of Health, Field Services Section, *Prior Authorization Study Project Final Report*, March 24, 1975, p. A.1.

[51] Stuart, "Utilization Controls."

hospital review; (2) review by the state; or (3) review by Professional Standards Review Organizations. Massachusetts and Illinois are two of the very few states that have developed concurrent review mechanisms independent of the hospital. Some states may prefer prior review to concurrent review. Others may just be unwilling or unable to perform the review function.

State Medicaid treatment of nursing homes also has aroused considerable criticism. The rapid growth of the nursing home industry and of abuses such as sale and leaseback arrangements, excessive interest payments, inflated rental costs, and frequent refinancing to minimize equity and increase the rate of return have been cited as evidence of the industry's capacity to manipulate state administrators. Although the nursing homes may have significantly influenced decision making in the early years of Medicaid, this influence appears to be waning with the rise in costs and public awareness. The extraordinary rise in Medicaid costs coupled with the widespread repercussions from scandals such as those in New York have forced states to limit nursing home reimbursement levels and to become increasingly concerned with enforcement of quality standards. Recent evidence that demand for nursing home beds exceeds the supply of available beds throughout the country suggests that states are not willing to pay at levels that would increase both the supply of beds and the profits of existing low-cost providers.[52]

Innovations in payment and regulation reflect the fiscal pressures operating on state governments. State tax revenues do not rise so rapidly as federal revenues, and state constitutions typically constrain government borrowing for operating expenses. Hence state governments are forced to control expenditures or to raise taxes. Many states have developed far more innovative administrative practices in reaction to fiscal pressure than the national government has done. Although some of these "innovations" undoubtedly reflect Medicaid's status as a "poor people's program," whose clients are deemed worthy only of second-class treatment, other innovations, especially those in provider payment, have provided valuable lessons for public policy.

---

[52] Scanlon, "A Theory of the Nursing Home Market."

LESSONS FOR NATIONAL HEALTH INSURANCE

Lessons for national health insurance from state behavior under Medicaid must be drawn with caution. Medicaid's structure has shaped that behavior, and it is not clear how states would perform if, for example, eligibility determination were less complex, if rates set by states applied to the entire population instead of to a vulnerable minority, or if services were not free. On the positive side, states apparently approach a national norm for population coverage, many states deal flexibly with rising costs, and some states are capable of administrative innovations. On the negative side, levels of coverage in some states are unacceptably low and many states have demonstrated persistent administrative deficiencies.

It appears that the responsiveness and flexibility of state government could enhance national health insurance administration if the risk of poor performance in some states can be minimized. The task, then, is to design a national health insurance plan that prohibits undesirable state performance while facilitating desirable state initiatives. Although this result is difficult to achieve, four measures can contribute to its achievement: the promulgation of national standards, population coverage that maximizes economic and political pressure for satisfactory performance, financing arrangements that promote cost-effective decision making, and reliance only on states that meet specified performance standards.

First, national standards can restrict state autonomy. The decline over time in state variations in Medicaid expenditures suggests that most states are willing to implement national objectives for insurance coverage for the poor. To reduce the remaining variation among states, it may be considered desirable for national government to set uniform minimum standards for eligibility and benefits across the nation. If consumer cost sharing is deemed inherently inequitable, it too can be nationally prohibited. Given past performance, uniform implementation of these national rules may well depend less on state resistance to national policies than on the complexity of those policies. The more complex the eligibility requirements are, for example, the less likely it is that state governments *or* the national governments will implement them uniformly and equitably.

Even if the national government sets uniform rules of eligibility and benefits, decisions on provider payment and regulation, on quality and utilization control, and on claims administration still will be left to the states. The states' interest in using these mechanisms to assure responsive and cost-effective service to the covered population will depend on two critical questions: What proportion of the population is affected and what are the states' financial responsibilities? If state payment policies affect only the poor, as in Medicaid, for example, policy makers cannot simultaneously control costs and maintain access. If, under national health insurance, states were to limit payments for only a segment of the population, providers could choose not to treat those persons for whom payments were limited.

Remedying this situation does not require implementing a single insurance program for all citizens; rather, remedying the situation requires that providers (both hospitals and physicians) receive the same rate of payment from all kinds of purchasers, regardless of their source of payment. For hospitals, uniform payments can be implemented through rate setting, in which charges set by the state government apply equally to all payers. Physicians may be required to participate in national health insurance and to accept rates set by the state government, or to forfeit any NHI reimbursement at all for those services. Similarly, patients wishing to receive services from nonparticipating physicians would be denied any reimbursement from the program. Adoption of these arrangements for national health insurance can simultaneously prevent discrimination against the poor and, by broadening the population affected by state action, increase pressure on state governments for efficient performance.

State policies can be made to apply to all state residents whether a state's role in national health insurance is to allocate funds under a national expenditure ceiling, to subsidize and regulate the purchase of private health insurance, or to operate a state insurance plan. In the last case, pressure for adequate state performance can be further enhanced if the state plan covers people who are not poor as well as the poor, an option we will consider below.

With respect to NHI financing arrangements, our concern is to assure that states making policy are sensitive to the fiscal consequences of their actions. The Medicaid experience reveals cost-consciousness in some states; but open-ended federal matching of state expenditures, Medicaid's current financing mechanism, is less likely than other mechanisms are to achieve this result. At the same time that open-ended matching provides substantial funding for the state, that mechanism also changes the price to the state for medical services versus other goods and services at all levels of expenditure. If matching rates are 50 percent, for example, states have an incentive to spend on medical care as long as a dollar spent provides benefits (relative to other goods and services) of fifty cents. Medicaid's approach was intended to encourage states to spend on health care for the poor, but in most states encouragement is no longer necessary. Furthermore, where provision of medical services remains inadequate, financing changes may not be the most efficient avenue to improvement. Thus, in designing a national health insurance program it is appropriate to adopt financing mechanisms that encourage decision makers to seek full dollar value for all dollars spent.

To achieve this result at both national and state levels, some plans have proposed that a national health budget be allocated among the states, which would then be responsible for allocating funds to providers. The success of this approach, proposed in the Kennedy-Corman bill, depends on the national government's willingness to stick to the budget it sets. If states could count on regular supplemental appropriations from Congress, they would have no incentive to stay within their budgets. Given past congressional reluctance to limit expenditures, continued escalation of expenditures might actually result from a budgeted approach.

Conversely, national responsibility for such an enormous budget might reduce congressional generosity. Recognizing that the leeway granted to some states would probably be sought by all, Congress might resist individual states' requests for supplementation. In such an event, states would be under pressure to spend carefully, even though NHI funds did not come directly from their treasuries.

States' cost-consciousness would increase if they were allowed or required to add their own funds to the national allocation. This approach—basically a block grant—shifts responsibility for resisting expenditure increases from the national government to state governments. Canada has recently replaced open-ended financing (similar to Medicaid's) with block grants for national health insurance. If it is assumed that a state's desired level of spending exceeds the amount of a national block grant, the more efficient a state is in allocation of national dollars, the less it is required to spend from its own resources. If this assumption is correct, the incentives for efficient allocation are strong. If the state wishes to spend less or no more than the block grant, however, it is free to do so. Although theoretically block grants could allow states to spend too little, a program's application to all state or provincial residents—as occurs in Canada—would reduce the likelihood of this result. Under universal application, the political pressure for sufficient expenditures is likely to be far greater than would be the case if programs were restricted to the poor.

If concern about insufficient expenditures remains, however, there are methods to prevent this problem. Closed-ended matching grants provide incentives for efficiency while reducing the possibility that states will spend too little. Closed-ending matching grants would reduce the price that states face for NHI services relative to the prices of other goods and services up to a specified level of total expenditures. Beyond that point, states would face the full price of NHI services. In contrast to the block grant, this approach has the advantage of requiring states to spend their own funds in order to receive national funds, thereby promoting state spending and, in all likelihood, assuring an acceptable expenditure level. At the same time, as is the case with the block grant, the ceiling on the national matching grants forces states to face the full cost of services at the margin and increases pressure for efficiency.

Combinations of block and matching grants also can be used to influence state expenditures. If it is assumed that state constituencies will demand at least an adequate level of basic services, block grants can be used to finance them. The national government can offer matching grants to those states that provide more than the basic level of services. To encourage service delivery while limiting national expenses, matching rates could vary with state income but be set at low levels in comparison with current Medicaid rates. For example, on top of a general NHI block grant, the national government might pay 20 percent of NHI expenses in wealthy states and up to 50 percent in poor states, instead of the current Medicaid rates of 50 percent to 83 percent. To cushion the effects of economic recessions, the matching rates also could vary with a state's unemployment rate.

Even with attention to population coverage and financial incentives, some states may not administer a health insurance program to the satisfaction of its residents, much less the national government. Nationally established health and other social policies generally have relied for their administration on all states, if they rely on any state. Although political pressure for such a "blanket" approach to state administration is strong, it may not be insurmountable. One approach to national health insurance is to establish a national program that states can opt out of if they demonstrate acceptable administrative capacity.[53] Waivers and research "demonstration" programs have been used to some extent to permit states greater flexibility in their Medicaid programs. The hospital cost containment bill proposed by the Carter administration and amended (though not enacted) by congressional committees would allow states to opt out of the national rate-setting program if they kept increases in the state's hospital revenues within a specified limit and met other explicit administrative criteria.[54] States could be encouraged to run their own programs by including appropriate incentives in federal-state financing arrangements.

A selective approach would protect against poor state performance only if the national government were willing to evaluate performance and impose sanctions on poor performers. The national government's record in this area is not encouraging. National policy makers may construe the option to turn to the states as an opportunity to pass the buck, as has been the case with the Medicaid program. Despite rising expenditures, national government has demonstrated considerable reluctance to aggressively monitor state Medicaid operations.[55] When

---

[53] Other analysts have advocated selective reliance on states in order to encourage better-than-average performance while discouraging unsatisfactory performance. For a review of these suggestions and problems in implementation, see Jerome T. Murphy, *State Education Agencies and Discretionary Funds: Grease the Squeaky Wheel* (Lexington, Mass.: D.C. Heath, Lexington Books, 1974), pp. 146–49, especially note 47.

[54] John K. Iglehart, "Carving Out a Role for the States in Controlling Hospital Costs," *National Journal* 10 (July 1, 1978): 1045–49.

[55] Robert Stevens and Rosemary Stevens, *Welfare Medicine in America: A Case Study of Medicaid* (New York: The Free Press, 1974), especially pp. 74–80, 137–39, and 237–59; John Holahan, William Scanlon, and Bruce Spitz, *Restructuring Federal Medicaid Controls and Incentives* (Washington, D.C.: The Urban Institute, June 1977).

national officials have become involved with the states, they have often been preoccupied with process regulation or with the specification of administrative procedures, with little regard to outcome.[56] And even when national officials have been dissatisfied with a state's procedures, they have been reluctant to enforce their own regulations.[57]

It may be possible to overcome these problems by structuring a program in which state administration is the exception rather than the rule and in which a state's entire population, rather than just the poor, is affected by deficient state performance. In such circumstances, a state's voters themselves might press to substitute national for unsatisfactory state operations.

Private Insurers

Administration of national health insurance by private insurers promises the greatest responsiveness to individual preferences of all administrative systems. A nationally administered system is intentionally uniform. A state-administered system allows variation according to state or local preferences, as expressed through the electoral system. But in all elections, some individuals' preferences prevail and others lose. In contrast, at least theoretically, the competitive market allows simultaneous satisfaction of different preferences. Each individual chooses products according to his or her own assessment of benefits in relation to costs. To stay in business, producers must respond to these preferences. With respect to national health insurance, the product would be a type and level of protection against the cost of illness, that is, an insurance policy. Insurers would offer an array of policies that reflected consumer preferences for insurance coverage. The result, proponents of the market approach argue, would be a more responsive and flexible system than any system that government could offer.[58]

---

[56] See, for example, National Governors' Conference, *Federal Roadblocks to Efficient State Government*, vol. 1, "A Sampling of the Effects of Red Tape," Washington, D.C., February 1977.

[57] See above, notes 7 and 8.

[58] This discussion draws extensively on a memorandum from Alain Enthoven to Secretary of Health, Education, and Welfare Joseph A. Califano, Jr., September 22, 1977, outlining the Consumer Choice Health Plan.

As with reliance on state administration, the desirability
of reliance on the market depends on the interests to which
insurers are actually responsive, the ability of the general
public to control insurance behavior, and the implications of
that behavior for equity and equality. The current market for
insurance raises problems on all counts. In the private sector,
responsiveness and accountability are largely functions of
purchasing power. Insurers are responsive to consumers whose
business they seek. They are publicly accountable to the extent
that consumers in general have information about the available products and have an opportunity to substitute a satisfactory product for an unsatisfactory one. Because consumers
vary in market power, both responsiveness and accountability
are limited and present insurance coverage is inequitable. The
next section describes the inequities in the current market and
indicates ways in which they could be mitigated in a market
structure for national health insurance.

THE CURRENT MARKET
FOR PRIVATE HEALTH INSURANCE

Variations in purchasing power, compounded by insurers'
incentives to limit their exposure to financial risk, have resulted in a division in the insurance market between large,
organized, relatively well-paid consumers, on one hand, and
the rest of the population on the other. Nontaxed employer
contributions to insurance premiums, the reduction in risk
associated with large numbers, and the sheer volume of premium dollars have given employees of large, unionized industries considerable advantage in the insurance market. Competition to insure these groups has led insurers to tailor benefits
to suit employer-employee preferences and to tailor rates exclusively to costs incurred by group members, that is, to
employ experience rating. Because of the age and economic
circumstances of employee groups, costs for such groups are
generally lower than costs for the rest of the population; experience rating therefore means lower premiums. Competition
to insure these groups and the groups' ability to hire experts
to oversee their insurance contracts also have tended to limit
insurers' profits and administrative costs, further restricting premium rates. The results have been relatively compre-

hensive insurance protection at relatively low cost for 75 percent of full-time workers, with terms most favorable for well-organized, well-paid employees of large firms.[59]

Although competition has led insurers to respond to variation among groups of insurers, it has not produced a flexible response to dealing with medical care costs. In part this situation is attributable to the nontaxable status of insurance premiums, which cushion the effect of medical cost inflation. The problem also stems from employers' reluctance to support actions such as utilization controls that employees might perceive as a reduction in benefits. This is particularly true where employers and their employees represent only a small share of an area's medical market. Providers can and have discriminated against insured individuals whose insurance companies have been aggressive in cost containment. Furthermore, in industries dominated by a few firms, most if not all employers share concern with employee satisfaction. Higher product prices as a result of rising insurance premiums therefore appear not to damage employers' competitive position in the market.[60] Thus, with the exception of some employers whose employees represent a significant share of an area's population,[61] employer concern with rising premium costs has produced more rhetoric than action.

People who cannot obtain insurance through employment are at a disadvantage in the current private insurance market. Blue Cross–Blue Shield plans offer individual insurance policies at a single rate for all individuals in the community, regardless of health status. Insurance companies, in contrast, can vary their rates with health status and can deny coverage

[59] Recent reviews of evidence on the private insurance market include S. Long and M. Cooke, "Discussion Paper: Financing National Health Insurance," January 6, 1978, prepared for National Health Insurance Advisory Committee; U.S. Congress, Congressional Budget Office, "Catastrophic Health Insurance," Washington, D.C., 1977; and Judith M. Feder, "Private Health Insurance and the Health Care Systems: Problems and Solutions," Report R–359, Government Research Corporation, Washington, D.C., September 15, 1975.

[60] See Feder, "Private Health Insurance and the Health Care System."

[61] Jon Kingsdale, "Labor and Management-Sponsored Innovations in Controlling the Cost of Employee Health Care Benefits," Council on Wage and Price Stability, *Federal Register*, September 17, 1976, pp. 40298–40326.

to high risks. Even in Blue Cross–Blue Shield, people in poor health are adversely affected by exclusions or waiting periods for preexisting conditions, which are common in individual policies. Furthermore, individual policies typically offer less comprehensive protection than group policies, particularly with respect to catastrophic protection. As a result of unorganized individuals' limited market power, their higher medical expenses, and the higher administrative costs associated with individual policies, these policies tend to be less comprehensive and more expensive than group policies.[62]

CHANGING THE MARKET
THROUGH NATIONAL HEALTH INSURANCE

By enacting Medicare and Medicaid, Congress declared that the inequities just described made the market unacceptable for protecting the old and the poor against the costs of illness. But public provision of insurance was not the only possible response to this situation. An alternative, most recently and comprehensively articulated by Alain Enthoven, would be a national health insurance program that addressed sources of inequity in the market.[63] Enthoven proposes the following: (1) specification of a minimum or basic package of benefits that all insurers must make available, with catastrophic coverage provided through a ceiling on out-of-pocket expenditures by the insurers; (2) more nearly equal distribution of purchasing power, by providing the poor with government-supplied vouchers equal to the cost of adequate insurance policies, and by providing people who are not poor with fixed tax credits equal to a share of that cost; (3) variation in vouchers and tax credits by actuarially determined risk category, to allow adequate purchasing power to individuals with a high risk of major expense; and (4) requirements that each insurer accept all people in an area who apply (open enrollment) and charge equal premiums to all persons in a specified risk category.

The objectives behind these requirements are clear: to allow

---

[62] See Long and Cooke, "Discussion Paper: Financing National Health Insurance," and Feder, "Private Insurance and the Health Care Systems."

[63] Memorandum from Alain Enthoven to the Secretary of Health, Education, and Welfare.

individual choice of coverage while assuring everyone, including the poor and the sick, access to adequate insurance protection. Whether responsiveness, equity, and equality can be compatible in practice remains an open question. Requirements for open enrollment and public subsidies that vary with risk are intended to eliminate current restrictions on insurance available to high-risk individuals. Without comprehensive specification of high risks—a complex and controversial task—these provisions will not eliminate rewards for avoiding high risks, both to insurers and to low-risk consumers who will face lower premiums in exclusive plans. In all likelihood, insurers and consumers therefore will seek to maintain selective membership.

One way to maintain selective membership is to restrict employee plans to current membership, for example, by claiming to be at the limits of administrative capacity. Another way to exclude people is to manipulate service availability. Thus, health maintenance organizations can make themselves inconvenient and unattractive to the elderly by offering poor service for chronic illness; or they can locate to attract a statistically low-risk population, for example, in a high-income suburb rather than an urban ghetto. To achieve similar effects, traditional insurers might restrict coverage to particular physicians, or to physicians in specified locations. It is unlikely that such actions would leave high-risk persons totally without insurance. But to the extent that the low-risk population can insure themselves separately from the high-risk population, the former would face lower rates than the latter. Thus, market responsiveness becomes inconsistent with equity.

The more detailed the actuarial categories and the more precise the relationship between public subsidies and actuarial status, the less likely inequity becomes. As Enthoven recognizes, however, detail and precision increase administrative complexity and increase the need for oversight of insurer and provider practices. Enthoven proposes to allow insurers to petition government for changes in rate structure associated with high-risk insurers. Although this procedure can reduce the necessity for exclusion, it may not reduce its convenience. Insurers may find it easier to avoid high risks as just described than to become involved in what may be lengthy and cumbersome administrative procedures. Insurer incentives and preferences similarly would be likely to overcome laws or regulations that prohibited exclusionary practices.

Concerns with equity do not necessarily prohibit a market approach. One solution to the problem just outlined is to establish a public plan—nationally or state administered—as one of the options in the market. CHIP offers a public plan as an option for people who are not poor. Here we are proposing that a public plan be optional, rather than compulsory, for the poor as well. People could use their vouchers to purchase a public plan if it was better than private policies available. Such a public backup plan could ensure the availability of adequate protection to all people regardless of the market, thereby setting a lower limit to inequality. In addition, by automatically enrolling individuals who have not purchased private protection by a specified date, a backup plan would assure universal coverage, thereby reducing the need for charity or locally supported care.

Public plans for the poor recognize explicitly what may be recognized as implicit in all NHI plans—persistent inequality between rich and poor. Even in proposals to cover all citizens by a single plan, as in the Kennedy-Corman plan, or in plans whose payment terms are to apply equally to all, economic resources are likely to create advantages in access to service. High-income areas that are now well served may be able to retain their advantage through the use of political influence, and side payments may enable the well-to-do to obtain special privileges. The appropriate policy question, then, is not whether a dual system is likely to exist, but whether it assures acceptable treatment of the poor relative to the better-off.

The performance of public plans is likely to be shaped by the political power of their beneficiaries, and this power will vary with the structure of the plan. Under the Long-Ribicoff-Waggonner proposal, membership in the public plan would be restricted to the poor; under CHIP and the 1979 Carter plan, other individuals and employers could choose to buy into the public program. By increasing the proportion of the population in a public program and by enhancing the political power of the poor with the influence of the middle class, the opportunity to buy into the public plan seems to offer greater potential for ensuring effective public administration. Further, the more efficient the public plan, the greater the competitive pressure it places on private plans. The result might be satisfactory and similar performance all around.

If, as suggested above, poor people also had the option to choose between public and private plans, as through use of Enthoven's voucher system, their ability to exercise economic power might also influence system performance. Whether purchasers can influence system performance, of course, depends on the degree to which public officials are held responsible for success in the marketplace, a condition that varies with the legislature's willingness to compensate for failure.

Beyond equity and equality, reliance on the market raises questions about flexibility in dealing with medical cost increases. Market advocates argue that a fixed subsidy for insurance, as provided by the voucher and tax credit, would encourage consumers to seek maximum benefits per dollar spent. In contrast to the current open-ended and tax-exempt or tax-deductible status of insurance premiums, the fixed subsidy would make consumers bear the full impact of the difference between insurance premiums and the subsidy. Proponents claim that increasing the costs consumers bear would increase consumer cost-consciousness, which, in turn, would stimulate insurers and providers to control the cost of medical care. The result then would be cost-effective organization and delivery of medical care, particularly through an expansion of health maintenance organizations.[64]

This argument has considerable theoretical appeal; in fact there is some evidence that the presence of a health maintenance organization puts pressure on traditional insurers (Blue Cross) to contain costs by controlling utilization.[65] Other evidence raises doubts about the probable extent of pressure to contain costs. In the purchase of insurance, consumers appear to be as concerned with comprehensiveness as with costs.

---

[64] Alain Enthoven and Walter McClure elaborated on these arguments at the Conference on Possible Effects of the Payment Mechanisms on the Health Care Delivery System, November 7–8, 1977, Skyland Lodge, Shenandoah National Park, Virginia, conducted by William R. Roy, M.D., of the St. Francis Hospital and Medical Center, Topeka, Kansas, under contract to the National Center for Health Services Research.

[65] Lawrence G. Goldberg and Warren Greenberg, "The Health Maintenance Organization and Its Effects on Competition," Staff Report to the Federal Trade Commission, July 1977.

Under Medicare, consumers have shown a marked readiness to supplement public with private insurance policies, whether or not supplemental insurance is cost-effective.[66] Such decisions are particularly likely when consumers have difficulty comparing and evaluating insurance policies, as is clearly true in the Medicare supplementary market. But even with improved information, decisions are likely to be based on the style as well as the cost of medical care. People may simply prefer the option to obtain whatever care they want when they want it to service by a closed panel of physicians as in a health maintenance organization. Reinforced by physician preferences for open fee-for-service practice, these people may continue to purchase traditional first-dollar insurance protection rather than join an HMO. Choices of this sort occur in the current system. But that system reflects existing open-ended subsidies of insurance and legal as well as political obstacles to HMOs. Behavior might change if subsidies and law were adjusted. Nonetheless, if many people maintain their current preferences, providers will not be forced to control the cost of services, and medical expenses will continue to rise.

This rise in medical costs is particularly likely if Congress should allow tax credits and vouchers to rise automatically with the cost of medical care. In such an event, subsidies would limit the extent to which individuals would bear the costs of their choices, and, as occurs in the present system, private choices would determine public expenditures. If Congress should choose instead to control national expenditures, it could set rates of increase in tax credits and vouchers without reference to medical cost increases, for example, allowing them to rise annually at the rate of increase in the overall consumer price index. With this approach, individuals would experience more directly the costs of the style of medicine they chose. This choice, however, could adversely affect the poor, who would be least able to supplement their public vouchers. If purchases by people who could afford to pay continued to cause the costs of medical care to rise, the value of the voucher would decline. With no backup plan, the poor's access to insurance coverage would diminish; with a backup plan, differences

---

[66] Judith Feder and John Holahan, *Financing Health Care for the Elderly: Medicare, Medicaid, and Private Health Insurance* (Washington, D.C.: The Urban Institute, February 1979).

would be perpetuated between medicine for the poor and for the better-off.

Policy makers, then, would face a choice between maintaining "second class" medicine for the poor or raising the voucher at the expense of cost containment. A decision to raise the voucher would limit inequalities between the poor and the well-to-do, but such action might achieve that goal at the expense of low- and middle-income taxpayers, whose access to insurance might simultaneously be reduced. In sum, if the market system allows costs to rise, inequality of some sort is likely to result.

This problem might be remedied if cost control were handled outside the market, that is, by government. National or state governments could set maximum rates for hospital and physician payment by which all insurers would have to abide. Insurers would retain autonomy in the design of benefit packages above a minimum. This proposal would permit responsiveness to individual preferences for insurance coverage, without allowing those preferences to generate unacceptable inequalities or to drive the costs of the system upward. By increasing consumers' sensitivity to prices, this system might provide greater public support for regulation than is present in the current system.

Conclusions

To choose among national, state, and market administration for national health insurance is to choose some policy objectives over others. When national government can achieve uniformity and control of administrative behavior, national administration emphasizes equal treatment of all citizens. But achieving control of a complex program is not a simple task. If policies are not amenable to relatively simple, easily applied rules, uniform decisions require extensive monitoring and evaluation. Monitoring and evaluation, in turn, impose a cost. As internal review expands, a program's capacity to respond to beneficiaries contracts. Although administrative decentralization may improve this situation, a national system's capacity to respond to geographic variations and to adapt to changing circumstances appears to be limited.

The risk, then, in relying on national administration is that too much may be expected and too little received. To prevent this outcome, the national government's responsibilities can be circumscribed. National government could establish limits on its expenditures for medical care and basic rules for expenditure use—specifically, minimum standards for eligibility and benefits. Operation of these standards and the establishment of other standards—for provider payment and regulation, quality and utilization control, and claims administration —can be delegated to the states or to the market.

The risk of this delegation is that responsiveness would outweigh equity, and that state administrators or insurance carriers would fail to respond to the very people to whom national health insurance matters most, the poor and the sick. Experience with state administration suggests that this risk is real but often exaggerated. Most states have implemented national objectives for Medicaid coverage and several states have been innovative in program design, particularly with respect to provider payment. Yet some states do continue to provide unacceptably low coverage and to administer programs so poorly as to jeopardize their effectiveness. To ignore these variations and rely fully on all states would undoubtedly risk program failure in some states.

In assessing this risk, it is important to remember that national health insurance need not adopt Medicaid's structure. Several policy changes could reduce the likelihood of poor state performance. To increase public interest and pressure for good performance, state policies could go beyond the poor to cover a state's entire population. To increase both national and state fiscal responsibility, open-ended matching grants could be replaced with more restrictive funding arrangements—budgeting, block grants, or closed-ended matching. Finally, uncritical reliance on all states could be replaced by selective reliance on states that perform well. State performance in areas such as service use, quality, and provider payment could be evaluated against national norms. National government would undoubtedly be reluctant to take over from a state performing poorly, but a state's voters themselves might seek national action if they were continually dissatisfied.

Risks associated with the market also could be mitigated by changing the environment in which insurers operate. Changes that reduce insurers' tendency to limit their liabilities include Enthoven's proposed requirements on benefits, enrollment, and premiums. But analysis suggests that these changes would not be sufficient to assure equity. It also might be necessary to make government responsible for cost containment activities and to make a public—national or state—insurance plan available alongside private plans in the marketplace. Taken together, these actions would reduce the likelihood of discrimination against the poor and the sick, while retaining the market's flexibility to respond to consumer preferences on price, comprehensiveness, convenience, and style of medical practice.

None of the policies proposed here would make adoption of an administrative structure for national health insurance a risk-free proposition. But policy choices made with the risks in mind are preferable to those made in ignorance. It is hoped that the options identified in this chapter will help policy makers cope with whatever risks they decide to take.

Chapter 2
PHYSICIAN REIMBURSEMENT

JOHN HOLAHAN

T HE choice of a method or methods of paying for physicians' services is one of the most important decisions to be
made in formulating national health insurance programs.
Payments to physicians currently account for 20 percent of
national health expenditures.[1] Moreover, physicians play a
critical role in determining use of many other services. Systems for reimbursement of physicians' services have been just
as important in recent years for Medicare, Medicaid, and other
third-party carriers; yet, little consensus exists today on appropriate methods of paying physicians.

Each component of a national health insurance program—
utilization controls, facility regulation, physician reimbursement, or whatever—should contribute to the overall goals of
(1) guaranteeing an adequate supply of services, particularly
to people whose access to services is now limited; (2) encouraging provision of high-quality service; and (3) restraining the
rising costs of health services through influencing the physicians' mode of delivery, choice of care setting, and mix of
services produced. Achieving all these objectives simultaneously is impossible. Increasing access of the poor to high-
quality services can be accomplished only at higher costs. Providing high-quality care with minimal incremental effect on
rates of inflation can be accomplished only at some sacrifice of
accessibility. Finally, achieving the objectives of equal access
and cost containment is to some degree inconsistent with the
goal of high-quality care. The chapter does not suggest new or
dramatic answers to this dilemma. Rather, the inconsistency
of these objectives serves to focus much of the analysis. Alter-

---

[1] R.M. Gibson and M.S. Mueller, "National Health Expenditures, Fiscal
Year 1976," *Social Security Bulletin*, April 1976.

73

native reimbursement strategies will help achieve some objectives but not others. The discussion highlights ways in
which different strategies would assist a national health insurance program in attaining any of these objectives.

The major choices in a physician payment scheme relate to
the method of payment and the level or rate of payment. The
primary methods of payment currently envisaged in this
country or abroad are fee-for-service, capitation, or salary.
Fee-for-service systems can be simply defined as those providing for separate payments to the physician by either the patient or a third-party payer for each unit of service provided.
The rate of payment under fee-for-service systems can be
controlled only by (1) the patients' ability and willingness to
seek substitutes or forgo services in lieu of payment, (2) fee
screens based on recorded histories of charges on a procedure-
by-procedure basis, or (3) negotiation of fee schedules by third
parties and physician associations. Fee-for-service is now the
dominant form of reimbursement for physicians in the United
States. Given its entrenchment, it is very unlikely that a different approach would be employed in this country under
natonal insurance.[2]

There is nevertheless considerable interest in salary and
capitation as alternative methods of reimbursement. Salary is
the second most common payment arrangement for physicians.
Salaried physicians practicing in general hospitals are primarily interns and residents, but also include pathologists,
radiologists, and anesthesiologists. Outside the hospital, salaried physicians practice in clinics, health maintenance organizations (HMOs), other group practices, neighborhood health
centers, government facilities such as Veterans' Administration hospitals, and recently the National Health Service Corps
(NHSC). From the public's perspective, salaried practice has
many desirable features, but it is unlikely to increase significantly as a form of physician reimbursement. This is largely
because reliance on salaries would require major changes in
the organization of physician services. Nonetheless, efforts to
increase the number of physicians who work in organized
practice settings and are remunerated on a salaried basis are
worth consideration.

---

[2] For an account of other countries' experience, see Theodore R.
Marmor, "The Politics of Paying Physicians: U.S., U.K., and Sweden,"
International Journal of Health Services 1 (1972).

The third method of physician reimbursement, capitation, is an arrangement under which lump sum payments are made directly to physicians in solo or small group practice for care of selected groups of patients, regardless of the number of units of service required for a specified period such as a year. In the United Kingdom, capitation payments are made directly to general practitioners in return for the delivery of ambulatory services to an enrolled patient population. This arrangement is generally unfamiliar to individual and small group practices in the United States. In this country, capitation payments are typically made on behalf of employees of large firms, and Medicare or Medicaid patients, to prepaid group practices or medical care foundations, both of which are forms of health maintenance organizations. Physicians in HMOs are paid on a fee-for-service or salaried basis, or through some type of income-sharing arrangement. Issues raised by these organizations will be dealt with in Chapter 3. This chapter addresses the possibility of using capitation arrangements for individual and small group practices. Possibilities include the British system for general practitioners, which provides a base salary plus capitation payments. The major advantages of capitation would be its incentive for efficiency and the elimination of many administrative tasks for both the physician and the national health insurance program.

Despite general agreement that fee-for-service will predominate under national health insurance, plans differ (1) in the extent to which they encourage physicians to enter practice modes in which other payment methods would apply, (2) in the type of controls placed on fee-for-service reimbursements, and (3) in the requirements or incentives to accept the charges allowed under the plan as payment in full. The differences will emerge from a brief examination of reimbursement procedures proposed by four national health insurance plans.[3]

Under the Comprehensive Health Insurance Plan (CHIP) proposed by the Nixon and Ford administrations, three population groups would be treated separately—the aged (Federal Health Insurance Plan—FHIP), employer-employee groups

---

[3] For a full description of NHI plans, see Saul Waldman, *National Health Insurance Proposals: Provisions of Bills Introduced in the 94th Congress as of February 1976*, U.S. Department of Health, Education, and Welfare (DHEW), Social Security Administration (SSA) (Washington, D.C.: U.S. Government Printing Office, 1976).

(Employee Health Insurance Plan—EHIP), and the poor and disabled (Assisted Health Insurance Plan—AHIP). Fee-for-service reimbursement is envisaged for most physicians, with fee schedules determined by state agencies. The program would classify physicians as full-participating providers, associate-participating providers, and nonparticipating providers. Full-participating providers would agree to accept reimbursement from the government as full payment for services rendered. In exchange, the program would bill eligible families for their cost-sharing liabilities. Associate-participating providers would accept reimbursement from the government as full payment for AHIP and Medicare patients and for the insured portion of the bill in the employee program, but would bill the patient for the uninsured portion of the latter plus any supplemental charge. Nonparticipating providers could not be reimbursed for any service. Providers in either the full or associated classification could not charge AHIP or FHIP beneficiaries more than the rates set by the states.

The Kennedy-Mills plan contained physician reimbursement provisions somewhat similar to those in the CHIP bill. In choosing to participate in the program, physicians would agree to accept payments set by government fee schedules in exchange for government collection of deductibles and coinsurance from the patient. Physicians who chose not to participate could collect the government share of the allowed fee from the government and bill patients for their cost-sharing liability plus any supplemental charges. In contrast to the provision of the CHIP proposal, physicians who chose not to participate in the Kennedy-Mills plan could charge the poor and aged more than the government-determined rates.

The Long-Ribicoff-Waggonner proposal would adopt a reimbursement system comparable to that employed by Medicare. "Usual, customary, and reasonable" (UCR) charges would be paid. As in Medicare, physicians could decide on a service-by-service basis to submit claims to the government and accept allowed charges as payment in full, or to bill the patient directly. In the latter case, the patient then would submit the claim to the program and receive reimbursement for the government-determined "reasonable" charge. If this charge was less than the physician's actual charge, the patient would be responsible for paying the balance to the physician. Individuals covered under the medical assistance component of the

Long-Ribicoff-Waggonner program designed for low-income individuals and families would not be required to pay amounts above the reasonable charge screen. For these patients, physicians would be required to accept reasonable charges as payment in full.

The Kennedy-Corman Health Security Plan proposes the most radical departure from current practices. Under this program, funds would be allocated to geographic regions for physician services, dental services, drugs, and the like on the basis of *expected per capita utilization* for each institution. Payments for physicians' services would come from a budget fixed in advance. Physicians and other private practitioners could choose to be paid on a fee-for-service, capitation, or salary basis, but allocations from the predetermined fund would be made first to providers accepting capitation or salary. Payments to physicians choosing fee-for-service would be limited by the predetermined budget, and if payments exceeded estimated levels, fees would be reduced. The likelihood of fee reduction is intended to provide strong incentives to physicians to accept capitation reimbursement or to enter prepaid group practices or medical care foundations.

The Kennedy-Corman plan also would mandate that professional practitioners such as pathologists and radiologists, whose practices are predominantly associated with a hospital and whose services are generally available to all patients of that hospital, should be compensated by the hospital. Because the cost of services by such specialists would be treated as a hospital expense, the plan strongly endorses and encourages salaried practice for those specialties. The Kennedy-Corman plan would provide both the strongest controls on levels of payment to physicians choosing fee-for-service reimbursement and the strongest incentives to physicians to choose practice modes in which they would be paid on a capitation or salaried basis.

The variety of proposed approaches to reimbursement reveals the lack of consensus on payment policy. The remainder of this chapter analyzes the choices policy makers face in implementing a fee-for-service system. Fee-for-service is emphasized not because that system is preferred but because large-scale displacement of it is extremely unlikely. The concluding sections discuss salaried and capitation arrangements.

Fee-for-Service Reimbursement

Under fee-for-service reimbursement, a physician's income depends on the quantity of services provided, the unit prices paid, and the costs of the services. The current system is widely criticized for placing few restrictions on a physician's ability to set prices and for not encouraging efficiency in the choice of treatment or method of production. Of all possible reimbursement systems, fee-for-service poses the greatest problem for people concerned with the control of health care costs. Recent evidence suggests that the quantity of services physicians provide depends in part on the physicians themselves, through their influence over patients' decisions. Many economists have argued that physicians can "create" demand;[4] others have responded that the empirical evidence presented thus far is consistent with a standard economic model in which patients respond to increases in quality, reductions in waiting time, and fewer delays in obtaining appointments by demanding more services.[5] They contend that there is no real evidence that physicians "create" demand.

The position taken here is that it is largely unimportant whether physicians "create" demand in a strict sense, or whether utilization rates respond to increased amenities, higher-quality services, or lower time prices. There is simply a great deal of evidence that medical services respond positively to increases in physician supply with little effect on money prices. The major policy question is the extent to which society should be willing to pay for additional services under NHI schemes that substantially expand coverage and reduce

---

[4] Robert G. Evans, "Supplier-Induced Demand: Some Empirical Evidence and Implications," in Mark Perlman, ed., *The Economics of Health and Medical Care* (New York: Halsted Press, 1974), pp. 163–64; Uwe Reinhardt, *Physician Productivity and the Demand for Health Manpower* (Cambridge, Mass.: Ballinger Publishing Co., 1975); Robert G. Evans, E.M.A. Parish, and Floyd Scully, "Medical Production, Scale Effects, and Demand Generation," *Canadian Journal of Economics* 6 (August 1973): 376–93; Victor G. Fuchs and Marcia J. Kramer, *Determinants of Expenditures for Physician Services in the United States 1948–1968* (Washington, D.C.: National Center for Health Services Research, 1972).

[5] Frank Sloan and Roger Feldman, "Monopolistic Elements in the Market for Physician Services," paper presented at the Federal Trade Commission Conference, June 1, 1977.

the cost of care to patients. If physicians could increase service utilization under national health insurance through "demand creation" or otherwise, it would become exceedingly difficult to control medical care expenditures.

This argument does not imply that physicians' incomes under fee-for-service systems are unaffected by the type of controls placed on rates. When there is no third-party coverage or when third-party coverage provides for indemnity payments (i.e., payment of fixed sums for specific services regardless of physician charges), rates of payment for physician services are controlled only by patients' ability and willingness to pay. Payment rates also can be controlled by fee screens based on average charges for each procedure over a previous period, as is currently done under "usual, customary, and reasonable" charge systems. Finally, payment rates can be controlled by fee schedules now negotiated between physician associations and insurance firms, or by state Medicaid programs; in principle, payment rates could also be set by state rate-setting commissions.

Setting up a method for controlling the level of physician fees solves only part of the pricing problem. Physicians do not always have to accept the allowed charge as payment in full. Under Medicare, for example, physicians can accept the allowed charge and collect full payment from the government less the deductible and coinsurance liabilities. The physician then collects cost-sharing liabilities from the patient. Or, the physician can bill the patient directly at rates above or below the Medicare-allowed level. (The patient then collects from Medicare the allowed amount less the deductible and coinsurance liabilities.) Other arrangements are used, or have been contemplated, in other nations. For example, in order to participate in the program, physicians could be required to accept the government's fee schedule as payment in full. The main point is that most methods for controlling physicians' charges envisage some way in which physicians are not bound by those controls for some patients or for some services. This issue, as will be seen later, is a critical policy choice under national health insurance.

In general, one can be encouraged by the incentives that fee-for-service systems provide for the delivery of high-quality care and for increasing access to care for the underserved.

Problems remain, however. If physicians can raise prices by increasing the quality of services they provide, fee-for-service systems encourage high-quality service perhaps more than any other reimbursement system. This statement assumes, of course, that patients can accurately assess the quality of care providers offer. To the extent that patients cannot gauge quality, fee-for-service may encourage provision of services which appear to increase quality but which do not really affect outcomes. If consumers use prices as indicators of quality, the incentives set in motion by fee-for-service systems become even more questionable. With these qualifications, however, fee-for-service systems seem likely to offer higher-quality care. These incentives would be muted to the extent that fee controls constrained the rewards to physicians who exerted extra effort.

Because fee-for-service systems reward physicians for additional units of service provided, these systems encourage physicians to see more patients than other payment schemes do (assuming fees exceed the costs of providing care). It appears, therefore, that equity of access would be enhanced by fee-for-service. But physicians' apparent ability to provide enough services and to charge higher fees in doctor-surplus areas makes relocation to underserved areas unnecessary. While physicians tend to have lower net earnings in urban areas than in rural areas,[6] incomes for physicians seem to be sufficiently high in urban areas that large-scale migration does not occur. Thus, although the basic incentives of fee-for-service systems seem to facilitate greater access, these systems do not appear to achieve that result.

The following sections analyze in detail the ways in which fee-for-service systems actually work. The main types of fee-for-service reimbursement systems—usual, customary, and reasonable charges, and fee schedules—are described, with particular attention to the methods they employ to control physician fees. Then we consider whether intended fee controls would work, first by exploring physicians' opportunities to opt out of program controls, and second by examining physicians' reactions to controls that do apply. Then we consider public policy options to deal with undesirable physician responses.

---

[6] *The Profile of Medical Practice* (Chicago: American Medical Association, 1976) p. 167.

USUAL, CUSTOMARY, AND REASONABLE CHARGES

Medicare reimbursements to physicians have been made on the basis of *usual and customary* charges [7] which limit reimbursements to the lowest of the following: a physician's actual charge, the physician's median charge in a recent prior period (usual), or the seventy-fifth percentile of charges in that same period by physicians in the same specialty and geographic area (customary). The principal advantage of usual and customary charge reimbursement is its broad acceptability to physicians. It virtually assures physicians of generous reimbursement over the long term by guaranteeing that fees will increase at relatively rapid rates. The system permits rate differences among physicians on the basis of quality, location of practice, or scope of service. The system also permits relatively rapid adjustments to procedural and technological changes. Many Medicaid programs and Blue Shield plans also have chosen this method to reimburse physicians, though often with different percentile limitations.

UCR systems have three main problems: They are administratively complex, they have inevitable inflationary consequences, and they reinforce what may be inappropriate price differentials. The administrative complexity of UCR systems is often underestimated. Determination of usual charges requires arraying all physician charges for each procedure performed. All excessively high or low charges are eliminated; the median charge for each procedure is identified and called the usual charge. All usual charges are then arrayed, and the seventy-fifth percentile is identified and called the customary.

Distinct customary charges may be calculated for different specialties and areas. Because physicians often do not have enough billings to calculate usual charges for all procedures, usual charges must be imputed on the basis of the more frequently performed procedures. The same must be done for customary charges when insufficient procedures exist. The usual and customary charge profiles calculated with a particular calendar year's data are typically used as screens in the

---

[7] The Medicare program has termed *usual* charges as *customary* and *customary* charges as *prevailing*. Medicaid and most Blue Shield programs use the terms *usual* and *customary*. Because the latter terminology is more frequently used, we have adopted it here.

following fiscal year. The actual charge is acceptable only if it does not exceed either the usual or the customary charge. In practice, the system has proven quite difficult to implement, in part because of the complexity of the definition of "usual" charges and the substantial amount of data manipulation required to calculate them.

Although usual and customary charges appear to provide strict limits on fees, in practice the system permits rapid escalation of fees. Technically, the usual and customary charge screens are updated annually through examination of the previous calendar year's billing behavior of physicians. Assuming that the system is enforced and that rates are annually updated, physicians always have a clear incentive to bill at a high rate. Submitting high actual charges will increase an individual physician's usual charge for the coming year. If replicated in the behavior of other physicians, this practice will increase the customary charge level used to set a ceiling on payment rates. Hence physicians have an incentive to bill not only at the maximum (allowable) screens, but actually at far higher rates.

This practice will not impose a financial burden on patients who bear no cost sharing, such as those covered by Medicaid. In Medicare, inflating actual charges above reasonable charge screens will impose a burden on patients when the physician (1) does not accept assignment and (2) actually collects the higher charge. The physician concerned with the patient's pocketbook may either accept assignment and submit bills in excess of reasonable charge screens, or bill the patient directly at a high rate but require payment of less than the full charge. The bill enters the physician's profile at the billed rate regardless of the amount collected.

It is possible, however, to introduce limits on charge increases into UCR systems. The first option is to limit the allowed rate of increase in usual and customary charge profiles. This would control the rate of increase in the program's unit costs. Medicare now follows such a procedure in applying an economic index adjustment factor to customary ("prevailing") charges. The major weakness of such controls is that relative values among procedures do not adjust as relative costs change. Moreover, relative prices among physicians are fixed, except for physicians whose own charges do not increase at the rate permitted by the state.

A second alternative is to define customary charges as a lower percentile than the seventy-fifth. If customary charges are defined, as, say, the fiftieth percentile of the distribution of usual charges, unit costs for medical services may be reduced substantially. The amount of expenditure reduction depends on the variance of the distribution for each procedure. If the variance is large, considerable reduction in program expenditures for medical services is possible. This approach would limit or reduce reimbursements made to physicians with particularly high charges; it also might discourage their participation in the program. If such physicians delivered a higher quality of care, their failure to participate in the NHI program would reduce the quality of service available to individuals covered under national health insurance.

The third option is to update physician profiles less often than annually. To maintain a system of usual and customary charges, profiles for each physician must be developed annually. When profiles are updated annually, physician's reimbursements for each procedure will increase at rates that depend on changes in usual and customary charges. If the profiles are not updated, increases in unit costs will occur only when the previous year's allowed charge was the actual billed charge, that is, when the actual charge was lower than the usual and customary. Otherwise, reimbursement rates would not increase, and the control method is identical to a freeze on reasonable charges.

With or without control mechanisms, usual and customary charge systems tend to sustain historical differences in charges and incomes among specialties and geographic areas —differences that may no longer be relevant. The profile of usual charges will be determined by a physician's own pricing behavior. The profile of customary charges will depend on pricing patterns of all physicians in the group, which may include physicians in widely differing specialties and geographic areas. The relative values given to different procedures will tend to change slowly and to reflect historical considerations, including the length of practice and the insurance coverage of a physician's clientele when the usual and customary charge system began.

FEE SCHEDULES

Some state Medicaid programs have recognized the administrative complexity and inflationary potential of a usual, customary, and reasonable charge reimbursement system. As an alternative, they have employed fee schedules—fixed sets of permissible charges for specific, well-defined procedures. Fee schedules are very often based on the California relative value schedule [8] (CRVS) or a similar relative value schedule that essentially gives the value of all procedures relative to some chosen standard procedure. For example, in the 1964 CRVS, a routine initial office visit by a new patient or a visit by a patient for a new but minor illness including history and examination is assigned a value of 2.0. An initial office visit with a complete diagnostic history and physical examination in the case of a new patient or a patient with a major illness, and including the initiation of diagnostic and treatment programs, is assigned a value of 6.0. Schedules will differ in the values given different procedures, but the principle is the same.

Once a system of relative values is established, the state then determines the price or conversion factor for the standard procedure and consequently determines all prices. The absolute level of fees can be quite generous, but typically fee schedules allow physicians little flexibility in setting fees and are generally regarded as a restrictive form of reimbursement. Several European countries prospectively determine the level of fees rather than reacting to the charge practices of physicians.[9] None uses a system resembling usual, customary, and reasonable charges.

Fee schedules have certain clear advantages over customary and prevailing systems. The principal advantage is that the fee schedule approach has much greater potential to control costs,[10] because the government at least gains controls over

[8] The Committee of Relative Value Studies, *1969 California Relative Value Studies* (San Francisco: California Medical Association, 1969).

[9] William Glaser, *Paying the Doctor Under National Health Insurance: Foreign Lessons for U.S.* (New York: Columbia University, 1976).

[10] Frank A. Sloan and Bruce Steinwald, "The Role of Health Insurance in the Physician's Services Market," *Inquiry* 12 (December 1975); John Holahan, "Physician Availability, Medical Care Reimbursement and the Delivery of Medical Services: Evidence from the Medicaid Program," *Journal of Human Resources,* Summer 1975.

unit prices. If the government were to structure relative values so that procedures were consistently priced relative to costs, it could also use fee schedules to control total expenditures without the statistical manipulations necessary to UCR controls. The government can freeze the fee schedule, reduce charges throughout the schedule, reduce some charges when a surplus of services exists while increasing or holding others constant, or permit a moderate rate of inflation. Because the rate of increase of conversion factors in a fee schedule is administratively determined, with the availability of government funds being one criterion for setting rates, the mechanism for freezing or reducing rates is inherent in the payment method.

Fee schedules also help achieve purposes other than cost control. Unlike usual and customary charge profiles, which reinforce what may be undesirable relative unit prices established over time, fee schedules permit the state to achieve certain redistributive objectives. Fee schedules can be used to change the relative values given different procedures and to redistribute income among specialties and among physicians in geographic areas.

The main difficulty with fee schedules is that they do not permit variation among physicians in absolute or relative fees. It is hard to incorporate adjustments to the fee schedule for higher-quality service because there are no tangible measures of quality. Higher absolute levels of fees could be permitted for board-certified relative to non-board-certified specialists. But this practice would not capture many aspects of quality that a market, and perhaps a UCR, system might reward. As a result, unusual effort may be discouraged. Ensuring that necessary care beyond the normal level of effort for a given procedure is rendered requires detailed procedure coding systems or an exceptions process—such as procedure code modifiers or separate reports justifying higher charges. Great detail in defining procedures permits physicians to respond to unsatisfactory rates of fee increase by shifting to higher-valued procedures. Physicians can use the procedure coding system to limit program control over fees. Frequent use of an exceptions process also undermines the fee schedule's capacity to control costs.

A second problem with fee schedules is that an NHI program might reimburse some physicians more than they would

have charged for certain procedures. This problem might be
avoided if fee schedules were used as the maximum permissible
charges rather than as the sole reimbursement rate. But the
program would then have to check all billings against the fee
schedule to establish individual reimbursement levels, thereby
eliminating one of the main advantages of fee schedules in the
first place.

Third, although administering a fee schedule is less complex and less costly than properly maintaining a usual and
customary charge system, the expense is not inconsequential.
Determining a schedule of relative values is an intellectually
demanding exercise, as one can quickly conclude from brief
perusal of a recent California relative value schedule. It is
necessary to survey periodically physicians' actual charges
or to rate a large number of procedures by the skill and time
required to perform them. In the latter case, committees,
including medical society officials, must be established to determine the relative value structure. As innovations occur and
the content of medical science changes, new procedures are
introduced and the relative values of others change. Methods of
changing the relative value structure must be established to
rapidly accommodate change. Other problems that arise in
usual and customary charge systems must also be addressed
in the administration of a fee schedule. Defining procedures,
for example, is itself a difficult task. Should the reimbursement for surgery apply to outpatient and inpatient visits before and after surgical services? Should supervisory care for
nursing home patients be reimbursed on a per visit or per
month basis? Committees must be convened for special rulings
on unusual cases.

Finally, an acceptable rate of increase in the schedule must
be determined. Possible criteria include wage rates, cost-of-
living indices, practice costs, and availability of government
funds. The rate of increase in conversion factors is critical
in the success of a fee schedule arrangement; either the rate
will be determined unilaterally by the government or it will
be negotiated between the government and medical societies.
The critical difference between fee schedules and usual and
customary charges—that annual rates of increase in fee
schedules are either administratively dictated or negotiated,

but not exogenously determined by physicians' behavior—necessitates implementation of a satisfactory process for updating the schedule.

REQUIRING PHYSICIAN PARTICIPATION IN NATIONAL HEALTH INSURANCE

Even if fee-for-service payment systems should limit what the national health insurance program would pay for services, these systems might not control what physicians charged their patients because insurance programs would not necessarily require physicians to accept the charges permitted by the NHI program as payment in full. National health insurance proposals differ in the degree to which physicians would be required to accept program-determined allowable charges as payment in full. The alternatives include such arrangements as assignment billing under Medicare, choice of participation status as proposed under CHIP and the Kennedy-Mills plan, or all-or-nothing arrangements like those employed by several European programs.

In Medicare's assigned billing arrangement, physicians can choose to accept or reject "assignment" on each individual procedure financed by Medicare. If "assignment" is accepted, the physician is spared the risk of noncollection, but the physician must accept as payment in full the reasonable charge for that procedure regardless of the actual charge billed. Under this arrangement, the patient pays the 20 percent cost-sharing amount on the reasonable charge (following payment of the deductible). A physician who bills on a nonassignment basis is responsible for billing the patient, who then is reimbursed by Medicare. Under the nonassignment alternative, Medicare still reimburses only 80 percent of the reasonable charge (following payment of the deductible), but the physician can bill and require the patient to pay the full amount of the actual charge—in which case, the patient share of the bill may exceed 20 percent. The patient's outlay is equal to 20 percent of the reasonable charge plus the full amount by which the actual exceeds the reasonable charge.

It is difficult to control fee increases under assignment billing arrangements because such arrangements permit physicians to shift costs to patients; that is, physicians can avoid limits on reasonable charges by refusing to accept assignment and, instead, billing patients directly at higher levels. Physicians clearly risk lower collection ratios, but this risk can be offset by the income from higher charges. Assignment billing also may permit and even encourage physicians to discriminate in their delivery of care to patients unable to pay higher amounts. The system encourages physicians to view patients differently, and to provide a higher quality and more comprehensive range of services to those able and willing to pay more than Medicare's reasonable charges. The major advantage of the assignment billing arrangement relative to the alternatives presented next is that it allows physicians to seek compensation for provision of higher-quality care.

An alternative to the assignment approach under national health insurance would be to require physicians to choose the terms of their participation in the NHI plan. Each physician could choose to accept rates determined by the government's fee schedule as full payment and to collect from the government. Alternatively, physicians could bill patients directly at levels constrained only by the patients' ability and willingness to pay. Patients would be reimbursed by the program in amounts equal only to the allowed fee less any cost sharing. Unlike the assignment approach, this system would not permit physicians to choose a billing method on a claim-by-claim basis. For example, it would not permit physicians to accept assignment on large bills, for which collection from patients might be difficult, and to refuse assignment on small bills for which the probability of collection is much higher. Instead, physicians would have to make a more drastic choice. They would have to trade off full collection of all bills (the advantage of dealing with the government) against the higher income on some share of their services (the advantage of direct patient billing). Dealing with government also has the advantage of eliminating physicians' responsibility for collecting cost sharing, thereby reducing their administrative tasks.

Most Canadian provinces employ this system. The plan pays physicians 85 percent to 90 percent of the fee schedule; physicians may choose to bill patients directly and attempt to collect the remaining 10 percent to 15 percent, but patients will be reimbursed only at the fee schedule level. In British Columbia, physicians may "extra bill" up to or above the fee schedule if they have obtained written consent of their patients. Extra billing is not common anywhere in Canada, and physician participation in the plans is high. The elimination of "bad debts" has had a very positive effect on physicians' incomes.[11]

The likelihood of physicians' full participation can be increased by limiting the amounts paid to *patients* who use nonparticipating physicians. The French national health insurance system employs this approach. Patients of physicians choosing to bill patients can collect only 60 percent to 80 percent of the fee schedule from the plan. As a result, all but 4 percent of physicians participate.[12] Even more stringent would be an all-or-nothing arrangement, in which patients received no reimbursement for services from nonparticipating physicians. All-or-nothing arrangements could take two forms: one would require physicians to opt in or out of the program for all their patients, essentially requiring that practices be either all public or all private. Another would permit physicians to participate for some of their patients and maintain a private practice in addition—a public and private option.

An all-or-nothing arrangement of the first kind is employed in Quebec; patients who consult nonparticipating physicians can receive no reimbursement for the plan. As a result, only 2 percent of the physicians do not participate.[13] A precedent for such an arrangement in this country exists in the public school system. All citizens support the public system through tax payments even if they choose to enroll their children in private schools. If this system is to be adopted for national health insurance, it is essential that the public system dominate the private. If the private system were to remain large, its members might capture control of the political process, perhaps causing limitations in funding of the NHI program.

The effect of any participation arrangement on the program's ability to control costs and provide access to high-quality care would clearly depend on how many physicians

[11] Robert G. Evans, "Beyond the Medical Marketplace: Expenditure, Utilization and Pricing of Insured Health Care in Canada" in Spyros Andreopoulos, ed., *National Health Insurance: Can We Learn From Canada?* (New York: John Wiley and Sons, 1975).

[12] Glaser, *Paying the Doctor Under National Health Insurance.*

[13] Ibid.

chose the full-payment alternative. Even with the least stringent approach, in which program reimbursement would be the same for participating and nonparticipating physicians, we would expect a higher percentage of participation than the current percentage of assigned claims under Medicare (about 51 percent).[14] Eliminating the claim-by-claim choice would increase the risk of the direct-patient-billing option, and thereby would reduce its appeal to physicians. Only physicians with a substantial upper-income clientele would be likely to choose direct patient billing. The proportion of such physicians would probably be greater here than in Canada, because U.S. incomes are higher. The percentage of participating physicians also would vary with the absolute level of physician charges, the specialty, or the type of services typically provided. The greater the proportion of participating physicians, the greater would be the program's ability to control charges and the less the physicians' opportunity or desire to discriminate against low-income persons.

Pressure to participate would obviously be greater under all-or-nothing arrangements, and greater if physicians had to choose between all-public or all-private practices. The latter option would have the most negative effect on physician incomes and autonomy, and therefore would be most strongly resisted. Because it also might inhibit patients' ability to obtain preferential treatment, high-income individuals might oppose this approach. This opposition makes enactment of the most restrictive arrangement, all-or-nothing with no private practice on the side, highly unlikely. Although political acceptance of the proposed all-or-nothing arrangement appears unlikely, it would, if enacted, offer greater potential for cost control than would more moderate arrangements. Given the tax burden inevitable with enactment of a national health insurance program coupled with the progressive income tax system, relatively few patients could afford the luxury of financing care outside the system. This would be particularly true if medical expenses were no longer tax deductible. Thus, even if physicians could operate public and private practices, private practice would probably be relatively small.

Even if political forces did not defeat enactment of an all-or-nothing arrangement, substantial pressure might be mounted

[14] Marion Gornick, "Ten Years of Medicare: Impact on the Covered Population," *Social Security Bulletin* 39 (July 1976):14.

to make fees under such an arrangement reasonably generous. Serious efforts toward unionization of providers of medical care might be expected, with serious threats of physician strikes against the system. Such threats might persuade the government to make substantial payment concessions in order to avoid disruption or widespread disaffection with the program. Equal access to the system would break down only if substantial numbers of physicians were able to practice successfully outside the system through treatment of the high-income population, or if side payments to physicians for preferential treatment became commonplace. If queue jumping through supplementary payments were to become an accepted, though illegal, procedure, objectives of equal access could be defeated. Evidence on which population groups most often appeared in queues should be simple to accumulate and should permit monitoring of such practices.

Despite their potential advantage, stringent participation arrangements could have adverse effects on the quality of care, particularly if fees were tightly controlled. Such arrangements would encourage physicians with excellent reputations to practice outside the program; as a result, their services would become unavailable to many people. Strict and binding controls on charges could discourage other physicians and result in a level of effort below that required to consistently maintain quality standards. Professional pride and medical ethics would operate to lessen these incentives. Physician responses to tight controls are treated in greater detail in the next section. Here it is sufficient to note that the threat to quality of care posed by tight controls could seriously threaten public acceptance of the national health insurance program. As a result, it is unlikely that strict participation arrangements will be adopted or, if they should be adopted, it is unlikely that fees will be rigidly controlled. All things considered, adoption of a more moderate participation arrangement seems more feasible and perhaps more desirable.

PHYSICIANS' RESPONSES TO FEE CONTROLS

Even if most physicians were to agree to accept government rates of payment, physicians' responses to fee constraints could impede cost containment. Unlike most providers of goods or services, physicians can influence the demand for their own services. If, in response to reduced fees, physicians could increase the volume of services they provided in order to maintain their real incomes, it is unlikely that a system of fee controls would be effective.

Analysis of physician responses to fee controls is complicated by the fact that physicians appear to be inefficient in allocating available resources and do not minimize the cost of service provision. Physicians apparently prefer to accept losses of income to using their time to organize efficiently various available inputs such as paraprofessional personnel and thereby minimize production costs. There is evidence that the efficiency of physicians' practices could be increased through less use of physicians' time and greater reliance on people with lower levels of training.[15] It can be argued, however, that use of less-skilled personnel and less physician time would reduce service quality. A reduction in inputs per unit of service (which would include substitution of less-skilled for highly skilled personnel) would reduce quality only if a less accurate diagnosis or a less appropriate treatment resulted. If there were no change in the accuracy of diagnosis and the appropriateness of treatment, efficiency would have increased. To summarize, physicians' responses will depend on trade-offs among four variables: income, leisure, practice efficiency, and service quality. Because research on physician behavior is relatively new, it is difficult to make accurate predictions about the effects of fee reductions.

Under a fee control system, physicians could maintain their current levels of income by increasing the number of services produced, by billing for more complex services than actually rendered, by shifting to a more remunerative mix of patients, or by adopting some combination of these methods. Increases in the delivery of services could be accomplished by reducing leisure, increasing practice efficiency, reducing the quality of the services provided, or some combination of the three. Physicians could also accept some loss of income from controls on charges in exchange for an increase in their leisure time. Or they could accept some loss of income but increase the volume

---

[15] For example, see Uwe Reinhardt, "A Production Function for Physician Services," *Review of Economics and Statistics*, February 1972.

of services provided by increasing practice efficiency or reducing service quality.

Clearly, options that maintain the quality and quantity of services are most socially desirable. Whether quality would be maintained probably would depend on how averse physicians are to providing low-quality care. If this aversion proved to be strong, and yet physicians desired to maintain current standards of living (that is, current levels of income and leisure), then increased efficiency could result from fee controls. Physicians would then respond by increasing their services without sacrificing quality.

Unfortunately, little empirical evidence exists on the effects of fee schedules on hours of work and numbers of services provided. Recent research on the effect of physicians' prices on hours worked suggests that physicians react to fee increases, when fees are at generally low levels, by increasing work effort. As fees increase further, hours of work stabilize and then decline. Vahovich[16] has estimated that for 23 percent of general practitioners, 21 percent of internists, and 31 percent of surgeons, increases in hourly earnings have the effect of reducing hours of work. It could well be that for such physicians, controls on charges would actually increase work effort. Vahovich also estimates that physicians at average income levels will not change work effort in response to small changes in earnings. Thus, controls on fees could have no effect or a slightly positive effect on hours of services provided by physicians.

The effect of fee controls on hours of work is not the same as the effect on the volume and mix of services provided. Through shortening visits or delegating tasks, physicians could increase their service volume without necessarily changing their hours of work. Interesting evidence on physicians' reactions to fee controls has been provided by the Canadian experience. Marmor[17] and Evans[18] cite evidence of increased billing in Canada following imposition of fee schedules in national health insurance. Evans in particular has found evidence of significant increases in per capita expenditures on physicians'

---

[16] Stephen G. Vahovich, "Physicians' Supply Decisions by Specialty: 2SLS Model," *Industrial Relations* 16 (February 1977).

[17] Theodore R. Marmor, "Can the U.S. Learn from Canada?" in *National Health Insurance: Can We Learn From Canada?*

[18] Evans, "Beyond the Medical Marketplace."

services when fee schedules were controlled. In Saskatchewan, between 1964 and 1971, physician fee schedules rose only 33.9 percent, while total expenditures on physician services increased by 62.3 percent. Three provinces, British Columbia, Manitoba, and Nova Scotia, allowed no increase in physician fee schedules from 1969 through 1971. In that two-year period, per capita expenditures on physician services increased by 18.5 percent in British Columbia, 23.8 percent in Manitoba, and 33.4 percent in Nova Scotia. Part of the increase was due to the establishment of fee schedules that exceeded actual fees. Some of the increase in per capita expenditures, however, also seemed to be the result of the provision of more services or the provision of, or billing for more, complex services than had been the case in earlier periods.

Physician responses to the Economic Stabilization Program (ESP) have recently been explored in studies at The Urban Institute.[19] The ESP was announced in August 1971 as part of the U.S. government's effort to slow the national rate of inflation. Beginning in July 1972, strict administrative controls were applied to Medicare's reasonable charges, that is, the amount Medicare pays physicians for any particular service.[20] Changes in physicians' billed charges to all patients were mandated to fall within specified guidelines. Price control authorities, however, relied on physicians' voluntary compliance coupled with patient complaints of price increases in excess of stated limits.

In order to assess ESP's impact on physicians' charges and on services provided to Medicare beneficiaries, claims data were assembled for a random sample of 1,396 general practitioners, 786 general surgeons, and 942 internists in California. The authors formed two sets of price indices for physicians' private charges and their Medicare reasonable fees. One set used base-year (1972) quantity weights to combine procedure-specific prices. (More than two hundred procedures were included in the calculations.) The second set used current-year quantity weights. This approach permits year-to-year shifts in

---

[19] John Holahan and William Scanlon, *Price Controls, Physician Fees and Physician Incomes* (Washington, D.C.: The Urban Institute, 1978). Jack Hadley and Robert Lee, "Toward a Physician Payment Policy; Evidence from the Economic Stabilization Program," *Policy Science* 10 (1978–1979) :105–20.

[20] In Medicare terminology, "reasonable" charges are the lowest of the actual billed charge, the customary charge, or the prevailing charge.

Table 3

PHYSICIANS' BILLED CHARGES AND MEDICARE
REASONABLE FEE PRICE INDICES IN CALIFORNIA
1972–75

	1972	*1973*	*1974*	*1975*
	Actual Charge	*Index (1972=1.000)*		
A. Base-Year Weights				
1. Billed charges				
General practice	$ 8.804	1.029	1.094	1.229
General surgery	14.986	1.027	1.092	1.225
Internal medicine	12.623	1.043	1.114	1.239
2. Medicare reasonable fees				
General practice	$ 8.073	1.011	1.024	1.098
General surgery	13.696	1.011	1.032	1.089
Internal medicine	11.569	1.017	1.042	1.107
B. Current-Year Weights				
1. Billed charges				
General practice		1.057	1.130	1.320
General surgery		1.072	1.139	1.315
Internal medicine		1.040	1.119	1.264
2. Medicare reasonable fees				
General practice		1.041	1.061	1.196
General surgery		1.058	1.080	1.182
Internal medicine		1.033	1.067	1.158

Sources: John Holahan and William Scanlon, *Price Controls, Physician Fees and Physician Incomes from Medicare and Medicaid,* The Urban Institute Publication URI 21800, April 1978, pp. 31–32, 44–45.

the mix of services provided. Table 3 shows the results of the calculations. Panel A presents the billed and reasonable charge indices computed with base-year weights. Panel B recomputes the indices with current-year weights.

Panel A suggests that ESP was reasonably successful in limiting the growth in physicians' billed charges. Medicare reasonable fees were even more constrained, presumably because they were under direct administrative control. When controls were lifted in 1974, the rate of increase more than doubled. This was the case for all three specialties studied. Panel B, conversely, suggests that ESP's impact on prices was perhaps not so dramatic. Physicians appear to have shifted to a higher-priced mix of services. For each of the three specialties, the 1972–73 price increase exceeded the ESP target of 2.5 percent per year. The 1974 and 1975 billed charge indices also suggest significantly greater jumps in prices than those reported by a constant weight index. These effects were even more dramatic for the Medicare reasonable fee index. For general practice and general surgery, the constant weight index understates real price increases by more than half. Thus, the figures reported in Panel B suggest that physicians were able to evade ESP price constraints by shifting to a more expensive mix of services.

Table 4 reports the numbers of services provided by physicians and gross payments made by Medicare to the sample physicians. Between 1972 and 1974, the number of Medicare services provided grew by about 10 percent per year for each specialty. In 1975, however, the number of services provided by general practitioners actually dropped. General surgeons' and internists' Medicare output continued to grow, but at much slower rates than during the previous two years. The evidence seems consistent with a demand-creation interpretation. The quantity of services provided went up when Medicare reasonable fees were under relatively tight controls, and fell off when controls were lifted and Medicare reasonable fees were free to increase, which they did. Finally, Panel B indicates that physicians' gross payments from Medicare were largely unaffected by the Economic Stabilization Program. If

Table 4

NUMBERS OF MEDICARE SERVICES AND GROSS MEDICARE PAYMENTS MADE TO PHYSICIANS IN CALIFORNIA, 1972–75

	1972	1973	1974	1975
		(Ratio to 1972)		
A. Numbers of Medicare Services (All Procedures)				
General practice	192,823	1.094	1.186	1.093
General surgery	40,257	1.109	1.214	1.230
Internal medicine	151,026	1.087	1.246	1.277
B. Gross Medicare Payments				
General practice	$1,742,408	1.119	1.258	1.303
General surgery	1,414,635	1.101	1.273	1.389
Internal medicine	1,773,577	1.129	1.347	1.513

Source: Holahan and Scanlon, *Price Controls, Physician Fees and Physician Incomes from Medicare and Medicaid*, pp. 68–70, 85–87.

anything, the end of ESP appears to have coincided with a slight slowdown in the rate of increase in payments. The California results in particular indicate a strong physician response to temporary price controls. What would have occurred under permanent controls is unknown.

Evans and Wolfsen have recently provided additional evidence from Canada to support the argument that physicans generate demand in response to fee controls.[21] But their evidence also suggests limits to this behavior.

As Table 5 shows, expenditures per capita for physician services increased at an average annual rate of 8.9 percent between fiscal 1972 and 1976. The average annual increase in the fee schedule in Canada during this period was 3.3 percent. A 3.9 percent increase in the physician supply contributed to the growth in expenditures. The most telling factor, however, is the 1.5 percent annual increase in services per physician. The result is an annual increase in utilization of 5.4 percent per capita. Some of this increase may be a response to shorter waiting time or more convenient access to care; the increase also could reflect more care provided to previously underserved populations. Evans and Wolfsen argue that the increase chiefly reflects creation of demand to offset fee controls. Despite controls on fee schedule increases and substantial growth in the supply of physicians, services per physician did not fall; as a result, utilization per capita, and thus expenditures per capita, increased.

Whatever the true explanation, it should be noted that medical expenditures per physician increased more slowly than did the Canadian consumer price index.[22] One would expect that if physicians did have target incomes, the targets would be, at a minimum, to maintain real incomes. Canadian physicians were clearly not able to do so. Chapter 3 of this book also presents evidence that real incomes of Canadian physicians have fallen in every province since the advent of national health insurance.

---

[21] Robert G. Evans and Alan D. Wolfsen, "Moving the Target to Hit the Bullet: Generation of Utilization by Physicians in Canada," paper presented at the National Bureau of Economic Research Conference on the Economics of Physician and Patient Behavior, Stanford, California, January 27–28, 1978, Table II.

[22] *The Economic Report of the President* (Washington, D.C.: U.S. Government Printing Office, 1978), p. 378.

Table 5

PERCENTAGE INCREASES BY PROVINCE, FY 1972–FY 1976, SELECTED FACTORS IN
MEDICAL CARE INSURANCE, AVERAGE ANNUAL RATES

	Provincial Medical Expenditure per Capita [1]	Provincial Medical Expenditure per Physician	Fee Schedule	Utilization per Physician [2]	Physicians per Capita	Utilization per Capita [3]	Physician Relative Income (1971) [4]
	(Percentage Increases)	(Percentage Increases)	(Percentage Increases)	(Percentage Increases)	(Percentage Increases)	(Percentage Increases)	(Percent)
CANADA	8.9	4.8	3.3	1.5	3.9	5.5	100.0
Newfoundland	13.6	6.2	5.5	0.7	7.0	7.7	97.0
Prince Edward Island	8.0	4.2	4.1	0.2	3.6	3.8	90.2
Nova Scotia	11.0	6.7	8.7	−1.8	4.0	2.1	86.0
New Brunswick	9.0	3.6	3.1	0.5	5.2	5.7	95.4
Quebec	10.2	4.0	—	4.0	6.0	10.2	95.0
Ontario	7.5	4.4	2.9	1.5	3.0	4.5	108.5
Manitoba	5.5	2.1	2.9	−0.8	3.3	2.5	99.5
Saskatchewan	10.0	5.5	5.8	−0.3	4.3	3.0	89.6
Alberta	6.1	4.0	4.1	−0.2	2.0	1.8	109.4
British Columbia	10.5	9.0	8.9	0.1	2.3	2.4	87.8

Source: Robert G. Evans and Alan D. Wolfsen, "Moving the Target to Hit the Bullet: Generation of Utilization by Physicians in Canada," paper presented at the National Bureau of Economic Research Conference on the Economics of Physician and Patient Behavior, Stanford, California, January 27–28, 1978, Table II.

1. Increase in provincial medical expenditure per physician multiplied by increase in physicians per capita.
2. Increases in provincial medical expenditures per physician divided by increase in fee schedule (with unity added to numerator and denominator, and rounded).
3. Increase in utilization per physician multiplied by increase in physicians per capita.
4. Average gross income of physician in province divided by national average gross income per physician.

The Canadian experience indicates that although generation of demand can be a problem, there are natural limits to it. It could be argued that patients probably would not submit to an increasing number of repeat visits, diagnostic tests, and surgical procedures year after year. It also seems unlikely that physicians would continually engage in the longer hours and task delegation necessary to continually expand services over an extended period of time. But the fact that physicians in Canada, faced with fee schedules and an increasing number of physicians, were unable to maintain real incomes does not mean that utilization per physician will not increase in the long run. Service utilization could continue to increase even in the long run, because of changing technology and changes in styles of practice. These rates of increase may be socially unacceptable even if they are not sufficient to maintain physicians' real incomes.

It is important to note, too, that increases in service provision would not be uniform across procedures. First, patients are more readily influenced to consume laboratory services than, say, to return for periodic reexaminations or to submit to risky procedures. Second, physicians' behavior is subject to certain ethical and quality constraints. Some medical procedures are vital for patient health; others are inherently interesting to physicians; still others may increase the likelihood of malpractice claims. Procedures of these types are unlikely to be affected by financial incentives.

Finally and perhaps most important, the relationship between fees and the marginal costs of service production is not uniform among all procedures. As a result, it is more lucrative for physicians to increase the provision of some services than of others. Hughes and others found that among surgical procedures, relative fees per hundred minutes of operating room time varied from 76.92 for hemorrhoidectomies to 29.88 for breast biopsies.[23] Blumberg found that specialists generated more revenue per hour on hospital visits than on office visits, because of the higher fees and the greater number of visits per hour.[24] In addition, the physician has lower overhead

---

[23] Edward Hughes, "Surgical Workloads in a Community Practice," *Surgery* 7 (1972) : 315–72.

[24] Mark S. Blumberg, M.D., "Rational Provider Prices: An Incentive for Improved Health Delivery," in George K. Chacko, ed., *Health Handbook* (Amsterdam: North Holland Publishing Co., 1978), p. 33.

expenses for services provided in a hospital. Clearly, this comparison assumes the hospital visits occur during regular rounds and do not require a special trip.

Blumberg concluded from a comprehensive survey of the literature that fees for many procedures did not reflect the relative costs of provision and, as a result, inappropriate incentives were widespread.

> Current relative values seem to favor procedures over more traditional physician activities such as history-taking and physical examinations. Laboratory and x-ray diagnostic studies are almost certainly overpriced on the average. Some surgical procedures are overpriced, but it is also likely that many are underpriced.[25]

Blumberg continues:

> There are many reasons why fees are not equated with costs. Some physician services had been systematically underpriced in times when physicians had considerable slack and there was little third party coverage. There was an attempt to encourage new patients through underpricing of initial office visits and complete physical examinations. In any event, the marginal cost to a physician for his time when he has slack is negligible and any marginal revenue is welcome. There are also reasons for systematic overcharges for some services by physicians. Newly developed procedures tend to have their relative value established soon after introduction. When technological improvements occur, the original high price is maintained even though production costs fall. The relative prices for health care services are extremely sticky. This is probably the main reason for the high profitability of diagnostic x-rays, electrocardiographs, blood chemistry tests and even injections.[26]

Limiting Creation of Demand

Policy makers are not without options to discourage or limit physicians' creation of demand for their services. Fees can be set to match the costs of efficiently produced services,

---

[25] Ibid., p. 50.
[26] Ibid., p. 49.

appropriateness of services used can be reviewed, broader definitions of services can be established, budgets for all physician services can be fixed, or fee increases can be tied to aggregate changes in physician incomes. Each option will be explored in turn.

Setting Fees in Relation to Costs. The first policy option is to structure fee schedules so that fees for all procedures reflect the costs of services when produced in a technically and economically efficient manner. The obvious difficulty with this option is that the cost of producing individual services in physicians' offices is extremely difficult to calculate. The method of producing services that is "optimal" in one practice setting may be completely infeasible in some other setting. Thus, structuring fees on the basis of costs in an economically efficient practice setting could prove inequitable elsewhere. The value of physicians' time is a cost-of-service provision, but this value varies considerably among physicians.

Despite the fact that precise determination of fee schedules is a formidable task, it is possible to make much better approximations of the relationship between fees and marginal costs than is now done. Reducing fees for most diagnostic services relative to other services would be an excellent first step. Several European countries pay the full fee for the first hospital or nursing home visit by a physician on a given day, and pay a substantially reduced fee for subsequent visits on the same day. Such a procedure should considerably reduce the incentives for "gang visiting."[27] Although establishing the "right" fee schedule poses many difficulties, it is not essential that fees be set in relation to cost from the very beginning. Undervalued or overvalued procedures would probably be reflected in utilization rates and could be periodically renegotiated in bargaining sessions.

Utilization Review. The second approach is to limit the provision of medically unnecessary and economically unwarranted services through utilization review. Utilization control through a variety of review mechanisms receives detailed attention in Chapter 9. This chapter only briefly discusses the merits of utilization review as a policy to reduce creation of demand for services by physicians. Utilization review basically involves comparing claims for services against preestablished norms or

---

[27] Glaser, *Paying the Doctor Under National Health Insurance.*

standards of appropriateness. When claims made for services exceed standards, physicians are required to provide information justifying the large number of services rendered. Inability to provide satisfactory evidence of the appropriateness of the service results in denial of payment. Utilization review has gained prominence as a mechanism for regulating the use of hospital inpatient care. It has not been applied on a large scale to ambulatory care, and there are a number of difficulties with such application.

First, national health insurance would pose the awesome task of establishing rigorous standards for many kinds of cases in which appropriate care will vary with the patient's age, medical history, and several other factors. Moreover, it is hard to find agreement among physicians on appropriate norms even for similar cases. Hence, utilization review might prove useful only for certain high-cost or high-frequency procedures for which the payoff is likely to be high and the potential for affecting utilization through economic incentives is likely to be low.

A second major problem in the implementation of utilization review as a mechanism for controlling health care costs is that incentives faced by the reviewing organization must be identical with those of the agency paying for services. The mandate of utilization review mechanisms in the past has not been merely to reduce the amount of excessive or unnecessary services provided, but to increase the quality of care for individuals whose care is inadequate. In the process of developing norms of appropriate care, standards can easily be set at a level which, in a resource allocation sense, is either too high or too low. If standards or norms are established by physicians as has been the case with Professional Standards Review Organizations, the decisions that will be made are likely to be based on medical, not economic, criteria. As a result, considerations of scarcity are likely to be ignored. Establishing standards of appropriateness that are neither too high nor too low requires consideration of both sets of criteria.

Finally, the costs of monitoring utilization patterns in ambulatory care settings are likely to be high relative to the savings from claims denials or services deterred. In contrast to inpatient care, for which the cost of a hospital stay is very large, ambulatory care typically consists of a large number of inexpensive discrete services. The resources required to make determinations of appropriateness are likely to be sub-

stantial despite the small average size (in dollars) of the claim.
Again this conclusion suggests a selective application of utilization review methods.

Global Definitions of Services. One important factor contributing to "demand creation" is the incentives generated by accepted systems of procedure coding terminology. One of the
most widely used systems, the California relative value schedule, has a large number of categories of office visits, laboratory
and radiological services, and surgical procedures. A physician
using the California RVS can bill for eight different types of
office visits for a new patient, twelve types of office visits for
an established patient, eight types of hospital visits, and seven
types of nursing home visits. The variety of office visits among
which the physician can choose are shown in Table 6. Each
will have a different fee attached.

Such narrow definitions of procedures can cause several
problems. First, the procedure coding terminology itself offers
physicians an effective means of raising their prices in a time
of controls. Physicians can react to controls on their charges
by billing more frequently for more expensive types of visits.[28]
Holahan and Scanlon found that procedure coding inflation
approximately doubled the actual rate of fee inflation during
the Economic Stabilization Program.[29] Second, treating ancillary services, which are intrinsic to the diagnosis in most
physician-patient encounters, as independent additional services encourages both inflated bills and more services.

One way to alter these incentives is to reduce substantially
the number of types of visits for which a physician can bill.
For example, in the extreme, a system could permit only one
charge for an office visit. The allowed amount could be calculated to be 10 percent or 15 percent below the cost of the
average visit plus the cost of the average number of tests
(using the median rather than mean value). The objective
is to set one fee and to assume that the excess cost to the
physician when the required services exceed the fee on average
will balance the windfall gains in simpler cases when the fee

[28] "Effects of the 1969 California Relative Value Studies on Costs of
Physicians' Services Under SMI," *Health Insurance Statistics* 69, by
W. I. Sobaski, SSA, Office of Research and Statistics, June 20, 1975.
[29] Holahan and Scanlon, *Price Controls, Physician Fees and Physician
Incomes from Medicare and Medicaid.*

Table 6

ALTERNATIVE OFFICE VISIT DEFINITIONS IN THE CALIFORNIA RELATIVE VALUE SCHEDULE

Office Visits

New Patient

90000	*Brief* evaluation, history, examination and/or treatment
90010	Initial *limited* history and physical examination, including initiation of diagnostic and treatment program
90015	Initial *intermediate* history and physical examination, including initiation of diagnostic and treatment program
90020	Initial *comprehensive* history and physical examination, including initiation of diagnostic and treatment program, adult
90021	Adolescent
90022	Late Childhood
90023	Early Childhood
90024	Infant

Established Patient

90030	*Minimal* service (e.g., injection, immunization, minimal dressing) (independent procedure) (See also 90700, 90705)
90040	*Brief* examination, evaluation and/or treatment, same or new illness
90050	*Limited* examination, evaluation, and/or treatment, same or new illness
90060	*Intermediate* examination, evaluation and/or treatment, same or new illness
90070	*Extended* reexamination or reevaluation
90080	*Comprehensive* reexamination or reevaluation, adult
90081	Adolescent
90082	Late Childhood
90083	Early Childhood
90084	Infant
90088	Periodic or annual examination, adult

exceeds the costs of services provided. An exceptions process would be established under which a physician who performed an unusually large number of tests or other diagnostic services could, upon evidence of the complexity of the case, receive a larger fee. The exceptions process should be sufficiently cumbersome for the physician that it would not be used routinely. Such an arrangement should cover an overwhelming majority of patient-physician encounters. It should be designed so that, over time, physicians would be treated equitably and, therefore, would find the system acceptable. Glaser reports that the French have gradually moved to simplify their procedure terminology, reimbursing for one office visit, one home visit, inclusion of twenty days of postoperative care after surgery, and the like.[30]

An alternative is to define different visit codes in time units; for example, a brief exam would equal fifteen to twenty minutes, and so on. Both the physician and patient would understand the meaning of the procedure coding terminology. A physician's ability to bill for more extended visits would be substantially reduced because patients would be better informed of the nature of the service. The increases in service complexity that have been associated with reclassification of services would be reduced. One problem in implementing this arrangement would be the treatment of time spent by ancillary personnel.

A final approach would be to adopt more all-inclusive procedure classifications or "case payments." Fees for surgical procedures could include all pre- and postoperative visits inside or outside the hospital, as well as all ancillary services. This practice is now common for maternity care and would be extended to other types of cases. Most of the incentives in the capitation schemes described earlier would apply to case payments. Physicians would face incentives to be efficient in their use of manpower and other resources, such as ancillary services, in the provision of care. Unnecessary services would be discouraged. Physicians would gain when a patient required few services and would suffer financially when the patient required a substantial amount of care. Cream skimming, or selection of "easy" cases, would be encouraged, and "difficult" cases would most likely be avoided. As in capitation arrangements, incentives also exist to sacrifice quality. Monitoring quality requires consumer information (if consumers have sufficient information, they can avoid physicians with reputations for poor-quality service), medical record audits, and a system of meaningful penalties.

Fixed Budgets. Another alternative to limit physicians' creation of demand for their services would be for the national health insurance program to establish a fixed budget for all

---

[30] Glaser, *Paying the Doctor Under National Health Insurance.*

physician services. Physicians would continue to be paid on a fee-for-service basis, but the total funds available for physician services would be established in advance. Note that the amount available for all physician services would be capped; individual physicians' earnings would be directly limited. Caps on individuals' incomes would provide obvious incentives to physicians to cease working after they had reached the maximum. Reimbursement for services would be determined by a fee schedule. If total billings exceeded the allocated budget, proportionate reductions in total payments to all physicians would be made. Physicians themselves, not the government, would bear the burden of excessive service provision. Such a system has been employed in the health insurance system in West Germany.[31]

Coupling fixed budgets with fee-for-service reimbursements presents several problems. First, the appropriate amount to be budgeted for physician services may be difficult to determine. The current level of expenditures for physician services provides no guidance because it is the dissatisfaction with current experience that created the need for reform. Setting appropriate budget levels for different parts of the country would require not only detailed information on morbidity and utilization patterns, but also informed judgments on the appropriateness of particular utilization patterns that deviate from acceptable norms. That is, urban areas should not receive larger budgets than rural areas on the basis of higher utilization rates if those higher rates reflect excessive provision of services where physician-population ratios are high.

Second, in a fixed-budget arrangement, all physicians would have an incentive to overprovide, because gains from overprovision would typically exceed the losses from the pro rata reductions. That is, those physicians responsible for excessive provision would be remunerated for those services, while pro rata reductions would apply to all physicians in proportion to total billings. The program or physicians themselves would have to carefully monitor utilization patterns to control unnecessary services and create equity in physician remuneration. Failure to monitor the system carefully would probably create resentment toward the program on the part of those

---

[31] William Glaser, *Paying the Doctor* (Baltimore: The Johns Hopkins Press, 1970).

physicians who had not abused it. This problem led to disenchantment with and abandonment of a fixed-budget system in West Germany.[32]

Third, an exceptions process would be necessary to treat unusual occurrences such as epidemics or natural disasters. It would also be necessary to establish a mechanism capable of equitably compensating physicians for events beyond their control, such as rapid increases in malpractice insurance costs.

Finally, if the budget allocated to physician services were clearly low, physicians would probably refer patients to other providers, most likely hospital inpatient and outpatient departments. Costs for the same services in these settings would probably be higher than costs for care in office settings. Thus these services must be carefully monitored, too. Alternatively, physicians might be less likely to participate in the program, thereby reducing the availability of private physician care and the value of national health insurance to the general public.

Fee Indexing. A variant of the fixed-budget approach is the tying of fee increases to aggregate changes in physician incomes (fee indexing). This approach avoids the allocation difficulties associated with the fixed budget by limiting rates of increase in current expenditures. Once a decision has been reached on a target rate of increase in physician incomes for the coming year, fee increases to provide for some share of the increase in incomes would be allowed. The balance of the increase in physician incomes would be expected to come from increased service provision. If utilization increases should exceed the anticipated rate, fees would be constrained even more in the next year. For example, the West German government entered into an arrangement in 1976 under which fees would rise by approximately 2 percent in 1976 and 4 percent in 1977, assuming utilization increased by no more than 6 percent and 4 percent respectively. If utilization should increase at faster rates, fees would be reduced so that the target rate of increase in ambulatory service expenditures was no more than 8 percent.[33] A comparable system has been formally adopted in

[32] Uwe Reinhardt, "Reimbursement for Ambulatory Physicians' Services in the Federal Republic of Germany," paper presented at Fogarty International Center Conference on Policies for the Containment of Health Care Costs and Expenditures, June 2–4, 1976.

[33] Glaser, *Paying the Doctor Under National Health Insurance.*

Quebec. In the rest of Canada, fee increases—both absolute rates of change as well as equalization among specialties—are informally tied to desired changes in incomes. According to evidence cited earlier, as well as information provided informally by Canadian officials, the system appears to have given the government effective control over "demand creation" by physicians.[34]

Linking of fee increases to target expenditures is likely to gain popularity as a method of budget control, but it has many of the problems of fixed budgets. The incentives facing the individual physician are different from those facing physicians in the aggregate. Under this system an individual physician has an incentive to provide a large number of reimbursable services, and a physician's income can exceed the target rate if the physician's rate of increase on total billing exceeds the average rate of increase. Similarly, physicians who increase their provision of services by less than the average rate of increase will receive income gains less than the target rate. Such an outcome would be desirable only if it forces physicians to establish formal procedures for monitoring the practice patterns of other physicians.

An indexing arrangement also requires accurate and timely data on physician incomes. In a fixed-budget arrangement, the rate of increase depends primarily on the government's ability and willingness to spend, rather than on target physician incomes. With a system tied to desired changes in incomes, relevant data must be made readily available to negotiators. Providing these data may be difficult, particularly if many carriers are permitted to operate. Indexing would be most feasible under NHI plans with a unified billing system.

Fee Structures and Equity Among Physicians

Fee levels and rates of increase are not the only elements of fee-for-service that affect cost, quality, and access. Equally important is the effect of the fee structure on the incomes of physicians in different medical specialties and in different geographic areas.

Specialty Distinctions. Should specialists receive greater fees for their services than primary-care physicians receive? Es-

---

[34] Conversation with Robert A. Armstrong, Director General of Canada's Health Insurance Program.

tablishing different fees for distinct specialties is a simple procedure in fee schedule arrangements, requiring the use of different conversion factors in certain parts of the schedule for different specialties or simply different fee schedules. Under UCR systems, customary ("prevailing" in Medicare terminology) charge profiles would be developed on a specialty-specific basis. Because specialists' charges are on average higher than those of primary-care physicians, the seventy-fifth percentile of the distribution also would be higher for specialists. Thus, specialty-specific customary charge profiles would raise fee screens for specialists and reduce them for primary-care physicians.

Although the mechanics appear straightforward, the justification for specialty distinctions is not. On one hand, it can be argued that physicians who have acquired additional years of training typically provide services of higher quality and should receive a just reward. On the other, higher fees for services that can be provided equally well by primary-care physicians simply permit a form of economic inefficiency in the system. Services of comparable quality are reimbursed at levels exceeding the level necessary to ensure their performance. Moreover, by contributing to higher incomes for specialists, distinct fee schedules may encourage an excessive number of physicians to choose a medical or surgical specialty. Administrative and equity problems also arise in the definition of specialties. Because specialty choice often is a matter of self-designation, distinct schedules also may encourage physicians simply to claim a particular specialty. Yet when board certification is required to establish a physician in a particular specialty, higher payment levels may be unfairly denied to older physicians who have years of experience performing the same services.

In general, it seems that different schedules permitting higher fees for specialists than for general practitioners are unwarranted. Specialists' incomes should tend to be higher simply because they perform more complex procedures. Higher fees for identical procedures would seem to be justified only when detailed evidence could be provided that a specialist's services were necessary, or that the expertise provided by the specialist contributed something "additional" to the product-accuracy of a diagnosis, appropriateness of treatment, and so on. In such cases, higher fees should be tied to some tangible measure of quality, such as board certification. It may be appropriate to limit coverage in such circumstances to services provided by specialists, or the program could establish differentials for selected procedures when there are likely to be real differences in the services provided.

The Medicare program does not require its carriers to distinguish between general practitioners and specialists. Carriers may establish separate reimbursement schedules for different specialties and may exercise considerable discretion in defining specialties for reimbursement purposes. The program has informally encouraged carriers to establish separate profiles for specialists on the grounds that higher charge screens will encourage specialists to participate and, as a result, higher-quality services will be available to Medicare beneficiaries. Physician associations have probably exerted considerable pressure in the same direction. The decision to recognize specialty differences also is available to the Medicaid program but at the state level. Roughly half the states have different reimbursement screens for specialists and general practitioners.

The same pressures toward favorable treatment of specialists would probably exist under national health insurance. With favorable treatment, several results can be predicted: participation of specialists and higher-quality care, excessive payments for relatively simple procedures performed by specialists, and higher program costs. Further, if specialization is encouraged by formal arrangements ensuring higher fees, the practice of primary-care medicine will be discouraged.

Location Distinctions. Should there be payment differentials for urban and rural physicians? The argument for different fee screens is as follows: Urban physicians have higher costs because they must pay higher prices for office space, higher wages for ancillary personnel, and the like; therefore fees should be higher in urban than in rural areas. Recognition of higher urban area costs in setting fees would result in increased participation by urban physicians and greater access for the population they serve. Encouragement of greater physician participation also might produce higher-quality care. Moreover, establishment of a single set of profiles for urban and rural physicians would result in unnecessarily generous payments to induce rural physicians to participate, and higher overall program costs.

The argument against differentiating fee screens for urban and rural physicians is that a uniform fee schedule or charge screens would encourage physicians to locate in rural areas.[35] It has been argued that because of a lack of general amenities and unavailability of colleagues in rural areas, incomes there must be higher to attract physicians. Raising fees in rural areas to levels existing in urban areas (or even higher), goes the argument, would encourage migration by raising incomes. It should be noted, however, that no relationship between fees and the supply of physicians has yet been established. Fees are higher in urban areas with large physician-to-population ratios than in the urban areas with smaller physician-to-population ratios or in rural areas with relatively few physicians, but the meaning of this information is elusive. These statistics are consistent with the hypothesis that physicians in urban areas with large physician-to-population ratios maintain adequate incomes through establishing high fees, through provision of more services per capita, or both. That is, large physician-to-population ratios lead to high fees, not vice versa. If this hypothesis is true, increasing fees in rural areas relative to fees in urban centers might have little effect on location decisions of physicians. Instead, such action would just increase the incomes of physicians already practicing in rural areas and raise program costs.[36] Fees that markedly constrained real incomes in urban areas, however, could have considerably different effects. Migration could occur if desired incomes could not be reached. Officials in Canada believe that some geographic redistribution is now occurring there because of the limits that country has imposed on relative fees. If this is true, then controlling the rate of growth in fees in real terms in urban areas could be more important than raising fees in rural areas.

The trend in Medicare and Medicaid has been for separate fee structures for urban and rural physicians. Medicare car-

[35] This argument has been made by Uwe Reinhardt in "Alternative Methods of Reimbursing Non-Institutional Providers of Health Services," paper presented to the Institute of Medicine Conference on Regulation in the Health Industry, January 7–9, 1974.

[36] The issue of incentives facing physicians in making specialty and location choices is treated in greater depth in Chapter 4 of this book.

riers have the option of establishing statewide fee schedules or permitting intrastate variations. The choice of the latter may reflect an objective of relating fees to the relative costs of practice, a lack of interest in manpower redistribution questions, or the political strength of urban physicians.

Salaried Reimbursement

Salary has many desirable features as a form of physician reimbursement. The most important is the potential administrative control it would provide over the costs of physicians' services. Salaried reimbursement also can be made attractive to physicians; it can guarantee incomes at acceptable levels (although one objective is to reduce salaries below those generated by fee-for-service) ; facilitate a regular work schedule; and provide a range of fringe benefits, such as vacation time, sick leave, pension plans, malpractice insurance, and Social Security. To the extent this option is attractive to physicians, it could be usefully employed to attract physicians to underserved areas. But reliance on salaries could also pose problems. First, salaries could have adverse effects on physician productivity. Second, the use of salaries would be really feasible only with relatively large-scale provider organizations having managerial hierarchies capable of monitoring performance of salaried employees. Such organizations are not now common. Third, salaried reimbursement could encourage the organization or unionization of physicians, with a consequent increase in their ability to bargain over rates of pay, hours of work, and the like. Such an effect could drastically restrict the government's ability to control health care costs through salaried reimbursement.

Salaried arrangements for physicians are similar to compensation arrangements for professionals in other fields—fixed payments for services rendered over a stated period of time, such as a year, independent, in the short term, of productivity or quality of performance. Salaries in other fields are typically adjusted over time, not simply for seniority and cost-of-living increases, but also for exceptional achievement according to a variety of performance measures. In medical practice, salaries could be adjusted for physicians who handled particularly heavy patient loads through additional hours of work, who were unusually efficient in their use of the capital or labor inputs of the organization, who delivered care of exceptionally high quality, or who did all these things. Salaries could be adjusted in the following year for exceptional current-year performance; systems employing current-year performance-related bonuses also could be implemented. A variety of criteria could be used as the basis for rewards, thereby fostering a system with substantial administrative control.

At first glance, salaried reimbursement would seem to allow greater control over costs than would the other methods of reimbursement. In practice, the incentives facing salaried physicians would in large part reflect the incentives facing the organization that employs them. If an organization were paid on a fee-for-service basis, the incentives filtering down to an individual physician might be quite different from those that would arise if the organization received capitation payments. Because the objective of implementing salary reimbursement would be to avoid the undesirable incentives of fee-for-service, this discussion assumes the presence of some form of budget limitation. Salaries could be set at whatever levels budgets permitted, and few incentives for overprovision of services would exist. Unlike the effects of fee-for-service, incomes of salaried physicians would not increase if they provided more services; in fact, income per unit of effort would decline. Nonetheless, given the lack of an immediate relationship of fees to output, cost control objectives could be thwarted if salaried physicians were less productive. Salaried reimbursement also may contain incentives for physicians to overuse other inputs and minimize their own efforts.[37] Low productivity would lead ultimately to a requirement for larger staffs, that is, for more physicians or aides, thereby negating the savings from controls on incomes. This result would be particularly likely when salary increases were tied only loosely to work effort. If adjustments to salaries over time were tied to desired behavior, however, salary reimbursement would probably not seriously affect levels of performance. Experience in other professions, where salary predominates as the system

---

[37] See Uwe Reinhardt, "Proposed Changes in the Organization of Health Care Delivery: An Overview and Critique," *Milbank Memorial Fund Quarterly*, Fall 1973; and Mark Pauly, "Efficiency, Incentives and Reimbursement for Health Care," *Inquiry* 7 (March 1970): 114–31.

of remuneration, suggests that the method can work quite well in inducing efficient performance.

Salary as a method of payment is at best neutral with respect to quality, unless salary increases or current-year bonuses are tied to quality of care provided. When provision of high-quality care is very important to the organization responsible for delivery of services, quality is likely to be critical in the evaluation of physicians' performance. In other environments, salary might not always encourage the additional effort required to produce high-quality service. Because higher-quality care will often require greater time input than lower-quality care does, higher-quality care may be less likely to occur if pay increases do not take this fact into account. Lower-quality care would be particularly likely to occur when the demand for physician services exceeded available supply.

The effect of salary on access to care is not obvious. Unless levels of payments were tied to numbers of patients seen, there would be very limited incentives under salaried arrangements for physicians to provide widespread access to the poor. As already noted, it has not been demonstrated that access to care objectives can be reached under fee-for-service arrangements. Physicians seem able to earn adequate incomes in areas with high physician-to-population ratios, even without seeking large numbers of the poor and disadvantaged as clients. If these people are to get care, specific organizational arrangements are necessary to serve them. More often than not, these organizational arrangements—prepaid group practices, Neighborhood Health Centers (NHCs), and the National Health Service Corps (NHSC)—pay physicians on a salary basis. Salaried arrangements can be an attractive inducement to physicians to locate in underserved areas; these arrangements reduce risks and eliminate managerial problems, such as collection of bills, inherent in caring for poor populations. Thus, when salaried payment is coupled with an organized practice designed to serve target populations, it can contribute to an enhanced capacity to care for the underserved.

The number of options for generating an increase in salaried practice is limited. The options fall into the general categories of direct subsidies of alternative modes of delivery, measures affecting the relative attractiveness of fee-for-service, and direct controls on payment for certain services.

Alternative delivery modes that could be encouraged through direct subsidization or public financing include health maintenance organizations (HMOs), Neighborhood Health Centers, and the National Health Service Corps. Health maintenance organizations are large-scale, multispecialty provider organizations that offer comprehensive health services to voluntarily enrolled consumers through annual contracts on a fixed price basis. Physicians are usually paid on a salaried basis. Considerable recent evidence supports the argument that prepaid group practices lead to fewer hospital admissions, substitution of ambulatory care for in-hospital care, and lower costs. The 1973 HMO Act was designed to provide greater financial support for the formation of HMOs, but in reality it placed several barriers to their development—open enrollment, comprehensive benefit packages, and community rating. Recent amendments to that act have eased some of these requirements, and HMOs may come to assume more importance in the health delivery system.

Federal support for programs such as Neighborhood Health Centers and the National Health Service Corps also could be increased. The Neighborhood Health Center program was initiated in 1965 by the Office of Economic Opportunity as a demonstration project in the War on Poverty. Neighborhood health centers were designed to provide comprehensive services to poor populations in areas with an inadequate supply of physicians and other medical resources. They were designed principally to serve the needs of the poor in the inner city, where substantial needs for services appeared to exist. There is some evidence that NHCs have both increased access of the poor to medical services and raised the quality of care available.[38] NHCs offer comprehensive benefits, community participation in decision making, outreach, and other features that make their services expensive relative to the services of private physicians. These features, although vital to the initial objectives of NHCs, are not central to the goal of delivery of medical services to the poor. The critical feature for our purposes is that physicians are paid on a salaried basis and that NHCs provide a center for delivery of ambulatory care services which can be made attractive to physicians. Practice on a

[38] Roger Reynolds, "Improving Access to Health Care Among the Poor— The Neighborhood Health Center Experience," *Milbank Memorial Fund Quarterly*, Winter 1976.

fee-for-service basis in poor neighborhoods presents physicians with several problems, including low fees, low collection rates, crime, lack of proximity to colleagues, and high start-up costs. Ambulatory care centers based on the NHC model with salaried reimbursement can offer physicians guaranteed incomes, physical safety, access to peers and other health workers, and shared administrative burdens.

The National Health Service Corps, which is somewhat oriented toward support of medical practice in rural areas, also offers reimbursement on a salaried basis. The NHSC, established by the Emergency Health Personnel Act Amendments of 1970, was designed to attract physicians to communities located in areas designated as having health manpower shortages. The National Health Service Corps differs from the Neighborhood Health Center program in that the corps is designed solely as a method to increase the delivery of medical services—not as a comprehensive approach to meet several interrelated needs of the poor. Communities must apply for assignment of corps personnel, document their need for medical manpower, and demonstrate their ability to provide support services and facilities necessary for establishment of a medical practice. The corps pays physicians and other health personnel on a salaried basis, with bonus payments up to $1,000 per month. The salary and bonus package is designed to provide corps physicians with incomes that are competitive with those of private practitioners in the same profession with equivalent training and time in practice. The program also provides one-time grants of up to $25,000 for support of costs of establishing a medical service, acquiring equipment, and the like.[39]

Increases in the financial support of these or comparable delivery mechanisms would be aimed principally at solving problems of access. Salaried reimbursement is employed in the NHCs and in the NHSC not strictly to minimize overprovision of services, but rather to provide incentives—specifically guaranteed incomes, fringe benefits, and reduced entrepreneurial and administrative tasks—for physicians to practice in relatively undesirable locations. Coupled with subsidization of the staffing and equipment requirements of an ambulatory

---

[39] House Report No. 94–266 of the Interstate and Foreign Commerce Committee, June 7, 1976, pp. 27–29.

care center, these incentives should significantly increase the attractiveness of practice in currently underserved areas.

Another method of increasing the proportion of physicians practicing on a salaried basis would be for government to reimburse for certain services only if provided by salaried physicians or to reimburse only the institution providing the service. In the United Kingdom and other West European nations, services provided in a hospital setting are performed only by salaried specialists employed by the hospital.[40] It is extremely unlikely that such a drastic change in accepted procedures for reimbursing for specialists' services would occur in the United States, and no such change has been seriously proposed.

Although the appeal of such a procedure would be enhancement of financial control, it is not clear whether such a change in the reimbursement of surgeons would reduce the number of surgical procedures performed. Fee-for-service reimbursement clearly provides inappropriate incentives, but financial gain is not the only cause of excessive surgery. Surgeons are obviously oriented toward surgical solutions to physical health problems. In view of the large supply of surgeons in this country, the extensive amount of surgery performed here might be expected to continue despite a change in method of payment; that is, the problem may be an excessive supply of surgeons, not the reimbursement method. National expenditures for surgery could be equally well controlled through limits on both fees and the number of surgeons.

A change in the methods of reimbursing surgeons seems very unlikely to occur, but the same does not necessarily hold for hospital-based specialists—radiologists, pathologists, and anesthesiologists. Prior to Medicare, these specialists were usually employed by hospitals on a salaried basis. During the debate over the Medicare-Medicaid legislation, hospital-based physicians successfully lobbied for individual determination of arrangements for personal services. As a result, many hospital-based physicians are reimbursed under Part B of Medicare for personal services separate from hospital billings under Part A for the institutional costs of the same services.[41] Hos-

[40] Glaser, *Paying the Doctor Under National Health Insurance.*
[41] Herman M. Somers and Anne R. Somers, *Medicare and the Hospitals* (Washington, D.C.: The Brookings Institution, 1967).

pital-based specialists now receive fee-for-service reimbursement and a number of different percentage arrangements as well as salary. Percentage arrangements tie reimbursements to total hospital billings for the department involved.

Several problems have emerged. The first is the obvious administrative burden of making separate determinations of professional and institutional service components. Second, the rapid introduction of new technology, particularly in pathology, has permitted charges for services rendered by particular departments to exceed costs, with the excess revenue contributing to operations of other hospital departments. Third, the payment arrangements appear to have produced very high incomes for hospital-based specialists,[42] both because of the level of hospital charges and because of the tying of each reimbursement arrangement to the number of services provided. For example, an arrangement based on a percentage of gross billings clearly encourages the performance of many tests. Even most salary arrangements tie incomes to volume of procedures. Reimbursement incentives are clearly not the only factor in determining the volume of services provided. Factors such as the Joint Commission on Accreditation of Hospitals requirements for accreditation and professional training and that commission's policy on referrals also are important.

Despite these problems, it is not clear that major steps will be taken toward salaried reimbursement. Radiologists, anesthesiologists, and pathologists view salaried employment by hospitals not only as a threat to their incomes but also as discriminatory treatment that demeans their professions in the eyes of other physicians. The American College of Radiology, the American Society of Anesthesiologists, and the College of American Pathologists fought strenuously for separate billing methods for personal services both in the 1965 debate over Medicare and in the recent hearings on the Talmadge amendments.[43] The Talmadge amendments, introduced in 1976, are the most recent legislative attempt to control payments for services of those specialists. The amendments would limit charges rather than mandate salaried arrangements.

---

[42] Arthur Anderson and Co., "Study of Reimbursement and Practice Arrangements of Provider-Based Physicians," unpublished, 1977.

[43] "Medicare and Medicaid Administrative Reform," Hearings before the Subcommittee on Health of the Committee on Finance, U.S. Senate, July 26–30, 1976.

> The charges of a physician or other person which are
> related to the income or receipts of a hospital or any
> subdivision thereof shall not be taken into considera-
> tion in determining his customary charge pursuant to
> subparagraph (A) to the extent that such charges ex-
> ceed an amount equal to the salary which would rea-
> sonably have been paid for such services to the physi-
> cian performing them if they had been performed in
> an employment relationship with such hospital. . . .[44]

This type of control would place some limits on charges, but
incomes and outlays for diagnostic services may not be drastically affected because the number of services provided—
referrals, hospital procedures, and the like—would not be
controlled.

Proposals like the Kennedy-Corman bill are more far-reaching, because they require hospitals to compensate professional
practitioners, such as pathologists and radiologists, who are
associated with a hospital and whose services are generally
available to patients of that hospital. Such proposals require
the hospitals to be concerned with the level of services provided and to enter into negotiations over rates of pay. Hospitals would most likely move to acquire salaried staffs in
those specialties. From the public perspective, such a structural
change seems very desirable. Prospects for legislative acceptance of such an arrangement seem poor, however, given the
strong preferences of the affected physicians and the success
physicians have generally had in winning battles over methods
of payment.

The most significant push toward increasing salaried payment of physicians could come quite indirectly. If rates of
increases in incomes of fee-for-service physicians were successfully constrained, fee-for-service reimbursement could become significantly less attractive. Physicians faced with high
costs of office space, equipment, auxiliary personnel, and malpractice insurance might find the burdens of practice management increasingly unattractive in a world with limitations

---

[44] U.S. Congress, Senate, *A Bill to Provide for the Reform of the
Administrative and Reimbursement Procedures Employed Under the
Medicare and Medicaid Programs and for Other Purposes*, Section 22.

on gross billings. Controls on physicians' incomes could conceivably come through fee schedules coupled with some of the limits on service provision discussed earlier. As noted in the discussion on limits to demand creation, tying annual changes in fees to changes in physicians' incomes in Canada has had salutary effects on the rate of increase in physicians' expenditures and on the geographic distribution of physicians there.[45] One might expect success in limiting fees also to increase physicians' interest in joining organizations that pay annual salaries and fringe benefits, guarantee regular hours, and so on.

Control over physicians' incomes might come through increases in the supply of physicians, who, faced with natural limits on their ability to generate satisfactory earnings, might opt for salaried practice and guaranteed incomes. Several economists have warned recently that an oversupply of physicians could have severe inflationary effects.[46] Because of physicians' influence on patients' decisions on hospital admissions, surgery, laboratory, X-ray services, and the like, increases in physician supply will probably lead to higher expenditures with little or no downward pressure on prices. In an interesting alternative argument, Starr has suggested that a large supply of physicians can result in pressure on physicians' incomes and make salaried forms of practice more attractive.

> The likely availability of large numbers of new doctors could greatly facilitate future efforts to change the medical system. Young physicians, just coming out of medical school without any prior attachment to private, fee-for-service practice, may be more readily attracted to new institutions and arrangements than older physicians [are]. There is some evidence that the new graduates, particularly women, are less interested than their predecessors in setting themselves up as solo entrepreneurs. But whatever their preferences, they may find it increasingly difficult to get started in private practice, which now, especially because of rising malpractice insurance rates and medi-

---

[45] Conversation with Robert Armstrong.
[46] See Reinhardt, *Physician Productivity and the Demand for Health Manpower*, and Evans, "Supplier-Produced Demand."

cal equipment costs, requires an investment beyond the reach of many young doctors. Instead, they may turn to neighborhood clinics, health maintenance organizations and other institutions that offer secure salaries.[47]

Starr argues that if an increase in the supply of physicians should lead to more acceptance of salaried reimbursement, negotiations with physicians over health insurance issues would be greatly facilitated and the threat or potential harm of physicians' strikes reduced.

The argument for increasing the supply is primarily political. We need more doctors who are not committed to private practice and an abundant supply of physicians to limit the economic power of the profession. At some point in the future, we may be forced into a confrontation with the medical profession over the maintenance of its privileges. Doctors' strikes over national health programs are not unheard of. At that point, it will be extremely useful to have more doctors than we need, instead of needing more doctors than we have. An expanding supply of physicians will not solve our problems, but it may create favorable objective conditions for the success of future efforts.[48]

Although Starr poses an interesting argument, two consequences of salaried practice make a deliberate strategy of increasing supply questionable. First, if, as was suggested earlier, salaried reimbursement reduces physician productivity or results in patient referrals to other providers, more practitioners may be required than are required under fee-for-service. In that case, expenditures for physicians' services could rise despite greater control over physicians' average net earnings. Second, while a large number of salaried physicians would weaken the potency of a strike by fee-for-service physicians, the possibility of strikes certainly does not evaporate. Salaried practice goes hand in hand with ties to centers or institutions and to peers, facilitating and indeed encouraging organization for bargaining over salary and terms of employment. If salaried reimbursement were to result in greater organization and

---

[47] Paul Starr, "Too Many Doctors?" *Washington Post*, 13 March 1977, p. 63.
[48] Ibid.

increased power in bargaining with government, the result might be little increase in control over incomes and expenditures for physicians' services.

Capitation Reimbursement

Capitation reimbursement is typically thought of as a system of reimbursing organizations. Because of their size, health maintenance organizations are usually able to pool a large number of risks and provide an insurance as well as a delivery function. Little consideration has been given to payment on a capitation basis to physicians in solo or group practices. Such arrangements are common, and indeed vital, components of the national health programs of the United Kingdom and the Netherlands. The Kennedy-Corman plan clearly encourages this physician payment system.

The usual advantages claimed for capitation reimbursement are more efficient organization and management of practice, less hospitalization, and fewer unnecessary services. This form of reimbursement, however, is unfamiliar to most individual and small group practices, and its implementation may be strongly opposed. Nonetheless, such a system would introduce incentives that could reduce hospitalization and discretionary services and eliminate many administrative tasks for both physicians and the program. As a result, the program could offer capitation rates that would increase the physicians' net income while decreasing program costs.

Several problems with such an arrangement can be identified. First, establishing appropriate capitation rates is extremely difficult. Regardless of how sensitive the capitation rates are (that is, regardless of disaggregation of expected medical expenditures by age, sex, race, education, and a host of other demographic variables), the health status of individuals in each cell will vary. Physicians can benefit from the capitation arrangement by examining all potential enrollees and selecting only the healthy. The only way to overcome this problem of cream skimming is to have mandatory open enrollment or to assign clients on a random basis. Unfortunately, both options would encounter intense physician and public resistance.

The second major problem is that capitation reimbursement will be unattractive to individual or small group practice physicians because they cannot limit risk by pooling a large number of patients. The state could absorb most of this risk by providing insurance against extraordinary events. For the scheme to remain desirable, the cost of insurance plus the capitation rate must be lower than per patient costs under fee-for-service. Defining the ordinary events which are covered by capitation and the extraordinary which are not is difficult yet critical. If too many events are defined as extraordinary, then the cost to the program for insurance is high and extraordinary cases will occur more frequently. Once a case is no longer covered by the capitation rate, the incentives facing the physician return to those of fee-for-service. If relatively few events are categorized as extraordinary, risks facing physicians increase and capitation tends to become unacceptable. One way to overcome the potential hardship of an extraordinary event would be to have the program reinsure providers by establishing cost thresholds per client per enrolled year. For example, services rendered to high-volume service users in a given year would be priced out in the fee-for-service market and if those services exceeded perhaps a $2,000 reinsurance threshold, the program would directly assume the burden of all costs in excess of $2,000.

The third problem is the need to include a wide range of services within the capitation rate to avoid adverse substitution effects. For example, allocating to primary-care physicians capitation payments designed to cover only primary-care services creates incentives for these physicians to refer to specialists, to hospitalize, and to overprescribe drugs. Substantial referral to specialists, use of hospital inpatient facilities, and prescription of drugs would economize significantly on the physician's own time, but markedly increase the cost of the program. The experience with capitation payments to general practitioners in the United Kingdom shows very high per capita rate of use of prescription drugs. The British reportedly have 2.7 filled prescriptions per capita compared with 2.0 per capita in the United States.[49] Under a system of capitation reimbursement, the use of specialists and hospital inpatient facilities might increase in the United States because of their availability. The existence of the problem demonstrates that capitation rates ideally should include specialists'

[49] Oden Anderson, *Health Care: Can There Be Equity?* (New York: John Wiley and Sons, 1975).

services, hospital inpatient care, and prescription drugs. Such a broadening of capitation reimbursement, however, increases the risk to physicians accepting capitation, and increases the importance and difficulty of insuring physicians against extraordinary costs.

Finally, physicians reimbursed on a capitation basis have an incentive to reduce the quality of care to minimize costs. Ideally, physicians would have to compete with one another and patients would choose among alternative physicians on the basis of price and their judgment of service quality. Whether patients are able to make accurate judgments on the quality of care is, of course, questionable. Capitation reimbursement could have adverse effects on the quality of care the poor in particular receive. For example, if the poor should prove less able than others to assess quality, physicians would be able to provide a lower quality of care to the poor because the risk of losing them as patients is less. Moreover, because the poor are more likely than others to frequently change their place of residence, physicians may be relatively unconcerned with the future consequences of inadequate care.

Quality of care could be monitored by combining two methods of quality assessment. First, physicians' practices could be monitored by examining turnover in the patients enrolled on a capitation basis. A high rate of voluntary disenrollment vis-à-vis other providers would indicate that some dimension of quality of care was unacceptable. Second, services under fee-for-service reimbursement could be directly monitored through the information supplied on invoices. Under a capitation arrangement, invoices, as well as diagnostic and therapeutic information, disappear. Physicians would be required continually to submit diagnostic and therapeutic information. Without that information it would be hard to assess the technical level of care provided. Random checks of medical records and a graduated scale of sanctions could be used to ensure that physicians submitted the required information.

Summary and Conclusions

Any reimbursement arrangement would have difficulty controlling costs, but some strategies seem better than others. A fee schedule system is preferable to usual, customary, and reasonable charge screens because fee schedules have much greater potential for controlling costs. By using fee schedules, a national health insurance program could maintain clear control over the absolute level of fees, determining them on bases such as the availability of funds or targets for physician incomes. Fee schedules would permit the program to achieve other objectives as well. Fee schedules could be structured to redistribute income among specialties and between urban and rural physicians and to quickly change the relative values given different procedures. Finally, the administration of a fee schedule would be less complex and less costly than properly maintaining a usual and customary charge system.

The second major issue concerns the type of provision for physicians to charge in excess of the fee schedule. Such a provision is usually considered necessary to assure a high level of physician participation. But arrangements that would make it relatively easy for physicians to opt out would severely hamper cost control objectives. It is clear that the assignment billing system used under Medicare undermines efforts to control costs. Assignment billing permits physicians to shift costs to patients. It also encourages physicians to provide a higher quality and more comprehensive range of services to those able and willing to pay more than the allowed fee. Systems that would require physicians either to accept the program's fee schedule or to forfeit any reimbursement would enhance the likelihood of participation and reduce discrimination against low-income persons. But these arrangements would probably encounter considerable opposition from both physicians and the well-to-do. If this opposition could be overcome, physicians, through organization and threat of service disruption, would probably demand and receive very generous fee levels.

Given these difficulties, the most effective strategy would probably be one which permitted physicians a direct-patient-billing option, but which also included strong incentives to accept the government fee schedule. Physicians would be required to choose either direct billing of the patient or billing of the government for that patient annually; billing the government would mean accepting the fee schedule as payment in full. The choice would be binding for all patients and for all procedures for that year. The government would guarantee prompt and certain payment if physicians billed the program, but would place full collection responsibility on physicians if they billed patients directly. Patients whose physicians chose direct billing would be reimbursed less than the fee schedule, perhaps 60 percent. Such penalties imposed on patients would place indirect pressure on physicians. This arrangement would discourage a two-class system and permit strong control over fees.

Controlling the level of fees solves only part of the problem. As noted earlier, physicians appear to be able to influence patients' decisions to use services and to increase reimbursements through manipulation of the procedure coding terminology. Several methods of limiting physicians' discretion have been suggested. First, fees should be structured so that they reflect the costs of services when produced in an efficient manner. The incentives for "demand creation" are strongest when fees exceed the marginal costs of provision. Although several problems with developing precise fee schedules were mentioned, much better approximations, particularly in diagnostic procedures and in-hospital services, can be made than now exist.

A second proposal to limit physicians' discretion is to reduce substantially the types of visits for which a physician can bill. A procedure coding system with a large number of visits and separate codes for a wide range of ancillary services permits physicians broad flexibility in setting rates and rewards the provision of several ancillary services during the course of a visit. Fee schedules should permit billing for a few widely different types of visits, each of which would include allowance for expected routine tests, or visits should be carefully related to and defined by the amount of time involved.

Third, indexing arrangements are attractive because they allow considerable program control costs. Indexing refers to tying of fee increases to aggregate changes in physician incomes. A portion of the increase in physician income would come from fee increases, the remainder from changes in service provision. If physicians' incomes should increase faster than the desired rate, fee increases the next year would be reduced. The main problem with such arrangements is that although incomes would be controlled in the aggregate, individual physicians would have clear incentives to maximize incomes. As a result, the system could break down or physicians could be forced to monitor carefully patterns of service delivery. Indexing schemes are now employed in West Germany and Canada. It would be premature to claim success in either country, but Canadian officials believe the system is working well there.

Although fee-for-service reimbursement would undoubtedly dominate under national health insurance, alternative arrangements would remain feasible for at least some physicians. Capitation reimbursement applied to individual physicians rather than to organizations appears to be too complex for widespread use. But salary reimbursement has many desirable features, primarily the control it permits over the cost of physician services. A serious limitation on the implementation of salaried reimbursement is the need for service delivery organizations responsible for and capable of monitoring performance and adjusting salaries over time. Most of the U.S. medical care delivery system is not now structured in that way. Such a major change would occur only if physicians were to become sufficiently disenchanted with fee-for-service reimbursement. This disenchantment might, in fact, occur following experience with controls of fees and incomes.

Short of such a major change in the system, the most promising reform would be the Kennedy-Corman proposal to require compensation by hospitals of professional practitioners, such as pathologists, radiologists, and anesthesiologists who are associated with a hospital and whose services are generally available to patients of the hospital. Coupled with fixed overall budget reimbursement of hospitals, that proposal would force hospital attention to rates of payment and to the level of services provided, thereby further encouraging cost containment.

Chapter 3
HEALTH MAINTENANCE ORGANIZATIONS

HAROLD S. LUFT
JUDITH FEDER
JOHN HOLAHAN
KAREN D. LENNOX

S INCE its promotion by the Nixon administration in the early 1970s, the health maintenance organization (HMO) has become perhaps the most commonly proposed solution to problems in the health care delivery system. The HMO's potential for efficient delivery of care and for responsiveness to consumer preferences has made it appealing to political activists concerned with such divergent issues as cost containment, consumerism, and limits on government involvement in the health care system. The HMO's popularity across the political spectrum explains its importance in national health insurance bills as different as the Kennedy-Corman bill and Alain Enthoven's Consumer Choice Health Plan.

The popularity of the HMO concept, however, does not justify its uncritical adoption in national health insurance design. Whether and how public policy should encourage the growth of health maintenance organizations depends on the extent to which experience with HMOs confirms widespread expectations for their performance. In the context of national health insurance, relevant experience includes not only the performance of operating HMOs, but the performance of public programs such as Medicare and Medicaid that have affected HMO development. The purpose of this chapter is to analyze this experience.

It is important to begin with a definition of the term *HMO*, which has come to mean many things to many people; then we will examine claims concerning HMO performance to date and the evidence supporting those claims. Much of the interest in HMOs is attributable to their purported cost savings. The evidence clearly indicates that costs of medical care are lower for HMO enrollees than for people with conventional health insurance. But the source of these cost differentials is not entirely clear. Utilization of hospital services is lower for HMO enrollees, but there is no conclusive evidence that HMOs reduce utilization or, if they do, how they do it. For instance, utilization may be lower because of subtle differences in enrollees or providers through self-selection. Although lower cost and utilization may have attracted interest in HMOs, to evaluate their desirability one must also examine other dimensions of performance, such as quality, consumer satisfaction, and long-term effects on the health care system. This chapter explores the evidence on each of these dimensions.

If, on balance, health maintenance organizations appear to be desirable, national health insurance proposals should incorporate mechanisms that facilitate HMO operations. Existing health financing programs—Medicare, Medicaid, and the Federal Employees Health Benefits Plan—demonstrate some of the mechanisms available and their likely implications for beneficiaries' use of HMOs. The authors analyze the experience of these health programs as they relate to health maintenance organizations, and speculate on the effects that different national health insurance programs would have on HMO growth and performance.

Definition of the Health Maintenance Organization

Reflecting its political origins, the term *health maintenance organization* has been used to refer to a variety of things. Some people use the term to mean the prepaid group practices that have existed for decades, such as the Kaiser-Permanente plan. In contrast, the federal HMO Act of 1973 restricts application of the term to organizations that comply with an extensive array of requirements. Individual as well as group practices can qualify as HMOs under the act, but many prepaid group practices have chosen not to seek federal qualification.

Each of these definitions is too narrow to permit comprehensive analysis of health maintenance organizations' potential role in the health care delivery system and in a national health insurance program. Taking all types of HMOs into account, in 1977, more than 6 million people were enrolled in 165 plans, most of them in group practices.[1] For purposes of analysis, we propose to define HMO in terms of its essential behavioral characteristics. The critical features are as follows:

1. The HMO assumes a *contractual responsibility* to provide or assure the delivery of a stated range of health services, including at least physician and hospital services.
2. The HMO serves an *enrolled, defined population.*
3. The HMO has *voluntary enrollment* of subscribers.
4. The HMO requires a *fixed periodic payment* to the organization that is independent of use of services. (There may be small charges related to utilization, but these are relatively insignificant.)
5. The HMO assumes at least part of the *financial risk* and/or *gain* in the provision of services.

Contractual responsibility implies that the HMO member has the legal right to medical care provided by the HMO. This situation contrasts with the conventional one in which the medical care provider has the right to decide whether to accept the patient and is under no obligation, other than an ethical one, to provide treatment. The existence of an *enrolled, defined population* means that the HMO knows its obligations and can estimate the probable demand for its services. The population is usually limited to a specified geographic area. *Voluntary enrollment* implies that consumers can choose not to participate in an HMO; mandatory enrollment would violate the assumption of responsiveness to consumers that enhances HMOs' desirability. The *fixed periodic payment,* independent of the quantity of services provided, implies that, for a given enrollee, the HMO does not gain any substantial revenue by providing more services. In fact, the fewer services the HMO provides, the more the HMO will increase its net revenue after expenses. (In the long run, of course, the HMO may gain more enrollees by offering more services, and it will

---

[1] U.S. Department of Health, Education, and Welfare (DHEW), Division of Health Maintenance Organizations, *Health Maintenance Organizations Third Annual Report to the Congress,* DHEW Publication No. (PHS) 78–13058, Washington, D.C., U.S. Government Printing Office, September 1977.

lose members if it noticeably underserves them.) At times
patients may be required to make small copayments related
to utilization, but these copayments are usually a small fraction of the cost of the service and the charges exist primarily
to reduce the monthly premium. Finally, *financial risk* implies
that the HMO will suffer or benefit financially from its decisions to provide services. The presence of risk creates the
incentives for cost containment that have made HMOs so
attractive.

This definition purposely allows considerable latitude for
HMOs' organizational characteristics. Note that the definition
did not specify any restrictions on the method by which individual physicians are paid or on whether services are offered
in a single group setting or dispersed over a large number of
practitioners' offices.

The two major types of health maintenance organizations
are prepaid group practices (PGPs) and individual practice
associations (IPAs). IPAs, often called foundations for medical care, sponsor prepaid programs and conduct peer reviews.[2]
Although there are many important exceptions, most prepaid
group practices pay their physicians on a salary or capitation
basis, and most individual practice associations are composed
of physicians in private offices who are paid on a fee-for-
service basis by the health maintenance organization. HMOs
also vary with respect to their reliance on part-time versus
full-time physicians, profit versus nonprofit orientation, extent
of consumer participation and control, centralization of administration, and ownership and control of facilities.

Health maintenance organizations also vary in the extent
to which they meet the five criteria of the overall HMO definition. The comprehensiveness of guaranteed services varies
widely among plans and beneficiaries. The Southern California
Kaiser Health Foundation Plan, for example, reported at least
five different basic benefit packages in 1971, with monthly

---

[2] Not all IPAs are foundations; nor are all medical foundations IPAs.
See Richard H. Egdahl, "Foundations for Medical Care," *New England
Journal of Medicine* 288 (March 8, 1973):491–98, and Richard H. Egdahl,
R.H. Taft, J. Friedland, and K. Linde, "The Potential of Organizations
of Fee-For-Service Physicians for Achieving Significant Decreases in
Hospitalization," *Annals of Surgery* 186 (September 1977):388–99.

premiums ranging from $7.82 to $16.00 per subscriber.[3] Groups also may purchase any combination of special coverage for eyeglasses, drugs, mental health care, and other benefits. Under some financing arrangements, an HMO enrollee's implicit benefit package may be more extensive than the plan's explicit coverage; for example, some Medicare and Medicaid recipients with HMO coverage retain eligibility for reimbursement for out-of-plan services, thus extending their financial coverage beyond the HMO.

The defined populations served by HMOs also vary widely. For instance, HMOs vary in size from 3,000 enrollees to more than 1 million enrollees. In some cases, enrollees are homogeneous populations, such as university faculty and staff members. In other cases, the population is heterogeneous. The geographic base of enrollment may be concentrated in a single town (such as Columbia, Maryland, or Marshfield, Wisconsin), or widely dispersed through several metropolitan areas (such as the Kaiser plans in California), or a large rural region (such as the San Joaquin Foundation, also in California). Furthermore, although the enrolled population at any time is known because of the capitation method of payment, enrollment may range from being quite stable to being very unstable. For instance, the turnover rate among middle-aged enrollees in the Kaiser-Oakland (California) plan is about 3.5 percent a year,[4] while in some prepaid group practices the turnover averages 75 percent a year.[5] Finally, the population enrolled on a capitation basis may be less than the HMO's total population, for some HMOs also treat patients on a fee-for-service basis. In some cases, the fee-for-service component is a minuscule fraction of the total (about 1.4 percent for Kaiser in 1970).[6] In other cases, the HMO operation is a sideline of a primarily fee-for-service practice; in the Marshfield Clinic,

[3] Anne R. Somers, ed., *The Kaiser-Permanente Medical Care Program: A Symposium* (New York: The Commonwealth Fund, 1971). An HMO must offer a rather extensive basic package to be federally qualified, but it also may offer some optional benefits.

[4] John L. Cutler et al., "Multiphasic Checkup Evaluation Study: 1. Methods and Population," *Preventive Medicine* 2 (June 1973):197–206.

[5] Lester Breslow, "Statement Prepared for Senate Permanent Subcommittee on Investigations of the Committee on Government Operations, March 12, 1975," in U.S. Senate, pp. 52–63.

[6] Somers, *The Kaiser-Permanente Medical Care Program*, p. 45.

134   *NATIONAL HEALTH INSURANCE*

for example, 85 percent of the income is from fee-for-service payment.[7]

The degree of freedom of choice in enrollment also varies, not because of requirements for membership, but because of limited access to other providers or modes of insurance. An HMO monopoly is particularly likely in underserved areas, such as inner cities and rural communities. This likelihood of an HMO monopoly increases wherever public financing programs, notably Medicaid, set reimbursement levels so low that many private practitioners refuse to accept public patients. For example, as of the mid-1970s, 45 percent of physicians in California refused to treat Medicaid patients, had already reduced their participation in Medicaid, or were planning to reduce their participation in the future.[8] When an HMO is the sole available provider, as a result of these or other circumstances, the public's freedom of choice is substantially weakened.

The fixed periodic payment is less uniform in practice than in theory. Health maintenance organizations may use cost sharing to varying degrees, and several types of cost sharing may be involved. Coinsurance requires the enrollee to be responsible for a certain fraction of the costs of specific services. Deductibles require the enrollee to pay the first "x" dollars of the cost of specific services. Coinsurance and deductibles may be combined so that, for example, the enrollee may pay the first $25, and 20 percent of all costs beyond the first $25. (This combination is more typical in conventional insurance plans than in HMOs.) California state employees are enrolled in HMOs that have coinsurance rates of zero, 20 percent, and 25 percent, and deductibles of zero and $2 per visit, or $25 per illness.[9]

---

[7] Joel H. Broida, "Macro and Micro Assessment of an Alternative Delivery System: The HMO: Methodology and Output," presented at American Public Health Association, Chicago, November 16–20, 1975.

[8] California Medical Association, Bureau of Research and Planning, "A Survey of Physician Participation in the Medi-Cal Program," *Socioeconomic Report* 15 (February/March 1975); idem, "Physician Dissatisfaction with Medi-Cal," *Socioeconomic Report* 15 (April 1975).

[9] Dave Dozier et al., "1970–71 Survey of Consumer Experience: Report of the State of California Employees' Medical and Hospital Care Program Prepared Under the Policy Direction of the Medical Advisory Council to the Board of Administration of the Public Employees' Retirement System," Sacramento, California, May 1973.

Some HMOs impose cost sharing by covering only a partial set of services for a fixed periodic payment. The Health Insurance Plan of Greater New York (HIP) provides physician services on a capitation basis, but enrollees must carry conventional health insurance coverage to pay for hospital costs.

Separation of hospital and physician financing also produces variation in HMOs' exposure to risk. HIP and other plans that use conventional insurance for hospital care are not at risk for hospital expenses. Even when an HMO is at risk for all services, risk can be allocated in a variety of ways among three functional (and sometimes legally distinct) parts of an HMO: (1) the "plan" that contracts with enrollees, (2) the physicians who provide medical services, and (3) the hospital that provides inpatient services. In some cases, the physicians bear essentially all the risk and reap all the rewards even though the mechanism may be indirect. In other cases the physicians may be paid a flat salary or a capitation rate that fixes their incomes in a given year. Even with this arrangement, however, the physicians have a long-term financial stake in the success of the plan.

This discussion suggests rather than exhausts the diversity of health maintenance organizations. Because variations can affect incentives and performance, they must be kept in mind in HMO evaluation. The following review of experience will identify influential variations wherever possible. It must be remembered, however, that every HMO has some unique features, and it is impossible to be sure to what extent the performance of a specific HMO relates to its general characteristics and to what extent its special features.

Claims and Evidence on HMO Performance

Health maintenance organizations are of interest to national health insurance planners because they are thought to behave in ways that distinguish them from the conventional medical care system. Specifically, this different behavior is seen as cost reducing and, therefore, as potentially offering a pattern for cost control in the system as a whole. Claims also are made concerning HMOs' emphasis on prevention of illness, the quality of care, and the satisfaction of consumers. In fact, it is difficult to evaluate one set of claims without also examining the other. An innovation that lowered cost by substantially reducing quality or consumer satisfaction is clearly inferior to one that can lower cost without such sacrifices. Thus, a discussion limited to specific dimensions of performance is not only incomplete but misleading.

As we evaluate HMO experience, two important caveats must be kept in mind. The first holds throughout this chapter: There have been no randomized, controlled experiments that involved the assignment of a representative group of people to a wide range of health insurance plans and health maintenance organizations. Therefore, while we can say that costs (or utilization, or satisfaction) are lower in one situation than in another, we cannot really determine if the differences are attributable to general characteristics of the plans, to unique features of the providers and administrators, or to subtle differences among the people selecting each plan. Later, it will be seen that, for some purposes, self-selection under national health insurance can be an advantage, and for other purposes, a disadvantage.

The second caveat relates to the availability of data. A recently completed comprehensive review of the published evidence on HMO performance indicates that available data vary in depth, breadth, and quality.[10] For example, there are more than fifty comparisons of hospitalization, but for some dimensions of performance only a single study is available. Furthermore, the literature frequently concentrates on a single HMO, thus limiting the information available about other organizations and settings. These limitations on evidence necessitate caution in conclusions.

HMO COSTS

Health maintenance organizations make intuitive sense as a means for cost control because they alter the usual economic incentives in medical care and give providers a stake in holding down costs. This observation proves particularly true when HMO incentives are compared with those in a system of extensive third-party reimbursement for providers. All the avail-

[10] Harold S. Luft, *Health Maintenance Organizations: Dimensions of Performance* (New York: Wiley-Interscience, forthcoming).

able evidence supports the view that the total cost of medical care (premium plus out-of-pocket costs) for HMO enrollees is lower than that for allegedly comparable people with conventional insurance coverage.[11] The lower costs are clearest for enrollees in prepaid group practices. The cost difference between PGPs and conventional insurance ranges between 10 percent and 40 percent. Costs for enrollees in individual practice associations also appear somewhat lower than for enrollees in conventional plans, although the difference is smaller.

An explanation of these cost differences requires further investigation. Total costs can be divided into the cost per unit of service and the number of services of each type provided by the system. Differences in total costs, then, theoretically could reflect differences in each of these elements. If lower HMO costs did reflect lower costs per unit, HMO input prices would appear to be lower, or HMO production more efficient. Because HMOs generally pay the going rate for the people they hire, and their physicians have earnings comparable to those in fee-for-service practice, we direct our attention to efficiencies in production.

The question of whether group practice leads to economies of scale has long been a subject of debate.[12] It is important to

---

[11] Harold S. Luft, "How Do Health Maintenance Organizations Achieve Their 'Savings'?: Rhetoric and Evidence," *New England Journal of Medicine* 298 (June 15, 1978):1336–43.

[12] Rashi Fein, *The Doctor Shortage: An Economic Diagnosis* (Washington, D.C.: The Brookings Institution, 1967), pp. 62–89; Herbert E. Klarman, "Economic Research in Group Medicine," in *New Horizons in Health Care*, proceedings of the First International Congress on Group Medicine, Winnipeg, Manitoba, April 26–30, 1970, pp. 178–93; Donald E. Yett, "An Evaluation of Alternative Methods of Estimating Physicians' Expenses Relative to Output," *Inquiry* 4 (March 1967):3–27; Uwe Reinhardt, "A Production Function for Physician Services," *Review of Economics and Statistics* 54 (February 1972):55–66; Richard M. Bailey, "Economics of Scale in Medical Practice," in Herbert Klarman, ed., *Empirical Studies in Health Economics* (Baltimore: Johns Hopkins Press, 1970), pp. 255–77; Larry J. Kimbell and John H. Lorant, "Production Functions for Physicians' Services," paper presented at the Econometric Society meeting, Toronto, December 1972; Larry J. Kimbell and John H. Lorant, "Physician Productivity and Returns to Scale," paper presented at the Health Economics Research Organization Meeting, New York, December 1973; and John H. Lorant and Larry J. Kimbell, "Determinants of Output in Group and Solo Medical Practice," *Health Services Research* 11 (Spring 1976): 6–20.

recognize that the issue here has little to do with the performance of HMOs as a unique organizational form; whatever
economies of scale exist should be equally obtainable by both
fee-for-service and prepaid medical groups. Unfortunately,
measurement of returns to scale is confounded by disagreement on measures of outputs or inputs and the paucity of
data available for analysis. Furthermore, the relatively small
size of most physician groups in the United States (more than
half the medical groups had only three or four physicians in
1975 and four-fifths had fewer than eight physicians) poses
difficulties in interpreting data relating to group size.[13]

Studies of economies of scale have reflected these analytical
problems and produced mixed results. Most agree that economies of scale may occur as practice size increases, but that
these economies peak at a relatively low scale, between two
and five practitioners. Whether productivity per physician
remains constant or even declines beyond that point is hard
to evaluate. Thus there is no real support for the claim that
large prepaid group practices realize substantial economies of
scale in ambulatory care.

Size has an effect on physician productivity as well as on
organizational output. There is a substantial body of theoretical literature that argues that the rewards for efficient
practice are inversely related to the size of the group, thereby
encouraging reduction in physicians' work effort as the size
of their practices rises.[14] While data problems exist here as
well, the empirical evidence suggests that physician productivity in ambulatory care is higher in small groups than in
large groups, whether the financing for the large groups is
prepaid or fee-for-service. Thus group size, not the unique
financial characteristics of the HMO, appears to be the critical
factor in physician productivity. The relationship between size
and productivity may reflect the attraction of different types
of physicians to solo, small group, and large group prac-

---

[13] American Medical Association, Center for Health Services Research
and Development, *Profile of Medical Practice*, 1975–76 ed. (Chicago:
American Medical Association, 1976).

[14] Joseph P. Newhouse, "The Economics of Group Practice," *Journal of
Human Resources* 8 (Winter 1973):37–56; and Frank A. Sloan, "Effects
of Incentives on Physician Performance," in John Rafferty, ed., *Health
Manpower and Productivity* (Lexington, Mass.: D.C. Heath, 1974), pp.
53–84.

tices. For instance, physicians in relatively large groups have been found to desire such benefits as longer vacations, more time for educational leave, and reduced patient loads.

The expensive part of medical care occurs in the hospital, so more efficient production of hospital services by health maintenance organizations could have a significant impact on total costs. Until recently, however, only the Kaiser plans and Group Health Cooperative of Puget Sound controlled their own hospitals. Data for Kaiser hospitals in California and Oregon, as well as the Group Health Cooperative of Puget Sound hospital, can be compared with data from a matched sample of hospitals of similar size in the same regions. The data show no consistent differences in cost per patient day, although lengths of stay are shorter, and thus costs per case are lower, in the HMO-controlled hospitals.[15] A detailed examination of hospital costs for people in Group Health Cooperative of Puget Sound and those in a comprehensive Blue Cross–Blue Shield plan in Seattle indicates that the hospital costs for the HMO members were about 25 percent lower. Almost all this difference, however, was attributable to lower utilization rates; the unit costs for drugs; X-rays, laboratory, and other services were comparable.[16] Lower hospital utilization among HMO enrollees is explored in the next section.

Health maintenance organizations also may increase their relative efficiency by avoiding duplication of facilities. It has often been pointed out that community hospitals compete for physicians by purchasing special equipment that subsequently is used at far less than capacity.[17] HMO-controlled hospitals should not face this problem; Kaiser, for example, appears to centralize its services and to have less duplication of facilities than do conventional hospitals.[18]

---

[15] Luft, *Health Maintenance Organizations*, Chapter 7.

[16] K.M. McCaffree et al., "The Seattle Prepaid Health Care Project: Comparison of Health Services Delivery," Chapter 3, "Comparative Costs of Services"; Grant No. R18 HS 00694, DHEW, HRA, National Center for Health Services Research, November 1976.

[17] Maw Lin Lee, "A Conspicuous Production Theory of Hospital Behavior," *Southern Economic Journal* 38 (July 1971):48–58; and idem, "Interdependent Behavior and Resource Misallocation in Hospital Care Production," *Review of Social Economics* 30 (March 1972):84–95.

[18] Harold S. Luft and Steven Crane, "Interhospital Resource Allocation in Health Maintenance Organizations and Conventional Systems of Hospitals," presented at the Joint National Meeting of TIMS/ORSA, May 1, 1979, New Orleans, Louisiana.

To summarize the evidence on costs, existing prepaid group practices clearly have been able to provide medical care for their enrollees at costs 10 percent to 40 percent lower than costs in conventional plans. Individual practice associations have experienced smaller differentials. The lower costs appear to stem from lower utilization rates, rather than from lower costs per unit of service. Finally, there are few economies of scale, but large systems such as Kaiser do appear to reduce duplication of facilities.

UTILIZATION OF SERVICE

In contrast to the relative paucity of data on costs, there is ample evidence on both inpatient and ambulatory care utilization by enrollees in health maintenance organizations and in conventional plans. Differences are likely to be concentrated in hospital rather than ambulatory care. Hospital use is easier to control. The consumer can directly initiate an ambulatory visit, but only a physician can authorize a patient's admission to a hospital. Furthermore, HMOs typically lower financial barriers to ambulatory usage and may attempt to substitute ambulatory for inpatient care.

The evidence supports the expectation of greater differences in hospital use than in use of ambulatory care.[19] A review of more than two dozen studies indicates somewhat more ambulatory visits for HMO enrollees, particularly those in individual practice associations, than for patients in the fee-for-service system. Differences are greater for hospitalization. Based on more than fifty observations over a twenty-five-year period, those studies with good data almost unanimously support the claim that enrollees in prepaid group practices have lower hospitalization rates than do people with conventional insurance. The results for individual practice association enrollees are more mixed. Average differences in utilization between enrollees in HMOs and people who rely on fee-for-service medical care are substantial, with about 30 percent fewer hospital days for enrollees in prepaid group practices and 20 percent fewer days for enrollees in individual practice

---

[19] Luft, "How Do Health Maintenance Organizations Achieve Their Savings?"

associations. The number of hospital days per enrollee is the product of admissions per enrollee and length of stay per admission. HMO enrollees have a somewhat shorter stay than do people in conventional plans, but most of the overall utilization difference stems from lower admission rates.

An explanation of these lower admission rates is critical to evaluating HMOs. If, for the moment, the impact of specific organizational incentives is ignored, there are two primary explanations: (1) that HMOs identify and screen out cases that really do not require hospitalization—the discretionary or "unnecessary" cases; and (2) that HMOs achieve a lower hospitalization rate without any apparent discrimination among cases according to obvious "necessity." If the first explanation holds, HMO desirability is confirmed on both cost and quality grounds. If the second explanation holds, then we must assess HMO experience with more caution to make sure that lower costs do not mean lower quality, and to investigate further the various factors that may explain the lower hospitalization rates in HMOs.

The best available data from a broad range of HMOs tend to support the second explanation rather than the first. HMOs do not achieve a disproportionate share of their lower admission rates by "reducing" surgical as opposed to medical cases; instead, admissions seem to be lower across the board. Similarly, although admissions for certain "discretionary procedures," such as hernia repair and hysterectomy, are lower in HMOs than in comparison plans, the figures for discretionary procedures do not appear disproportionately lower than the figures for all surgery. Unfortunately, the measures of "discretionary" care are rough approximations that mask the fine distinctions in patient care. It is highly likely that many so-called discretionary admissions are actually essential, and that many "nondiscretionary" admissions are actually optional.

Recognizing the complexities of evaluating admissions and assuming a scattering of discretionary cases in all patient categories, we find four possible, but not mutually exclusive, interpretations of the reasons for lower hospital admissions in HMOs: (1) Rather than reducing admissions for cases the literature has identified as "discretionary," an effective HMO reduces admissions that case management reveals as "discre-

tionary." Although it may be almost impossible to define
categories of discretionary medical diagnoses in the aggregate,
a good physician can, if pressed, triage patients on a one-by-one
basis and decide who really needs admission and who can be
treated on an ambulatory basis. (2) HMOs may undertreat,
or traditional providers overtreat, nondiscretionary cases.
Data on outcomes, necessary to test this hypothesis, have not
been used extensively to compare HMOs and traditional fee-
for-service practice. (3) Self-selection among HMO enrollees
may result in lower admission rates; that is, better health or
greater aversion to hospital admissions among HMO enrollees
may contribute to the differential between HMO and fee-for-
service admission rates in so-called nondiscretionary categories. (4) HMOs may provide preventive care that reduces
the occurrence of health problems that require hospital admissions. Evidence is not yet available for comprehensive evaluation of these hypotheses, but evidence does exist with respect
to self-selection and preventive care.

Factors Affecting Consumer Selection of an HMO

People are not randomly assigned to health maintenance
organizations or to conventional medical care plans. HMO
enrollees generally choose HMO membership over other delivery options. Critical to HMO evaluation are the implications
of this self-selection for HMO performance.

The HMO literature about self-selection has been somewhat
ambivalent. The theory of consumer preference (often identified in this instance as the "risk-vulnerability hypothesis")
argues that people most concerned about the expected costs
of medical care will choose the HMO option. In fact, HMOs
have been concerned that self-selection on this basis through
open enrollment periods will leave them with those people
who are sickest. Conversely, it has been argued that low HMO
utilization rates prove that HMO members were healthier at
the time they chose to enroll. Beyond an individual's perceived
risk, choice of enrollment in an HMO also may reflect particular attitudes toward illness and medical care. We will
explore evidence on each of these questions.

The risk-vulnerability hypothesis has been treated in several
ways. The simplest studies examine the correlation between

HMO enrollment and demographic factors (e.g., age, sex, and marital status) and conclude that people who join health maintenance organizations are likely to be older than people with conventional medical care plans, to be married, and to have young children.[20] But other studies do not indicate any statistically significant differences between HMO members and people with conventional third-party coverage.[21] A second level of analysis compares perceived measures of health status for HMO members and nonmembers. Perceived health status can be measured through direct questions concerning health status or by specific questions concerning chronic and acute illness. Some studies have indicated no differences in perceptions of health status.[22] Others that have focused on chronic and acute conditions indicate either no differences or mixed results, with HMO members reporting more of certain types

[20] Richard L. Bashshur and Charles A. Metzner, "Vulnerability to Risk and Awareness of Dual Choice of Health Insurance Plan," *Health Services Research*, Summer 1970, pp. 106–13; A. Taher Moustafa, Carl E. Hopkins, and Bonnie Klein, "Determinants of Choice and Change of Health Insurance Plan," *Medical Care* 9 (January/February 1971):32–41; Clifton Gaus, "Who Enrolls in a Prepaid Group Practice: The Columbia Experience," *Johns Hopkins Medical Journal* 128 (January 1971):9–14; and Robert W. Hetherington, Carl E. Hopkins, and Milton I. Roemer, *Health Insurance Plans: Promise and Performance* (New York: Wiley-Interscience, 1975).

[21] Richard Tessler and David Mechanic, "Factors Affecting the Choice Between Prepaid Group Practice and Alternative Insurance Programs," *Milbank Memorial Fund Quarterly/Health and Society* 53 (Spring 1975): 149–72; Klaus J. Roghmann et al., "Who Chooses Prepaid Medical Care?: Survey Results from Two Marketings of Three New Prepayment Plans," *Public Health Reports* 90 (November/December 1975): 516–27; Avram Yedidia, "Dual Choice Programs," *American Journal of Public Health* 49 (November 1959):1475–80; and Clifton R. Gaus, Barbara S. Cooper, and Constance G. Hirschman, "Contrasts in HMO and Fee-for-Service Performance," *Social Security Bulletin* 39 (May 1976):3–14.

[22] Odin W. Anderson and Paul B. Sheatsley, *Comprehensive Medical Insurance: A Study of Costs, Use, and Attitudes Under Two Plans*, Health Insurance Foundation: Research Series No. 9, 1959; Tessler and Mechanic, "Factors Affecting the Choice Between Prepaid Group Practice and Alternative Insurance Programs," p. 160; Gaus, Cooper, and Hirschman, "Contrasts in HMO and Fee-for-Service Performance," p. 8. S.E. Berki et al., "Enrollment Choice in a Multi-HMO Setting: The Roles of Health Risk, Financial Vulnerability, and Access to Care," *Medical Care* 15 (February 1977):95–114.

of illnesses and no differences in other measures.[23] These results indicate that HMO enrollees report somewhat more chronic illness.

Roghmann and associates provide data relating more explicitly to the risk-vulnerability hypothesis by examining out-of-pocket medical expenses of people who later chose to stay with conventional coverage or to join various prepaid plans.[24] Although differences in total expenditures were not statistically significant, families who stayed with Blue Cross–Blue Shield (BC–BS) averaged lower total expenditures ($281) than did those who joined prepaid plans ($332). Moreover, families who stayed with BC–BS had statistically significant and lower expenses for physician, laboratory, and X-ray services. Another study, by Wells and Roghmann, shows that in the year *prior* to the opportunity for dual choice (arrangements whereby enrollees periodically have the opportunity to choose the plan, HMO or conventional, they like best) the hospitalization rate for people who left BC–BS to join the prepaid group practices was only half the rate for people who stayed with BC–BS.[25] Thus, prior to the opportunity for choice, people choosing HMOs had higher expenditures for physician care and laboratory and X-ray services, and substantially lower expenditures for hospital care.

This behavior is consistent with the incentives facing individuals in a dual-choice situation. In most cases, choices are offered to an employee group which has already established patterns of medical care and relationships with particular physicians. People having good relationships with their physicians are unlikely to give them up to join a prepaid group practice.[26] Patients currently under treatment also would not be expected to switch physicians. (There is no issue if the choice

---

[23] Tessler and Mechanic, "Factors Affecting the Choice"; Dozier et al., "1970–71 Survey of Consumer Experience"; Roghmann et al., "Who Chooses Prepaid Medical Care?"; Hetherington, Hopkins, and Roemer, *Health Insurance Plans*; Gaus, Cooper, and Hirschman, "Contrasts in HMO and Fee-for-Service Performance"; and Berki, "Enrollment Choice in a Multi-HMO Setting."

[24] Roghmann et al., "Who Chooses Prepaid Medical Care?"

[25] Sandra M. Wells and Klaus J. Roghmann, "GM Inpatient Utilization Before and After Offering Prepayment Plans," paper presented at 105th Annual Meeting of the American Public Health Association, Washington, D.C., October 1977.

[26] Berki et al., "Enrollment Choice in a Multi-HMO Setting."

is between a conventional insurer and an individual practice association that includes those physicians.) People who have no close relationship with a physician or who perceive substantial financial benefits from the prepaid group practice are thus the most likely ones to enroll in the organization.

What are the advantages an HMO offers individuals already covered by conventional insurance? Conventional coverage offered in dual-choice situations usually includes reasonably comprehensive hospitalization benefits which, with the exception of maternity coverage, are comparable to HMO protection. Conventional coverage also might include some copayments, but we doubt that many people would be sufficiently sensitive to them to change plans. The major financial advantage HMOs offer their enrollees, then, is the coverage of ambulatory visits. Enrollment in an HMO is therefore most likely to occur among people who anticipate a large number of ambulatory visits.

Differentials in coverage for maternity care also appear to affect the choice of an HMO, and, in turn, hospital utilization. In the multiple-choice situation in Rochester, New York, Blue Cross–Blue Shield offered only $155 toward maternity costs that averaged $850 to $1,000, while the prepaid plans offered complete coverage. The subsequent general fertility of Blue Cross members was 30.9 births per 1,000 women ages fifteen to forty-four, while the rates in three prepaid plans were 75.1, 81.5, and 148.8.[27] The differential is probably due to self-selection. Contrary to the apparent effect, self-selection for HMO enrollment on the basis of high maternity benefits may help rather than hurt health maintenance organizations. The maternity benefits attract young married couples who typically have low hospitalization rates, both for themselves and their children.[28] The cost to the HMO for attracting such people is the few hospital days involved in a delivery. If these people

---

[27] Richard P. Wersinger, *The Analysis of Three Prepaid Health Care Plans in Monroe County, New York, Part III: Inpatient Utilization Statistics, January 1, 1974–December 31, 1974* (Rochester, N.Y.: University of Rochester School of Medicine and Dentistry, Department of Preventive Medicine and Community Health, October 1975).

[28] DHEW, HRA, National Center for Health Statistics, "Persons Hospitalized by Number of Episodes and Days Hospitalized in a Year—United States—1972," *Vital and Health Statistics*, series 10, no. 116, DHEW Publication No. (HRA) 77–1544.

stay members, this cost may provide a worthwhile investment. Offering optometry, dental care, and preventive services also may attract a relatively healthy population.

Lower hospital admission rates for HMOs also might reflect members' tendency to leave the plan or to obtain care outside the plan if they seek hospitalization, because hospitalization is frequently a matter of discretion. It is not uncommon for a patient to disagree with a physician and to seek second, third, or fourth opinions until the desired response is obtained. If such a patient is an HMO enrollee and the HMO encourages its physicians to avoid hospitalization, then the patient may well seek care outside the HMO, or, in a dual-choice situation, switch coverage at the next open enrollment period. Because of low overall incidence of hospitalization in the population, a relatively small number of "switchers with hospitalization in mind" can have a substantial effect on hospitalization rates. Unfortunately, this phenomenon is difficult to measure, and no evidence is available on its occurrence.

Self-selection in HMO membership has important consequences for the evaluation of HMO performance. If the lower hospital utilization and associated lower costs of health maintenance organizations are a function of their membership rather than their structure or financial incentives, then expectations about the effect of HMO expansion may require substantial adjustment. Rather than promoting efficiency in the overall delivery system, increased HMO membership might simply alter the distribution of medical costs. The expansion of dual choice and of HMOs might draw low users of hospital care into HMOs and leave high users in conventional insurance plans. If frequency of use reflects health status, the result would be concentration of medical costs among the sick, rather than the distribution of risk that insurance is supposed to promote. Conversely, if differential utilization patterns merely reflect preferences for different styles of medical care, the concentration of costs among high users of hospitals might be considered desirable. Finally, if HMOs attract persons who are high users of some services and lower users of other services, average costs and their distribution may remain comparable between HMOs and the fee-for-service system. At present we do not have enough evidence to determine which result would predominate if HMOs were to become more widely available.

Use of Preventive Services

Studies concerning the provision of preventive services can be divided into two groups that appear to have contradictory findings.[29] The first group supports the hypothesis that the HMO enrollees receive more preventive services than do people with conventional health insurance.[30] The second group suggests that there are no differences in the use of preventive services or that the HMO enrollees receive even fewer services than do people with conventional coverage.[31] In fact, the two sets of studies are not really in conflict. With a few exceptions,

---

[29] Harold S. Luft, "Why Do HMOs Seem to Provide More Health Maintenance Services?" *Milbank Memorial Fund Quarterly: Health and Society* 56 (Spring 1978):140–68.

[30] Committee for the Special Research Project in the Health Insurance Plan of Greater New York, *Health and Medical Care in New York City* (Cambridge, Mass.: Harvard University Press, 1957); Joy G. Cauffman, Milton I. Roemer, and Carl S. Schultz, "The Impact of Health Insurance Coverage on Health Care of School Children," *Public Health Reports* 82 (April 1967):323–28; Lester Breslow and Joseph R. Hochstim, "Sociocultural Aspects of Cervical Cytology in Alameda County, California," *Public Health Reports* 79 (February 1964):107–12; Lester Breslow, "Do HMOs Provide Health Maintenance?" paper presented to Delta Omega, San Francisco, California, November 7, 1973; Hetherington, Hopkins, and Roemer, *Health Insurance Plans*; Diana Barbara Dutton, "A Casual Model of the Use of Health Services: The Role of the Delivery System," unpublished doctoral dissertation, Massachusetts Institute of Technology, February 1976; Doris P. Slesinger, Richard C. Tessler, and David Mechanic, "The Effects of Social Characteristics on the Utilization of Preventive Medical Services in Contrasting Health Care Programs," *Medical Care* 14 (May 1976):392–404; J.E.F. Hastings et al., "Prepaid Group Practice in Sault Ste. Marie, Ontario; Part I: Analysis of Utilization Records," *Medical Care* 11 (March/April 1973):91–103; P.K. Diehr et al., "The Seattle Prepaid Health Care Project: Comparison of Health Services Delivery," Chapter 2, "Utilization: Ambulatory and Hospital," Grant No. R18 HS 00694, DHEW, HRA, National Center for Health Services Research, November 1976.

[31] Gordon H. DeFriese, "On Paying the Fiddler to Change the Tune: Further Evidence from Ontario Regarding the Impact of Universal Health Insurance on the Organization and Patterns of Medical Practice," *Milbank Memorial Fund Quarterly: Health and Society* 53 (Spring 1975):117–48; Norman Fuller and Margaret Patera, *Report on a Study of Medicaid Utilization of Services in a Prepaid Group Practice Health Plan*, DHEW Public Health Service (PHS), Bureau of Medical Services, January 1975; Gaus, Cooper, and Hirschman, "Contrasts in HMO and Fee-for-Service Performance"; Diehr et al., "The Seattle Prepaid Health Care Project."

the different results can be explained by focusing not on the distinction between HMO versus other coverage, but on the presence or absence of coverage for preventive visits. Such coverage is almost universal with HMOs, but it is rare with conventional insurance. Thus, those studies that involve a comparison between HMO enrollees and people with conventional insurance coverage (the first group above) are actually testing two variables: (1) an HMO health maintenance effect, and (2) the differential financial coverages for preventive care. In the few instances in which the third party covers preventive visits (the second group of studies), the second (insurance) variable is held constant and there appears to be little or no HMO health maintenance effect. In fact, studies comparing HMO enrollees with people having conventional coverage for preventive services typically have ambiguous results; the HMOs provide more preventive care of some types and less of others. These results may reflect recent skepticism in the medical community concerning the efficacy of many "preventive services," such as tests, screenings, and check-ups.[32]

In sum, HMO experience does not allow firm conclusions on the reasons for HMO enrollees' lower rates of hospital utilization and the organizations' resulting lower overall costs. Aside from evidence that lower utilization is not a function of preventive care, HMO experience is consistent with several hypotheses: (1) that HMO incentives and controls reduce all types of unnecessary hospital admissions; (2) that HMOs attract enrollees who tend to use hospital services less frequently than the conventionally insured population; and (3) that HMOs provide too little care. Evidence on the third hypothesis is considered in the review of evidence on HMO quality and member satisfaction, which follows.

Quality of Care

Improved health status or outcome is the ultimate objective of medical care. Unfortunately, outcomes are very difficult

---

[32] Morris F. Collen et al., "Multiphasic Checkup Evaluation Study: 4, Preliminary Cost Benefit Analysis for Middle-Aged Men," *Preventive Medicine* 2 (June 1973):236–46; Stuart S. Sagel et al., "Efficacy of Routine Screening and Lateral Chest Radiographs in a Hospital-Based Population," *New England Journal of Medicine* 291 (November 1974): 1001–04; A.L. Cochrane and P.C. Elwood, "Screening: The Case Against It," *Medical Officer* 121 (January 31, 1969): 53–57.

to measure. Health services researchers, therefore, rely on other measures of medical care quality, such as the presence of "appropriate" resources (structural measures) and the use of "appropriate" procedures for given cases (process measures).[33] There is unfortunately little evidence that structure, process, and outcome measures correlate well with each other or with what people might recognize as "quality." [34] Despite these limitations, all three measures are used here to review the quality of care in HMOs.

Although furthest removed from outcomes, structural measures are the most visible indices of quality of care. The available data generally support the argument that health maintenance organizations have resources at least as good as the resources of the conventional system.[35] HMOs tend to have higher proportions of more highly trained physicians and are more likely to use accredited hospitals. There are, however, a number of important exceptions. Some HMOs have not been able to get ready access to the "better" hospitals and others apparently have chosen not to emphasize specialists and accredited, nonprofit facilities. Moreover, there is nothing in a health maintenance organization's direct financial incentives to promote structural quality, other than the possible advantages structural quality offers in attracting physicians or enrollees.

With respect to organizational characteristics, there is little evidence that HMOs enhance quality of care. Despite frequent claims, there is no indication that group practice really leads to more informal consultations among physicians.[36] Group practice does seem to encourage more time for continuing education, but there is little evidence that such programs make a difference in the delivery of care; they may well just be a fringe benefit. Finally, group practice is not essential to peer

[33] Avedis Donabedian, "Evaluating the Quality of Medical Care," *Milbank Memorial Fund Quarterly* 44 (July 1966, Part 2):166–203.

[34] Robert H. Brook, "Critical Issues in the Assessment of Quality of Care and Their Relationship to HMOs," *Journal of Medical Education* 48 (April 1973, Part 2): 114–34; and Robert H. Brook, *Quality of Care Assessment: Comparison of Five Methods of Peer Review* (Washington, D.C.: National Center for Health Services Research and Development, U.S. Government Printing Office, 1973).

[35] Luft, *Health Maintenance Organizations*, Chapter 10.

[36] Paul B. Guptill and Fred E. Graham II, "Continuing Education Activities of Physicians in Solo and Group Practices: Report on a Pilot Study," *Medical Care* 14 (February 1976): 173–80.

review; physicians in group practice do have the advantage of physical proximity, but individual practice associations and fee-for-service practice allow the development and use of practice profiles for evaluating physicians.

The average HMO therefore appears to offer care comparable or somewhat superior to the "average" fee-for-service practitioner, but not superior to that of the "better" conventional settings.[37] Although HMOs tend to score higher than conventional practitioners when process measures (especially laboratory tests and procedures) are used, this differential appears to reflect comprehensiveness of coverage rather than organizational characteristics. Large prepaid group practices often exhibit higher quality than do average fee-for-service providers, but the quality is not higher than what large fee-for-service groups provide. The HMO financial structure, therefore, does not appear to be critical to performance.

Outcome measures are most useful in quality evaluation, but the available studies focus on narrowly defined mortality-morbidity measures or on broad outcomes such as disability days. The early Health Insurance Plan studies showed lower prematurity and mortality rates for HMO enrollees.[38] Few subsequent studies offer as conclusive evidence in any direction. In general, the available data suggest that outcomes in HMOs are much the same as those in conventional practice.

In sum, while the quality question remains unresolved, there is no evidence that HMOs achieve their utilization and cost savings by offering substantially lower quality care than does the fee-for-service system and, in fact, there is some suggestion of higher quality in health maintenance organizations.

Consumer Satisfaction

No generally accepted framework exists for evaluating satisfaction. One approach focuses on feelings people have about

[37] Luft, *Health Maintenance Organizations.*

[38] Sam Shapiro, Louis Weiner, and Paul Densen, "Comparison of Prematurity and Perinatal Mortality in a General Population and in the Population of a Prepaid Group Practice Medical Care Plan," *American Journal of Public Health* 48 (February 1958):170–85; idem, "Further Observations on Prematurity and Perinatal Mortality in a General Population and in the Population of a Prepaid Group Practice Medical Care Plan," *American Journal of Public Health* 50 (September 1960):1304–17; idem, "Patterns of Medical Use by the Indigent Aged Under Two Systems of Medical Care," *American Journal of Public Health* 57 (May 1967): 784–90.

various aspects of medical care, such as access, information transfer, quality, and humaneness; each is treated as a separate dimension and no effort is made to combine them. Another approach identifies and measures behavioral correlates of satisfaction or dissatisfaction, such as use of out-of-plan services and withdrawal from the plan.

The most important features of HMOs for which evidence on consumer satisfaction is available are access, financial coverage, continuity of care, communication, and perceived quality.[39] Among a broad range of access measures, prepaid group practices offer shorter office waiting times, but longer waiting periods to obtain an appointment. The relative value of these two measures of access will vary among individuals. The PGP pattern is probably best for people with routine problems that can be scheduled, such as checkups and periodic visits for chronic conditions. People with "semi-urgent" acute problems who can afford the time to wait in the office are more likely to prefer fee-for-service practitioners and the guarantee of eventually seeing their own physicians.

It is not surprising that financial coverage is the feature of health maintenance organizations that members like most. HMO members almost universally express greater satisfaction with the financial coverage provided by their HMOs than do people with other insurance coverage.

HMOs and fee-for-service arrangements also seem to differ with respect to physician-patient relationships.[40] Prepaid group practices appear to offer less continuity of care when that care is measured by consumer identification with a single physician. But when care is measured in terms of continuity within a system having the patient's records, a group may be able to provide more continuity of care. The first measure would seem to produce biased results. One of the main reasons people give for not joining a PGP is an existing close tie to a physician; those who do enroll therefore are much less likely to have had a close relationship with a physician. Hence a measure of consumer identification with a single physician may reflect consumer experience before joining an HMO and underlying preferences rather than consumer experience with the HMO itself.

---

[39] Luft, *Health Maintenance Organizations.*
[40] David Mechanic, *The Growth of Bureaucratic Medicine* (New York: Wiley-Interscience, 1976).

In medical care, communication between physician and patient is vital. Overall, people enrolled in prepaid group practices seem less happy with their communication with physicians than do fee-for-service patients or people enrolled in individual practice associations. PGP enrollees generally express more dissatisfaction with the information physicians give them than with the physicians' solicitation of information from them. The general view is that PGP physicians are less willing than individual practitioners to spend time with patients. Physicians in prepaid group practices also are reported to be dissatisfied with the degree of communication they have with their patients.[41]

Assessments of interactions with staff members other than physicians appear to be more mixed, with some prepaid group practices judged to be just as good as or better than the fee-for-service setting. This somewhat surprising result, given expectations that PGPs might be bureaucratic and impersonal, is perhaps understandable in terms of shorter waiting times in the office and, therefore, reduced patient interaction with support staff.

The second approach to measuring consumer satisfaction assumes, logically enough, that an "important indicator of consumer satisfaction might be the extent to which PGP subscribers continue to use services outside the plans in preference to the corresponding services available to them within the plans."[42] In fact, there is substantial evidence of a negative correlation between outside utilization and expressed satisfaction. The data on outside utilization reflect a reasonably consistent pattern. Between 5 percent and 10 percent of prepaid group practice members are regular outside users, while a comparable proportion of different members each year use an occasional service outside the plan. Overall, outside use accounts for 7 percent to 14 percent of all services members receive. If outside use represents dissatisfaction, which it does to some degree, the extent of outside use is comparable to the proportion of members reporting substantial dissatisfaction in interviews.

---

[41] David Mechanic, "The Organization of Medical Practice and Practice Orientations Among Physicians in Prepaid and Nonprepaid Primary Care Settings," *Medical Care* 13 (March 1975):189–204.

[42] Avedis Donabedian, "An Evaluation of Prepaid Group Practice," *Inquiry* 6 (September 1979):3–27.

The dual-choice arrangements available to most HMO members offer what may be the best single *objective* measure of overall satisfaction.[43] The impressive record of long-term growth in the HMO share of given enrollee groups implies that the levels of dissatisfaction are relatively low and have an insignificant effect on membership. Among every group of new enrollees, a small proportion, perhaps 5 percent to 10 percent, find that they really do not like the HMO. Such people probably become high users of outside services and eventually leave the plan. Over time, additional people become dissatisfied for one reason or another and leave. These withdrawals, however, are more than offset by withdrawals of people from conventional plans who join health maintenance organizations.

The coexistence of dissatisfaction and continued and growing HMO membership reflect the multiple factors affecting the choice of a health care plan. In the dual-choice setting, people who joined a health maintenance organization obviously felt that it was the best option available to them. In making that decision, they weighed the various factors, such as financial coverage, premiums, perceived quality, and access. For some people, the benefits of the HMO option outweighed the costs. The costs nevertheless continue to exist and when opinions are solicited, dissatisfaction is likely to be expressed. Hence, HMO members like the short waits and financial coverage, but are dissatisfied with the amount of time it takes to get an appointment, their inability to see their usual physician for urgent visits, and the limited communication and warmth in their patient-physician relationship. People would like the plan to improve all the characteristics that bother them while maintaining its low costs. However, when people are offered, through open-enrollment periods, the alternative of improving access and physician-patient interaction versus the price differential associated with conventional coverage, most choose to stay in the HMO.

---

[43] Several assumptions must be made when interpreting these data. First, they measure people's choices only among the available alternatives, and none of the options may be very satisfactory. Second, behavior often falls far short of the predictions of rational models. In particular, there appears to be a great deal of inertia, so that once in a plan, people stay there unless drastic changes occur. Over time, however, one can expect that a plan which its enrollees consistently dislike will lose membership. Third, people must have a basis for comparison and although most HMO members have some experience with traditional practice, most members of conventional plans have never tried HMOs.

Evidence on consumer satisfaction, then, like evidence on other elements of HMO experience, is not clear-cut. It seems fair to conclude that HMO costs tend to be lower than fee-for-service costs for broadly comparable populations; that lower costs primarily reflect lower hospital utilization; and, that, although we cannot identify the causes of these lower rates, they appear to be neither a product of poor-quality care nor a source of significant consumer dissatisfaction.

Models for Incorporating HMOs Under National Health Insurance

Available evidence indicates that health maintenance organizations offer advantages in medical care delivery that a national health insurance program would want to promote. Policies toward payment of HMOs under national health insurance appear to be critical to achieving this objective. Although current health financing programs (such as the Federal Employees Health Benefits Program) include some oversight of HMO qualifications, each has a different approach to payment. The FEHBP, which offers HMO enrollment as one of several insurance options, employs a payment mechanism that encourages competition among plans and, concomitantly, enhances the attractiveness of health maintenance organizations. The program makes the same dollar contribution regardless of the plan chosen by the insured.[44] The fact that the patient bears the full financial burden of more expensive plans would favor HMO enrollment in most areas. Under the FEHBP, it is assumed that beneficiary cost-consciousness and competition will assure reasonable rates.

Medicare, in contrast, offers no market for insurance plans. Instead, it treats HMOs as providers of care rather than as an insurance plan and has applied traditional provider payment methods to HMOs—fee-for-service for physicians and cost reimbursement for hospitals.[45] Efforts to shift to some

---

[44] The FEHBP will pay 75 percent of the individual plan's premium or 60 percent of the average premium of six large insurance plans, whichever is lower. In most cases the 60 percent figure is lower resulting in uniform FEHBP contributions across plans.

[45] Judith Feder, *Medicare: The Politics of Federal Hospital Insurance*, (Lexington, Mass.: D.C. Heath, Lexington Books, 1977), pp. 82–87.

form of capitation reimbursement, authorized since 1972, have involved Medicare in complex calculations of appropriate rates.

These alternative approaches to payment, reinforced by other features of the programs, have had very different consequences for HMOs. The FEHBP has successfully stimulated HMO enrollment. In 1976, roughly 8 percent of federal employees were enrolled in HMOs, more than double the proportion of HMO enrollees in the general population.[46] In contrast, fewer than 2 percent of Medicare subscribers were enrolled in HMOs in 1977.[47] Although this low participation rate reflects in part the fact that HMOs find the elderly less desirable than other age groups as enrollees, the low participation rate also reflects the restrictiveness and complexity of capitation rates under Medicare. Because Medicare and the federal employees' program have had considerable experience with health maintenance organizations, the next section explores in some detail the lessons to be drawn from both groups' experience for incorporating HMOs under national health insurance.[48]

---

[46] Enrollment rates were 7.5 percent for federal employees and approximately 3 percent in the general population in 1977. Figures obtained from "Annual Report of Financial and Statistical Data for Fiscal Year Ended June 30, 1976, for Civil Service Retirement, Federal Employees Group Life Insurance, Federal Employees Health Benefits and Retired Federal Employees Health Benefits," Bureau of Retirement, Insurance, and Occupational Health, U.S. Civil Service Commission (CSC), Table D6, p. 34; and from "National HMO Census Survey, 1977," Washington, D.C. Group Health Association of America, Inc., 1978.

[47] "HMO-GPP Enrollment Totals Through December 1977"; enrollment statistics obtained from the Division of Group Health Plan Operations, Health Care Financing Administration (HCFA).

[48] Medicaid is not discussed here despite the fact that its involvement with HMOs has been much greater than Medicare's has been. Because Medicaid is a state-administered program and policies differ among states, a review of the whole range of policies in several states is beyond the scope of this chapter. Medicaid beneficiaries typically have less freedom of choice of provider, both because they are less mobile and relatively isolated from most physicians and because low Medicaid fees have often discouraged physician participation. As a result, Medicaid seems to have developed a unique set of problems: unethical marketing practices, low-quality care, and financial scandals. However, several of the problems Medicaid faces, such as how to reimburse for care and how to regulate, are very similar to those of Medicare, and the Medicare discussion will cover the critical issues. We also have not examined the federal HMO program established by the 1973 HMO Act and subsequent amendments because that program is basically concerned with supply subsidization and regulation.

THE FEDERAL EMPLOYEES
HEALTH BENEFITS PROGRAM

The Federal Employees Health Benefits Program has been a strong advocate of prepaid health plans. The 1959 Federal Employees Health Benefits Act authorized the Civil Service Commission to provide health benefits to its employees, annuitants, and dependents. A "multiple-choice" approach is used; Blue Cross–Blue Shield, Aetna, employee organization plans, individual practice plans, and group practice plans all are permitted to offer health coverage. As HMOs continually develop throughout the states, more plans are negotiating with the FEHBP to tap the large pool of potential federal enrollees. In 1973, 7.2 percent of almost 9 million federal employees were enrolled in twenty-six plans. By 1976, approximately 8 percent of federal employees were enrolled in forty plans; total enrollment reached 760,434 of 9.5 million employees that year.[49] The number of HMOs in which the FEHBP offers enrollment has subsequently increased dramatically, to seventy-eight plans by January 1978, and negotiations are under way to offer several additional plans at a later date.[50]

In 1978, total biweekly premium charges for all comprehensive plans ranged from $11.55 to $25.79 for self and $33.13 to $62.03 for self and family.[51] The FEHBP views the wide range of premiums and benefit packages offered as an important aspect of the program.[52] The offering of several diverse comprehensive plans and governmentwide Blue Cross–Blue Shield and Aetna plans provides considerable consumer choice. To increase competition among plans, and thereby maximize choice to the employee, the FEHBP also maintains a policy of qualifying as many comprehensive plans as possible with-

---

[49] "Annual Report of Financial and Statistical Data for Fiscal Year Ended June 30, 1973," and "Annual Report of Financial and Statistical Data for Fiscal Year Ended June 30, 1976," Bureau of Retirement, Insurance, and Occupational Health, CSC.

[50] Interview with senior Comprehensive Health Plans Office official, Bureau of Retirement, Insurance, and Occupational Health, CSC.

[51] "Federal Employees Health Benefits Program 1978 Monthly Health Benefits Rates," Bureau of Retirement, Insurance, and Occupational Health, CSC.

[52] Interview with senior Comprehensive Health Plans Office official, Bureau of Retirement, Insurance, and Occupational Health, CSC.

out limiting the number of plans offered by location or plan type.[53]

Ironically, unlike most large employers, the FEHBP is not required under the dual-choice provision of the HMO Act to offer a federally qualified HMO. But the FEHBP prefers to have as many participating HMOs as possible and relies on consumer preferences and competition to guarantee quality of care. Although requirements for FEHBP participation are in many ways not so strict as those for qualification under the HMO Act, federally qualified HMOs also must meet certain additional FEHBP requirements. The FEHBP, for example, requires HMOs to have physicians representing three specialties.[54] To date, the FEHBP has turned down one federally qualified HMO for not meeting these additional requirements.[55]

The FEHBP has a two-step process of determining reimbursement for benefits offered by comprehensive plans. The first step is the calculation of premium rates, and the second, the determination of the employee's share of the premium. The FEHBP establishes premiums on the basis of a community rate or an experience rate. Experience rating essentially results in reimbursement for costs and therefore does not offer the usual HMO incentives to control utilization and costs. The FEHBP therefore discourages this mode of payment, although it would lower rates to HMOs with particularly healthy members. Currently, only a handful of HMO plans have experience-rated premiums that are negotiated annually.

The more common approach to payment under the FEHBP is community rating—use of the HMO's rate to the general community. Although federal procurement regulations limit items included under the rate and both the Government Accounting Office and the Civil Service Commission have the authority to audit HMOs for compliance, the FEHBP generally accepts an HMO's community rate if it is approved by

---

[53] Ibid.

[54] "Guidelines for Comprehensive Medical Plans Seeking Approval to Participate in the Federal Employees Health Benefits Program." Comprehensive Health Plans Office, Bureau of Retirement, Insurance, and Occupational Health, CSC.

[55] Interview with senior Comprehensive Health Plans Office official, Bureau of Retirement, Insurance, and Occupational Health, CSC.

the state insurance department.[56] The FEHBP operates on the principle that competition among plans will assure reasonable rates. Patients bear the full burden of rate excesses and are expected to respond to excess by changing plans.

The FEHBP permits adjustment of rates according to family size, with per capita premiums set higher for individuals in order to attract families into HMOs. This practice is justified on the grounds that as long as total revenues received from an employee group are based on a pure community capitation rate, loadings according to family composition are acceptable within the community rate concept. Self and family rates cannot be based on employee group population characteristics and utilization rates. The FEHBP allows for additional loadings and adjustments to reflect differences in coverage and special circumstances for the FEHBP enrollees.[57] For example, adjustments are made for extra benefits, coverage of dependent children, employees on leave without pay, and late payment of premiums.

The second step in FEHBP payment is allocation of the premium between the government and employee. Once the gross premium for self only and the premium for self and family are determined, the government will contribute either 75 percent of the premium in question or 60 percent of the average premium charge for the six largest plans, whichever amount is lower.[58] In almost all cases the 60 percent figure is lower, making federal contributions uniform across plans. For 1978, the maximum government biweekly contribution for self-only enrollment was $10.98 and for family enrollment, $26.69. The employee is responsible for the remainder of the premium charge which, in 1978, ranged from lows of $2.89 and $8.08 to highs of $41.81 and $35.34 for self only and for self and family, respectively.[59]

The FEHBP's 60 percent of average premium charges are based on the premiums of the following six plans: Blue Cross–

[56] Interviews with Office of the Actuary official, Bureau of Retirement, Insurance, and Occupational Health, CSC.

[57] "Instructions for Development of 1978 Federal Rates from Community Rates," Bureau of Retirement, Insurance, and Occupational Health, CSC.

[58] 5 U.S.C. 8906 and 5 CFR Section 890.501—Section 890.503.

[59] "1978 Federal Employees Health Benefits Program Bi-Weekly Premium Rates for Postal and Non-Postal Employees," Bureau of Retirement, Insurance, and Occupational Health, CSC.

Blue Shield and Aetna (the two governmentwide plans), American Postal Workers Union Plan and the National Association for Letter Carriers Plan (the two employee organization plans with the largest number of enrollees), and Kaiser Northern California and Kaiser Southern California (the two largest comprehensive medical plans). Because most government contributions are based on these six plans, an overstatement of actual costs (if there are large profits or unjustified expenses) of any one of the plans will affect government contributions to all plans and thus the total expenditures of the FEHBP.[60] The average premium charge based on data from these six plans may also overstate "average costs" in low-cost geographic areas and understate them in high-cost areas.

Despite these risks of what may be considered excessive payments, FEHBP accepts as reasonable whatever rates the market sets. The FEHBP's policy of paying a partial and fairly uniform amount across plans allows employees to exercise free choice of plans but places on them the full burden of additional payments for more expensive plans. This policy is expected to make employees cost-conscious. Moreover, this policy coupled with the FEHBP's policies of information dissemination, open enrollment, and community rating, is expected to produce active competition between health maintenance organizations and traditional insurers. The intention is to minimize costs without "cream skimming" (i.e., enrolling a relatively healthy population) or sacrificing quality.

MEDICARE

The FEHBP's relatively simple approach to payment stands in marked contrast to Medicare's complex reimbursement rate determinations. Unlike FEHBP, Medicare does not establish a market for insurance plans, one type of which is the health maintenance organization. Instead, the program is the insurance plan and HMOs are one type of provider. For fee-for-service physicians, hospitals, and other providers, designers

---

[60] Recent investigation by the U.S. Government Accounting Office (GAO) has questioned the premiums quoted for federal employees by Kaiser plans. See "Civil Service Should Audit Kaiser Plans' Premium Rates Under the Federal Employees Health Benefits Program to Protect the Government," U.S. GAO Report HRD 78–42, January 1978.

of the Medicare program took great pains to adopt payment mechanisms consistent with (and often more generous than) pre-Medicare practices. Such courtesies were not, however, extended to HMOs. Rather than adopting the HMO capitation mechanism, Medicare required that HMOs adopt the fee-for-service or cost reimbursement arrangements used by traditional providers.[61]

Until 1972, Medicare would pay for care provided by HMOs only by one of these two methods; Medicare also paid separately for physician (Part B) and hospital (Part A) care. Alternatives to fee-for-service and cost reimbursement methods have been introduced and are discussed later, but the two original methods are still in effect. Under both of these original arrangements, payments for all Part A services and any Part B services not provided by the HMO are made directly to the hospital, nursing home, or other providers of those services. Under the fee-for-service method, bills for Part B services are submitted to area carriers, and services are paid at a rate of 80 percent of reasonable charges after deductibles are met. Under the cost reimbursement option, per capita payments are made on interim basis but are adjusted retroactively following the HMO's submission of actual cost and utilization reports to Medicare.

The separation of payment for hospital and physician services and the use of cost-based or fee-for-service reimbursement are counter to the basic concept of a health maintenance organization. This approach to reimbursement does not provide for a fixed capitation rate, will not reimburse for available but unused services, and provides no financial incentives for an organization to keep costs low or to control utilization of services by its Medicare beneficiaries. Furthermore, under cost-based reimbursement, plans do not assume financial responsibility for emergency services, urgently needed services, or services received outside the HMO, because Medicare reimburses these services on a fee-for-service basis. The Medicare enrollee is free to use and be reimbursed for Medicare-covered services received from providers other than the HMO. Although this approach maintains freedom of choice of provider, reimbursing the beneficiary for care from several pro-

---

[61] For a more thorough analysis of the legislative development, see Feder, *Medicare*, pp. 82–7.

viders may result in duplication of services and higher costs. Removing financial responsibility from the plan to provide all necessary services removes incentives to control unnecessary out-of-plan utilization and to seek the least expensive means for providing care. Finally, cost reimbursement does not allow HMOs to exercise their primary tactics for attracting enrollees—reducing cost-sharing obligations or offering additional benefits.

In the short term, these cost reimbursement policies may hold Medicare payments below probable capitation levels. Cost reimbursement over any significant time period, however, will not provide the incentives necessary to control HMO costs, unless Medicare beneficiaries remain a relatively small share of HMOs' total enrollment.

As a result of these program features, few health maintenance organizations have contracted with Medicare under the original reimbursement options, and few elderly people are enrolled in prepaid groups. In 1977, thirty-five prepaid plans contracted directly with Medicare under the original reimbursement option (Section 1833 of the Social Security Act) for reimbursement of Part B services, and provided care to approximately 440,000 elderly persons.[62] The rate of HMO enrollment among the elderly is roughly half the rate for the rest of the population.[63]

Recognition that Medicare discouraged HMO enrollment led to congressional authorization of the new approach to reimbursement in 1972, through an amendment to the Social Security Act (Section 1876). The legislative history of that amendment reveals the difficulty of setting an HMO rate in the absence of a market. Unlike the FEHBP, which relies on the insurance market to control rates, the Medicare program and its overseers in Congress have been preoccupied with establishing a payment rate that covers, but does not substan-

---

[62] "HMO-GPP Enrollment Totals Through December 1977," table obtained from the Division of Group Health Plan Operations, HCFA.

[63] Enrollment rates were 1.7 percent for Medicare and approximately 3 percent in the general population in 1977. See enrollment statistics in "HMO-GPP Enrollment Totals Through December 1977," table obtained from the Division of Group Health Plan Operations, HCFA, and "National HMO Census Survey, 1977," Group Health Association of America, Inc., Washington, D.C., 1978.

tially exceed, the costs of delivering care. As a result, rate determination remains quite complex.

Under the 1972 amendment, plans meeting the Medicare definition of an HMO can be reimbursed for both Part A and Part B services. Although the prevailing payment mechanism remains restrictive, with payments made on a cost basis retroactively adjusted according to services rendered, the amendment allows HMOs that meet additional special size and experience requirements to be paid for both services on a risk basis. HMOs choosing this option are required to provide all Part A and Part B services available to persons residing in the area served, to offer an open-enrollment period, and to assume financial responsibility for all services rendered to Medicare enrollees. The Medicare beneficiary is "locked into" the plan until the next open-enrollment period; Medicare will not reimburse enrollees for care received outside the HMO (except emergency services).

Annual capitation rates for at-risk HMOs are equal to the adjusted average per capita cost (AAPCC) to Medicare for services delivered to Medicare beneficiaries in the area who are not enrolled in health maintenance organizations. Although interim payments are made in advance, calculations of AAPCC are made and rates adjusted after the year in which services are delivered. Plans receive a maximum of half the difference between operating costs and the AAPCC, up to 20 percent of nonmember costs.[64] Savings in excess of 20 percent of the AAPCC are recaptured by the Medicare trust funds, and any deficits are absorbed by the HMO or carried forward to be offset against future savings.

An HMO is permitted to return its share of the savings to Medicare beneficiaries and thus encourage elderly enrollment in HMOs by lowering supplemental premiums, by covering deductible and coinsurance amounts, or by increasing benefits. It cannot, however, make cash refunds to beneficiaries.[65] If HMOs do not choose to return savings to beneficiaries, they can keep the money, expand capacity, fund another HMO location, or return savings to providers in terms of increased salaries.

As of 1978, only one plan, Group Health Cooperative of

---

[64] Commerce Clearing House, Inc., *Medicare and Medicaid Guide*, paragraph 13,965.

[65] Ibid.

Puget Sound in Seattle, had contracted with Medicare on a risk basis.[66] A retroactively adjusted capitation rate and shared savings appear to be an insufficient incentive for HMOs to seek Medicare enrollees. As a result, new proposals have surfaced for Medicare reimbursement. Most prominent is a proposal to pay HMOs 95 percent of their adjusted average per capita cost and to allow them to retain whatever savings they actually accomplish. Plans would be obligated, however, to use these savings to improve benefits or to reduce cost sharing for elderly beneficiaries.

Like previous Medicare policies, this proposal reflects Medicare's ambivalence in dealing with health maintenance organizations. At the same time that policy makers seek to offer HMOs financial incentives to enroll the elderly, they are anxious to avoid allowing what might be seen as the excessive profits that would occur if HMOs engaged in cream skimming. To limit the size of the HMO payments, Medicare has tied them to fee-for-service costs for an allegedly comparable population. To limit the attractiveness of potential profits, Medicare has imposed constraints on HMOs' use of savings. Not only do these limitations require detailed auditing, but also they may be insufficient to achieve the intended objectives.

First, present methods of calculation of the adjusted average per capita cost are extremely crude. The government's actuary determines per capita area cost by compiling non-HMO Medicare claims within a health maintenance organization's service area. To compare equitably an individual HMO's costs with area costs, actuarial adjustments are made for age, sex, race, disability status, and institutional status. These variables, however, are not sufficient to control for both obvious and subtle differences in factors affecting health service utilization patterns. Other variables likely to be highly correlated with the elderly's use of health service would include the presence and kind of chronic illness, Medicaid eligibility, availability of private insurance, conversion and open-enrollment status, income, education, marital status, and living ar-

---

[66] "HMO-GPP Enrollment Totals Through December 1977," table obtained from the Division of Group Health Plan Operations, HCFA. Seven other HMOs contracted on a nonrisk basis under the 1972 combined Parts A and B reimbursement option. Including Puget Sound, these plans provided care for approximately 20,000 Medicare beneficiaries.

rangements. Control for all these variables requires extensive
data and careful analysis. Failure to control for the most important of them, however, results in crude estimates of the
AAPCC, which in turn may cause gross errors in estimating
the cost of caring for the HMO population.

The second problem in Medicare policy is the effect of controls on HMOs' use of savings, that is, the difference between
costs incurred and Medicare payments. Currently, HMOs that
choose the risk option must share their savings with the government but they may use their share as they wish. The proposed change in reimbursement would prohibit HMOs from
earning profits or net income on their Medicare enrollees.
HMOs could avoid savings by increasing their service costs,
either in fact (by expanding facilities, staff, or salaries) or in
fiction (by shifting overhead to Medicare enrollees). And expanding enrollment might offer some economies of scale,
improving HMOs' ability to market to the non-Medicare population. But it is not clear that these possibilities offer HMOs
sufficient reward for expanding elderly enrollment. The current approach, which limits the amount of savings HMOs can
keep but does not restrict the use of savings, may therefore be
preferable.

Medicare's difficulties in setting rates that are "just right"
offer important lessons for national health insurance, because
NHI programs that eliminate insurance markets will undoubtedly face the same problem. An NHI program could assume a cautious posture and reimburse HMOs on a cost basis,
or at some percentage of fee-for-service, and permit the HMO
to retain none of the savings. In following this course, national
health insurance would discourage further HMO development
and forfeit the benefits that HMO competition with the fee-
for-service sector would bring. The alternative—paying HMOs'
unadjusted rates equal or close to fee-for-service costs—would
certainly encourage HMO growth by assuring healthy profits.
This practice, however, might lead to widespread cream skimming and increases in program costs.

An ideal NHI reimbursement policy would strike a balance
among three objectives: (1) incorporating incentives for
HMOs to grow by permitting retention of savings when they
result from efficiency; (2) encouraging HMOs to use savings
to reduce premiums, deductibles, and coinsurance payments or
to increase benefits and thus aid their enrollees; and (3) re-

ducing government expenditures. Provisions requiring HMOs to return all the savings to beneficiaries or to the government are obviously inappropriate. Increased sophistication in calculating capitation rates, such as Medicare's AAPCC, also is necessary. Several of the relevant variables mentioned earlier should be controlled for and a schedule of rates established. It is not necessary to control for every determinant of utilization. Cream skimming has costs as well as benefits. Beyond some point, it probably does not pay a health maintenance organization to "fine-tune" its enrollment practices. Policies such as open enrollment also restrict an HMO's ability to limit its risks through patient selection.

Failure to accurately calculate capitation rates under nonmarket programs leads to two types of problems. If capitation rates are too low relative to the costs of care for an individual or a group, the HMO will be forced to "cream" low-cost enrollees or to provide inadequate service. If open enrollment results in too many high-cost enrollees for a particular HMO, that organization will ultimately fail. If capitation rates are too high relative to the costs of care, the HMO will receive substantial profit. Some of the savings can be returned to the beneficiary in the form of lower cost sharing or greater benefits. The problem arises when the savings result not from greater efficiency but from enrollment of low risks. The program's costs for the low-risk individuals may actually have been lower under fee-for-service arrangements.

A similar problem can occur under the FEHBP market arrangement, but the calculation of capitation rates is much simpler and the beneficiary is more likely to bear the burden of mistakes. The question of who can best bear that burden, of course, is an important equity issue. In the market arrangement, the program attempts to set a rate below the costs of care under all available insurance arrangements. The insured then chooses among plans and bears the full financial burden of choosing more expensive coverage. If the program establishes a benefit level that is too low for a particular individual or group, supplementary payments for coverage will be necessary. If the program establishes a benefit level that is too high relative to the costs of coverage for a particular individual or group, HMOs and insurance carriers can reduce cost sharing, increase benefits, or retain the difference as profit. The government can reduce the likelihood of these actions by lowering its payment level, thereby shifting the burden of financing expensive coverage to individuals or groups who want or need them. The nonmarket approach, for example, Medicare, is characterized by a marked unwillingness to shift this burden; as a result, the government bears the consequences of mistakes in setting capitation rates. Because high-cost beneficiaries cannot supplement government capitation rates to obtain coverage, one of two things happens: Either beneficiaries receive no care from HMOs but instead receive care in the more costly fee-for-service sector, or the program pays more for care in HMOs than it would for fee-for-service care, again increasing costs.

Role of HMOs in Four National Health Insurance Plans

Contracting arrangements are only one of many features of a national health insurance plan that will affect HMO viability and growth. Other important features include the comprehensiveness of benefit packages, the method of eligibility determination, the presence of deductibles and coinsurance, the methods of paying fee-for-service physicians, and tax treatment of insurance premiums. In order to explore the combined effect of these factors, this section examines the prospects for HMOs under four NHI plans—the Nixon-Ford Comprehensive Health Insurance Plan (CHIP), the Long-Ribicoff-Waggonner Catastrophic Health Insurance Plan, the Kennedy-Corman Health Security Plan, and the Enthoven Consumer Choice Health Plan.

COMPREHENSIVE HEALTH INSURANCE PLAN— NIXON-FORD

CHIP comprises three separate plans. For the employed population, the key feature of the CHIP proposal is mandated employer coverage of employees with a broad, but not total, basic benefit package including both deductibles and coinsurance. In CHIP's Assisted Health Insurance Plan (AHIP), low-income and nonemployed people would be covered through a comparable package financed in part by premiums and in part by federal and state governments. Finally, CHIP's Federal Health Care Insurance Plan (FHCIP) for the aged would replace Medicare and involve only minor changes from that program. Under all three plans, prepaid group practices and individual practice associations would have to cover the mandated basic benefits and be reimbursed only on a capitation basis, with copayment as authorized by the Department of Health, Education, and Welfare.

Under CHIP's Employee Health Insurance Plan (EHIP), the mandated benefit package would substantially improve coverage from any employees. For instance, only 70 percent of employed wage and salary workers currently have regular medical benefits and only 37 percent have major medical coverage.[67] Expansion in benefits also would probably mean an increase in premiums. This increase would substantially reduce the premium differential that currently leads many employees to reject an HMO option. HMOs might be able to offer a basic benefit package without copayments at premiums comparable to conventional insurance premiums for basic benefits alone. If so, HMO enrollment would clearly be a better buy for employees than conventional insurance would be. Employee choice would nevertheless be limited by the fact that CHIP (like the existing HMO Act) would require employers to offer coverage in only one prepaid group plan and one individual practice association, where they are available in the community. If there were several HMOs of each type in an area, this provision not only would limit choice but also would reduce the portability of coverage if workers were to change jobs in the same locale. This provision also could lead to controversy over which particular HMO should be allowed to market in a given employee group.

The continued use of tax deductions for employer and employee premium payments under EHIP would maintain the current subsidization of more expensive plans. HMOs tend to have lower total enrollee costs than do conventional carriers, but these costs often are reflected in a combination of higher premiums and lower out-of-pocket costs. The tax subsidy of premiums (especially when combined with current increases

---

[67] Martha Remy Yohalem, "Employee-Benefit Plans, 1975," *Social Security Bulletin* 40 (November 1977):19–28.

in the standard deduction and proposals for a 10 percent adjusted gross income floor for medical deductions) makes plans with premiums more attractive than plans with out-of-pocket payments. If conventional insurers moved toward more comprehensive packages and lower copayments under EHIP, however, their utilization rates and premiums would probably rise. In contrast to HMOs, higher premiums for conventional insurance would not be offset by lower out-of-pocket costs. Thus even though tax subsidies continued to favor more expensive plans, HMOs would gain competitive advantage.

In its reliance on the market (albeit somewhat distorted by the subsidies and limited choice), EHIP resembles the Federal Employees Health Benefits Program approach to HMO contracting. The plans for the poor (AHIP) and the aged (FHCIP), however, are closer to the Medicare model and require that the federal government set HMO capitation rates. Enrollees under these two plans also would have the option of electing coverage under an approved prepaid group plan or individual practice association. If PGP or IPA coverage were selected, the state or federal government would pay the plan an amount equal to the average cost of coverage to the government under the regular state-administered AHIP or FHCIP, whichever was applicable. Government payments would be equal to the average cost of care, less average deductible and coinsurance obligations. While the proposal is not specific, this payment would be comparable to Medicare's adjusted average per capita cost. Because of the high cost-sharing requirements, for traditional insurance, particularly under AHIP, HMOs probably would attract more elderly enrollees than they have done under Medicare. What is perhaps more important, CHIP would not adopt Medicare's restrictions on either the capitation rate (through the adjusted average per capita cost) or on the use of savings. If capitation rates were not adjusted for population characteristics related to likely service use, the incentives to enroll low risks would be considerable. Low-risk people could cost the government more if they joined HMOs than if they remained in the fee-for-service system. In AHIP, HMO cream skimming would make the state plan more and more costly, increasing the rewards to HMOs, and, concomitantly, increasing public expenses.

Such a situation would be less likely to occur under FHCIP. Because FHCIP is national in scope, HMO enrollment would have less effect on public plan costs and on capitation rates than would be the case under the state-administered AHIP. Failure to adjust the national rate for geographic variations in cost, however, would pose other problems. In high-cost regions, the capitation payment might be barely sufficient to cover costs, while in low-cost regions it would be excessive. This approach seems a substantial step backward from Medicare's adjusted average per capita cost, which incorporates geographic variables.

Under the CHIP proposal, fee-for-service physicians choosing to participate in the program would have to accept the state fee schedule as payment in full for all patients. Nonparticipating physicians would have to accept the state fee schedule for AHIP and FHCIP, but could charge more for EHIP beneficiaries. If participation rates were low, physicians might try to avoid serving the poor, and HMOs could become the only option for large segments of the urban poor. If the poor had little or no choice of providers, HMOs might not provide care of acceptable quality. This problem is less likely to occur with respect to the elderly, for two reasons. First, the aged are geographically more evenly distributed than the poor, and thus the elderly are less likely to be in areas where an HMO provides the only source of care. Second, as indicated above, joining a prepaid group practice requires changing physicians, and the elderly, who are often under the care of and have strong attachments to particular physicians, are less likely to make such a change.

CATASTROPHIC HEALTH INSURANCE PLAN— LONG-RIBICOFF-WAGGONNER

The Long-Ribicoff-Waggonner proposal would establish a federally financed program of catastrophic health insurance benefits designed to coordinate coverage with a revised Medicaid program (the Medical Assistance Program) and with conventional private basic health insurance. As an alternative to adopting the federal program, employers could establish their own catastrophic plans. This plan has a provision for pooling risk, but it may be limited to only very large benefits levels. Thus plans could be effectively experience-rated.

The financing provisions of this proposal would give employers strong incentives to establish their own plans, and to pay considerable attention to their cost-effectiveness. The federal program would be supported by 1 percent payroll tax (using the Social Security wage base) ; 50 percent of the contribution would count as a federal tax credit, rather than as a business deduction. If a firm established its own plan, it would receive a tax credit based not on its actual premium payment but on the actuarial average for catastrophic health insurance costs in the state. Given the better-than-average health of most employee groups, most firms could opt for private coverage and receive a tax credit substantially greater than 50 percent of the payroll tax. The lower the actual premiums paid, the more the firms could retain from that tax credit. The probable result would be enhanced competition, and competition should stimulate interest in HMOs.

Interest in health maintenance organizations is particularly likely because the proposal would require carriers to offer a basic health insurance package to cover services that form the deductible of the catastrophic plans. HMOs might cover these services more cheaply than conventional insurance could. Basic insurance packages as well as the Medical Assistance Program for low-income people (which would replace Medicaid) could allow some coinsurance and deductibles. Given these cost-sharing provisions, the Long-Ribicoff-Waggonner proposal appears to offer a definite place for the marketing of HMO coverage. The proposal, however, does not even mention dual choice, but existing HMO Act provisions would probably apply. Moreover, nothing is said about Medicare and Medical Assistance Plan enrollments in HMOs, so they are not precluded. Still, the Long-Ribicoff-Waggonner proposal would not encourage HMO development in the manner that CHIP would.

HEALTH SECURITY PLAN—KENNEDY-CORMAN

The Health Security plan is the most explicitly pro-HMO proposal. Its stated intent is to restructure the delivery system by replacing fee-for-service physician payment with salaries and capitation payments under a top-down budgeting process.

Unlike most other NHI bills, which seek to encourage cost-consciousness through consumer cost sharing, the Kennedy-Corman plan focuses most of its attention on providers. Ironically, the result might in fact be less HMO development under Kennedy-Corman than under other bills.

Given the comprehensive benefit package and the absence of cost sharing, it is reasonable to question whether people would join HMOs if this proposal were enacted. It is difficult to imagine many people leaving their customary providers to join a prepaid group practice, unless the group already had an outstanding reputation in the community. It is important to remember from our earlier review that the evidence on enrollment choice is that even with substantial cost savings, people with good patient-physician relationships will not switch into PGPs. For those without established relationships, the potential savings under Kennedy-Corman are limited. Not only would the plan have no cost-sharing gap that HMOs could fill, but also HMOs could offer very few extra benefits with which to attract members. People who did not belong to HMOs could get mental health and dental benefits at no cost from organizations formed exclusively for these services. The only benefit for which HMOs might have an advantage would be outpatient prescription drugs for acute conditions, hardly a large cost. Thus, even if the costs of a prepaid group practice were quite low relative to its capitation payments, these savings could not be passed on to potential enrollees. The probable result would be limited HMO development, which is consistent with experience in Canada under similar conditions.[68]

The strongest incentives for HMO development under Kennedy-Corman would be the budgeting system for provider payment. A national health budget would be prospectively established and these funds allocated to regions on a per capita basis with some recognition of current levels of regional expenditures. These allocations are to be adjusted to reduce regional disparities over time. The regional board or "Health Security Agency" would then use similar bases to divide its funds among health service areas, which would then pay local providers. In that allocation, HMOs would receive priority over fee-for-service providers. If, during a given year, funds allocated for fee-

---

[68] Eugene Vayda, "Prepaid Group Practice Under Universal Health Insurance in Canada," *Medical Care* 15 (May 1977):382–90.

for-service providers were less than billings, their fees would be reduced in an amount proportionate to the volume of services billed. HMOs would receive capitation payments for ambulatory care equal to the average costs in the local areas. If an HMO had its own hospital or nursing home, it would receive an annual budget for those services. If it arranged for institutional services through other providers, those providers would be reimbursed on a per patient-day basis. An HMO would be entitled to 75 percent of any savings resulting from lower utilization of institutional services by its enrollees compared with similar population groups. As an alternative, an HMO could receive a capitation payment for institutional care and if there were savings, the HMO could keep the entire amount.

Given the expectation of increasingly tight regional budgets, health care providers would have an incentive to join or to form HMOs to get the guaranteed capitation payments and to avoid the vagaries of the residual fee-for-service budget. (Substantial funds would be set aside to finance the development of organized provider systems.) As noted earlier, because of the absence of cost sharing and the comprehensiveness of the benefit package, it may be difficult to entice people to enroll in prepaid groups. But this difficulty does not exist for individual practice associations, in which patients can remain under the care of their own physicians. IPAs require no change in the style of practice for either physicians or patients. Only the source of payment would differ; the local medical foundation rather than the local health security agency would allocate funds to individuals providers.

This change in source of payment could have several significant consequences. First, physicians might be more willing to cooperate with a medical society individual practice association than with a government agency. Second, the IPA might choose to be responsible for institutional services in the area; in fact, there are strong incentives for this to happen. It would allow hospitals to escape from budget negotiations with the local agency and, instead, to deal with the IPA on whatever basis the two could agree upon. Third, the IPA could reallocate funds from hospitals to physicians in order to maintain professional incomes and practice styles. (At current expenditure levels, a 1 percent reduction in hospital expenditures could provide a 2 percent increase in physicians' revenues.) Fourth, if the fee-for-service sector were to disappear into IPAs, there would be no "standard for comparison" against which to evaluate capitation rates.

Despite the greater potential for individual practice associations with enactment of the Kennedy-Corman bill, there is one possible situation in which prepaid group practices would prosper. Because capitation rates would be based on average community costs of care in this plan, the incentives for HMO cream skimming would be substantial. As noted in the discussion of Medicare reimbursement policies, adjustments for differential risks are not simple. Because of centralized control over marketing and enrollment, prepaid group practices are more likely to be successful at cream skimming than are individual practice associations. (PGPs have central formalized marketing and enrollment procedures, whereas IPAs are more likely to rely on individual physicians, who have different incentives from those facing the organization.) Widespread cream skimming would soon lead to segmentation of the insurance market. As market segmentation developed, PGP capitation rates would significantly exceed costs because enrollees are relatively healthy. Prepaid group practices can attract enrollees if they can offer better service than either the fee-for-service sector or individual practice associations. By increasing their costs somewhat but keeping within capitation rates, PGPs could offer shorter waiting times for appointments, access to hospital care, more amenities, and so on. Fee-for-service providers or individual practice associations would be left serving older, poorer, and less healthy members of the population.

If capitation rates reimbursed prepaid group practices excessively, insufficient funds would be available for fee-for-service or individual practice associations because the budget would be fixed. The rationing envisaged by the system would therefore disproportionately affect access among the very population the plan was designed to serve more adequately. Eventually, fee-for-service providers and individual practice associations could successfully argue that the system was failing to provide necessary care. The probable result would be supplemental budget appropriations, which would defeat the program's cost containment objective. Ironically, the success of prepaid group practices would be inconsistent with cost containment.

Unfortunately, if individual practice associations were to overwhelm prepaid group practices following enactment of the Kennedy-Corman bill, the prospects for cost containment would be equally dim. If most physicians were to form individual practice associations, each area's Health Security Agency would face a single provider group. The IPAs could claim that the available funds were insufficient to provide adequate quality medical care. The agency would find it difficult to contradict this claim, both because it would not be directly involved in patient care, and, more important, because there would be no competing providers to demonstrate that care could be provided within the allocated budget. If the agency attempted to blame the National Health Security Board, the stage would be set for local physicians to mobilize consumer pressure on Congress to raise the total health care budget.

Even greater pressure would be likely if the Health Security Board attempted to redistribute resources from high-expenditure to low-expenditure areas. Given the difficulties in measuring need, individual practice associations in high-cost areas could argue persuasively to their representatives that the reallocation was unfair and detrimental to the health of their constituents. Again, there would be no local groups able to provide evidence to the contrary. In such an event, the Kennedy-Corman proposal could discourage organized systems of medical care associations and enhance the power of the medical profession to resist resource reallocations.

CONSUMER CHOICE HEALTH PLAN—ENTHOVEN

Alain Enthoven's Consumer Choice Health Plan (CCHP)[69] was designed to stimulate competing delivery systems and insurance coverage through financial incentives for consumers. In a number of important ways it was modeled on the Federal Employees Health Benefits Program and has many of the strengths and weaknesses of that program. The proposal would replace all tax deductions for health insurance with tax credits (and vouchers for the poor) if people enrolled in approved

---

[69] Alain C. Enthoven, "Consumer-Choice Health Plan," *New England Journal of Medicine* 298 (March 23, 1978) :650–58 and (March 30, 1978): 709–20.

plans. The tax credits were designed to be less than the cost of enrollment in reasonably comprehensive, efficient health maintenance organizations. Because premiums and all but catastrophic out-of-pocket medical costs would not be tax deductible, people wanting more expensive coverage or delivery systems would be paying the full marginal costs of those choices. Employers could still contribute to the cost of premiums, but the treatment of such contributions as taxable income would remove the current incentives to prefer expensive health care fringe benefits over the equivalent value of wages. Medicare would be retained, with benefits increased to the basic level proposed in the Consumer Choice Health Plan; beneficiaries would be allowed to use the actuarial value of their benefits (or the adjusted average per capita cost) for fee-for-service coverage or a qualified HMO. Increases in the adjusted average per capita cost would be tied to the consumer price index, effectively reducing purchasing value over time and shifting Medicare to a system like that of the Federal Employees Health Benefits Program.

Although CCHP resembles the FEHBP, the former does include precautions against cream skimming. A health care actuary would define categories based on age, sex, family size, disability status, and other factors; tax credits and vouchers would be adjusted accordingly. Thus, premiums (and tax credits) would be higher for high-risk people, so plans would have little incentive to exclude them. As noted previously, however, more refined adjustments might be necessary to assure this result. In addition, plans would have to be community-rated within their market areas for each actuarial category. This feature would prevent the establishment of preferred-risk groups with lower premiums. More important, the requirement that plans be community-rated within a *local* area would end the regional cross-subsidization of medical care costs. Employee groups would have greater incentives to seek cost-effective plans, and local health systems agencies would realize that approval of more beds in the area would imply higher premiums for its residents. (Enthoven's proposal would allow subsidies based on regional differences in actuarial costs to be equalized over time.)

Promoting choice among plans (with requirements on minimum benefits) is the central feature of the Enthoven proposal.

A government agency would manage an annual open-enrollment period the same way the Civil Service Commission over-
sees the Federal Employees Health Benefits Program. People
would receive comparable statements about each plan's benefit
package, financial status, history of utilization, quality, and
accessibility. Furthermore, the agency would review promotional material for accuracy. Direct service plans, such as prepaid group practices, might specify a maximum enrollment
level and might have the agency randomly, or otherwise impartially, select people who could join. "Gaming," switching
into full-coverage plans only when one expects substantial
medical costs, is a potential problem. CCHP would try to reduce this by (1) setting the tax credit high enough to cover
a good basic plan, (2) allowing plans to reject open-season
applicants who are hospitalized or already pregnant, and (3)
imposing penalties for frequent switchers, such as refusing
to reaccept people who had switched from their previous plan
within a five-year period or adding a surcharge to their
premiums.

While CCHP is rather explicit in its means to promote
consumer choice among plans, it is much less explicit concerning the development of alternatives to fee-for-service. Enthoven is rather leery of promises of increased federal support
for the creation of new health maintenance organizations. He
argues that such support traditionally has been accompanied
by excessively stringent regulation—thus reflecting the bureaucracy's tendency to avoid the small probability of a failure
even at the expense of a more likely success. Furthermore,
CCHP assumes that direct promotion of HMOs should not be
necessary because of their potential for cost savings and
implicit competitive advantage. For instance, commercial carriers might find it profitable to establish new HMOs, and
employer-union groups would find HMOs more advantageous
under CCHP. Moreover, supporters of CCHP argue that this
plan would be merely an attempt to reinstate "fair market
competition" in the medical delivery system. Yet it can be
argued that the proposal should include more funds for the
start-up costs of new HMOs and for other transition costs.
More funds would be particularly important for the development of prepaid group practices, the type of HMO with the
clearest potential for lower costs. The start-up costs of a new
HMO can be substantial, both in terms of personal effort and

financing. Given the risks, for-profit companies are unlikely to make major investments unless the potential profits are substantial.

While some prepaid group practices have done very well in the past, an important distinction must be made between the type of competition that has taken place and the heightened competition CCHP would promote. In a sense, PGPs have been able to compete with and out-maneuver conventional carriers because countermeasures by the latter have been difficult to implement in the face of relatively small HMO penetration. Conventional insurers have not been able to band together to compete with HMOs and, besides, HMOs have taken a small share of the market. For instance, although the Kaiser share of specific employee groups may be as high as 60 percent to 70 percent, it enrolls only 10 percent to 15 percent of the total state population in California. Because conventional carriers can only attempt to influence practice patterns across large geographic areas, they cannot respond effectively to such concentrated competition. If CCHP were to result in a broadly based HMO penetration, the conventional carriers might be able to join forces and become more competitive.

In CCHP's competitive atmosphere, individual practice associations (or the so-called Health Care Alliances, which involve each area's most cost-effective providers)[70] could be a particular threat to prepaid group practices. If such HMOs were to develop and threaten to control utilization, it would become very difficult for prepaid group practices, with their more limited choice of providers, to use cost differences as a bargaining advantage. Such a situation seems to have occurred in Hawaii, where both Kaiser and the local Blue Shield plan have comparable utilization rates and stable market shares. It is unlikely that new PGPs could effectively enter that market. Although Enthoven is concerned about the potential for an individual practice association to use its monopoly power to fix prices, an IPA is more likely to use predatory pricing techniques to keep competing prepaid group practices from enter-

---

[70] Paul M. Ellwood, *The Health Care Alliance*, Excelsior, Minnesota, Interstudy. Under the Health Care Alliance scheme, an insurer identifies the most cost-effective physicians and hospitals in an area. The insurer can then offer a low-cost prepaid package to those people who agree to limit themselves to care by the selected cost-effective providers.

ing the market unless short-term assistance is given to the potential groups.

Ways in which conventional carriers might reduce their costs, other than by sponsoring their own health maintenance organizations, remain to be examined. A carrier can lower its costs by cutting administrative costs, by paying providers less for given services, by attempting to change provider practice patterns by refusing reimbursement for certain things (e.g., tonsillectomies), or by altering its benefit package. Providers are unlikely to accept any substantial differences in fee schedules, and changes in practice patterns are unlikely to occur for some carriers in an area and not others. Professional ethics would lead physicians to identify a specific procedure as required or discretionary in particular cases, rather than saying it is reasonable care for an Aetna, but not for a Blue Cross, patient.

Carriers can, however, alter their benefit package to exclude certain services, such as elective surgery, maternity, and eye examinations. If they do this, then the market can easily become segmented as single people decline maternity benefits, those with perfect vision refuse optical coverage, and so on. In general, people who feel less need for medical care may buy packages with larger deductibles, constrained only by the mandatory $1,500 maximum out-of-pocket. Although market segmentation may be acceptable from an efficiency perspective, it does run counter to the idea of risk spreading and may eventually become politically unattractive. Various modifications to the CCHP proposal could reduce some of this market segmentation. The example, however, demonstrates that NHI plans can have unexpected and undesirable effects.

Summary and Conclusions

HMOs are a major innovation in medical care delivery that must be considered in the design and implementation of national health insurance options. The available evidence concerning HMO performance is sufficiently favorable to lead many analysts to argue for HMO promotion under national health insurance. Total medical care costs are substantially lower for HMO enrollees than for the general population and these lower costs are attributable to lower hospitalization rates. The reasons for this lower hospitalization are less clear. The major factor is lower admission rates, but admissions do not appear differentially lower for surgical cases or even particular types of surgery often identified as being discretionary. While the lower admission rate for HMO enrollees might imply less care than is medically appropriate, there is little evidence that the quality of care in HMOs is poor or that HMO enrollees have worse health outcomes. A second explanation, that HMOs provide much more preventive care, which leads to less illness, is not supported by the data. Two major alternative explanations remain: (1) that HMOs provide the appropriate level of care, and the conventional system too much; and (2) that utilization differences are attributable to the self-selection of different types of people into HMOs and into the conventional system.

Although the true situations may be represented by a combination of these explanations or some other, unexplained mechanism, their potential importance motivates our investigation of alternative policies toward HMOs. The current federal policies are represented by Medicare and the Federal Employees Health Benefits Program. Medicare emphasizes cost reimbursement for HMOs; for those HMOs wishing to be at risk, complicated formulas are required to compute the capitation payments and savings must be shared with the Medicare program. The implicit assumption seems to be that HMOs might skimp on services in ways that beneficiaries will not be able to detect or should not be allowed to tolerate. The FEHBP is rather different. It provides a fixed contribution that the consumer can allocate to any of a broad selection of alternative plans. The implicit assumption is that consumers can evaluate health insurance and delivery options. If consumers choose a system that costs less because it does less, or costs less because it attracts people who need (or desire) fewer services, they can keep the "savings."

The Medicare model seems most appropriate if there is a real concern that HMOs will underserve their enrollees, jeopardize their health, and pocket the profits. Conversely, the FEHBP model is most appropriate if one believes that HMOs are responsive to consumer needs and provide reasonable levels of appropriate quality care. The implications of the self-selection hypothesis are also very different. The Medicare program seems to assume that cost differences attributable to differences in enrollee needs or preferences should be largely recaptured by the government. The FEHBP model encourages the identification of such differences and allows the market to determine its allocation between consumer and provider or insurer.

All of the available studies of HMO performance have dealt with relatively isolated programs within the context of a highly diversified health insurance market generally not conducive to HMO development. (For instance, the dual-choice provisions of the 1973 HMO Act are only beginning to be exercised, let alone studied.) Thus, any projection of HMO performance under alternative NHI schemes must not only extrapolate from current experience with established HMOs, but also imagine their behavior in the context of a market environment drastically altered by national health insurance. Some of the proposals, such as CHIP, give little attention to HMOs, but set up an environment and incentives that, perhaps inadvertently, may substantially encourage HMO development. In contrast, the Kennedy-Corman proposal includes specific policies to promote HMOs and, in particular, prepaid group practices. Some of the other aspects of the proposal, however, eliminate most of the incentives for consumers to join HMOs and may inadvertently strengthen the power of the medical profession in resisting government budgetary controls.

The potential for such unintended consequences should be the most important message of this chapter. A relatively simple set of scenarios can be developed by emphasizing the role of incentives inherent in the NHI plan and the likely responses by providers, insurers, and consumers. Add a bit of Murphy's Law (if something can go wrong, it will), and the projected results of implementation may be quite different from those initially desired. Furthermore, given the gaps in our knowledge about HMO performance, the potential for surprising outcomes is still greater under national health insurance.

Chapter 4
PHYSICIAN SUPPLY AND DISTRIBUTION

JACK HADLEY

P ARTLY because national health insurance bills rarely include explicit health personnel provisions, the implications of the various proposals for the health labor force often are overlooked. The various configurations of eligibility rules, benefits, and payment mechanisms, however, could very well have different effects on provider remuneration. To the extent that shifts in earnings influence physicians' career choices, then each of the bills would indeed influence the supply and distribution of health personnel.

It also seems reasonable to assume that those proposals that do not explicitly address labor force issues would implicitly delegate that responsibility to a companion set of federal and state legislation. From fairly modest beginnings in 1963, federal involvement in the education and training of health professionals has grown considerably. The Health Professions Educational Assistance Act of 1976 (PL 94–484) provides the Department of Health, Education, and Welfare (DHEW) with an extensive array of financial, regulatory, and direct intervention mechanisms for affecting not only the aggregate supply, but also the distribution, of health personnel.

Figure 1 summarizes policy options available to influence the physician. The eligibility and benefits provisions of a national health insurance bill are targeted primarily at the health services consumer, who indirectly influences physicians' career decisions through the demand for services. Physician payment mechanisms, which include fee-for-service (with alternative fee-setting rules), capitation, salary, and various forms of financial subsidy or penalty, are aimed at the practicing physician. Hospital reimbursement also affects physician distribu-

Figure 1

OPTIONS IN HEALTH PERSONNEL POLICY

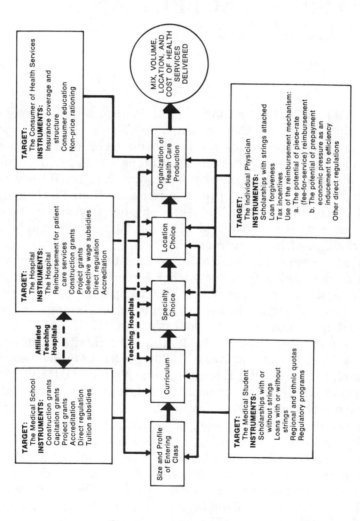

SOURCE: Adapted from Jack Hadley and Uwe Reinhardt, "The Supply of Graduate Medical Education Positions by Specialty," in Kerry Kilpatrick, ed., "Policy Analysis for Physician Manpower Planning: The Supply of and Demand for Graduate Medical Education Positions," DHEW, Public Health Service (PHS) Health Resources Administration (HRA), Bureau of Health Manpower, 1977, p. 24.

tion through influence on graduate training programs. Finally, both the medical student and the medical school are potential targets for policy intervention.

Given the magnitude and importance of the health labor force in the delivery system, the effects of a national health insurance plan on labor force supply and distribution should be a critical part of evaluating that scheme. Accordingly, this chapter aims to describe and evaluate what appear to be the three principal policy options for influencing physician supply and distribution: altering provider earnings, directly intervening in physician supply and distribution, and manipulating the financing and organization of the education sector. Pertinent to the first are the following questions: How responsive are providers to financial incentives? How large might payments have to be to attain desired objectives? What mechanisms could be used to alter relative earnings? Included among the direct intervention options are changes in immigration and licensure laws, explicit allocation or regulation of health personnel, direct provision of services by public (federal) authorities, and imposition of various limits or ceilings on career choices. The final set of options focuses on the financing and organization of educational activities, with particular attention to the variety of individual and institutional grants, loans, and scholarships available. Consistent with the general theme of this book, this chapter focuses not only on the potential consequences or outcomes of the various options, but also on the factors that might prevent policy makers from effectively implementing their chosen actions. We also shall look at lessons from the Canadian and other foreign experiences with personnel policy and the health labor market.

Issues of Physician Supply and Distribution

Until recently, the dominant issue with respect to the health labor force was the physician shortage, and indeed shortages of most types of medical care personnel. It was precisely this concern that prompted the federal government to provide both institutional and student support to expand training. This policy appears to have been most successful; in fact, Congress has officially declared the current situation to be one of physician sufficiency.[1]

Unfortunately, labor force policy issues appear to have at least one thing in common with the Hydra of Greek mythology: when one issue is put to rest, several more take its place. Most prominent among these are the problems of maldistribution among medical specialties, geographic areas, and community sizes.[2] Although optimal distributions have yet to be determined, most authorities believe that specialty maldistribution consists of too few primary-care physicians, especially general and family practitioners, too many surgeons, and possibly too many hospital-based specialists. Physicians also are thought to be scarce in rural areas and low-income neighborhoods of large cities. Finally, the southeastern, north central, and mountain regions of the country seem to have too few physicians, at least relative to other regions.

Two other issues are, ironically, consequences of earlier policy responses to the perceived physician shortage. One is our increased dependence on foreign medical school graduates (FMGs). The other is possible inflation in the cost of medical care because of an excess supply of physicians. Although the goal of reducing the number of FMGs is usually shrouded in concern over the quality of care, a cynic might view this concern as a form of tariff protection for a domestic industry, that is, U.S.-trained physicians.[3] Similarly, it has been pointed out that even under very conservative assumptions about future growth in the numbers of domestically trained physicians and total population, the United States will have a large increase in the aggregate physician-population ratio.[4] This

---

[1] U.S. Congress, *The Health Professions Educational Assistance Act of 1976*, PL 94–484, 94th Congress, 2nd session, 90 Stat. 2243.

[2] Implicit in the policy of expanding physician supply was the belief that market forces would eventually allocate new physicians to shortage areas and specialties. The maldistribution issue was explicitly identified when comparisons of 1963 data with 1975 data indicated only insignificant changes in physician distribution. See Eli Ginzberg, "Physician Shortage Reconsidered," *New England Journal of Medicine* 275 (July 14, 1966):85–87, for an early discussion of the link between aggregate supply and distribution.

[3] See Robert G. Evans, "Does Canada Have Too Many Doctors?— Why Nobody Loves an Immigrant Physician," *Canadian Public Policy* 2 (Spring 1976):147–60.

[4] Uwe Reinhardt, *Physician Productivity and Health Manpower Policy* (Cambridge, Mass.: Ballinger Publishing Co., 1975), p. 5.

becomes a problem if the increase in physician supply does little to redress physician maldistribution or leads to socially undesirable increases in total medical care expenditures.

The next three sections of this chapter investigate the major policy options for addressing these issues—altering physicians' financial incentives, directly intervening in the delivery system, and influencing medical education. The implications of each policy for physician supply and distribution and the problems likely to arise in implementation are addressed. Then recommendations for health labor force policy under national health insurance are made. Whether such policies are integrated into a single national health insurance bill or are allocated to separate health labor force legislation is not critical. It is vital, however, that the link between the two be recognized and taken into account.

Altering Physicians' Earnings

This section addresses two questions. First, given that a national health insurance plan will affect physicians' incomes and fees, what are the likely consequences for physician supply and distribution? Second, what are the implementation problems likely to arise in attempting to manipulate physicians' financial incentives? In addition to whatever direct personnel provisions an NHI plan may contain, physicians' earnings will be affected by at least four other components of the plan: covered benefits, population eligibility, patient cost sharing (coinsurance and deductibles), and method(s) of physician reimbursement. Other chapters explore these issues in greater detail; this section begins with a brief summary of the range of possible provisions in a plan.

Most so-called comprehensive plans, such as the Nixon-Ford Comprehensive Health Insurance Plan (CHIP) or the Kennedy-Corman bill, would cover all hospital inpatient and most physicians' services without limits on either quantities used or locus of care. Because approximately 80 percent of the population under age sixty-five currently have some type of hospital insurance,[5] this kind of coverage would affect pri-

---

[5] U.S. Department of Health, Education, and Welfare (DHEW), Public Health Service (PHS), Health Resources Administration (HRA), *"Health: United States 1976–1977,"* DHEW Publication No. (HRA) 77–1232, p. 365.

marily the demand for office services. About 62 percent of the population under age sixty-five had coverage for office and home visits in 1974.[6] Furthermore, existing insurance coverage is highly correlated with income. Together, these facts imply that demand for services would increase most for office-based physicians' services by lower-income populations. Catastrophic plans, such as Long-Ribicoff-Waggonner, would trigger public coverage for hospital and physician services only after some expenditure or use ceiling is reached ($2,000 family medical expense and sixty days of hospital care per year, for example). But these plans also tend to include more comprehensive coverage for low-income populations. Plans vary with respect to coverage of drugs, preventive services, maternity care, well-child care, dental care, and nursing home stays. To the extent that any plan expands existing coverage, the incomes of providers of covered services will be enhanced.

Population eligibility provisions vary from universal eligibility in a single plan (Kennedy-Corman), to universal eligibility over multiple plans (CHIP), to mandatory enrollment for only some populations (Long-Ribicoff-Waggonner). The last-named plan would expand the Medicaid program to cover a larger population under uniform eligibility standards; this plan also would permit voluntary enrollment in private insurance for the population which was neither poor nor aged. Obviously, the broader an NHI plan's eligibility provisions, the greater effect the plan will have on the demand for services.

A plan's cost-sharing features are primarily intended to offset some of the demand increases that expanded coverage and eligibility would stimulate.[7] Cost sharing can vary considerably. CHIP, for example, includes under its employment plan a $150 deductible per person (plus a separate $50 deductible for drugs), a 25 percent coinsurance rate above the deductible, and maximum liabilities of $1,050 for individuals and $1,500 for families. Both the federal plan for the elderly (FHCIP) and the state-assisted health plan for the poor (AHIP) have income-contingent deductibles, coinsurance rates, and maximum liabilities. Even at very low incomes, the bill would impose a 10 percent coinsurance rate up to a maximum liability

---

[6] Ibid.

[7] Another feature that contributes to the same end is controls on utilization, discussed in Chapter 9 of this book.

of 6 percent of income. As income increases, however, all three cost-sharing components would increase as well. Conversely, the Long-Ribicoff-Waggonner plan would rely primarily on a fixed copayment of $3 for each of the first ten outpatient physician visits per family eligible under Medicaid or Medicare. Services provided under the catastrophic portion of the plan would have no cost sharing. At the other extreme, a plan may have no cost sharing (Kennedy-Corman or the Canadian system, for example). Cost sharing probably would not impose a greater out-of-pocket burden, on average, than exists under the current array of private and public insurance. Hence, demand for physicians' services probably would increase, relative to current demand.

Finally, a system's physician reimbursement features critically determine the effect of that system on physicians' incomes. Several key reimbursement elements can be combined in almost any pattern. These include the following:

1. Distribution of physicians among fee-for-service, salary, and capitation payment modes;
2. Payment under a fixed fee schedule or freedom to set fees individually;
3. Option to bill some or all patients over and above any plan-set fees;
4. Voluntary, mandatory, complete, or partial participation in a plan that limits fees;
5. Fee uniformity across patients covered by different insurance plans; and
6. Fee uniformity across medical specialties and geographic areas.

If it is assumed that fee-for-service reimbursement will continue to predominate, then a system with no constraints on what physicians could charge would lead to higher incomes in all specialties and areas. Constraints on fees paid by public insurance plans would penalize physicians who treated persons covered by such plans. But fee schedules that are uniform across the entire population should benefit physicians who treat low-income and rural patients more than other physicians.

Overall, then, the ultimate impact of the reimbursement system selected on physicians' incomes is extremely difficult to predict. As Canadian evidence cited later will suggest, it is not even clear that physicians' real incomes would rise under national health insurance. The effects on incomes by medical specialty and geographic area are even more difficult to estimate. In addition, no politically feasible plan can control physicians' hours of work or productivity, two of the main determinants of physicians' earnings.[8]

Although exact predictions are impossible, the next section assumes that national health insurance would affect physicians' incomes, and investigates the potential impact of national health insurance on aggregate physician supply and distribution. Then the section explores possible implementation problems that might arise under various approaches to using physicians' earnings as a policy tool.

THE RELATIONSHIP BETWEEN PHYSICIANS' INCOMES AND THE SUPPLY DISTRIBUTION OF PHYSICIANS

Aggregate Physician Supply

At any particular time, the aggregate supply[9] of patient-care physicians depends on the number of graduates of U.S. medical schools, the inflow of graduates of foreign medical schools, and the rate of exit from active practice. Very little is known about influences affecting the FMG inflow (although the rate of entry of FMGs is clearly sensitive to immigration laws) or the exit of physicians from active practice. Since the early 1960s, however, the growth in the number of U.S. medical school graduates has been the dominant factor affecting the current and projected size of the aggregate stock of practicing physicians. Between 1965 and 1977, medical school enrollment increased by almost 80 percent, from 32,428 students to

---

[8] The relationships among physicians' hours of work, fees, productivity, and incomes will not be explored in detail here. For further discussion see Frank A. Sloan, "A Microanalysis of Physicians' Hours of Work Decisions," in *The Economics of Health and Medical Care*, Mark Perlman, ed. (New York: John Wiley and Sons, 1974); Frank A. Sloan, "Physician Supply Behavior in the Short Run," *Industrial and Labor Relations Review* 28 (July 1975):549–69; and Stephen G. Vahovich, "Physicians' Supply Decisions by Specialty: 2SLS Model," *Industrial Relations* 16 (February 1977):51–60.

[9] Aggregate supply is defined as all active, nonfederal, patient-care physicians, including residents.

58,266.[10] By 1990, the supply of U.S.-trained physicians per 100,000 population is projected to reach 188.9, an increase of more than 40 percent over the 1970 level.[11]

What effect might an exogenous increase in physicians' incomes have on these trends? First, studies of medical school application rates show a positive and statistically significant relationship between physicians' incomes (or the rate of return to becoming a physician) and the number of applicants.[12] Even though the number of applicants persistently exceeds the number of available first-year medical school places, fluctuations in the rate appear to be related to medical school capacity.[13] Government, both federal and state, has played a significant role in expanding training capacity, partly in response to the perceived shortage of physicians, but also in response to increased public demand for entry into the medical profession.[14]

---

[10] Jack Hadley, Frank Sloan, Robert Lee, and Roger Feldman, "Financing Medical Education: Issues and Options," Final Report, The Urban Institute Working Paper 5925-3, Washington, D.C., June 30, 1978, p. 115.

[11] DHEW, PHS, HRA, Bureau of Health Manpower, "Supply and Distribution of Physicians and Physician Extenders," GMENAC Staff Paper, Publication No. (HRA) 78-11 (1978). Because of changes in the immigration laws in 1977, almost no growth in the supply of foreign medical graduates is expected.

[12] Roger Feldman and Richard Scheffler, "The Supply of Medical School Applicants and the Rate of Return to Training," *Quarterly Review of Economics and Business* (Spring 1978):91–98; and Frank A. Sloan, "The Demand for Higher Education: The Case of Medical School Applicants, *Journal of Human Resources* 6 (Fall 1971):466–89. In every study that has computed the rate of return to becoming a physician, choice of a physician's career has been at least as profitable as the next best alternative. See, for example, Stephen T. Mennemeyer, "Really Great Returns to Medical Education," *Journal of Human Resources* 13 (Winter 1978):75–90; Cotton M. Lindsay, "Real Returns to Medical Education," *Journal of Human Resources* 8 (Summer 1973):331–48; Frank A. Sloan, "Lifetime Earnings and Physicians' Choice of Specialty," *Industrial and Labor Relations Review* 24 (October 1970):47–56; and Frank Sloan and Cotton M. Lindsay, "Real Returns to Medical Education: Comment and Reply," *Journal of Human Resources* 11 (Winter 1976): 118–30.

[13] Thomas D. Hall, "An Economic Model of Medical School Behavior," Ph.D. dissertation, Department of Economics, University of California, Los Angeles, 1975.

[14] In 1976, state governments contributed 21.3 percent, and the federal government 37.1 percent of medical schools' revenues. Hadley et al., "Financing Medical Education," p. 130.

In general, then, there is little doubt that increases in physicians' incomes would exert expansionary pressure on the aggregate supply of physicians. The more interesting and difficult question is whether further growth in the number of physicians is desirable. In particular, what implications does an increased supply have for geographic and specialty distribution and total expenditures for medical care?

Specialty Distribution

Statistical research on physicians' specialty and location decisions is voluminous. Fortunately, there are several comprehensive and recent literature reviews available, so a detailed assessment of all studies is unnecessary here.[15] Not surprisingly, the results are diverse, and almost every study can be criticized for data or methodological weaknesses. As with all empirical research, it also must be remembered that inferences can be made with confidence only concerning specific conditions investigated by the study. Thus, radical institutional changes may well nullify research findings.

Given these caveats, this and the following section on geographic distribution describe changes in distribution over the past ten years and compare these changes with shifts in physicians' incomes and in aggregate physician supply. Then the limited statistical evidence on the influence of incomes and reimbursement is summarized.

Table 7a describes aspects of physician specialty distribution in 1965–67 and 1974–75. One point to note is the continued decline in the proportion of general practitioners, which decreased by 34 percent in the period covered (from 31.1 percent to 20.6 percent). The proportion of physicians in the other specialties category, however, increased by more than 50 per-

---

[15] See, for example, Human Resources Research Center, *Specialty and Location Choices of Physicians*, Final Report of Grant No. 359 from the Robert Wood Johnson Foundation (1975); Institute of Medicine, *Medicare-Medicaid Reimbursement Policies*, Final Report of Contract No. SSA–PMB–74–250, Social Security Administration, DHEW (March 1976); Elliot Long, *The Geographic Distribution of Physicians in the United States*, Final Report of Grant No. NSF–C814, National Science Foundation (Minneapolis: Interstudy, January 1975); Jack Hadley, *Models of Physicians' Specialty and Location Decisions*, Technical Paper No. 6, National Center for Health Services Research, DHEW (October 1975); DHEW, HRA, Bureau of Health Resources Development, *Factors Influencing Practice Location of Professional Health Manpower: A Review of the Literature*, Publication No. (HRA) 75–3 (July 1974).

cent, from 10.7 percent to 16.7 percent of all active patient-care physicians. The proportions of physicians in each of the other specialties listed also grew by between 4 percent and 17 percent.

The trend in the specialty distribution of physicians in training, however, looks quite different. The largest decrease occurred in the other category, while the largest increase was for general and family practitioners. For the two largest specialty areas, internal medicine and surgery, the former grew by 68 percent, compared with 18.4 percent for the latter. In fact, the proportion of physicians training for surgical specialties actually declined over the period.

Changes in specialists' net incomes appear to be somewhat related to these trends in specialty distribution. The three specialty groups that experienced reduced shares of physicians in training (surgical specialties, psychiatry, and other specialties) also had the smallest increases in net incomes. Internal medicine, which had the second greatest increase in share of trainees, also ranked second in net income growth. The only anomalous shift occurred for obstetrics-gynecology, which increased its share of trainees very slightly (by 8 percent), but had the greatest growth in net income.

Because average net incomes mask possible variations in hours worked and case loads, Table 7b presents data on net income per hour, average fee for an initial office visit, hours per week, and patients per week, by specialty, for two years, 1970 and 1974. Comparing the change in the distribution of trainees with changes in income per hour reveals that surgical specialties and psychiatry, which lost trainees relative to other specialties, had the smallest increases in both net income per hour and average fee. General and family practice, pediatrics, obstetrics-gynecology, and medical specialties all increased their shares of physicians in training and also had relatively large gains in net income per hour and average fees. The only anomaly is anesthesiology, which had the biggest jump in income per hour but only very small growth in the share of residents.

Tabular data of this sort are at best suggestive, because it is impossible to control or adjust for changes in other factors that might influence specialty choice and income levels. Unfortunately, there have been only two multivariate statistical analyses of physicians' specialty choices, and both were based on outdated and otherwise deficient information on physicians'

Table 7a

PHYSICIANS' INCOMES AND NUMBERS OF PHYSICIANS IN PRACTICE AND TRAINING, BY SPECIALTY, 1965-67 AND 1974-75

(Percentages in parentheses)

Year	General and Family Practices	Internal Medicine and Medical Specialties	Surgery and Surgical Procedures	Pediatrics	Obstetrics-Gynecology	Psychiatry	Anesthesiology	Other
1965-67								
Number in active practice (1967)[1]	64,279 (31.1%)	32,520 (15.7%)	42,827 (20.7%)	11,455 (5.5%)	13,630 (6.6%)	12,711 (6.1%)	7,416 (3.6%)	(10.7%)
Number in training (1967)[1]	645 (1.5%)	8,184 (19.2%)	11,233 (26.4%)	3,121 (7.3%)	2,528 (6.0%)	3,345 (7.9%)	1,200 (2.8%)	(28.9%)
Net income (1965)[2]	$23,218	$24,673	$33,018	$22,032	$27,771	$24,984	$28,215	$29,879
1974-75								
Number in active practice (1975)[3]	48,206 (20.6%)	40,908 (17.5%)	50,483 (21.5%)	13,970 (6.0%)	16,273 (0.9%)	14,479 (6.6%)	9,944 (4.2%)	(16.7%)
Number in training (1975)[3]	3,064 (5.7%)	13,774 (25.7%)	13,298 (24.8%)	4,576 (8.5%)	3,469 (6.5%)	3,384 (0.3%)	1,547 (2.9%)	(19.6%)
Net income (1974)[4]	$44,727	$51,340	$60,510	$42,112	$61,693	$41,258	$54,365	$54,582
Ratio of 1974-75 to 1965-67 (Ratio of Percentages in Parentheses)								
Number in active practice	.75 (.66)	1.26 (1.11)	1.18 (1.04)	1.22 (1.09)	1.194 (1.05)	1.226 (1.08)	1.341 (1.17)	(1.56)
Number in training	4.75 (3.8)	1.68 (1.34)	1.18 (.94)	1.47 (1.16)	1.37 (1.08)	1.01 (.80)	1.29 (1.04)	(.68)
Net income	1.93	2.08	1.83	1.91	2.22	1.65	1.93	1.83

Note: Percentages may not total 100 percent because of rounding.

Sources: 1. J. N. Haug and G. A. Roback, *Distribution of Physicians, Hospitals, and Hospital Beds in the U.S., 1967* (Chicago: American Medical Association, 1968), p. 50.

2. Zachary Dyckman, "Study of Physicians' Income in the Pre-Medicare Period—1965," DHEW, SSA, Office of Research and Statistics, DHEW Publication No. (SSA) 76–11932 (Washington, D.C.: U.S. Government Printing Office, 1976), p. 45.

3. Louis J. Goodman, *Physician Distribution and Medical Licensure in the U.S., 1975* (Chicago: American Medical Association, 1976), p. 66.

4. Sharon R. Henderson, ed., *Profile of Medical Practice 1977* (Chicago: American Medical Association, 1977) p. 184.

Table 7b

PRACTICE CHARACTERISTICS BY SPECIALTY, 1970 and 1974

Year and Specialty	Percentage of Physicians in Residency Training, by Specialty	Hours per Week	Patients per Week	Average Annual Net Income	Net Income per Hour	Average Fee, Initial Office Visit
1970						
General Practice	2.4	54.1	171.5	$33,859	$13.01	$ 8.46
Medical Specialties	20.2	55.2	127.2	40,251	15.45	17.81
Surgical Specialties	25.1	54.6	123.4	50,701	19.60	14.72
Obstetrics-Gynecology	5.2	59.1	125.6	47,094	16.60	14.23
Pediatrics	7.2	54.2	163.4	34,799	13.35	9.95
Psychiatry	6.5	45.1	46.5	39,896	19.15	32.64
Anesthesiology	2.8	54.4	—	39,432	15.72	—
1974						
General Practice	5.7 [a]	49.7	177.2	44,727	18.97	12.03
Medical Specialties	25.7	51.7	124.7	51,390	21.02	23.11
Surgical Specialties	24.8	51.9	119.6	60,510	24.70	18.87
Obstetrics-Gynecology	6.5	52.9	131.8	61,693	24.61	22.07
Pediatrics	8.5	48.4	140.2	42,112	18.28	14.49
Psychiatry	6.3	44.1	48.3	41,258	18.74	41.39
Anesthesiology	2.9	48.9	—	54,365	23.91	—

Ratio of 1974 to 1970

General Practice	2.38	.92	1.03	1.32	1.46	1.43
Medical Specialties	1.27	.94	.98	1.28	1.36	1.30
Surgical Specialties	.99	.95	.97	1.19	1.26	1.28
Obstetrics-Gynecology	1.25	.90	1.05	1.31	1.48	1.55
Pediatrics	1.18	.89	.86	1.21	1.37	1.46
Psychiatry	.97	.98	1.04	1.03	1.03	1.27
Anesthesiology	1.04	.90	—	1.38	1.52	—

[a] Physician-in-training data are for 1975.

Sources: J. N. Haug, G. A. Roback, and B. C. Martin, *Distribution of Physicians in the United States, 1970* (Chicago: American Medical Association, 1971), p. 54; Goodman, *Physician Distribution and Medical Licensure in the U.S.,* 1975, p. 66; and Henderson, *Profile of Medical Practice,* 1977, pp. 131, 135, 145, 158, and 184.

incomes. Sloan found that significantly more residents enrolled in training programs in specialties with the greatest historical lifetime earnings patterns.[16] The quantitative impact of an increase in earnings, however, was estimated to be exceedingly small. Hadley investigated the specialty choices of a group of physicians who graduated from medical school in 1960.[17] Using mean net incomes by specialty and state to approximate individuals' income expectations, he found that only physicians choosing internal medicine tended to pick that specialty over a lower-income alternative. For general practice and surgery, the alternative specialty had a higher income; for all six other specialties, income was not a statistically significant variable.

Based on this limited evidence, it appears that any relationship that may exist between income and specialty choice is probably weak. Therefore, any policy to manipulate physicians' incomes to influence specialty distribution would be expensive and slow to affect aggregate specialty distribution. Moreover, this research also indicates that policy makers probably should focus on distribution of services provided, rather than on the distribution of specialists. Apparently an increasing number of physicians are providing services outside their designated specialties.[18] Furthermore, a fee-for-service reimbursement system could exert powerful incentives on all physicians, not just those in training, to alter the mix of care provided. Finally, there is evidence that physicians do increase the supply of a particular procedure when its profitability is increased by a higher fee or lower costs.[19]

---

[16] Sloan, "Lifetime Earnings."

[17] Jack Hadley, "A Disaggregated Model of Physicians' Specialty Choices," in Richard M. Scheffler, ed., *Research in Health Economics: An Annual Compilation*, vol. 1 (Greenwich, Conn.: JAI Press, 1979).

[18] Richard J. Reitemeier et al., "Participation By Internists in Primary Care," *Archives of Internal Medicine* 135 (February 1975):255–57; Charlotte L. Rosenberg, "How Much General Practice by Specialists?" *Medical Economics* (September 15, 1975):131–35; Edward F.X. Hughes et al., "Time Utilization of a Population of General Surgeons in Community Practice," *Surgery* 77 (March 1975):371–83.

[19] See George N. Monsma, "Marginal Revenue and the Demand for Physicians' Services," in Herbert Klarman, ed., *Empirical Studies in Health Economics* (Baltimore: The Johns Hopkins Press, 1976); and William A. Glaser, *Health Insurance Bargaining: Foreign Lessons for Americans* (New York: Halsted Press, 1978), Chapters 5, 6, 11, 14, and 15.

Geographic Distribution

The concern over the geographic distribution of physicians has three components: inequities among states or regions, inequities between urban and rural areas, and inequities between high- and low-income urban areas. Unfortunately, although the last two components tend to be the main concern of policy makers, most of the available evidence on the effects of physicians' earnings on their locational choices concerns the first component. In fact, no pertinent evidence is available on the last component. Accordingly, most of the data and studies discussed here bear only on the general issues of whether income or reimbursement influences locational behavior. Specific analyses of the relationships between financial incentives and intraurban or urban-rural distributions will require new data.

Figure 2 depicts the number of active, nonfederal patient-care physicians per 100,000 population in 1975 plotted against three measures of physicians' financial opportunities: per capita income, physicians' average net income, and average net income per hour. Panel A clearly shows that census divisions with higher per capita incomes tend to have higher physician-population ratios, a common result in analyses of physician distribution. Yet Panels B and C suggest that both total net income and net income per hour are inversely related to the number of physicians per 100,000 population, that is, the higher the physicians' remuneration, the lower the number of physicians. Causal inferences cannot be drawn from this chart, however, because these data reflect the influences both of physician supply and of demand for medical care. In fact, the small variation in net income per hour across census divisions suggests that current incentives for physicians to relocate may be small. The greater variation in mean annual net income may simply compensate for regional variations in patient loads and hours worked.[20]

---

[20] According to survey data collected by the American Medical Association in 1975, the number of patient visits per physician per week varied by more than 70 percent between census divisions with the smallest and largest patient loads (New England, 106.2 patient visits per physician per week, and East South Central, 181.9 visits per week). Total annual hours varied by almost 14 percent, or more than six average work weeks per year (Middle Atlantic 2,228 hours per physician per year, and East South Central, 2,536 hours). Sharon R. Henderson, ed., *Profile of Medical Practice 1977* (Chicago: American Medical Association, 1977), pp. 133, 137, and 147.

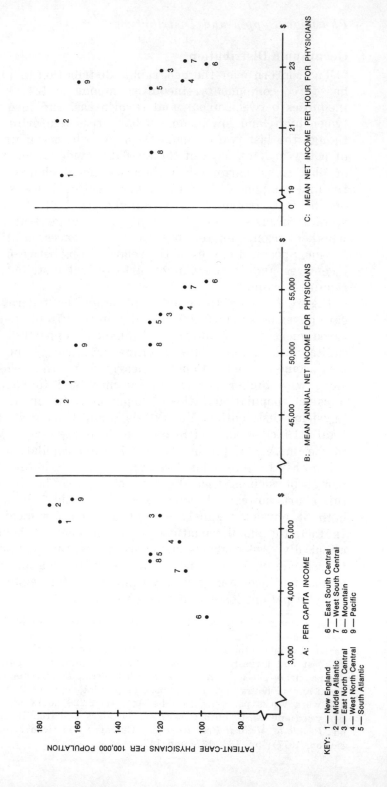

Figure 2

PHYSICIAN DISTRIBUTION AND FINANCIAL VARIABLES
BY CENSUS DIVISION, 1974–75

Table 8 examines changes in physician distribution, physicians' mean annual net income, and per capita income by census division between 1967 and 1975. Several points are noteworthy. First, the rate of growth in the number of patient-care physicians per 100,000 population was quite low, averaging about 1 percent per year. Thus, this period provides little information on the potential effects of the projected rapid growth in aggregate physician supply. Second, the physician-to-population ranking of census divisions remained unchanged, except for the East North Central area which slipped from fourth to sixth position. Third, 1967 is similar to 1975 in that the number of physicians per 100,000 population is positively related to per capita income and negatively related to net physician income. Finally, the bottom panel of Table 8, which computes the ratio of 1975 values to 1967 values, indicates that census divisions in which the proportion of physicians grew more rapidly than average also had greater increases in both net physician income and per capita income.

This point becomes clearer when census divisions are combined into two groups of four areas (Table 9). The rate of growth in the number of physicians per 100,000 population was about 44 percent larger in the high-growth census divisions than in the low-growth areas. Net physician income and per capita income also grew at higher rates, by almost 40 percent and 12 percent, respectively.

Similar comparisons between metropolitan and nonmetropolitan areas suggest that financial incentives may be less influential in shifting physicians between different types of areas than among census divisions. Table 10 shows that in 1965, the number of active, nonfederal patient-care physicians in metropolitan areas was almost four times the number in nonmetropolitan areas. Metropolitan area net income per hour was about 12 percent greater, but cost-of-living adjustments would undoubtedly move this difference toward zero. By 1975, there were almost six times as many physicians in metropolitan areas, an increase since 1965 of about 50 percent.[21] However, the ratios of annual and hourly net incomes had remained essentially unchanged.

Studies of physicians who choose to enter or to leave rural practice reveal that the conditions of employment, such as

---

[21] Nonmetropolitan areas also showed a decline in the number of physicians per 100,000, from 73.6 to 70.4. The ratio in nonmetropolitan areas increased from 123.2 to 130.9.

Table 8

PHYSICIAN DISTRIBUTION AND INCOME, BY CENSUS DIVISION, 1967 AND 1975

Year and Census Division	Patient-Care Physicians per 100,000 Population	Net Income[1] per Physician	Number of Patient-Care Physicians	Population (in millions)	Per Capita Income
1967					
Middle Atlantic	163.69	$24,587	60,112	36.72	$2,809
New England	158.63	24,512	17,896	11.28	2,778
Pacific	149.15	26,178	37,659	25.24	2,866
East North Central	114.35	23,256	44,497	38.91	2,781
South Atlantic	109.93	26,867	32,168	29.26	2,212
Mountain	109.41	25,575	8,725	7.97	2,287
West North Central	106.86	28,175	17,143	16.04	2,496
West South Central	95.67	26,671	18,093	18.91	2,099
East South Central	85.30	22,077	10,963	12.85	1,846
Ratio of High to Low Values	(1.92)	(1.28)			(1.55)
1975					
Middle Atlantic	168.50	47,688	63,032	37.40	5,477
New England	167.15	46,261	20,421	12.21	5,280
Pacific	160.33	50,858	45,529	28.39	5,502
East North Central	119.26	54,166	48,980	41.07	5,232
South Atlantic	122.43	54,396	41,708	34.06	4,647
Mountain	122.12	49,522	11,948	9.78	4,583
West North Central	112.21	53,637	18,940	16.87	4,826

West South Central	103.04	57,724	21,735	21.09	4,429
East South Central	95.74	58,371	13,052	13.63	4,006
Ratio of High to Low Values	(1.76)	(1.22)			(1.37)
Ratio of 1975 to 1967					
Middle Atlantic	1.029	1.939	1.049	1.019	1.950
New England	1.054	1.887	1.141	1.083	1.901
Pacific	1.075	1.943	1.209	1.125	1.920
East North Central	1.043	2.329	1.101	1.055	1.882
South Atlantic	1.114	2.025	1.297	1.164	2.101
Mountain	1.116	1.936	1.369	1.227	2.004
West North Central	1.050	1.904	1.105	1.052	1.933
West South Central	1.077	2.164	1.201	1.115	2.110
East South Central	1.122	2.644	1.191	1.061	2.170

[1] Data on net income per physician are for 1965 and 1974.

Sources: Henderson, *Profile of Medical Practice, 1977*, p. 190; Goodman, *Physician Distribution and Medical Licensure in the U.S., 1975*, pp. 14–15; Haug and Roback, *Distribution of Physicians, Hospitals, and Hospital Beds in the U.S., 1967*, p. 9; and Dyckman, "Study of Physicians' Income in the Pre-Medicare Period—1965," pp. 89–90.

Table 9

RATIOS OF 1975 TO 1967 VALUES FOR PHYSICIAN
DISTRIBUTION, PHYSICIAN INCOME, AND PER
CAPITA INCOME, BY CENSUS GROUPS

	Patient-Care Physicians per 100,000 Population	Net Physician Income	Per Capita Income
Higher-Growth Areas	1.089	2.29	2.065
East South Central			
Mountain			
South Atlantic			
West South Central			
Lower-Growth Areas	1.062	1.92	1.95
Middle Atlantic			
New England			
East North Central			
West North Central			
Ratio of Higher-Growth Areas to Lower- Growth Areas	1.435	1.40	1.12

Source: Computed from Table 8.

practice pace, opportunities for vacations and time off, collegial
contact, and access to facilities, tend to be more important in
their decisions than do earnings opportunities.[22] Earning satisfactory incomes probably can be thought of as a necessary, but
not sufficient, condition for rural practice. Average physician
earnings across communities of different sizes are very similar,
suggesting that with the exception of extremely remote or
sparsely populated areas, inadequate earnings opportunities
may not be a problem.[23] It is also interesting to note that varia-

[22] J. Warner and D. Aherne, 1974 Profile of Medical Practice, American
Medical Association, Chicago, 1974: R.L. Parker and T.G. Tuxill, "The
Attitudes of Physicians Toward Small Community Practice," Journal of
Medical Education 42 (April 1967):327–44; B.L. Bible, "Physicians'
Views of Medical Practice in Non-Metropolitan Communities," Public
Health Reports 85 (January 1970):11–17; R. Crawford and R.L. Mc-
Cormack, "Reasons Physicians Leave Primary Care Practice," Journal
of Medical Education 46 (April 1971):263–68.

[23] According to a 1975 survey of physicians conducted by the DHEW's
Health Care Financing Administration, physicians in areas with between
51 and 100 physicians per 100,000 population had the lowest average
net incomes, $49,850. Physicians in areas with between 151 and 200
physicians per 100,000 population had the highest net incomes, $56,872.
These data have not been adjusted for cost-of-living differences.

Table 10

PHYSICIAN STATISTICS FOR METROPOLITAN AND NONMETROPOLITAN AREAS, 1965 AND 1974

Variables	Metropolitan		Nonmetropolitan		Ratio of Metropolitan to Nonmetropolitan		Ratio of 1974 to 1965	
	1965	1974-75	1965	1974-75	1965	1974-75	Metro-politan	Nonmetro-politan
Number of patient-care physicians	189,211	235,994	48,271	40,076	3.92	5.89	1.25	.83
Hours per week	53.2	51.4	56.0	53.9[a]	.95	.95	.97	.96
Weeks per year	47.5	47.2	47.7	47.3	.99	.99	.99	.99
Total hours	2,527	2,426	2,671	2,550	.95	.95	.96	.95
Average annual income	$27,093	$52,756	$25,673	$48,824	1.06	1.08	1.95	1.90
Average income per hour	$ 10.72	$ 21.75	$ 9.61	$ 19.15	1.12	1.14	2.03	1.99

[a] Hours data are for 1975.

Sources: Henderson, *Profile of Medical Practice, 1977*, pp. 134, 138, 187; DHEW, HRA, Bureau of Health Manpower, "Supply and Distribution of Physicians and Physician Extenders," DHEW Publication No. (HRA) 78–11, pp. 42–43; and Dyckman, "Study of Physicians' Income in the Pre-Medicare Period," pp. 68–70.

tions in hours are not so great as might have been expected. Given the variations in patient loads, these observations imply that a fast practice pace rather than long hours worked is the more objectionable aspect of rural locations.

This conclusion may be deceptive, however. Achieving just the right physician-patient balance in rural settings is difficult. In communities with relatively few physicians, the addition of another physician could significantly cut patient loads, while simultaneously antagonizing already established physicians. Understanding of this situation might well discourage physicians from considering rural locations. In fact, the best solution to situations of this sort might be to increase the productivity of physicians already on the scene, perhaps with the addition of new types of health personnel. Another factor that ought not to be overlooked in the discussion of financial incentives is the generally high income tax rate most physicians face. Physicians at high income levels may prefer nonpecuniary (and thus nontaxable) forms of professional returns.

Some evidence on the impact of financial factors on location choice may be gleaned from the experiences of various loan forgiveness and direct subsidy programs for inducing physicians to locate in rural practices. A survey of experience in the eleven states with the oldest programs (eleven to twenty-nine years) revealed that a total of 658 physicians repaid their loans by practicing in a rural area. [24] This figure is equivalent to three physicians per state per year. No effort was made to identify physicians who would have chosen rural practice in the absence of the forgiveness program.

Between 1965 and 1972, about 30,000 medical and dental students received Health Professions Assistance Program Loans. As of May 1973, only 183 recipients (62 physicians and 121 dentists) had chosen the rural service repayment option, and of that total, 137 stated (in response to a questionnaire) that they would have chosen rural practice even without loan cancellation.[25]

Although these figures are hardly overwhelming, the trend

---

[24] U.S. Senate, "Health Professions Educational Assistance Act of 1974," Report on S.3585 (Washington, D.C.: U.S. Government Printing Office, September 3, 1974), p. 216.

[25] U.S. Senate, "Health Manpower Legislation 1975," Report on S.989, Part 1 (Washington, D.C.: U.S. Government Printing Office, July 31, 1975), p. 769.

in participation seems to be increasing. Between May 1973 and June 1975, DHEW reported that loans to 139 physicians had been partially cancelled as a result of practice in shortage areas; an additional 245 physicians had signed agreements to practice in shortage areas in return for loan repayment. Of the latter group, the amounts to be repaid to DHEW ranged from $300 to $20,000; the average was $3,600.[26] Given the average debt amounts and relatively liberal buy-out provisions of the various programs, it is not surprising that the impact of the loan program on rural practice has been minimal. A recent study, however, indicates both growing indebtedness and growing interest in practicing in underserved areas.[27]

Canadian data on physician distribution show trends similar to the U.S. experience. In 1960, prior to the adoption of universal physician insurance in any of the provinces, physicians' net incomes ranged from $12,589 in Quebec to $17,754 in Alberta; the population per physician ranged from 758 in British Columbia to 1,314 in New Brunswick.[28] Income in the most remunerative province was roughly 41 percent higher than that in the least remunerative province. At the same time, the most physician-rich province had 73 percent more physicians per capita than the least (excluding Newfoundland). By 1973, the spread of net incomes had been reduced to about 30 percent, but the range of physician availability remained quite high—a 64 percent difference. It appears that although physicians' incomes increased substantially in the poorest provinces, the fact that incomes increased in all provinces effectively diluted any redistributional spillovers. It is also interesting to note that the stock of physicians increased substantially over this period as well, from 117 physicians per 100,000 population to 151 per 100,000. (Medical school capacity roughly doubled, and net immigration increased so much that foreign-trained physicians constituted 30 percent of the Canadian stock.) Again, there appears to have been little spillover to distribution.

---

[26] Ibid., p. 771.

[27] DHEW, PHS, HRA, "Medical School Indebtedness and Career Plans, 1974–75," Publication No. (HRA) 77–21, p. 99.

[28] Data on earnings of physicians in Canada are reported annually in "Earnings of Physicians in Canada," published by Health and Welfare Canada, Health Economics and Statistics Directorate, Health Programs Branch.

With regard to intraprovincial distribution, John R. Evans notes that "manpower studies in the provinces with the most favorable ratios [of physicians] to population have shown major inequities of regional distribution and many communities have been identified that are underserved, particularly in the sparsely populated areas."[29] One study found that between 1968 and 1974, rural areas in three prairie provinces (Alberta, Manitoba, and Saskatchewan) experienced more rapid improvement in the population per physician ratio than did metropolitan areas.[30] In Ontario, however, the populous southern portion of the province gained relative to the rural north.[31] Without more comparable time-series data in other provinces, it is hard to draw firm conclusions.

The Ontario experience with special programs (e.g., education opportunities, start-up practice grants, and guaranteed minimum incomes) to encourage physicians to locate in rural areas appears to have been somewhat more successful. Between 1969 and 1973, 178 doctors were located in 95 communities designated as underserved.[32] Indenture programs in Canada, however, have generally been unsuccessful.[33]

Econometric studies of the relationships between physicians' incomes, reimbursement, and supply have investigated distribution across political units. (No studies of reasons for physicians' choices of location in urban or rural areas or movement among urban areas in the United States have used recent

---

[29] John R. Evans, "Health Manpower Problems: The Canadian Experience," in *Manpower for Health Care,* papers of the spring meeting, Institute of Medicine, (Washington, D.C.: National Academy of Sciences, May 1974), p. 93.

[30] Noralou P. Roos, Michael Gaumont, and John M. Horne, "The Impact of the Physician Surplus on the Distribution of Physicians Across Canada," *Canadian Public Policy* 2 (Spring 1976):178. It should be noted, however, that rural areas were defined as places other than major cities, so these areas may not exactly correspond to the more narrow concept of underserved areas. Moreover, some of the improvement was due to declining populations in rural areas.

[31] W.B. Spaulding and N.U. Spitzer, "Implications of Medical Manpower Trends in Ontario, 1961–1971," *Ontario Medical Review* (September 1972):527–33.

[32] John R. Evans, "Health Manpower: Issues and Goals in Canada," *Pan American Health Organization Bulletin* 8 (1974):309.

[33] William S. Hacon, "Health Manpower in Canada," paper presented at the Northeast Canadian/American Health Seminar, Montreal, Quebec, March 1975.

data on physicians' incomes or reimbursement.) Although definitions vary and the data quality is far from ideal, several studies have found income to have a positive effect on the number of physicians in a state.[34] The one study that used post-Medicare data estimated that, on average, a 1 percent increase in sole proprietor physicians' earnings would increase the number of active, nonfederal physicians in a state by 1.65 percent.[35]

Two other studies have investigated the number of physicians in an area as a function of average reimbursement for physicians' services. Fuchs and Kramer, using 1966 data for thirty-three states, found that the estimated average price for an office visit was positively and significantly related to the number of physicians per 100,000 population.[36] Ramaswamy and Tokuhata estimated an identical model for sixty Pennsylvania counties in 1972.[37] Using more reliable data (claims submitted to Pennsylvania Blue Shield), they also found a positive and significant relationship between the average price of a service and the number of nonfederal physicians per 100,000 population.

---

[34] Frank A. Sloan, "Economic Models of Physician Supply," Ph.D. dissertation, Harvard University, Department of Economics, 1968; Lee Benham, Alex Maurizi and Melvin V. Reder, "Migration, Location and Remuneration of Medical Personnel: Physicians and Dentists," *Review of Economics and Statistics* 50 (August 1968): 332–47; M.W. Lee and R.L. Wallace, "Demand, Supply, and the Distribution of Physicians," Report No. 5, *Studies in Health Care*, Dept. of Community Health and Medical Practice, University of Missouri, 1970; and Jeffrey L. Harrison and G. Donald Jud, "A Regional Analysis of Physician Availability," presented at Southern Economic Association, Houston, Texas, November 8, 1973.

[35] Harrison and Jud, "A Regional Analysis of Physician Availability," Table 3.

[36] Victor R. Fuchs and Marcia J. Kramer, "Determinants of Expenditures for Physicians' Services in the United States, 1948–68," National Center for Health Services Research and Development, DHEW Publication No. (HSM) 73–3013, DHEW, Health Services and Mental Health Administration, December 1972.

[37] Krishnan Ramaswamy and George Tokuhata, "Determinants of Expenditures for Physicians' Services in Pennsylvania: Differences Across Counties, 1972: An Econometric Analysis," presented at the Joint Statistical meetings of the American Statistical Association, the Biometric Society and the Institute of Mathematical Statistics (Business and Economic Statistics Section) at Atlanta, Georgia, August 28, 1975.

More recently, several econometric studies of Canadian physicians' location choices have been completed. These analyses were based on far more accurate data on physicians' incomes obtained through provincial and federal health insurance and internal revenue agencies. In a study of metropolitan versus nonmetropolitan location choices of new physicians in the province of Nova Scotia, Brown found that the probability of a physician's locating outside the Dartmouth-Halifax area was positively related to the earnings of general practitioners (GPs) already in the community and to the individual physician's own earnings in the first full year after establishing practice.[38] Based on Brown's coefficients, one would predict that a 10 percent increase in GPs' gross earnings (about $3,760) would increase the probability of nonmetropolitan practice by 4.1 percent, that is, from .653 to .678. An equivalent payment to a new GP would increase the probability from .653 to .671. This estimate suggests that increasing payments only to new physicians to practice in nonmetropolitan areas would be a far more efficient way to achieve this end than supplementing the earnings of all physicians, but in neither case is the predicted impact large.

Another study analyzed physician supply response in Quebec over the five years following the introduction of universal and comprehensive health insurance in 1970.[39] Data provided by the Regie de l'Assurance-Maladie du Quebec permitted quarterly identification of each physician's location and gross payments from the Regie.[40] Thus, it was feasible to track both new physicians' first locations and established physicians' relocations. During this period, Quebec experienced a phenomenal increase of 36 percent in the number of active physicians.[41]

[38] Murray G. Brown, "Analysis of Physician Practice Location Decisions in Nova Scotia," paper presented at the Operations Research Society of America meeting, Las Vegas, Nevada, November 1975.

[39] Charles Berry et al., "A Study of the Responses of Canadian Physicians to the Introduction of Universal Medical Care Insurance: The First Five Years in Quebec," final report, Mathematica Policy Research, Princeton, New Jersey, February 28, 1978.

[40] The Regie de l'Assurance-Maladie du Quebec is an agency of the Quebec provincial government. Its primary function is to process and to pay all claims submitted by Quebec physicians for payment for services provided to persons covered by the provincial insurance plan.

[41] Active physicians are defined as physicians receiving more than $5,000 per quarter in gross payments from the Regie.

The number of physicians per 100,000 population increased at a compound annual rate of 7.6 percent per year, from 104.5 in 1971 to 140.2 in 1975.

The province was divided into sixty-four physician market areas in order to investigate how physician distribution had changed after Medicare and in order to discover what influence gross payments had had on migration behavior. Using Lorenz curves to examine the change in distribution, it was found that there had been a small movement towards greater equalization.[42] More interesting, perhaps, is the finding that general practitioners were distributed more evenly than specialists, both at the beginning and end of the observation period. This finding provides further evidence of the important link between physicians' specialty choices and their geographic distribution.

The effect of gross payments on migration was investigated using multivariate regression analysis. Again, there were distinct differences in the reactions of general practitioners and specialists. For the GPs, gross payments had a positive effect on in-migration, a negative effect on out-migration, and a greater impact on new GPs than on GPs already in practice. For the average market area, a 1 percent increase in gross payments to general practitioners was estimated to result in a 3.4 percent increase in the number of GPs. For specialists, however, the results were contrary to expectations, indicating that an increase in specialists' gross payments was associated with a net decrease in the number of specialists. This finding suggests the greater importance of nonmonetary factors (access to hospital facilities, large patient populations, and collegial contacts) to specialists' location decisions.

Finally, Hadley analyzed interprovincial data on physicians' net incomes and the number of active, fee-practice physicians between 1958 and 1976.[43] Again, income had a positive effect on the number of physicians in a province. Further

---

[42] A Lorenz curve plots the proportion of the population in each market area against the proportion of physicians. Perfect equality is defined as a 45-degree line, that is, a market area with 10 percent of the population also has 10 percent of the physician stock. Inequality is then measured in terms of the deviation of the actual plot from the 45-degree line.

[43] Jack Hadley, "Canadian Evidence on the Income Elasticity of Physician Supply," The Urban Institute Working Paper 1225–02, Washington, D.C., October 1979.

calculations indicated that the long-term cost per additional physician attracted to an average province is about $55,000 per year (in 1976 U.S. dollars).

These last three studies suggest that, at least in Canada, physicians do respond positively to financial incentives in making their location decisions. Furthermore, two of the studies indicate that general practitioners are probably more responsive than specialists are to such inducements in choosing among locations of different population sizes. Whether such is the case for all primary-care physicians requires further research because of the difference between the specialty designation systems of the United States and Canada. Finally, the efficiency or cost of a financial incentives policy depends on the extent to which additional payments can be directed only to new physicians or to potential relocators.

In general, then, the evidence supports the premise that financial incentives can be used to influence at least some aspects of physicians' locational choices. Unfortunately, none of the prior research has used high-quality data that are both recent and representative of U.S. physicians. Thus, there are no good quantitative estimates of how influencial and how costly financial incentives policies might be. At the least, it appears that attempts to use financial variables in a strategy to redistribute physicians should include carefully planned data collection and evaluation plans to monitor possible adjustments in financial incentives.

SOME POTENTIAL IMPLEMENTATION PROBLEMS

If policy makers were to choose to use financial incentives to help attain redistribution objectives, several difficult issues would need to be addressed: selecting a method for actually manipulating earnings, deciding which physicians are to be affected, and determining the proper dose of financial incentive. This section discusses each of these tasks.

Methods of Altering Physician Earnings

The level of a physician's earnings depends on how the physician is paid, what reimbursement rate is used, and, to a lesser extent, who pays (patient, private insurance company, or government). Chapter 2 examines the impact of alternative reimbursement methods on provider behavior; the focus here is on how readily physicians' incomes could actually be influenced under alternative reimbursement methods. Three approaches will be discussed: fixed fee schedules (CHIP, Kennedy-Corman); usual, customary, and reasonable reimbursement (Long-Ribicoff-Waggonner); and various lump sum payments, such as salary, bonus, practice subsidy, or capitation payment (Kennedy-Corman).

Fixed Fee Schedules. Altering physicians' incomes through a fixed fee schedule would appear to be relatively simple. Because gross income is the product of the fee schedule times the quantity of services provided, however, inability to control the latter may easily thwart attempts to alter *relative* earnings across locations and specialties. The problem is not so much an inability to raise the incomes of physicians in shortage areas and specialties as it is an inability to limit the earnings of other physicians. A central issue is whether physicians can "create enough demand" to compensate for the fixed fees.

Some evidence of the effects of fee schedules on physicians' incomes is available from Canadian experience. It is frequently argued that conversion to a national health insurance system with universal eligibility, generous benefits coverage, and limited patient cost sharing would lead to explosive growth in physicians' earnings. The impact of Medicare and Medicaid in the United States is cited as an example. Similarly, several observers of the Canadian health care system have highlighted sharp jumps in physicians' earnings following conversion to Medicare in Canada. For example, Evans says that "the single most prominent influence of health insurance in Canada has been to increase the earnings of health providers." [44] Wolfe and Badgley point out that physicians' net earnings prior to Medicare grew at apparently high rates (8.1 percent per year between 1960 and 1970), and then

---

[44] Robert G. Evans, "Beyond the Medical Market Place: Expenditures, Utilization and Pricing of Insured Health Care in Canada," in S. Andreopolous, ed., *National Health Insurance: Can We Learn From Canada?* (New York: John Wiley and Sons, Inc., 1975).

jumped even higher upon conversion to the physician insurance program.[45] Marmor and Tenner present data that indicate a 28.8 percent average increase in physicians' net incomes for the two years ending with the first full year of provincial participation in Medicare.[46] The average increase for the immediately preceding two years was 13.7 percent.

According to a Canadian official, much of the observed increase was both intentional and transitory,[47] reportedly reflecting a desire to reduce disparities among specialties and locations by raising payments to lower-income physicians. Further, Gellman has argued that senior executives in Canadian industry and government experienced earnings increases of between 6 percent and 8 percent per year in the years prior to 1969, thus implying the physicians' income increases were not substantially out of line with the general experience.[48]

Table 11 provides a closer look at this experience by examining not only changes in physicians' earnings, but also changes in the stocks of physicians and in expenditures for physicians' services by Canadian province. Data cover various years between 1958 and 1976, depending on when Medicare was implemented in each province. Annual compound rates of growth are presented for four-year intervals both before and after Medicare was implemented in each province. In order to eliminate the once-for-all effect of converting to Medicare, the transition year was excluded from one set of calculations. All financial data are stated in 1970 dollars.

Probably the most striking numbers in this table are the negative rates of growth in physicians' net real incomes in the post-Medicare years. If the transition year is excluded from the calculations, the rates of growth are negative in every province, ranging from —2.37 percent to —6.56 percent per

---

[45] Samuel Wolfe and Robin F. Badgley, "How Much Is Enough? The Payment of Doctors—Implications for Health Policy in Canada," *International Journal of Health Services* 4 (1974):245–64.

[46] Theodore R. Marmor and Edward Tenner, "National Health Insurance: Canada's Path, America's Choices," *Challenge* (January 1977):19.

[47] Personal communication from Robert Armstrong, Director General, Health Insurance, Department of Health and Welfare, Ottawa, Canada.

[48] D.D. Gellman, "Medicare, Medical Income Disparities, and Fee Schedule Changes: Facts, Fallacies, Problems and Positions," *Canadian Medical Association Journal* 105 (September 18, 1971):655.

year. Panel B indicates that the stock of active, fee-practice physicians grew at extremely high rates, both before and after Medicare. Annual increases are between 2 percent and 10 percent per year with most greater than 5 percent per year. In the United States, by contrast, the physician stock grew at between 1 percent and 2 percent per year over this period. Finally, Panel C shows that expenditures for physicians' services grew more rapidly in the pre-Medicare years than in the post-Medicare period. It also illustrates the major impact of the transition year on calculations of average annual expenditure increases. Excluding the transition year reduces the growth rates in every province but one and, in some cases, by as much as a factor of four or five. It appears then that while expenditures continued to grow at a moderate rate, the increases were due primarily to the large, planned expansion in the number of physicians.

Additional data on expenditures for physicians' services in Canada and the United States reinforce the picture presented by Table 11.[49] In 1960, the United States spent about 16 percent more of its GNP for physicians' services than did Canada (1.14 percent and 0.98 percent, respectively). By 1971, when Canada fully implemented Medicare, the gap between the two countries closed by more than half, to 7.6 percent. Following conversion to Medicare, however, the share of Canadian GNP going to physicians dropped dramatically, to 1.09 percent in 1976. Over the same time period, the United States, which has neither fee controls nor universal and comprehensive health insurance, increased its spending for physicians' services to 1.75 percent of GNP, about 60 percent more than Canada spent.

Reinhardt has pointed out that physicians in Quebec generally own neither X-ray nor laboratory facilities, and therefore cannot resort to increased diagnostic testing as a means of maintaining earnings.[50] Such is not the case in West Germany, however, where ownership of such facilities is quite

---

[49] Jack Hadley, John Holahan, and William Scanlon, "Can Fee-for-Service Reimbursement Coexist with Demand Creation?" *Inquiry* 16 (Fall 1979).

[50] Uwe E. Reinhardt, "Health Manpower Policy in the United States," paper presented at the Bicentennial Conference on Health Policy, University of Pennsylvania, Philadelphia, November 1976, p. 37.

Table 11

ANNUAL COMPOUND PERCENTAGE RATES OF GROWTH IN PHYSICIANS' NET INCOME, THE SUPPLY OF PHYSICIANS, AND EXPENDITURES FOR PHYSICIANS' SERVICES BY CANADIAN PROVINCE, BEFORE AND AFTER MEDICARE, 1958–75

	ALB	BC	MAN	NB	NF	NS	ONT	PEI	QUE	SAS
Date Medicare Implemented	July 1, 1969	July 1, 1968	April 1, 1969	Jan. 1, 1971	April 1, 1969	April 1, 1969	Oct. 1, 1969	Dec. 1, 1970	Nov. 1, 1970	July 1, 1962
Transition Year	1970	1969	1969	1971	1969	1969	1970	1971	1971	1963
A. Net MD Incomes (1970 dollars)										
Pre-Medicare	4.78	1.10	2.97	2.64	2.65	2.24	2.82	1.70	0.55	−2.42
Post-Medicare (Includes transition year)	−4.90	−1.57	−1.63	−6.41	−2.46	0.80	−5.62	−7.46	−5.77	−2.33
(Excludes transition year)	−5.70	−2.37	−6.21	−6.56	−3.62	−3.16	−6.15	−5.20	−4.92	−3.74
B. Physician Stock										
Pre-Medicare	9.92	9.62	5.74	10.59	9.92	8.95	7.70	7.20	7.07	2.34
Post-Medicare (Includes transition year)	5.52	8.34	5.78	8.96	7.53	8.44	5.71	5.47	8.90	6.30
(Excludes transition year)	5.10	8.06	4.11	5.77	5.63	6.05	4.70	6.10	5.87	4.05

C. *Expenditures*
(1970 dollars)

Pre-Medicare	13.35	8.67	5.89	8.65	10.31	7.55	9.49	7.56	5.00	N/A
Post-Medicare (Includes transition year)	3.41	6.61	4.57	3.13	5.30	9.11	3.23	0.22	3.42	2.62
(Excludes transition year)	2.41	5.78	—0.82	0.51	0.93	3.59	1.74	4.46	2.08	2.13

Note: Four-year periods before and after implementation of Medicare in each province.

Sources: Health and Welfare Canada, *Earnings of Physicians in Canada* and unpublished statistics from Health and Welfare Canada.

Table 12

HEALTH CARE STATISTICS, PROVINCE OF QUEBEC, CANADA, 1971–74

(Figures in parentheses are index numbers, with 1971 = 100).

	1971	1972	1973	1974
1. Per capita cost of physician services	$ 45.4 (100)	$ 49.9 (110)	$ 56.1 (124)	$ 59.4 (131)
2. Average number of physician services paid for, per capita	5.34 (100)	5.76 (108)	6.41 (120)	6.66 (125)
3. Average cost per service	$ 8.50 (100)	$ 8.65 (102)	$ 8.75 (103)	$ 8.93 (105)
4. Average remuneration per physician:				
a. All general practitioners	$33,047 (100)	$32,217 (97)	$34,236 (104)	$36,379 (110)
b. Group of 1,850 full-time GPs	$47,409 (100)	NA	$49,938 (105)	NA
c. All specialists	$43,645 (100)	$44,376 (102)	$46,827 (107)	$47,597 (109)
d. Group of 2,770 specialists	$53,586 (100)	NA	$56,132 (105)	NA
5. Consumer price index (Canada)	100	105	113	124
6. Physicians per 100,000 population	116 (100)	128 (110)	136 (117)	140 (121)

Sources: Government of Quebec, Regie de l'Assurance—Maladie du Quebec, *1974 Annual Statistics,* various tables. Lines 4b and 4d from A. P. Contandriopolous (1976), Table 1, p. 165. Reproduced from Uwe Reinhardt, "Health Manpower Policy in the United States," paper presented to the Bicentennial Conference on Health Policy, University of Pennsylvania, November 1976, p. 36.

common and where physicians have openly admitted having used such procedures as an income maintenance device.[51] Tables 12 and 13 illustrate the comparative situations. Most would agree that the U.S. situation is more likely to approximate the German than the Quebec experience. Finally, two studies of Ontario physicians suggest that they have increased service levels in response to declining real incomes (due to general inflation), but that the rate of increase slowed in response to upward fee revisions in 1974.[52]

---

[51] Ibid., p. 39.

[52] Carolyn J. Tuohy, "Medical Politics After Medicare: The Ontario Case," *Canadian Public Policy* 2 (Spring 1976):198.

Table 13

A. AVERAGE GROSS REVENUE PER PHYSICIAN RECEIVED FROM SICKNESS FUNDS, WEST GERMANY, 1950–74

Year	Gross Revenue from Funds per Physician	Gross Revenue from Sickness Funds per Physician, Divided by Gross National Product per Capita	Gross Revenues from Funds Earned by all Physicians, as a Percentage of Gross National Product
	Deutsche marks		%
1950	14,700	7.0	0.46
1960	44,469	8.1	0.63
1965	72,995	9.2	0.70
1970	122,204	10.8	0.80
1974	199,623 [a]	12.4	0.97

[a] Estimated.

Source: G. Wollny, "Arzthonorar Und Bruttosozialproduct," *Die Ortskranken-kasse,* (October 1, 1975) Table 2, p. 718. Reproduced from Reinhardt, "Health Manpower in the United States," p. 38.

B. MIX OF SERVICES REIMBURSED PER "CASE",[b] LOCAL SICKNESS FUNDS, WEST GERMANY, 1965–74

Service Category	Fourth Quarter 1965		Fourth Quarter 1974		Percentage Change 1965–74
	Deutsche marks	%	*Deutsche marks*	%	%
Consultations	7.70	31.2	7.31	20.0	− 5.1
Visits	2.06	8.3	1.55	4.2	− 24.8
Minor medical procedures	7.53	30.5	10.42	28.5	+ 38.5
Medical supplies	1.33	5.4	1.69	4.6	+ 27.1
Diagnostic procedures	2.56	10.4	9.13	25.0	+256.6
X-ray procedures	2.45	9.9	4.65	12.7	+ 89.8
Total per "case"	24.68	100.0	36.59	100.0	+ 48.3

[b] "Case" in this context means "patient treated by a given physician during the quarter" and is not to be confused with a medical case.

Source: Th. Siebeck, "Zur Kostenentwicklung der Krankenversicherung," *Die Ortskrankenkasse* 7 (April 1976), Table 11, p. 276. Reproduced from Reinhardt, "Health Manpower in the United States," p. 38.

Although the Canadian experience supports the notion that physicians' earnings can be limited through fee schedules (plus a sharp increase in the number of providers and limited access to laboratory and X-ray facilities), it also suggests that physicians can resort to political means to reach income goals. In particular, an increasingly explicit component of the agreement between provincial governments and the physicians' union is that fees be set so as to attain acceptable (to the physicians) lifetime earnings across specialties and locations.[53] Thus, physicians in low-earnings activities are permitted larger fee increases than are other physicians, but all physicians are entitled to increases large enough to maintain parity with other occupations. In effect, although incentives have been increased to persuade physicians to choose shortage activities, disincentives have not been imposed on physicians in "overdoctored" areas or surplus specialties. Rather, physicians' generally comfortable and prestigious positions have become institutionalized.[54]

It appears, then, that fee schedules can be used to alter relative earnings, particularly when those schedules are implemented through a negotiation process. The most likely way to accomplish this purpose is to equalize fees across geographic areas and specialties, presumably somewhere near the upper end of the existing fee distribution. (This approach was used in Quebec.) Physicians in high-volume, low-fee practices might gain substantially.[55] Given physicians' opportunities to generate additional services through devices such as procedure

---

[53] Ibid., p. 200; Milan Korcok, "Medical Dollars and Data: Collection and Recollection. Part II Medicare Benefits Statisticians," *CMA Journal* 112 (March 22, 1975):773–77; Evans, "Does Canada Have Too Many Physicians?" p. 150.

[54] In fact, physicians located in overdoctored areas or surplus specialties might be quite pleased to see public policy used to move physicians away from their locations and specialties. In this context, it is not at all surprising that surgical specialists in the United States now support *reducing* the number of surgical residency training positions.

[55] A potentially important consequence of increasing fees and incomes for such physicians may be reduced work loads. This situation could be especially troublesome if physicians were to set their patient loads in order to attain a "target" income. Reduced patient loads would dissipate much of the desired gains in access to physicians. The general issue of how physicians' hours of work and patient load decisions will respond to redistribution-oriented payment plans warrants careful attention.

coding terminology changes, increased diagnostic testing, and more frequent follow-up visits, however, areas and specialties of physician adequacy may be able to continue to absorb disproportionate numbers of physicians, even in the face of a growing physician supply.

To become truly effective, it appears that negotiations over fees must ultimately expand to include physicians' incomes and explicit distributional objectives. Then the negotiation process would give providers themselves a share of the responsibility for redistribution. Tuohy refers to this process as moving toward "corporate accommodation" between physicians and provincial governments.[56] As such, the establishment of the negotiating mechanism and agenda may turn out to be a more effective policy tool than is the manipulation of fixed fees per se.

Usual, Customary, Reasonable (UCR) Reimbursement. As specified in the Long-Ribicoff-Waggonner bill, UCR reimbursement is usually associated with preserving disparities in fees across areas and specialties.[57] UCR could, however, reduce disparities in relative physician earnings in two ways. First, imposing uniform reimbursement methods and rates for both Medicare and Medicaid should increase the earnings of physicians treating Medicaid patients. Many states with large Medicaid populations currently reimburse physicians on the basis of fee schedules that are generally well below Medicare's "reasonable" amounts.[58] The extent of the increase would depend on the size of the existing gap in fees and the proportion of Medicaid patients in physicians' practices.

Second, the Long-Ribicoff-Waggonner bill would increase the importance of Medicaid patients to physicians by legislatively

[56] Tuohy, "Medical Politics After Medicare," p. 200.

[57] Pierre de Vise, "Physician Migration from Inland to Coastal States: Antipodal Examples of Illinois and California," *Journal of Medical Education* 48 (February 1973):141–51; Institute of Medicine, "Medicare-Medicaid Reimbursement Policies," final report, submitted to the Subcommittee on Ways and Means, supported by DHEW Contract No. SSA–PMB–74–250.

[58] The Medicare "reasonable" charge for a specific procedure is the lowest of the physician's usual charge, the customary charge in the reimbursement area, and the actual charge billed. The reasonable charge is the amount in fact credited to the physician. (Chapter 2 of this book discusses physician reimbursement.)

expanding the size of the eligible population.[59] This action would probably have the double-barreled effect of increasing the demand for physicians' services by the near poor or working poor and of shifting current Medicaid patients away from generally more expensive institutional providers, such as hospital emergency rooms and clinics.

Like the fixed fee schedule system, UCR probably would have few options for constraining physicians' earnings in sufficiently served areas and specialties. Public authorities could conceivably manipulate fee screens (points along fee distributions used to determine usual and customary charges) to further affect relative physician earnings. In fact, Senator Talmadge proposed such action in his 1976 bill to amend the Medicare and Medicaid programs.[60] The potential ability to constrain physicians' earnings is limited also (at least in the Long-Ribicoff-Waggonner proposal) by the existence of a largely private system for the population which is neither aged nor poor, and by the continued option physicians have of refusing to assign bills of nonpoor Medicare patients.[61] Finally, physicians' response would depend on whether they are income maximizers. If they are not, their ability to earn satisfactory incomes in desirable surroundings without a large government presence might mean that UCR reimbursement would have little redistributive impact.

In the short term, fixed fee and UCR reimbursement (as envisaged in the bills under examination) could have similar effects in terms of shifting relative physicians' earnings by area and specialty. But the fixed fee approach, which would involve establishing fee schedules and negotiating procedures, might require a much greater start-up effort. Over time, however, the fixed fee system seems to offer the policy maker more

---

[59] Recent research indicates that the physician's decision to treat Medicaid patients is positively related to the Medicaid fee. See Frank A. Sloan, Jerry Cromwell, and Janet B. Mitchell, *Private Physicians and Public Programs* (Lexington, Mass.: D.C. Heath, Lexington Books, 1978); Frank A. Sloan and Bruce Steinwald, "A Time Series Cross-Section Analysis of Hospital Demand for Inputs," work in progress, Department of Economics, Vanderbilt University.

[60] U.S. Senate, "Medicare Medicaid Administrative and Reimbursement Reform Act," S.3205, 94th Congress, 2nd Session, 1976.

[61] A physician accepts assignment of a Medicare claim by agreeing not to charge the patient a fee above the reasonable fee determined by Medicare. (See Chapter 2 of this book.)

ways to alter earnings and distributions, precisely because the negotiating forum exists. Further, establishing negotiating activities at the state or regional level (probably with some state cost sharing and public accountability) should improve identification of shortages and monitoring of physicians' responses with respect to hours worked and patient loads.

The Canadian experience, particularly in Quebec, suggests that, in switching to a fee schedule, physicians would probably garner a large one-time gain.[62] Establishing a government-provider dialogue, however, would help to identify concerns and, it is hoped, to resolve them cooperatively. Although a centrally administered UCR system would avoid much of the costly and difficult start-up phase of the fee schedule system, the UCR system might ultimately prove a much less flexible redistribution mechanism.

Lump Sum Payments to Physicians. The Kennedy-Corman bill would authorize lump sum payments (presumably by the government) to physicians practicing in certain locations or specialties.[63] Such payments would take the form of single or periodic bonuses, salary supplements, subsidies for purchasing equipment or renting space, tax credits or deductions, or guaranteed minimum incomes. The question of how the earnings of such physicians are altered is answered directly: they receive checks (or reduced tax liabilities). The difficult questions relate to identifying shortage areas and specialties, identifying physicians who practice in designated activities, deciding on the necessary size of the payment, and measuring the effects of the policy on physicians' effort.

The United States has had virtually no experience with bonus programs for physicians, but some data are available from programs in Ontario, Canada, and in the United Kingdom. The former appears to have been quite successful in placing physicians in underserved (predominantly rural) areas. Of 203 physicians assigned since October 1969, 177 were still on assignment in December 1973.[64] The program offers as

---

[62] Korcok, "Medical Dollars and Data," p. 777; Evans, "Beyond the Medical Marketplace," 1975, p. 160.

[63] Similar authority was included as part of the Health Professions Educational Assistance Act of 1976 (PL 94–484).

[64] W.J. Copeman, "177 of 203 Doctors Stay in Underserved Areas," *Ontario Medical Review*, December 1973, pp. 774–77.

financial incentives a guaranteed net annual professional income of $33,000 or an incentive grant of $20,000 paid over four years in declining installments.[65] Other features of the program include provision of adequate housing and clinic facilities by the local community, emphasis on group practice, and careful matching of physicians and communities. Slightly more than half of the physicians (111) chose the incentive grant. More than 80 percent are married and, as might be expected, the majority (108) are less than thirty years old. No analysis of the independent impact of the financial incentives is presented, nor are any cost data provided.

In the United Kingdom, any area that has at least 2,500 or more unassigned patients remaining after all physicians in the area have been assigned their 2,500 patients each is designated a shortage area.[66] All general practitioners working in areas so designated for a period of at least three consecutive years were eligible for the basic "designated area" allowance (initially $935 and, as of 1974, $1,145). The allowance was payable for every year of designation, as well as for a concessionary period of two years after the designation was dropped. Since 1970, a higher allowance, $1,675, has been paid to practitioners in areas with at least 3,000 unassigned patients.

An early analysis of this program indicated that the bonus was too small, relative to physicians' incomes, to have any effect. Between 1966 and 1970, the number of designated areas increased from 241 to 320. In 1968, twice as many areas were added to the designated list as were dropped. Since 1970, designated areas have been doing better, apparently because of the constantly growing supply of physicians and the disincentives against opening practices in so-called restricted areas.[67] Physician surveys suggest that the small size of the inducement payments made them relatively unimportant in comparison to the importance of previous contacts with an area.[68]

---

[65] The financial payments are $5,000 less for locating in an underserved area in southern Ontario.

[66] J.R. Butler and R. Knight, "The Designated Areas Project Study of Medical Practice Areas," Health Services Research Unit, University of Kent at Canterbury, June 1974.

[67] The disincentive is ineligibility for payment by the National Health Service.

[68] Butler and Knight. "The Designated Areas Project Study," pp. 15–16.

The British experience also revealed two potential administrative problems: the fundamental task of identifying and monitoring underserved areas, and the strong incentive for physicians currently practicing in a designated area to keep the area designated. If the bonus payment were increased in order to attract physicians, the incentive for existing physicians to discourage new practitioners would become even stronger. Conversely, if allowances were granted only to new physicians, physicians already in an area would no doubt complain, legitimately, about the inequity of rewarding new practitioners who may have low practice volumes.

A concern that might arise in the United States is that a lump sum bonus might discourage physicians from vigorous bill collection and efforts to build a busy, successful practice. For example, a continuing puzzle with many National Health Service Corps (NHSC) practices is their relatively low productivity.[69] Table 14 compares data on patient visits for the National Health Service Corps with data for roughly comparable private practitioners. Although factors such as physician age, office staffing, and patient uncertainty regarding NHSC practices doubtless contribute to the marked differences, NHSC physicians do receive salaries independent of their productivity.

Two empirical studies have examined the effects of nonpractice incomes on physicians' hours or weeks worked. In both cases, work effort declined to some extent as nonpractice income increased.[70] Most physicians in these studies, however, were in private practice and probably none received payments of the type contemplated here.

---

[69] The National Health Service Corps (NHSC) was established by the Emergency Health Personnel Act of 1970 (PL 91–623) to deal with the problem of maldistribution of health care personnel in the United States. The preamble to the authorizing legislation states the purpose as ". . . to authorize the assignment of commissioned officers of the Public Health Service (PHS) to areas with critical medical manpower shortages to encourage health personnel to practice in areas where shortages of such personnel exist. . . ." The NHSC has responded by placing health professionals in areas with critical shortages and by helping these areas develop the capability to independently attract and retain health professionals.

[70] Sloan, "Microanalysis of Physicians Hours of Work Decision"; and Vahovich, "Physician Supply Decisions."

Table 14

PHYSICIAN PRODUCTIVITY IN NHSC SITES
AND IN PRIVATE PRACTICE

Practice or Site	Average Annual Billable Visits per Practitioner
I. *ALL 80 NHSC SITES SURVEYED IN 1975:*	3,595
a. *BY AGE OF SITE*	
30 sites in existence for 2 years or longer	3,581
22 sites in existence between 1 and 2 years	3,571
28 sites in existence less than 1 year	2,805
b. *BY SIZE OF SITE*	
39 sites with one NHSC practitioner	3,568
39 sites with two NHSC practitioners	3,318
2 sites with three NHSC practitioners	NA
c. *BY YEAR OF SURVEY*	
24 sites surveyed in 1974	3,826
the same 24 sites surveyed in 1975	3,726
d. *THE MOST PRODUCTIVE 12 SITES*	4,337
II. *ROUGHLY COMPARABLE DATA FROM PRIVATE PRACTICE*	
a. *PRIVATE PRACTITIONERS IN NONMETROPOLITAN AREAS*	
General Practice:	
Office visits (162.8 visits per week x 47.8 weeks per year)	7,782
Total visits (212.4 visits per week x 47.8 weeks per year)	10,152
Internal Medicine:	
Office visits (90.0 visits per week x 47 weeks per year)	4,230
Total visits (144.2 visits per week x 42 weeks per year)	6,777
All Physicians:	
Office visits (127.5 visits per week x 47 weeks per year)	5,993
Total visits (175.9 visits per week x 47 weeks per year)	8,267

Table 14

PHYSICIAN PRODUCTIVITY IN NHSC SITES
AND IN PRIVATE PRACTICE—Continued

Practice or Site	Average Annual Billable Visits per Practitioner
b. *PRIVATE PRACTICES IN DHEW-DESIGNATED SHORTAGE AREAS*	
Family and General Practice— North Central States:	
Office visits (125.3 visits x 47 weeks per year)	5,889
Family and General Practice— Southern States:	
Office visits (192.9 visits x 47 weeks per year)	9,066

Sources: Reproduced from Reinhardt, "Health Manpower Policy in the United States," p. 53. Lines Ia to Id—Written Communication from U.S. Congress, Congressional Budget Office, September 20, 1976. Lines IIa—American Medical Association, *Profile of Medical Practice 1974*, Tables 55, 57, and 60. (Data are for 1973). Lines IIb— Held and Reinhardt (1975), Table 9.

Policy makers still may want to employ such payments to induce physicians to make certain career choices. The fact that work effort declines may simply reflect the reality that it is more expensive to provide medical services to certain populations in certain areas. It is important for authorities to be aware of this potential effect, however, and not to be taken aback if subsidized physicians should prove to carry smaller than average case loads.

If reduced effort is unacceptable, some type of monitoring system seems inevitable. How such a system would be set up, particularly for solo practice physicians in remote areas, is not at all clear. In the case of the National Health Service Corps, program officials find it difficult to explain variations in work loads across sites, even though elaborate data reporting systems have been established.

Because extensive monitoring systems could be very costly, it is vital to study carefully the effect of paying practice subsi-

dies at the time such a policy is implemented. Appropriate baseline data should be collected on patient loads, hours worked,
and weeks worked. Longitudinal samples of physicians, some
of whom receive subsidies, should be maintained. A careful
evaluation using samples of physicians should provide good
estimates of whether the allegedy negative impact on effort
was being held to acceptable levels.

If the levels proved too high, policy makers would have to
consider whether subsidies could be made contingent upon attaining certain work loads, and whether the accuracy of reported effort levels was verifiable. Clearly, such monitoring
would be easier under a unified fee-for-service system because
bills submitted could be used to measure work load. But it is
important to avoid creating incentives for physicians to provide otherwise unneeded services. If these implementation
problems, should they exist, cannot be solved, other methods
of addressing distribution issues should be used.

Identifying Shortage Areas and Specialties

Any attempt to alter physician distribution will involve
identifying areas and specialties deserving public support.
This requirement is explicit in bonus or lump sum payment
system, such as the one proposed by the Kennedy-Corman
bill. Proponents of UCR reimbursement plans would have to
decide whether to vary fee screens by specialty or location.
Fixed fee schedule proponents face this problem indirectly,
because procedure-specific fee levels obviously will influence
relative specialty earnings, and procedure frequencies vary
among specialties. Inasmuch as substantial transfers of funds
could hinge upon the designation of a shortage area or specialty, the designation process itself becomes critical.

Some experience has been gained from current legislation
requiring the secretary of Health, Education, and Welfare to
designate shortage areas, populations, and facilities with respect to various types of personnel.[71] Some headway has been
made with respect to populations or facilities, but the primary
focus in geographic areas has been almost entirely on the
county. The usual approach is to rank counties on the basis of
a single criterion, such as infant mortality, physician-popula-

---

[71] Health Professions Educational Assistance Act of 1976 (PL 94–484),
Section 332.

tion ratio, or dentist-population ratio. Some value of the ranking criterion is selected as a cutoff point, and all counties below that value are designated shortage areas.

Using surveys of both physicians and households, studies by Kleinman and Wilson and by Reinhardt and Held have examined the validity of this ranking.[72] Data for respondents in shortage counties were compared with responses from other nonmetropolitan counties. The physician survey examined patient loads, hours worked, and waiting time to appointments. The household survey included several measures of health status plus information on medical care utilization. In both cases there were no significant differences in most of the variables compared. When information from the lowest quartile of shortage counties was compared with that from other nonmetropolitan areas, however, areas designated as shortage counties did appear to be worse off.

Part of the problem is the lack of generally accepted definitions of shortage, adequacy, or surplus. Research on ways to make such assessments is just beginning; moreover, even if valid methods were available, the data requirements for implementing them are likely to be substantial. Public authorities can look forward to repeating the exercise periodically to keep up with population and provider migration, and with changing economic conditions.

Given the potential benefits to both providers and residents of living in a shortage-designated area, it is reasonable to expect heavy political pressure on behalf of adopting a generous cutoff point or of granting designations through an exceptions procedure. Public authorities who find themselves supported by neither the strongest methodologies nor the best data may have difficulty resisting political pressures.

The obvious danger is that the shortage area net would be too large, and that any supplementary payment system would result in excessive program costs. At the same time, within the shortage area counties, the distance between the best-off and

[72] Joel C. Kleinman and Ronald W. Wilson, "Are Medically Underserved Areas Medically Underserved?" *Health Services Research* 12 (Summer 1977):147–62; Philip J. Held and Uwe E. Reinhardt, "Health Manpower Policy in a Market Context," paper presented at the annual meeting of the American Economic Association, Dallas, Texas, December 1975.

worst-off is likely to be so great that the redistributive impact of the program on the truly needy areas could be minimal. Moreover, under any system of area designation, particularly at the level of small political units, severe boundary problems may exist.

Regardless of the designation scheme ultimately selected, program administrators also would have to deal with the problem of identifying physicians actually practicing in those areas. Professional addresses are easy enough to verify, but how should physicians with multiple offices be handled, and how could one verify that the patients treated are actually shortage area residents? These problems are likely to be most severe in metropolitan areas where certain neighborhoods are identified as shortage areas. In effect, the desire to ensure equitable health care by disaggregating areas and populations as finely as possible conflicts with the administrative problem of permeable boundary lines.

The problem of identifying shortage specialties is both more complex and more straightforward than the problem of designating physician-shortage areas. There is general agreement that there should be more primary-care physicians; that, ideally, primary-care physicians should constitute about half of all patient-care physicians; and that there are too many surgeons and surgical specialists. There is much less agreement about what primary care is as it relates to constituent specialties and, even more important, as it relates to services and procedures. There is also disagreement about whether the problem concerns too much surgery rather than too many surgeons. If the payment system is keyed to self-designated specialty assignments, it is easy to foresee largely artificial responses in specialty designations to differences in specialty earnings.[73]

---

[73] For example, when Quebec instituted its Medicare program in 1970, general practitioners experienced relatively large income gains compared with those of specialists, primarily because the prior private insurance plan had paid GPs at rates lower than the rates at which it had paid specialists. In the first year after Medicare, the number of GPs in Quebec jumped 11 percent (Robert A. Armstrong, "Canada's Health Insurance Programs," paper presented to the Association of University Programs in Health Administration, Carleton University, Ottawa, Ontario, June 1973). It is unlikely that droves of GPs were attracted to Quebec from other locations, or that specialists decided to forgo their sophisticated training. More likely, this statistic reflects the fact that a large number of GPs previously had identified themselves as specialists.

Because of this problem, some NHI proponents suggest requiring board certification as an entry condition to specialties. The Kennedy-Corman bill, for example, proposes limiting surgery to board-certified surgeons, but the bill also essentially "grandfathers" all physicians currently doing surgery in good standing into the eligible class. Furthermore, this type of restriction is clearly in the economic interest of the affected specialty, and may actually further restrict access to services by people who have relatively poor access to physicians. Another problem is that board certification does not distinguish subspecialties within a broad specialty area, such as pediatrics or internal medicine. Finally, most recent U.S. medical school graduates have chosen to seek board certification almost as a matter of course.[74] Imposing explicit financial incentives will simply push the proportion closer to 100 percent.

Because the ultimate objective is to alter the relative frequencies with which particular services are provided (for example, to encourage more preventive services, fewer tonsillectomies, more office visits, and fewer hospital visits), it would seem far easier administratively to rely on the rates at which those services are reimbursed as the mechanism for adjusting their provision. Numerous studies in this country and abroad have shown that physicians do respond to financial incentives of this sort.[75] Once the claims-processing system was established, the data provided would enable relatively close monitoring of how frequently services were being performed. This process would seem to be simpler and more responsive than trying to verify what physicians had which specialties and whether physicians were actually providing services consistent with their specialty identification.

Determining Appropriate Payment Levels

Given existing data and knowledge about the determinants of physicians' specialty and location decisions, it is hard to estimate how large the fee or earnings increases would have to be to adjust physician distributions to desired configurations. In principle, the income differential between an isolated

[74] Edithe J. Levit, Melvin Sabshin, and Barber C. Mueller, "Trends in Graduate Medical Education and Specialty Certification," *New England Journal of Medicine* 290 (March 7, 1974):545–49.

[75] Monsma, "Marginal Revenue"; Glaser, *Health Insurance Bargaining*; and Wolfe and Badgley, p. 118.

rural area and a suburban area, for example, would have to be sufficiently large to compensate a physician for the decreased amenities, reduced access to colleagues, possibly longer and more intensive hours of work, and the value of whatever other nonpecuniary factors influence this choice. Similar considerations would govern the determination of specialty payments. One reasonable certainty is that small payments of the size involved in past loan forgiveness programs will not have much impact. Furthermore, the size of payments necessary to induce changes is likely to vary across locations, geographic regions, and medical specialties.

This is not to say that careful econometric research could not provide estimates of required payment levels. Retrospective analyses of physicians who recently entered practice coupled with prospective data from physicians currently in training could provide reasonable baseline information. The problem with most prior research is that the available data did not permit exploring sensitivity to financial incentives.

In light of these considerations, one can only say that the payment system should be flexible enough to allow for both cross-sectional and intertemporal variations and, at the same time, include mechanisms for monitoring changes in physician distribution. Such mechanisms would be essential for assessing physicians' responses to the payment system and for making appropriate adjustments in payment levels. Any monitoring system must identify changes in distribution beyond those that would have occurred without policy intervention. This identification is vital for evaluating the effectiveness of the financial incentives.

Because payment systems have other objectives in addition to affecting physician distributions, and because payment systems would probably be subject to budgetary constraints, the lump sum payment approach appears to offer the most flexibility in setting and adjusting payment levels. This is the case precisely because this approach, at least as envisaged in the Kennedy-Corman bill, would be concerned only with matters of physician distribution. Therefore, including such a fund or account in a national health insurance bill would appear to be beneficial regardless of the method chosen for reimbursing physicians for services. If a fixed fee system were used to alter physicians' relative earnings in the context of an overall limit on payments to physicians, however, the fee schedule could have a substantial effect because of its ubiquity.

Direct Intervention Strategies

The second of the three general sets of policy options for affecting physician supply and distribution is direct intervention. Direct intervention refers to a variety of legal-institutional options, such as changes in immigration and licensure laws, explicit regulation or allocation of physicians, imposition of upper limits on entrants to locations or specialties, public delivery of services, and development of new types of delivery institutions. The broad and vaguely delineated authority that the Kennedy-Corman bill would grant to the proposed Regional Health Boards could very well encompass measures of this sort. Furthermore, the trend in health personnel legislation, such as the Health Professions Educational Assistance Act of 1976, is definitely toward a greater regulatory and interventionist role.

Because this set of policies could result in significant changes in rules or institutional structure, evidence based on prior research conducted under a different institutional structure is not directly applicable. Therefore, this section focuses on possible administrative problems, internal inconsistencies, or political liabilities of various alternatives. Each of the various options just listed will be discussed in turn.

IMMIGRATIONS LAWS AND FOREIGN MEDICAL SCHOOL GRADUATES

Changes in immigration laws are clearly directed at reducing the flow of foreign medical school graduates into the United States. The Health Professions Educational Assistance Act of 1976 eliminated preferential immigration treatment for FMGs on grounds of shortages of skilled personnel, and imposed several restrictive conditions on foreign physicians desiring to enter the country as either immigrants or exchange visitors (graduate trainees). Complete enforcement of the law could cause serious disruption of patient-care services in those hospitals that are heavily dependent on FMGs. In recognition of this consequence, the DHEW secretary granted a blanket waiver to all hospitals for 1977.

Given the expectation that the overall stock of physicians in the United States is expected to continue growing as a result of past U.S. medical school expansion, and given the consensus that simply expanding supply will do little to improve specialty or geographic distributions, the move toward limiting the supply of FMGs is well taken. Although this action may lessen the problem of a potential oversupply of physicians, it also may exacerbate existing distributional problems. FMGs do not enter the same specialties, practice in the same locations, or serve the same populations in the same proportions as U.S. graduates. FMGs are more likely than U.S. graduates to choose institution-based specialties such as anesthesiology, radiology, or psychiatry, and they are more likely to locate in metropolitan areas. In some areas, they make up a substantial proportion of both hospital and total physicians.[76] For example, in 1967, FMGs constituted about 35 percent of all physicians in New York City; 33.8 percent in Youngstown, Ohio; 38.5 percent in Jersey City, New Jersey; 27.2 percent in Chicago; and 28.8 percent in Cleveland.[77] In 1973, FMGs made up more than 45 percent of hospital-based physicians in Standard Metropolitan Statistical Areas in eight states.[78]

Although hard evidence is difficult to come by, FMGs appear to be the principal source of physicians employed by public hospitals in many of these areas. As such, they are likely to be responsible for a major portion of the medical care received by low-income people whose only source of care for both inpatient and ambulatory problems is the local public hospital. For example, in 1974, hospital residents provided 1,031,000

[76] Beverly C. Martin, ed., *Socioeconomic Issues of Health, 1975–76* (Chicago: American Medical Association, 1976), pp. 66–67.

[77] Chris N. Theodore and James N. Hang, *Selected Characteristics of the Physician Population, 1963 and 1967* (Chicago: American Medical Association, 1968) Table 32.

[78] Martin, *Socioeconomic Issues of Health*, p. 65; U.S. House of Representatives, *Health Professions Educational Assistance Act of 1976, House Report 94–266 to accompany H.R. 5546*, 94th Congress, 2nd Session, 1976, p. 5398.

outpatient physician visits (half of these in emergency rooms) in municipal hospitals in Brooklyn, New York.[79] Ninety-three percent of the residents staffing those hospitals were foreign medical graduates.

What effects will the reduced flow of FMGs have on the institutions and people now dependent on them? To the extent that institutions attempt to maintain the current numbers of physicians on their staffs, stipends for residents and full-time physicians almost certainly will increase. Public hospitals will have to attract increased numbers of U.S. graduates or physicians already in practice away from their current activities, and increased salaries would presumably be the principal mechanism used. In the face of rising input costs, however, greater efforts might be expected toward substituting nonphysicians for physicians, possibly toward increased pressure on government to make nonhospital, ambulatory care more readily accessible to low-income populations.

Hospitals facing tight budget constraints might attempt to adjust for lower staff levels by shortening hours, closing facilities, or increasing waiting times. Such practices probably would be unacceptable to populations affected, and strong reactions through various political mechanisms could be anticipated.

It is ironic that one of the arguments in favor of reducing dependence on FMGs is that they presumably provide lower-quality care, inasmuch as a major consequence of restricting immigration could be no care at all for people with no alternatives. From the perspective of implementing national health insurance, the important lesson is to anticipate and plan for the adverse distributional consequences of fewer FMGs. Blanket waivers to hospitals as applied during the first year of the Health Professions Educational Assistance Act of 1976 do not solve the problem, but merely perpetuate it.

LICENSURE LAWS AND ENTRY LIMITS

A second method of institutional intervention might focus on existing licensure laws. It has been suggested that condi-

---

[79] Edward F. X. Hughes, "Residency Distribution: The Need for Partnership," testimony before the Senate Subcommittee on Health, Hearings on S.989, September 30, 1975.

tions for licensure be made more restrictive in areas with apparent physician surpluses, thereby increasing the incentive for physicians to locate in relatively physician-poor areas. For several reasons, this approach would probably be both ineffective and inappropriate. Theoretically, licensure requirements are designed to measure physician competence. If there were to be a wide range in the ease with which a license could be obtained, applicants might sort themselves among states roughly on the basis of ability, the best-qualified applicants tending toward the most physician-rich states and vice versa for the least-qualified applicants. Second, geographic maldistribution is largely an intrastate problem, so statewide licensure would not affect the issue. Similarly, licensure examinations are not likely to become specialty-specific, so these exams would have little influence on specialty distributions. Finally, it is not at all clear that it is possible to substantially reduce flows of physicians into more popular states through licensure barriers. Several economic studies of physician migration indicate that licensure barriers have not been effective in impeding physician mobility.[80]

If health planners were to extend the licensure concept to the physician distribution process, they might attempt to impose upper limits on the numbers of physicians of a particular specialty who would be permitted to practice in an area. Presumably, areas would be defined in such a way as to uncover intrastate variations in physician availability. A system of this kind has been used in the United Kingdom, where the penalty for locating in certain areas is ineligibility for payment under the National Health Service; such a system also is under consideration in Canada.[81] This type of regulation is appealing because it is passive rather than active; it does not direct or coerce physicians into areas or specialties against their will, but simply imposes a constraint on what is now primarily an unconstrained process.

Such intervention, however, is subject to serious problems. Probably foremost among these is how to set the upper limit.

---

[80] Sloan, *Economic Models of Physician Supply*, p. 358; Benham et al., "Migration, Location and Remuneration of Medical Personnel," p. 337.

[81] Maurice Leclair, "The Canadian Health Care System," in *National Health Insurance: Can We Learn From Canada?* Spyros Andreopolous, ed. (New York: John Wiley and Sons, 1975), p. 88; Evans, "Health Manpower Problems: The Canadian Experience," pp. 98–99.

Would separate limits be set for each specialty and then summed? How would nonphysician resources, physician productivity, and physician age distribution be taken into account? Would areas with medical centers that provide highly specialized care for out-of-area populations be exempted from the general rules? How would the limits be changed over time as population, technology, and other nonphysician medical care inputs change? Contemplating the answers to these questions is discouraging.

A second problem concerns who would make the determinations. Local planners might not have the technical capacity. Nor would they have an incentive to impose strict limits if nonlocal third parties were responsible for a large share of the financing. Regional or federal agencies might have difficulty obtaining adequate data (as, in fact, might local planners). Furthermore, administrative or judicial procedures would doubtless be established through which areas could appeal their limits if those areas considered them too low. In view of the frustrations health planners, economists, physicians, and other professionals have experienced in attempting to determine the right number of physicians, it would be most surprising if a judge and jury could do better.

Finally, aside from the various administrative problems described above, there is little reason to think that limits would necessarily induce physicians to choose either shortage locations or primary-care specialties. Any limits set would probably be placed somewhere near the upper end of existing physician-population ratios. As a result, a large number of reasonably well served locations (for example, growing small cities) could continue to absorb physicians, and the policy would not necessarily have much impact on either isolated rural or low-income urban areas. Thus, although such a policy might constrain the numbers of physicians in the best-served areas, it also might do little to improve access for the areas most in need of physicians' services.

DIRECT ALLOCATION OF PHYSICIANS

If one cannot be sanguine about the effectiveness of negative or passive regulation, the logical alternative might seem to be direct regulation. In its simplest form, this regulation might

be thought of as a physician draft. Proponents argue that
because medical students receive substantial public subsidies
over the course of their education, they should be obligated to
some form of repayment. Furthermore, in order to preclude
a system in which the wealthy buy their way out while the
poor become indentured, this repayment should take the form
of mandatory service, presumably in areas that are currently
underserved.

Probably the first thing to be said about this proposal is
that it has little chance of legislative passage. In 1975, health
personnel bills containing physician draft provisions were
defeated in the Senate and House, even though they were
sponsored by Senator Kennedy and Congressman Rogers. The
reasons for defeat are easy to ascertain. Many people feel that
to single out physicians for mandatory public service would
be unfair. At a more practical level, it is legitimate to ask
whether drafting physicians would be an effective means of
providing services. Even if a physician were sent to an underserved area, serious concern might arise about how many and
what kinds of services would be provided by an uncommitted
individual serving under coercion. (Conceptually, the concerns
are similar to those raised in the debate over the performance
of enlisted men versus draftees in the military. In the context
of highly skilled professional services, these concerns may be
magnified.)

The question of when such service would be required is also
relevant. If the service were to follow completion of residency
training, many physicians trained in various specialties would
be delivering primary-care services. If the service were to be
rendered immediately after medical school, many physicians
would be inadequately prepared for "front-line" medicine. In
either case, it would almost certainly be necessary to have an
institutional superstructure of offices, equipment, aides, and
so on to minimize the transition costs associated with the
high rate of turnover.

Finally, imposition of a physician draft would most likely
affect both the quantity and quality of applicants to medical
school. Even if incomes during mandatory service were comparable to those earned by physicians in practice, the net
nonpecuniary return to becoming a physician would certainly
be lower. Exactly what the effect would be is hard to estimate.
It could be expected, however, that the applicants of highest

ability also would have the best alternative opportunities, and these applicants therefore would be most likely to pursue other careers.

A less drastic form of direct allocation is a semivoluntary organization like the National Health Service Corps, which has two basic goals: a short-term objective to redress the imbalance of personnel resource distribution by placing providers in scarcity areas, and a longer-term objective of encouraging these providers to locate their practices in those areas permanently. To meet these objectives, Congress appropriated a total of $110.5 million during the program's first five funding cycles (1973–74 through 1977–1978). About 4,700 medical students received NHSC scholarships over that period.[82] Current benefits include $6,750 annually for living and educational expenses, plus full tuition and fees charged by the medical schools.

The NHSC is called semivoluntary because enrollees voluntarily apply for scholarships or loans with forgiveness options while in training. But once awards are made, recipients incur an obligation of one year of full-time clinical practice in a health personnel shortage area for each year or less of scholarship support received. Loans may be forgiven at a rate of $10,000 per year for each year of service. The minimum service obligation that could be incurred is two years. The service obligation is satisfied only by employment in the National Health Service Corps, the Indian Health Service, or the Bureau of Medical Services, which are components of the Health Services Administration.

Of all NHSC scholarship recipients through 1977-78, 1,619 have graduated from medical school and are now deferred for internship or residency training, 281 are currently in their service period, and 26 have completed their service obligation.[83] Based on the current distribution of awards, the largest group to begin service obligations will approach 1,000 physicians in 1980 and 1981. In 1977, the NHSC had assigned approximately 850 persons to NHSC and the Bureau of Community

---

[82] DHEW, HSA, "National Health Service Corps, First Annual Report to Congress, 1977." Support for the NHSC increased substantially in 1978–79. Scholarship awards were made to 2,703 medical and osteopathic students. The average award was $11,000. *The Blue Sheet*, Washington, D.C., November 1, 1978, p. RN–4.

[83] DHEW, HSA, "National Health Service Corps, First Annual Report."

Table 15

NATIONAL HEALTH SERVICE CORPS
Facts and Figures, 1975-78

	1975	1976	1977	1978
Output				
Number of persons served (in thousands)	398	492	566	728
Sites staffed with at least one assignee	248	331	398	668
Number of assignees	488	596	690	1,289
Physicians	313	395	465	694
Dentists	74	95	106	210
Other	101	106	119	385
Cost (in $ millions)				
Authorized	$16	$30	$34	$47
Appropriated	$20	$15 [a]	$25	$40
Patient fees collected and returned to Treasury	$2.0	$4.3	$4.5	$1.6
Efficiency Measures				
Cost per visit	NA	$15	$16	$17
Retention rate	30%	38%	47%	48%
Funding (in $ millions)				
Field obligations	NA	NA	$25.4	$42.6
Program support obligations	NA	NA	3.3	4.1
Labor Force				
Field positions	551	701	701	1,425
End-of-year field strength	488	596	690	1,425
Program support managers	NA	NA	103	118
Average cost per field assignee	$31,100	$32,700	$36,000	$42,000

[a] Includes $5 million appropriated in 1975 for obligation in 1976.
Source: DHEW, HSA.

Health Services Grant program sites. The NHSC retention rate beyond the period of obligation was 47 percent.[84] Whether this rate will be applicable to future groups cannot be determined.

Tables 15 and 16 provide additional data on National Health Service Corps sites. The Department of Health, Education, and Welfare has estimated that if the NHSC were to be the primary vehicle for meeting critical health personnel needs by

---

[84] Ibid.

1990, approximately 5,000 physician assignees would be required.[85] Although this number represents almost a fivefold increase over the current size of the corps, the NHSC still would absorb no more than a small fraction of the total stock of patient-care physicians in the United States. If half of the NHSC physicians fulfill their obligations and drop out of the program in any given year, NHSC obligations will be required from about 15 percent of future medical school classes in order to maintain staffing.[86]

A detailed exploration of whether the National Health Service Corps is the best mechanism for meeting medical care distribution objectives clearly exceeds the scope of this chapter, but several observations can be made. First, in order to attract recruits and improve retention rates, the NHSC has been flexible in permitting assignees to select practice sites. As a result, the distribution of physicians engaged in NHSC prac-

Table 16

PROJECTED NHSC FIELD STRENGTH AND TYPE OF PLACEMENT, 1979-83

	1979	1980	1981	1982	1983
Total placement sites staffed	743	843	943	1,043	1,143
Total assignees	1,725	3,120	4,144	4,713	4,938
Breakdown of assignees by type of placement					
Corps sites (community-sponsored)	716	815	918	975	1,048
Centers (grant- and facility-sponsored)	659	1,718	2,450	2,798	2,793
State and local health department-sponsored	190	270	370	470	570
Prisons	67	125	180	235	290
Other state and state mental hospital placement	93	192	226	235	237
Percentage urban (projected)	15%	20%	25%	30%	35%
Percentage rural (projected)	85%	80%	75%	70%	65%

Source: DHEW, HSA.

---

[85] DHEW, PHS, "Levels of Support for National Health Service Corps (NHSC) and NHSC Scholarship Programs," memorandum to the Assistant Secretary for Health, March 1978.

[86] Ibid.

tices is exceedingly uneven, with few located in the southeastern states. If assignment policy should become more restrictive, the financial inducement for prospective recruits might have to increase commensurately.

Second, NHSC sites tend to have relatively low productivity; as a result, visits are relatively costly. Data from the twelve most productive NHSC sites in 1975 indicate average annual billable encounters per practice of 4,337.[87] The median figure for annual office encounters for solo-private-practice, non-metropolitan, primary-care physicians ages thirty to thirty-five was estimated to be 6,627.[88] Cost per visit was $7.56 in the private practice sites, compared with about $15 for the NHSC (see Table 15).

Many factors may explain these differences: natural selection of private practices into the most productive and financially viable locations; unwillingness of local populations to give up traditional sources of care; salaried reimbursement of NHSC physicians, as opposed to fee-for-service reimbursements of private practices; differences in the style and quality of care delivered; and continual practice-building and start-up periods because of turnover in NHSC physicians. The relative importance of these factors must be determined before a decision can be made on whether to make the NHSC a key component of federal health personnel policy. Some problems can be dealt with by changing program structure (e.g., offering productivity bonuses for NHSC physicians) but others, such as patient nonacceptance, may be fatal to the NHSC program.

If the NHSC serves as a provider of last resort in areas which, under current insurance and reimbursement systems, cannot support private practices, then the apparent low productivity/high cost may be an inevitable component of efforts to redistribute care. In this respect, the NHSC would be much like other public programs (e.g., power, transportation) that subsidize services to rural residents. Whether this subsidy is desirable for medical care is clearly a political decision.

---

[87] Reinhardt, "Health Manpower Policy in the United States."

[88] David Emery, Dan Calvin, and Allen Dobson, "An Analysis of NHSC Economic Performances for Quarter 3 FY 1975," Working Paper No. 3, Office of Policy, Evaluation, and Legislation, HSA, DHEW, February 1976, Table II–1.

DEVELOPMENT OF NEW SERVICE INSTITUTIONS

The last type of institutional intervention to be considered here may be called, for lack of a better term, the ambulatory-care institutional approach. This generic term can apply to any number of institutional settings for delivering care. Current examples of ambulatory-care institutions might include Area Health Education Centers; National Health Service Corps sites; Neighborhood Health Centers (NHCs); and group practices, both prepaid and fee-for-service. The first is primarily a network of private providers tied into medical education centers for purposes of referrals, spot backup, and continuing education. The next two are federally operated, direct-care institutions. The last, of course, is generally a purely private entity organized on either a for-profit or nonprofit basis.

The major premise underlying the ambulatory-care institutional approach is that independent, solo medical practice is not the best mode of practice for providing care in underserved areas, either rural or urban. Professional isolation, lack of control over hours, heavy patient loads, and inadequate facilities are frequently cited as reasons why physicians forgo rural practice. In some urban areas, physical safety may pose an additional problem, but an overwhelming patient load, low fees, and probably low collection ratios appear to be the main deterrents to new practice.[89] (We assume that ability to pay would be covered by a national health insurance plan.)

In contrast to a draft or obligatory service plan, physicians who would staff ambulatory-care institutions would be voluntarily recruited and presumably would have some commitment to serving the institution's clientele. Expected earnings no doubt would have to be competitive with private practice alternatives. However, if national health insurance in effect were to enfranchise low-income people through universal eligibility, and if ambulatory-care institutions were to carry full patient loads, such institutions should be able to generate most of their own revenues without having to cope with the administrative burdens of eligibility determination.

Almost by definition, ambulatory-care institutions would be

---

[89] National Health Council, *1976 National Conference on Health Manpower Distribution*, (New York: National Health Council, Inc., June 1976), pp. 46–52.

located in areas lacking alternative sources of care (except for public hospitals). As a result, the potential for the "Medicaid mill" phenomenon (high-volume, low-quality care) may be high. To help guard against this phenomenon, some local government control, preferably with a degree of financial clout, should be built into the general ambulatory-care institutional model. Local involvement also should reduce the problem of bureaucratic rigidity frequently characteristic of centralized programs. (Both quality of care and general "responsiveness" to patients' needs should be higher under a system in which patients have the option, through universal eligibility, to seek care elsewhere.) [90]

In many ways the Office of Economic Opportunity-sponsored Neighborhood Health Centers, if shorn of the financing and eligibility problems inherent in a grant-supported program, serve as a valuable guide to the potential of an expanded ambulatory-care institutional concept. A detailed cost-finding analysis of six NHCs found average costs for physician and primary-care services comparable to costs in both hospital outpatient and prepaid group practice settings. [91] The availability of such centers appears to have increased the use of ambulatory services by the poor to a level comparable with the national average for all persons. [92] The quality of care and patient satisfaction have been found to be quite acceptable. [93] At least two studies have suggested that NHCs provide a substitute source of care for hospital ambulatory and inpatient facilities. [94] As such, NHCs could help increase efficiency in

[90] R. Fein, "An Economist's View of the Neighborhood Health Center as a New Social Institution," in *Neighborhood Health Centers*, R. Hollister et al., eds. (Lexington, Mass.: D.C. Heath, 1974), pp. 192–93.

[91] G. Sparer and A. Anderson, "Cost of Services at Neighborhood Health Centers—A Comparative Analysis," in *Neighborhood Health Centers*, pp. 184, 186.

[92] M.A. Strauss and G. Sparer, "Basic Utilization Experience of OEO Comprehensive Health Services Projects," in *Neighborhood Health Centers*, p. 232.

[93] M.A. Morehead, R.S. Donaldson, and M.R. Seravalli, "Comparison Between OEO Neighborhood Health Centers and Other Health Care Providers of Ratings of the Quality of Health Care," in *Neighborhood Health Centers*, pp. 257–73.

[94] S.S. Bellin, H.J. Geiger, and C.D. Gibson, "Impact of Ambulatory Health Care Services on the Demand for Hospital Beds," in *Neighborhood Health Centers*, pp. 309–16; L.I. Hochheiser, I. Woodward, and E. Charney, "Effect of the Neighborhood Health Center on the Use of Pediatric Emergency Departments in Rochester, New York," *Neighborhood Health Centers*, pp. 317–24.

delivering medical care. Finally, although any program's impact on health is hard to identify, a study of Baltimore communities receiving comprehensive health care services found a 60 percent drop in the incidence of rheumatic fever between 1960 and 1970.[95]

Would ambulatory-care institutions be as efficient as purely private, for-profit alternatives? Ambulatory-care institutions should not be expected to duplicate private practices for at least two reasons. First, they would be treating generally less affluent populations and second, they might have to offer higher compensation to employees to make up for intrinsically less desirable practice locations. In part, higher compensation would take the form of a more elaborate institutional arrangement, perhaps more extensive ancillary support and more time off. The key point is that although ambulatory-care institutions are likely to be more expensive than private, office-based practices, they are less expensive than hospital emergency rooms or outpatient departments. A frequent complaint of hospital-based ambulatory care is that much of it is provided by residents who are training for a non-primary-care specialty. Ambulatory-care institutions would have the advantage of being staffed by a mix of physicians who have completed their training and whose specialties are appropriately matched to the type of care they are providing. No doubt there would be some poorly run ambulatory-care institutions as well as some highly efficient and responsive ones. But if the failure rate for new, for-profit business ventures is any guide, this mix would be more or less par for the course.

Where would ambulatory-care institutions be located? A major assumption here is that the private sector, if left to itself, would not respond adequately to the potential demand for medical care in areas that are currently underserved. Because the demand for care in these areas could easily outstrip society's ability or willingness to provide it, some type of allocation process appears necessary.

Basically two approaches, one active and the other passive, exist. The active approach would establish some formula for ranking areas on the basis of need and allocate resources accordingly (per the shortage area designation already discussed). The requirement that DHEW designate underserved

[95] Leon Gordis, "Effectiveness of Comprehensive Care Programs in Preventing Rheumatic Fever," *New England Journal of Medicine* 289 (August 16, 1973), pp. 331–35.

areas for the purpose of eligibility for HMO planning grants and for NHSC physicians provides some experience with the active approach. Given the difficulties of defining both need and underservice and of collecting appropriate data at a highly centralized level, however, the indices developed do not appear to be very discriminating.

The passive approach might involve a grant application process and, in effect, rely on needy areas identifying themselves. This process would place a burden on local areas to prepare applications, perhaps no trivial requirement. But because local involvement might be a vital element in successful establishment and operation of an ambulatory-care institution, the application process might be an important first step for creating local involvement. Furthermore, to the extent that a network of Health Systems Agencies was developed under the Health Planning Act, these decentralized public agencies could provide needed technical assistance. On the grounds that local involvement is important and that local sources are better able to identify underserved populations, a grant process appears preferable to a process involving shortage area designation.

In sum, of the methods of direct intervention reviewed here, the one that appears to have the best chance of resolving the current geographic maldistribution of physicians is the direct subsidization (at least initially) of ambulatory-care institutions. Other methods such as a physician draft, prohibitions on physicians' locating in sufficiency areas, or modifications to licensure laws appear to be either ineffective or politically unfeasible. At some level of costs, of course, ambulatory-care institutions also would be politically unfeasible. A major objective of an ambulatory-care institutional program would be to develop incentives for encouraging organizational efficiency. These might include a bonus system, net revenue sharing, or cost sharing with the local jurisdiction. Although this task is not trivial, some progress toward achieving it should be possible over time, provided adequate information systems and feedback mechanisms are explicitly recognized parts of the structure.

Most of this section has been devoted to mechanisms for dealing with spatial distribution, in part because the processes that determine geographic and specialty distributions are different and thus require different approaches. In addition, because it is hard to regulate effectively what physicians do once they are in practice or to monitor whether their specialty designations correspond to the procedures and treatments they perform, intervention into the specialty distribution process should be directed at the educational system. These direct intervention policies are discussed next as part of the general consideration of policies affecting medical education.

Methods of Influencing Medical Education

Most public policies thus far established in the area of physician supply and distribution have been aimed at medical education. Federal involvement began with the Health Professions Educational Assistance Act of 1963, which provided loans for medical students. At that time and subsequently when federal health personnel legislation was modified prior to 1976, the chief policy problem was the physician shortage. Accordingly, loans to medical students were supplemented by capitation payments to medical schools which agreed to expand class sizes, special teaching grants, and capital expansion subsidies. State support also encouraged expansion of medical school capacity. Of the thirty-five new medical schools opened between 1960 and 1975, all but seven are state-owned. As has been already discussed, the objectives of increasing both capacity and numbers of applicants have been achieved. In fact, there is some concern that targets may have been overshot.

Recent federal policy affecting medical education is embodied primarily in the Health Professions Educational Assistance Act of 1976. Like its predecessors, this law continues capitation payments to medical schools, but changes the eligibility conditions for payments. First, the requirement that class size be expanded has been dropped, but schools must maintain first-year enrollments and nonfederal funds at current levels, and the incentive to expand still exists. The more interesting condition, however, is that schools must allocate a certain proportion of all residency training programs in affiliated teaching hospitals to primary-care specialties (defined as general and family practice, general internal medicine, and general pediatrics). Target proportions are 35 percent for 1978, 40 percent for 1979, and 50 percent for 1980. (Data for 1976, which were not available until 1978, showed that 47.5 percent of filled first-year residencies were in primary-care specialties.[96]) If medical schools in the aggregate reach these targets by a certain date, individual medical schools need not comply. This incentive to provide primary-care residencies is supplemented by authorizations to make project grants for the development and support of teaching programs in primary-care specialties. Finally, direct aid to medical students (loans and scholarships) is expanded through the Health Educational Assistance Loan program and the National Health Service Corps scholarship program. As already noted, the former has a forgiveness option for service in areas designated by DHEW as medically underserved.

Although the Health Professions Educational Assistance Act of 1976 also contains provisions affecting other health occupations and training institutions, the following are the law's major approaches to influencing physician distribution through the educational system: capitation, block, or project grants to medical schools and teaching hospitals; and direct financial aid to medical students with various outcome-connected repayment or eligibility conditions. Not surprisingly, institutional policies are aimed primarily at influencing specialty choice, while individual policies are aimed at altering locational decisions. The reasons are fairly straightforward. Medical schools and teaching hospitals have little control over locational choices, which may not be made until several years after completing training, but to the extent that different specialties require distinctly different training, control over educational inputs may be an effective way of influencing specialty choices.

INSTITUTIONAL FINANCIAL OPTIONS

Block Grants

A block grant is simply a lump sum payment which does not depend on the level of a particular activity within the recipient institution. Congress, for example, might decide to grant every medical school $500,000 per year, regardless of the school's enrollment, faculty size, service activities, or

---

[96] *Directory of Accredited Residencies, 1977–78* (Chicago: American Medical Association, 1978).

research program. Or every teaching hospital might receive an annual grant which would be independent of the nature or size of its teaching program. The logic underlying this type of grant is that individual institutions know best how to deal with perceived problems in medical education. Further, there may be extensive variation among institutions as to the best way to deal with these problems. These factors imply that social objectives will be efficiently achieved by allowing each institution to "do its own thing." The choices of specific methods to influence specialty or location decisions, for example, would be left to the discretion of the individual institution.

An unrestricted block grant, however, is an inefficient method of achieving specific policy goals because of the multiplicity of objectives and activities within medical schools and teaching hospitals. Institutions would use unrestricted grant funds to expand all activities, regardless of stated public policy objectives for physician supply and distribution. A further problem is that evaluating the effects of such grants and trying to determine whether social objectives were in fact being addressed would be extremely difficult. Primarily for these reasons, no pure, unrestricted block grants are being funded under the Health Professions Educational Assistance Act of 1976. Earlier legislation built a block-grant component into the formula for computing maximum capitation grants, but this provision was deleted in 1972.[97]

Two types of restrictions might be imposed on income grants. One is that an institution must satisfy some threshold or side condition to receive a grant. An example of such a restriction is the set of conditions imposed by the 1976 health professions legislation on medical schools' receipt of capitation grants. The second type of restriction would limit the use of grant funds to a limited set of activities, for example, programs to encourage primary care. The first type of condition allows institutions flexibility in deciding both how to satisfy the target condition and how to use the block-grant funds. Whether the threshold condition is met will depend on how consistent the condition is with preexisting institutional priorities and on how costly (financially, administratively, and philo-

---

[97] In 1966, each medical school was eligible to receive a block grant of $12,500 plus a variable grant based on enrollment. Between 1967 and 1971, the block-grant component was increased to $25,000.

sophically) it is to satisfy the target. Institutions that already exceeded the threshold would receive a pure bonus. Others might consider the cost of adjustment too high relative to the size of the grant. As a result, the all-or-nothing nature of income grants with side conditions is inequitable because of its differential treatment of institutions which either just miss or just exceed the specified targets.

Limiting the use of funds to broadly specified activities may not produce the desired effects. Since a block grant does not alter the relative costs of any two activities, trade-offs are still possible. For example, cross-subsidization could be based on revenue sources other than the grant. In theory, expansion of activities other than the one supported by the grant could be restricted. Administratively, however, such action would be extremely complicated because it would require detailed monitoring and verification of all of an institution's programs.

Capitation Grants

In general, capitation payments could be made to medical schools or teaching hospitals. As long as institutions' use of capitation grants is unrestricted, these grants will be treated as general revenues. Conditions that an institution must satisfy to receive a capitation grant may be keyed to an institution's inputs (total enrollment, total faculty, or enrollment or faculty in a particular program or department) or tied to institutional outputs (total number of graduates or number of graduates choosing primary care). Most of the conditions imposed by the Health Professions Educational Assistance Act of 1976 are of the first type, but the requirements for primary-care residencies in affiliated teaching hospitals stretch considerably the medical school's administrative authority.

Even if capitation grants are made without conditions, per head payments create incentives for increasing the number of units (students, residents, or faculty) involved in the grant computation, as long as the cost to the institution of adding one more unit is less than the additional revenue generated. If conditions are imposed, the institution also must consider the costs—financial and nonfinancial—of meeting the conditions. If the total costs exceed the net revenue generated by the grant, the institution will be better off refusing the grant. If a particular condition is thought to be particularly onerous, "rich" institutions are more likely than others to forgo the grant even if financial benefits still exceed costs. As a result, the burden of meeting such requirements will probably be inequitably distributed.

Between 1965 and 1976, medical schools had to meet enrollment expansion conditions to qualify for capitation payments. Because capitation payments are made for all enrollees, not just for additional places, any assessment of the cost of capitation payments per additional physician must take into account the cost of all capitation payments, not just the cost of payments made for added graduates. One set of estimates places the cost to the federal government at almost $60,000 per extra physician.[98] For graduates covered by the Comprehensive Health Manpower Act of 1971 (PL 92-127), which was more generous than earlier legislation, the cost was more than $80,000 per net increase.

Unconditional capitation grants or those requiring only enrollment expansion probably have only minor effects on either specialty or geographic distributions. Unless the demographic composition of the additional students differs markedly from the demographic composition of other students, increased medical school enrollments are unlikely to result in changes in medical students' career choices. Since the mid-1960s, the proportions of female and minority medical students have increased, but this increase appears to have resulted from broader social forces rather than from capitation grants per se. Similarly, payments made to teaching hospitals on the basis of the total number of house staff should not differentially affect the number of primary-care residencies offered or the geographic distribution of residency training positions.

Linking capitation grants to the satisfaction of specific input conditions by the institutions receiving the grants assumes that encouraging use of the particular input will lead to increased production of the desired output. If the condition is stated too broadly or vaguely, however, institutions may nominally comply with little or no real adjustments. Such compliance appears to have occurred with respect to conditions for the proportion of first-year residencies in primary care that were part of the 1976 act. In 1974, the number of first-year positions offered in primary-care specialties (family practice,

[98] George E. Wright, Jr., "The Efficiency of Federal Subsidies to Medical Education," *Health Manpower Policy Discussion Paper Series*, University of Michigan, Ann Arbor, April 1974.

general practice, internal medicine, obstetrics-gynecology, and pediatrics) was 8,372, 44.8 percent of all first-year positions in affiliated hospitals.[99] Two years later, the number offered was 10,497, 54 percent of first-year positions in affiliated hospitals.[100] Thus the condition specified for fiscal year 1980 has already been met. Yet if too narrow conditions are specified, schools may find compliance too difficult or costly, or resources may be used inefficiently.

From an institution's perspective, the all-or-nothing nature of conditional capitation grants makes them both inequitable and unstable. For example, schools or hospitals that just fell short of the requirement would be penalized by the full amount of the grant, while those that just satisfied the condition would be rewarded to the same degree as institutions that surpassed the condition by a wide margin. Capitation grants are unstable because factors affecting an institution's ability to meet a condition may not be fully within the institution's control. For example, teaching hospitals that are affiliated with a school but not under that school's direct administrative control might be unwilling to meet specialty mix conditions for their residency programs, particularly if doing so brought no direct gain to the teaching hospital. Further instability is created by the fact that once the perceived social need (e.g., an inadequate number of primary-care physicians) has been met, the grant presumably would be terminated. There is little room to fine-tune or to make marginal adjustments over time when the capitation grant and the condition are not functionally related.

Capitation payments to medical schools based on the number of graduates who *make certain decisions* appear to have several advantages over grants that require institutions to meet side conditions. First, this option would require the government to specify *what it is that society wants more of.* Second, this option creates the incentive for medical schools to produce the desired output efficiently and leaves the decision about methods in the hands of the schools themselves. Third, schools are rewarded in proportion to their contribution toward meeting social objectives. Fourth, compliance is entirely voluntary

---

[99] *Directory of Accredited Residencies, 1975–76,* (Chicago: American Medical Association, 1976).

[100] *Directory of Accredited Residencies, 1977–78.*

and does not lead to confrontations over meeting current targets. The amount of the capitation payment can be raised or lowered over time in accordance with perceived social needs. The amount of adjustment and even the initial size of the capitation payment are difficult to assess in advance, but medical schools' responsiveness and the required grant sizes should soon become evident once the program is in effect.

A possible problem with this approach—indeed, with any financing options directed at medical schools—is that undergraduate medical education is fairly far removed from the individual physician's entry into practice. There is little firm evidence that medical school structure or organization per se influence specialty or location decisions.[101] (There is evidence, however, that students' personal characteristics are relevant and that student body composition varies significantly among medical schools.)

Capitation grants could be based on the number of graduating medical students who enroll in a primary-care residency within a specified time period, such as three years. Attrition from primary care over time would remain a problem, but such attrition may not be the medical school's responsibility. Some risk would be involved, though, because schools might decide to invest resources to expand primary-care faculty or facilities, and then receive less capitation money than expected when graduates failed to enter primary-care residencies. This possibility might reduce the acceptability of such a financing system to the affected institutions.

A system of capitation payments to teaching hospitals based on the number of residents in primary-care specialties should encourage expansion of primary-care training. Experience with federal support of residency training in psychiatry and family practice, although not identical with training in primary-care specialties, suggests that the number of positions offered and filled is sensitive to financial incentives.[102] Because hospitals could use primary-care capitation funds to cross-subsidize non-primary-care training, it may be necessary

---

[101] Jack Hadley, "Models of Physicians' Specialty and Location Decisions," Technical Paper No. 6, National Center for Health Services Research, HRA, DHEW, October 1975; Human Resources Research Center, "Determinants of Physician Specialty and Location Choices," Final Report on Grant 3330 from the Robert Wood Johnson Foundation, 1978.

[102] Hadley et al., "Financing Medical Education," pp. 103–04, 122–26.

either to restrict the number of non-primary-care positions or to limit the total number of house staff positions.[103]

The amount of capitation support provided to medical schools in 1974 was about $125 million. If federal project-grant support for family practice residencies is counted, the total rises to about $147.8 million. If these funds were distributed among all filled primary-care residencies, a capitation payment of slightly more than $6,200 per primary-care position filled would be provided. If payments were to exclude first-year positions on the grounds that many non-primary-care specialties treat one year of primary-care training as a prerequisite, the available budget could support payments of about $9,600 per position in primary-care residencies in the years following the first. The effect that such payments would have on the number of positions offered and filled depends on what restrictions are placed on residencies in non-primary-care specialties, and on the sensitivity of students and teaching hospitals to financial incentives. Firm evidence on the latter is not currently available.

Categorical Grants

The last type of institutional grant to be discussed is the project or categorical grant. Unlike either capitation or conditional block grants, which depend on production of certain outputs, a categorical grant is much more likely to support a set of inputs in the production process. For example, the Health Professions Educational Assistance Act authorizes grants to support family medicine, general pediatrics, and general internal medicine departments or programs in medical schools, and to support family practice residencies in teaching hospitals. Judging from the experience of residences in family practice, which increased from about 435 first-year positions offered in 1971 to 1,959 such positions in 1976[104] (due in large part to support provided by grants authorized in the 1971 Health Manpower Act), one may expect categorical grants to be quite effective. Figure 3 illustrates the dramatic effect of these grants in family medicine. Of course, this growth also coincides with a substantial growth of interest in family medicine.

---

[103] Roger Feldman and Sunny Yoder, "Financing Graduate Medical Education: An Economic Analysis of Public Policy Options," unpublished paper, Department of Economics, University of North Carolina, 1978.

[104] *Directory of Accredited Residencies, 1977–78,* and *1972.*

Figure 3

POSITIONS OFFERED AND GRANTS AWARDED FOR FAMILY MEDICINE RESIDENCIES
BY DHEW REGION, 1972–73 to 1976–77

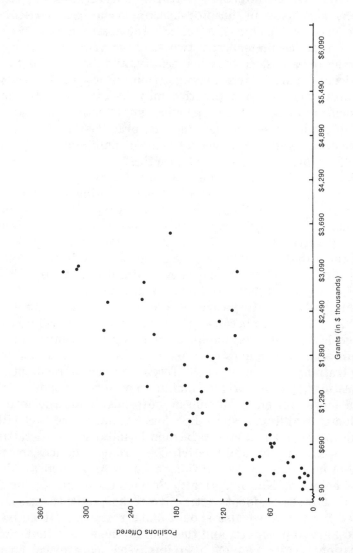

Note: Each point represents a DHEW region in one of the five years for which data were available. Only positions in hospitals receiving grant awards were tabulated.

Sources: Positions offered—Directory of Approved Internships and Residencies, annual issues, 1972-73 to 1975-76. Grant awards —"Health Professions Grants for Training in Family Medicine by Institution, Fiscal Year and DHEW Region," unpublished data, Bureau of Health Manpower, 1977.

Why there should be such interest in family medicine is itself a question of interest. Has there been a major shift in values, from an era of scientific medicine to one of community medicine? Is the interest a natural market response to apparent surpluses in hospital-based specialties, particularly those in surgical areas? After all, the training required for family practice is generally two to three years less than the training for a hospital-based specialty, and demand for family physicians, particularly among group practices, appears to be substantial. (Group practice may be attractive to young physicians because it can provide an effective institutional way of avoiding several low-income, practice-building years.) Is the development of a specialty called family medicine a way of adding prestige to general practice?

The answers to these questions are important for two reasons. First, simply creating residency training positions will not necessarily fill them. In fact, some specialties, such as radiology and pathology, have persistently experienced vacancy rates of about 25 percent. Second, the only way to guarantee that positions will be filled is to limit the mix and total numbers of other specialty training positions. This is what the current law attempts to accomplish. Thus, to the extent that ambulatory-care residencies are "unprofitable" to teaching hospitals because they are not fully reimbursed, categorical grants may be an efficient way to compensate for the differential revenues granted by inpatient and ambulatory-care training programs. The difference in reimbursement may be justified, particularly if ambulatory services can be provided more efficiently outside of hospitals. Thus the locus of graduate training, especially for primary-care activities, should perhaps be expanded beyond hospital walls, to settings such as satellite or affiliated clinics, group practices, or possibly to new types of institutions such as Area Health Education Centers or National Health Service Corps sites. The factors that make residents attractive to hospitals (e.g., service traded for training) also should make residents attractive to clinics, group practices, and the like. To the extent that purely educational costs cannot be reimbursed, categorical grants could be used to supplement revenues from patient care.

The main premise underlying categorical grants is that by specifying production inputs, in this case a training program, one can control the output produced. Whether this premise is true depends on how flexible graduate training really is. If there is high substitutability among physicians with apparently different specialty training, categorical grants and other attempts to influence medical education may not succeed in actually altering the mix of physicians' services provided to the population. If we assume that manipulating the reimbursement system is also ineffective, the remaining alternative is to impose stricter control on hospital admitting privileges, ownership of X-ray equipment, and ownership of labs. Because these drastic measures would no doubt meet stiff political resistance, be difficult to enforce, and probably impose costs on patients as well, they should be turned to only as a last resort.

Therefore, research should be undertaken to investigate what happens to physicians who pass through family medicine residencies. What kinds of services do they provide? Whom do they treat? What referral networks are established? How do they divide their time between office and hospital practice? How are these decisions affected by reimbursement methods and rates? Until these questions are satisfactorily answered, support of specialized medical education programs and payments to schools based on the numbers of certain types of graduates may do little more than change our nomenclature for certain physicians.

INDIVIDUAL FINANCING OPTIONS

The rest of this section is devoted to individual financing mechanisms and their impact on supply and distribution. These include various combinations of loan and scholarship plans, which may vary in terms of eligibility, maximum amounts, and pay-back conditions (interest rates, length of pay-back period, start of first payment, forgiveness provisions). Although such plans could be used to influence specialty choices (e.g., by making eligibility or pay-back terms a function of specialty choices), their main goal heretofore has been to induce physicians to change location decisions. Accordingly, the discussion here focuses on the use of these plans to achieve this goal. Questions to be posed are these: What types of students would subscribe? How large a loan would be needed to alter location decisions? What effects would individual financing options have on applicant behavior? What potential impediments do various plans face?

The 1976 act included several individual financing provisions. Two already described are the National Health Service Corps Scholarship program and the Health Educational Assistance Loan program. Both of these have strong links to service in the National Health Service Corps, other federal programs, or private practice in medically underserved areas. In addition, the act authorizes a conventional, subsidized loan program without forgiveness provisions and scholarships for special purposes. These two programs emphasize financial need as a criterion for receiving a loan or scholarship.

Financial aid for medical students is now frequently discussed in the context of substantial increases—to between $12,000 and $15,000 per year—in medical school tuitions. (Such fees approximate the full-cost level, which is currently subsidized predominantly by public funds.) An apparent objective of federal scholarship and loan programs is to increase students' financial liabilities and to allow repayment in kind through service in locations that probably would not otherwise be selected. One possible consequence of this policy might be a sharp reduction in size and a change in composition of the medical school applicant pool, for the following reasons: First, a person decides to apply to medical school perhaps six to ten years before he or she enters practice. At the time the person makes the application decision, the size of the prospective financial liability may loom quite large relative to the prospect of repayment in kind several years in the future. Second, the extent to which service repayment is viewed as a nonpecuniary burden will reduce the attractiveness of a medical career. Third, economic research has indicated that the number of applicants is also sensitive to financial rates of return.[105]

Therefore, depending on the size of the increased liability, the following changes might be expected in applicant pools: (1) The total number of applicants would decline, as both low-income and high-ability students switch to alternative careers. (The latter presumably would have the best opportunities in other professions.) (2) The number of applicants who would

---

[105] Sloan, "The Demand for Higher Education"; Roger Feldman and Richard Scheffler, "The Supply of Medical School Applicants and the Rate of Return to Training," *Quarterly Review of Economics and Business*, Spring 1978, pp. 91–98.

in fact be willing to serve in shortage areas might increase; to a large extent, this group might include people who would have practiced in shortage areas anyway. (3) Applicants who have the resources to finance their own medical education might make up a larger share of the pool. (4) To the extent that medical schools would attempt to maintain quality standards, a shift might be expected toward a larger proportion of students from high-income backgrounds, because such backgrounds are usually associated with good grades and test scores.

Of persons who entered medical school, who would be most likely to assume loans or scholarships with forgiveness provisions? Acceptance would doubtless be inversely related to family income; well-off students would have greater access to locations deemed more desirable while poorer medical students would be induced to practice in less desirable areas. Of the seven medical schools receiving more than ninety-nine NHSC scholarship awards between 1973 and 1977, two schools with predominantly nonwhite enrollments, Meharry and Howard, ranked first and third. The other five schools were private institutions and had annual student expenses exceeding $4,500.[106] The second group of students likely to assume such loans, probably with eagerness, would be persons who would locate in less desirable areas even without financial inducement. For these physicians, the forgiven amounts would represent lump sum transfer payments, and the net gain to society would be minimal.

How large a liability is necessary to induce shifts in location decisions? In principle, the forgiven amount should be large enough to compensate physicians for the extra costs, both financial and nonpecuniary, of practicing in a shortage area rather than elsewhere. This amount obviously will vary from individual to individual, and also will depend on out-of-pocket costs—chiefly tuition, other direct expenses, and living costs that exceed the student's private resources. In order for the incentive to work, there has to be a strong, latent demand for loans which previously had been constrained by low ceilings on loanable amounts. If this demand fails to materialize, either because of changes in applicant mix or because of continued subsidization of medical school tuitions, simply raising

---

[106] "1977 National Health Service Corps Report to Congress," DHEW, PHS, HSA, National Health Service Corps (mimeographed).

ceilings on loan amounts may induce few net changes. In 1974–75, 66.9 percent of medical students responding to a survey of indebtedness reported an anticipated total mean debt of $11,573.[107] Because of this level of debt, and because of the current program's requirement for a minimum of two years' service, the options available under PL 94-494 may prove to be a bargain only for the borrower who already has a strong interest in shortage area practice. Unless all students' financial liabilities increase markedly, only students with a strong predisposition toward practicing in underserved areas or with extreme financial need will exercise the forgiveness option or apply for NHSC scholarships.

Some evidence on the question of the relationship between size of anticipated indebtedness and interest in shortage area practice is provided by the DHEW survey of medical students' anticipated indebtedness in 1974–75. As Table 17 shows, interest in shortage area practice was positively related to debt size. But within each debt category, it also was positively related to a small or rural area hometown. Thus, the independent effect of indebtedness is hard to separate from the influence of hometown size. Also, a medical student's expression of interest in shortage area practice is very different from actual choice of such a practice.

Another critical assumption of the loan-forgiveness/obligated-scholarship approach is that the implied higher educational cost cannot be passed forward to patients in the form of higher fees. In most markets, competitive forces might be expected to keep fees at efficient levels, so that higher-cost producers (new physicians with large educational debts) would not be able to charge higher prices and still attract clients. Unfortunately, as has been amply demonstrated elsewhere, competitive market forces in the area of physicians' services cannot be counted on to control prices. The extent to which costs may be passed on, of course, depends on the nature of the reimbursement system and on the ability of physicians to induce demand. (These issues are discussed in Chapter 2.)

Another perhaps undesirable consequence of increasing financial liability is that it may increase the incentive for physicians to enter higher-income specialties, which are gen-

---

[107] *Medical Student Indebtedness and Career Plans*, DHEW Publication No. (HRA) 77–21, September 1976, p. 11.

Table 17

INTEREST IN SHORTAGE AREA PRACTICE AMONG MEDICAL STUDENTS
BY ANTICIPATED INDEBTEDNESS AT GRADUATION, 1974–75

Medical Students	No Debt		Debt < $10,000		Debt > $10,000		All Debt Levels	
	Total	%	Total	%	Total	%	Total	%
Total	2,273	41.4	2,475	48.0	2,235	54.3	6,983	47.9
Hometown Size								
Large city	1,064	38.8	1,001	45.0	994	50.5	3,059	44.6
Medium or small city	860	38.4	982	46.5	751	51.9	2,593	45.4
Small town or rural area	340	57.1	490	57.1	486	65.6	1,316	60.3

Source: DHEW, *Medical Student Indebtedness*, p. 99.

erally not the primary-care specialties. Such a development not only would aggravate the problem of dealing with specialty distribution per se, but also might make it more difficult to attract physicians to rural areas, because the higher-paying specialties tend to be hospital-based. It is interesting to note that the growth of federal loan programs between 1963 and the present has largely coincided with the decline in primary-care specialties, perhaps because these loans make longer training (and thus entry into hospital-based specialties) more feasible.

As was described earlier, experience with loan forgiveness as a means of inducing physicians to enter shortage area practices has not been good. In those state programs that have been relatively successful, an important element appears to have been recruitment of students among persons who were potentially interested in practicing in such areas and who might not have considered medical practice—and then smoothing those persons' transition from training to practice. In other words, the institutional arrangement for identifying and locating potential entrants may be more important than financial incentives per se. (Of course, it is difficult to untangle the extent to which these success stories resulted in *net* additions to the local physician stocks.) Thus, development of such an institutional network, perhaps through the types of ambulatory-care institutions described in a previous section, should be an important component of a program to increase physician availability in shortage areas.

In general, it is inefficient to attempt to influence long-term distribution goals by manipulating medical education. Little firm evidence exists that general medical training has any effect on physicians' practice behavior or location choices. It takes a long time, too, for educational institutions to alter their training programs, so policies aimed at them run the risk of being very unwieldy. Changes in policy emphasis or cutbacks in public funding could leave medical schools and teaching hospitals with difficult readjustment problems. Controlling the specialty mix and total number of residency training positions—a difficult task—would more directly affect the specialty distribution of future physicians than would manipulation of medical education. It would take many years, however, before a meaningful change occurred in the specialty mix of all physicians as a result of such control.

The use of loan and scholarship programs to influence physicians' locational choices is probably more efficient than institutional financing policies. First, the burden on the educational institution is likely to be smaller than the burden under a program of institutional grants. Second, some physicians in training face significant financing barriers and, consequently, may find obligated loans or scholarships very appealing. Third, scholarship and loan amounts should be easy to adjust as perceived maldistributions change. Finally, the subsidy provided by the loan or scholarship is limited to new entrants into a shortage area. At the same time, of course, the caveats raised in the preceding sections about shortage area designation, equity, and financial self-sufficiency of practices staffed by quasi-indentured physicians still apply.

Recommendations

This chapter has attempted to identify and evaluate how alternative strategies, both within and outside a national health insurance plan, might affect physician supply and distribution. In general, physician supply and distribution can be influenced by three types of policies: (1) altering financial returns to practicing various specialties or locating in certain types of areas; (2) directly intervening into the delivery system through regulatory and legislative actions or direct provision of services by public authorities; and (3) influencing the medical education system.

The main conclusion drawn from reviewing the specific policy options is that parts of all three general approaches ought to be used in efforts to influence total physician supply and specialty and geographic distributions. The reason lies, in part, in the interdependencies among personnel policy and other features of a national health insurance system, especially physician reimbursement and eligibility determination. For example, the feasibility of using financial incentives to influence specialty and location distributions depends on the nature of the reimbursement system. Or, the workability of new forms of delivery institutions, lumped under the general rubric of ambulatory-care institutions, may be determined largely by the extent to which, and conditions under which, potential users are covered by national health insurance. There-

fore, one cannot conclude that any particular approach dominates in terms of either probable outcome, implementation
ease, or implicit costs.

The second factor underlying the general conclusion is that,
in most cases, the available evidence is too ambiguous to support clear-cut inferences. This fact alone suggests a pluralistic
policy which pursues several options, evaluates their operations and consequences, and adjusts accordingly. Such an approach is further buttressed by the following arguments: (1)
supply and distribution are dynamic processes, influenced
by population shifts and technological changes as well as the
factors already enumerated; and (2) the ability to identify
optimal quantities and distributions of physicians is more of
an art than a science. Hence, future personnel policy should be
flexible, in order to respond to data systems and research
programs that can monitor physician supply and distribution
and the availability of multiple policy levers.

As was emphasized in the beginning of this chapter, the
fact that a particular NHI plan focuses on financing, reimbursement, benefits, and eligibility does not mean that it would
have no impact on physician supply and distribution. In fact,
the conditions of reimbursement and eligibility are critical
components of any policy to influence the physician labor force.
For this reason, rather than for its specific personnel provisions, the approach taken by a plan like the Kennedy-Corman
proposal seems best suited to implementing a policy for re-
distributing physicians and physicians' services over specialties
and locations. Universal eligibility without regard to socioeconomic characteristics, uniform fee schedules across a geographic area, and the combination of the reimbursement and
personnel distribution authorities within a single administrative structure are key features of this bill relating to physician
supply and distribution issues. Plans like those proposed by
CHIP and the Long-Ribicoff-Waggonner bill would give physicians the option to charge higher fees for certain classes of
patients, presumably their more affluent ones. As long as such
patients have the ability to "bid away" physicians from treating lower-income patients or certain populations, such as rural
residents, not covered by the plan, any positive incentives to
redistribute physicians are unlikely to be successful.

A second key characteristic of the Kennedy-Corman type
of plan (a characteristic shared in part by CHIP) is an em-

phasis on the fee schedule as the principal tool of physician reimbursement. Although establishing such a schedule initially would no doubt be arduous and complicated, and some, perhaps most, physicians would reap financial windfalls in converting to a fee schedule, over the long term the fee schedule approach provides several important policy tools. First, as the Canadian experience has shown, the process of fee negotiation itself establishes a forum in which issues of supply, distribution, quality of care, and utilization review, as well as fee levels, may be considered as legitimate agenda items. Given the potential ability of physicians to induce demand, the importance of a cooperative, self-regulating posture by providers should not be underestimated. Second, the fee schedule provides powerful support for other, more direct efforts to influence supply and distribution, such as adjusting medical education financing. Third, a natural byproduct of the fee schedule approach and its attendant billing system is the data necessary to monitor the quantity and distribution of services provided as well as physicians' specialty and location distributions. Again, the Canadian experience demonstrates that such data are vital for monitoring system performance and essential in the negotiating process.

A third salutary feature of the Kennedy-Corman approach is the combination of reimbursement and resource development authorities within a single administrative structure. The existence of such a structure should facilitate the use of multiple policy levers to attain physician distribution goals.

Obviously, this discussion does not imply that Kennedy-Corman is necessarily the "best" approach overall. The key characteristics discussed above clearly could be incorporated into modified versions of other bills. Similarly, other, less desirable aspects of the Kennedy-Corman bill may well be modified. It is hoped, therefore, that the substantive comments about how national health insurance might influence the physician labor force will be the main lesson drawn from this chapter. Accordingly, the concluding subsections of this chapter sketch specific recommendations that might serve as components of a physician supply and distribution policy under national health insurance. The underlying assumptions about policy objectives are these: (1) Both the aggregate supply of physicians and the capacity of the medical education sector are adequate; (2) there are too few physicians (or, more accurately, physicians' services) available to populations in certain rural and low-income urban areas; and (3) the proportion of physicians practicing primary care (general and family practice, general internal medicine, and general pediatrics) is too low.

AGGREGATE SUPPLY POLICIES

The belief that the aggregate supply of physicians is adequate stems largely from the observation that growth in supply has had little effect on geographic or specialty distribution. Most of this growth stemmed from two factors, relaxed immigration barriers and federal subsidies to medical schools. Therefore, in order to stabilize, or perhaps even reduce, the flow of new physicians into the U.S. medical care system, the following measures appear to be appropriate: First, restrict the entry of graduates of foreign medical schools, except for educational or research activities. (This is already an explicit component of the Health Professions Educational Assistance Act of 1976.) Second, phase out medical school subsidies that encourage expanding class sizes and developing new facilities.

Again, the 1976 act moves toward tying medical school capitation payments to attaining specified targets for the proportion of first-year residency training positions in primary-care specialties. As was discussed above, the all-or-nothing nature of the implicit penalty and the problems of translating first-year residencies into a final specialty distribution suggest that this feature of the bill should be modified. (This problem is discussed more fully in the next section.)

Two potential consequences of these actions should be anticipated. First, some hospitals may be disproportionately affected by the reduced flow of foreign medical graduates. Therefore, areas served by these hospitals should be given high priority with regard to any compensatory distributional policies. Second, medical schools should be expected to increase tuitions in the face of reduced public subsidies. To the extent that maintaining equity of access to physician careers also is a public objective, a system of loans and scholarships based on financial need should be established to encourage medical school applications from low-income individuals.

GEOGRAPHIC DISTRIBUTION

Problems in geographic distribution reflect the belief that too few physicians are practicing in certain rural and low-income urban areas. Several financial and direct intervention policies were considered: using the payment system to increase the earnings of physicians practicing in shortage areas, subsidizing shortage area practices (e.g., by forgiving education loans or granting bonuses), changing licensure and regulatory conditions, and directly providing services by public authorities. Each of these policies suffers from one or more potential implementation problems, such as identifying shortage areas, determining appropriate payment levels, or monitoring physician effort. The following considerations, however, might be useful in developing an appropriate geographic distribution policy.

Efforts to increase physicians' earnings in shortage areas should be coupled with attempts to constrain earnings in sufficiency areas. Reimbursement based on a fee schedule, if it applies to the majority of patients treated, may be the best way to alter relative earnings. In the short term, a fee schedule may be hard to implement because of the need to set initial fee levels, interspecialty fees, and interarea fees. Over time, however, the process of negotiating fees establishes a forum for discussing maldistribution and relative earnings with physicians.

Existing loan forgiveness programs appear to have too little financial clout to affect distribution. Further, even if average indebtedness were increased and buy-out provisions stiffened, the indentured service aspect of forgiveness programs makes it unlikely that many physicians would remain to practice in shortage areas after completing their service obligations. In addition, solo private practice may not be an appropriate institutional mode for providing physicians' services in shortage areas. Heavy patient loads, inadequate backup, lack of collegial contacts, inability to control hours, and the like are frequently cited as reasons for leaving or forgoing practices in shortage areas.

Therefore, altering practice arrangements should be encouraged through the reimbursement system and through a program of grants and loans. One class of alternatives might consist of multiphysician arrangements, such as Neighborhood

Health Centers, Area Health Education Centers, rural medical clinics, or small group practices or partnerships. Because some areas may be too small or too isolated to support an additional full-time physician, the second class of alternatives should focus on increasing the productivity of existing physicians, particularly through the use of specially trained ancillary personnel. (This subject is discussed in detail in the next chapter.) To encourage efficiency in organizing and operating prospective ambulatory-care institutions, grants and loans should be provided only for various start-up expenses. Under a system of uniform fees for all patients and broad eligibility for services, centers should be required to be self-supporting. As a result, the definitions of reimbursable providers may need broadening to include nonphysicians, in some circumstances, as well as institutional providers.

Finally, data systems should be established to monitor both physician productivity and geographic distribution. The requisite data can be easily generated as byproducts of a fee-for-service reimbursement system.

SPECIALTY DISTRIBUTION

Problems in specialty distribution relate primarily to the shortage of primary-care physicians. This problem is thought to reflect, in part, the structure of the medical education system, which traditionally has emphasized specialty practice. Therefore, one set of potential policies should focus on inducing both medical schools and teaching hospitals to alter their teaching programs. From a somewhat different perspective, the problem may be seen as a maldistribution of types of services (e.g., too many operations and radiological procedures, and not enough preventive or health maintenance visits). Thus, any attempt to alter the distribution of specialists in training should be supplemented with a fee schedule to encourage or discourage certain procedures. Ultimately, policy makers may want to consider limiting access to or ownership of certain types of capital equipment, such as operating rooms, X-ray facilities, and laboratories.

Primary emphasis should be on using fee schedules to encourage desired services and to discourage services thought to be oversupplied. To legitimize such activities, changes in fees should be executed in close consultation with provider representatives. Study groups should be established to examine the feasibility, limits, and conditions under which access to or ownership of certain capital equipment might be curtailed. Again, consultation with provider groups is essential.

Second, the current capitation system for medical schools should be phased out because the condition tying capitation to the national percentage of residency training positions in primary care is too vague and easily influenced by nominal changes in residency programs. If future reimbursement systems continue to treat inpatient services more generously than ambulatory services, however, some direct support may be necessary to compensate for reimbursement bias. This support could take the form of project or categorical grants for primary-care teaching and residencies, or a modified capitation scheme that would make payments to a medical school for each graduate entering a first-year primary-care residency, or to a teaching hospital for each physician completing a primary-care residency. (Completion could be defined as "becoming board eligible.")

Finally, any specialty and geographic distribution policy should be flexible. Flexibility means using multiple programs to achieve policy objectives and developing accurate and up-to-date data systems for monitoring changes in the distribution of both physicians and medical care services. These data are essential for evaluating individual programs' effects and making gradual realignments among the set of potential policy tools.

Chapter 5

NEW HEALTH OCCUPATIONS: NURSE PRACTITIONERS AND PHYSICIANS' ASSISTANTS*

DOROTHY L. ROBYN
JACK HADLEY

ALL major national health insurance proposals directly consider policy toward physicians, at least with respect to payment methods. By contrast, policy toward members of health occupations who work with physicians receives little explicit attention.[1] For example, the Nixon-Ford administrations' CHIP bill provides for the participation of nurse practitioners (NPs) and physicians' assistants (PAs) when certain conditions are met: when the NP or PA (1) works under the supervision of or as the agent for a physician, (2) has met specified training or certification requirements, (3) is authorized to perform services under the state law, and (4) is reimbursed indirectly through the supervising physician or employing organization. The Kennedy-Corman bill states that health maintenance organizations (HMOs) should em-

---

* The authors would like to thank several persons who read an early draft of this chapter and provided many helpful comments: Dolores L. Farr, American Nurses' Association; Thomas R. Godkins, P.A., University of Oklahoma Health Sciences Center; O. Marie Henry, R.N., D.N.Sc., U.S. Department of Health, Education, and Welfare (DHEW); Karl R. Katterjohn, P.A.–C, George Washington University Medical Center; Jerry L. Weston, Sc.D., DHEW; and Martha L. Wilson, American Academy of Physicians' Assistants.

[1] This chapter also does not consider dentists, chiropractors, optometrists, podiatrists, or members of other health-related occupations and professions who are generally eligible to establish independent practices. The supply, distribution, and reimbursement issues pertinent to these people are similar to those discussed in earlier chapters on physicians.

ploy nurse practitioners and physicians' assistants to the extent possible, and calls for funds to train such persons. The Long-Ribicoff-Waggonner bill is silent with respect to nurse practitioners and physicians' assistants, stating merely that under the Catastrophic Insurance and Medical Assistance Plans, payments to and standards for providers would be handled as they are under Medicare.

This chapter discusses several issues important to developing a comprehensive health personnel policy under national health insurance. The two relatively new occupations of nurse practitioner and physicians' assistant around which we focus our discussion were selected because of their potential substitutability for physicians in providing many health and medical care services. It is precisely this relationship to physicians that raises issues of NP/PA supply, distribution, and reimbursement. Although there are important differences between NPs and PAs, we nevertheless group them together here for expositional convenience.[2] Accordingly, our inferences should not be interpreted as applying specifically or only to nurse practitioners and physicians' assistants, but rather should be taken as conclusions referring to persons in the broad class of health occupations who assist and/or substitute for physicians in providing health and medical care services.

Interest in promoting nurse practitioners and physicians' assistants stems from their potential for reducing health care costs and improving access to care. Qualified NPs and PAs can carry out a specific set of functions traditionally performed by physicians. Generally, a nurse practitioner or physicians' assistant can be trained in twelve months to two years, compared with five to eight or more postcollege years for a physician; their training costs are approximately one-fourth to one-third the total cost of training a physician.[3]

---

[2] Some differences between nurse practitioners and physicians' assistants should be pointed out. All NPs must be graduates of registered nurse programs and thus are fully qualified to engage in traditional nursing activities such as counseling and health teaching, which are complements to medical care services provided by physicians. NPs include persons trained in a number of specialty areas such as family nurse practitioners (PRIMEX), pediatric nurse practitioners, and geriatric nurse practitioners. In contrast, PAs may have only a high school diploma, some college education, or a college degree, and they are trained specifically to assist physicians in providing medical care.

[3] DHEW, Health Resources Administration, National Center for Health Services Research, "Nurse Practitioners and Physicians' Assistants Training and Deployment Study," September 30, 1976.

In turn, their salaries are considerably lower than physicians' earnings, and this fact implies cost savings to society.[4] Precisely because it costs less to maintain a nurse practitioner or a physicians' assistant in the field, these persons can provide primary care in areas lacking the resources to support a physician. Accordingly, many NP and PA training programs prepare and orient graduates to work in areas where physicians have been unwilling to serve. Overall, the use of these new health personnel is envisaged as a means of improving the health care system by increasing access to primary care, particularly in rural, underserved areas, and by reducing the costs of medical care while still providing high-quality care.

In the decade since the new health occupations first emerged, nurse practitioners and physicians' assistants have demonstrated their potential for improving health care delivery. But with only about 14,000 nurse practitioners and 8,000 physicians' assistants practicing in a field that employs approximately 340,000 physicians and 900,000 nurses, the aggregate impact of these personnel has been limited.[5] As will be explained later in the chapter, some federal and state policies have intentionally shaped and constrained development of these new health occupations, while other government policies have affected their development in unintended ways.

The general objective of this chapter is to examine the policy implications of national health insurance for nurse practitioners and physicians' assistants. Four specific questions motivate the analysis: (1) Using quality of care, cost, and access to care as criteria, how well have nurse practitioners and physicians' assistants performed? (2) Should national health policy encourage the expansion of these health occupations? (3) What is their optimal supply? (4) What are the impediments to expanded use of NPs and PAs?

---

[4] Annual earnings of PAs and MEDEX, former military medical corps personnel, were $15,196 in 1976. Richard M. Scheffler, "The Supply of and Demand for New Health Professionals: Physician's Assistants and Medex," Executive Summary of Contract No. 1–44184, Bureau of Health Manpower, DHEW, 1977.

[5] The estimate of NPs was made in a personal communication with Dr. O. Marie Henry, Division of Nursing, Bureau of Health Manpower, DHEW, April 2, 1979. The figure for PAs comes from the American Academy of Physicians' Assistants, personal communication with Ms. Lynda Geary, April 2, 1979.

Development of the NP and PA Occupations

Physicians have been delegating tasks to nonphysicians for years. What is new about the new health occupations, however, is the development of formal institutions that train and accredit individuals to assume a range of tasks traditionally performed by the physician. Thus, nurse practitioners and physicians' assistants can serve as both substitutes for and complements to physicians. Duke University initiated the country's first PA program in 1965 to relieve overworked physicians in underserved rural areas. That same year, the first NP program, specializing in pediatric health care, was initiated at the University of Colorado. In subsequent years, the University of Washington established a MEDEX program, which is PA training for Vietnam veteran medical corps personnel, while Cornell and the University of North Carolina began PRIMEX programs to train family nurse practitioners.

A 1971 Department of Health, Education, and Welfare (DHEW) White Paper called for widespread training and use of nurse practitioners and physicians' assistants.[6] President Nixon's Special Health Message of 1971 strongly endorsed the policy as well. In direct response, funding support for NPs and PAs moved from its experimental base to the ongoing programs authorized in the national health professions' education legislation.[7] Federal support to train and promote the use of these personnel has exceeded $65 million since 1969. Current annual support is approximately $25 million.

Federal subsidization promoted a rapid proliferation of NP and PA training programs. Fifty PA training programs currently operate, graduating 1,200 to 1,500 PAs annually. More than two hundred NP programs currently produce about 2,000 graduates a year.

Nurse practitioners and physicians' assistant training programs vary considerably in length and content. Because NP programs are restricted to individuals already licensed as registered nurses, NP programs tend to be shorter than PA programs. Depending on a nurse's prior training and experience, NP training ranges from nine to twenty-four months, and includes both classroom and clinical instruction. PA pro-

---

[6] DHEW, "Towards a Comprehensive Health Policy for the 1970s," 1971.

[7] The Health Professions Educational Assistance Act of 1976 (PL 94–484) and the Nurse Training Act of 1975 (PL 94–63).

grams also tend to admit individuals who have worked in health/medical fields or have earned a degree in a medical-preparatory area. Generally, PA training spans twenty-four months and incorporates classroom and clinical practice phases of approximately equal length. MEDEX programs are the most notable exception to this PA model; the classroom phase of MEDEX training is reduced, with students devoting most of the training period to a "preceptorship" with a single physician—usually one serving in a rural shortage area. Common to all NP and PA programs is the focus on primary-care skills: taking a history; performing physical exams, simple diagnostic lab tests, and basic treatment for common illnesses; and providing emergency care in common situations.

The legal status of NPs and PAs varies by state. Nurse practitioners, by virtue of their being registered nurses, are licensed to practice under the nurse practice act of individual states. Most states have amended these acts to recognize formally the expanded duties NPs perform. Physicians' assistants are not licensed, but forty-four states have enacted legislation permitting PAs to practice under the supervision of a physician.

Expansion of the NP and PA Occupations

EVIDENCE ON NP AND PA PERFORMANCE

Performance of nurse practitioners and physicians' assistants to date provides the best basis for deciding whether or not to expand these occupations. Numerous studies have attempted to analyze the impact of these personnel on health care delivery. Two reports sponsored by the National Science Foundation's Research Applied to National Needs (RANN) Division provide an excellent evaluation of that body of research.[8] These and subsequently reported research findings are quite consistent. They are summarized below in terms of

---

[8] Eva D. Cohen et al., *An Evaluation of Policy Related Research on New and Expanded Roles of Health Workers,* Office of Regional Activities and Continuing Education, Yale University School of Medicine, October 1974; Gary L. Appel and Aaron Lowin, *Physician Extenders: An Evaluation of Policy-Related Research* (Minneapolis: Interstudy, January 1975).

the threefold objective of the nurse practitioner and physicians' assistant occupations: maintaining the *quality of care,* while *reducing medical care costs* and *increasing access to primary care in underserved areas.*

Quality of Care

The quality of care provided by nurse practitioners and physicians' assistants is at least as high as the care rendered by physicians for that range of skills NPs and PAs are trained to use.[9] This judgment is borne out by two "objective" measures of quality—degree of concurrence between physicians and NPs/PAs regarding diagnosis and recommended treatment,[10] and experimental studies comparing outcomes of patients randomly assigned to physicians and to NPs/PAs.[11] NPs and PAs tend to "err" on the side of caution, but with no resulting loss in quality of care.[12] Studies of patient satisfaction further reinforce this conclusion.[13] Patients are no less

[9] E. Cohen et al., *An Evaluation of Policy Related Research,* p. 116; Appel and Lowin, *Physician Extenders,* pp. 10–11.

[10] Burris Duncan, Ann N. Smith, and Henry K. Silver, "Comparison of the Physical Assessment of Children by Pediatric Nurse Practitioners and Pediatricians," *American Journal of Public Health* 61 (June 1971) 1170–78; Eric J. Hamersten, W.D. Stanhope, and A.W. Horseley, "The Effects of Physicians' Assistants on Patient Care," University of Oklahoma Health Sciences Center, 1973 (mimeographed); Charles C. Henriques, Vincent G. Virgadamo, and Mildred D. Kahane, "Performance of Adult Health Appraisal Examinations Utilizing Nurse Practitioners-Physician Teams and Paramedical Personnel," *American Journal of Public Health* 64 (January 1974):47–53.

[11] David W. Gordon, "Health Maintenance Service: Ambulatory Patient Care in the General Medical Clinic," *Medical Care* 12 (August 1975); M.C. Meglen, "Final Report of Cost-Effect Potential of a New Maternal and Infant Care Health Team," University of Mississippi, Jackson, 1976 (mimeographed); Jane C. Record, Arnold V. Hurtado, and Joan E. O'Bannon, "Quality of PA Performance at a Health Maintenance Organization" in *The New Health Professionals,* Anne A. Bliss and Eva D. Cohen, eds. (Germantown, Md.: Aspen Systems Corporation, 1977).

[12] Duncan et al., "Comparison of the Physical Assessment of Children"; Anthony L. Komaroff et al., "Protocols for Physicians' Assistants," *New England Journal of Medicine* 290 (February 7, 1974):307–12.

[13] Evan Charney and Harriet Kitzman, "The Child-Health Nurse (Pediatric Nurse Practitioner) in Private Practice: A Controlled Trial," *New England Journal of Medicine* 285 (December 1971):1353–58; Eugene C. Nelson, Arthur R. Jacobs, and Kenneth G. Johnson, "Patient Acceptance of Physicians' Assistants," Dartmouth Medical School, 1974 (mimeographed).

satisfied with the care they receive from NPs and PAs than with the care received from physicians, and in some cases patients prefer the former. Although studies have not generally considered the reasons for the high level of satisfaction, it appears that patients respond favorably to the quality of the treatment itself, as well as to the tendency for nurse practitioners and physicians' assistants to spend more time with patients and to create a more relaxed atmosphere in which patients feel comfortable asking questions they might regard as too trivial for a physician.

Cost Saving

Nurse practitioners and physicians' assistants have demonstrated their potential to reduce medical care costs, but in practice they have not yet achieved significant savings.[14] Unit cost savings can result from greater productivity, measured by the increase in the number of patient visits, services provided, or patients served in a practice employing an NP/PA. Productivity studies show that NPs and PAs can, without consulting a physician, handle more than two-thirds of all patients who present themselves for primary-care treatment.[15] Of the remaining one-third, many can be handled through phone consultation with the physician. Potentially, one NP or PA can increase by approximately 70 percent the productivity of a solo-practice physician.[16] In practice, physicians appear to underuse NPs and PAs or to use them inefficiently, so that actual productivity increases brought about by one NP or PA have ranged between 10 percent and 40 percent.[17] Given the

---

[14] Cohen et al., *An Evaluation of Policy Related Research*, p. 119.

[15] Paul D. Lairson, Jane C. Record, and Julia James, "Physician Assistants at Kaiser: Distinctive Patterns of Practice," paper presented at the annual meeting of the American Public Health Association, November 1972; Walter O. Spitzer et al., "The Burlington Randomized Trial of the Nurse Practitioner," *New England Journal of Medicine* 290 (January 31, 1974) :251–56.

[16] Frederick L. Golloday, Marianne Miller, and Kenneth R. Smith, "Allied Health Manpower Strategies: Estimates of the Potential Gains from Efficient Task Delegation," *Medical Care* 11 (November/December 1973); Louis R. Pondy, Jeffrey M. Jones, and John A. Braun, "Utilization and Productivity of the Duke Physician's Associate," *Socio-Economic Planning Science* 7 (1973) :327–52.

[17] Appel and Lowin, *Physician Extenders*, pp. 19–21.

costs of training NPs and PAs, these health workers are cost-effective to society only when productivity gains are at the upper end of that range.[18]

Two studies reported subsequent to the RANN evaluation have yielded favorable results on NP/PA cost savings. An evaluation of PA cost-effectiveness in the Kaiser-Portland HMO concluded that each physicians' assistant saved the system at least $15,000 annually by providing outpatient care otherwise rendered by a physician, with still greater savings possible through more efficient use of PAs.[19] Another study found that for two sites served by ambulatory clinics staffed by nurse practitioners and physicians' assistants, utilization of hospitals (number of admissions and duration of stay) was lower than for two matched control sites without clinics.[20]

Not generally considered are the indirect savings NPs and PAs may produce by legitimizing the notion of physician delegation of tasks. It also has been hypothesized that because NPs and PAs tend to spend more time with patients than physicians can generally afford to, patient compliance with medical instructions may improve and better self-care result.[21] If this hypothesis is correct, complications and subsequent hospitalizations could be reduced. If this reduction were to lead to a gradual realignment of roles in health care delivery, considerable long-term cost savings would be implied.[22]

Access to Care

Although the emergence of nurse practitioners and physicians' assistants has not produced unambiguous savings in health care costs, the use of these personnel does appear to have increased access to care. Overall, 63 percent of NPs and

---

[18] Ibid., p. 40.

[19] Jane C. Record and Joan E. O'Bannon, *Cost Effectiveness of Physicians' Assistants*, DHEW, Bureau of Health Manpower, and Kaiser Foundation Health Services Research Center, Portland, Oregon, 1976.

[20] C.E. Anderson et al., *A Site-Specific Study of Physician Extender Staffed Care Centers* (The MITRE Corporation: McLean, Va., February 1977).

[21] Letter from Dolores L. Farr, American Nurses' Association, Inc., Washington, D.C., October 25, 1977.

[22] Appel and Lowin, *Physician Extenders*, p. 40.

PAs are practicing in primary-care settings.[23] For PAs trained in MEDEX programs, this figure is close to 90 percent.[24]

Evidence on geographic location of NPs and PAs, while also favorable, is less complete. Overall, the percentage of NPs and PAs practicing outside standard metropolitan statistical areas exceeds the percentage of physicians located in those areas and is even greater than the percentage of the total population living in those areas.[25] MEDEX graduates locate in rural areas at almost double the rate of other types of PAs and NPs, generally as part of solo-physician practices. Other PAs and NPs tend to practice in clinics, hospitals, and other organized care settings.[26]

IMPEDIMENTS TO NP AND PA PERFORMANCE

Although the performance of NPs and PAs over the past decade has been shown to be good, several factors have significantly impeded more effective and efficient use of these personnel. The single greatest obstacle has been the reimbursement policy of third-party payers. Under Medicare, NP/PA services performed outside an institutional setting are eligible for reimbursement only if (1) the supervising physician is on the premises, and (2) the services are ones traditionally delegated

---

[23] Stephen B. Morris and David B. Smith, "The Diffusion of Physician Extenders," Working Paper No. 1, "The Physician Extender Reimbursement Study," DHEW, Social Security Administration (SSA), Office of Research and Statistics, 1977 (mimeographed); Richard M. Scheffler, "Characteristics of Physicians' Assistants: A Focus on Specialty," *The P.A. Journal: A Journal for New Health Practitioners* 5 (Spring 1975): 30–41; Judy A. Light, Mary Jane Crain, and Donald W. Fisher, "Physicians' Assistant: A Profile of the Profession, 1976," *The P.A. Journal: A Journal for New Health Professionals* 7 (Fall 1977):109–123.

[24] National Council of MEDEX Programs, *A Progress Report on MEDEX Programs in the United States*, University of Washington MEDEX Program, 1974.

[25] Richard M. Scheffler, *Factors Affecting the Employment of Physician Assistants and MEDEX: Preliminary Report No. 1*, University of North Carolina at Chapel Hill, January 1977; Morris and Smith, "The Diffusion of Physician Extenders."

[26] Morris and Smith, "The Diffusion of Physician Extenders."

by the physician.[27] The latter caveat implies that even if the physician is present, Medicare does not reimburse nurse practitioners or physicians' assistants for carrying out duties normally performed by the physician—precisely those duties for which they were trained in federally subsidized programs. (NP/PA services provided in institutional settings are reimbursable under Medicare because the salaries of the health personnel may be included as part of the institution's reasonable costs.)

Because Medicare recipients constitute a sizable percentage of the population in many rural and other medically underserved areas, the federal government's reimbursement policy often has made it financially prohibitive for nurse practitioners and physicians' assistants to work in precisely those areas where they are most needed. Ironically, this policy has been particularly damaging to efforts by the federal government's National Health Service Corps to place NPs and PAs in shortage areas. The policy also has worked against federally subsidized clinics set up under the Appalachian Regional Development Act of 1965, which rely heavily on the services of these health workers to serve isolated rural areas. According to congressional testimony, some of these clinics would have been forced to close without reimbursement for care provided to the large number of Medicare eligibles they serve.[28] To forestall closing of the clinics, Titles XVIII and XIX of the Social Security Act were amended in 1977 (PL 95-210) to enable rural health clinics to qualify for reimbursement of services they provide in areas with a health personnel shortage. These services can be provided by NPs or PAs with periodic review by physicians who have arranged with the clinic for conducting such reviews. Medicare reimbursement for NP/PA services in underserved urban areas is not affected by these amendments.

In contrast, the federal government's Medicaid regulations

---

[27] Memorandum, "Medicare Regulation Which Prevents Reimbursement Claims for Services Unless a Physician is Physically Present," from Director, Bureau of Health Insurance, SSA, to the Assistant Secretary for Health, U.S. Public Health Service (PHS), July 30, 1976.

[28] Statement of Donald W. Whitehead, Federal Cochairman, Appalachian Regional Commission, "Medicare Reimbursement for Physician Extenders Practicing in Rural Health Clinics," hearing before the Subcommittee on Health of the U.S. House of Representatives Ways and Means Committee, 95th Congress, 1st Session, February 28, 1977.

do permit reimbursement of nurse practitioners and physicians' assistants, if an individual state so chooses; so far, fourteen states have decided to permit such reimbursement. Commercial and private insurers follow the government's practice of reimbursing for NP/PA services provided in institutional settings. For services in noninstitutional settings, the meager available evidence suggests that these insurers have no common policy, but typically reimburse physicians without explicitly recognizing that a portion of the services was provided by auxiliary personnel.[29]

One reason for the federal government's reluctance to reimburse nurse practitioners and physicians' assistants has been the lack of consistency among states in laws and regulations governing NPs and PAs.[30] State legislation has impeded use of these personnel, particularly PAs, in more direct ways as well. A number of states fail to recognize PAs legally, thereby virtually precluding PAs from practicing in those states. Restrictive requirements for physician supervision have limited PAs' ability to practice in rural and remote settings. Even in an office setting, the time saved by having a physicians' assistant treat a patient is often lost when both must wait for the physician to "see" the patient, to comply with supervision requirements. Cumbersome regulations, such as the need for a detailed job description, serve to discourage physicians from hiring a nurse practitioner or a physicians' assistant. At the same time, the scope of duties that state laws permit physicians to delegate is often so vague or narrowly defined as to make hiring a PA seem unprofitable or even risky from the standpoint of malpractice threat.

Problems of state legislation hamper nurse practitioners less than they hamper physicians' assistants, for all but three states have revised their nurse practice acts to incorporate the ex-

---

[29] For further discussion of the reimbursement policy of private and commercial insurance companies, see Ruth S. Hanft, "Reimbursement for the Services of Physician's Assistants Under Federal and Private Insurance," in *Intermediate-Level Health Practitioners*, Vernon W. Lippard and Elizabeth F. Purcell, eds. (New York: The Josiah Macy, Jr., Foundation, 1973); Stephen B. Morris, "Third Party Payment for the Service of the Assistant to the Primary Care Physician," in Ann A. Bliss and Eva D. Cohen, eds., *The New Health Professionals* (Germantown, Md.: Aspen Systems Corporation, 1977).

[30] U.S. Senate, Committee on Finance, *Social Security Amendments of 1972* (Washington, D.C.: U.S. Government Printing Office, 1972).

panded nursing duties that NPs perform. In two of the three
remaining states, NPs can practice under a delegatory provision of the medical practice act.[31] Nurse and medical practice
acts, considered together, do not require physician supervision
of NPs in the performance of traditional nursing services.
The acts do require, however, that duties traditionally within
the physician's domain (diagnosis and treatment) be performed only when such duties are delegated by a physician.[32]

Lack of reimbursement plus the legal and regulatory problems described above account in part for a third impediment,
reluctance of physicians to hire nurse practitioners or physicians' assistants, despite physicians' endorsement, in principle,
of the concept of delegating duties to NPs/PAs. Low physician
demand also results from poor exposure to the NP/PA concept.
Medical school training typically provides little or no contact
with such personnel. With fewer than 22,000 NPs and PAs
practicing in a work force of 340,000 physicians, it is not
surprising that physicians gain little exposure in the field.
Although employment of NPs and PAs has generally been
found to be profitable to those practices that hire them,[33]
physicians do not necessarily recognize the potential financial
benefits. Even an awareness of the potential for profit does
not guarantee that a physician will want to hire an NP or PA.
Many physicians may be uncomfortable with the notion of
delegating duties they are accustomed to performing themselves. For others, the necessity of taking on a supervisory
role would not offset the financial gain or the freedom to
concentrate on more challenging aspects of their work.

IMPLICATIONS OF NATIONAL HEALTH INSURANCE FOR EXPANDING NP AND PA SUPPLY

In light of the performance record of nurse practitioners
and physicians' assistants, does the prospect of national health

[31] Interview with Anna Kuba, Coordinator on State Boards of Nursing,
American Nursing Association, September 7, 1977.

[32] Virginia C. Hall, "The Legal Scope of Nurse Practitioners Under
Nurse Practice and Medical Practice Acts," in Bliss and Cohen, eds.,
The New Health Professionals.

[33] Cohen et al., *An Evaluation of Policy Related Research*, p. 117.

insurance call for an expansion of these occupations? Several considerations are pertinent. First, national health insurance would most likely increase the demand for health care services. The amount of increase would depend on the particular NHI legislation implemented, but the experience from Medicare and Medicaid demonstrates that when financial barriers to obtaining care are reduced, some increased demand for medical care results. One legitimate response to this likely increase is to expand the number of NP and PA providers.

Second, as financial barriers to obtaining care are removed, the specific lack of primary care in some areas stands to frustrate the NHI goal of improved access to care. Despite a reimbursement policy that has to some extent discouraged provision of primary care, NPs and PAs have demonstrated their ability to provide this care.

The main argument against expanding the number of nurse practitioners and physicians' assistants is the expected increase in the supply of physicians, which was discussed in the preceding chapter. This projected increase in the number of physicians could mean that NPs and PAs would glut the market or be used by physicians even less efficiently than at present. In either case, employment of NPs or PAs could cease to be a cost-reducing measure.

Some argue that an increase in the number of physicians will mean more employment opportunities for nurse practitioners and physicians' assistants, because physicians will increasingly desire to delegate a portion of their tasks. This possibility seems unlikely, however, given physicians' apparent reluctance to hire NPs and PAs and the slow-to-change attitudes underlying this reluctance. A more reasonable prediction, and one shared by most NP/PA educators, is that a sizable increase in physician supply bodes ill for nurse practitioners and physicians' assistants, who function more as substitutes for than complements to physicians. The fact that medical care standards are traditionally physician-defined gives physicians considerable power to exclude potential competitors with less training. Consumers' lack of information about and inability to judge the quality of the health care they receive compound this problem.

Even if physicians were willing to hire large numbers of nurse practitioners and physicians' assistants, expansion of these occupations is not necessarily desirable. If hiring a nurse practitioner or a physicians' assistant simply results in a physician's cutting back on his or her own work load, taxpayers might receive little benefit in return for their subsidy of NP and PA training. This problem might be particularly acute if the national health insurance program were to reimburse employers for NP/PA services at the same rate as for physician services.

Changing the policy toward foreign medical school graduates (FMGs), which was discussed in the preceding chapter, should offset, in part, the detrimental effects on NPs and PAs of more physicians. The director of one PA program reported that some hospitals are already looking to replace FMGs with PAs.[34] In explanation, he cited hospitals' increasing need to compete for patients, and patients' more favorable reaction to PAs than to FMGs with whom they face a language barrier. If the supply of American-trained physicians were plentiful, hospitals would no doubt prefer them to PAs, but hospitals that rely on FMGs often do so precisely because they are unable to attract other physicians (given the facility's location and/or patient population). Even a greatly expanded supply of physicians may do little to change that phenomenon.

Health maintenance organizations provide another opportunity for NP/PA employment. HMO administrators have a clear financial incentive to be efficient, a fact that presumably has led to their current use of nurse practitioners and physicians' assistants. To the extent that national health insurance might foster the HMO delivery concept, demand for NPs and PAs should expand naturally. Because the potential productivity gains appear to be greatest for NPs and PAs in group settings,[35] this development seems particularly appropriate.

Even considering the decline in the number of foreign medical school graduates and the interest of HMOs in nurse practitioners and physicians' assistants, doubt remains as to whether these personnel have any immediate cost-savings value, given the increasing physician supply. Perhaps the greatest benefit of NPs and PAs is their potential, over the long term, to bring about a realignment of providers' roles in

---

[34] Interview with Karl Katterjohn, Acting Director, George Washington University Physician Assistant Program, July 7, 1977.

[35] Appel and Lowin, *Physician Extenders*, p. 29.

health care delivery. Such a development would have profound implications for the cost of medical care. It is apparent that much of the primary care provided by physicians could be done just as well by individuals with considerably less education and training, and hence at less cost to society. Thus, to restrict NP/PA expansion would reinforce the inefficiency of a system in which physicians are the near-exclusive providers of medical care.

Overall, then, it seems desirable to expand the number of nurse practitioners and physicians' assistants. But this expansion should take place gradually and be coordinated with policy decisions affecting the number of physicians so as to avoid a situation in which NPs or PAs are employed unproductively or not employed at all. A gradual expansion of the NP/PA supply also would give state laws and regulations a chance to catch up with developments in these new occupations, and thus permit more efficient utilization of these personnel.

Hence it seems desirable to focus the deployment of nurse practitioners and physicians' assistants on underserved areas that could not attract or retain a physician. A strategy that emphasizes NP/PA deployment in areas where physicians have been unwilling to practice is less likely to encounter opposition from state medical societies than would other deployment strategies. At the same time, such a strategy would require the most ambitious changes in state legislation, because this strategy necessarily calls for minimal physician supervision of NPs and PAs and for broad definition of duties physicians can delegate. Such changes will not come easily.

Implementation Issues

REIMBURSEMENT OF NPS AND PAS

Third-party reimbursement is a key factor in achieving the desired supply of nurse practitioners and physicians' assistants and in encouraging their optimal use. If an NHI system should adopt the predominant Medicare philosophy (in general, services are reimbursable only if delivered by a licensed physician), NPs and PAs would be prevented from assuming a significant role in the health care delivery system. Physicians would find it financially disadvantageous to hire a nurse practitioner or a physicians' assistant, and states would have little incentive to adopt or alter legislation to permit more effective use of those health personnel. Although, as already mentioned, the 1977 Social Security Act Amendments permit reimbursement of services provided by NPs and PAs in rural health clinics with only physician review, these changes affect only a small proportion of the population.

The general issue is whether to reimburse all nurse practitioners and physicians' assistants under national health insurance, regardless of practice location or mode. Three arguments have been made against universal reimbursement for services provided by NPs and PAs. One focuses on the potential for fraud and abuse by physicians in urban areas. Medicare regulations prohibiting NP/PA reimbursement were instituted in the early 1970s in response to evidence that some physicians were making substantial profits by hiring paraprofessionals to provide services to Medicare patients at lower costs to the physician than the reimbursement rates. Misuse of NPs and PAs by so-called Medicaid mills is a similar concern. Altering the reimbursement method to eliminate the potential for windfall profits to physicians, however, seems more appropriate than a policy of denying reimbursement altogether.

A second argument against universal reimbursement for NP/PA services is that reimbursing only for these services in underserved areas would help attack the maldistribution of medical care services. But this problem also might be approached through a differential reimbursement structure covering all nurse practitioners and physicians' assistants but reimbursing for their services more generously in shortage areas than elsewhere. Moreover, a policy to reimburse for all services provided by NPs and PAs would encourage states to adopt less restrictive laws and regulations regarding physician supervision of these personnel and the scope of duties physicians can delegate. Such legal and regulatory changes are essential to permit NPs and PAs to function effectively in rural and remote areas.

The third argument against universal reimbursement of nurse practitioners and physicians' assistants is that adding more providers to the health care delivery system in nonshortage areas might result in provision of unnecessary medical services and thus in added costs. This dilemma was posed earlier in this chapter. It is not clear to what extent employment of nurse practitioners and physicians' assistants represents a saving or a cost to the current system. Without a more coherent policy on physician supply, base fee schedules, and total physician fees generated, physicians can use NPs and PAs in nonshortage areas primarily to provide additional and possibly unnecessary services. As a result, employment of NPs and PAs could become a net expense to the health care system.

Yet, clearly, use of these personnel offers *potential* cost savings through bringing about a more efficient delivery system. Achieving this potential, however, is substantially impeded if reimbursement policy fails to recognize NPs and PAs as bona fide providers of care in any setting. If the federal government continues to subsidize NP/PA training programs, it seems desirable to accompany the subsidy with a policy to provide third-party reimbursement to all NPs and PAs. If accompanied by a coordinated and efficient policy on physician supply and reimbursement, this action could represent a significant step toward achieving substantial long-term savings through more efficient health care delivery in all geographic areas. Although the need to direct NPs and PAs toward shortage areas argues for reimbursing their services only in those areas, a policy of differential reimbursement seems a better approach to this problem.

RATE OF REIMBURSEMENT

If a national health insurance program should qualify NP/PA services for reimbursement, the issue then becomes the rate of reimbursement. Two views predominate: (1) full reimbursement at the same rate paid to physicians for performing the same service; (2) reimbursement at some fraction, such as 80 percent, of the rate paid to a physician.

Congress tends to support fractional reimbursement because it views employment of NPs and PAs as a cost containment measure.[36] There are three arguments against fractional re-imbursement. First, because the "usual and customary" basis for reimbursing physicians generally means lower fees in rural areas, fractional reimbursement of NPs and PAs serves to en-trench that disparity. Second, it is claimed that a two-price policy implies to patients that NPs and PAs provide inferior care. Because NPs and PAs tend to work in underserved areas, it is feared that fractional reimbursement would lead to a two-class system of medical care. In the absence of empirical evi-dence, it is impossible to know if patients do in fact perceive care that costs less as inferior and, more important, whether such a perception reduces the efficacy of the treatment. Third, fractional reimbursement diminishes the incentive for physi-cians to hire NPs and PAs. The strength of the incentive is a function of the reimbursement rate selected. Schweitzer and Record recently estimated that a 46 percent reimbursement rate is the point at which physicians would break even in hiring a nurse practitioner or physicians' assistant,[37] but such a rate assumes efficient use of the NP or PA by the physician. Physicians unfamiliar with NPs and PAs would probably perceive a higher break-even point.

What are the arguments in favor of full reimbursement?

---

[36] U.S. Senate, Committee on Finance, p. 228. By congressional man-date, the Office of Policy Planning and Research, Health Care Financing Administration (HCFA), is conducting "The Physician Extender Reim-bursement Study" to determine the impact of various Medicare reim-bursement rates on program cost and physician demand for NPs and PAs. Participating physician practices are randomly selected to use one of three reimbursement rates—100 percent, 80 percent, or 62 per-cent. (For a description of the study, see Morris and Smith, *The Diffusion of Physician Extenders*, pp. 155–60.) Results of the experiment will be available for policy planning in 1979. The general applicability of the results will be limited because of the small number of practices HCFA has been able to enlist and the high degree of expected physician and NP/PA mobility. For discussion of this problem, see "Physician Extender Reimbursement Under Title XVIII of the Social Security Act (Medicare)," memorandum prepared by Winston J. Dean, Program Analyst, Office of Policy Development and Planning in the Office of Assistant Secretary for Health, DHEW, for the Health Resources Ad-ministration (HRA) Work Group, February 28, 1977.

[37] Stuart O. Schweitzer and Jane C. Record, "Third-Party Reimburse-ment for New Health Professionals in Primary-Care: An Alternative to Fractional Reimbursement," paper presented to a conference sponsored by the National Rural Center on "Nurse Practitioners/Physician Assis-tants: A Research Agenda," Airlie, Virginia, June 21–22, 1977.

First, if we assume that employment of NPs and PAs is a desirable goal, full reimbursement offers physicians a financial incentive to hire these personnel. Second, full reimbursement reflects the view that equal services should carry equal prices, thus emphasizing to the consumer that care provided by nurse practitioners and physicians' assistants is of no lower quality than care provided by physicians. Third, full reimbursement avoids the administrative problems of trying to determine how much of a particular service was performed by the NP/PA and how much by the physician. Most physicians now charge patients the full rate for services performed by NPs and PAs, so full reimbursement also has the advantage of being the system already in use.

The chief drawback to full reimbursement is its potential cost, an inevitable result of providing physicians with a financial incentive to hire nurse practitioners and physicians' assistants. Some patients also may object to full reimbursement on this basis, in recognition of the fact that although the service is of equal quality, it costs considerably less to provide.

A third approach to reimbursement potentially offers more advantages than either the full or fractional approach. Under this approach, the patient pays the same price whether the service is provided by an NP/PA or a physician, but the price for a service is based on the cost at which it can be most efficiently provided.[38] For example, if NPs and PAs are qualified to take a throat culture, then the price for providing that service would reflect the fact that it is a task physicians could delegate. Physicians could continue to perform throat cultures themselves, but they would be reimbursed no more than a nurse practitioner or physicians' assistant for doing so. This policy would presumably encourage task delegation and increase practice efficiency.

The advantages to such an approach are direct. Patients would benefit from the reduced fees charged for relatively routine diagnostic and treatment services. At the same time physicians would have an incentive to use NPs and PAs to provide these services, thereby reserving physician time for more complex procedures.

Possible drawbacks are less clear. Third-party payers would have to develop lists of tasks that physicians could and could

---

[38] For a more detailed description of this general approach, see ibid.

not delegate. This problem could be minor, because many states now require detailed NP/PA job descriptions for physicians wanting to hire those personnel. A potentially more serious drawback is the effect this approach to reimbursement would have on physicians who are not in a position to hire a nurse practitioner or physicians' assistant, either because no NP/PA is available or because the physician's practice is too small to justify an additional employee. It seems unlikely that physicians will tolerate significant income reductions. Thus, their response may be either to hire an NP/PA and "create" enough additional demand to pay his or her salary, or to perform a greater number of complex, profitable services to compensate for any income losses in performing routine tasks. (Chapers 2 and 4 discuss the details of problems in setting and using fixed fee schedules to pay for physicians' services.)

Although the drawbacks to charging for health services on the basis of the most efficient means of production are significant, the basic idea seems sound. It has been found that approximately two-thirds of the primary-care physician's duties could be delegated to a nurse practitioner or physicians' assistant; such delegation could represent a substantial alteration of physicians' fee schedules. Physicians oppose fractional reimbursement because it would restrict their potential profit from hiring a nurse practitioner or physicians' assistant. By contrast, reduction of fees for services that NPs or PAs could provide would increase the costs of not hiring a health professional, and thus from the physicians' perspective, is far more objectionable than fractional reimbursement.

Given physicians' probable opposition to making fees reflect the degree to which tasks could be delegated, only moderate changes in this direction can be expected. As a compromise, full reimbursement might be employed only in medically underserved areas and fractional reimbursement elsewhere. Such a policy is primarily a cost-serving strategy, but it also provides an incentive for NPs and PAs to practice in needy areas.

A final approach to reimbursement, distinct from the methods (fractional, full, modified full) just described, is cost-based reimbursement, under which third parties reimburse for the actual cost of having a nurse practitioner or physicians' assistant provide a given unit of service. The major advantage of this approach is its potential for cost savings, but this advantage is offset by the same basic drawbacks associated with fractional reimbursement: the administrative difficulty of determining the actual cost of the portion of a task performed by the NP or PA, and the potential for a two-class system of health care delivery. Even the potential cost savings under cost-based reimbursement may be elusive. The experience of Medicare and Medicaid with cost-based reimbursement of hospitals suggests that, over time, this approach may create an incentive to increase costs. (Chapter 6 on paying hospitals discusses this problem.)

DIRECT VERSUS INDIRECT REIMBURSEMENT

From the standpoint of economic theory, it is irrelevant whether nurse practitioners and physicians' assistants are reimbursed for their services directly or indirectly through a supervisory physician or facility. Theoretically, as long as the service provided is reimbursable, the NP or PA could receive an equivalent income in the form of a salary or wage paid by the employer. In practice, however, indirect reimbursement has considerable economic, legal, and symbolic importance. Indirect reimbursement permits physicians to realize higher incomes from the development of the NP and PA occupations. More important, indirect reimbursement guarantees that the role of NPs and PAs in health care delivery will be one of dependence on physicians.

Physicians' assistants, whose role is universally defined by state statutes to involve physician supervision, have not fought for direct reimbursement. They believe that their occupation can best make political headway by keeping a "low profile," that is, by accepting a status of formal dependency on the physician, and focusing on having state regulatory bodies both expand the scope of duties considered delegatable and relax the requirements for physician supervision. Nurse practitioners, by contrast, have lobbied for direct reimbursement, maintaining that the existence of nurse practice acts removes NPs from a position of dependence on physicians.[39] In line with

---

[39] Statement of Anne Zimmerman, President of American Nurses' Association. "Medicare Reimbursement for Physician Extenders Practicing in Rural Health Clinics," Hearing before the Subcommittee on Health of the U.S. House of Representatives Ways and Means Committee, 95th Congress, 1st Session, February 28, 1977, pp. 61–65.

this belief, NPs have recommended that mandated physician supervision be replaced by a provision for reimbursable physician consultation.[40]

The underlying issue, then, is the nature of the working relationship between physicians and NPs/PAs. Overall, it seems unnecessary and undesirable for federal law to require any greater degree of physician supervision or delegatory responsibility than is needed to comply with state law. Additional federal requirements are unnecessary because states tend to be, if anything, overly restrictive in their supervision requirements; they are undesirable because excessive requirements for compliance with federal regulation could cause patients covered under national health insurance to be handled less efficiently than other patients. It seems sufficient to require simply that physicians, NPs, and PAs satisfy the legal and regulatory requirements regarding supervision or delegatory authority that apply in the state in which they practice.

By the same token, the reimbursement mechanism should not prevent nurse practitioners and physicians' assistants from functioning as autonomously as state law allows. Inasmuch as physicians' assistants clearly function under physician supervision, indirect reimbursement is arguably inappropriate only for nurse practitioners, especially those who are self-employed. The major obstacle to direct reimbursement is physician opposition. Physicians maintain that they are ultimately responsible for the actions of all nurse practitioners. NPs dispute this claim, but no NP has ever been sued for malpractice, so the question has not been legally resolved.

Aside from the legal issues, there are significant arguments against the direct reimbursement of nurse practitioners and physicians' assistants and the recognition of these people as independent providers that direct reimbursement would represent. One argument is that allowing NPs and PAs to practice independently could compromise quality of care by effectively reducing their contact with physicians and the learning that takes place through that contact. A second argument is that direct reimbursement of NPs and PAs would open the door to similar treatment of many other groups in the health care system, such as therapists and technicians. If health care providers can generate significant increases in the demand for

---

[40] Ibid.

their services, direct reimbursement could add substantially to the cost of health care in this country.

Ultimately, the direct versus indirect reimbursement issue will no doubt be resolved politically; hence direct reimbursement is unlikely to come about. Given physicians' control over the way other NHI policy toward NPs and PAs will be set—requirements for physician supervision, for example—nurse practitioners' fight for direct reimbursement might prove not only futile, but even counterproductive.

CERTIFICATION AND LICENSURE

Next to reimbursement, the issue on which NHI policy can most influence the use of nurse practitioners and physicians' assistants is in the granting of credentials and licenses. Much has been written about the benefits of standardizing certification and licensure procedures,[41] but that literature will not be treated here. Proposed solutions to the general problem include certification and licensure on a national, regional, or institutional basis. The issue seems largely an academic one. Because traditionally licensure has been a state function and certification a professional function, significant departures from these arrangements are highly unlikely. Nevertheless, if third-party reimbursement of NPs and PAs is to come about, some federal policy with respect to certification and licensure is necessary.

At minimum, it seems reasonable for the federal government to require that state licensure meet certain standards and then accept the credentials of nurse practitioners and physicians' assistants who are certified or licensed in their states. Nurse practitioners now have a national licensure examination to become registered nurses before entering NP training. Pediatric NPs also have a national certifying examination and other NP specialties have similar examinations to qualify for excellence in practice. Federal policy should encourage greater standardization and adoption of these exams as the basis for state certification or licensure. Physicians' assistants now have

---

[41] Harris S. Cohen and Winston J. Dean, "To Practice or Not to Practice: Developing State Law and Policy on Physician's Assistants," *Milbank Memorial Fund Quarterly: Health and Society* (Fall 1974):349–76; Winston J. Dean, "State Legislation for Physician's Assistants, A Review and Analysis," *Health Services Reports* 88 (January 1973):3–12.

national certifying examinations, and thirty-one states currently recognize the national PA examination as the basis for certification. The American Academy of Physicians' Assistants is attempting to make such recognition mandatory in all states. In endorsing the legislation to amend Medicare reimbursement, then DHEW Secretary Joseph A. Califano, Jr., recommended that DHEW set certain standards which nurse practitioners and physicians' assistants would be required to meet; this suggestion is a change from the department's previous position.

Perhaps a bigger problem with state regulation is the tendency to overrestrict what NPs and PAs can do. The National Commission on Certification of Physicians' Assistants plans to work with the Federation of State Medical Boards of the United States to develop model legislation to reduce this problem. The American Nursing Association also hopes to develop such model legislation.

TRAINING

Although no NHI legislation is likely to address the training of nurse practitioners and physicians' assistants directly, accompanying health professions' education legislation would do so. Several issues are pertinent. Most important is the question of continued federal subsidization of NP/PA training programs. Three arguments can be used to justify continued subsidization. One is that private decisions would result in a less than optimal supply of NPs and PAs, because social returns to NP/PA training exceed private returns or because imperfect access to loans reduces the number of trainees below the optimum.

The second argument focuses on distributional imperfections, by location, practice mode, or specialty. These maldistributions might stem from imperfect information or from the fact that salaries do not accurately signal social demands. Therefore, to the extent that subsidizing particular kinds of training in specified locations helps move private distributional decisions toward socially desirable outcomes, subsidization may be called for.

Third, because careers in the NP/PA field are relatively new, it can be argued that public support is needed to expedite the establishment of training programs. Ultimately, the demand for NP/PA training could be expected to stimulate an equilibrating supply of training positions. Response might be slow, however, because most training institutions are non-profit, because people lack knowledge of NP/PA careers, and because those people who do want the training programs are too scattered to exert much influence. Of these three general arguments, only the first—that private decisions would result in a less than optimal NP/PA supply—implies continued subsidization over the long term; yet improved access to loans would reduce the need to continue subsidies. The other two arguments are clearly directed at smoothing the short-term transition to a new and presumably more desirable equilibrium.

How large a subsidy is called for? A priori, this question is almost impossible to answer exactly. Theoretically, the size of the subsidy depends on several unobservable factors, such as individuals' rates of time preference (the willingness to forgo current income in return for higher future incomes), expectations of future earnings and costs, and attitudes towards risk and uncertainty. Further, much is unknown about the future demand for NPs and PAs. How will the institutional structure change? What reimbursement system will evolve, and where will relative earnings of NPs and PAs and physicians settle?

Given these difficulties, it seems that a desirable course of action is to establish an administrative structure which can accurately monitor the supply and distribution of NPs and PAs and which maintains the flexibility to alter subsidy rates in response to changing supplies of and demands for medical care. The health sector is among the most dynamic and rapidly changing parts of our economy. Thus, little would be gained from adopting policies and administrative structures predicated on the notion of identifying and moving to a static equilibrium. Therefore, the major emphasis should be on establishing a system for identifying and monitoring changes in health personnel employment, earnings, hours, and (for trainees) expectations regarding these important variables. Such a system would enable policy makers to assess the effectiveness of changes in subsidy policies (and in other factors affecting NPs and PAs) with much greater accuracy than at present.

DEPLOYMENT

As previously discussed, providing first-contact primary care in areas unable to support a full-time physician may be a principal role of a nurse practitioner or physicians' assistant. The MEDEX program emphasizes this role, and this role follows the tradition of visiting nurse programs like the Frontier Nursing Service of Eastern Kentucky. Areas most frequently mentioned in this context are isolated rural communities and urban neighborhoods characterized by difficult access to (or relative underutilization of) medical care. This shortage-area delivery model would have a nurse practitioner or physicians' assistant provide a substantial amount of relatively routine primary care such as children's checkups, prenatal care, and chronic disease maintenance independent of a physician. But the NP/PA would have prompt access to a physician through a telecommunications link—at minimum, a telephone, but ideally, through equipment for relaying data, for example, from remote EKG or EEG equipment. In acute-care cases, the NP/PA might act as a coordinator, arranging transportation, alerting facilities and personnel at a destination point, and providing interim care for the patient. More elaborate delivery models envisage NPs and PAs functioning as part of an organized medical care team based in ambulatory medical care institutions such as group medical practices, health clinics, or neighborhood health centers.

What policy changes are necessary if nurse practitioners and physicians' assistants are to play the role just described? As already indicated, supervision requirements in many states will have to be relaxed, and the scope of medical duties that physicians can delegate to NPs and PAs broadened. Because these changes fall under state authority, the federal role may be limited. Reimbursement is the area in which federal policy will be most important in achieving deployment of NPs and PAs to underserved areas. It may well be desirable to reimburse NPs and PAs who serve in these areas at a higher rate than elsewhere. Experience has shown that financial incentives are relatively ineffective in attracting physician providers to rural areas, but financial incentives might work in the case of NPs and PAs because their earning potential is considerably lower than that of physicians. Moreover, rural service offers a nurse practitioner or physicians' assistant the opportunity for more professional autonomy.

Higher reimbursement for NPs and PAs practicing in underserved areas would probably encourage some physicians in these localities to employ these personnel, but because these physicians often carry heavy patient loads, many might not be willing to take on the additional supervisory responsibilities. Therefore, the most feasible method for employing NPs and PAs may be through public or quasi-public facilities such as Area Health Education Centers, Neighborhood Health Centers, or National Health Service Corps sites—facilities which are capable of using NPs and PAs efficiently and which have the explicit objective of serving populations with poor access to medical care. Where such facilities should be located and how the right number of NPs and PAs is to be determined are difficult questions for health planners and facility regulators. Making NP/PA services available, particularly for currently underserved populations, may require the direct attention of NHI planners.

Changes in policy affecting NP/PA training programs also may be considered as a way to increase NP/PA service in underserved areas. For example, MEDEX graduates tend to practice in rural primary-care settings in greater numbers than do NPs or PAs. This experience supports the feasibility of targeted recruitment and placement of students to serve in particular practice settings. Similarly, PA program directors have observed that the best predictor of whether PA graduates will go to work permanently in a shortage area is whether they received some training experience in such a setting. Encouragement of this aspect of NP/PA training seems highly desirable.

PHYSICIANS' ATTITUDES

Physicians' reluctance to hire nurse practitioners and physicians' assistants remains a major impediment to expansion of this health field which, ideally, a national health insurance system could address. Much improvement could result indirectly from policy changes regarding reimbursement and certification. Other sources of this reluctance may be more difficult to penetrate.

Medical school education currently gives students little team training experience or instruction in personnel supervision. As a consequence of this training deficiency, many physicians later demonstrate little skill in employing even the traditional medical aides, to say nothing of their inability to use NPs and PAs productively.

A few university-based PA programs have succeeded in combining some core medical school and PA classes. Among physicians who are trained in such a setting, the tendency to hire PAs is apparently much higher than average. This approach offers much promise, because it also is efficient from the university's standpoint to reduce replication of core courses taught in more than one training program.

In the field, as in medical school, exposure leads to acceptance. Of physicians who take on an NP/PA apprentice, a large proportion become permanent converts. These physicians then serve as models for others in the community to follow. Nurse practitioners and physicians' assistants are innovations to the health care system. Research shows that physicians generally will adopt an innovation of any kind—a new drug, a piece of equipment, and the like—only after receiving word-of-mouth recommendation from another physician. As a result, the diffusion process is necessarily a gradual one. Physicians in large urban practices are most likely to adopt innovations, so the emphasis on NP/PA deployment in rural areas has perhaps slowed the diffusion process. Not surprisingly, physicians who serve as "opinion leaders" for the surrounding physician community play a particularly important role, so enlisting the leaders' involvement in NP/PA apprenticing and placement seems particularly important to speeding diffusion.

Conclusions

The first decade of experience with nurse practitioners and physicians' assistants demonstrates one thing clearly—much primary health care can be provided, with no loss in quality, by personnel with considerably less education and training than physicians have. This fact has profound implications for potential cost savings in the delivery of health care. Less clear is whether this potential for cost savings can be realized in the near term, given the tendency for physicians to use NPs and PAs inefficiently or else to reduce their own work loads.

Policy makers face a dilemma. If the primary effect of employing auxiliary personnel is to reduce physicians' work effort, the public may be receiving little direct benefit from its subsidization of NP/PA training, and NP/PA expansion may be a net cost to consumers. Because the need to contain costs has been a prime stimulus to national health insurance proposals, expansion of the supply of nurse practitioners and physicians' assistants may not be justified. At the same time, whatever their direct effect on the total supply of health care services, these personnel are contributing to a gradual realignment of roles in the health care delivery system. Movement away from a physician-dominated delivery system is essential if significant long-term cost savings are to result. Because NHI policy will permanently shape the character of the health care system, this long-term potential of NPs and PAs seems all the more important. Thus, for NHI policy planners, the most acceptable resolution of the dilemma seems to be a compromise, that is, to continue expanding the numbers of NPs and PAs at the current, gradual rate, but to do so within the context of policies that will permit NPs and PAs eventually to assume a more significant role in health care delivery.

Reimbursement policy is the vital link between national health insurance and these new health occupations. Providing third-party reimbursement for NP/PA services is essential if these health workers are to be accepted and used more fully. Reimbursement of NPs and PAs at the same rate as physicians are reimbursed is also desirable; equal reimbursement would both provide a needed incentive for physicians to hire NPs and PAs and avoid the problems of a two-class system of medicine implied by fractional reimbursement. To be consistent with cost-saving objectives' however, full reimbursement must be used in conjunction with a fee schedule in which prices reflect whether tasks are routine and delegatable. Only by making it unprofitable for physicians not to delegate routine tasks can long-term realignment of medical care delivery roles be encouraged.

Certification and licensure policy is the second direct link between national health insurance and new health occupations, but the federal government's role is more limited in this case than in the previous one. By restricting federal reimbursement to states where nurse practitioners and physicians' assistants meet certain minimum requirements, the federal government can encourage higher and more uniform state standards. But the real need is for policy to encourage less restrictive state laws that permit NPs and PAs to exercise their full potential as physician substitutes.

Other desirable policy options relate to legislation that would accompany adoption of a national health insurance program. Most important is the need for continued subsidization of NP/PA training programs and for encouragement of medical school programs that give medical students more exposure to NPs and PAs.

Given the limited numbers of nurse practitioners and physicians' assistants that will be produced at the current (and recommended) rate of training, it seems advisable to use these people primarily to reduce the physician maldistribution problem. One possible approach is to reimburse for NP/PA services performed in underserved areas at a higher rate than the rate used elsewhere, an incentive directed less at NPs and PAs than at potential physician employers. But the private market often is unresponsive to the demand for care by the needy, so it may also be necessary to couple development of the NP/PA occupations with new institutions for delivering care. Neighborhood Health Centers, Area Health Education Centers, and the National Health Services Corps may serve as appropriate models on which to build. Using NPs and PAs to deliver a defined set of primary-care services and to serve as a point of entry into the larger medical care system may help avoid the establishment of a two-class delivery system.

Even assuming that the kinds of policy changes just recommended take place, much uncertainty remains about what the demand for nurse practitioners and physicians' assistants will be. Any significant increase in the role of health maintenance organizations in delivering health care would probably augment demand for NPs and PAs. But the degree to which physicians can be persuaded to hire these health personnel or to use them efficiently once hired is less predictable. This uncertainty confirms the need to develop the NP and PA occupations gradually, and underlines the necessity for an administrative structure able to fine-tune and monitor this development. Judging from experience, the research community will continue to evaluate the effects that employment of these health personnel has on quality, cost, access, and other aspects of health care delivery. It is important for persons monitoring these effects to remember that the greatest value of nurse practitioners and physicians' assistants may not be their immediate contribution to increased health services, but rather their long-term contribution to realignment of roles in the health care delivery system.

Chapter 6
HOSPITAL PAYMENT

JUDITH FEDER
BRUCE SPITZ

W HEN governments purchase hospital services, hospital revenues become a matter of public policy. Theoretically, that policy should reflect the value to society of hospital care versus other publicly purchased goods and services, but this has not been true in American experience. Under Medicare and Medicaid, the government typically promises to pay hospitals the costs they incur in delivering care to program beneficiaries. With payment guaranteed, hospitals and their medical staffs develop and deliver services as they see fit with little regard to costs. Similarly, patients whose care is paid for by the government consume services with little regard to price. There has been little consideration of whether the benefits of hospital care are worth their full costs.

Open-ended access to public funds has encouraged rapid and continual increases in hospital expenditures. Resulting increases in hospital program costs have reduced the government's capacity to spend in other social service areas. In spring 1977, the Carter administration declared this situation intolerable: "The voracious appetite of hospital charge increases can no longer be permitted to devour revenue needed for child health and other pressing health needs of the aged and disabled." [1]

Dissatisfaction with hospital inflation predates the Carter administration. Numerous proposals for new approaches to

---

[1] Joseph A. Califano, Jr., Secretary of Health, Education, and Welfare, Statement before the Subcommittee on Health and the Environment, Committee on Interstate and Foreign Commerce and the Subcommittee on Health, Committee on Ways and Means, House of Representatives, May 11, 1977, p. 4.

hospital payment, both for national health insurance and for present payment programs, have been made in recent years. Because national health insurance bills have not yet been refined through the legislative process, they suggest the objectives rather than the specifics of alternative payment policies. Their primary objective is to eliminate open-ended payment by limiting payments in advance of service delivery. Thus, both the Ford-Nixon administrations' Comprehensive Health Insurance Plan (CHIP) and the Kennedy-Mills bill of 1974 propose that payments to hospitals be prospectively set (i.e., set in advance), by the states under federal regulation in the former plan and directly by the federal government in the latter. These proposals do not specify the constraints they would impose on payment, but the Kennedy-Corman bill would set individual hospital budgets in advance within a national budget for health expenditures.[2]

Other proposals for change in the present hospital payment system, notably the Talmadge bill[3] and the Carter administration bill,[4] emphasize prospectively set limits on payments, but they vary in the degree of constraint imposed and in the scope of their application. Although the Long-Ribicoff-Waggonner bill for catastrophic health insurance endorses the present Medicare-Medicaid reimbursement approach,[5] its payment provisions, if enacted, would most likely reflect the changes in that approach now under consideration.

Proposals for change represent widespread rejection of retroactive cost-based or "reasonable cost" reimbursement and the open-ended financing it provides. Dissatisfaction with retrospective cost-based hospital payment is far from new—this type of payment has been called inflationary from the moment of its adoption by government programs. Academic journals and

---

[2] For a summary of proposed national health insurance legislation, see Karen Davis, *National Health Insurance: Benefits, Costs, and Consequences* (Washington, D.C.: The Brookings Institution, 1975), Chapter 5.

[3] Senator Talmadge introduced his amendments as S.3205 in the 94th Congress, 2nd Session; a revised bill was introduced in the 95th Congress as S.1470.

[4] "President's Hospital Cost Containment Legislation," *Congressional Record—House*, April 25, 1977, pp. H3530–H3535.

[5] Davis, *National Health Insurance.*

legislative records abound with proposals for alternative approaches, and public and private payers have experimented with their use. But these efforts appear to have had little effect on hospital or program expenditures. Understanding why this has been the case is essential to effective change. This chapter is intended to provide that understanding.

Our analysis is based on the premise that deciding payment policy is a political process, involving several public and private groups with different interests and capacities to influence outcomes.[6] Our conclusion is that the failure of payment policy to control hospital costs reflects the resilience of provider influence in the payment process. Despite changes in payment methods, professional "judgment" and interests continue to dominate the determination of appropriate levels of government expenditures.

To explain what has happened and to derive lessons for the future, this chapter traces the origins of present payment criteria and outlines the political and technical weaknesses in the efforts to change these criteria. It then explores the Canadian and United Kingdom experiences with national health insurance to identify the opportunities and problems in using different criteria for government payment—notably, criteria that treat resources as finite, force trade-offs between hospital and other expenditures, and permit governments to contain hospital costs.

Principles of "Reasonable Cost" Reimbursement

Despite a statutory promise not to interfere in hospital industry practices,[7] federal payment policy has had a major impact on hospital financing. The Medicare payment method (followed by Medicaid) was based on principles promoted by the American Hospital Association (AHA) and their then-

---

[6] Although issues and problems reflect the peculiar characteristics of medical care, the process through which they are resolved is common to most if not all social policy. For comparative policy analysis across nations as well as issues, see Arnold J. Heidenheimer, Hugo Heclo, and Carolyn Teich Adams, *Comparative Public Policy: The Politics of Social Choice in Europe and America* (New York: St. Martin's Press, 1975).

[7] 42 U.S.C. sec. 1395.

affiliated insurers, Blue Cross.[8] These principles stated that hospitals should be paid the costs of service delivery as determined retrospectively according to specified rules. Both the government and the hospitals believed that cost reimbursement provided greater equity and accountability than did payment of charges, the method used by commercial insurers and some Blue Cross plans. With this decision, the government intended simply to endorse prevailing hospital practice. But Medicare's and Medicaid's adoption of cost reimbursement significantly increased the portion of hospital revenues earned in this way.[9] Hence, the principles and incentives behind what was deemed "reasonable cost" reimbursement became major determinants of hospital revenues and expenditures.[10]

The principles behind cost reimbursement were shaped by the political pressures and concerns that surrounded enactment of Medicare and Medicaid.[11] By choosing cost reimbursement, program strategists sought to gain the hospital industry's cooperation in legislation. In defining costs, program administrators sought the hospital industry's cooperation in implementation. Hospitals exerted considerable pressure on administrators for liberal definitions of "allowable" costs and liberal calculations of the government's share of these costs. Although constrained by congressional reluctance to raise taxes, program administrators were anxious to assure

---

[8] The following history of Medicare payment principles is more fully developed in Judith M. Feder, *Medicare: The Politics of Federal Hospital Insurance* (Lexington, Mass.: D.C. Heath, Lexington Books, 1977).

[9] Klarman cites an American Hospital Association report of an increase of 75 percent or more in the volume of services paid for on a cost basis. See Herbert E. Klarman, "Reimbursing the Hospital—The Differences the Third-Party Makes," *Journal of Risk and Insurance* (December 1969):563. Elsewhere the authors of this chapter have compared the share of expenditures reimbursed on a cost basis in 1965 (roughly 53 percent) with the share in 1974 (roughly 68 percent), and found an increase of 28 percent. Bruce Spitz and Judith Feder, "Hospital Reimbursement" in *Altering Medicaid Provider Reimbursement Methods* (Washington, D.C.: The Urban Institute, 1977), pp. 55–56.

[10] The issue addressed here is not whether cost reimbursement is more or less inflationary than charge reimbursement, a question that has received some attention in the literature. Either system will be inflationary to the extent that providers can independently set the terms of payment. This discussion outlines the way that independence has been encouraged under the predominant cost system.

[11] See Feder, *Medicare*, especially Chapter 4.

hospital participation in Medicare and Medicaid. Accordingly, these administrators agreed with the hospitals on two payment principles: Payment should treat all hospitals "fairly" and equitably, and payment should assure beneficiaries quality or "mainstream" medical care.

Equity and quality concerns produced a commitment to pay each hospital its incurred costs. Although both the AHA and Congress recognized that one hospital's costs could be "excessive" relative to other hospitals' costs, cost differences were treated as a result of differences in quality and intensity of care. On these grounds, Congress promised that hospitals' incurred costs would be paid, "however widely they may vary from one institution to another." [12] Concern that all hospitals should receive similar treatment reinforced this approach. Program administrators and their advisers rejected as "inequitable" payment methods such as group averages that would pay some hospitals less and some more than their actual costs.

Equal treatment, however, went beyond actual costs. In some areas, policy makers were willing to pay more than actual costs to avoid the "inequity" of paying some hospitals less than others. If Medicare provided accounting options to accommodate hospitals with inadequate records or technical capacity, all hospitals could take advantage of them. If Medicare payments allowed one hospital to pay off a debt, Medicare payments should allow another hospital to accumulate internal capital. If working capital, investment capital, or unaccounted-for nursing costs were a problem for one institution, "fairness" dictated that all institutions should benefit equally from the solution. Equity meant that payment options designed to solve fiscal problems of some institutions should be available to all, whether or not the problem applied. The result was an upward bias in hospital payment.

Concern with "mainstream medicine" and quality care had a similar effect. If government financing was to replace charity care, it was argued, the government had to cover the full cost of care for its beneficiaries. The expected result was an increase in hospital revenues. The conventional wisdom of the period when Medicare and Medicaid were established—the mid-1960s—was that more revenue meant more and better

---

[12] Excerpts from Report of the Committee on Finance, U.S. Senate, to Accompany H.R. 6675, 1965, pp. 35–36, in Health Insurance Benefits Advisory Council, *New Members Background Book*, 1968, Part I.

services, and that hospital growth and development were in the public interest. People who questioned the identity of hospitals' interests with public interest, or doubted that more was necessarily better, were a small minority. In deference to the prevailing point of view, as well as to pressure from the hospital industry, allowable costs were liberally defined and apportioned—and justified as promoting quality care.

Payment policy that treats each hospital's incurred costs as "reasonable," equitable, and supportive of quality care has had two major consequences. First, this policy has provided financial resources for individual hospitals to spend as they see fit, and has thereby encouraged an upward spiral in hospital expenditures. Second, it has established standards of adequate and appropriate hospital payment that have been almost impossible to challenge.

Medicare and Medicaid increased hospital revenues and freedom to spend in several ways. First, these government programs paid the costs incurred for services previously delivered to the poor and the elderly as charity care, or not previously delivered at all.[13] Such payment increased hospitals' revenues and guaranteed that whatever hospitals spent in the delivery of care would be reimbursed by the government. Second, because government payment includes interest and depreciation, government payment has assured a return on investment in hospitals and thereby improved hospitals' access to capital markets.[14] Third, rules for calculating allowable costs and government's appropriate share encouraged hospitals to manipulate their accounts to maximize revenues.[15] The re-

---

[13] Hospital stays provided without charge fell from 17 percent of hospital stays before Medicare to 3 percent after Medicare. The number of days with charges incurred rose 50 percent. Regina Lowenstein, "Early Effects of Medicare on the Health Care of the Aged," reprinted from *Social Security Bulletin* (April 1971), Department of Health, Education, and Welfare (DHEW), Social Security Administration (SSA), p. 3.

[14] On capital financing, see Paul B. Ginsburg, "Resource Allocation in the Hospital Industry: The Role of Capital Financing," *Social Security Bulletin* 35 (October 1972):20–30; David E. Marine and John A. Henderson, "Trends in the Financing of Hospital Construction," *Hospitals, Journal of the American Hospital Association* 48 (July 1, 1974): 13; and John K. Iglehart, "Stemming Hospital Growth—The Flip Side of Carter's Cost Control Plan," *National Journal* 9 (June 4, 1977): 843–52.

[15] On accounting methods and manipulation, see Feder, *Medicare*, Chapter 4, and Bruce Spitz and Judith Feder, "Hospital Reimbursement," pp. 40–42 and 58–63.

sult has been rapid and continual increases in hospital revenues and expenditures.[16]

Hospital expenditures reflect the incentives of the several parties who shape their behavior. Physicians who use hospitals stimulate expenditures in three ways.[17] First, because they do not bear the costs of hospital resources they employ, physicians have no reason to consider the actual costs of hospital services. Hence they tend to order service, like diagnostic tests, whose costs may exceed their benefits. Second, for the same reason, physicians are likely to substitute hospital inputs for their own inputs, whose costs they *do* bear. In this way, they may increase total expenditures while reducing their own production costs.[18] Third, physician income and prestige are tightly linked with their degree of specialization, which is in turn closely related to expansion of hospital technology. As Redisch argues,

> The growth of technological applications in health care has interacted with the current orientation of medical training programs in a feedback mechanism that is leading the health care system down an explosive path. The new high cost hospital technology necessitates specialization and fosters narrow professionalism among new physicians. That is, for reasons relating to income, prestige and the way that modern medicine is practiced, new physicians are drawn away from a primary care, office-based setting and toward the practice of specialized medicine within an urban, institutionalized setting. This trend toward medical specialization in turn creates even greater demands from physicians to induce hospitals to adopt still more technology, completing the cycle and starting it anew.[19]

---

[16] On revenue and spending increases following the introduction of Medicare and Medicaid, see Karen Davis, "Hospital Costs and the Medicare Program," *Social Security Bulletin* 36 (August 1973):18–36. For history of hospital cost inflation, see Executive Office of the President, Council on Wage and Price Stability, "The Problem of Rising Health Care Costs," Staff Report, Washington, D.C., April 1976; and John K. Iglehart, "Medical Cost Quandary," *National Journal* 7 (September 20, 1975):1319–28.

[17] See Michael A. Redisch, "Cost Containment and Physician Involvement in Hospital Decision-Making," SSA, Office of Research and Statistics (photocopied).

[18] Ibid., pp. 9–13.

[19] Ibid., p. 31.

Hospital administrators respond to these demands because of their interest in attracting and retaining prestigious medical staff and in operating a large and sophisticated institution.[20] As long as their costs are reimbursed, hospitals have no reason to resist growth in the number or types of services provided.

Patients and communities reinforce hospitals and physicians in these biases. Just as insurance removes an individual's responsibility to pay for the services he or she consumes, insurance also removes a community's responsibility to pay for the services available to it. Insurance premiums and taxes are typically collected from more than one community; hence each community has an incentive to increase services available to its residents at the expense of nonresidents.

The result is a continual increase in the number and type of hospital services that constitute hospital care, and correspondingly greater increases in the price of a day in the hospital than in the consumer price index.[21] As hospital expenditures absorb an increasing proportion of the federal budget and the gross national product,[22] policy makers and health professionals increasingly ask, Is hospital care worth the price? Answers must distinguish between two sources of hospital inflation. In one category are expenditures that represent waste and inefficiency, either for the medical care system as a whole or within individual hospitals. These expenditures include construction and maintenance of unnecessary hospital beds, inappropriate reliance on hospitals versus other delivery settings, duplication of expensive equipment, and unnecessary

---

[20] For theories of administrators' behavior, see Philip Jacobs, "A Survey of Economic Models of Hospitals," *Inquiry* 11 (June 1974):83–97; and Karen Davis, "Economic Theories of Behavior in Nonprofit, Private Hospitals," *Economic and Business Bulletin* 24 (Winter 1972): 1–13.

[21] See Redisch, "Cost Containment and Physician Involvement in Hospital Decision-Making"; and U.S. Congress, Senate, Committee on the Budget, *Hearings on the First Concurrent Resolution of the Budget, Fiscal Year 1978*, vol. 3, 95th Congress, 1st Session, 1977, Statement of Dr. Stuart Altman, especially pp. 109–10.

[22] Iglehart, "Medical Cost Quandary," p. 1319; Altman, in *Hearings*, p. 107.

or harmful service delivery.[23] In 1977, the Department of Health, Education, and Welfare (DHEW) estimated that elimination of these and other inefficiencies could reduce total U.S. hospital costs more than $5 billion or about 16 percent.[24]

Even if a health insurance program could eliminate inefficiencies and limit covered services to those that provide some positive value, however, a second category of hospital expenditures would still pose a resource allocation problem. To the extent that individuals are insured and hospitals are paid incurred costs, hospital administrators, physicians, communities, and patients have every reason to seek expansion of services as long as they provide some positive benefits; no one has any incentive to compare benefits to costs. As a result, the resource or opportunity costs of hospital expenditures on services will exceed the benefits derived. In other words, people will sacrifice more in other goods and services than hospital care is worth.[25]

Recognition of these problems has not produced solutions. Incurred costs remain the predominant basis for hospital payment, and resources continue to pour into hospital services.

---

[23] For discussion of duplication and excess, see National Academy of Sciences, Institute of Medicine, "Controlling the Supply of Hospital Beds," Washington, D.C., 1976; Walter McClure, *Reducing Excess Hospital Capacity*, prepared for Bureau of Health Planning and Resources Development, (Minneapolis: Interstudy, 1976); Clifton R. Gaus and Barbara S. Cooper, "Technology and Medicare: Alternatives for Change" (typewritten); National Academy of Sciences, Institute of Medicine, "Computed Tomographic Scanning: A Policy Statement," Washington, D.C., 1977; Howard A. Hiatt, "Protecting the Medical Commons—Who Has the Responsibility?" *The New England Journal of Medicine* 293 (1975):235–41; A.L. Cochrane, *Effectiveness and Efficiency: Random Reflections on Health Services* (London: The Nuffield Provincial Hospital Trust, 1972); and U.S. House, Committee on Oversight and Investigations, *Getting Ready for National Health Insurance: Unnecessary Surgery*, 94th Congress, 1st Session, 1975.

[24] Joseph A. Califano, Jr., statement, p. 9. The Social Security Administration estimated 1976 expenditures for hospital care at $30.4 billion. Robert M. Gibson and Marjorie Smith Mueller, "National Health Expenditures, Fiscal Year 1976," *Social Security Bulletin* 40 (April 1977):11, Table 4.

[25] For development of this argument, see Clark C. Havighurst and James F. Blumstein, "Coping with Quality Cost Trade-Offs in Medical Care: The Role of PSROs (Professional Standards Review Organizations)," *Northwestern University Law Review* 70 (March–April 1975): 6–68.

The persistence of the problem is directly related to the second consequence of cost reimbursement—entrenchment of its principles as a standard for appropriate hospital reimbursement. Based on equity and quality, and officially characterized as "reasonable," reimbursement for costs that hospitals incur has acquired a legitimacy that, for both analytical and political reasons, has been difficult to overcome.

The analytical problem is the difficulty of developing objective measures of hospital outputs and production costs. If we could specify what a hospital produces, what we want it to produce, and what efficient production should cost, we would have an objective standard against which to evaluate costs that hospitals incur. But this specification is extremely complicated. Hospital production traditionally has been measured in terms of patient-days or admissions, measures that fail to account for differences in the kinds of patients a hospital admits (its case mix) or in the level of care it provides (intensity). A more specific measure, like diagnosis-specific admissions, gives more information but fails to allow for differences in patient conditions and differences in intensity of treatment. As a student of hospital production explained, if we find differences in hospital expenditures for the same diagnosis, we need to know whether that difference is a function of the unit price of services, the number and type of services provided, the clinical condition of the patient, or some combination of these.[26] Unless we can distinguish among the factors that constitute output and determine their appropriate costs, we cannot define efficient production of quality care.

Inability to define efficiently produced quality care presents a political problem. Without a definition of the desired output, it becomes extremely difficult to challenge a hospital's claim to the "reasonableness" of the costs it incurs. Equity and quality, with which cost reimbursement was initially justified, provide a rationale for continuation of this reimbursement policy. Hospitals challenge as "inequitable" any payment methods that fail to take into account the particular circumstances of each institution or that treat some institutions better than others. Furthermore, the hospitals argue, payment restrictions would threaten hospitals' capacity to deliver quality care to

---

[26] Discussions with Marcia Goldfarb, National Center for Health Services Research. For a general discussion of problems in defining hospital output, see Sylvester E. Berki, *Hospital Economics* (Lexington, Mass.: D.C. Heath, Lexington Books, 1972).

government beneficiaries. When payers lack an objective standard and appropriate data to challenge these claims, providers retain the upper hand against proposals to limit revenues.

Hospital dominance is reinforced by two facts: (1) the hospitals' ability to opt out of the public system when the government pays for care for only part of the population; and (2) the influence of hospital interests versus public interests in the policy process. With Medicare and Medicaid programs, the government constantly faces the threat that hospitals will refuse to treat government-financed patients or will provide them "second-class" care. The importance of Medicare and Medicaid revenues makes it unlikely that many hospitals will refuse to serve government patients. But for political purposes, an industrywide hospital boycott is unnecessary. Refusal to participate by a few prominent hospitals would probably suffice. This threat is believable and therefore effective.[27]

Even without this threat, policy makers tend to be more responsive to the particular interests of providers than to the general interest of taxpayers and consumers.[28] The hospital industry and the medical profession, both of whom benefit from maximum payment with minimum control, are readily mobilized for political action to protect their interests. Acquiescing in those interests imposes costs, primarily in rising medical expenditures and taxes, without regard to the health benefits derived. But because those costs are widely distributed among consumers and taxpayers for whom medical care is only one of many concerns, it is difficult to mobilize people for political action.[29] Congressional committees or government officials who have competing program objectives and want to avoid raising taxes may attach greater concern to controlling costs and may, therefore, challenge hospital interests. But these groups, too, feel greater pressure from the hospital industry than from the public at large, and thus often acquiesce in the industry's interests. Persistent vigilance by the hospitals and intermittent pressure on behalf of taxpayers and con-

---

[27] On government-hospital bargaining, see Spitz and Feder, "Hospital Reimbursement," pp. 84–88.

[28] James Q. Wilson, "The Politics of American Business Regulation," in James McKie, ed., *Social Responsibility and the Business Predicament* (Washington, D.C.: The Brookings Institution, 1974).

[29] Ibid.

sumers have combined to perpetuate reimbursement of "reasonable" costs.

This set of circumstances poses a dilemma for public policy. On one hand, policy makers are dissatisfied with a payment mechanism that delegates resource allocation decisions to providers (thereby inducing inflation that inhibits access to care for the uninsured), requires continual increases in taxes and premiums for the working population, and limits alternative use of the public and private resources. On the other hand, policy makers seek an undefinable goal of payment for efficiently produced quality care. Because an undefinable goal is analytically and politically indefensible, ostensibly "new" approaches to payment have had little effect on expenditures. The following account illustrates how and why these approaches have produced such meager results.

Approaches to Hospital Cost Containment

RESTRICTING ALLOWABLE COSTS

When payers are worried about rising payments under cost reimbursement, their first recourse is to restrict definitions of costs deemed "allowable" and to refine accounting methods by which hospitals allocate costs among payers. Although policy makers treated hospitals liberally in designing Medicare and Medicaid payment procedures, then and later they have restricted payments as they found such action politically feasible.[30] Their actions reflect three objectives: (1) restriction of payment to costs related to patient care; (2) avoidance of government program subsidy of the general population; and (3) elimination of specific cases of obvious excess and gross exploitation of program funds, particularly for personal gain.

In operational terms, restriction of reimbursement to patient-related activities has meant disallowance of costs associated with basic research and with non-patient-related activities (gift shops, parking lots, public cafeterias, etc.) plus special arrangements with respect to payment for physicians' teaching activities. Medicare and Medicaid have tried to avoid cross-subsidies (1) by refusing to pay for nonbeneficiaries' bad debts and for charity care and (2) by replacing the predominant method of allocating a hospital's costs (on the basis

---

[30] Feder, *Medicare*, Chapters 4 and 6.

of an average patient-day) with allocation according to a ratio of beneficiary charges to total charges. In what officials themselves have characterized as piecemeal efforts to control abuse, Medicare and Medicaid have imposed limits on payment for purchases from related organizations, franchise fees, advertising costs, return on capital investments, and depreciation. Furthermore, they have established as a general principle that hospitals should not spend more for the items they purchase than a "prudent buyer" would pay—that is, the going market price.[31]

Although disallowances and exclusions do somewhat restrict hospital revenues, their potential for overall cost containment is limited by two factors: the leeway in hospital accounting and the capacity of hospitals to absorb constantly rising revenues in allowable categories. In the absence of uniform accounting requirements, hospitals have many opportunities for accounting manipulation; they can distribute overhead and set charges in ways that increase Medicare and Medicaid liabilities. Evidence from Medicare cost reports indicates that hospitals have used these opportunities with the result that "the Medicare program subsidizes a portion of the care provided to non-Medicare patients in these hospitals."[32] The government has responded to this tendency by restricting accounting options;[33] but this practice limits rather than eliminates opportunity for maneuver.

Even without manipulation, specific disallowances have a limited impact on costs because of their narrow focus. Restrictions can inhibit specific abuses, but they do not address the uncontrolled expansion of labor and capital resources—both in quantity and price—devoted to patient care.[34]

[31] Ibid., Chapter 6; Commerce Clearing House, *Medicare and Medicaid Guide,* paragraph 5852.

[32] Fred J. Hellinger, "Hospital Charges and Medicare Reimbursement," *Inquiry* 12 (December 1975):313–19. On accounting manipulation, see Spitz and Feder, "Hospital Reimbursement," pp. 58–63. In general, the extent to which government programs subsidize other patients or vice versa depends on the size and proportion of these patients to total patient population and the identification of program-specific services.

[33] Feder, *Medicare,* Chapter 6.

[34] Altman, statement in *Hearings,* p. 110; and Stuart A. Altman and Joseph Eichenholz, "Inflation in the Health Industry—Causes and Cures," in Michael Zubkoff, ed., *Health: A Victim or Cause of Inflation?* (New York: Prodist, for the Milbank Memorial Fund, 1976), p. 15, Table 5.

DIRECT REGULATION

Recognizing these problems, policy makers have turned to direct regulation of hospital activity. This regulation takes two forms. First is the regulation of hospitals' facility and service expansion by designated state and local planning agencies. In an effort to contain costs, public and private third parties have refused to reimburse some or all hospital costs associated with expenditures that planning agencies have disapproved. Second, public and private third parties have instituted oversight and review of services provided in the hospital. Utilization review requirements and the emergence of Professional Standards Review Organizations (PSROs) represent attempts by public and private third-party payers to avoid payment for and to inhibit delivery of inappropriate or unnecessary care. Detailed analysis of these regulatory mechanisms is beyond the scope of this chapter. Questions about mechanisms' effectiveness relate not only to regulators' general incapacity to override the interests of the regulated,[35] but also to regulators' particular incapacity in cases in which regulation occurs in the absence of resource constraints. As former DHEW official Stuart Altman has observed,

> . . . unless payment changes are made, the fledgling efforts underway in health planning, certificate-of-need, and PSR [O]'s are likely to fail. To expect supply regulators to continuously stand in the way of more sophisticated and new services which the medical community believes are necessary and the patients through their third parties have the means to pay for is asking the impossible. Only when there are constraints on the availability of funds to providers can we expect meaningful discussions to take place about what services are really necessary and how important it is that there be better access to particular types of care.[36]

---

[35] Roger Noll, *Reforming Regulation: An Evaluation of the Ash Council Proposals*, a staff paper, Studies in the Regulation of Economic Activity (Washington, D.C.: The Brookings Institution, 1971). For extension of this analysis to certificate of need and PSROs, see Clark Havighurst, "Regulation of Health Facilities and Service by 'Certificate-of-Need,'" *Virginia Law Review* 59 (1973):1143–1232; and Havighurst and Blumstein, "Coping with Quality Cost Trade-Offs in Medical Care."

[36] Altman, statement in *Hearings*, p. 115.

Some early evidence to support this argument comes from hospitals' responses to capital expenditures or certificate-of-need (CON) regulation; as measured to date, restrictions on bed expansion have been offset by hospital investment in equipment and other facilities. As a result, CON regulation had little or no effect on hospital costs.[37]

INCENTIVE REIMBURSEMENT

As policy makers have recognized the obstacles to effective regulation in the face of "powerful incentive systems whose rewards and penalties encourage precisely the opposite results of those sought by the program," [38] a third approach to cost containment has received considerable attention. This approach is "incentive reimbursement," that is, incorporation into hospital payment of incentives for efficient delivery of care. Although this concept has broadened into "prospective reimbursement"—payment set in advance—historical differences in emphasis make it appropriate to consider the two concepts one at a time.

Incentive reimbursement came to prominence in the hospital payment field almost immediately after Medicare and Medicaid expanded the application of cost reimbursement. According to conventional wisdom, no system could be more likely to encourage inefficiencies, waste, and uncontrollable costs than the one that had been adopted. Accordingly, in the health field a cry arose for incentives to encourage efficiency in hospital reimbursement. The result was "experimentation" with reimbursement "incentives" in both the private and public sectors.[39]

Evidence from 1967 to 1972, when these experiments were at their height, reveals the limitations of the incentive approach. First, proponents of incentive reimbursement ignored the absence of consensus on definitions of output and quality,

---

[37] David S. Salkever and Thomas W. Bice, *Hospital Certificate-of-Need Controls: Impact on Investment Cost and Use* (Washington, D.C.: American Enterprise Institute for Public Policy Research, 1979).

[38] Charles L. Schultze, *The Politics and Economics of Public Spending*, (Washington, D.C.: The Brookings Institution, 1968), pp. 104–05.

[39] For a discussion of these developments and the government's response, see Feder, *Medicare*, Chapter 5.

without which the concept of "efficiency" is meaningless. In advocating attention to incentives, Charles Schultze emphasizes that

> . . . the development of incentive systems requires that particular attention be paid to the careful specification of objectives and the measurement of performance in the light of these objectives. We must, after all, first decide what it really is that we wish to provide rewards for or penalties against before we can devise positive incentive schemes or modify existing ones.[40]

In authorizing Medicare reimbursement experimentation, the House Ways and Means Committee called attention to this problem, particularly with respect to quality of care.[41] Without measures and definitions of both output and quality, an absolute decline in total costs might indicate (1) an improvement in efficiency (production of the same quality of output at less cost), (2) a decline in output, or (3) a deterioration in quality. Unfortunately, as noted above, such measures and definitions were not available at the time. In the absence of any detailed specification of desired outcomes, proponents of incentive reimbursement tended to assume that "efficient" production would follow incentive rewards.

Second, incentive schemes assumed (1) that hospitals function under a unified and hierarchical organizational structure in which administrators control organizational production, and (2) that administrators have a stake in minimizing costs. The first assumption ignores the dispersion of decision-making authority in the hospital. Because hospital administrators are dependent on their medical staffs, administrators may control only a small proportion of hospital activities. Administrator interest in financial rewards or sanctions may have little effect on the key decision makers, the physicians.[42]

Even the assumption that administrators respond to mone-

---

[40] Schultze, *The Politics and Economics of Public Spending*, p. 106.

[41] U.S. Congress, House, *Report of the Committee on Ways and Means on H.R. 1: Social Security Amendments of 1971*, 92nd Congress, 1st Session, House Report No. 92–231, May 26, 1971, pp. 80–81.

[42] On the influence of physicians on hospital expenditures, see Redisch, "Cost Containment and Physician Involvement in Hospital Decision-Making."

tary incentives is open to question. Administrators derive prestige and professional advancement from the size and reputation of their institutions and their medical staffs. As former Medicare official Irwin Wolkstein has observed,

> The success of a hospital in its administration may be measured not merely by hospital efficiency but also by the completeness of hospital facilities, the fame of its staff, and the wealth of its patients. None of these is necessarily highly correlated with efficiency. . . .[43]

The ability to test whether incentive reimbursement schemes could overcome these obstacles was significantly limited by a third problem—the voluntary nature of the incentive experiments. Neither private Blue Cross plans nor Medicare and Medicaid could require hospitals to participate in alternatives to reasonable cost reimbursement, so incentive schemes were designed to avoid both political conflict and analytical complexity. Accordingly, these schemes focused on hotel, more than medical, services in hospitals; evaluated performance within each hospital rather than for the community as a whole; and were restricted to reliance on positive incentives or financial rewards rather than the more powerful tools of limits or sanctions. These rewards had only limited appeal. Administrators facing a choice between full cost reimbursement and, under an incentive scheme, a share in any savings below a target, would have little reason to prefer the latter. Inasmuch as all revenues in nonprofit institutions go to hospital expenses, hospital administrators have little reason to prefer saving money in order to spend it, rather than simply spending money and receiving full cost reimbursement.[44]

---

[43] Irwin Wolkstein, "The Legislative History of Hospital Cost Reimbursement," in DHEW, SSA, Office of Research and Statistics, *Reimbursement Incentives for Hospital and Medical Care: Objectives and Alternatives*, Research Report No. 26, 1968, p. 14.

[44] For further discussion, see Katherine G. Bauer and Paul M. Densen, "Some Issues in the Incentive Reimbursement Approach to Cost Containment: An Overview," Health Care Policy Discussion Paper No. 7, May 1973, Harvard Center for Community Health and Medical Care, Program on Health Care Policy, Boston, Massachusetts. Students of incentive schemes found that administrative interest in acquiring the expertise and leverage of outside consultants was a more important stimulus to participation in experiments than were financial rewards.

Finally, expectations of the effectiveness of financial rewards in a single year ignore the continuing nature of reimbursement negotiations. Hospital administrators, like government contractors in other fields, take a long-term view of the reimbursement process. For example, if reimbursement is based on a target, hospital administrators are as much concerned with the level of the target as with any reward they might gain from performance below target. Performance too far below target would reduce the administrators' capacity to negotiate a higher target in future years.[45]

In sum, "incentive reimbursement" posed narrow or imprecise objectives and offered few, if any, real incentives to achieve them. Partly as a result of their awareness of these problems, Medicare officials approached experimentation cautiously and undertook very few experiments of this nature.[46] Those they initiated had little or no effect on costs and thus confirmed the inadequacies of voluntary incentive reimbursement.[47]

PROSPECTIVE PAYMENT

Rising hospital costs and the ineffectiveness of highly touted solutions have stimulated more rhetoric than action by the federal government over the past decade. But state governments responsible for Medicare expenditures and regulation of Blue Cross premiums and Blue Cross plans themselves have tried to go beyond "incentive reimbursement" in their efforts to restrain hospital reimbursement. From the mid-1970s, the research branch of the Medicare program has encouraged evaluation and further development of payment methods.[48]

---

[45] See, for example, Katherine G. Bauer and Arva Rosenfeld Clark, "New York: The Formula Approach to Prospective Reimbursement," Harvard Center for Community Health and Medical Care, March 1974, p. ix and p. 33. For similar observations on defense contracting, see J. Ronald Fox, *Arming America: How the U.S. Buys Weapons* (Cambridge, Mass.: Harvard Business School, 1974), pp. 240–47.

[46] See Feder, *Medicare*, Chapter 5.

[47] For a comprehensive review of the incentive experiments, see Carol McCarthy, "Incentive Reimbursement as an Impetus to Cost Containment," *Inquiry* 12 (December 1975):320–29.

[48] For Social Security's role and ongoing experiments, see John K. Iglehart, "Government Searching for a More Cost-Efficient Way to Pay Hospitals," *National Journal* (December 25, 1976):1822–29.

These efforts come under the rubric of prospective payment, which is broadly defined as payment set in advance.

Prospective payment is expected to contain costs by limiting payer obligations in advance and by encouraging efficient funds management by hospitals. Retrospective reimbursement has neither of these features. But as a former Medicare official observed, prospective reimbursement is a mechanism not a policy.[49] Experience to date reveals that a change in timing does not in itself eliminate from hospital payment the choices associated with "reasonable costs." Although payers and regulators have a variety of objectives, they frequently commit themselves to payment "reasonably related to the efficient production of services of good quality." [50] We have repeatedly observed that this output remains hard to define, and therefore hard to attain. As a result, third parties and regulators tend to define "reasonable" in terms of hospitals' actual cost experience, to accept the structure of the existing delivery system, and to address only incremental changes in hospital behavior that seem particularly outrageous.[51]

Payers' ability to contain even these increments is restricted to the share of hospital costs that their payment scheme covers.[52] As long as there are multiple payers with separate and different payment arrangements, hospitals can play payers off against each other—that is, shift costs that one does not cover onto others.

Prospective payment methods can be divided into two broad types, the formula or target budget approach and the budget review and negotiation approach.[53] Variations of the first

[49] Quoted in Feder, *Medicare*, Chapter 6.

[50] Katherine G. Bauer, "Improving the Information for Hospital Rate Setting," Harvard Center for Community Health and Medical Care, Report Series R-45-15, September 1976, p. 11.

[51] For analysis of existing prospective reimbursement schemes and their limitations, see Katherine G. Bauer, "Hospital Rate Setting—This Way to Salvation?" *Milbank Memorial Fund Quarterly* 55 (Winter 1977):117-58.

[52] For estimates of those shares, see ibid., p. 126.

[53] For comprehensive treatment, see ibid.; William L. Dowling, "Prospective Reimbursement of Hospitals," *Inquiry* 11 (September 1974): 163-80; Paul J. Feldstein and John Goddeeris, "Payment for Hospital Services: Objectives and Alternatives," Health Manpower Policy Studies Group, School of Public Health, The University of Michigan, Ann Arbor, December 1976; and Susan S. Laudicina, "Prospective Reimbursement for Hospitals: A Guide for Policymakers," Department of Public Affairs, Community Service Society of New York, October 1976.

method have appeared in New York State's rate-setting program, Medicare's Section 223, the Talmadge amendments to Medicare, the Economic Stabilization Program, and the cost containment legislation proposed by the Carter administration. With the formula or target budget approach, hospital payment in the coming year is based on cost or revenue experience in an earlier year projected forward for inflation. The base-year experience may be either that of each individual hospital or an average of several hospitals, and the target set may be a payment ceiling or an actual rate. The primary advantages of this approach are its administrative control and the simplicity of a statistical method; its disadvantages are its tendency to perpetuate the base distribution of resources and its limited capacity to respond to particular circumstances.

Alternatively, payment may be set by budget review and negotiation. With this approach, the payer or regulator reviews and evaluates each hospital's proposed expenditures, and a final budget is negotiated and approved. The budget review method allows review of resource distribution and individual treatment of hospitals; but at the same time it poses a considerable administrative burden on regulators and offers hospitals an opportunity to exert political pressure.

Features of the formula and budget review methods can be combined.[54] A budget review system can use statistical norms as guidelines or triggers for review; formulas can incorporate standards for resource allocation. Moreover, a formula can be used to set an aggregate limit on expenditures for a group of hospitals and individual budgets can be negotiated within that limit. Finally, proposed budgets can be reviewed periodically, such as every three to five years, with a formula applied between reviews. The objectives of the combination are to enhance control, to minimize administrative burdens, and to provide flexibility in resource allocation.

Regardless of approach, all reimbursement mechanisms require political choices about seemingly technical points, including definition of covered costs, limits on payment, exclusions from payment ceiling, treatment of inflation, revenue offsets, units of payment, and appeals and adjustments. These issues are discussed in the following paragraphs.

---

[54] Dowling, "Prospective Reimbursement of Hospitals," p. 174.

Covered Expenditures

This issue addresses the choice of expenses to be included in either a base budget or an approved budget that patient revenues could appropriately cover. In essence, this decision relates to "allowable costs" and, as such, broadly determines the liberality or restrictiveness of third-party payment. Specifically, prospective payers must decide whether to allow revenues to cover bad debts, charity care, research, professional education, and working and investment capital.

The treatment of capital expenditures has been the area of greatest controversy in determining covered costs. Capital has been handled in two ways. Hospitals have sought and sometimes received an automatic allowance for technological change —or "intensity factor"—in addition to otherwise allowable expenditures. Although this allowance enhances a hospital's flexibility, it does not cover capital and operating costs of major capital investment. Reimbursement for major investment depends on review of proposed changes in facilities and services by the payment regulator or by the state agency charged with health planning and facilities regulation.

The distinction between payment and planning poses several complications. In determining the "need" for or desirability of hospital expansion, planning agencies have rarely taken costs into account. Conversely, payment regulators tend to be less concerned with socially desirable facility development and distribution than with controlling expenditures. Both perspectives are desirable in payment determination, but frequently they have not been integrated. How the planning and payment bureaucracies interact greatly affects payment determinations.[55] Once a hospital receives planning agency approval for a change in services or facilities, its position before the payment regulator is significantly enhanced. Thus, if the planning agency has failed to consider the cost implications of the

---

[55] For discussions of planning and rate setting, see Drew Altman, "Connections Between Hospital Rate Setting and Planning in Maryland and Rhode Island," Harvard Center for Community Health and Medical Care, Report Series R–45–6, June 1976; Katherine G. Bauer and Drew Altman, "Linking Planning and Rate-Setting Control to Contain Hospital Costs," Harvard Center for Community Health and Medical Care, October 24, 1975; and Conference on State Rate Setting, Social Security Administration (SSA), Office of Research and Statistics, Division of Health Insurance Studies, Sterling, Virginia, November 8–9, 1976.

change, the payment regulator may be compelled to approve an investment for which the costs outweigh the benefits. Even when planners have considered costs, the division in regulatory responsibility presents opportunities for hospital manipulation. Thus hospitals have been known to present one set of cost estimates for planning agency approval and a higher set for purposes of payment determination.[56]

In practice, payers and planners have dealt with each other differently in different states. In New York, the payment agencies accept approval by a planning agency as justification for increasing reimbursement, but payment agencies still must determine how much the increase should be. In Maryland, though, payment regulators have refused to reimburse for changes that planning agencies have approved. In Rhode Island, planners develop priorities for expenditures for the state as a whole within spending limits negotiated between payers and the hospitals.[57] Unless the two regulatory responsibilities are smoothly integrated, efforts to contain costs can be undermined.

Limits on Payments

Closely related to the payer's or regulator's decision on expenditures to reimburse is the decision on how much to pay. Determination of expenditure levels entails several elements. First is the choice of a standard for desirable, or efficient, performance. As discussed earlier, an ideal standard would specify the inputs and costs for a specific intensity and quality of care delivered to a specific population. Comprehensive evaluation of hospital performance in relation to this standard requires abundant data. Katherine Bauer has identified the following areas of importance.

- Scope of service offered by hospital(s), including service complexity and physician specialist mix;
- Burden of illness brought to the hospital(s) for care, for example, diagnostic case mix, case complexity, patient age, and income characteristics;
- Nature, volume, and timeliness of services rendered;

---

[56] Discussion among state rate setters at SSA Rate-Setting Conference.

[57] See Katherine G. Bauer and Arva Rosenfeld Clark, "Case Studies in Prospective Reimbursement for the Social Security Administration," evaluations of rate-setting experiments on contract from the Social Security Administration; and Drew Altman, "Connections Between Hospital Rate Setting and Planning."

- Prices hospital(s) must pay for necessary labor and non-labor inputs;
- Efficiency of service delivery in terms of flexible staffing in relation to volume changes, internal management controls, and the like;
- Appropriateness of patient care rendered in relation to patient needs and population needs;
- Quality of care rendered;
- Duplications in facilities and services (especially high-technology services) in hospital service areas or regions and gaps in access;
- Trends in per capita utilization and per capita expenditures for hospital services in the region, and their relationship to total health care utilization and expenditures; and
- Outcomes to patients and populations in terms of health and well-being.[58]

No payment process comes close to meeting these requirements, either in theory or in practice. With problems ranging from the absence of uniform hospital accounting and reporting procedures to the lack of consensus on the contribution of medical care to patient health, it is not clear that any payment process will ever approach these requirements. So how can hospital payments be limited? One answer is to avoid complex evaluation by basing expenditure limits on the government's willingness or capacity to spend, rather than on hospital performance. Prior government commitments to equity, quality, and "reasonableness," however, lead to exceptions in the application of these limits. Pressed to justify their ceilings, payers resort to hospital comparisons to define efficiency and quality. They arrange hospitals in groups according to size, location, educational role, case mix, or other factors assumed to assure similar output; they analyze hospitals' cost experience on a service, department, or other basis; they establish a statistical norm as a ceiling or screen; and they reject costs exceeding the norm in the formula method and review those costs in the budget review or negotiation approach.[59]

Hospital comparisons present several problems, including, first, a decision about the basis for classification. If classification is based on the simplest characteristics of hospitals, such as size and location, hospitals complain that the nature of their

---

[58] Bauer, "Improving the Information for Hospital Rate Setting," p. 24.
[59] See Bauer, "Hospital Rate Setting—This Way to Salvation," p. 137.

case mix, intensity of services, and educational activity are being inadequately considered and that therefore they are being compared with dissimilar hospitals. On this basis, hospitals contest their classification and related payment limitations, and press payers for adjustments.[60]

To deal with this problem, payers and regulators have developed more sophisticated classifications and standards for evaluating particular costs, including (1) minimum occupancy criteria for operating costs;[61] (2) Maryland's "target bed" estimates for determining capital payments;[62] and, still developing, (3) comparison of costs according to case mix.[63] Better data affect hospital-payer bargaining by giving payers defensible grounds for withstanding hospital claims for additional payment, but this advantage is gained at a cost. Detailed data requirements both complicate administration and raise problems of data availability and accuracy. Evaluation of cost-reporting systems has revealed inaccuracies in discharge diagnosis data resulting from communication problems [64] and from discrepancies in judgment and classification.[65] Bauer summarizes data problems:

> Researchers and analysts who work with both the Medicare cost reports and the cost/budget reports used for rate setting find that hospitals usually report the dollars they spend and receive completely and well, but that they report the other half of the cost

[60] See, for example, testimony on behalf of the Association of American Medical Colleges, p. 104, in U.S. Congress, Senate, Committee on Finance, *Medicare-Medicaid Administration and Reimbursement Reform*, 94th Congress, 2nd Session, July 1976. For similar problems in Canada, see Karin A. Dumbaugh, "Hospital Information Systems in the Province of Quebec," Harvard Center for Community Health and Medical Care, Report Series R–45–2, January 1976.

[61] Bauer, "Hospital Rate Setting—This Way to Salvation," pp. 140 and 142.

[62] See Harold A. Cohen, "Experience of a State Cost Control Commission," p. 411, in Michael Zubkoff, Ira E. Raskin, and Ruth S. Hanft, eds., *Hospital Cost Containment* (New York: Prodist, for Milbank Memorial Fund, 1978).

[63] Bauer, "Hospital Rate Setting—This Way to Salvation," pp. 144–45 and Laudicina, "Prospective Reimbursement for Hospitals," pp. 36–39.

[64] Diane Rowland, "Data Rich and Information Poor; Medicare's Resources for Prospective Rate Settings," Harvard Center for Community Health and Medical Care, Report Series R–45–12, July 1976, p. 78.

[65] Dumbaugh, "Hospital Information Systems in the Province of Quebec," p. 45.

equations—their input and output statistics—quite unevenly.

Inconsistencies of definition are one major source of unreliability. For example, unless the instructions that accompany the forms are highly specific, reasonable people can and do differ in their interpretations of what may constitute "major" versus "minor" equipment, "short term" versus "long term" loans, etc. The completeness and accuracy with which particular measures of activity are reported also leave much to be desired. Even the basic denominator of all inpatient cost comparisons, a hospital's bed complement, is not always reported consistently.[66]

How far payers and regulators must go in collecting and improving data is related to what standard is adopted for adequate hospital payment. Less information may be necessary to support or defend a limit on government expenditures than to guarantee "efficient production of quality care"—hence the significance of the choice of program goals both to cost containment and administrative costs.

The second problem with comparisons is that they are insufficient to set a ceiling on costs. The problem stems from two sources: the inappropriateness of the norm and the norm's responsiveness to hospital behavior. On the first point, Feldstein and Goddeeris have maintained the following:

If, as many observers suggest, the present situation is one in which considerable unnecessary duplication of facilities and services exists, then the average costs of providing some hospital services (even if each hospital is internally efficient) do not represent the minimum cost at which those services could be provided.[67]

Furthermore, the divergence between minimum and average costs may increase if average costs become a ceiling.

_____

[66] Bauer, "Improving the Information for Hospital Rate Setting," pp. 28–29.

[67] Feldstein and Goddeeris, "Payment for Hospital Services," p. 50.

Ceilings based on statistical averages (and typically even statistical cost functions) rise as hospitals use more resources. If the mean cost experience of a group of hospitals becomes the ceiling, hospitals have an incentive to move toward it. Any savings to third-party payers therefore depend on the distribution of liabilities among institutions above and below the mean, and on the length of time it takes for hospitals to adjust their expenditures or their accounting practices to the average. Furthermore, because such ceilings are often set not at the mean but at the mean plus a percentage of the mean, the mean is likely to increase at the specified percentage rate. Finally, to the extent that hospitals obtain resources outside reimbursement to finance expansion, even this specified percentage rate is likely to be pushed upward. Once expansion occurs, the mean will reflect it and the ceiling will move upward.[68] For these reasons, ceilings based on hospital industry performance cannot limit hospital costs.

Exclusions from Ceilings

Whatever ceilings are set, prospective payers face pressure to treat some expenditures separately, that is, to leave them outside the ceiling. On the broadest level, decisions have been made to distinguish between routine and ancillary costs. Ceilings have most commonly been applied to routine costs, on grounds that they are subject to administrative control, relatively uniform across different types of hospitals, and outside the controversial area of physician behavior. Medicare's Section 223, for example, imposes ceilings on routine but not ancillary costs. Exception of ancillary costs both reduces control over a critical segment of hospital costs and allows hospitals to shift overhead costs from routine to ancillary services in order to avoid ceilings.[69] Dissatisfaction with these results

---

[68] For discussion of hospital responses to this approach, see ibid., pp. 51–52; Dowling, "Prospective Reimbursement of Hospitals," p. 174; and J. Michael Fitzmaurice, "An Evaluation of Alternative Systems for Establishing Hospital Reimbursement Limits Under Medicare," presented at the American Public Health Association Annual Meeting, October 1976 (photocopied).

[69] "Highlights of the Health Insurance Benefits Advisory Council Meeting," Washington, D.C., May 10–11, 1976 (typewritten), p. 23.

has led New York to extend ceilings to ancillary costs[70] and has put pressure on Senator Talmadge to include ancillary costs in his proposed amendments to Medicare and Medicaid.[71]

Hearings on the 1976 Talmadge amendments revealed the importance of inclusions and exclusions to both payers and hospitals. On grounds that specified expenditures reflected differences in hospital output, the Talmadge proposal excluded from its proposed limit on routine costs expenditures related to capital, direct hospital education, intern and resident salaries, and energy to heat and cool the hospital plant. The Ford administration reacted with concern that the proposed ceiling applied to only 35 percent of a hospital's expenditures as compared with application to 50 percent under the existing Medicare Section 223 ceiling. Hospitals, conversely, applauded the exclusion from ceilings of costs "beyond the control of the administration of an institution," and advocated further exclusion of energy costs and of malpractice insurance premiums.[72]

The application of screens and ceilings raises extremely controversial questions for the treatment of hospitals' wages and salaries. Unlimited payment policies allow hospitals to pass on wage increases to third-party payers. Over the past several years, the gap in earnings between hospital workers and other wage earners in the economy has diminished and hospitals have increased their employment of relatively highly paid, highly skilled personnel.[73] Payers or payment regulators who try to constrain wage and salary increases become involved in wage and salary negotiations. Payers might want to ignore wages and salaries in setting a payment ceiling, or they might want to tie hospital and salary increases to general wage and salary increases in the economy. In either case, if what results is a relatively tight constraint, payers are likely to be

---

[70] "Evaluation of Blue Cross and Medicaid Prospective Reimbursement Systems in Downstate New York," Final Report, June 1976, DHEW–OS–74–248, Principal Investigator, William Dowling, Department of Health Services, School of Public Health and Community Medicine, University of Washington, p. I–7, note 3. New York's payment method is under litigation at the time of writing.

[71] Commerce Clearing House, *Medicare and Medicaid Guide,* Update No. 207, June 10, 1977, p. 1.

[72] *Medicare-Medicaid Administrative and Reimbursement Reform,* pp. 31 and 126.

[73] Altman and Eichenholz, "Inflation in the Health Industry," p. 19.

under considerable pressure from hospital unions for exceptions and adjustments. Hospital administrators, who will try to avoid being squeezed between payer and union pressure, may well support union demands. Evidence on the strength of union pressure comes from the Carter administration's decision to exclude wages and salaries from its proposed ceiling on hospital revenues.[74] Enacting such a proposal is likely to undermine cost containment. Evidence from Canada, discussed later, suggests that the government must address appropriate labor costs if it wants to contain hospital costs.[75] Because any exclusion allows continued inflation, cost control requires that all expenditures must be subject to cost ceilings.

Inflation Index

Once payers determine acceptable or allowable costs at a particular time, they must decide whether and how to adjust for inflation in a hospital's purchases between the moment of decision and the time expenses are incurred. The percentage or index chosen can range from flexible to restrictive. Inflation indices can be defined specifically for the goods and services hospitals purchase (their unique "market basket"), related to the consumer price index, or set at a level chosen as "reasonable" by policy makers. Similarly, an index can be generally applied or varied by location and other factors.[76] The more closely the index is tied to hospital experience, the less it serves to bring hospital increases in line with the rest of the economy. In the most absurd instance, an index based on hospital inflation serves only to support unabated rates of increases in hospital expenditures.

---

[74] On labor pressure, see John K. Iglehart, "And Now It's Carter's Turn to Try to Control Costs," *National Journal* 9 (April 9, 1977):556. See also testimony of the American Hospital Association, pp. 126–27 in *Medicare-Medicaid Administrative and Reimbursement Reform.*

[75] On Canada's experience, see Lewin and Associates, Inc., *Government Controls on the Health Care System: The Canadian Experience,* Washington, D.C., January 31, 1976, pp. 3–41—3–47; and Robert G. Evans, "Beyond the Medical Marketplace: Expenditure, Utilization and Pricing of Insured Health in Canada," in Spyros Andreopoulos, ed., *National Health Insurance: Can We Learn From Canada?* (New York: John Wiley and Sons, 1975), pp. 147–48.

[76] See Feldstein and Goddeeris, "Payment for Hospital Services," pp. 39–40.

Revenue Offsets

Having arrived at an acceptable level of expenditures, payers next confront acceptable revenues, beginning with consideration of hospital income other than patient revenues. The issue is whether such income should reduce (offset) allowable patient revenues. The issue arises particularly with respect to hospital endowments, which hospitals can use to cover expenses that regulators or payers have disallowed as excessive, or expenses such as luxury services that are not appropriately covered by patient revenues. Although use of endowment for luxury services may be entirely appropriate, use of endowment for capital expenditures inhibits cost containment. Even if the investment is initially financed independently of reimbursement (for example, through philanthropy), investment puts pressure on payers and regulators to include operating costs in later payment. To avoid this pressure, it is appropriate to discourage independent endowment support. Maryland does this by reducing approved hospital revenue levels by income earned from endowments.[77] Exceptions may be allowed for approved capital expenditures.

Units of Payment

Payers must next decide whether and how to set units of payment. Payers can set overall revenue limits ("global" budgets), departmental budgets, or line-item budgets. Alternatively, they can establish rates per person or family (capitation), per episode of illness, per case or stay, per day, or per service. The unit chosen has major consequences for hospital behavior and for payer liability and oversight.[78] If payment is based on a unit of output, such as per day or per service, hospitals have an incentive to increase the quantity of units provided and reduce the quantity of inputs, or intensity of care. This incentive was recognized in the course of the Economic Stabilization Program (ESP), and its Phase IV proposals substituted payment per admission for the earlier per diem method.[79] This lesson was incorporated in the 1977 Carter

---

[77] Cohen, "Experience of a State Cost Control Commission," p. 417.

[78] For the implications of each, see Dowling, "Perspective Reimbursement of Hospitals."

[79] Altman and Eichenholz, "Inflation in the Health Industry," pp. 24–25.

administration proposal.[80] Problems of manipulation, however, still exist.

> Thus, for example, if a policy focused on reducing the cost per admission, the pattern of admissions could be shifted towards lower cost case-types; or, case-specific average stays could be reduced to a point that reduced the quality of care. Either of these would be masked by aggregate data on cost per admission. The measured result of the policy would be that which was sought, but the real effect would be increased unnecessary hospital admissions and/or undesired reductions in the quality of care.[81]

Budget and capitation methods present similar problems. Proposals to overcome them include setting different rates for different diagnoses and types of cases,[82] or different rate structures for different types of institutions.[83] But these methods pose other difficulties—cumbersome data requirements, potential data manipulation, and payer involvement in the details of hospital management.[84] Because no unit of payment can combine complete control of provider behavior and administrative simplicity, the choice of a unit of payment requires a compromise.

Appeals and Adjustments

Once payers or regulators have decided what costs to cover, applied their screens or ceilings, and fixed units of payment, the process would seem to be complete; but this is not the case. Under both approaches, hospitals have recourse to administrative and judicial review for decisions they consider unjust or restrictive; and both methods must deal with experience that differs from premises on which payment decisions

[80] "President's Hospital Cost Containment Legislation," *Congressional Record—House*, April 25, 1977, pp. H3530—H3535.

[81] John Rafferty and Mark Hornbrook, "The Hospital Cost Containment Problem," Division of Intramural Research, National Center for Health Services Research, October 1976, pp. 18–19.

[82] Dowling, "Prospective Reimbursement of Hospitals," p. 169.

[83] Judith R. Lave, Lester B. Lave, and Lester P. Silverman, "A Proposal for Incentive Reimbursement for Hospitals," *Medical Care* 11 (March–April 1973): 79–90.

[84] On problems, see Laudicina, "Prospective Reimbursement for Hospitals," p. 37.

were based. Unanticipated experience in two areas—change in the volume of services produced and inaccurate cost estimates related to capital expenditures—has created difficulties.

Changes in hospital output, whether a product of intent or circumstances, make an enormous difference to hospital revenues. Budgets or rates based on one set of volume assumptions may be excessive or inadequate if volume changes, but determining what adjustment to make is a complex problem. A hospital has both variable costs and fixed costs (costs that do not vary with patient volume). If volume increases, fixed costs are divided among more patients and average fixed costs per patient decrease. Unless average costs are distinguished from marginal costs (the costs associated with the admission or discharge of each patient), hospitals can benefit inappropriately or suffer unduly from volume changes. Thus, for example, Phases II and III of the Economic Stabilization Program assumed a constant average total cost per patient-day. The result was payment in excess of costs for hospitals whose volume increased. This policy created an incentive to expand hospital use, contrary to the goal of containing unnecessary or excessive provision of services. Similar problems have arisen in Connecticut and New York, offsetting savings from payment limits.[85]

To avoid this problem, payers have attempted to distinguish between average and marginal costs and have adjusted payment to reflect the latter. This approach was proposed in ESP's Phase IV but was never implemented.[86] It was incorporated in the Carter administration's 1977 cost containment proposal.[87] Unless measures are precise, however, payers may face a choice between fixing payment regardless of volume changes, thereby potentially squeezing or overpaying some

---

[85] In Connecticut, volume increases eliminated savings; see Iglehart, "Government Searching for a More Cost-Efficient Way to Pay Hospitals," p. 1827. In New York, volume increases offset but did not eliminate savings; see Dowling, "Evaluation of Blue Cross and Medicaid Prospective Reimbursement Systems in Downstate New York," pp. I-49—I-51.

[86] Altman and Eichenholz, "Inflation in the Health Industry," pp. 22–24.

[87] The 1977 Carter legislation, like ESP's Phase IV, established a zone of no adjustment within which changes in volume do not affect allowed revenues. Outside that range, the bill required positive and negative adjustments, reflecting marginal cost assumptions, up to a point.

hospitals, or providing "escape valves" from cost containment.[88]

In the second area of contention, inaccurate estimates of costs associated with approved capital expenditures, if a payer or regulator approves reimbursement for a capital investment on the basis of capital and, more important, operating cost estimates that later prove too low, a decision has to be made on whether to cover the additional costs. This situation is quite similar to government appropriations and the cost overrun problem in government contracting. Contractors and hospitals have an incentive to provide low cost projections in order to get plans approved. Once the project is underway, purchasers and regulators have an investment in its completion. Rather than "cut their losses," they tend to pay extra costs as they occur.[89]

The problems for hospital payers and regulators, like government contracting officials, are the difficulty of accurately projecting future costs, dependence on the industry or contractors for data, and political difficulty in terminating payment. But, unlike defense contractors, for example, hospitals are not dependent on a single source for financial support. Hospitals can turn to their communities if third parties or regulators turn them down. Maryland Cost Commissioner Harold Cohen has made this argument to fellow payment regulators. The general attitude, he said, tends to be that if hospitals spend the money, payers have to cover it. "Punishment" is considered inappropriate. But with this approach, he argued, no one is protecting the public purse. The alternative regulators should pursue is to turn the hospitals down and let them seek philanthropic donations, just as universities do. As Cohen and his colleagues recognized, their capacity to take this course is a function of their political support.[90]

---

[88] For volume increases exceeding 15 percent, the 1977 Carter proposal made no upward adjustments; for volume decreases greater than 15 percent, allowed revenues were to be reduced by the full average cost per admission. H.R. 6575, Title I, Section 113. The combination of allowances provides some flexibility while setting explicit limits on payer responsiveness.

[89] For experience in defense contracting, see Fox, *Arming America: How the U.S. Buys Weapons.* Observations on rate-setting experience come from rate setters' comments at the Conference on State Rate Setting.

[90] Discussion at SSA Conference on State Rate Setting.

Adjustments and appeals mechanisms can destroy the cost containment capacity of any reimbursement system. If expenditures are to be contained, government officials must be willing and able to refuse to pay beyond a preestablished point. This refusal will result in financial stress and, in some instances, bankruptcy. This result is to be expected; when excess supply exists in normal economic markets, some economic failure is inevitable.

Impact of Prospective Payment

Prospective payers address the question of how much to pay hospitals not once but several times. Each of the decisions outlined above, albeit technical in appearance, requires a choice about whether to be liberal or restrictive in hospital payment. If payers make these decisions inconsistently—allowing concessions in one area to compensate for restrictions in another—their entire effort may be undermined. Unless payment decisions are consistently restrictive, costs cannot be contained.

In fact, evaluations reveal that prospective payment has not contained costs. Although statistical limits or screens appear to be more successful than subjective review, differences between costs in prospectively paid hospitals and other hospitals generally have not been statistically significant. Even if they had been, "the magnitude of savings [1 percent to 3 percent] per year that could be attributed to the systems would not even approach bringing hospital cost increases into line with inflation in other sectors of the economy." [91]

Although payers' skills and information have become more sophisticated since these evaluations were made,[92] factors that

---

[91] Clifton R. Gaus and Fred J. Hellinger, "Results of Hospital Prospective Reimbursement in the U.S.," presented to the International Conference on Policies for the Containment of Health Care Costs and Expenditures, The John E. Fogerty International Center, June 3, 1976, pp. 16–17. It is important to note, however, that quantitative analysis was inhibited by difficulty in isolating the effect of prospective payment schemes from other factors, like the Economic Stabilization Program, affecting hospital costs.

[92] Rate setters are emphatic on this point and contrast "first generation" with later payment mechanisms. At the Social Security Administration Conference on State Rate-Setting, one rate setter even argued that no one had really become serious about constraining payment until the mid-1970s, and no rebuttal was made.

inhibit the effectiveness of prospective payment persist. First, lack of uniformity among payers allows hospitals to play one payer off against the other. As they have done with Medicare, hospitals can use their capacity to shift costs as a bargaining tool, thereby inhibiting restrictive measures;[93] or they can actually shift costs from the restrictive to open-ended payers.

Second, payers cannot take or uphold consistently restrictive measures unless supported by their constituencies or clients. Thus far, that support has been decidedly limited. Private third parties have only recently begun to experience pressure from purchasers to control costs. For most of their history, insurers have simply passed cost increases along to purchasers in higher premiums.[94] As for the government, Congress has provided only intermittent pressure for restrictions on Medicare payment,[95] and has been reluctant to enact proposals to restrict all hospital payment. State legislatures also frequently fail to support payment restrictions.[96] Furthermore, as a result of commitments to equity and efficiency embodied in state and federal laws and regulations, the courts sometimes overturn the restrictive decisions that are actually made.[97] As long as payers and their constituencies are more committed to equity among hospitals and open-ended assurance of quality than they are to limiting costs, providers will continue to dominate the payment process. One set of data will be challenged by another, payers will be forced to seek a level

---

[93] This was the major argument against the Ford administration proposal to put a ceiling on cost increases for Medicare.

[94] See John K. Iglehart, "Medical Cost Quandary," *National Journal* 7 (September 20, 1975):1319–28; idem, "Government Searching for a More Cost-Efficient Way to Pay Hospitals"; and "Labor and Management Sponsored Innovations in Controlling the Cost of Employee Health Care Benefits," Council on Wage and Price Stability, prepared by Jon Kingsdale, *Federal Register*, September 17, 1976, pp. 40298–40326.

[95] Iglehart, "Medical Cost Quandary," p. 1320; and Feder, *Medicare*, Chapter 6.

[96] Rate setters' comments at Conference on State Rate Setting and Iglehart, "Government Searching for a More Cost-Efficient Way to Pay Hospitals," pp. 1826–27.

[97] On legal actions, see Commerce Clearing House, *Medicare and Medicaid Guide*, paragraphs 27,818 and 27,941. On court's overturning New York's adoption of ESP wage-price guidelines, see Dowling, "Evaluation of Blue Cross and Medicaid Prospective Reimbursement Systems in Downstate New York," p. I–69.

of precision that is beyond both theoretical and technical capacity, and decisions to limit funds will be overturned to appeal. Regardless of the payment mechanism, expenditures are likely to equal incurred costs.

The lessons of this experience are clear. If we want to control expenditures on hospital care, we have to change payment objectives, consolidate market power, and choose the payment mechanism least subject to provider manipulation. Further evidence on the importance and difficulties of this course comes from Canada's experience with hospital payment under national health insurance.

THE CANADIAN EXPERIENCE

Canada's national health insurance system differs from our present mix of public and private insurance.[98] Hospital insurance is universal in Canada, with expenses shared roughly fifty-fifty between provincial and federal governments. Hence, market power is less dispersed than in the United States, and all payment is public. In addition, although the hospitals are privately owned, the government has greater legal authority over hospitals' structure and behavior than is true in this country. Nevertheless, patterns of hospital expenditures and the political issues they raise have been similar in Canada and the United States. The Canadian federal and provincial governments' responses to these issues both parallel and extend lessons from our own experience.

In both the United States and Canada, hospital expenditures have been rising steadily, and in both countries the rate of increase has speeded up with the expansion of government

---

[98] This account of the Canadian system is based on Andreopoulos, ed., *National Health Insurance: Can We Learn From Canada?*; Robin F. Badgley, Catherine A. Charles, George M. Torrance, *The Canadian Experience with Universal Health Insurance*, draft, Department of Behavioral Science, University of Toronto, 1975; Lewin and Associates, Inc., *Government Controls on the Health Care System*; and an interview with the Director General of Canada's health insurance program, Robert Armstrong.

financing.[99] By the late 1960s, however, increases had become a burden to both levels of government. The federal government began to look for ways to reduce its share of payment [100] and provincial governments sought to limit their liabilities to providers.[101] Their reactions suggest the following principles in the politics of hospital payment:

1. *The objectives of government payers outweigh the significance of particular payment methods in determining program expenditures.*

The Canadian government never used retrospective cost reimbursement. From the beginning of their program, provincial governments have reviewed and approved hospital budgets in advance of expenditures. With a uniform accounting system and large data requirements, government payers have reviewed hospital activities line by line, examining and limiting individual input costs for hospital activities.[102] These reviews gave the governments a means to control individual hospital expenditures.

---

[99] On hospital inflation in Canada, see Evans in Andreopoulos, ed., *National Health Insurance: Can We Learn from Canada?*, especially pp. 137–51. For comparisons of Canadian and U.S. experience, see Stuart H. Altman, "Health Care Spending in the U.S. and Canada," in ibid., especially pp. 198–99. Altman reports the annual rates of increase in expense per patient-day at 12 percent for the United States and 11 percent in Canada for 1963–71. Cost per day was considerably lower in Canada than in the United States ($62 vs. $92 per day in 1971) and utilization rates were considerably higher in Canada. As a result, the levels of spending are approximately equal in the two countries.

[100] Lewin and Associates, Inc., *Government Controls on the Health Care System*, pp. 1–24—1–29. Conversations with Canadian Health Insurance Director General Robert Armstrong indicate that the cost-sharing dispute has been settled. Federal contributions for hospital and medical insurance and postsecondary education will be tied in part to a fixed percentage of income tax revenue and in part to a three-year moving average of the gross national product.

[101] Lewin and Associates, Inc., *Government Controls on the Health Care System*, pp. 3–4—3–9.

[102] For discussions of payment mechanism, see Maurice LeClair, "The Canadian Health Care System," in Andreopoulos, ed., *National Health Insurance: Can We Learn from Canada?*, p. 57; Evans in ibid., pp. 135–37 and 151–55; Lewin and Associates, Inc., *Government Controls on the Health Care System*, pp. 3–2 and 3–3. The limitations of this mechanism, noted by both LeClair and Evans, are discussed later in this chapter.

But the governments did not use this mechanism to control costs. Expenditures rose rapidly, at a rate comparable to that in the United States.[103] Why? As in the United States, the introduction of government hospital insurance reflected a commitment to reducing financial barriers to medical care and a belief that the more resources devoted to care, the better the system would be. Hence, despite the availability of a payment control mechanism, provincial governments tended to finance whatever costs hospitals incurred.[104]

As already noted, governmental perspectives began to change in the late 1960s. Cost increases became unacceptable. As Canadian governments responded to this situation, they demonstrated a second principle of payment:

> 2. *Some payment mechanisms are more conducive to cost containment than others.*

Once cost containment became a goal, line-item budgeting proved insufficient to its achievement. Because the data on input costs were not related to hospital outputs, the system did not facilitate measures of "efficiency." As Evans explained:

> When the need arises to make estimates of the full costs of particular activities in Canadian hospitals, or the relative costs of hospitals engaged in similar activities, the data require vigorous massage to yield approximate answers.[105]

Even when challenges to individual hospitals were possible, line-item review involved the governments in detailed disputes with the hospitals about where cuts should be made, a time-consuming and heated process.[106]

To reduce this problem as well as to encourage "efficient" and "flexible" management, Canadian governments shifted

---

[103] Altman, "Health Care Spending in the U.S. and Canada," pp. 198–99.

[104] Lewin and Associates, Inc., *Government Controls on the Health Care System*, pp. 3–4; Badgley, *The Canadian Experience with Universal Health Insurance*, p. 200; Evans, in Andreopoulos, ed., *National Health Insurance: Can We Learn from Canada?*, p. 151.

[105] Evans in Andreopoulos, ed., *National Health Insurance: Can We Learn from Canada?*, p. 134 and pp. 152–53.

[106] LeClair, in ibid., p. 57.

from line-item to "global" budgeting.[107] Instead of limiting
individual input costs, this approach limits total costs. The
"global" limit may be based on line-item review or on a level
of increase in expenditures deemed acceptable by the provincial government. Within the limit, hospitals can allocate
dollars as they see fit.

As researchers in this country have found, it is extremely
difficult to evaluate the impact of changes in payment mechanisms on hospital costs. In Canada, evaluation is complicated
by the introduction of medical insurance in the late 1960s and
by reductions in federal funds for capital expansion. Separating the effects of these changes from the effects of reimbursement changes is virtually impossible. Even in combination,
however, the effects do not appear considerable. By some
measures, increases in expenditures appear to have slowed,
at least temporarily. Recent reports from Canada suggest,
however, that slower rates have not been maintained. No one
would conclude that the change in payment mechanisms has
in itself controlled costs.[108] As argued earlier, global ceilings
do not eliminate choices as to desirable and acceptable hospital expenditures. Hence, the third principle:

---

[107] On the shift, see Lewin and Associates, Inc., *Government Controls
on the Health Care System*, pp. 3–3 and 3–6—3–7; and LeClair, in
Andreopoulos, ed., *National Health Insurance: Can We Learn from
Canada?*, pp. 57–58.

[108] Data reported in Lewin and Associates, Inc., *Government Controls
on the Health Care System*, pp. 1–16, show a slower rate of increase in
operating expenditures per capita for 1970–72 than for 1961–72; rates
of increase in expenditure per day slowed for some provinces but not
for Canada as a whole. Data to 1973, however, do not suggest a general
downward trend in either measure (*Annual Report 1974–1975: Hospital
Insurance and Diagnostic Services*, Health and Welfare, Canada). In
June 1977, the Canadian government reported the following percentage
increases in hospitals' *total* operating expenditures:

1961–1971	1972	1973	1974	1971–1974
13.7 (annually)	10.8	12.1	23.7	15.4 (annually)

Of the increase in 1974, the Canadian government estimated that 60.18
percent was related to increases in salaries and wages per hours of work,
25.27 percent to cost and volume of supplies per day, 2.87 percent to
paid hours of work per day, 6.90 percent to population growth, and 4.78
percent to patient days per capita. Tables supplied by Health Programs
Branch, National Health and Welfare, Canada, June 1977.

3. *No method of payment eliminates the necessity for political choices on how much to spend.*

The several ways in which ceilings can allow hospitals leeway have already been elaborated.[109] Faced with continuing cost increases, several provinces have tried to restrict that leeway by explicitly refusing to increase budgets for increases in inpatient or outpatient volume, for increases in delivery of laboratory and radiology services to inpatients, or for expansion of the services hospitals offer. In addition, these provinces have imposed moratoria on construction and renovation; they have required bed closings; and they have lowered the rate of budget increase deemed acceptable.[110]

Whether these decisions have been generally undercut by year-end adjustments is not clear. It is clear, however, that these decisions have been undercut in the specific area of labor costs. Political commitment to contain costs has not extended to limits on wage and salary increases. This important gap provides a fourth and concluding principle:

4. *Neither objectives nor methods for cost containment eliminate political conflict.*

Hospital cost inflation can reflect increases in wages and prices for a given quantity of inputs and increases in the quantity of labor and nonlabor inputs. In the United States and Canada, the contribution of different components has varied over time but in the former, changes in the price and quantity of inputs have, on average, contributed about equally to inflation. In Canada, however, increases in price—particularly the price of labor—have far exceeded increases in resource use, and are responsible for most of Canada's recent expenditure increases.[111] Global budgets do not solve this problem; instead they shift the focus on labor pressure from hospital administrators to the government. Canadian governments have been unable to withstand the pressure for large increases

---

[109] On the provinces' retroactive adjustments, see Lewin and Associates, Inc., *Government Controls on the Health Care System*, pp. 3–30—3–31.

[110] Ibid., pp. 3–6—3–9.

[111] For a comparison of the United States and Canada, see Altman, "Health Care Spending in the U.S. and Canada," in Andreopoulos, ed., *National Health Insurance: Can We Learn from Canada?*, pp. 200–201. On rising labor costs, see Evans, in ibid., p. 147; and Lewin and Associates, Inc., *Government Controls on the Health Care System*, pp. 3–5.

in wages and salaries for hospital employees. Hence, they have
financed wage-salary increases incompatible with the overall
ceiling on costs. Success in one province strengthens labor's
hand in other provinces, and increases among one set of
employees generate pressure for increases throughout the
health sector and the economy as a whole. The results are
continuing increases in hospital expenditures.[112]

This history is not encouraging. The Canadians have broadly
applied measures with which we in the United States have
only experimented, and they have been unable to control hospital expenditures. But by telling us what will not work, the
Canadian experience should help us focus on the real issues
and choices. As Medicare officials recognized long ago,

> . . . there seem to be no magic bullets that will control
> medical costs without direct or indirect restriction on
> physicians and providers, control program costs in
> face of rising medical costs without disadvantage to
> the beneficiary, or insulate the beneficiary from ris-
> ing medical and program costs without increased cost
> to the general taxpayer or the social security contrib-
> utor. What must be faced in evaluating . . . policy is
> the hard trade-off of interests involved in adopting
> alternative policies.[113]

Consequences of Cost Containment

The limited experience in Canada and the United States
with restricted payment provides little information about
what would happen if cost containment actually worked.
Resource constraints have been advocated on grounds of
excess in the system; implementation of these constraints is
intended to eliminate or reduce that excess. Ideally, we would
expect such constraints to reduce capital investment, in both

---

[112] Lewin and Associates, Inc., *Government Controls on the Health Care
System*, pp. 3–41—3–46; and discussion with Canadian officials.

[113] "Background Material for the Council's Intended Discussion of
Medical Costs," Staff Memorandum for the Health Insurance Benefits
Advisory Council (HIBAC), HIBAC Agenda Book, January 10–11, 1970,
quoted in Feder, *Medicare*, Chapter 6.

facilities and in equipment; to introduce resilience in wage settlements; to inhibit inappropriate or unnecessary use of the hospital (for example, for services that could be performed outside the hospital, that provide little if any benefit, and that actually do harm); and overall, to assure a more rational distribution of resources. But reality often departs significantly from the ideal. Assume for the moment that a payment mechanism restricted hospital revenues to levels below current expenditures, that revenues could not be manipulated, and that hospitals lacked alternative resources. What departures from the ideal might be expected? An answer comes from theoretical propositions about provider behavior and from experiences in the United Kingdom, where hospital revenues and expenditures have been constrained through a national budgeting system.[114]

Responses to resource constraints are likely to reflect two independent factors: (1) the relative incidence of restrictions across hospitals and (2) behavior patterns or incentives of hospital administrators and physicians. Unless resource allocation reflects norms for efficient and effective service delivery, responds to changing circumstances, and is extremely precise, constraints will probably affect both efficient and inefficient hospitals and necessary as well as unnecessary services. As argued earlier, this fact has posed a major obstacle to imposing cost constraints. British experience suggests that the problem is political as well as technical. Despite considerable and unjustifiable inequities in resource distribution among regions,[115] the British government did not use its power to change resource distribution until some twenty years after taking control of the system.

---

[114] On the British payment system, see Michael H. Cooper, *Rationing Health Care*, (New York: John Wiley and Sons, 1975); Michael H. Cooper, "Health Costs and Expenditures in the United Kingdom," and A.J. Culyer, "Discussant's Comments," Chapter 5 in Teh-Wei Hu, ed., *International Health Costs and Expenditures*, DHEW, Public Health Service, National Institutes of Health, DHEW Publication No. (NIH) 76–1067, 1976; and Odin W. Anderson, *Health Care: Can There Be Equity? The United States, Sweden and England.* (New York: John Wiley and Sons, 1972). On hospital expenditure increases in England relative to those in the United States and Sweden, see ibid., p. 226.

[115] Cooper, *Rationing Health Care*, pp. 60–72.

On the appointed day (July 5, 1948) resources were allocated to reflect the old order and it has since proved extremely difficult to radically change them. As Enoch Powell once remarked, "Once the butter is in the dog's mouth, it can only be scraped out at the risk of being bitten. . . ." To put right disparities in one region or specialty would have involved the "political odium of being seen to reduce expenditure" in another.[116]

In 1971, the British government overcame these obstacles and changed its budget allocation system to reduce regional disparities.[117] Although the new method is a substantial improvement, political choices within regions will remain, as will technical problems of defining need and performance and responding to changes in population and circumstances.

Allocation of resources within hospitals is a function of professional values and incentives. With resources constrained, physicians could be expected to give priority to more serious cases. The U.K. experience generally confirms this expectation.[118] But such broad criteria for rationing do not necessarily produce patterns of efficient and effective use of the hospital. Studies of British hospital use have identified substantial unnecessary hospitalization and considerable variation in length of stay for the same diagnosis.[119] Cooper observes:

> Whilst it is true that doctors have to adjust their aggregate demands so that they are consistent with available resources, clinical freedom means that they are individually neither adjusting from nor to a common base line or conception of need.[120]

Physicians' adjustments are influenced by methods of physician payment as well as by professional ethics and hospital resources. Payment systems may be neutral with respect to

---

[116] Cooper, "Health Costs and Expenditures," p. 94.

[117] Cooper, *Rationing Health Care*, p. 71, and Alan Maynard, "Health Care Planning in the United Kingdom," prepared for a Conference on Policies for the Containment of Health Care Expenditures, Fogarty Center, DHEW, May 1976.

[118] Cooper, *Rationing Health Care*, p. 91.

[119] Ibid., pp. 53–59.

[120] Ibid., p. 56.

use, as with salaries, or may encourage particular kinds of use, as with fee schedules. Furthermore, where supply restrictions require rationing, physician behavior may be influenced by side payments offered by patients who wish to jump queues. Unless side payments were prohibited by law and the law enforced, the result would be differences in treatment for the poor versus the well-to-do.

As this discussion suggests, any evaluation of the effect of resource constraints cannot treat the hospital sector in isolation. Cost savings and patterns of hospital use must be carefully analyzed, for reductions in the delivery of hospital services may not mean overall reduction in service. To the extent that ambulatory care replaces hospital care, total cost savings will be less than reductions in hospital expenditure. Although substitution of ambulatory care may be entirely appropriate, savings could be eliminated altogether if ambulatory services become excessive and expensive—as, for example, when physicians buy and use expensive capital equipment in their offices to avoid constraints on hospital expenditures.[121]

In sum, effective resource control is not identical with efficient resource allocation. This limitation may be less of a problem in conditions of excess, but it is a problem nevertheless. It must be recognized that payment controls can encourage but not assure particular changes in the system. The direction of change will be influenced not only by hospital payment policy, but by other policies affecting health service delivery—including physician payment, utilization review, and direct regulation of facilities and equipment.

Conclusions

The recent preoccupation with hospital expenditures and cost containment is predicated upon empirical appraisals of the adequacy of this country's hospital sector. The conclusion reached repeatedly is that the system is not only adequate but excessive: The United States has more beds than it needs, more high technology than it can use, and more hospitalization and surgery than it can safely endure.

---

[121] John K. Iglehart, "The Cost and Regulation of Medical Technology: Future Policy Directions," *Milbank Memorial Fund Quarterly* 55 (Winter 1977):32–33.

This excess is a direct result of the public and private commitment to absolute hospital equity and mainstream medicine or quality of care. The resulting payment systems have placed most decisions regarding cost, quality, and utilization in the hands of the hospitals, leading to enormous increases in hospital expenditures and misallocation of resources. So long as the government clings to the principles of absolute equity and provider-determined quality, hospital expenditures will never reflect their value to society vis-à-vis other publicly purchased goods and services.

No change in payment policy can control costs without political conflict, but some changes can enhance the government's capacity to resist hospitals' demands. Improving the government's bargaining capacity under national health insurance requires (1) that policy makers change their payment objectives, (2) that national health insurance adopt the payment method least subject to provider manipulation, and (3) that payment be uniform across all payers in order to consolidate payers' market power.

The current objectives of equity among hospitals and "mainstream" care should be replaced with objectives of relative equity and satisfactory care. Equity in payment must go beyond hospitals to equity among hospitals, patients, taxpayers, and the community as a whole. Appropriately defined, equity requires that benefits and costs of hospital care be considered simultaneously and in relation to alternative use of funds. As long as consumers' payment responsibility is limited, decisions on resource distribution must become a public responsibility.

Open-ended commitments to finance whatever the medical and hospital industry define as the "best" in medical care must be replaced by commitment to finance satisfactory care fairly. As Gerald Rosenthal has argued:

> This emphasis on the best that the system can do has led to concentrating descriptions of the health care system on attributes which tend not to be widely available and indeed *not widely achievable* within any realistic, available resource constraints. . . .
>
> Alternatively, little attention has been paid to describing the floor of care. The concentration on the

best that the system does has diverted attention from
the *worst* that it does. . . .[122]

By providing funds for use at providers' discretion, the present financing system allows continual elaboration of the best
without assuring general availability of the good. To achieve
equitable assurance of benefits for controllable costs, it is
necessary to substitute commitment to finance a "true floor"
of quality care.[123]

Changes in payment objectives must be accompanied by a
change in payment methods. Reimbursement that continually
reflects autonomous hospital expenditure decisions is clearly
inconsistent with expenditure control and efficient resource
allocation. Despite the inefficiencies that the "reasonable cost"
reimbursement system has produced, political acceptance of
a new system requires that national health insurance take
current aggregate hospital expenditures as a starting point.
The new reimbursement system should concentrate on controlling the rate of increase in expenditures in coming years.
Initially, this goal can be achieved most easily if policy makers
accept each hospital's current level of revenues, establish a
ceiling on the rate of increase in all hospitals' revenues for
the coming year, and subject all hospital expenditures to the
revenue ceiling. If these ceilings are to limit hospital expenditures, payments to individual hospitals cannot be affected by
expenditures hospitals incur after the adoption of a national
health insurance program. Ceilings based on average hospital
performance are therefore undesirable. Instead, rates of increase should be tied to some independent measure of acceptable expenditure increases (for example, the consumer price
index less the medical care component of that index). If all
sources of expenditure are to be controlled, publicly established revenue ceilings should apply to all purchasers of hospital care, private as well as public, and revenues earned independent of patient care (from endowments or services like
parking lots or gifts shops) should be counted toward the
ceilings. To prevent provider manipulation and encourage efficient management, hospitals' total expenditures—on ancillary

---

[122] Gerald Rosenthal, "Setting the Floor: A Missing Ingredient in an
Effective Health Policy," *Journal of Health Politics, Policy and Law* 1
(Spring 1976):2–3.
[123] Ibid.

as well as routine services—cannot be allowed to exceed approved revenues. To minimize hospitals' capacity to avoid ceilings by manipulating their volume of services, payments should be tied to admissions, not days of care. Total revenues should not be increased to finance increases in admissions that exceeded a predetermined range.

These actions would close the loopholes in existing payment systems, and would place extremely tight limits on hospital revenues and expenditures. Because they would freeze the existing distribution of resources, such stringent controls could not be imposed over a long period of time. But their adoption at the beginning of a national health insurance program could shift negotiations between the government and the hospital industry from debates on how much to tighten expenditures to debates on how much to loosen expenditures. Such a shift could enhance the government's bargaining power and give public policy makers, rather than providers, the advantage in negotiations.

Over time, the rigid payment system should be replaced with a payment system that would allow shifts in the existing distribution of resources. Nationally set limits on national expenditures should remain, but the mechanism for allocating expenditures to individual hospitals should change. A national budget for hospital care could be prospectively set, apportioned to the states by the federal government, then apportioned to localities or individual hospitals by the states. To simultaneously establish public control and allow managerial flexibility, it seems most appropriate to fix global budgets for hospitals and allow hospitals to spend within those budgets as they see fit. With this budgeting approach, limits would be set by the level of government that faced the broadest cost-benefit trade-offs, represented the largest range of interests, and wielded the most comprehensive authority. Furthermore, setting budgets from the top down would establish fiscal constraints at every level of decision making while allowing those closest to hospital operations to decide where funds should be spent.

If allocation responsibility is totally separated from fiscal responsibility, we will recreate the current situation in which health planning works at cross purposes with the financing of health care. Unless states and localities bear some costs of hospital care, they may have greater interest in promoting expansion of the federal budget than in operating efficiently and effectively within that budget. A state's ability to gain an exception or special rate of increase would be limited by competition for federal dollars among other states and with other users of federal dollars. But the degree of conflict over these dollars could be reduced by including state and local payment obligations in any financing scheme. If states or local communities wanted to spend more on hospital care than their NHI obligations required, they should be allowed to do so. But they should only do so with the understanding that they were obligated for future operating, as well as capital, costs of any investment they undertook.

Delegating the allocation function to the state does not eliminate the constant necessity for political choice. Apportionment procedures will be one long political bargaining session: Will a hospital's performance be reflected in its budget? What costs will be covered? What ceilings will be imposed? What will be the recourse for adjustments and appeals? And what will happen given imminent bankruptcy of a hospital? These difficult and controversial questions cannot be reduced to technical rules. Nor can budgets be assumed to produce efficient outcomes. Experience with budgets in the United Kingdom reveals that long-standing patterns of resource distribution are difficult to change. Political power of particular communities and hospitals will undoubtedly influence any resource allocation system adopted. Furthermore, it should be recognized that budgeting for hospitals alone will not automatically control total medical costs. To the extent that ambulatory care replaced hospital care, total cost savings would be less than savings in hospital costs. Although substitution of ambulatory care might be entirely appropriate, savings could be eliminated altogether if ambulatory services became excessive and expensive. The fact that budgeting does not assure efficiency, however, should not obscure its advantage over other payment systems. In contrast to other systems—especially "reasonable cost" reimbursement—budgets do not preclude efficient outcomes. Instead, budgets create pressure to face rather than ignore the difficult choices expenditure control requires.

Chapter 7
HOSPITAL REGULATION

ANDREW B. DUNHAM

A LTHOUGH a national health insurance program has yet to be adopted in the United States, all levels of government regulate the growth of health facilities, and each major NHI proposal either implicitly or explicitly includes facility regulation as one of its cost control mechanisms. The success of any NHI program in controlling costs will depend in part on how well facility regulation works. Indeed, effective cost control policies may prove to be a necessary precondition for the passage of a national health insurance program. It is useful, therefore, to examine the current operation of facility regulation, to consider ways that regulation might change and problems that regulation might encounter under various NHI programs, and to analyze the implications for facility regulation in the future.

This chapter opens with a brief discussion of the dynamics of the hospital care system without controls and of the problems that facility regulation is supposed to address. It then describes the range of workable control instruments. The third section describes the operation of facility regulation, analyzes the impact thus far, and describes provider response to regulation. Finally, the chapter analyzes how facility regulation might interact with other control mechanisms, instituted in conjunction with or separately from national health insurance, and how the statutory and structural changes under various proposed NHI programs would alter the operation and effects of regulation.

The Problem

Public controls on capital investment and services are the predominant form of existing federal and state policies for containing the cost of medical care. Although rising medical care costs in general have caused concern, the increase in hospital costs has been particularly alarming. Increases in medical care prices have exceeded the rise in the consumer price index, but hospital costs have been outstripping other health service expenditures.[1] Hospital care is the largest single component of medical care, accounting for 40 percent of all health spending in 1976 and amounting to $55.4 billion.[2] The importance of the hospital in modern medical care is growing, and the control of hospital costs is an essential part of controlling medical costs.

Rising costs are usually believed to flow from problems in the organization of the market for hospital services. Consumers face only a fraction of a hospital bill at the point of use. Hospitals get about 90 percent of their revenue from third parties, who usually reimburse hospitals on the basis of costs. The predominance of cost-based reimbursement and the ability of providers to generate demand for their services[3] mean that virtually every community hospital can strive for expansion to "full service" status. The risk of expansion has involved little more than an occasional confrontation with a recalcitrant Blue Cross plan administrator or state insurance commission, and certainly not severe financial losses. Because hospitals depend on their staff physicians as the prime source of patients, a liberal response to staff demands for new facilities, equipment, or personnel is essential. A hospital that cannot keep or attract staff cannot survive. Furthermore, with the "discretionary financial power"[4] provided by growing insurance coverage, expansion of service can be undertaken without accompanying efforts to increase efficiency of daily operations. With their nonprofit status guarding them from financial or stockholder pressures, institutional providers have little reason to sacrifice autonomy for the sake of efficiency

[1] Robert M. Gibson and Marjorie Smith Mueller, "National Health Expenditures, Fiscal Year 1976," *Social Security Bulletin* 40 (April 1977): 19–20.

[2] Ibid., p. 3.

[3] Milton I. Roemer, "Bed Supply and Hospital Utilization: A Natural Experiment," *Hospitals* 35 (November 1, 1961):36–42.

[4] Martin A. Feldstein, *The Rising Cost of Hospital Care* (Washington, D.C.: Information Resources Press, 1971).

by entering into shared-service arrangements or other forms of interhospital coordination.

This market structure allows and indeed encourages provider investment decisions that lead to a series of problems: surplus capacity and unnecessary duplication of facilities, excessive use of services and facilities, excessive adoption of high technology, costly care that only marginally improves medical treatment, and some poor-quality care.

The facility surplus is the most obvious and commonly cited problem. The national hospital bed occupancy rate is less than 75 percent, even though large hospitals can operate efficiently at much higher rates. "Experience in several areas has shown that bed occupancy rate of 90 percent or more can be achieved for non-maternity beds in large hospitals without sacrificing the quality of care."[5] Because the cost of maintaining an empty bed is estimated to be almost two-thirds the cost of a bed in use, the large number of surplus beds greatly increases the cost of hospital care.[6] It has been estimated that 100,000 of the nation's 930,000 short-term, acute-care beds are unused and thus unnecessary.[7]

Although the bed surplus is the most publicized problem, hospitals also have acquired other unneeded facilities and services. Technological innovations are usually introduced in large hospitals, then in other large hospitals, and eventually in smaller and smaller hospitals.[8] As more hospitals acquire a

---

[5] Institute of Medicine, "Controlling the Supply of Hospital Beds," National Academy of Sciences, Washington, D.C., October 1976, p. 12.

[6] Robert S. Powell, Jr., *Bureaucratic Malpractice: Hospital Regulation in New Jersey* (Princeton: The Center for Analysis of Public Issues, 1974), p. 59.; see also Institute of Medicine, "Controlling the Supply of Hospital Beds," p. 15; and U.S. Congress, Senate, 95th Congress, 1st Session, Subcommittee on Health and Scientific Research of the Committee on Human Resources, "The Hospital Cost Containment Act of 1977: An Analysis of the Administration's Proposal," prepared by the Congressional Budget Office (Washington, D.C.: U.S. Government Printing Office, June 1977), p. 33.

[7] U.S. Congress, House of Representatives, 93rd Congress, 2nd Session, Report by the Committee on Interstate and Foreign Commerce, Report No. 93–1382, September 26, 1974, "National Health Policy, Planning and Resources Development Act of 1974," p. 27. See also Institute of Medicine, "Controlling the Supply of Hospital Beds."

[8] For complete discussion, see Louise B. Russell, "The Diffusion of New Hospital Technologies in the United States," *International Journal of Health Services Research* 6 (1976):557–80.

particular service, the average utilization rate tends to drop. For example, "of almost 800 hospitals in the United States equipped for closed heart surgery, over 90 percent did fewer than one case per week, and 30 percent had done none in the year studied." [9] Those idle facilities are costly. The Institute of Medicine points out that unnecessary facilities increase the overall demand for trained personnel, and drive up salaries, further increasing the costs of medical care.[10]

It is now generally accepted that the availability of facilities increases utilization without lowering price. More beds mean that more patients are admitted for longer stays. According to Roemer's Law, supply can create its own demand.[11] Thus not only are the empty beds unnecessary, but many occupied beds are also surplus in that they are being used unnecessarily. Limiting the availability of facilities and services should constrain the amount of hospitalization and the use of specialized procedures, thus producing savings in both capital and operating costs.[12]

Facility regulation also is expected to deal with the problem of high-technology, high-cost medical care. The previous discussion dealt with facilities that are unnecessary because they provide no benefits for patients. But rapid advances in medical technology have led to creation of new, costly, and capital-intensive methods of treating medical problems. Gaus and Cooper estimate that what they call the "technology factor" has accounted for 47 percent of the increase in expenses per patient day between 1967 and 1976.[13] Some of the

---

[9] Howard Hiatt, "Protecting the Medical 'Commons'—Who Has the Responsibility?," in *The National Leadership Conference on America's Health Policy* convened by the *National Journal*, Rep. Paul Rogers, and Rep. Dan Rostenkowski, at the Hyatt Regency, Washington, D.C., April 29–30, 1976, pp. 19–24.

[10] Institute of Medicine, "Controlling the Supply of Hospital Beds," p. 15.

[11] Roemer, "Bed Supply and Hospital Utilization."

[12] Note that this conclusion is tenable even if Roemer's Law on the availability effect is rejected. Even if facility controls did not reduce demand, such controls could necessitate rationing as demand expands while capacity is limited. As a result, the total volume and costs of services would be reduced.

[13] Clifton Gaus and Barbara Cooper, "Technology and Medicare: Alternatives for Change," paper presented at the Conference on Health Care Technology and Quality of Care, Boston University Policy Center, Boston, Massachusetts, November 19–20, 1976.

technological "advances" may have no medical value at all; even those procedures that clearly are beneficial need to be examined to see if the benefits are worth the costs. To cite an example given by McClure, if a $50 test gives a 95 percent certainty of diagnosis, is it worthwhile to administer a $250 test to get 97 percent certainty? [14]

Concern about the declining marginal utility of medical expenditures is mounting. Carlson and others have proclaimed "the end of medicine is near." [15] One does not have to agree with their arguments to recognize that spending more money on high-technology medicine is often not the most effective way of improving health. Facility regulation could slow and reduce the spread of expensive technologies.

Finally, it should be noted that the maintenance of surplus capacity and the spread of technologies are not only expensive, they are actually dangerous. Some facilities need to be used frequently if the physicians and staff associated with them are to acquire and maintain optimal experience and skill.[16] Because of proliferation of services, many hospitals perform only a few specialized operations; concentration of special services in a few medical centers produces safer and less expensive care than does diffusion of services. Thus facility regulation is supposed to ensure the development of services only where utilization would permit high-quality care.

Policy Responses

The predominant policy response to these problems in the late 1950s and early 1960s was health planning. Planning mechanisms were supposed to rationalize the system—control costs, improve distribution, and maintain quality—by preventing unnecessary proliferation of facilities and equipment,

---

[14] Walter McClure, "The Medical Care System under National Health Insurance: Four Models," *Journal of Health Politics, Policy and Law* 1 (Spring 1976):32.

[15] Rick J. Carlson, *The End of Medicine* (New York: John Wiley and Sons, 1975) p. 2; see also Ivan Illych, *Medical Nemesis: The Expropriation of Health* (New York: Pantheon Books, 1976).

[16] See, for example, "The 11th Report of the Human Renal Transplant Registry," *Journal of the American Medical Association* 226 (December 3, 1973): 1197.

by encouraging regionalization, and by promoting sharing and coordination at the local level. The program initiatives through which planning processes were developed—particularly Comprehensive Health Planning and Regional Medical Programs—were tied to the principle of voluntary cooperation rather than public control. But participating providers had little or no incentive to relinquish their autonomy, so the market conditions just described were not significantly altered by voluntary planning. Thus it is hardly surprising that cooperative solutions did not emerge and that problems persisted.

In the early 1970s, increased public control, in the form of financial and legal sanctions, was added to health planning. Because provider decisions tended to produce excessive capital expenditures, public or publicly supported agencies were authorized to evaluate proposals and to determine whether the new facility or service was really "needed." Public control involved the legal prohibition of disapproved capital expenditures or the financial sanction of reduced payments to facilities that generated capital expenditures in spite of government disapproval.

Financial sanctions over capital expenditures were authorized in 1972 by Section 1122 of the Social Security Act.[17] The secretary of health, education, and welfare may contract with the states to perform reviews of proposed capital expenditures and to reduce payments under Titles VI, XVIII, and XIX of the Social Security Act to any facility that undertakes a capital expenditure which has not been approved by the reviewing agency. More specifically, capital costs (interest, depreciation, and return on equity) are not included as "allowable costs" for federal reimbursement under the Medicare, Medicaid, and Maternal and Child Health Programs unless the project has been approved. This payment withholding may continue as long as the secretary deems necessary. The secretary may, however, overrule a state's decision and make full payment if he decides that a reduction would discourage an effective and efficient provider or would otherwise hinder operation of federal programs. Participation in the Section

---

[17] 1972 Amendments to the Social Security Act, PL 92–603, Section 1122 (42 U.S.C.A. 1320a–1).

1122 program is optional for states; by 1975, thirty-nine states were participating.[18]

A number of states added controls (similar to public utility regulation) that prohibited health facility expansion without state certification. In 1964, New York passed the first certificate-of-need (CON) legislation, requiring health facilities to get state approval before making any major capital expenditures. By 1974, twenty-nine states had certificate-of-need programs.[19]

The federal government then passed the "National Health Planning and Resources Development Act of 1974," [20] requiring all states to develop a certificate-of-need program if they did not want to lose federal funding under some sections of the Public Health Services Act. The legislation authorized more than two hundred Health Systems Agencies (HSAs) to review and make recommendations on all major capital expenditures in the area. A state agency would make the final determination of whether to grant a certificate of need. If the state agency does not follow the local HSA recommendation, it has to explain its reasons in writing. Although the certificate-of-need programs were to be developed and operated by the states, the programs had to meet certain federal requirements. In particular, acceptable state laws were required to have sufficient sanctions (license forfeiture, injunctions, civil or criminal penalties) to assure the DHEW secretary that uncertified construction would not take place. Withholding payment was not, by itself, sufficient.

Although the federally mandated state certificate-of-need laws would seem to make Section 1122 review unnecessary, financial sanctions may still be used in some situations. First, it will be several years before all states have federally approved certificate-of-need programs, and until a state has an operating program, Section 1122 review is the only important sanction available. Even if all states were to have certificate-of-need programs, though, Section 1122 could be applied to expenditures and facilities not covered by state laws. Federal regulations also can be expanded (e.g., to cover physicians'

---

[18] Jack Wood, ed., *Topics in Health Care Financing* 2 (Winter 1975): 93, Appendix C.

[19] Ibid.

[20] PL 93–641; Act of January 4, 1975, 88 Stat. 2225 et seq. 42 U.S.C.A. 300 K.

offices) in less time than would be required to change all state laws. Thus, Section 1122 review continues to be a potentially useful policy tool.

There is a significant difference between regulatory activities that respond to the initiative of the providers on the basis of a determination of "need," and control that operates within a relatively fixed sum and must compare needs and set priorities. In 1977, the Carter administration proposed a limit—less than one-third of current investment levels—on the total amount of capital expenditures that would be allowed in each state. Such a tight cap would significantly alter the behavior of facility regulators. They would have to choose between projects, and would have to reject on average two-thirds of the dollar volume they now approve.[21] The fixed cap would obviously have a greater impact on hospital investments than the current open-ended project reviews have had.

Review of proposals initiated by health providers is not the only possible form of capital expenditures control. Control also has been exercised through public programs that supply capital funds for construction and modernization. Over the past thirty years, the Hill-Burton program has provided $4.5 billion to hospitals approved by a state planning agency.[22] The more hospitals depend on public financing for capital expenditures, the more powerful this control mechanism can be. Increasingly, however, hospitals are depending less on direct grants from government and philanthropy, and relying more on their own reserves or on deficit financing for capital funds. An American Hospital Association survey of hospitals reporting construction completed in 1968 indicated that 32 percent of the funding came from government grants and appropriations.[23] A 1975 survey showed that government grants and appropriations made up only 21 percent of hospital capital funds.[24] Between 1968 and 1975, the share of philanthropy decreased from 20 percent to 9 percent.

[21] Congressional Budget Office, "Hospital Cost Containment Act," p. 42.

[22] Judith R. Lave and Lester B. Lave, *The Hospital Construction Act* (Washington, D.C.: American Enterprise Institute for Public Policy Research, 1974), p. 14.

[23] Pat N. Groner, "Study Shows Changing Pattern of Financing," *Hospitals* 46 (March 1, 1972):135–37.

[24] Sallie Manley and Susan Ashby, "Sources of Funding for Construction," *Hospitals* 46 (June 19, 1977):59–63.

Yet the importance of public money for hospital capital formation has not been reduced. Medicare alone paid health facilities about one billion dollars for depreciation and interest in 1977.[25] The shifts in sources of funding emphasize the important role reimbursement mechanisms currently play in capital expenditures. If national health insurance or other controls (e.g., President Carter's capped budget proposal) were to significantly reduce hospital revenues so that hospitals could not generate their own reserves or attract funds through borrowing, then government-provided capital could be a crucial device to control the total size, distribution, and mix of capital expenditures.

Government monopoly of the supply of capital would give the greatest degree of control over capital expenditures. Canada has tried this approach with mixed results. The Canadian provinces review the capital budgets of hospitals, and they provide a large proportion of the capital funds. For example, Quebec provides all of the funding for large projects and Ontario provides two-thirds. In the 1960s, the provincial governments were quite permissive in funding facility expansion, but as financial pressures on the public budget increased, the strictness of project review also tightened. The more limited the government's budget became, the tighter were the constraints on facility expansion. Some Canadian provinces even imposed complete moratoria on new construction and expansion.[26]

Public monopoly of capital funds not only allows greater public control over the size of the total investment, but also allows control over the site and the type of investment. Regulatory programs like Section 1122 or certificate of need can only prevent unneeded investments. If providers do not propose capital expenditures, the regulators cannot generate the investments in the services or in the places where they are needed. Monopoly control of capital, in contrast, would allow government initiation of capital investment as well as government rejection of investments that others propose.

---

[25] *Special Analyses, Budget of the United States, Fiscal Year 1978* (Washington, D.C.: U.S. Government Printing Office, 1977), p. 215.

[26] Lewin and Associates, Inc., *Government Controls on the Health Care System: The Canadian Experience* (Washington, D.C.: January 31, 1976).

The Operation and Impact of Facility Regulation

REGULATING FACILITIES
BY CERTIFICATE OF NEED

On one level, the task of project review is not particularly difficult. Providers develop a proposal and submit it for review. Planners appraise the proposal and recommend approval or denial. Fulfilling the letter of the law—reviewing applications and making recommendations—is easy; agencies have been doing it for years.

It is extremely difficult, however, to make a substantive review that really determines the "needs" of an area, decides whether a particular project will help meet those needs, evaluates whether the proposed project is the best way to meet those needs (or whether the provider is the best one—or even a capable one—to carry out the project), and finally decides whether the project is worth the cost. Going through the process of reviewing projects is easy; actually determining "need" is so hard as to be, in practice, impossible. Facility regulation as currently practiced by Section 1122 and certificate-of-need agencies cannot produce optimal results.

Local planning agencies have always found it difficult to control costs. First, planning agencies have been funded at too low a level to meet all their responsibilities. The early Comprehensive Health Planning agencies often were financially dependent on the very providers they were supposed to influence.[27] The National Health Planning Act of 1974 eliminated that problem by prohibiting provider funding; this act also authorized more federal money to the local agencies. But the appropriations have never equaled authorizations, and the funding is still limited. Indeed, at whatever level HSAs are funded, they still would not be able to fully accomplish all their tasks. There are too few skilled personnel to inventory all the health resources and needs of the area, to provide technical expertise to other groups, to draw up a health plan and an annual implementation plan, to review and make recommendations on all capital expenditure projects, and to review the appropriateness of all the health facilities in the area every

---

[27] J. Joel May, "The Impact of Regulation on the Hospital Industry," Center for Health Administration Studies, University of Chicago, May 1974, (mimeographed).

five years.[28] Planners in the Miami area HSA reported that if deciding on "appropriateness" meant reviewing every service in every hospital in the area, they could not adequately perform that task even if they had no other responsibilities.

There is, in fact, a serious national shortage of trained, skilled personnel to fill HSA positions. In 1976, Joel May, Director of the Graduate Program in Hospital Administration at the University of Chicago, said it was unlikely that "sufficient manpower for these purposes can be identified or trained in the near future." [29] A survey of HSAs supported this statement; remarkably enough, 68 of the 134 HSAs surveyed had no staff members with expertise in data gathering and analysis, and 28 had none with expertise in planning. Moreover, the HSAs surveyed were the ones that DHEW had designated as operational—presumably the agencies that were best developed and prepared.[30]

Given their limited staff, expertise, and time, HSAs must decide how best to allocate their efforts. They must decide, for example, whether to choose to develop a detailed plan rather than to review projects. Even within project review, they must decide what types of projects to emphasize. Bicknell and Walsh reported that in Massachusetts the planners concentrated on beds, and "the closer, technically more sophisticated scrutiny was normally reserved for bed related applications." [31] The uneven development of criteria and data that Lewin and Associates found indicates that Massachusetts is not atypical in this respect, and that agencies have had to concentrate their efforts on certain subjects.

The limited availability and poor quality of data constitute another constraint within which HSAs must operate. Planning agencies typically spent several years just making an inventory of the health resources available in the area. "The inability to obtain complete and reliable data on a regular basis

---

[28] PL 93–641, Section 1513 (a–g).

[29] J. Joel May, "Will Third Generation Planning Succeed?" reprinted from *Hospital Progress*, March 1976, n. p.

[30] Office of Health Resources, Opportunity, Health Resources Administration (HRA), Public Health Service (PHS), DHEW, "Project Summary: Board and Staff of Health Planning Agencies," DHEW Publication No. HRA 78–609, p. 12.

[31] William Bicknell and Diana Chapman Walsh, "Certificate-of-Need: The Massachusetts Experience," *New England Journal of Medicine* 292 (May 15, 1975):1057.

is one of the most crippling problems facing review agencies, particularly at the local level." [32] This deficiency means that many state and local areas have reviewed projects without systematic data, particularly for projects involving specialized beds, equipment, and services. Even when information is available, it is often out of date: "Seventy-nine percent of the states and nearly half of the area agencies were relying on acute care utilization data at least two years old." [33] The data on future costs are even worse. Lewin and Associates concluded that "agencies are unable to differentiate between efficient and inefficient health resources." [34] With information scarce or out of date, it is difficult to produce meaningful need projections or to develop a plan that can be used in project review. A study of the U.S. comptroller general found that some states and localities were reviewing projects with no plan at all, and that most did not have a plan that was useful in regulatory decision making. [35]

More important than the lack of data and staff resources is the state of the art of health planning and, more generally, the state of medical evaluation. There is no accepted methodology for establishing the "need" for even the most common services, much less for new or infrequently used procedures. Should projections of bed "needs" be based on current utilization rates, on health maintenance organization (HMO) rates (which are 10 percent to 60 percent lower), or on some other standard? If excess hospitalization exists, employing current utilization rates for projections simply projects excess utilization into the future. In this respect, a program like President Carter's 1978 hospital regulation bill that would tie construction to occupancy levels could, at best, only reduce the number of beds that were unnecessary because they were unfilled. It would not deal with beds that were unnecessarily filled; indeed, it would provide an incentive to fill beds.

The magnitude and the impossibility of the job HSAs are expected to perform should be clear. Determining the value

---

[32] Lewin and Associates, Inc., *Evaluation of the Efficiency and Effectiveness of the Section 1122 Review Process: Part I* (Washington, D.C.: September 1975), p. III–32.

[33] Ibid., p. IV–17.

[34] Ibid., p. VI–2.

[35] Comptroller General of the United States, *Comprehensive Health Planning as Carried Out by States and Areawide Agencies in Three States* (Washington, D.C.: U.S. Government Printing Office, 1974).

of medical procedures is very difficult. Because of the paucity of controlled, random clinical trials in medicine, new procedures can be introduced and become standard practice, even though later they may be shown to have no medical benefits. Even when procedures are shown to have medical benefits for some patients, a true determination of "need" would require an estimate of how generally applicable such benefits are. For a variety of reasons—including the lack of clinical trials, the natural and admirable tendency of doctors to try procedures if there is any hope of favorable outcome, and the placebo effect—appraisals of procedures are rare and difficult. Yet if HSAs are to carry out their mandate of certifying need properly, these issues must be addressed. HSAs are, in fact, put in the position of determining what the proper practice of medicine ought to be. For example, in deciding how many institutional renal dialysis units are needed in an area, planners must decide how many patients can appropriately use home dialysis (a much less expensive treatment), even though physicians seriously disagree on precisely that question, and the estimates vary widely.[36]

Ultimately, determining the "need" for medical facilities is not a question of gathering the best data and employing the proper planning methodology to arrive impartially at objective standards. Facility control is, and must be, a political question. That is, planning must establish priorities and decide on trade-offs between competing values; it is impossible to reach an objective and absolute determination of the need for a new service. As Walter McClure has said, "the quality, quantity and style of medical care are indefinitely expansible. The medical care system can legitimately absorb every dollar society will make available to it."[37] Thus most proposed projects are "needed" in the sense that they will be used and will presumably benefit patients. The question that ought to be asked is not whether they are needed but whether they are worth their cost—whether they are desirable when compared with alternative ways to use resources.

For example, even if a large number of underutilized beds existed in a particular area, a newly developed and growing

---

[36] Christopher Blagg and Tom Sawyer, "Letters to the Editor," see *New England Journal of Medicine* 289 (September 6, 1973):537, and the reply from Eli Friedman in ibid.

[37] McClure, "Medicare Care System," p. 32.

suburb might have no nearby hospital. The suburb might need better access to medical care, but this need must be balanced against increased costs in the area as a whole if more beds were added to an already overbuilt market. More data and improved planning methods can help clarify the issues and illuminate the alternatives in this case. For example, we need to know how much more a new hospital would cost the region and how decreased travel time would affect health status and consumer satisfaction. But the final decision is not technological but political: How much are we willing to pay to improve access for inhabitants of that suburb? Obviously, different people will have different answers to that question. There is no correct answer or even best answer, and the issue can be resolved only through the political process.

The current emphasis on plans and professional determination of need therefore misses the basic issue: the making of choices. Because state and local planning agencies do not operate under a fixed, or even a limited, capital budget, they are not forced to consider whether one project is more useful than another, or whether there might be a cheaper way of obtaining particular results. They *can* consider such issues, but they are not required to do so. It is quite possible, and indeed it sometimes happens, that an agency approves every proposal that comes before it. After all, as has been mentioned, most projects are "needed" in some absolute sense. Without a budgetary limit, therefore, agencies have little reason to restrict projects.

Many observers have blamed the poor record of past health planning on the "capture" of the planning agencies by the providers. The 1974 Planning Act does require a consumer majority on the local Health Systems Agency board, but it also requires at least 40 percent provider participation. Studies have shown that consumers tend to be less active than providers, so the boards often end up provider-dominated despite a consumer majority. This is particularly true of specialized committees like project review. Moreover, consumer members of HSA boards often are selected as representatives of special interest groups which are more concerned about their particular goals than about controlling costs. For example, representatives of senior citizen groups are likely to push for more services rather than fewer, because their members are high users who bear little of the tax and insurance costs for their care.[38]

The problem, however, is not so much numbers as interests. Unless regulatory boards contain individuals or groups who have a real interest in controlling costs and facility growth, regulation is unlikely to be effective. The present system of local HSA review and state regulation in a context of multiple financing does not establish a concentrated stake in effective regulation. State and local government officials may be more concerned about costs than HSAs, because their governments must help finance Medicaid expenditures. The capacity of government officials to participate in HSAs has been restricted by the 1974 National Health Planning Act, so cost concern is likely to be more effectively expressed at the state level. Groups who have a role in paying for medical care, like Blue Cross, unions, or large employers, presumably have an interest in cost control. But they have been neither heavily represented on local boards nor particularly active. For example, a survey of 134 HSAs revealed that only 5 percent of the providers were health care insurers.[39]

Given the composition of planning boards, they should not be expected to be interested in controlling costs. Many planners see their role as improving distribution of facilities, even at the risk of increasing costs. Thus Lewin and Associates reported that fewer than one-half of the state agencies identified cost control as a primary goal and one-fifth of the local agencies said cost control was not a goal at all.[40]

Even if payers were present and active, facility regulation as now structured would achieve less than optimal results. There is evidence that consumers in some areas have been more cost-conscious than this analysis would predict.[41] But even cost-conscious regulators are unlikely to decide against a new project unless they operate under some financial con-

---

[38] For a fuller discussion of community support, see Ray Elling, "The Hospital Support Game in Urban Centers," in Eliot Freidson, ed. *The Hospital in Modern Society* (Glencoe, Ill.: Free Press, 1963).

[39] Office of Health Resources Opportunity, "Project Summary," p. 11.

[40] Lewin and Associates, Inc., *Evaluation of the Section 1122 Review Process*, p. IV-7.

[41] Drew Altman, "The Politics of Health Care Regulation: The Care of the National Health Planning and Resources Development Act," *Journal of Health Politics, Policy, and Law* 12 (Winter 1978):560–80.

straints. The marginal cost of a new facility to Blue Cross, to a union, or to taxpayers is smaller than the facility's impact on the total bill for medical care. As already noted, agencies will tend to approve a project because they do not have to face the full financial consequences of that approval. Nearly 75 percent of the states and areas in the Lewin study had "approved hospital beds in excess of 105 percent of their published need projections for five years hence." [42] Until funds are clearly limited, the balance of competing values that is an essential part of facility regulation will remain tilted towards costly approvals.

THE RESULTS OF FACILITY REGULATION

The foregoing analysis is supported by the fact that the published studies using national data do not report favorably on the effectiveness of certificate-of-need programs. At best, the studies indicate that such programs have had little impact on hospital investments, and apparently there have been some perverse effects. Although some case studies of state certificate-of-need programs have concluded that the program in question had an impact on hospital investment,[43] other case studies have found CON to be ineffective.[44] This conflict indicates there may be a wide variation among the states. Case studies that use the number of projects denied certification as an indicator of success, however, implicitly assume that the projects

---

[42] Lewin and Associates, Inc., *Evaluation of the Section 1122 Review Process*, p. IV–7.

[43] See, for example, William J. Bicknell and Diana C. Walsh, "The Certificate-of-Need: The Massachusetts Experience," *The New England Journal of Medicine*, May 15, 1975, 1054–61; Alan Reider, John R. Mason, and Leonard Glantz, "Certificate-of-Need: The Massachusetts Experience," *American Journal of Law and Medicine* 1 (March 1975): 13–40; and G. Stuehler, "Certificate-of-Need: A Systems Analysis of Maryland's Experience and Plans," *American Journal of Public Health* 63 (November 1973).

[44] Eleanore Rothenberg, *Regulation and Expansion of Health Facilities: The C/N Experience in New York State* (New York: Praeger, 1976); Powell, *Bureaucratic Malpractice;* Anne Somers, *State Regulations of Hospitals and Health Care: The New Jersey Story*, Research Series No. 11 (Chicago: Blue Cross Reports, July 1973); Bonnie Lefkowitz, "Health Planning and Certificate-of-Need Regulation in Maryland" (mimeographed), Harvard University, June 1975.

would actually have been built if it had not been for agency denial. This assumption is simply not true.[45] Further, although an agency may deny some projects, the overwhelming majority of proposed projects are approved. In a national sample, only 5 percent of all hospital proposals were denied.[46]

Nevertheless, the very existence of a reviewing agency may persuade some providers not even to bother to apply for approval of expansion, so for this reason, too, approval rates are not really the best indicator of program success. Unfortunately for facility regulation, national studies seem to confirm the impression that planning and regulatory agencies have not significantly affected facility growth. To avoid the problems of descriptive case studies, David Salkever and Thomas Bice used cross-sectional analysis of state data to develop sets of regression estimates for the net effect of certificate-of-need regulation.[47] They found that although the number of hospital beds was indeed reduced in states with such regulation, no reduction in total capital growth had occurred in those states when they were compared with states without certificate-of-need regulation. Apparently hospitals had merely shifted their investments from beds to other facilities. Salkever and Bice concluded that certificate-of-need regulation does not "reduce the total dollar volume of investment; [CON only] alters its composition." [48] Joel May found a similar pattern of changed investment in his study of local health planning agencies, the old 314(b) CHP agencies that antedated HSAs.[49] Fred Hellinger also found that total invest-

[45] Carolyn Harmon, "The Efficiency and Effectiveness of Health Care Capital Expenditures and Service Controls: An Interim Assessment," in Herbert H. Hyman, ed., *Health Regulation* (Germantown, Md.: Aspen Systems Corporation, 1977), pp. 45–6.

[46] Lewin and Associates, Inc., *Evaluation of the Section 1122 Review Process*, p. I–21, Table I–17.

[47] David Salkever and Thomas Bice, "The Impact of Certificate-of-Need Controls on Hospital Investment," paper presented to Center for Health Administration Studies Workshop, October 8, 1975, University of Chicago.

[48] Ibid., p. 1.

[49] J. Joel May, "The Impact of Regulation on the Hospital Industry" (mineographed), May 1974, draft, University of Chicago; see also his "The Planning and Licensing Agencies," in Clark Havighurst, ed., *Regulating Health Facilities Construction* (Washington, D.C.: American Enterprise Institute for Public Policy Research, 1974), pp. 47–68.

ment was not decreased by certificate-of-need controls.[50] He noted that hospitals anticipated the advent of controls by actually increasing their investments immediately before the controls took effect, so at least in the short term, the program resulted in more, not less, hospital investment.

None of the published studies has examined the net impact of certificate-of-need programs on costs. As already noted, the total effect on costs can be ambiguous, if savings from reducing the bed supply are balanced by an increase in other investments. In a report to DHEW, Salkever and Bice used several different models to estimate the effect of certificate-of-need programs on costs. They concluded that the controls had no strong impact, either positive or negative, on total hospital costs.[51]

These conclusions may be too pessimistic for some states. The case studies mentioned earlier indicate that some states are doing a better job controlling costs than others. In the study by Lewin and Associates, six states consistently ranked at the top of their "effectiveness" scales.[52] States differ markedly in their statutory provisions,[53] in the financial and staff support they provide for facility regulation[54] and in their political climate and acceptance of regulation. Other preliminary analyses also indicate that certificate-of-need programs have significantly different effects in different states.[55] Some differences among states would undoubtedly persist under national health insurance, but the degree of difference would

---

[50] Fred J. Hellinger, "The Effect of Certificate-of-Need Legislation on Hospital Investment," draft of article that appeared in *Inquiry*, June 1976.

[51] David Salkever and Thomas Bice, "The Impact of Certificate-of-Need Controls on Hospital Investment, Costs, and Utilization," final report to the National Center for Health Services Research, DHEW, Contract No. HRA–106–74–57.

[52] The six states are New York, Ohio, Indiana, Connecticut, Michigan, and Georgia. Lewin and Associates, Inc., *Evaluation of the Section 1122 Review Process*, p. IV–24.

[53] Lewin and Associates, Inc., "Nationwide Survey of State Health Regulations," Contract No. HEW–05–73–212, September 16, 1974.

[54] Lewin and Associates, Inc., *Evaluation of the Section 1122 Review Process*, p. III–37.

[55] Donald R. Cohodes, "Certificate-of-Need Controls and Hospitals: An Outcome Assessment" (mineographed, n.d.); Andrew Dunham, "The Impact of Certificate-of-Need Regulation," address to the Center for Health Administration Studies Workshop, University of Chicago, May 18, 1978.

be affected by other features of the program, particularly the source of financing.

PROVIDER RESPONSES TO REGULATION

Facility regulation, like most regulatory programs, produces some perverse or unanticipated consequences. The "wise guy" effect, in which the regulated alter their behavior to get around or overcome the regulatory constraints, has produced some unwanted results. The first has already been mentioned: increased investment just before controls take effect. According to Hellinger, providers apparently rush to make investments "while they still can." [56] Investment might increase after regulation as well. For instance, certificate-of-need regulation could protect hospitals from competition if regulators turned down applications for new facilities. This action might encourage investment by reducing the risk that high costs would invite entry from lower-cost competition. A certificate-of-need program also enhances the availability of investment funds from the commercial capital market, because potential lenders or investors view the franchise-like character of the certificate of need as protecting the hospital's ability to generate an adequate cash flow.

Along with some tendencies to stimulate investment, a certificate-of-need program can change the type and site of investments. It has already been noted that hospitals shift from beds to plant, because beds are scrutinized more closely and are denied more often.[57] There is also evidence of a shift toward unregulated settings. The furor over CAT scanners has revealed that some scanners have been put in doctors' offices (or bought by doctors and leased to hospitals) to avoid facing a project review. The shift to unregulated settings is sure to continue, and indeed would grow stronger if facility control were stricter.

Another way to avoid review is to disaggregate projects so that they fall below the threshold for review. For example, if the state threshold is $100,000, the hospital could make several smaller purchases instead of a single investment that

[56] Hellinger, "The Effect of Certificate-of-Need Controls."
[57] Lewin and Associates, Inc., *Evaluation of the Section 1122 Review Process*, p. I–10, Table I–9.

would require a certificate of need. Although the total cost might be raised by such a maneuver, the hospital would avoid the regulatory limits.

Another possibility is that providers will bypass the application process altogether or will simply ignore a denial and proceed with construction anyway. At present, there is no way to estimate the extent of such practices, and because agencies currently approve most applications, there are few cases in which ignoring the law would be an issue. Providers have, on occasion, proceeded with plans after approval was denied under Section 1122 review, and such cases might become more common if for some reason the facility agencies became more restrictive.

The threat of indirect financial sanctions is not always sufficient to inhibit a hospital; a hospital can proceed with its investment and either give up the revenue of the disallowed costs or pass the costs on to other payers. Because the federal government provides about 40 percent of hospital revenues, and because capital costs are a fraction of total costs for services, this strategy is quite possible, particularly if the facility is only lightly used by federal patients.

Even with stronger sanctions, compliance still would be problematic. First, an effective deterrent requires that there be a reasonable chance of detecting noncompliance. Health Systems Agencies have no systematic method of monitoring hospital behavior to know what new services and facilities have been added; HSAs do not even follow up the denial of a certificate to see if the denial has been respected. Detection of noncompliance is not the end of the issue either, for the proper authorities must still be notified of the noncompliance and they must be sufficiently interested to take action.

The functioning of Section 1122 illustrates some of the difficulties involved in enforcing regulation or applying sanctions. DHEW's Bureau of Health Planning and Resources Development is responsible for the regulations governing the Section 1122 review process. The programs administering Titles V, XVIII, and XIX of the Social Security Act, however, have the responsibility of determining the amount of actual withholding that may occur following a determination by one of the department's regional health administrators that reimbursement should be withheld.[58]

---

[58] Letter from Colin C. Rorrie for Harry Cain II, Director, HRA, PHS, DHEW, January 31, 1977.

Three federal agencies, therefore, share responsibility for various expenses. In the case of Medicaid or Maternal and Child Health Programs, the federal agency is supposed to inform the state agency of a denied capital expenditure, and the state agency (or its intermediary) is supposed to reduce payments. For Medicare payments, the federal agency is supposed to inform the fiscal intermediaries, who are then to reduce payments. Obviously there is considerable potential for delay or simple failure to communicate denials and, hence, there is potential for failure to reduce payments. For example, in response to some inquiries for this book, the acting regional Medicaid director of one federal region commented that "as far as we can determine, none of the states in (our) Region— have received reduced payments from the federal government because of Section 1122." In contrast, the Social Security Administration's program officer for the same region announced that two projects had been completed despite denial of certification. (No reimbursements, however, had been withheld to reinforce the denial of certification.) The potential for noncommunication is also supported by the fact that many fiscal intermediaries, in response to our inquiries, said "to our knowledge" or "as far as we know" no denials had occurred in their regions. One region's officer pointed out that Section 1122 regulation was just a minuscule part of the region's program and did not warrant a major data collection or enforcement effort.

State certificate-of-need laws reduce the likelihood of noncompliance, but do not eliminate the possibility. Federal regulations setting national standards for state certificate-of-need programs require stronger sanctions than merely withholding payments. But sanctions such as license forfeiture, injunctions, or civil or criminal penalties may not create a sufficient deterrent either. For example, Virginia's law, which calls for a $1,000 fine if expansion is undertaken without a certificate of need, is probably too weak to prevent investments. Yet states that have stronger sanctions are unlikely to invoke them. Some states' laws allow forfeiture of the license for the whole facility if an uncertified investment takes place. Shutting down a hospital that is providing needed care simply because it added an uncertified CAT scanner is an extreme response—and unlikely to be used. DHEW's difficulties thus far in enforcing quality standards suggest that closing a facility because of violations is not very likely.[59] Hence we conclude that some providers will continue with their investment plans despite regulatory controls.

Finally, regulation that encourages or permits the construction or expansion of ambulatory facilities or other supposedly more efficient forms of care such as health maintenance organizations may actually increase health costs in the short term. According to Roemer's Law, the fact that the old, less efficient facilities continue to exist means they will continue to be used. Duplication and excessive utilization of facilities will result. This situation has been reported in Canada, and Feldstein has found evidence in the United States supporting this point.[60] If regulators try to restrict the growth of more efficient delivery modes, however, they merely perpetuate costly and inefficient health facilities. Unless providers can be persuaded to close down some facilities once they are replaced by more efficient delivery systems, local health costs may not be reduced at all.

The Future of Facility Regulation Under National Health Insurance

National health insurance might change the operation of facility regulation in two ways: (1) NHI could change the dynamics of medical care providers, and so change the pressure on regulators; and (2) NHI could directly change the authority, procedures, incentives, and behavior of the regulators. Because facility regulators traditionally have not used all the authority they had, the more interesting changes national health insurance might bring involve changing the will or political climate for control, rather than altering the statutory authority.

National health insurance is likely to increase demand for medical care. Past government financing programs—Medicare, Medicaid, and the recent amendments adding renal dialysis to Medicare—have all increased demand for medical

---

[59] Judith M. Feder, *Medicare: The Politics of Federal Hospital Insurance* (Lexington, Mass.: D.C. Heath, Lexington Books, 1978).

[60] Martin S. Feldstein, "Hospital Cost Inflation: A Study of Non-Profit Price Dynamics," *American Economic Review* 61 (December 1971): 853–72.

care, and consequently have increased pressures for facility expansion. Any NHI program enacted could be expected to reduce the financial barriers of at least some consumer groups to at least some services. The extent of barrier reduction would depend on provisions involving deductibles, coinsurance, needs tests, populations covered, and services included. But the important point is that NHI probably would further reduce whatever constraints are now imposed by patients' financing.

As a result, restrictions on the expansionary dynamics of the medical care market will have to come from the supply side, including, of course, physicians, who control most hospital demand. The supply restrictions could take several forms: more extensive peer review through utilization review; Professional Standards Review Organizations (PSROs); development of HMOs; and finally, new payment methods that would increase provider incentives for low-cost care. These developments could take full effect in conjunction with national health insurance or, as appears to be happening, without adoption of a major NHI program.

FACILITY REGULATION AND OTHER CONTROL MECHANISMS

Health Maintenance Organizations

There is considerable evidence that health maintenance organizations involving group practice and salaried physicians use significantly fewer hospital resources than does the fee-for-service delivery system. A general reduction in utilization rates to HMO levels, estimated as at least 10 percent and maybe as much as 30 percent lower than fee-for-service levels, would obviously reduce pressures to build more hospital beds. (Kaiser has only 2.2 beds per 1,000 population served, compared with a 1976 national average of 4.5.) Reduced utilization involves not only beds but certain services. By reducing utilization (and revenue) of hospitals, extensive HMO coverage would reduce both the incentives and the financial ability of hospitals to expand. Because a growing amount of construction is financed by hospital revenues or borrowing, and availability of capital affects facility construction,[61] extensive HMO

---

[61] Paul Ginsburg, "Resource Allocation in the Hospital Industry: The Role of Capital Financing," *Social Security Bulletin* 35 (October 1972): 20–30.

coverage would be an important and effective form of facility control.

Unfortunately, there is little reason to believe that HMOs with group practices and salaried physicians are going to expand rapidly. Although HMOs were the "cornerstone" of the Nixon health strategy and also have been favored by Senator Edward Kennedy, HMO development in the last few years has been slow. Their slow development is often attributed to peculiarities in the HMO Act of 1973, but it is also true that physician organizations have opposed and continue to oppose the concept and development of health maintenance organizations.

There is little reason to expect HMOs to replace fee-for-service reimbursement under national health insurance. Marmor and Thomas observe that although physician payment methods under NHI programs throughout the world are very diverse, there is always a "remarkably close resemblance to what physicians were used to before the program began." [62] It is interesting in this light that no NHI bill, not even the Kennedy-Corman Health Security plan that promotes HMOs, proposes to eliminate fee-for-service payment methods. The medical foundation form of HMOs (in which physicians still receive a fee for each service) is clearly less effective in reducing facility utilization than are HMOs with salaried physicians.[63] Indeed, the method of paying physicians may be the key factor in utilization rates.[64]

If we can judge from experience, HMO development is unlikely to eliminate pressure for facility control. HMOs are developing too slowly to effect a significant restructuring of the medical system soon. Moreover, the form many will take, including the fee-for-service HMO, probably would not effectively reduce utilization, and hence would not significantly reduce either the demand for facility services or the ability of facilities to expand.

---

[62] Theodore R. Marmor and David Thomas, "Doctors, Politics, and Pay Disputes: Pressure Groups Politics Revisited," *British Journal of Political Science* 2, Part 4 (October 1972):437.

[63] Clifton Gaus, Barbara Cooper, and Constance Hirschman, "Contrasts in HMO and Fee-for-Service Performance," *Social Security Bulletin* 39 (May 1976):3–14.

[64] Richard Foster, "HMO: A Synthesis of the Evidence of Use," paper presented at the Center for Health Administration Studies Workshop, University of Chicago, April 1977.

Although HMOs may not make the task of regulators any easier, certificate-of-need regulation could have a negative impact on HMOs. At best, the need to get approval to build new facilities or to expand existing ones places one more barrier to the development and growth of this delivery method. At worst, an HSA or state agency hostile to HMOs could significantly delay or even prevent the formation or expansion of prepaid practice. Even when regulators are favorably disposed toward HMOs, difficulties will occur. For example, should an HMO be allowed to build a surgical unit? If certification were granted, the overall costs in the area would probably increase, because the inpatient facilities already there would continue to exist. But if certification were denied, not only would cheaper forms of care be prevented, but the HMO's ability to compete and grow would be hindered.

Utilization Review

In theory, utilization review could change the practice of medicine and significantly reduce hospital utilization (and revenue). There is evidence that extensive review does indeed reduce utilization rates.[65] Therefore, extension of coverage by Professional Standards Review Organizations to the whole country, whether coupled with national health insurance or not, might reduce pressure for construction of new facilities. The impact would probably be greater on some services than on others, because the standards for some services may be stringent enough to control the expansionary demand. For example, if guidelines called for extensive use of home dialysis, and if these guidelines were enforced through reduced payment mechanisms, there would be fewer requests for certificates of need for institutional dialysis units.

In general, however, utilization review by itself probably would not greatly reduce utilization or facility growth. Empirical evidence indicates that any measurable reduction resulting from utilization review thus far has been small, certainly not on the order of the reduction effected by HMOs. Because this evidence comes from areas that have been rela-

---

[65] Congressional Budget Office, *Expenditures for Health Care: Federal Programs and Their Effects* (Washington, D.C.: U.S. Government Printing Office, August 1977).

tively favorable to peer review, the figures may actually be upper limits and therefore may not be duplicated when PSROs are extended to other parts of the country.[66] The standards developed by PSROs have not restricted the ordinary practice of medicine in the area, partly because the standards are developed by local physicians. This practice allows physicians to institutionalize the local practice of medicine in the standards: For example, if there are a large number of surgeons in the area (and a large number of surgeries), the PSRO would probably produce standards that allow a high surgery rate. As Havighurst and Blumstein have pointed out, PSROs are likely to produce standards that favor quality over cost control.[67] To continue the example given earlier, PSRO-generated standards for home dialysis would probably approve more institutional dialysis than a cost-conscious decision maker would.

The development of utilization standards might marginally improve facility control in one way: The development and publication of utilization rates for various services and equipment could provide added justification to facility regulators to deny requests. Indeed, the use of PSRO standards would considerably reduce the work load of HSAs. Yet use of these standards would not be beneficial if, as Havighurst and Blumstein suggest, the standards are lax. Moreover, it should be reemphasized that facility regulators have in the past approved expenditures that would increase facilities beyond their own published need standards. At best, standards offer only a political tool that could facilitate denial; by themselves, standards will not provide the political will to control growth. Regulation is a political problem, not a technical one.

Payment Mechanisms

The effect of payment mechanisms on facility growth is hard to forecast. We do not know what method might be incorporated into an NHI bill or how that method would be administered; indeed, several bills explicitly call for experi-

---

[66] Richard Krieg, "Utilization Review," University of Chicago, December 1976 (mimeographed).

[67] Clark C. Havighurst and James F. Blumstein, "Coping with Quality/Cost Trade-Offs in Medical Care: The Role of PSROs," *Northwestern University Law Review* 70 (March-April 1975):6–68.

mentation. But restrictions on capital funds are absolutely central to facility growth. As long as facilities could generate revenues that exceeded expenditures, could borrow capital, or could receive philanthropic donations, they would benefit from expansion and would propose capital expenditures. And without a significant change in the political climate, these expenditures would continue to be approved. Conversely, payment mechanisms that restricted the availability of funds would reduce the number of proposals for additional facilities and thereby control facility growth regardless of what facility regulators did.

For an example, let us return to the problem of renal dialysis. When Medicare began to cover treatment of end-stage renal disease for all patients regardless of age (following enactment of the 1972 amendments to the Social Security Act), demand for renal dialysis jumped and institutions began plans to expand their services. Dialysis at home is feasible for a significant proportion of the affected population and is far cheaper than hospital dialysis. Because of deductibles and coinsurance, however, home care costs the patient more than institutional treatment does; moreover, physicians get higher remuneration for care they give in institutions. The demand for institutional services, then, is quite high, and if the planning agency were simply to respond to demand, there would be more facilities and much larger program costs than are theoretically necessary. But a local planning agency (or state agency) has little reason to prevent institutional care. The physicians want it, the patients want it, and the federal government pays for it. Alternatively, if the payment mechanisms were to provide for free care at home, plus stiff patient deductibles and lower physician fees for institutional care, demand for institutional care would drop dramatically.

For another example, a Wisconsin HSA planner told us that for some years his office had spent a great deal of time and effort reviewing proposals for new or expanding nursing homes. Then the state reduced its Medicaid reimbursement for nursing home care, and suddenly old applications were withdrawn and no new ones were proposed. Clearly, reimbursement is a key to facility control.

Reimbursement policies could have beneficial effects other than merely reducing the number of applications. If a state has both facility and rate regulation, and if there is a close relationship between them, facility regulators can get a much better idea of the operating costs of a proposed project. Facility regulators depend chiefly on providers for information on how much a new service or facility will cost, both for capital and operating expenses. A Maryland HSA planner asserted that providers were coming in with a low estimate of operating costs and then going to the rate regulators with a higher figure. Where they exist, budget or rate review agencies can provide a more accurate estimate of costs and thereby improve facility regulation. A Lewin study noted that of the six states that ranked highest on their effectiveness scales for project review, all but one had some form of rate regulation as well.[68]

Yet the causal connection is not certain. Certificate-of-need programs, by legitimizing new services, could make it harder for rate regulators to control costs. The connection Lewin and Associates noted could simply reflect the fact that some states are more serious about controlling health care costs, have a greater political commitment to controls, and so have more regulatory programs. It is probably the political commitment, not the number or interaction of programs, that determines effectiveness. And it should be remembered that reimbursement policies are as likely to fuel investment as to control costs. Certainly the experience of Medicaid, Medicare, and renal dialysis does not justify reliance on reimbursement policies to control investment.

Capped Capital Budget

A probable change in facility regulation, either in conjunction with or before the adoption of national health insurance, is the addition of a lid or cap on the total amount invested. As mentioned earlier, a cap would create incentives for tougher facility review, less investment, and presumably lower cost increases. An investment lid would force regulators to make determinations of relative rather than absolute need, and hence would force them to make choices. Establishment of a lid on total investment is a necessary change if facility regulation is to become a significant cost control mechanism.

---

[68] Lewin and Associates, Inc., *Evaluation of the Section 1122 Review Process*, p. IV–25.

Having said this, the limitations on a capped capital budget should be noted. The capped budget, at least as proposed by the Carter administration, would not control all investments, only those investments in health institutions that are large enough to meet the certificate-of-need trigger criterion. We must expect, therefore, that hospitals would occasionally divide their investments into smaller discrete units that singly would not require certification; and we must expect a shift of investment to unregulated settings like physicians' offices. These two tendencies would reduce the total impact of the regulation. The Congressional Budget Office's estimate of the savings by 1982 under the capped budget is clearly optimistic. It assumes no compensatory growth either in investments not requiring certification, or in investments outside hospitals.[69] Yet even if the projected $9.5 billion savings in 1982 are unrealistic, and even if the number of small projects doubled and considerable investment occurred in physicians' offices, capping the investment budget would still greatly reduce capital expenditures.

Another difficulty associated with a capped budget—the problem of political pressures on behalf of powerful interests —must be addressed. State and local agencies forced to operate within tight investment constraints would experience considerable pressure, and there is no reason to expect that resource allocation under such circumstances would prove ideal. Moreover, a capped budget would not solve the problem of inadequate investment in underserved areas. In fact, that problem might be exacerbated as the few projects that were proposed for underserved areas were forced to compete for certificates of need with the many proposals from overserved but politically powerful areas. There is little reason to believe that the greatly limited investments would go where they were most "needed." Large teaching hospitals have great community influence, and suburban areas tend to be more politically effective than the inner city. As Marmor and associates have pointed out, "the political process is unlikely to right the distributive wrongs of the economic marketplace when a similar set of actors dominate both."[70]

---

[69] Congressional Budget Office, "Hospital Cost Containment Act," p. 40, Table 4.

[70] Theodore R. Marmor, Donald Wittman, and Thomas Heagy, "The Politics of Medical Inflation," *Journal of Health, Politics, Policy and Law*, vol. 1, no. 1, p. 81.

FACILITY REGULATION WITH NHI PROGRAMS

This section examines how particular provisions of various national health insurance proposals would affect and be affected by facility regulation. The analysis here proceeds bill by bill, but it should be clear that most of what is said about the probable results of legal changes in facility regulation does not depend on the particular bill. For example, only the Kennedy-Mills bill would provide authority for regulators to close down existing facilities, so the administrative and political difficulties of actually using that power are discussed only in relation to that bill. Yet any NHI program that had such power would encounter similar difficulties in actually putting that regulation into effect.

Kennedy-Corman

The Kennedy-Corman bill would substantially extend the scope and authority of certificate-of-need and Section 1122 regulation. Kennedy-Corman's Section 53 would require all participating providers to get certificates of need for new construction or enlargement. The paragraph specifically includes ambulatory-care facilities, which in the past have generally not been covered. The proposal also would expand the sanction of Section 1122 review, because virtually all payments to providers would be reduced in the event of uncertified capital expenditures.

The proposed extension of control to ambulatory facilities has been extremely controversial. When DHEW was writing the regulations for the National Health Planning and Resource Development Act to define the required coverage of state certificate-of-need laws, an early draft included coverage of large physician group practices. Strong objections were made to this expansion of coverage, and eventually surgi-centers were the only ambulatory-care facilities included. Further objections to office coverage were raised in congressional consideration of amendments to the planning act in 1978.

Unless NHI regulations could overcome physicians' opposition, coverage of physicians' offices would be left to the states. Most state laws do not cover such facilities at present. Therefore, before controls could be extended to physicians' offices, state legislatures would have to act, a time-consuming and controversial process. A small number of aggressively regulatory states might extend coverage to physicians' offices, but experience suggests that most states would not exceed federal requirements.

Even if federal or state governments were to expand certificate-of-need coverage to ambulatory facilities, no similar expansion would occur in actual regulatory review activities. The Health Systems Agencies and state agencies that must perform certificate-of-need regulation are already overburdened. One-fifth of all physicians were in a group practice in 1972,[71] so the addition of just group practice ambulatory facilities to the regulatory responsibilities of HSAs would immensely increase their task. HSA staffing and resources are unlikely to increase commensurately. Confronted with responsibilities far beyond their resources, the HSAs would still have to choose where to concentrate their efforts. Although obvious attempts to circumvent hospital controls—CAT scanning has already been mentioned—might attract regulators' attention, regulators most probably would continue to focus primarily on hospitals, particularly hospital beds.

The Kennedy-Corman bill would make virtually all payments to facilities through a single source—a newly established Health Board. If the indirect sanctions of Section 1122 review were invoked, none of the costs of construction would be reimbursed. Because providers would not be able to make up the loss from other sources as they now can, the effectiveness of Section 1122 review should increase. Facilities that under current arrangements were willing to bear the partial loss of revenue might be deterred from making capital expenditures.

The most important impact of the Kennedy-Corman bill on the regulators would come not from the sections dealing specifically with facility regulation but with the method of payment and the capped budget. This bill calls for the budget to be split up both by function and by geographic area, and mentions the health service areas set up by the Health Planning and Resources Act of 1974 (PL 93–641). If there were to be a single capped budget for health facilities within a single health service area, the pressures and incentives facing the

---

[71] Milton Roemer and William Shonick, "HMO Performance: The Recent Evidence," *Milbank Memorial Fund Quarterly: Health and Society*, vol. 51, no. 3, Summer 1973.

Health Systems Agency in making its initial certificate-of-need review and recommendations would be significantly changed. If the cap should indeed be fixed, the addition or expansion of a facility in an area would directly affect all other facilities in the area. The providers would be competing among themselves for a share of the budget, and any increase in expenses or services by one provider would be partially borne by other providers. In addition, both consumers and providers would know that health dollars spent in one area for one service (e.g., a new coronary unit in a suburban hospital) would reduce the amount of health dollars available for other services in other areas. This would be the case even if the area's cap could be adjusted upward during the year or for the next year because of new facilities and services. As long as there was some constraint on the budget, both consumers and providers would have an interest in controlling facility growth—in other facilities.

Such a situation would dramatically change the political support for restrictive review by HSAs. Currently, incentives for restricting growth are inadequate. The local area that acquires the facilities benefits, while a large portion of the costs is borne by others (federal taxpayers). Local costs (taxes and insurance premiums) are diffuse enough that demand for cost control is limited. Providers may have some interest in restrictive review (e.g., if there is a bed surplus, the addition of more beds may depress occupancy rates in the area) but that interest is weak. Today providers can make up most of the revenue lost from oversupply, and only rarely have they been actively involved in enforcing restrictive regulation.

Under a Kennedy-Corman Act, both providers and consumers would have a clearer stake in restricting facility expenditures they considered unnecessary, so denials of certificates of need should be more frequent. All along, the main difficulty in facility regulation has not been a lack of authority, but a lack of will to use that authority. By providing incentives to local regulators to use their regulatory power, the Kennedy-Corman plan should give the regulators the will to deny projects, and hence improve the impact of facility regulation.

The local Health Systems Agency would not, however, have final authority over issuing a certificate of need; that authority would remain at the state level. A state's interest in controlling growth and costs would depend on its financial responsibilities. If an NHI program shifted all health expenditures to the national budget, a state might seek to boost its share of the budget rather than to control its expenses. If a state were to certify facilities and services in the state as "needed," the federal government might feel pressure to supply sufficient funds to pay for them. If the federal government resisted such pressure, however, the federally determined budget would probably constrain certificate-of-need approvals. In addition, and perhaps even more important, that budget could restrict actual payments to providers, thereby making expansion more difficult and less rewarding.

Kennedy-Mills

Of all the NHI bills, the Kennedy-Mills bill proposes the most drastic change in facility regulation. Kennedy-Mills would amend Section 1122 so that only those facilities and services that had been approved in writing by the state and local planning agencies could be included in the determination of prospective budgets. This provision would extend certificate-of-need regulation beyond regulation of new capital expenditures to all existing facilities. In effect, it would allow forfeiture of licenses.

If enacted, this proposal would, of course, generate tremendous opposition from health care providers. Providers were strongly opposed to the provision in the Health Planning and Resources Act requiring HSAs to review the "appropriateness" of facilities, even though the appropriateness review carried no legal sanctions. Section 1513(g) of this act requires each HSA to review the appropriateness of all institutional health services in its area at least every five years. As we have already noted, a complete and thorough review of all health facilities is beyond the administrative capabilities of Health Systems Agencies. To be manageable, the review therefore has to be selective. Even a restricted review could not be performed for all facilities at once, but would have to take place over an extended period. Thus, at a minimum, the certification (or "de-certification") of all health facilities, as envisaged by Kennedy-Mills, would probably take place gradually.

In reality, denials of appropriateness of existing facilities are even less likely than denials of proposed capital expenditures. The reasons are political. Following their review of Canadian health regulation, Lewin and Associates concluded, "It is extremely difficult to close hospital beds once they are operating." [72] They found that several provinces had tried to close unneeded beds, or to convert them to other uses, but "despite the overwhelming authority of the government over hospitals, these efforts, like those in Ontario, have had mixed results." [73] Still, the Canadian provinces did manage to close some facilities. The political difficulties of closing existing hospitals can also be seen in the problems New York City has had in trying to deal with its fiscal crisis. New York's certificate-of-need law was the first state law to allow review of existing institutions to determine if they are "needed," but the state has demonstrated considerable reluctance to use that authority. This experience suggests that providing authority to close facilities will not quickly solve the problems of duplicate and unnecessary facilities, and even over the long term may have only limited results.

Comprehensive Health Insurance Plan (CHIP)

The Nixon-Ford administrations' bill would greatly increase the sanctions behind Section 1122 review. Section 302(a) of CHIP would amend Section 1122 of the Social Security Act to eliminate payments for services provided by disapproved facilities, not just the costs associated with the disapproved capital expenditure. The CHIP bill also proposes that insurance carriers should not make payments for services in the disapproved facility.

The CHIP bill therefore would extend Section 1122 review so that no payments should be made by third-party payers for services in disapproved facilities. Although this heavy sanction, if regularly enforced, would ensure that virtually no disapproved capital expenditure would be undertaken, it would not affect the basic operation of the regulators. It would provide no incentives for regulators to disapprove more facilities than they have in the past.

---

[72] Lewin and Associates, Inc., *Canadian Experience*, p. 5.

[73] Lawrence Lewin, Anne Somers, and Herman Somers, "State Health Cost Regulation: Structure and Administration," *The University of Toledo Law Review* 6 (Spring 1975):670.

CHIP proposes one administrative requirement that would certainly be costly and might actually weaken Section 1122 review. Section 302(b)(3) of CHIP states that exclusion of payment shall begin after the secretary of DHEW has notified individuals under insurance plans who might reasonably be expected to seek services in the facility involved and after the secretary has notified the state and prepaid and employer plans that can reasonably be expected to provide services in the facility. Because such notification would be difficult and time consuming, there might well be cases for which adequate notification would not have occurred and for which Section 1122 sanctions would therefore never take effect. At minimum, this administrative requirement would be a costly addition to facility regulation. The benefits from the new procedure are unclear, and the result could be serious impairment of the program.

Long-Ribicoff-Waggonner

Facility regulation is not specifically mentioned in the Long-Ribicoff-Waggonner bill, so the existing regulatory mechanisms would continue to operate. Some evidence on the likely results of combining catastrophic coverage with the existing regulatory structures is provided by the Social Security Administration's operation of the End Stage Renal Disease Program. To cope with the increased demand for dialysis and transplant facilities that the program produced, the Social Security Administration set up its own "facilities review" network just for kidney dialysis and transplant facilities, and required all plans for new services or expansion of old services to get prior approval. The network was established to control both cost and quality. Seldom-used facilities have relatively high mortality rates. In addition, SSA did not want to leave supply decisions to local planning agencies because with federal money available to pay most of the costs of new facilities, local HSAs would have little or no reason to deny projects. It was feared that without federal controls, every HSA would get its own dialysis and transplant units.

This experience with a federally funded catastrophic plan sharply illustrates the difficulties of federal financing coupled with local regulation. Under the Long-Ribicoff-Waggonner scheme, local areas would have few incentives to restrict the supply of facilities. The federal government, which does have financial incentives to restrict supply, does not have the authority to do so under either certificate-of-need laws or Section 1122 review. Although it was possible to set up a separate review within SSA just for renal dialysis units, imposing federal review on all facilities following enactment of a comprehensive catastrophic insurance package not only would be very burdensome, but also would have to essentially duplicate the existing planning network.

Yet some restriction on the quite predictable growth of facilities providing federally funded treatment for catastrophic illnesses would be needed. Catastrophic insurance would greatly increase inflationary pressures and, indeed, would immensely exacerbate one of the problems facility regulation is supposed to control: the spread of new, costly, and comparatively inefficient technologies. Local and state review probably could not control this expansion. If patients faced "free care" (above a certain amount), they would demand facilities and services to provide that care. And they would have not only financial incentives but sometimes life-and-death incentives to get facilities and services in their area. If adequate federal dollars were available, and if there were no restrictions on what could be approved, facility regulation, as currently performed by state and local agencies, could not be expected to restrain the growth of new facilities.

Conclusion

Analysis of specific legislative proposals highlights the elements of national health insurance necessary to make facility regulation work. The first requirement is a capital financing policy that would limit and force choices. Second, and perhaps equally important, is a requirement that regulators—from the HSAs through the federal government—have a financial stake in limited growth. Third is a statutory design for a certificate-of-need program that offers enough scope and sanctions to deter undesirable behavior. And last is the availability of regulatory resources sufficient to perform the required tasks. Experience thus far encourages skepticism about whether these conditions would in fact be met under national health insurance. If they should not be met, however, the prospects for effective facility regulation are indeed dim.

Chapter 8
PATIENT COST SHARING

DOUGLAS CONRAD
THEODORE R. MARMOR

P ATIENT cost sharing, the direct payment by consumers of some share of the costs of medical care at the time of use, has been a topic of controversy throughout the continuing American national health insurance debate. Cost sharing has received particular attention in recent months as observers have become increasingly concerned with the inflationary potential of national health insurance and increasingly pessimistic about the probable success of regulatory efforts. The debate over costs has enhanced the appeal of all measures promising economy; as a result, many national health insurance proponents have taken pains to show how their provisions for patient cost sharing would avoid excessive use of medical services, thus combining widened insurance coverage with economy measures. The theoretical appeal of a policy should not, however, obscure potential problems in implementation of that policy. This chapter identifies and explores problems likely to arise if national health insurance should put cost sharing into effect.

The three types of cost sharing are deductibles, coinsurance, and copayment. Deductibles require a patient to pay all costs up to a specified maximum, such as the first twenty-five dollars of a hospital stay. With coinsurance, the patient's liability is fixed as some percentage of a medical bill. Copayments, in contrast, are fixed charges per unit of service, for example, two dollars per office visit. Coinsurance and copayment obligations can be unlimited or kept within some specified maximum or percentage of income.

A variety of approaches to cost sharing are included in past and current national health insurance proposals. A num-

ber of plans—particularly the major risk insurance proposal
of Martin Feldstein, the Nixon-Ford administrations' Comprehensive Health Insurance Plan (CHIP) and the Kennedy-
Mills proposal of 1974—propose cost sharing as a central
policy tool for containing medical costs while expanding insurance coverage. The CHIP bill offers perhaps the most
comprehensive approach to cost sharing. Individuals qualifying for the Employee Health Care Insurance Plan (EHIP)
would face a $150 deductible with a $450 family maximum and
25 percent coinsurance. The maximum out-of-pocket payments would be $1,500 per family. Families and individuals
covered by the Assisted Health Care Insurance Plan (AHIP)
would face a schedule of premiums, deductibles, coinsurance
rates, and limits to liabilities that increased with income.
Deductibles would begin at zero and rise to $50 for prescrip-
tion drugs and $150 for all other services for individuals with
incomes greater than $7,000 and families with incomes greater
than $10,000. Coinsurance rates would begin at 10 percent for
the lowest income class and rise to 25 percent for the two
highest classes. Liability for expenditures would be limited
to 6 percent of income for individuals with incomes less than
$1,750 and families with incomes less than $2,500. Maximum
liability would increase to 15 percent of income for individuals
with incomes greater than $5,250 and families with incomes
greater than $7,500.

The Kennedy-Mills plan proposes a $150 per person deduct-
ible with a $300 maximum per family, 25 percent coinsurance,
and maximum per family liability of $1,000. No cost sharing
would be imposed on individuals with incomes less than $2,400
or families with incomes less than $4,800. Individuals and
families with incomes above these levels would be liable for
cost sharing, and maximum liabilities would increase with
income. For example, maximum liability for a four-person
family with an income between $4,800 and $8,800 would equal
25 percent of the difference between their income and $6,800.

Other plans give cost sharing a prominent role, but clearly
not as a device for restraining demand. The Long-Ribicoff-
Waggonner bill, for instance, prescribes large deductibles—
sixty days of hospital care and $2,000 worth of medical ex-
penses—but at the same time attempts to induce beneficiaries
to supplement or pay all of these amounts through health
insurance coverage.

Finally, some plans—the Kennedy-Corman plan and the Dellums bill, most strikingly and explicitly—reject cost sharing as a major means of cost containment, on grounds that substantial patient cost sharing is both an inequitable way to restrain medical care use and an ineffective mechanism for reducing inflation in the health industry's most inflationary sector—the hospital.

Clearly a wide range of cost-sharing mechanisms have been proposed. In examining the problems of putting any patient cost-sharing plan into effect, this chapter particularly attempts to anticipate gaps between proposals and performance. It is assumed that cost sharing would deter some service use and thus *could* affect the cost of national health insurance. Hence the chapter concentrates on exploring the practical consequences of employing complicated cost-sharing provisions within a national health insurance program. It is hoped that understanding the actual forms of cost-sharing policies when implemented will contribute to more realistic policy assessment.

The chapter first reviews the range of arguments for and against cost sharing. Then it considers the administrative feasibility of cost sharing, examining particularly the complicated provisions for relating cost sharing to family income, the main device most NHI proposals offer for making sure that rationing of care by patient costs would not fall disproportionately on lower-income families. The main concern is to discover if these provisions can be put into effect, and at what price in administrative complexity and dollars. The chapter then investigates the possibility of private supplementation of national health insurance, that is, the purchase of private insurance to cover costs that patients would be required by national health insurance to share (as well as some uninsured services). The more extensive the supplementation, the less that patient cost sharing under national health insurance would affect the use of service under an NHI program.

Cost-Sharing Arguments: Pro and Con

Several arguments can be used to justify patient cost sharing. First, it is most often advocated as a way to make consumers cost-conscious—discouraging unnecessary use of services while encouraging search for inexpensive care. The assumption is that consumers will use more health services when their out-of-pocket costs are low. When a third party pays all of a physician's or hospital's bill, the services are free to recipients, so they can be expected to use more services than would be the case if a price were attached. According to this reasoning, the demand for free care is limited only by transportation costs, the cost of lost time (in wages or leisure), and the pain sometimes associated with the consumption of medical care. The conclusion is that cost sharing would reduce the total amount of care demanded and might lead to a substitution of less expensive forms of care.

The effect of various levels of cost sharing on demand for health services will depend on how well the population is insured for particular services before enactment of national health insurance and how responsive individuals are to charges for those services. Newhouse, Phelps, and Schwartz have completed an extensive review of available research on the demand for hospital and ambulatory care and have used that evidence to estimate the costs of different NHI cost-sharing arrangements.[1]

They estimate that an NHI plan with a coinsurance rate of 25 percent could increase demand for hospital inpatient services by as much as 8 percent, depending on the current configuration of coverage. An NHI plan offering full coverage could increase demand for inpatient services from 5 percent to 15 percent. Given current hospital occupancy rates, the authors argue that the capacity of the system would not be seriously strained. Thus, barring successful control through other mechanisms, increases in demand for inpatient services would probably be reflected in utilization. Because current hospital inpatient services (including inpatient physician services) already account for approximately 55 percent of health service expenditures, however, even these small percentage increases would be quite important.

Because insurance now covers ambulatory services less comprehensively than it covers hospital care, the percentage change in ambulatory service demand generated by national

---

[1] Joseph Newhouse, Charles E. Phelps, and William B. Schwartz, "Policy Options and the Impact of National Health Insurance," *New England Journal of Medicine*, June 13, 1974, pp. 1345–59.

health insurance would be considerably greater than the changes in demand for inpatient services. Newhouse and associates project the demand for ambulatory services to increase by 75 percent under a full-coverage plan and by 30 percent under a plan with a 25 percent maximum coinsurance rate. They estimate demand for ancillary services to increase by about half, or about 35 percent to 40 percent, under a full-coverage plan and by about 15 percent under a plan with a 25 percent coinsurance rate.

Increases in *demand* for ambulatory services, however, would probably not be translated into increases in *utilization* because of existing supply constraints. Newhouse and associates conclude that without cost sharing, the demand for ambulatory care would dramatically increase, and that other rationing devices, with their own cost implications, would have to be imposed. Cost sharing for ambulatory care, they argue, is the only alternative to delays in obtaining appointments, increased waiting time, reductions in time physicians devote to individuals, and higher physician fees. These researchers assume Americans would not tolerate such rationing devices and would press for expansion of ambulatory services. Thus they conclude that cost sharing must be seriously considered as a measure for restraining the growth of ambulatory medical expenditures.

A second justification for cost sharing is that it makes the medical system easier to "police." According to this argument, cost-conscious patients can limit abuses such as unnecessary laboratory tests and X-rays, excessive referrals to other practitioners within a clinic, and excessive prescribing of drugs. These well-publicized abuses are easily perpetuated when patients bear none of the financial costs of care. Without cost sharing, the burden of monitoring the appropriateness of care is borne almost entirely by third-party payers, whose efforts to control abuse thus far appear decidedly ineffective. By limiting such abuses, cost sharing would contribute to national health insurance's political acceptability as well as to cost containment goals.

In this connection, it should be noted that in some West European countries, patients pay almost a quarter of the costs of ambulatory medical visits, not primarily to restrain medical inflation, but to remind patients about the costs of using medical services, particularly those services for which use is typically initiated by patients (such as individual psychotherapy or eyeglasses). It may be that such services are particularly suited to continued financial participation by patients. That question thus far has been peripheral to discussion of national health insurance in the United States, but the matter is directly relevant to the issues of implementing complex provisions of cost sharing and estimating private supplementation.

A third argument in favor of cost sharing is that it would permit NHI plans to cover a broader range of services than would otherwise be possible. Cost sharing is but a single example of a general search for ways to reduce public insurance program costs in reaction to a growing sensitivity to the size of the federal budget. Cost sharing is said to offer a method of reducing third-party program expenditures that is fairer than other prominent alternatives, such as rigid limits on benefits that exclude certain infrequently needed services or deny payment for hospital care beyond a fixed number of days. Cost sharing could be designed to apply only to routine services and thus be broadly shared among beneficiaries, thereby avoiding the effects of measures that fall most heavily on persons with severe but specific needs for services. Theoretically, cost sharing also could be related to family incomes, with little or no sharing of costs for low-income families and increasingly greater shared costs as income rises.

In response to these arguments in favor of cost sharing, there seems little doubt that cost sharing would deter utilization, perhaps substantially, for *some* services, but it is less clear that cost sharing would deter utilization equitably or efficiently. To begin with the equity question, programs with uniform deductibles or coinsurance rates impose relatively greater burdens on low-income families than on high-income families. As a result, it is argued, use of medical services varies not solely with illness but also with income.

Karen Davis has provided evidence that Medicare's equal cost-sharing terms have supported continuing discrimination by income affecting the elderly's access to medical care.[2] Enterline and associates have argued that the absence of cost sharing in Canadian national health insurance has eliminated this

---

[2] Karen Davis, *National Health Insurance: Benefits, Costs and Consequences* (Washington, D.C.: The Brookings Institution, 1975).

problem and in fact has redistributed physician services toward the poor.[3] These views have led some NHI planners to reject cost sharing as a major policy tool and others to propose tying cost sharing to family income levels. Unless cost sharing is linked to income, increasing access to medical care for persons currently underserved—one of the major stated aims of national health insurance—is unlikely.

As for the efficiency of cost sharing, authorities disagree. A further problem is that if cost sharing is to control costs, providers must collect cost-sharing payments and consumers must adjust their level of utilization. If cost-sharing payments proved difficult to collect, as might be the case with low-income populations, or if cost sharing had significant deterrent effects on utilization, the incomes of physicians and other providers would suffer. Physicians might well respond by increasing their delivery of services they initiate to compensate for any reduction in incomes. Because these problems are discussed in Chapter 2, however, they will not be elaborated upon here.

Some argue that patients have insufficient knowledge to make rational calculations of benefits and costs of their medical choices (can patients judge what is "unnecessary" care?), and that physicians and other providers who presumably possess adequate information are only indirectly affected by the prices facing consumers. Cost sharing, it is argued, might deter people, especially the poor, from seeking necessary care early, thereby adversely affecting health and leading to greater use of services in the long run.

Having presented just the outlines of the cost-sharing debate, this chapter now turns not to the details of the debate but rather to a precondition of that debate—an assessment of whether cost-sharing proposals can be put into effect as their designers intend. If they cannot, debate about the consequences of cost sharing is premature if not irrelevant. Two arguments against cost sharing pose the most serious obstacles to its use as a cost control mechanism. The first is a claim that administration of patient cost sharing in a national program would be extremely costly and perhaps unworkable, particularly if the system should attempt to minimize inequities by linking cost sharing with income. Second, it is argued that

---

[3] Philip E. Enterline et al., "The Distribution of Medical Services Before and After 'Free' Medical Care—The Quebec Experience," *New England Journal of Medicine* 289 (May 31, 1973):1174–78.

individuals and groups would purchase supplementary insurance to cut their out-of-pocket expenses at the time of service use, thereby undermining cost containment objectives. The remainder of this chapter reviews the evidence supporting and opposing each of these views.

Administrative Implementation of Cost Sharing Under National Health Insurance

Implementation of patient cost sharing would impose several kinds of costs. Uncertainty about coverage, for example, can lead to actual loss of benefits. A beneficiary can be uncertain about the services or expenses that count toward a deductible, the point at which a deductible is met, the copayment or coinsurance associated with a particular service, or the claims payment—patient or program—at a given time. Beyond uncertainty are actual administrative costs: The patient has to keep track of bills, the provider has to bill and collect from two sources, and finally, the program has to process claims.

Obviously, the actual costs of cost sharing—and the determination of who will bear them—depend on a plan's specific terms. Opponents of cost sharing, particularly opponents of income-related cost sharing, argue that the more complex the terms, the more reason to question whether cost sharing is administratively feasible. To assess the validity of this concern, this section addresses a specific set of administrative issues: (1) claims processing and collection when cost sharing is not related to income and (2) methods of income determination in an income-related system.

Even without income determinations, claims processing for cost sharing involves several detailed steps. For each claim it may be necessary to determine patient eligibility, service coverage, medical necessity, the "reasonableness" of the charge, satisfaction of the deductible, any limits on out-of-pocket expenses, and the amount of copayment or coinsurance. Although these tasks are numerous and complex, they are currently being performed by both public and private third-party payers for the bulk of the population. Some payers undoubtedly perform better than others, but the tasks themselves are clearly feasible.

A national health insurance plan, however, could increase the detail involved in one or more claims-processing decisions —for example, eligibility, medical necessity, or provider charges. If claims processing were handled by a multitude of carriers (either as underwriters or government agents), considerable variation in the determination of patient liability would probably result. Variation of this sort has occurred in determining charges under Medicare.[4] The result is that, contrary to the statute's intent, different program beneficiaries pay different cost-sharing amounts. Processing could be centralized to avoid this result, but centralized processing would probably slow claims payments. In either case, mistakes are inevitable. Although these mistakes might be no more severe under national health insurance than under current insurance arrangements, they might well attract more attention. These problems do not suggest that cost sharing is infeasible, only that it would compound the problems a new program like national health insurance would have to confront.

The collection of cost-sharing payments would depend on the national health insurance program's approach to claims payment. When physicians bill patients, who, in turn, submit claims for reimbursement under commercial insurance plans, cost-sharing payments are collected as part of the total bill. Whatever collection problem exists applies to the total charge and is not unique to the cost-sharing portion. To reduce collection problems, Blue Cross–Blue Shield has introduced a different approach to paying claims. Providers submit bills to and receive payment from the plan, but the insurer's payment usually does not cover any cost-sharing payments. When cost sharing is required, the provider must bill the patient as well as the insurer. In addition to having to bill twice, the provider also must wait until the third party pays the claim to know the patient's cost-sharing obligation. To avoid these burdens, physicians might decide to bill all patients directly and try to avoid serving anyone who appeared to pose a financial risk.

Credit mechanisms have been proposed for national health insurance that would reduce collection burdens and associated

---

[4] Charlotte F. Muller and Jonah Otelsberg, "Interim Research Findings on Physician Reimbursement Under Medicare," Department of Health, Education, and Welfare (DHEW) Contract No. 600–76–0145, Center for Social Research, City University of New York, 1978.

access problems. The health credit card, suggested in both the Kennedy-Mills and CHIP bills, would allow patients to "charge" their entire expenses. The program—or carrier—would pay to the provider the full charge, including the patient cost-sharing portion, and then collect the cost-sharing portion from the patient. By shifting the collection burden to the program, proponents of the health card seek not only to reduce barriers to access but also to encourage physicians to accept reimbursement from the program as payment in full. This transfer to the public sector of the collection task would increase the visibility of the administrative costs of patient cost sharing.

The credit card's capacity to achieve its objectives at reasonable administrative cost is open to question. Carriers would be required to take on collection responsibilities with which they have had no experience, to have the reserves available with which to advance credit, and to absorb bad debts. Carriers may be reluctant to undertake these responsibilities, and there is no reason to assume that they would perform them more efficiently than providers have done.

An even greater problem posed by the credit card is the proposed treatment of beneficiaries who defaulted on their cost-sharing obligations.[5] Following commercial practice, the NHI bills propose to deny credit to persons who default. Carriers would be responsible for identifying and notifying these persons. Once credit was withdrawn, providers would be responsible for collecting whatever cost-sharing payments defaulters incurred. As a result, not only would the administrative burden imposed by the credit card increase, but also providers would inherit the very collection tasks the card was intended to eliminate. Inasmuch as defaulters are estimated to make up as much as 15 percent of the population,[6] it is appropriate to consider whether the credit card ultimately would raise more problems than it would solve. Alternative approaches to credit are presented in the following discussion of income-related cost sharing.

---

[5] For a detailed discussion of these issues, see "National Health Insurance Administrative Alternatives—Option Papers for the Secretary; Healthcard," Memorandum from the Commissioner of Social Security to the Assistant Secretary for Planning and Evaluation, DHEW, January 10, 1975.

[6] Ibid., pp. 3–4.

The most striking feature of income-related cost sharing is that it has never been tried before. To minimize program administrative costs, a national health insurance program would probably retain the current system of income determination for individuals whose income is now determined by a government agency. This practice, which follows the assumptions of actuary Gordon Trapnell,[7] would reduce the incremental costs of administering national health insurance. Even with this conservative assumption, however, approximately 26 million new income determinations would be required under the CHIP bill. To put this task into perspective, consider the 8 million income determinations that the current welfare programs—AFDC and SSI—together now require.[8] Using the estimates of the Social Security Administration with some adjustments, the incremental administrative costs of income testing proposed under CHIP would have cost about $740 million in 1975.[9] This amount is approximately equal to the total costs of administering Medicare during fiscal 1975. The real resource costs of implementing just this aspect of national health insurance cost sharing are obviously not trivial. Nevertheless these costs are only a small fraction—less than 1 percent—of total expenditures. Clearly, the desirability of these administrative expenses depends on the amount of savings in total expenditures cost sharing might produce.

The question of which time period to use for determining beneficiary income is important for program administration. Generally, income-related cost sharing is designed to distribute progressively the burden of out-of-pocket medical expenses across socioeconomic groups. To enhance redistribution, cost-

---

[7] Gordon Trapnell, *A Comparison of the Costs of Major National Health Insurance Proposals*, prepared for the Office of the Assistant Secretary for Planning and Evaluation, DHEW, September 1976.

[8] "National Health Insurance Administrative Alternatives—Option Papers for the Secretary; Income Determinations," Memorandum from the Commissioner of Social Security to the Assistant Secretary for Planning and Evaluation, DHEW, January 10, 1975, p. 1.

[9] This figure was derived from reference estimates in Comptroller General, *Report to the Congress: Potential Effects of National Health Insurance Proposals on Medicare Beneficiaries* (Washington, D.C.: U.S. Government Printing Office, February 24, 1977). We assumed salary costs per staff-year of $12,307, fringe benefit and other costs per income determination of $7.18, approximately 26.7 million independent income determinations per year, and 1/600 staff-years per income determination.

sharing obligations ideally would be based on a measure of permanent income rather than current income, which is subject to random, transitory disturbances. Out-of-pocket medical costs, however, pose an immediate consumer budgeting problem, which suggests reliance on a measure of current income.

There are several ways to measure current income. One is the face-to-face interview, or means test, which is currently employed for welfare and Medicaid. Given the number of income determinations required, however, this approach appears to be prohibitively expensive for national health insurance. The Social Security Administration estimated that to obtain initial income declarations for CHIP, this approach for 39 million filing units would cost at least $1.5 billion and require more than 65,000 employee-years. Costs would rise if changes in income and family status were incorporated during the year.[10]

It may be reasonable to continue the interview approach for the population on welfare, but it seems advisable to consider alternatives for the rest of the population. CHIP proposed that each person not on welfare who wanted to establish eligibility for lower-than-standard premiums or cost-sharing payments should file an application with the appropriate authorities. (Normally these applications would be taken by providers and forwarded to the public agency.) Subsequent declarations of income during the calendar year would be recorded by state or federal income tax authorities, and income tax forms would provide for year-end refund claims related to national health insurance premiums and cost-sharing payments.

Income-related cost-sharing rates for the entire population not on welfare could be established on the basis of the previous year's income as reported to the Internal Revenue Service (IRS). The IRS, or the NHI administration agency using IRS data, could inform individuals of their cost-sharing obligations for the coming year, based on their previous year's tax returns. To avoid hardship for families with fluctuating incomes, an exceptions process could be introduced. Choosing the criteria for exceptions would require a balance between two program objectives: avoiding excessive financial burdens for

---

[10] "National Health Insurance Administrative Alternatives—Option Papers for the Secretary; Income Determinations," p. 1.

beneficiaries and maintaining an acceptable administrative workload. In considering a similar option, the Social Security Administration noted that defining "significant variance" between current and previous year's income—that is, variance that warrants a change in cost-sharing obligations—as a positive or negative 20 percent would minimize the frequency of exceptions.[11] The credit card could be used to minimize burdens on beneficiaries. Rather than denying credit to defaulters, the IRS could add unpaid cost-sharing payments to income tax obligations at each year's end.

Reliance on the income tax system has several advantages. First, this method of determining income requires far less time and fewer personnel than the interview method. Second, it builds on an established, unstigmatized mechanism for income determination, the Internal Revenue Service, rather than developing a new and perhaps duplicative system. Third, it simplifies administration for the carriers. Because they could accept the IRS determinations of patient income levels, they would not have to make detailed income investigations or eligibility queries. The complexity of employing different cost-sharing terms for each beneficiary, however, would remain.

Involving the Internal Revenue Service, however, would pose several policy choices.[12] First is the definition of income employed. If the national health insurance program were to determine cost-sharing obligations on the basis of taxable income, it would reinforce inequities created by loopholes and subsidies in the income tax system. To avoid this result, cost-sharing rates could be based on gross incomes, an alternative approach that is itself not free from problems.

Second is the issue of comparability of IRS and NHI filing units. The "family" unit on which maximum cost-sharing liabilities are based may not correspond to the unit filing an income tax return. If two persons who were married to each other filed separate returns, for example, the IRS would not identify them as a family unit. Combining returns to correspond to NHI categories might constitute an unwieldy task. It may therefore be necessary to make NHI cost-sharing terms correspond to IRS filing units.

A third problem with reliance on the IRS is the burden it might pose on the tax-collecting agency. Using the tax system

---

[11] Ibid., p. 3.
[12] Ibid.

to handle individuals in default would lower the direct costs of collecting cost sharing, as an upward adjustment of withholding taxes could be used to "collect" the amount in default. However, one must weigh the political and administrative consequences of employing the income tax mechanism in a nontax function against the potential savings in direct administrative costs. By involving itself in the collection of NHI cost sharing, the IRS might become a party to litigation in cases in which default is challenged by program beneficiaries.

Another risk to the IRS approach is the possibility that individuals might choose to underreport their income and defer their cost-sharing obligations, particularly if a credit card were used to provide easy credit. The Social Security Administration has noted that

> . . . secondary uses of tax data may create incentives detrimental to the integrity of the basic system. IRS personnel contend that the basic declaration of income could be strongly influenced by external incentives encouraging the underreporting of income. Although the accuracy of this contention cannot be evaluated, current estimates indicate that income is now underreported by 20 percent.[13]

It is not clear how realistic concerns of this kind are; they could simply reflect the reluctance of agency personnel to take on new and different tasks. In any case, they must be addressed if an NHI program is to use the IRS as a monitoring agency for cost sharing. Even if the IRS were able to collect all debts retroactively, the administrative burden and the credit demanded of the program could be so great as to raise questions about the fiscal integrity of a national health insurance program. In addition, such extensive use of credit might eliminate the deterrent effect of cost sharing. Such a risk must be considered in deciding the amount of credit the program should make available.

In sum, using the tax system to determine cost-sharing obligations appears feasible but poses political risks. If through insufficient monitoring the Internal Revenue Service should allow taxpayers to shirk their cost-sharing obligations under national health insurance, not only would the integrity of the

---

[13] Ibid., p. 2.

NHI program be undermined, but also compliance with the entire income tax system could be jeopardized. Policy makers should weigh these contingencies in appraising income-related cost sharing.

Private Supplementation of National Health Insurance

The principal argument against extensive use of cost sharing is that many individuals and families would buy supplementary insurance policies. Such policies would pay the deductibles and coinsurance, as well as extend coverage to services such as drugs or dental care that were not included in the national health insurance plan. Extensive supplementation of the first kind would work against the efficiency and cost-containing objectives of cost sharing. If persons who bought supplementary policies were to face little or no cost sharing at the time of service use, they would have little or no incentive to consider the cost of the service or of alternatives. Moreover, individuals who purchased supplementary policies could be expected to have higher incomes than those who did not. Thus, widespread supplementation would contribute to inequities in access; the wealthy would face lower prices at time of use than would the poor.

A basic principle of insurance is that one seeks to insure against events that are unlikely to occur but are very costly when they do. Supplementary insurance policies that cover deductibles, coinsurance, and, in some cases, uncovered services probably would not meet this criterion. In most cases, price would exceed the expected medical payments from the supplementary policies, sometimes by a wide margin. This apparent economic irrationality has led to the argument that significant supplementary insurance purchases would occur only if the current system of tax subsidies for private insurance were permitted to continue. This section argues, on the contrary, that supplementary insurance might thrive for other reasons, including pressure in the unions' collective bargaining process and the public's general aversion to risks.

To identify areas in which supplementation is likely, we first describe the current structure of the U.S. insurance industry. We then consider possible reasons for supplementation under national health insurance. Empirical evidence regarding the purchase of supplementary insurance under national health insurance in Canada and Medicare in the United States is presented.

U.S. PRIVATE HEALTH INSURANCE INDUSTRY

The private health insurance industry in the United States includes many competing firms and broadly covers the population for hospital, surgical, and some physician services. Table 18 summarizes private health insurance coverage in 1976. Although gross enrollment has grown steadily for hospital, physician, and other types of care over the past decade, the percentage of expenditures met by private health insurance has grown steadily only for physicians' services and for other types of care. In 1974, private health insurance met the following proportions of consumer expenditures, broken down by type of care: 77 percent for hospital care, 50.6 percent for physicians' services, and 7.4 percent for all other types of care.[14]

This pattern of coverage reflects both relatively little market penetration by private insurers beyond hospital and physician care, and little depth of coverage. Insurance companies generally offer policies for physician services performed outside a hospital with relatively high coinsurance and deductibles. Economically, such policies lower actuarial cost by shifting to the insured the liability for the low-risk and relatively discretionary component of medical care expenses. Unless NHI were to substantially alter the demand or cost conditions for covering these expenses, there would be little reason to expect supplementation in these areas.

It is useful to note the areas in existing coverage that offer the greatest potential for expansion. First, dental care coverage is probably the fastest-growing form of private health insurance, estimated net enrollment having increased approximately elevenfold between 1965 and 1974.[15] Perhaps more important, from the standpoint of our interest in tracing the

[14] Marjorie Smith Mueller and Paula A. Piro, "Private Health Insurance in 1974: A Review of Coverage, Enrollment, and Financial Experience," *Social Security Bulletin* 39 (March 1976) :18.
[15] Ibid., pp. 3–20.

Table 18

ESTIMATES OF NUMBER OF PERSONS COVERED BY PRIVATE
HEALTH INSURANCE AND PERCENTAGE OF POPULATION
COVERED, BY AGE AND SPECIFIED TYPE OF CARE

(December 31, 1976)

Type of Service	All Ages		Under Age 65		Ages 65+	
	No. ('000s)	%	No. ('000s)	%	No. ('000s)	%
Hospital	164,235	76.8	149,643	78.5	14,592	62.8
Physician:						
Surgical	162,179	75.8	149,262	78.3	12,917	55.6
In-hospital visits	155,548	72.7	145,470	76.3	10,078	43.4
X-ray and laboratory exams	150,897	70.6	142,942	75.0	7,955	34.2
Office and home visits	124,124	58.0	118,522	62.2	5,602	24.1
Dental Care	46,578	21.8	45,808	24.0	770	3.3
Prescribed Drugs (out-of-hospital)	150,222	70.2	145,440	76.3	4,782	20.6
Private Duty Nursing	147,311	68.9	142,668	74.8	4,643	20.0
Visiting Nurse Service	145,863	68.2	140,841	73.9	5,022	21.6
Nursing Home Care	70,422	32.9	65,560	34.4	4,862	20.9

Note: Health Insurance Association of America estimates included in the *Social Security Bulletin* table are excluded here, but they are roughly similar to the SSB estimates.

Source: Marjorie Smith Carroll, "Private Health Insurance Plans in 1976: An Evaluation," *Social Security Bulletin* 41 (September 1978), Table 1, p. 4.

mechanism by which supplementation probably would occur under national health insurance, of the 5 million to 8 million beneficiaries added in 1975 alone, the majority obtained dental insurance through new benefits added in collective bargaining. Despite the rapid growth of dental coverage in the past decade, Table 18 reveals that only 24 percent of the population who are not elderly currently have dental coverage. Thus this area offers considerable room for expansion, but that fact by itself does not imply that high growth rates will continue.

Although Table 18 indicates that out-of-hospital prescription drug coverage is widespread in the United States, private insurance actually meets only about 7 percent of all prescription drug expenses. As discussed in Chapter 11, the high net enrollment probably reflects the inclusion of these benefits within most major medical policies, but the low fraction of expenses covered reflects the use of deductibles and coinsurance, plus the limited coverage of the elderly. Clearly there is considerable potential for more intensive coverage of existing enrollees, but the extent of such benefit expansion is hard to predict.

Finally, a significant gap exists in current policies for cash benefits for short-term disability not related to work. Insurance and sick leave provisions together cover little more than one-third of the potential income loss due to illness.[16] There is substantial scope for expansion in income replacement, to increase the number of beneficiaries (extensive) and the depth of protection (intensive). One might predict greater growth in the number of beneficiaries, because even with less than 100 percent protection, income replacement is subject to moral hazard—that is, having the insurance is likely to encourage the occurrence of the insured event.

Several factors that have contributed to the growth of insurance coverage would undoubtedly affect supplementation under national health insurance. Group policies now constitute a substantial share of all private insurance sold. Because of the potential role of group policies in supplementation, it is important to understand group policy structure. Group plans are less costly than individual policies because of (1) economies of scale in terms of administrative function such as marketing, underwriting, and processing claims; and

---

[16] Daniel N. Price, "Cash Benefits for Short-Term Sickness, 1948–1972," *Social Security Bulletin* 37 (January 1974):19–30.

(2) reduction of risk through minimization of adverse selection by individuals. Insurers have difficulty getting adequate information for estimating the expected losses of particular individuals. Not only is it costly for insurance companies to acquire the information, but insured people have an incentive to understate their own risk.

To compensate for this problem, the insurer asks a surcharge. This surcharge is mitigated in the group policy for three reasons: (1) Because of the law of large numbers, insurers can price a group policy with better foresight than they can price individual policies. (2) Because individuals presumably do not choose among employment opportunities solely on the basis of the health insurance contract offered, the risk of adverse selection is diversified in the group setting. (3) In the case of an employee group policy, the very fact of employment is a signal of reasonably low health risk.

Income also affects the purchase of health insurance. In families with an employed head, the enrollment rate for private health insurance is 41 percent among those with incomes below $3,000, as compared with 98 percent for those with incomes greater than $15,000. The data do not allow us to separate independent effects, but income and coverage are linked by the following factors: (1) the fact that demand for insurance increases with wealth as well as with income; (2) the availability of Medicaid to the poor as a substitute for private health insurance; and (3) the positive relationship between income level and tax subsidies for purchase of private health insurance.[17]

Tax subsidies generally favor income tax payers in relatively high brackets both because of the increasing marginal rates of income taxation and the larger volume of insurance purchased by higher-income families. (It is not clear to what extent the latter results from the marginal tax subsidy or causes it.) Mitchell and Vogel estimate that the tax subsidy for deductions from personal income tax for unreimbursed medical expenses rises gradually until adjusted gross incomes of $15,000, thereafter increasing more rapidly with income. Despite the fact that no one can deduct his or her medical

---

[17] Charles E. Phelps, "Statement Before the Subcommittee on Public Health and the Environment," in *National Health Insurance Implications*, Hearings before the Subcommittee on Public Health and Environment House Committee on Interstate and Foreign Commerce, 93rd Congress, Sessions 1 and 2, 1974, pp. 357-61.

expenses from taxable income until expenses exceed 3 percent
of income, the effect of progressive income taxation is to
render the tax subsidy regressive with respect to income.
Table 19 illustrates the distribution of the tax subsidy for
employer and employee contributions to health insurance premiums by income class. (The table excludes deductions for
unreimbursed medical expenses, in order to highlight the subsidy only to purchase health insurance.) Karen Davis has
estimated total subsidies for 1975 at $3.4 billion due to em-
ployer premium contributions and $2.7 billion due to personal
income tax deductions (the latter includes deductions for
individual premium payments and for unreimbursed medical
expenses in the ratio of six to thirteen).[18]

Table 19

TAX SUBSIDIES FOR HEALTH INSURANCE
PREMIUMS, BY INCOME CLASS

Family Income, 1969	Tax Reduction per Family due to Employer Contribution Exclusion, 1969	Adjusted Gross Income, 1968	Tax Reduction per Taxpayer due to Deductions for Individual Pre-mium Payments, 1968
Less than $1,000	$12.10	Less than $1,000	
$ 1,000 —	19.58	$ 1,000 —	
2,000 —	21.13	2,000 —	$ .61
3,000 —	24.28	3,000 —	1.17
4,000 —	26.50	4,000 —	1.88
5,000 —	29.44	5,000 —	2.44
6,000 —	38.65	6,000 —	3.72
7,000 —	37.70	7,000 —	3.80
8,000 —	29.57	8,000 —	5.07
10,000 —	37.18	9,000 —	6.28
15,000 —	46.98	10,000 —	9.51
25,000 —	58.81	15,000 —	11.98
		20,000 —	16.55
		25,000 —	25.91
		50,000+—	29.54

Source: The table is constructed from Tables 2 and 6 in Martin S. Feldstein
and Elizabeth Allison, "Tax Subsidies of Private Health Insurance:
Distribution, Revenue Loss and Effects," Health Care Policy Discussion Paper No. 2, Harvard Center for Community Health and
Medical Care, Program on Health Care Policy, Boston, Massachusetts, October 1972, pp. 5 and 13.

[18] Davis, *National Health Insurance.*

Tax subsidies have encouraged insurance coverage. The total tax subsidy for employer and individual premium contributions to health insurance actually exceeds the administrative costs of health insurance (measured as total earned premiums minus benefits paid).[19] In other words, the cost of insurance to the consumer net of the subsidy is on average actually less than the expected benefits. Thus the purchase of medical care by insurance is cheaper than out-of-pocket purchase. This fact helps explain the purchase of coverage beyond what would be expected if insurance simply served to spread risks.

If such subsidies were to continue under national health insurance, one would expect "upper-end" coinsurance burdens to be privately insured. As for supplementation for first-dollar deductibles, net loading costs (e.g., administrative costs and profit, as a fraction of expected benefits) are appreciable even in the presence of tax subsidies. What private insurance supplementation does occur can be expected to cover a broader range of services in greater depth as the income level of the individual increases, because the tax subsidy is regressively distributed with respect to income. Supplementation also is likely to be concentrated in group insurance plans.

The current structure of the private health insurance market raises important questions about how and where supplementation would develop under national health insurance. Currently, private health insurance makes substantial use of deductibles and coinsurance, and offers only limited benefits for drugs, dental care, or income replacement. The most obvious explanation of this pattern is that the value of insuring such benefits does not exceed the costs, despite group insurance and tax subsidies. If this is true in the absence of national health insurance, why should we expect private insurance to cover these services once national health insurance exists?

In assessing the probable extent and character of private supplementation under national health insurance, at least four issues require review. First, to the extent that an NHI plan reduces patients' out-of-pocket expenditures, two effects would follow: (1) The use of medical care services would be less sensitive to costs of care; and (2) certain services would be in

---

[19] Phelps, "Statement before the Subcommittee on Public Health and the Environment."

greater demand because of national health insurance's effects on relative medical care prices. Reducing patients' sensitivity to the price of care encourages increases in hospital charges, professional provider fees, and other prices. The consumer could gain by purchasing a supplementary policy against the financial risk created by this price change if the premium (net of expected medical payment) was less than the benefits derived from insurance.[20] Reduction of the out-of-pocket price for hospital and physician care increases the demand for services that normally accompany this care. It is plausible to predict that coverage of hospital and physician services will increase the demand for drugs and for replacement of the income losses due to illness. Consequently, the private demand for insuring such expenses might increase, suggesting a range of supplementation even if national health insurance were to cover part of these services.

Second, national health insurance would alter the distribution of income. The configuration of premiums, payroll taxes, corporate income taxes, and personal income taxes that now finance both private and public health insurance probably would be quite different from the financing of national health insurance. The incidence of the tax and premium burden also would probably be quite different; that is, some income groups would gain and others would lose. The demand for insurance of uncovered benefits would increase if the increase in demand by those who gained exceeded the reduction in demand by those who lost. (Clearly, if, on balance, incomes net of taxes and premiums declined, then demand for supplementary insurance could fall.)

Third, if national health insurance preempted the private health insurance market, the range of market opportunities to insurance entrepreneurs would narrow considerably. Firms would have an incentive to search out alternative productive activities once national health insurance was enacted. If they found better methods of calculating risks and administering claims, the new coverage would be marketable even if demand

---

[20] In the case where the NHI carrier (whether underwriter or fiscal intermediary) and the supplementary insurer were the same, the company could derive economies by jointly processing NHI and supplementary claims for a given health care episode. The dampening effect of coordinated processing on administrative cost would enhance the marketability of supplementary policies.

for that coverage did not increase. It is certainly reasonable to expect the search for new opportunities to be concentrated in areas closely related to previous insurance coverage—drugs, dental care, and income replacement.

The fourth rationale for supplemented insurance relies less on economic calculation than on the visibility of benefits from collective bargaining.[21] If a substantial range of fringe benefits were removed from the bargaining table, union representatives would be pressured to replace those benefits with an equivalent set. Thus, benefits that were less desirable before the advent of national health insurance might be included afterward.

Supplementation would occur only if at least one of these four factors assumed importance. All else being equal, the demand for supplementary policies would be greater with tax subsidies than without them. In the absence of tax subsidies, supplementation would occur if these factors proved great enough to compensate for the reduced demand for insurance following the elimination of tax subsidies. For example, the importance to union representatives of the "visibility" of fringe benefit packages must be great enough to compensate for the lessened economic attractiveness of including them. The same would be true for changes in risk aversion, income, and so on.

EVIDENCE FROM CANADA

This section examines insurance supplementation in Canada following enactment of national health insurance. This particular natural experiment on a national scale suggests the direction and magnitude of the private insurance sector's response under institutional arrangements roughly similar to those in the United States. Before further discussion, two characteristics of Canadian policy need to be mentioned. First, Canadian national health insurance offers very comprehensive benefit coverage; in addition, there are no deductibles or

---

[21] William Vickrey, "Comment: Group Health Insurance as a Local Public Good" in Richard N. Rosett, ed., *The Role of Health Insurance in Health Services Sector* (New York: National Bureau of Economic Research, 1976), pp. 113–14.

coinsurance on covered services. Thus supplemental insurance is not needed to cover cost-sharing liabilities. The supplemental insurance market is limited to drugs, dental care, private hospital rooms, and income replacement. Private insurance by law may not provide supplemental coverage of an NHI benefit.

Second is the Canadian treatment of health insurance premiums. In Canada, employee premium contributions to voluntary, nongovernment medical care plans are treated as a legitimate medical expense for tax purposes. Medical expenses, which are defined to include expenses for drugs, dental care, hospital/medical care, eyeglasses, and health insurance premiums, are deductible on either of the following bases: (1) One can take the standard $100 deduction for medical expenses and charitable contributions, or (2) one can deduct an amount equal to total unreimbursed (by private or public plan) medical expenses minus 3 percent of net income. Employer premium contributions are treated as a legitimate business expense, and thus are deducted from taxable corporate income. As in the United States, payments an employer makes to a group sickness or accident plan are not regarded as taxable to the employee. But when the plan begins to pay benefits, the employee pays tax on all benefit payments that exceed accumulated premiums that the employee has paid into the plan. If the employee paid no share of the premium (the employer having paid it all), the result would be the same as if the employer simply gave the employee taxable income to pay for medical care. In contrast, disability insurance premiums are treated differently, with neither premiums nor benefits taxable to the employee, so there is a tax incentive for these disability benefits.[22]

In sum, the Canadian tax treatment of the employee's premium contribution is virtually identical with the U.S. treatment of such contributions. But, in contrast to the United States, the employer premium contribution to voluntary health insurance plans in Canada receives only a small implicit tax subsidy. Thus, to the extent that we can observe private supplementation in Canada, given only a small tax subsidy to employer premium contributions, we predict (on the tax effect alone) that even greater private health insurance supplemen-

---

[22] W. Gassira, personal communication, February 14, 1977.

tation would occur under national health insurance in the United States than has occurred in Canada.

Table 20 documents key dates in the development of Canadian private and public coverage. These dates are significant for understanding the relationship between the private market and national health insurance. Canada's national health insurance program developed in two stages: the implementation of hospital coverage between 1956 and 1961 and enactment of the physicians' services component in 1968.

Table 20

KEY DATES IN THE DEVELOPMENT OF CANADIAN NATIONAL HEALTH INSURANCE

Date	Event
1956	Federal government offered program of conditional grants toward half the cost of basic hospital services if majority of provinces with a majority of population agreed to implement universal, publicly administered programs.
1961	By this year, all provinces had established hospital care plans and had excluded private carriers except for insuring differential cost of private or semiprivate rooms.
1962	Saskatchewan implemented government-operated, compulsory medical care insurance.
1963	Alberta adopted an insurance company-operated medical care insurance plan (based on an intercompany risk pool), which offered basic medical insurance to all willing to buy it, with premiums for low-income persons to be paid either partially or totally by the government.
1968	Implementation of federal conditional grants was begun to share provincial costs of physicians' services.
1971	By this date, all provinces had established a universal medical care insurance plan.

Figures 4 and 5 show the relatively rapid growth in private health insurance, particularly group medical and major medical policies, in the period after NHI hospital coverage was enacted.[23] Interestingly, supplementary hospital coverage not only was maintained, but experienced gradual growth during this period.

---

[23] The extent of the private market is understated in these figures and in Figure 6 since the Canadian Association of Accident and Sickness Insurers 1960–75 data omit subscribers of Blue Cross and Blue Shield Plans.

Figure 4
NUMBER OF INSURED PERSONS IN CANADA, 1950–75

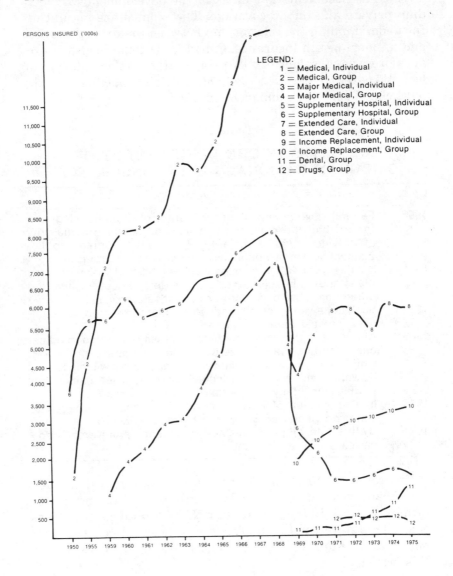

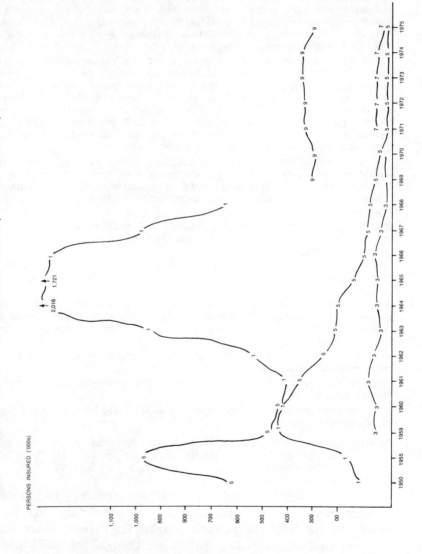

Figure 5

INDIVIDUAL COVERAGE ONLY, IN CANADA, 1950–75

Explanatory Notes to Figures 4 and 5

1. From 1962 on, information distinguishes between supplementary and comprehensive major medical contracts. Part of the swing to major medical coverage was accomplished by rewriting existing surgical and medical coverages into broader, more comprehensive contracts. Notice that our major medical categories total supplementary plus comprehensive coverage.

2. Until 1962, our medical category is for medical coverages only. It should be noted that the number of persons insured for medical expense is almost equal to the number covered for surgical expense, and either category provides a rough estimate (because of the large majority being covered simultaneously for surgical and medical expense) of the number of persons covered for both medical and surgical. After 1962 the medical column is defined to include all persons insured for surgical and medical simultaneously, plus those with surgical only and medical only.

3. As of 1964, Trans Canada Medical Care Plans first began reporting individual and group medical-surgical contracts separately, so there is a possible error in pre-1964 comparisons of group vs. individual coverage. However, the *total* of the two categories should be accurate for both periods.

4. Beginning in 1965, the medical category includes figures from the British Columbia Medical Plan and the Alberta Medical Plan, both of which are voluntary, but Saskatchewan Medical Care Insurance Plan is excluded because it is compulsory.

5. As of 1967, the figures from the Ontario Medical Services Insurance Plan, which is voluntary, are included in the medical-surgical category of our table.

6. After 1968, when the federal Medical Care Act was enacted, the medical-surgical category of the Survey of Voluntary Health Insurance is discontinued, because the previous variety of voluntary medical care plans began to erode.

7. After 1968 only "supplementary" major medical is included for the major medical categories.

8. For 1970 extended care benefits are explicitly included in the major medical category.

9. The extended care category overlaps substantially with the class previously called "major medical."

Source: Canadian Association of Accident and Sickness Insurers (CAASI), "Survey of Voluntary Health Insurance in Canada 1960–75," Toronto, unpublished data.

In the post-1968 period the pattern of private health insurance changed. With the addition of physicians' services benefits to the NHI package, the market for private insurance was reduced substantially. But, even though the NHI plan required no cost sharing, private insurance remained and some benefits grew. Supplementary hospital policies declined but were largely offset by the emergence of extended care plans in the private sector. Major medical and basic group medical policies diminished after 1968. Most of the growth in private health insurance during this time was concentrated in drugs, dental care, extended care, and income replacement. Roughly 6 million Canadians, 30 percent of the population, have purchased extended care policies. Subscribers to income replacement plans have increased from 2.0 million in 1969 to 3.3 million in 1975. Group dental and drug plans covered approximately 1.3 million and 300,000 persons, respectively, in 1975.[24]

Figure 6 provides information on the changes in private insurance premiums written in Canada before and after the two stages of NHI implementation. The total for all group insurance (line 16) indicates that the volume of private premiums has grown dramatically both before and after national health insurance.[25]

Income replacement policies (the benefit that is subsidized by the tax system) now dominate the supplementary insurance market. Income replacement policies are believed to yield benefits clearly in excess of their costs, but it is hard to determine how extensive income replacement—and thus total supplementation insurance—policies would have become in the absence of the subsidy. Yet the tax subsidy for income replacement policies existed before national health insurance was enacted, and income replacement policies were not important then. This fact suggests that the tendency toward supplementation is independent of the tax system.

The desire to supplement can be explained by any or all of the hypotheses proposed earlier: change in relative prices, income, or supply factors; or replacement in the collective bargaining process. The latter hypothesis is particularly persuasive in light of evidence from Canada. When medical insurance was introduced there between 1968 and 1971, Canadian employers shifted funds to provide additional benefits rather than to reduce health and welfare fringe benefits.[26] Similar collective bargaining arrangements are in place in the United States, and the same incentives would encourage the provision of supplementary benefits in this country, par-

---

[24] CAASI, "Survey of Voluntary Health Insurance in Canada."

[25] Inflation in consumer prices accounts for some of this growth and these figures have not been deflated. Nonetheless, substantial real growth in premiums and persons covered has occurred.

[26] Lewin and Associates, Inc., *Government Health Care Systems, the Canadian Experience: Supplementary Health Insurance in Canada,* HRP–0009349 (Washington, D.C.: National Technical Information Service, 1976).

Figure 6

CHANGES IN THE VOLUME OF PRIVATE INSURANCE PREMIUMS IN CANADA
BEFORE AND AFTER ENACTMENT OF NATIONAL HEALTH INSURANCE
(in millions of Canadian dollars)

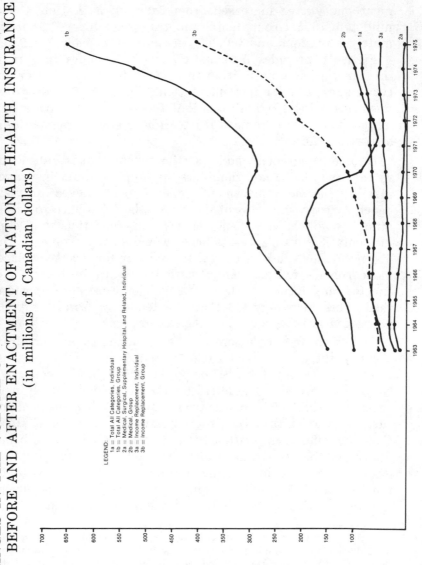

LEGEND:
1a = Total All Categories, Individual
1b = Total All Categories, Group
2a = Medical, Surgical, Supplementary Hospital, and Related, Individual
2b = Medical, Group
3a = Income Replacement, Individual
3b = Income Replacement, Group

ticularly if the United States should retain its tax subsidies to private insurance. In addition, because the purchase of supplementary policies increases with income, the income distribution of the out-of-pocket burden of health care consumption will be partially reversed from that intended by the framers of income-related cost-sharing proposals.

Failure to examine the Canadian evidence on private supplementation could easily lead one to overemphasize the importance of tax incentives for private health insurance. Indeed, if the Canadian data teach us one thing, it is that factors *other than* the tax subsidy to employer premiums (the largest component of United States tax subsidies) are driving the general trends in supplementation. A competing explanation for the broad trends in supplementation should begin with the strong pressures on union leadership to maintain the size of health and welfare fringe benefits.

In anticipating the private purchase of policies covering deductibles and coinsurance in the United States, policy makers must remember that the outcome would still depend largely on the value of those policies relative to their costs. Policies designed to cover large deductibles and coinsurance might be more or less economically rational than the Canadian income replacement, dental care, or extended care policies. It is hard to tell a priori because many factors are involved: the size of the deductible, the maximum liability, the tax subsidy, and so on. The Canadian evidence suggests, however, that analysts cannot ignore the role of negotiation over fringe benefits.

U.S. EXPERIENCE WITH PRIVATE INSURANCE

The experience of the elderly with private insurance to supplement the Medicare program provides further evidence on supplementation. In contrast to the Canadian NHI program, Medicare employs deductibles and coinsurance and leaves several services uncovered. In addition, most private insurance coverage is purchased by the elderly as individuals, or through senior citizens' groups that are not employment-related. Hence the economies of employee group purchase and generous tax subsidies are not present. The costs of supplementary insurance coverage, therefore, are very likely to exceed their expected benefits. Two questions must be asked if supplementation occurs: What motivates the purchase of supplementary insurance, and why is private insurance purchased in the presence of a public insurance program that was not purchased before its enactment? In drawing inferences from the Medicare program for other population groups, one must be cautious because of differences in health risk and income of the population groups.

Table 21 shows the time trend of net enrollment as a percentage of total aged population. Private health insurance is presented in separate columns for hospital and surgical care. During the first full year of Medicare, individuals cut back on private insurance coverage, but thereafter they steadily increased coverage for hospital and surgical care. Even so, the share of per capita personal health care expenditures of all types met by private health insurance remained virtually constant between 1967 and 1975, ranging only between 5.9 percent (1967) and 5.2 percent (1972). In 1975, private health insurance paid 5.4 percent of the elderly's expenses.[27]

This relatively small and consistent percentage reflects the limited services covered by private insurance policies for the elderly. Beyond hospital and surgical services, coverage is quite limited. Because out-of-hospital services represent almost half of the elderly's health expenses, a major gap in insurance protection exists. In 1975, less than one-third of the elderly had coverage for physician home and office visits; about one-fourth had coverage for visiting nurse services; about one-fifth had coverage for nursing home care, out-of-hospital prescription drugs, and private duty nursing; and about 3 percent had coverage for dental care. Statistics on other services are not generally available. The limited available information on insurance policies currently offered suggests that insurers offer benefits for services not covered by Medicare (custodial care in nursing homes, drugs, home nursing, dental care, vision and hearing aids, etc.) far less frequently than they offer benefits for noncovered costs of covered services (hospital and physician care). Insurance for hospital care generally covers the Medicare deductible and

[27] Robert H. Gibson, Marjorie Smith Mueller, and Charles R. Fisher, "Age Differences in Health Care Spending, Fiscal Year 1976," *Social Security Bulletin* 40 (August 1977): Table 5.

Table 21
TIME SPREAD OF NET ENROLLMENT
AS A PERCENTAGE
OF TOTAL AGED POPULATION

Year	Hospital Care Percentage Enrolled	Surgical Care Percentage Enrolled
1962	54.1	46.2
1967	45.0	44.1
1970	51.4	46.7
1972	56.4	52.9
1974	57.9	54.0
1976	62.8	55.6

Source: Data for 1962–74 are from Marjorie Smith Mueller and Paula A. Piro, "Private Health Insurance in 1974," *Social Security Bulletin* 39 (March 1976): Table 6, p. 8; for 1976, Marjorie Smith Carroll, "Private Health Insurance in 1976," *Social Security Bulletin* 41 (September 1978): Table 1, p. 4.

coinsurance, but not the costs beyond what Medicare covers. Insurance for physicians' services (predominantly in-hospital) is more difficult to characterize. In 1967, about two-thirds of Blue Cross–Blue Shield individual policies reportedly paid Medicare's deductible, while somewhat more covered the 20 percent coinsurance. It is not clear how many policies then or now covered physician charges that exceeded the level Medicare deems reasonable.[28]

Previous assessments of supplementation may have underestimated the likelihood of first-dollar coverage. Keeler, Morrow, and Newhouse[29] estimate that only 11 percent of eligible Medicare beneficiaries have purchased private insurance against the Part B deductible for physician services. The authors argue that in the absence of special tax subsidies, private insurance supplementation of deductibles for out-of-hospital services would be negligible under national health insurance. We suggest caution in using Keeler's evidence to

[28] The preceding paragraph was based on Judith Feder and John Holahan, *Financing Health Care for the Elderly: Medicare, Medicaid, and Private Health Insurance* (Washington, D.C.: The Urban Institute, February 1979).

[29] Emmett B. Keeler, Daniel T. Morrow, and Joseph P. Newhouse, *The Demand for Supplementary Health Insurance, or Do Deductibles Matter?*, R–1958–DHEW (Santa Monica: The Rand Corporation, July 1976).

forecast first-dollar supplementation under national health insurance. First, the sample from which the 11 percent figure is constructed is limited to Part B enrollees who were not hospitalized in 1969. Although that group is numerically large (80 percent of enrollees), its financial risk for health losses is clearly less than the risk for enrollees who were hospitalized, since the latter presumably would use more ambulatory services as a byproduct of hospital episodes. Keeler and his associates concede that 11 percent may be an underestimate, but additional data are required to determine the degree of understatement.

Keeler, Morrow, and Newhouse present direct evidence from the Current Medicare Survey for 1970 which is consistent with greater than 11 percent supplementation against the Part B deductible: 38 percent of Medicare Part B beneficiaries meeting the $50 deductible used private insurance to pay all or part of the deductible or coinsurance amounts, while 14 percent of those not meeting the deductible did so.

The small size of the Part B deductible plays a crucial role in these writers' conclusions regarding first-dollar coverage. Even granting the rough accuracy of the 11 percent figure, a $50 deductible is quite small, particularly to a nonhospitalized population. If deductibles ranged from $150 to $450, the implications for national health insurance would be very different.

In sum, it appears that enactment of Medicare did not lead to new areas of insurance coverage. On the contrary, insurance coverage is concentrated on the cost sharing for covered services, often not including open-ended or catastrophic expenses. First-dollar coverage is expensive to administer because it consists of a large volume of small claims. When first-dollar coverage is offered in individual policies, for which marketing costs are high, a large percentage of the premium dollar goes to administrative costs rather than to benefits.

What, then, explains supplementary insurance purchases by the elderly? Turning to answers offered above, the popularity of such insurance can perhaps be explained in terms of a change in the absolute and relative success of health services to the elderly and higher disposable incomes. The expansion of employment-related group benefits extending into retirement also would have an effect.

The Current Medicare Survey and unpublished figures from the Health Interview Survey of the National Center for Health Statistics show that supplementary private insurance enrollment as a proportion of the eligible population over age sixty-five increases with income level. Table 22 illustrates this finding for private hospital and surgical care insurance by family income.

The positive relationship between percentage enrollment and family income reflects the close tie between income and demand for insurance, the tax subsidy for individual premium payments, and the positive relationship between labor force participation and, therefore, employer premium contribution and resulting family income. Supplementary demand is weakened by Medicaid buy-in arrangements for the purchase of private health insurance among eligible, low-income elderly. But even with Medicaid, almost 40 percent of elderly persons with incomes below $3,000 purchased supplementary policies.

Caution must be exercised in using the Medicare experience to predict probable supplementation of coinsurance and deductibles under national health insurance. The elderly may be more averse to risk than are younger people, and may have less information to make cost-effective choices in the complex supplementary market. Furthermore, as consumers supple-

Table 22

PRIVATE HEALTH INSURANCE, PERCENTAGE OF PERSONS AGE 65+, CIVILIAN NONINSTITUTIONAL POPULATION, ENROLLED BY SERVICE TYPE AND BY FAMILY INCOME, 1974

Family Income	Private Hospital Insurance, Percentage Enrolled	Private Surgical Insurance, Percentage Enrolled
Less than $3,000	39.7	35.6
$3,000–$4,999	55.1	50.3
$5,000–$6,999	67.5	63.4
$7,000–$9,999	69.9	65.8
$10,000–$14,999	70.3	65.2
$15,000+	68.3	65.4

Source: Unpublished estimates from Marjorie Smith Mueller.

menting Medicare, the elderly are in a position different from
the position younger people would occupy under national
health insurance. The availability of Medicare—financed
through taxes paid by the working population—frees income
for persons reaching age sixty-five who previously purchased
private health insurance. Although these people could use this
income in a variety of ways, its continued use for health insurance is not surprising. Under a national health insurance
program, younger people might be paying (or having paid
for them) as much for national health insurance, through
taxes and premiums, as they now pay for private health insurance. Hence supplementation could be less likely. Finally,
it is important to recognize that most elderly people have not
purchased (or have not been able to purchase) supplementary
health insurance for physician office visits, a service for which
cost sharing may have its greatest deterrent effect. This fact
suggests that such policies might not arise under national
health insurance.

Even allowing for these considerations, the widespread
purchase of insurance policies for which premiums exceed
the expected return suggests substantial aversion to risk
among the elderly population.

Conclusions

In sum, cost sharing, even in its most complex form, appears
to be feasible, but difficult to administer and increasingly
expensive when tied to the income of insurance beneficiaries.
Private insurance supplementation would probably be significant under national health insurance, particularly in a plan
that assumed large amounts of patient cost sharing. Should
extensive private supplementation of national health insurance
occur, however, it would vitiate the constraint on the use of
service that patient cost sharing would be expected to have
under a national health insurance program.

Reliance on cost sharing to control service use under national health insurance makes sense only under two conditions:
(1) that cost sharing can be effectively administered and (2)
that people do not buy private insurance to pay for whatever
services national health insurance does not cover. In this
chapter, we explored the administrative feasibility of income-

related cost sharing, the most equitable cost-sharing arrangement. If this arrangement were to be operated in conjunction with the income tax system, we concluded that it would be workable. There is some risk in this approach, however. Poor administration of NHI cost sharing could undermine public confidence not only in national health insurance but in the entire income tax system. This risk should be considered carefully in assessing cost sharing's desirability.

Supplementation poses what may be more serious obstacles than administration to cost sharing's effectiveness. Neither Canadian national health insurance (which has no cost sharing for covered services) nor Medicare (which is limited to the elderly) is directly analogous to the NHI plans with major deductibles now under consideration in the United States. But experience in Canada and in this country under Medicare suggests that factors other than the cost-effectiveness of risk spreading or the incentives created by a tax subsidy drive the purchase of supplementary insurance. These factors include the effects of national health insurance on employees' and employers' disposable incomes, on the public's attitude toward insurance, on insurance market practices, and, perhaps most important in the American context, on collective bargaining. In our view, strong pressures on union leadership to maintain the size of health and welfare fringe benefits make supplementation particularly likely. The higher the cost sharing an NHI plan imposes, the greater the likelihood of supplementation. If policy makers fail to take the likelihood of private supplementation into account before adopting an NHI plan, their expectations for cost sharing as a cost containment device are unlikely to be realized.

Cost sharing nevertheless remains a potential source of NHI financing. Whether this is a sensible form of financing is a question quite separate from the effectiveness of cost sharing as an allocative device.

Chapter 9
UTILIZATION CONTROLS
BRUCE STUART

U TILIZATION presents one of the more perplexing dilemmas to surface in the debate over national health insurance. Presumably the main reason for enacting a national plan would be to improve access to medical care—not to create new barriers. Yet fiscal conservatives and liberals alike realize that medical resources are limited relative to human wants, and that some mechanism is necessary to allocate limited services among potential users. But here agreement ends. Should the allocation be based on a patient's ability to pay? Should some other form of private rationing be employed? Should the plan rely on direct regulatory controls such as prior authorization or concurrent review?

Over the past ten years, variations on each of these allocation methods have been recommended in NHI proposals presented to Congress. In general, the most comprehensive and administratively centralized plans, such as the Kennedy-Corman Health Security proposal, rely on direct regulatory controls and "non-price" rationing (queuing). The tax credit and catastrophic expense approaches exemplified by the Brock and Long-Ribicoff-Waggonner bills emphasize patient cost sharing. The Nixon-Ford administrations' Comprehensive Health Insurance Plan (CHIP) and some of the newer mixed strategies employ all three methods.

No amount of formal analysis can tell us which is "best," for the choice of approach depends as much on ethical precepts as on the technical issue of control effectiveness. Nonetheless, it is important to understand the operational implications arising from the selection and implementation of one form of utilization control over another. It is not enough to argue that the "right to health care" requires one approach and "free enterprise" medicine another. Nor is it sufficient to rank policy options on the assumption that each would operate as originally designed. There are simply too many steps between initial concept and ongoing operating for policy development to be viewed in static philosophic or technocratic terms.

The adoption of national health insurance would entail countless new rules and regulations affecting benefits, recipient eligibility, quality of care, provider characteristics, and reimbursement as well as the actual use of health services. It is naive to expect that policies in each area would mesh smoothly to meet overall program goals. Some policies would prove mutually incompatible, others would be unnecessarily duplicative, and still others would be hampered by the inability or unwillingness of program administrators to follow through with planned implementation procedures.

To avoid such pitfalls, it is necessary first to establish priorities among policy objectives and to identify realistic boundaries for control activities. Traditionally, the term "utilization control" has denoted policies that reduce utilization, particularly "unnecessary" utilization. Here a broader definition is employed. As noted throughout this book, the chief objectives of national health insurance would be to expand access to quality medical services and at the same time to restrain the rising costs of health care. The first objective suggests that utilization should be increased, at least for certain parts of the population. The second implies a need for expenditure or budget control. But since the level of expenditure is a product of quantity (use) times price, expenditures, too, are affected by utilization patterns.

Viewed in these terms, a utilization control policy for national health insurance should serve two functions: to promote an aggregate level of use consistent with a given budget constraint, and to promote a distribution of services that satisfies the egalitarian intent of the legislation. Although the two functions are conceptually separable, fulfilling one will tend to increase the difficulty of achieving the other. For this reason there is some debate about which should be given priority. The order in which the two aims are presented here reflects a widespread concern voiced by NHI advocates and opponents alike that the current rate of increase in health expenditures cannot and should not be maintained. Because this concern is likely to be embodied in the final legislation, this chapter places primary emphasis on activities that suppress rather than promote the use of health services.

Emphasis also is put on regulatory rather than on incentive approaches to control. The importance of patient cost sharing and other economic inducements in controlling the use and provision of health services is fully treated in Chapter 8, so that subject will only be touched upon in this chapter. But there is another reason for stressing the regulatory approach to utilization control here. Passage of a national plan would magnify all the objective circumstances favoring direct controls: increased budgetary pressures, expanded potential for fraud and abuse, and uncertain provider reaction if resources were indeed constrained. Almost fifteen years of experience under Medicare and Medicaid provide ample evidence that large federal programs develop a "regulatory imperative" in matters too complex for simple incentive approaches.[1] A similar development could be expected under national health insurance even if specific regulatory activities were not spelled out in the original enactment. From a political standpoint, the regulation of utilization patterns is a moot issue. The degree of intervention remains an open question.

Current Utilization Controls

Medicare and Medicaid represent the only experience this country has had with large-scale public programs to subsidize personal health expenditures, and it is only natural that there should be a similarity between current Medicare/Medicaid regulations and the methods of utilization control now proposed for national health insurance. The Medicare and Medicaid controls fall into two main categories: *prescriptive* regulations requiring that all transactions be carried out in a specific manner, and *proscriptive* regulations forbidding certain private transactions (leaving other options open).

The first major prescriptive regulation was the tripartite Medicare requirement for certification, recertification, and

---

[1] See, for example, the Commerce Clearing House, *Medicare and Medicaid Guide* (updated biweekly). The three current volumes plus year-by-year "New Development" binders provide some 15,000 pages of regulations, guidelines, interpretations, and judicial findings related to these two programs.

utilization review of institutional services. Designed to ensure
the appropriateness of inpatient care through peer pressure
and the threat of retrospective payment denials, the application of these control mechanisms (except perhaps for skilled
nursing home care) is now generally regarded as a failure.[2]
The controls did, however, provide an experiential basis for
development of more suitably targeted and enforceable prescriptive regulations. The results thus far (not all successful
by any means) have included such federal or state requirements as prior authorization, on-site concurrent review,
patient/provider "lock-ins" (under which a patient must use
a specified provider), mandatory second surgical opinions,
pretreatment screening, and new claims review techniques.

Proscriptive control mechanisms have undergone similar
development. The specific regulations are far too numerous to
recount. Examples include the threat of civil prosecution to
curb such program abuses as "gang visits" to nursing home
patients (during which a physician sees dozens of patients
in a short period of time, providing little or no service in each
case) ; "Ping Pong referrals" in shared health facilities
(automatic specialist referrals and re-referrals without regard
to medical necessity) ; and "family sweeping" by physicians
specializing in home visits (when all members of a given
family are treated for the same or similar illness, again without regard to medical necessity).

One of the clearest examples of how these developments have
shaped current thinking on national health insurance can be
seen in the prescriptive regulation that mandates review by
a Professional Standards Review Organization (PSRO) of all
inpatient admissions and lengths of stay for publicly supported
patients. Even though the efficacy of PSRO review has yet to
be demonstrated, this approach to utilization control already
has the widespread support of NHI advocates of all political
persuasions. Expansion of PSRO review activities under national health insurance would be required by the Kennedy-
Corman Health Security plan, which the American Federation

---

[2] See U.S. Congress, Senate, Committee on Finance, *Medicare and
Medicaid: Problems, Issues and Alternatives*, Report of the Staff, 91st
Congress, 1st Session, February 9, 1970, pp. 105–12; and Judith Feder,
"Professional Peer Review: SSA and the Practice of Medicine," in
Medicare: The Politics of Federal Hospital Insurance (Lexington, Mass.:
D.C. Heath, Lexington Books, 1977).

of Labor–Congress of Industrial Organizations supports, and by the Fannin National Health Standards bill, backed by the U.S. Chamber of Commerce. Other NHI proposals incorporating PSRO review requirements include the Long-Ribicoff-Waggonner catastrophic expense plan, the Nixon-Ford CHIP proposal, and several additional bills sponsored by Ketchum-Lagomarsino, Young, Matsunaga, and Lujan.

Similarities in statutory requirements are but one indicator of the importance of understanding the Medicare and Medicaid experience with utilization control. Equally significant are the lessons about what administrators do with a given set of controls once they are enacted. The development of PSRO review provides a case in point. Although the structure of review (admissions certification and concurrent review, provider profile analysis, and medical evaluation studies) was established by the Bennett amendment to the Social Security Act in 1972, implementation remains in a state of flux. Under current timetables, it will be several more years before all regional PSROs are fully operational. Moreover, the implementation of mandated procedures varies widely among the organizations granted conditional operating status. Some of this variation is due to administrative laxity, some to unforeseen logistical problems, and some to the fact that no two PSROs interpret the regulations identically. To complicate matters, the regulations themselves are constantly being rewritten and expanded through the traditional processes of administrative rule making, congressional oversight, judicial review, and legislative amendments. The result is an endless cycle of new implementation guidelines, extended timetables, and changes in interpretation and regulatory response leading to further governmental initiatives.

If PSROs were to become a major tool to control utilization under national health insurance, this regulatory dynamic would take on added significance because the current base of PSRO operations would have to be expanded considerably and because health providers and consumers would have a greater stake in the results. The same would be true, of course, for any other broad-based control option. In every case, an understanding of the regulatory process, from initial implementation through private reaction and governmental counteraction, is necessary before a final judgment can be made about the potential outcome or desirability of one approach versus another.

Internal Systems of Regulatory Control

The suppressive and promotional objectives of NHI utilization policy differ substantially from plan to plan, as do the
complementary objectives related to eligibility, benefits, and
reimbursement policy. Such differences would undoubtedly
affect the timing and depth of regulatory intervention. A
common paradigm of policy choices, however, applies to the
entire range of NHI proposals.

The paradigm is displayed in the framework shown in
Figure 7. Although no NHI proposal has outlined a control
system in precisely these terms, the six basic components—
surveillance, standard setting, assessment, targeting, intervention, and evaluation—are useful in exploring the functions
and linkages common to all utilization policy decisions. Program surveillance is designed to document the current status
and observable trends in medical utilization and delivery
patterns. The purpose of standard setting is to establish program utilization and delivery objectives. Assessment and
targeting are the related processes of comparing actual patterns to desired outcomes and assessing priorities for intervention. Intervention itself involves implementation of specific
techniques designed to move the system toward the desired
outcome. Evaluation is intended to provide an ongoing analysis
of the system's internal effectiveness and its external relationships with other control mechanisms. The whole process is
iterative to the extent that evaluation leads to a redefinition
of surveillance methodology, program standards, or targeting
and intervention strategies.

No analytical framework, however sophisticated and integrated, can substitute for the political decision-making
process. Analysis cannot preclude implementation of ineffective or even harmful utilization control policies, but analysis
can help explain the consequences of faulty regulatory design.
Such understanding is particularly important now because
of the checkered history of efforts in this area, and because
of the broadened impact that any system of regulatory controls would have under national health insurance.

When previous controls have failed, several related causes
have been to blame. For example, the lack of success of the
early utilization review requirements may be attributed to
the failure to include necessary components in the system.

Figure 7
PROGRAM STRUCTURE AND UTILIZATION CONTROLS

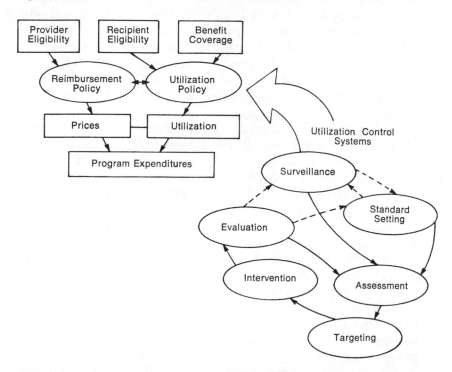

Note: Solid arrows indicate direction of primary decision variables.
Broken arrows indicate formal feedback loops.

Although the original utilization review regulations paid some attention to standard setting, targeting, and intervention, they did not address the issues of surveillance and program evaluation. In fact, most of the limited surveillance activities conducted by the Social Security Administration, state Medicaid agencies, and program intermediaries were kept separate from the utilization review process.[3] This separation not only jeopardized the credibility of the established standards, but also made evaluation impossible. The lack of evaluation, in turn, deprived the "system" of a vital feedback loop for correcting deficiencies in standards, targeting, and intervention techniques.

A full complement of system components is a necessary condition for any single component to work effectively, but it is not a sufficient condition. A weak component or inadequate integration among otherwise strong components will have deleterious effects, as will failure to structure control activities in a dynamic context. The utilization control system must, of course, be compatible with the regulatory and structural boundaries of the entire program, but it must also be designed to accommodate future changes in those boundaries. To date, controls have been simply grafted onto health financing programs with little attention paid to the impact on medical prices, supply decisions, or even consumer and provider willingness to participate in the program. Similarly, little attention has been given to the impact that changes in these variables have on control performance. Are the effects of utilization control the same under conditions of stable prices and rapid inflation? Does it matter if a small or a large percentage of the population receives its services from prepaid group practices? Failure to compensate when outward conditions change may have a marked influence on the effectiveness of control operations.

This list of shortcomings is not meant to suggest that agencies empowered with regulatory control under national

---

[3] A surveillance system of sorts, the Medicare Analysis of Days of Care (MADOC), was developed in 1969 and implemented in 1970, but according to Judith Feder in *Medicare*, ". . . institutions found fault with the system and did not use it, and BHI [the Bureau of Health Insurance] showed no interest in imposing it on them." See also Diane Rowland, "Data Rich and Information Poor: Medicare's Resources for Prospective Rate Setting," Harvard Center for Community Health and Medical Care, Boston, Massachusetts, Report Series R–45–12, July 1976.

health insurance would blindly repeat past mistakes. Much has been learned since utilization review requirements were first promulgated in 1965. The following sections highlight this experience. The six internal control components enumerated earlier provide the analytical context. Emphasis is placed on factors related to deficiencies in control design (missing or weak components and inadequate linkages). It is not particularly fruitful at this stage to target the analysis to individual NHI proposals. With the exception of tax credit proposals, the bills themselves contain very similar statutory control provisions. The general implications for national health insurance are examined on the assumption that the most important aspects of control development would occur after enactment.

Utilization Surveillance

The first phase in any system of utilization control is an initial cataloguing and periodic reporting of program statistics related to utilization and provision of medical services. This activity establishes the reference points for all further aspects of the control process. It provides the baseline data necessary for standard setting, targeting, and intervention strategy, and is an essential ingredient in program evaluation. Utilization surveillance also can aid in other program management functions such as budget analysis and forecasting. Given these roles, surveillance and reporting systems would doubtless develop under any form of national health insurance. The approach chosen would depend on the scope of control activities, data acquisition and processing costs, confidentiality requirements, and program managers' needs for reporting formats and timing.

Analysis of the available options involves three interrelated steps: assessment of data requirements, choice of appropriate data sources and collection methods, and determination of reporting format. Although literally dozens of so-called "health information systems" are in operation today, the surveillance and utilization review (S/UR) subsystem of the Medicaid Management Information System (MMIS) will serve as a point of departure to show how these steps have been handled in the past and how they might be employed in the future.

Surveillance and utilization review is one of six computerized subsystems of the Medicaid Management Information System.[4] It is designed to collect, store, and report on virtually all Medicaid transactions involving delivery and receipt of covered medical services. Data routinely collected include patient identifiers; provider identifiers; primary and secondary diagnoses; and services delivered by category, date, number, and location. Fifteen states have implemented MMIS and thirty-two more are developing such systems.[5] The system itself is large and expensive. Hardware and software requirements for handling literally millions, in some cases billions, of individual inputs are immense. Although this investment is designed to produce a number of standardized outputs and specialized reports, the rationale for the system as a whole is couched in such phrases as "gaining an overview of program operations" and "improving management efficiency." Given such general objectives, surveillance and utilization review programs have tended to collect (if routinely reported) the entire spectrum of utilization data obtained through Medicaid claims-processing activities. The system, in other words, determines "data needs" more on the basis of what can be collected than on how the data will ultimately be used.

The S/UR method may be accused of processing data elements which in all likelihood will never be used. If a prime objective of utilization control systems is to increase the cost-effectiveness of medical delivery and utilization, it stands to reason that the control system itself should be cost-effective. Unused data are a wasted expense. This line of argument, however, presupposes both a basic stability in program dimensions and a thorough understanding of the complex interrela-

---

[4] The other components of MMIS are (1) the recipient subsystem, (2) the provider subsystem, (3) the claims-processing subsystem, (4) the reference subsystem, and (5) the management and administrative reporting subsystem. For a description of all subsystem components see the U.S. Department of Health, Education, and Welfare (DHEW), Social Rehabilitation Services, Medical Services Administration, *Medical Assistance Manual*, Sections 7–71–40 through 7–71–60, effective June 10, 1974.

[5] DHEW, Health Care Financing Administration, Medicaid Bureau. *Data on the Medicaid Program: Eligibility, Services, Expenditures: Fiscal Years 1966–78*, Publication No. (HCFA) 78–24523, p. 97.

tionships affecting supply and demand decisions within the health sector. It may well be the case, for example, that hospital overutilization is the most serious problem control authorities now face. But what if government attempts to solve this problem merely result in an equally uneconomic compensatory adjustment in the delivery of ambulatory care? Unless the surveillance mechanism is geared to track changes in ambulatory utilization, program managers will get a signal indicating successful intervention when such was not the case. It is on this point that limited surveillance mechanisms, such as PSRO hospital profiling activities, are most vulnerable.

Unfortunately, not enough is known at this stage to tell whether the risks of such potential "false positives" outweigh the additional costs of systemwide surveillance. Nor, incidentally, is the appropriate depth of surveillance known. Current PSRO profiles, for example, concentrate on length of hospital stay rather than on specific inpatient service data. Control authorities cannot be certain that any "savings" obtained in reduced lengths of stay are not at least partially offset by increased service intensity within the confines of shorter stays. Of course, there is no inherent reason why PSRO profiling activities could not be expanded under national health insurance, and indeed this expansion has been specifically recommended in several NHI proposals.

The risk of drawing erroneous policy conclusions from inadequate data bases is a problem for any health financing program. As size and degree of market penetration increase, so do these risks. Not only does the dollar magnitude of errors increase, but also the potential for error itself rises as government regulation induces undetected compensatory changes in provider and recipient behavior. The decision to implement a broad-based surveillance system is similar to the choice an individual faces when buying insurance. The less uncertainty policy makers are willing to tolerate regarding future utilization patterns, the more likely that such a surveillance system will be "purchased."

Whichever system is chosen, the data collected must be valid and accurate. Policy decisions based on unreliable information may lead to serious biases in utilization standards and intervention mechanisms. But reliable utilization data are generally expensive to obtain on an ongoing basis unless they are already being collected for some other purpose. If the NHI plan were to reimburse providers on a fee-for-service or procedure cost basis, a strong argument could be made for tying surveillance activities to the claims payment function as is currently done in the MMIS system.

The data inputs in surveillance and utilization review are obtained directly from the claims-processing subsystem which collects and tabulates claims information from all participating providers and recipients of service. The surveillance is based on a complete census so there is no sampling bias, and the system is program-specific so that surveillance statistics are not contaminated by the inclusion of nonrecipient usage patterns. Furthermore, the integration of the S/UR and claims payment functions ensures that utilization data have been checked for accuracy through internal edits, exceptions reporting, and manual follow-up and verification.

These procedures do not guarantee completely accurate data.[6] Every collection system is subject to error, but a case can be made that processed claims data are likely to be more accurate than is similar information collected in other ways because of the monetary (reimbursement) implications to the provider and payer. Both parties have a stake in the veracity of all data elements directly or indirectly related to payment; these elements include demographic information necessary for eligibility determination, procedures performed, service costs or charges, and even diagnostic breakdowns in instances when payers screen service procedures against diagnosis as a check on medical necessity. The one real drawback to using claims data for utilization surveillance is the limited information typically contained on claims forms. Most current claims-processing systems provide scanty information on provider and recipient characteristics, and no information at all on eligible persons who fail to use the program. These problems are not insurmountable. Even now MMIS systems have the capability to interface provider and recipient eligibility files with S/UR profiles. Moreover, under national health insurance, uniform claims forms could, if necessary, require more information than is now collected.

An alternative to basing the surveillance system on claims data is to rely on private abstracting services. Professional

[6] See Avedis Donabedian, *A Guide to Medical Care Administration*, vol. 2, *Medical Care Appraisal-Quality and Utilization* (Washington, D.C.: The American Public Health Association, 1969), p. 50.

Standards Review Organizations are entrusted with review authority, but just recently they have been provided with operating funds to perform their own routine data collection and processing.[7] Most PSROs still contract with hospital abstracting services, Blue Cross, or private computer companies to provide the necessary regional surveillance information standardized according to the uniform hospital discharge data set (UHDDS).[8] Acquiring the data in this way can be more economical than would be the case if the PSRO did its own collecting and processing, but there are four serious drawbacks to this approach. First, because the data are not processed internally, the PSRO has no way to judge their reliability. As a result, it is difficult for the organization to set minimum standards of validity and accuracy of data even if it wished to do so. Second, there is good reason to question the accuracy of diagnostic and procedural information obtained through the abstracting process. A recent study conducted by the Institute of Medicine found that principal diagnoses are erroneous, on average, more than 33 percent of the time for sampled discharge abstracts used by four of the nation's largest hospital abstracting services. Comparable data for principal service procedures are in error nearly 25 percent of the time.[9]

A third problem is data validity. Even the largest abstracting service, the Commission of Professional and Hospital Activities, covers only a portion of the hospitals in any given region.[10] Because the smallest and largest institutions are

[7] See James Sorensen and Paul Ertel, "Management Information Systems and the Cost of Systematic Peer Review," in Paul Ertel and M. Gene Aldridge, eds., *Medical Peer Review: Theory and Practice* (St. Louis: C.V. Mosby Co., 1977), pp. 260–69.

[8] See DHEW, Public Health Service (PHS), Health Resources Administration (HRA), "Uniform Hospital Abstract: Minimum Basic Data Set," *Vital and Health Statistics*, series 4: Documents and Committee Reports, no. 14, Publication No. (HRA) 75–1450 (August 1974) and DHEW, Office of the Assistant Secretary for Health, Office of Professional Standards Review, *Program Evaluation Plan: Professional Standards Review Organization*, by Martin A. Baum et al., September 1975.

[9] Institute of Medicine, *Reliability of Hospital Discharge Abstracts* (Washington, D.C.: National Academy of Sciences, February 1977), p. 24.

[10] In 1974, for example, only 243 of 2,052 hospital service areas in the country were Professional Activity Service (PAS) "full coverage" areas, and nearly half of these were in the five states of Michigan, Indiana, Ohio, Illinois, and Wisconsin. *PAS Reporter* 12 (February 25, 1974):4.

typically excluded, systematic bias in the resulting profiles is a strong possibility. Abstracting services provided by Blue Cross are less susceptible to this bias, but because the data are obtained from claims files, they are usable only in areas where Blue Cross is the fiscal intermediary for the public programs. In regions where a state agency or some other insurance carrier acts as intermediary, Blue Cross data are inappropriate because they systematically exclude utilization information for the recipient groups of most concern.

Some of these problems could be rectified under a uniform national surveillance policy. Hospitals participating under national health insurance could be required, for example, to subscribe to an abstracting service. New and tougher standards for data verification could be imposed. All participating abstracting services could be required to employ standardized coding and reporting formats. Even if the issues of accuracy and validity of hospital inpatient data were resolved, however, there is a fourth drawback: The abstracting services are currently not equipped to survey ambulatory utilization. The U.S. National Committee on Vital and Health Statistics has recommended a basic data set for ambulatory care, but implementing this or a similiar abstract format would be expensive and time consuming.[11]

Such efforts might prove necessary if an NHI plan were to reimburse providers on a non-service-related basis (e.g., capitation or salary for practitioners and predetermined budgets for health institutions). But, if fee-for-service and cost reimbursement prevail, as seems likely,[12] a claims-based surveillance system is the best alternative. Movement in this direction is already under way as states develop Medicaid Management Information Systems capable of providing the UHDDS information necessary for PSRO review. Assuming

[11] DHEW, PHS, HRA, National Committee on Vital and Health Statistics, "Ambulatory Medical Care Records: Uniform Minimum Data Set," *Vital and Health Statistics*, series 4, no. 16. Publication No. (HRA) 75–1453, 1974. See also discussion in J.H. Murnaghan, ed., "Ambulatory Care Data: Report on the Conference on Ambulatory Care Records," *Medical Care* 11 (Supp. 1973):2.

[12] For a discussion of the various reimbursement mechanisms recommended under current NHI proposals, see DHEW, SSA, Office of Research and Statistics, *National Health Insurance Proposals: Provisions of Bills Introduced in the 94th Congress as of February 1976* by Saul Waldman, Publication No. (SSA) 76–11920.

the PSRO review would be incorporated under national health insurance, the pressure for expanded MMIS development could be expected to continue under federal, if not state, auspices.

Whatever form the NHI surveillance system should take, not all the data amassed would be worth reporting routinely. Similarly, some reporting formats would prove more useful than others. The decision of what to include and exclude and how to do it can be simplified by placing the issue in the context of the three generic reporting formats in use today. The first and most common format consists of cross-sectional summaries in which patterns of recipient utilization, provider treatment, or specific service usage are arrayed at given points in time. The reports typically take the form of cumulative frequency distributions in which percentile rankings are assigned to each element or group of elements within the array. The PSRO length-of-stay profiles are of this type. The surveillance and utilization review generates two forms of cross-sectional reports: summary profiles of service utilization rates among recipients grouped by demographic and medical characteristics, and treatment profiles of service delivery for specific diagnoses. When interfaced with program eligibility files, surveillance and utilization review can profile utilization rates for persons eligible for service as well as for actual recipients of service.

The second type of reporting format tracks utilization and provision patterns over time, typically, again, by cumulative frequency distribution. Surveillance and utilization review routinely generates historical profiles both for program recipients and providers. Few PSROs employ this reporting format for the simple reason that they lack the necessary data-processing capability. When historical trends or comparisons are desired, the information must be individually tabulated from sequential cross-sectional summaries.

Both periodic cross-sectional and longitudinal reports are useful for gaining an overview of program operations. The former are particularly valuable for identifying aberrant patterns of care at a particular time. The latter help identify potential program abusers and help track systematic changes in utilization and provision characteristics that may prove correlated to governmental regulatory activities. Moreover, simple statistical manipulations of reporting format can be designed to produce measures of program norms and variances for each type of recipient, provider, diagnosis, and treatment category entering the information system. The norms and variance measures may then be used in the standard-setting process to establish acceptable ranges of behavior.

For relatively simple systems, these two reporting formats may be adequate. But as the number and complexity of behavioral patterns subject to review and standard setting increase, the surveillance system must be able to produce a third category of outputs known as exceptions reports. Exceptions reporting is the key to the utilization assessment and targeting function described later. In essence, it simply represents a method of comparing actual patterns of behavior against predetermined standards. If the individual input falls outside the relevant standard, it is screened out for special review or targeted for intervention. Exceptions reporting can be done manually, but this practice makes sense only when the standards are broadly defined and inputs are few.

Automated exceptions reporting is an integral part of surveillance and utilization review. Not only does the system periodically identify exceptions through the use of screens in the cross-sectional and historical profiles, but also it can report exceptions at the time data are entered into the system. The distinction in timing is important. Although monthly or quarterly reporting is useful in formulating policy and planning decisions, such reporting is too infrequent to help in day-to-day management of a utilization control program. Successful management requires active monitoring and enforcement of control procedures, which are possible only if the system has on-line reporting capabilities.

The linkage of surveillance and monitoring provides yet another reason why surveillance and utilization review may be considered as a prototype for NHI information processing, even if the national health insurance program were merely to continue current PSRO review functions. If an NHI program should go further and institute active review of ambulatory care, home health services, or long-term care, the value of automating all three basic reporting formats into an integrated system would increase exponentially. Indeed, at this level, failure to implement a sound management information system would negate any effort to influence utilization patterns under national health insurance.

Standard Setting

The process of establishing rules, standards, and guidelines is the lifeblood of government regulatory agencies. From fly parts in peanut butter to noise levels in jet aircraft, there is literally no significant aspect of production or consumption over which government has failed to make some pronouncement of "what ought to be." Medical care is no exception. The structure of the industry today is as regulated as any in the American economy. Methods of delivery and utilization of medical services are equally subject to government purview. Even standard setting itself is subject to guidelines imposed by the government, as may be seen in the 1972 PSRO amendment.

It is extremely unlikely that enactment of national health insurance would lessen the government's authority or disposition to impose standards on medical service delivery and utilization. Most NHI proposals, however, leave the issue of standard setting organizationally unsettled. A majority of bills would grant PSROs implicit authority to establish medical standards for length of stay and service provision, but would leave the Department of Health, Education, and Welfare residual power to direct PSRO operations. A few proposals such as the Kennedy-Corman bill would establish separate administrative agencies charged with advisory authority over quality and service utilization. The tax credit proposals apparently would place the most stringent limits on government authority, in that all contain clauses prohibiting "federal supervision and control over the practice of medicine, the manner in which services are provided, the selection or compensation of officers and employees of providers of service, or the operation of providers of services." [13] The Medicare statute contains similar language with respect to the practice of medicine, and the language has not prevented second-order or once-removed control of the standard-setting process.

These provisions notwithstanding, it is impossible to infer from the bills themselves how the administration will interpret and implement vague and general standard-setting objectives. There is a whole continuum of possibilities. At minimum, standard setting might be used simply as a device for establishing indicators of program performance. Assessment of performance need not imply judgment on the overall appro-

---

[13] Ibid., pp. 171, 771–78.

priateness, quality, and cost of utilization and delivery patterns under national health insurance. But assessment might be used as a driving wedge to obtain public authority to change what are seen as inappropriate patterns of usage. In such an event, standard setting would assume a more active role. At the extreme, standard setting might devolve into a direct conduit for regulatory intervention, as is the case, for example, of the authority wielded by such agencies as the Federal Drug Administration, the Environmental Protection Agency, and the Occupational Safety and Health Administration. Once again, prediction is hazardous, but at least the implications of these various options may be usefully explored.

The first step in standard setting is to define terms. What is meant by "appropriate" or "necessary" treatment? What is "equitable" distribution of services? At what level is the "quality" of care to be judged sufficient? When do "cost constraints" enter the equation? The establishment of standards or objectives for these various factors makes sense only within the context of overall program goals. Stated crudely, a program of "Cadillac" medicine for all citizens would imply different utilization standards from those of a program designed to provide only the most essential services to people in dire need. In the first instance, "appropriate" utilization conceivably could incorporate any treatment with the slightest positive marginal value in terms either of caring or curing. In the latter case, marginal value would have to exceed some (presumably high) limit before treatment could be considered appropriate. This dichotomy is legitimate to a point, but the division of goals is simplistic. Establishing minimum standards does not obviate the need to consider budget constraints. In fact, the more comprehensive the program adopted, the more likely that pressure would build to impose maximum limits on utilization. The effects of such pressure can already be seen in the Medicare and Medicaid experience.

The Title XVIII and XIX amendments specify that only "necessary" medical services are to be reimbursed. During the early years of program operations, medical necessity was defined in terms of individual practitioners' certification and recertification procedures. Because practitioners differed in their views of what constituted necessary or appropriate treatment, there was no operational standard other than an attempt to avoid outright fraud. Recognition of this fact and the presumed abuse of the privilege among certain providers led to the imposition of more stringent requirements under the PSRO amendment. Now the criteria for necessity and appropriateness incorporate regional norms and standards for care (at least for inpatient length of stay). But what was true for the individual practitioner is now true for each of the 203 PSRO regions. Prevalent modes of practice have simply been grandfathered into the system.

Are model patterns of care appropriate as a base for standard setting? The oft-repeated differences in lengths of stay for similar cases treated in hospitals located in eastern and western parts of the United States raise some doubt. If a mean length of stay of 11.2 days is appropriate for a Medicare appendectomy in the West, can an average stay of 16.1 days for the same procedure in the Northeast be judged necessary?[14] Or perhaps a stay of 16.1 days is appropriate, in which case all earlier discharges represent underservice. A variety of cross-national,[15] cross-country,[16] and cross-system[17] comparisons of

---

[14] Marian Gornick, "Medicare Patients: Regional Difference in Length of Stays, 1969–1971," *Social Security Bulletin* 38 (July 1975):16. In a later study by the same author, "Medicare Patients: Geographic Differences in Hospital Discharge Rates and Multiple Stays," *Social Security Bulletin* 40 (June 1977), it was noted that a substantial portion of the difference in lengths of stay among Medicare beneficiaries in hospitals in the East and in the West is offset by higher admission rates in the latter region. However, this would not be a factor in surgical operations such as appendectomies, for which a single admission may be presumed to solve the problem.

[15] See, for example, J.P. Bunker, "Surgical Manpower, A Comparison of Operations and Surgeons in the United States, England, and Wales," *New England Journal of Medicine* 285 (January 1970):135–44, and E. Vayda and G.D. Anderson, "Comparison of Provincial Surgical Rates in 1968," *The Canadian Journal of Surgery* 18 (January 1975):18–26.

[16] See, for example, Clifton Gaus, findings presented before the National PSRO Advisory Council, March 9, 1976, reported in "Hospital Costs, Stays Vary Widely Across U.S.," *American Medical News* 19 (March 22, 1976), and John Holahan, *Physician Supply, Peer Review and Use of Health Services in Medicaid* (Washington, D.C.: The Urban Institute, 1976).

[17] See, for example, the studies reviewed in Milton Roemer and William Shonick, "HMO Performance: The Recent Evidence," *The Milbank Memorial Fund Quarterly: Health and Society* 51 (Summer 1973):271–317; Edward F.X. Hughes et al., "Utilization of Surgical Manpower in a Prepaid Group Practice," *Surgery* 77 (March 1975):371–83, Clifton Gaus et al., "Contrasts in HMO and Fee-for-Service Performance," SSA Office of Research and Statistics, December 30, 1975 (mimeographed); and Council on Wage and Price Stability, *Employee Health Care Benefits*, preliminary draft printed in the *Federal Register*, September 17, 1976, Part III, pp. 40312–15.

hospital stays and other medical procedures have yielded similar differences and raised the same fundamental question.

There is little point in seeking an answer by using dictionary definitions to judge the necessity and appropriateness of actual utilization patterns. Most dictionaries define necessary as "indispensable, logically unavoidable, inevitable, absolutely required." Such terms would imply standards of utilization far stricter than those imposed in the past or contemplated for future programs. Conversely, the Medicare definition of "reasonable and necessary for the diagnosis or treatment of illness or injury, or to improve the functioning of a malformed body member," [18] is loose enough—as experience has shown—to justify almost any recognized medical procedure. Attempts to put the Medicare standards into effect have, of course, led to numerous ad hoc proscriptive regulations.[19] But with the possible exceptions of length-of-stay and level-of-care requirements, providers and beneficiaries have been relatively free to seek or employ whatever quality and quantity of treatment they see fit, constrained only by physical access and availability of resources.

The fact that utilization standards under Medicare (and typically under Medicaid and private insurance as well) are not subject to specific quality and cost restrictions has several important implications for national health insurance. First, the lack of standards places the burden of cost containment on other control techniques such as reimbursement ceilings, direct benefit reductions, limits on eligibility, and increased patient cost sharing. Under certain conditions, these techniques can indeed reduce utilization rates, but they may do so in a way that (1) conflicts with other program objectives (e.g., eliminating financial barriers to access or reimbursing providers on the basis of a "fair" rate of return), (2) has unintended side effects (e.g., providers' dropping their program affiliation), or (3) produces a regulatory structure that is inefficiently targeted to the problems at hand.

A second implication is that unconstrained utilization standards foster an inherently inequitable benefit structure in which patients living in areas with abundant medical resources are provided, in effect, with better "policies" than are people

---

[18] *Medicare and Medicaid Guide*, p. 1452.
[19] Ibid., "Exclusions from Coverage," pp. 1451–1531.

living in poorly endowed regions.[20] The same is true within a given region for people who have access to the "best qualified" practitioners and facilities as compared with people who do not. Although medical services would be rationed according to physical availability and access even under the most comprehensive NHI plans, the chosen plan need not legitimize either substandard or luxury care through the payment mechanism. Avoiding these inequities, however, requires operational definitions for "substandard" and "luxury" services and the definitions in turn become the limitations in the standard-setting process.

The third and perhaps most obvious implication is that utilization standards unconstrained by cost and quality considerations are an open invitation to program abuse. The irony here is that the term "abuse" itself has no meaning without reference to program standards. If standards are not defined, it is logically impossible to identify, let alone correct, abusive behavior. In practice, limits on acceptable behavior or performance are always implied if not explicitly stated, but the use of implicit standards virtually guarantees haphazard administration.

Given the advantages, could explicit statements of program restrictions be expected to arise either during NHI deliberations or through postenactment developments? The political prospects are uncertain, for the issue would place Congress and the Carter administration in a classic dilemma. Presumably the population as a whole would be better off if both a floor and a ceiling were placed on the quality and quantity of medical services that could be reimbursed for any given diagnosis or course of treatment. The floor would provide insurance against substandard care; the ceiling would be an expression of the social value or opportunity cost of spending government funds for health services as opposed to some other purpose. The distance between ceiling and floor could be designed to reflect the inexact nature of medical science and the peculiarities of individual cases. Nonetheless, the ceiling would impose a maximum short of the "best possible care"

---

[20] Karen Davis, "Equal Treatment and Unequal Benefits: The Medicare Program," *Milbank Memorial Fund Quarterly: Health and Society* 53 (Fall 1975):449–88.

for the simple reason that at some point the aggregate value of financing additional quality exceeds its social cost.[21]

The dilemma arises from the fact that it is in no individual's own interest to have a limit placed on reimbursable services at the time that individual desires or needs these services. As under a community-rated insurance policy, the utilization experience of one citizen under national health insurance would have an imperceptible impact on the tax (or premium) he or she pays. Collectively, therefore, individuals would tend to undervalue the benefits derived from this type of budget ceiling. It is problematic whether Congress can overcome this tendency, but the budgetary experience with Medicare and Medicaid should at least provide an impetus for tighter control.

On another level is the question of whether the ceilings and floors could be operationally defined in the form of specific utilization standards. The PSRO experience suggests that it is possible to establish diagnosis-specific standards for inpatient length of stay. With the data-processing capability of a claims-based surveillance and utilization review system, it should be feasible to develop national standards for certain categories of ambulatory care and inpatient service intensity. In all cases, however, there is an implicit assumption that the characteristics of "appropriate" utilization can be quantified. If the characteristics cannot be expressed in terms of number of visits, days of care, intensity of treatment, or specific service provisions, the standards will be nothing more than elastic

---

[21] A basically similar approach has been suggested by J.P. Newhouse and V. Taylor, "The Economics of Moral Hazard: Further Comment" (Santa Monica, California: The Rand Corporation, 1970). Known as variable cost insurance (VCI), the plan would categorize medical providers into expense classes (Newhouse and Taylor restrict their analysis to hospitals but the concept could be applied to all providers). Indemnification to patients would be tied to the average for each class; patients choosing more expensive care would have to make up the difference out of pocket, while those choosing care that costs less than the average would receive a monetary bonus. The plan, however, is based on the dubious assumption that quality of care varies directly with price within each class of provider. The cost and price of care will vary systematically with quality only if providers operate under competitive conditions that ensure maximum economic efficiency and preclude monopoly profits. Although the VCI proposal is designed in part to produce competitive conditions, the reimbursement methodology assumes that these conditions already exist.

rules, which continue to allow substantially different benefits to different provider and recipient groups.

The main complicating factor is the issue of quality. Does, for example, one day of hospitalization in a large university teaching hospital imply the same degree of quality as a day in a small rural institution? Or is a visit to a board-certified orthopedic surgeon the same as a visit to the local general practitioner? Clearly not. How then can the appropriate standards be developed? One method is based on the traditional notion that levels of skill and competence may be objectively tested and minimum guidelines imposed. Licensing requirements for practitioners and medical facilities establish such minimum standards; so do private accreditation and certification procedures. From the very beginning, public funding of personal health services has been tied to qualification requirements: licensing in the case of medical vendor payments under public assistance, institutional accreditation under Medicare, and board certification for surgery under the proposed Kennedy-Corman Health Security bill. Such standards establish the "who" but not the "how." They have certain implications for utilization floors but not for ceiling standards.

Determining the "how" and "how much" requires a different approach. It must be granted that even with minimum qualification standards, practitioners will display different levels of skill, utilize different procedures, and effect different health outcomes among their patients. Certain aspects of medical and health practice will never yield to adequate quantification as far as standard setting is concerned. Yet much of what is considered qualitative in health care delivery has a quantitative analogue. The day spent in a prestigious university hospital is different, largely because the facilities and staff are quantifiably different. The specialized care that is rendered, the tests performed, even the prescriptions written will reflect these differences—and reflect them in terms that are amenable to the establishment of quantitative standards.

Once the potential for quantification is established, the next step is to determine an appropriate standard-setting process. There are two basic approaches. The first can be designed as the "top-down" approach and entails the derivation of standards from an explicit statement of program objectives. Despite the logic of this approach, it has been rarely employed.

Historically, utilization standards have been determined by the groups (medical practitioners in particular) to whom the guidelines are to apply. This second, "bottom-up," approach has a basic disadvantage in that the standards established may be unrelated to or at odds with the program's objectives for budgetary control, distribution of services, or even quality of care. Nonetheless, the "bottom-up" approach is implicit in every NHI proposal that incorporates PSRO or related utilization review mechanisms. Desirable or not, the development of future standards under NHI will be strongly influenced by this fact.

There are variants on the "bottom-up" standard-setting process. The first and most common method operates through review procedures based on implicit medical criteria. Hospital utilization review committees typically establish utilization standards in this way. Although the selection of cases may be determined by explicit criteria (such as length of stay, evidence of pathology, or past indications of physician competence), the consensus of the committee will depend on the personal opinions of its members. Implicit criteria represent the basis for standard setting under the rapidly expanding programs for second surgical consultation. PSROs also rely on implicit criteria to establish de facto ranges of acceptable variation around statistical norms during concurrent review.

In each case, the primary advantage is one of flexibility. If a standard is not predetermined, it can be readily adjusted to meet the contingencies of a particular situation. Such flexibility, however, is purchased at a high price. The process tends to be costly in professional time. It promotes existing inequities in program benefits to the extent that reviewers in different settings systematically apply different criteria of appropriateness to otherwise identical cases. Similarly, the process provides few guards against capriciousness in standard setting at any given site. Finally, the process makes it almost impossible to monitor accountability and may invite collusion between the reviewer and the one reviewed.[22] In sum, a utiliza-

---

[22] Active collusion may not be so serious a problem as implicit collusion when reviewer and reviewee have a continuing and close relationship. It has been noted, for example, that the implicit criteria employed by nurse coordinators and physician advisers in hospitals participating in the On-Site Concurrent Hospital Utilization Review program of the Utah Professional Review Organization (UPRO)—a PSRO prototype—

tion standard based on implicit criteria is very close to a contradiction in terms.

The alternative is to make the criteria explicit and to apply the same standards in all similar situations. The difficulty comes in determining when the situations are indeed similar enough to warrant the application of a given standard. This consideration is important but its importance should not be overdrawn. Every patient is unique in terms of having a particular combination of hereditary traits, past medical history, cultural and personal attitudes, and current symptoms and prognosis. But this fact does not mean that practitioners and facilities treat each case as a universe unto itself. The application of standardized diagnostic and treatment procedures has always been the rule rather than the exception. The fact that providers use different techniques is scarcely an argument against applying the same explicit criteria to similar cases. It is an argument for typing standards to common combinations of patient characteristics and attendant protocols, and for applying some form of exceptions procedure to handle truly unusual circumstances.

Experience with explicit utilization standards has been limited. The PSRO length-of-stay norms are explicit criteria but only in the crudest sense. For any given inpatient episode, the final PSRO standard will reflect both the length-of-stay norm and whatever implicit criteria the admitting physician, nurse coordinator, and physician adviser bring to the case. In fact, the length-of-stay norm is not a standard at all but rather an initial bargaining point. Given current PSRO operating procedures, bargaining may be necessary because the statistical norms are not specific enough to reflect the characteristics of the patient under review, and because length

---

in the early 1970s resulted in just 47 cases of certification withdrawal of a total of 34,000 cases monitored by UPRO; Jay Winsten, "The Utah Professional Review Organization as a Prototype for PSROs" in Richard Green, *Assuring Quality in Medical Care* (Cambridge, Mass.: Ballinger Publishing Company, 1976). Such a low "rejection rate" implies either that the standards were so loose as to accommodate virtually any treatment request or, more likely, that attending physicians, nurse coordinators, and physician advisers were able to reach acceptable compromises in all but a minuscule number of cases. The problem, of course, is that when the standards are implicitly determined on a case-by-case basis, the line between compromise and collusion is very thin indeed.

of stay is both a complement to and a substitute for other aspects of the inpatient episode that are not captured in the norms themselves. To transform the norms into workable explicit standards would require further disaggregation of patient characteristics, incorporation of specific treatment variables, and elimination or curtailment of the bargaining process. Such a move would be equivalent to establishment of standardized medical protocols or algorithms.

Standards based on inpatient protocols have been devised and implemented in various Experimental Medical Care Review Organization projects in New Mexico, Utah, Hawaii, Oregon, and Virginia.[23] Alternative approaches have been suggested by Hirsch, Payne and Lyons, and Decker and Bonner.[24] Roos and associates have recently developed a method of employing protocols based on data obtained through claims-processing files.[25] The feasibility of using explicit protocols to assess ambulatory care has been examined by the Joint Committee on Quality Assurance and the American Society of Internal Medicine.[26]

The one factor distinguishing most of the work on protocol development is an emphasis on medically "optimal," rather than typical or adequate, care. From the providers' standpoint, this emphasis is only natural, given a concern for technical competence and professional excellence (and perhaps

---

[23] See, for example, B. Becker and P. Bonner, *Criteria in Peer Review* (Cambridge, Mass.: Arthur D. Little, 1974); and Institute of Medicine, *Assessing Quality in Health Care: An Evaluation* (Washington, D.C.: National Academy of Sciences, November 1976).

[24] See, for example, E.O. Hirsch, "A Problem and Objective Oriented Approach to Patient Care Evaluation," *New England Journal of Medicine*, vol. 292, 1975; B.C. Payne and T.F. Lyons, *Method of Evaluating and Improving Personal Medical Care Quality: Episode of Illness Study and Office Care Study* (Chicago: American Hospital Association, 1973); and Decker and Bonner, *Criteria in Peer Review.*

[25] N. Roos, P. Henteleff, and L. Roos, "A New Audit Procedure Applied to an Old Question: Is the Frequency of T&A Justified?" *Medical Care* 15 (January 1977):1–18.

[26] C.E. Osborne and H.C. Thompson, "Criteria for Evaluation of Ambulatory Child Health Care by Chart Audit: Development and Testing of a Methodology," *Pediatrics* 65 (1975): 4, Part 2, Supplement; and DHEW, National Center for Health Services Research, "Medical Care Appraisal and Quality Assurance in the Office Practice of Internal Medicine," by R.C. Hare and S. Barnoon, Publication No. (HSM) 110–70–420, July 1973.

not incidentally, a concern that anything less could lead to restrictions or reimbursable services). But as has already been emphasized, the best possible care implies a level of resource use that exceeds the most liberal interpretation of a social optimum and the deepest recesses of the public purse. The question of how closely NHI standards should reflect "optimal" or "adequate" utilization is a political issue. The question, however, presupposes that a technology exists for quantifying desired rates of medical service usage when, in fact, this technology is still in a developmental phase.[27]

Assessment and Targeting

Defining a standard-setting methodology is one thing; determining which standards to implement at what time and for what purpose is quite another. The standards themselves are not the final outcome of the utilization control process; nor do they provide operational guidelines on how to reach the desired outcome. The development of such guidelines would involve NHI administrators in three additional stages of analysis: (1) an assessment of existing problems, (2) an analysis of the feasibility of intervention, and (3) an accounting of the costs and benefits associated with alternative intervention mechanisms.

The assessment function presupposes that utilization standards are intended to do more than simply justify current practices, and that standards and surveillance data are statistically comparable to such a degree that both the type and extent of misutilization may be routinely reported. The process would

---

[27] One of the most serious problems noted by R.H. Brook, ("A Skeptic Looks at Peer Review," *Prism*, October 1974, pp. 29–32) is that when explicit criteria are employed there is a tendency to produce a "laundry list" of acceptable procedures. If all providers and all possible treatments were subject to specific protocols this outcome might well be inevitable, given the sheer size of the task. However, as is argued in the next two sections, it rarely pays to target utilization controls on a universal basis. With selectivity in targeting it is possible to devote the time necessary to develop workable protocols. The same holds true for most of the other shortcomings with the explicit criteria approach noted by Palmer in "Choice of Strategies," in *Assuring Quality Medical Care*, pp. 68–71.

be straightforward except for the fact that policy makers invariably interpret utilization standards in light of the political and technical feasibility of successful programmatic intervention. This interpretation may be practical, but it places the policy maker in the predicament of attempting to assess program performance when the results of the assessment determine the criteria by which that assessment will be made.

A solution is possible only if the process is conducted over time. Because short-term adjustments in utilization patterns are typically subject to the most severe political and technical constraints, any standards imposed in the near future would have to be relatively conservative. As the time frame lengthens, more radical departures from the status quo can be planned. This distinction in timing is exemplified by the "bottom-up" and "top-down" approaches discussed earlier. Current applications of the bottom-up approach have tended to minimize political conflict through reliance on short-term "practical" solutions (i.e., consonant with the usual practices of most if not all providers), but this muting of conflict has been accomplished at the expense of drafting long-range objectives. Indeed the bottom-up approach ensures a future composed of successive short-term adjustments in which program perspectives never extend beyond the next immediate horizon.

As noted previously, most control authorities now rely on some variation of the bottom-up method to establish utilization standards. There is no inherent reason, however, why a different approach could not be employed under national health insurance in some future period. The major impediment may not be political at all. Instead, the main problem lies in the fact that so little effort has been expended in analyzing which type of provision and utilization patterns might be desirable five or ten years hence that it is obviously going to be some time before meaningful long-range objectives and attendant standards can be developed.

Short-term program assessment and targeting of utilization controls is another matter. Even if the ultimate destination is unknown, one may reasonably project that plan administrators will find enough room for improvement (or at least alteration) in current patterns of care to keep the authorities who set standards and handle controls busy for years to come. Moreover, the economic issues that must be considered before utilization controls are imposed are basically the same whether targeting is designed to meet short- or long-term goals. In both cases, controls logically should be imposed only if there is a reasonable expectation of a positive net return. When alternative control mechanisms are feasible, the decision of which to employ should be designed to maximize the net return.

One approach to assessing net returns is shown in the accounting framework in Table 23. The benefits and costs of regulatory intervention are first separated according to their potential for measurement in dollar values. For those that can be so measured, there is a further disaggregation between effects that are direct consequences of the control mechanism and indirect effects that are at least one step removed from control operations as such. Once monetary values have been determined and properly discounted to present value in the case of benefits and costs arising in the future, it is theoretically possible to calculate a benefit-cost ratio for each of the controls under consideration. Because the ratios capture only monetary effects, however, it may be necessary to adjust the ratios to reflect intangible benefits and costs.[28] Once this process is accomplished, the single control or combination of controls with the highest positive net yield would be chosen for implementation.

There are many practical and methodological problems in applying benefit-cost analysis to health programs in general and to utilization controls in particular.[29] These difficulties may help explain why there have been so few formal attempts to measure the benefits and costs associated with specific control activities. Nonetheless, an examination of the literature generally available to policy makers clearly demonstrates that failure to adopt this general approach to targeting can lead

---

[28] Critics of benefit-cost methodology tend to focus on the impossibility of measuring intangibles to discredit the entire approach. It is true that some past users of benefit-cost analysis (particularly the Defense Department and the U.S. Army Corps of Engineers) have tended to treat intangibles rather cavalierly. But there is no reason why intangibles cannot be given as much weight in the final decision as more measurable components are given. Indeed, the whole point of benefit-cost analysis is to provide an explicit accounting of *all* the variables germane to a particular decision.

[29] See in particular, Herbert Klarman, "Application of Cost-Benefit Analysis to the Health Services and the Special Case of Technological Innovation," *International Journal of Health Services* 4 (1974):325–52.

to serious miscalculations of the potential effectiveness of control. Several of the most common analytical errors and their implications are described here.

The first is a failure to consider all possible control options. The benefit-cost approach is useful not only in deciding whether to go ahead with a control program but also in deciding what form the intervention should take. Many controls, for example, can be applied either to providers or recipients. The controls also may be selectively targeted to certain individuals, facilities, or specific classes of service. The point is that if potentially important options are not addressed, the wrong control may be implemented or the control mix may prove suboptimal. These problems may be seen, for example, in the implementation of second surgical opinion programs and PSRO concurrent review activities.[30]

Second is the failure to adequately enumerate control costs. It is common, in fact, to find recommendations for specific utilization controls that make little or no reference to costs at all.[31] Some forms of control may have rather low direct administrative costs but high deadweight and indirect costs, while others will exhibit the reverse. In either case, a failure to account for all costs will give an unwarranted upward bias to the results. In past studies, the most common omissions have

---

[30] In the case of second surgical consultation plans, the major impetus for growth appears to have been the widely publicized programs developed by the United Storeworkers Union and AFSCME District 37 in New York City. (See the Council on Wage and Price Stability, *Employee Health Care Benefits*, pp. 40298–326). But with the exception of the Massachusetts Medicaid plan (which requires second consultations only for eight selected surgical procedures), the numerous union and Blue Cross second-opinion plans that have been developed in the past two years have invariably covered all prospective surgeries despite evidence that the approach is probably not cost-effective unless selectively targeted. The same is even true for PSRO concurrent review procedures. Congress mandated concurrent review without any clear indication that this appoach to utilization control was more effective than other methods. Moreover, despite growing evidence that selectivity in targeting is more cost-effective than universal review, most PSROs continue to review all Medicare and Medicaid admissions.

[31] See, for example, the arguments for second surgical consultation requirements under Medicare and Medicaid posed by the Moss Committee in 1976 (*Report on Cost and Quality of Health Care*).

been capital costs, deadweight losses, and indirect costs in general. For ongoing programs, nonrecurrent development and capital expenses may be legitimately considered as sunk costs, but if the program is to be replicated, these expenses will have to be met and should, therefore, be included in the cost estimate. Deadweight losses are almost never considered, probably because they affect people being controlled rather than control authority itself. But they are true costs, as any physician who must go through a prior authorization request, or any patient who must undergo a second set of presurgical diagnostic tests, knows well enough. Indirect costs are frequently ignored because they are the most difficult to estimate prospectively. To date no one has empirically analyzed the impact of utilization controls on other regulatory functions. Some work has been done in identifying likely or appropriate substitutes for inappropriate utilization, but most control agencies still operate as though a denied benefit is a net saving, even if the patient undergoes some alternative (and not costless) treatment.

This last example points up a third class of analytical failings, namely, inadequate accounting of control-related benefits. For perhaps obvious reasons, control agencies have a tendency to overstate the actual level of benefits produced through their activities. One of the easiest ways to exaggerate benefits from a utilization review process is to count all current service denials as program savings. The procedure is unjustified for two reasons: because providers (or recipients) may make multiple requests for service, in which case the same benefit is counted more than once,[32] and because some services may be denied which, in fact, are appropriate. Control authorities also have shown a tendency to overstate future benefits from control activities both with respect to payment denials and resource savings. For example, it is common simply to extrapolate current denial rates into the future without considering the facts that current rates may be artificially high due to

---

[32] See, for example, the treatment of control-related benefits (payment denials) in Robert Brook and Kathleen Williams, "Evaluation of the New Mexico Peer Review System 1971 to 1973," *Medical Care* 14, Supplement (December 1976), and California Department of Health, Field Services Section, "Prior Authorization Study Project Final Report," Sacramento, The Department, March 24, 1975.

"Hawthorne effects" [33] or that future rates may be expected to decline as recipients and providers learn to adjust their behavior to accommodate the regulations.[34] In terms of future resource savings it may be true, for example, that fewer hospital beds would be necessary if the average length of stay were lowered, but the full measure of program savings would occur only if the beds were actually retired. Even if excess beds were retired, the savings would have to be discounted to present value to obtain an accurate estimate of current benefits.

Yet there are two types of potential benefits from utilization control that are rarely considered. Just as substitutes for disallowed procedures must be treated as program costs (these expenditures would not have occurred in the absence of control), so too must complements of disallowed procedures be counted as program benefits. A reduction in the number of physician visits can be expected to result in fewer prescriptions, referrals, laboratory tests, and other procedures. A surgery not performed saves more than the hospital's charge and the surgeon's fee. It lowers the demand for anesthesiology, for other inpatient services not included in the hospital room charge, and for postdischarge services including physician follow-up, further tests, drugs, medical supplies, home health services, and various types of therapy.

In addition, it should be noted that Table 23 incorporates benefits derived from raising utilization rates to floor standards as well as from lowering them to ceiling standards. PSRO guidelines implicitly recognize the benefits from improved quality, but because neither PSROs nor the other control

---

[33] The distinction between transitory and permanent program impacts is particularly important for newly implemented control procedures because provider or recipient behavior may be influenced by the fact that controls have just been imposed (the Hawthorne effect) as much as by the characteristics of the control procedures themselves. For this reason alone, short-term benefits may be expected to decline over time as, for example, when Blue Cross of New Jersey implemented its Approval by Individual Diagnosis Program. See D.R. Bailey and D.C. Riedel, "Recertification and Length of Stay," *Blue Cross Reports* 4 (July 1968).

[34] A change in recipient or provider behavior may be legitimately considered as a control-related benefit in future years *only* to the extent that the behavioral pattern is contingent on a continuation of the control. If the pattern were to persist without the control, then clearly there are no benefits to continued regulation.

authorities have designated minimally acceptable service levels, measurement is effectively precluded. Only when such standards have been developed can the significance of these control-related benefits be ascertained.

A fourth common failing in present techniques for targeting utilization controls relates to the intangible benefits and costs of control. Although several types of intangibles are listed in Table 23, others could be added. As noted, the effect of controls on innovation (both organizational and clinical) could be positive or negative depending on control design, incentive structure, and enforcement procedures. In any case, they have typically been ignored. The medical consequences of control, however, have received considerable attention. In general, authorities opposed to control have emphasized the costs associated with the denial of necessary and appropriate treatments, while those favoring controls have emphasized the medical or iatrogenic consequences of providing unneeded treatment. Both problems will arise no matter how fine-tuned the control. Whether they cancel each other out is an empirical question requiring further research.[35]

A final point regarding targeting should be stressed even though it is relegated to a footnote in Table 23. In a prospective analysis of the benefit and cost outcomes of any control process, some impacts will be relatively certain, others probabilistic, and still others highly uncertain. The degree of precision in forecasting will generally decline as the decision variables become further removed in space and time from the initial implementation decision. In other words, although control costs under the direct authority of the regulatory agency may be quite predictable in the short term, direct benefits will be less so, and indirect benefits and costs will be least predictable. Similarly, even direct control costs will become increasingly less certain as the time horizon of control activities lengthens.

---

[35] In one sense, this issue is akin to quality control in manufacturing settings. Because every production process, industrial or medical, is going to result in a certain percentage of "rejects," the question can be reduced to one of defining acceptable quality control levels. In industry, the problem is purely economic. In medicine, it is both economic (e.g., the direct monetary cost of treatment and indirect costs of production lost through illness) and psychological (e.g., the human costs in pain, suffering, and ultimately death).

Table 23

BENEFIT AND COST CONSIDERATIONS IN TARGETING UTILIZATION CONTROLS

Potential Benefits[1]	*Potential Costs*[1]
A. Direct Benefits	A. Direct Costs

1. Reductions in program outlay for inappropriate service use (i.e., lowering service use to ceiling standards)	1. Nonrecurring outlays for control administration
	  a. Research and development costs
	  b. Training and implementation costs
	  c. Capital outlays

a. Marginal cost savings by type of service
  b. Effects over time (permanent or transitory)
  c. Discounted future savings in real resources (personnel, capital, other)
	2. Recurring outlays for control administration
	  a. Data acquisition costs
	  b. Data processing costs
	  c. Office and equipment rental
	  d. Professional and clerical personnel
	  e. Supplies and office maintenance
	  f. Contract service expenses

2. Increases in program outlays for appropriate service use (i.e., bringing utilization up to floor standards)	3. Deadweight costs
	  a. Time costs to recipients (delays in waiting time and treatment scheduling)
	  b. Time costs to providers
	  c. Monetary costs to providers to meet control requirements

a. Marginal expenditures by type of service b. Effects over time (permanent or transitory)	B. Indirect Costs
B. Indirect Benefits	1. Compensatory changes in delivery system a. Offset to A(1) benefits if recipients utilize inappropriate substitutes

1. Compensatory changes in delivery system
  a. Reduced use of service complements under A(1) above
  b. Reduced use of substitute services under A(2) above
  c. "Halo effects" in provision of appropriate services to nonprogram recipients	

2. Compensatory changes in program administration	

  a. Reduced burden of cost control on other regulatory mechanisms

3. Gains to the economic system
  a. Reduction in employment losses associated with A(1) above
  b. Employment gains associated with A(2) above

C. Intangible Benefits
  1. Health consequences
    a. Reduction in iatrogenic consequences of inappropriate service use
    b. Improvement in health status if floor standards are maintained
  2. Patient and provider education
  3. Effects on innovation
    a. Organizational improvements in treatment delivery
    b. Increased emphasis on cost-saving clinical research

D. Transfer Benefits (no net resource savings)
  1. Lower taxes reflecting program expenditure savings)

  b. Offset to A(2) benefits for increased use of inappropriate complementary services
  c. "Ceiling effects" as providers and/or recipients treat ceiling standards as de facto floors
  d. Loss of production from unused capacity

2. Compensatory changes in program administration
  a. Increased burden on other regulatory agencies (i.e., increased cost of claims processing)

C. Intangible Costs
  1. Health consequences
    a. Losses associated with delay or denial of necessary or appropriate services
  2. Participation rates
    a. Drop in provider participation in program due to control activities
    b. Drop in recipient participation in program (losses associated with reduction in A[2] benefits)
  3. Effect on innovation
    a. Reduction in clinical or organizational innovation because of control activities

D. Transfer Costs (no net resource cost)
  1. Incidence of control costs outside program boundaries
    a. Higher service prices to nonrecipients
    b. Higher taxes to cover control costs

---

[1] Not all benefits and costs listed may arise from the imposition of a specific control. Some values may be weighted according to probability of occurrence.

If these factors are ignored (as too frequently happens), the resulting benefit-cost ratios will be imbued with an unwarranted degree of precision. In the case of truly uncertain events, the best that can be done is to consider the sensitivity of the estimates to alternative specifications of the uncertain event (it may not change the final outcome). Some impacts may be known in probabilistic terms (based, for example, on previous experience with similar controls), in which case the probabilities of alternative outcomes can be used as weights in the benefit or cost calculations.

As each of these examples demonstrates, the process of targeting utilization controls is very complex. The apparent success of some past and present control efforts is due less to careful preparatory analysis than to luck and a counterbalancing of errors. With the exception of the PSRO concurrent review program, however, most forms of regulatory intervention have been conducted on a small scale where errors have had a relatively minor impact on the health financing and delivery system. One must be less sanguine about the prospects under national health insurance where the impact of targeting errors could assume major proportions.

Intervention

The purpose of utilization control is to correct perceived deficiencies in observed patterns of provision and usage. The success of the endeavor will depend on the type of tools the policy maker has on hand, the method and timing of implementation, and the monitoring and enforcement of control procedures. Counting subtle distinctions, intervention strategies are unlimited, but they may be classified into some ten basic options according to degree of governmental coercion. The least coercive strategies include two forms of moral suasion designed to induce voluntary change in provider or recipient behavior: (1) public pressure through disclosure and "jawboning" and (2) institutionalized peer pressure. Potentially more coercive are four methods of tying reimbursement to "approved behavior": (3) prior review, (4) prior authorization, (5) concurrent review, and (6) postdelivery denial of payment. The most coercive options are administrative and judicial: (7) restrictions placed directly on recipient utilization and/or provider delivery, (8) cancellation of program affiliation, (9) payment retrieval proceedings and civil penalties, and (10) criminal prosecution.[36]

These options are not mutually exclusive. Indeed, most programs of utilization control employ several simultaneously or in sequence, depending on the seriousness of the problem. Here they will be analyzed separately in order to judge their potential usefulness in NHI control systems. The discussion is necessarily brief, but each option is examined from the perspective of political feasibility, administrative requirements, and economic effectiveness. In each case, experience is used as the basis for discussion. If an intervention option has been extensively employed in the recent past, it may be considered politically acceptable in the near future (although not necessarily desirable). If serious problems of management and enforcement or lack of cost-effectiveness have plagued past efforts, they will undoubtedly occur again, even granting the value of hindsight. These issues are difficult to address given the paucity of methodologically sound studies of past control performance, but it is possible to reach tentative conclusions with regard to the relative if not absolute consequences of alternative approaches.

MORAL SUASION

All programs of utilization control, whether voluntary or compulsory, contain elements of moral suasion. In general, however, the concept of changing behavior through public or peer pressure implies that other sanctions will not be used— at least not immediately. The distinction between the two types of pressure is open to debate, but typically, public pressure has a punitive tone, whereas peer pressure has an educational connotation. There is no direct evidence that the former approach has had any significant impact on behavior, but the

---

[36] Not included in this list are other program policy variables (benefit structure, eligibility criteria, reimbursement levels and methods) which also affect, albeit indirectly, the appropriateness of medical utilization. These policy variables are treated elsewhere in this volume.

latter has had a clear and pervasive effect on the quality of medical services and the manner in which they are delivered.[37]

It was peer pressure, not organized public opinion, that led to professional licensure with its emphasis on minimum educational and technical qualifications. The American College of Surgeons (ACS) relied on peer pressure to gain acceptance for its "minimum standard" hospital approval program developed from trial applications in 1918 and 1919. As the precursor to accreditation by the Joint Commission on Accreditation of Hospitals (JCAH), the ACS approach emphasized the educational value of staff review and analysis of inpatient medical treatment. Now known as medical audit, these review procedures are still designed to educate (pressure) staff physicians to meet high standards. Both retrospective and concurrent utilization review and some of the new approaches to "health accounting" are based on a similar premise that physician performance can be measurably influenced through peer evaluation.

The question, however, is not whether peer pressure can lead to improved quality, but whether this mechanism offers any real assurance that the suppressive objectives of utilization control will be met. Experience suggests not. The utilization review requirements under Medicare and Medicaid, for example, invited hospital staff physicians to develop their own standards. The fact that hospitals procrastinated at every stage of the utilization review process (in setting up committees, in developing criteria, and in imposing standards), strongly implies that it was not in the providers' interests to have a workable system.[38] Peer pressure works only when peers have a positive stake in the outcome. It is unlikely that any utilization control program introduced under a national health insurance program would provide such positive stakes whether the standards were formulated by providers or imposed from above.

But if peer pressure alone is an unsatisfactory utilization

---

[37] Peer pressure is used here to refer to medical practitioners, not patients, but peer pressure among patients also plays a role in medical consumption habits as evidenced by different utilization patterns among persons classed according to cultural heritage.

[38] See, for example, *Medicare and Medicaid: Problems, Issues and Alternatives,* p. 107 and references on Committee on the Evaluation of Delivery and Utilization of Service staff reports contained in Feder, *Medicare,* p. 71.

control, a minimal degree of peer group acceptance is necessary for control to be effective. Unfortunately, there is considerable confusion on this point arising from failure to distinguish between incentives and sanctions, on one hand, and approval and acceptance on the other. Approval of utilization control implies that there is some independent incentive (goodwill, prestige, financial gain, etc.) to reach the control objective. Acceptance implies only that the consequences of not meeting the objective are seen to outweigh all other considerations. Because utilization controls (at least the suppressive variety) appear to provide few positive incentives to individual providers or patients, it is necessary to gain acceptance through the imposition of sanctions which, in effect, raise the price of failure to meet control objectives.

PAYMENT DENIALS

The most obvious way to raise the price of failure is to do so literally—through the threat of payment denials. All four methods of making payment contingent upon meeting utilization standards have extensive applications. Prior authorization arrangements tie payment directly to formal pretreatment approval by the fiscal intermediary or government agency on a case-by-case basis. More than half of the state Medicaid programs currently employ this review mechanism for certain medical services. The requirements range in scope from two or three selected services in states such as Illinois and Indiana to coverage of most major services in California and Oregon.[39] Prior authorization is relatively uncommon in the private sector but has been applied under a limited number of dental insurance plans.[40] The approach is not just an American phenomenon. National health plans in the Netherlands, Italy, and and Luxembourg require prior authorization for specialty services and prosthetics. Prior authorization for hospital care also is required in the Netherlands, Italy, and Belgium.

The popularity of prior review has risen rapidly in recent years. There are two basic types. The first is just an extension of covered benefits to include, at the patient's request, a second

---

[39] For a more complete discussion, see Stuart, "Utilization Controls," pp. 65–80, and *Medicare and Medicaid Guide*, "State Charts," pp. 6501–6619.

[40] See, for example, Council on Wage and Price Stability, *Employee Health Care Benefits*, p. 40304.

medical opinion before treatment is undertaken. This voluntary approach is typified by the growing number of Blue Cross second surgical consultation programs. In 1976, New York became the first state to require that all private health insurance carriers offer second-opinion benefits, and just recently Medicare has provided such coverage on a voluntary basis. The second mechanism is mandatory prior review in which the service will not be reimbursed unless a second opinion is obtained. (The patient, however, need not accept the second opinion.) Massachusetts enacted a law in 1976 requiring mandatory second surgical opinions for eight selected surgical procedures under the state's Medicaid program.[41] All surgeries are subject to such review under the employee health benefits plans of the United Storeworkers of America and AFSCME District 37 in New York City.[42]

Tying payment to concurrent review is now the most extensive method of utilization control practiced in this country. Concurrent review actually is a mixture of prior review and authorization techniques applied to successive stages in the treatment process. As mandated by PSRO regulations, an inpatient admission must be certified to ensure payment up to the length-of-stay checkpoint assigned by the nurse coordinator. Payment for services rendered beyond the checkpoint requires further review and certification. Although all hospitals serving Medicare, Medicaid, and Maternal and Child Health patients must follow these procedures, the experience with concurrent review prior to the PSRO amendment is limited to a few Experimental Medical Care Review Organization projects in California and Utah.[43]

---

[41] The eight procedures are (a) tonsillectomy and/or adenoidectomy; (b) cholecystectomy; (c) hemorrhoidectomy; (d) hysterectomy; (e) disc surgery/spinal fusion; (f) joint cartilage surgery/menisectomy; (g) submucous resection/rhinoplasty/repair of nasal septum; and (h) excision of varicose veins. See "Special Edition," Health Care Foundation of Western Massachusetts *Newsletter* 4 (February 1977):2.

[42] Council on Wage and Price Stability, *Employee Health Care Benefits*, pp. 40300–40303.

[43] See, for example, Katherine Bauer, "Containing Costs of Health Services Through Incentive Reimbursement: Some Approaches by Third Party Payers," *Cases in Health Services*, Harvard Center for Community Health and Medical Care, series no. 4, December 1973; E. Brian, "Foundation for Medical Care Control of Hospital Utilization: CHAP-A PSRO Prototype," *New England Journal of Medicine* 288 (April 26, 1973); and Jay Winsten, "The Utah Professional Review Organization as a Prototype for PSROs."

Posttreatment review is the final method of utilization control based on the threat of payment denial. Approaches vary among users. Before PSROs were implemented, fiscal intermediaries had the power to deny reimbursement after the fact for services deemed unnecessary by a hospital utilization review committee. The Social Security Administration took the same tack in its wholesale review and disallowance of nursing home services in the early 1970s.[44] Virtually all public and private health financing programs with computerized claims payment systems employ some form of posttreatment screening. In the public sector, posttreatment review can still lead to payment denial for any services not subject to PSRO concurrent review or for services in cases involving fraud and abuse.

From a practical standpoint, any of these four approaches could be implemented under an NHI plan. Administrative requirements would be most complex for concurrent review, but this system already is well into the implementation stage. Postpayment review is a natural concomitant to surveillance activities and would require little additional administrative machinery. A system of prior authorization would entail significant administrative expenditures, but the plan could rely on the experiential base developed at the state level. Of the four approaches, prior review is the least costly because the only administrative task is seeing that reviews take place.

Enforcement procedures are straightforward for all but concurrent review, under which, as mentioned previously, there is no "arms length" relationship between reviewer and reviewee. Provider acceptance might be a significant political issue during congressional debate, but opposition could be expected to subside unless the utilization control measures deviated substantially from past practices. If a major departure were considered desirable, the only practical solution would be to phase in new regulations and sanctions over time.

In fact, a major departure from past practices might be desirable for both administrative and economic reasons. The only legitimate rationale for a control system based on prior authorization, prior review, or concurrent review is the imprecision of utilization standards. All three of these controls

---

[44] U.S. Congress, Senate, Special Committee on Aging, Subcommittee on Long-Term Care, *Nursing Home Care in the United States: A Failure of Public Policy*, 93rd Congress, 2nd Session, December 1974, pp. 30–34.

are designed to eliminate the risk of nonpayment to the provider (or recipient). But given explicit standards, one can argue that the risk *should* rest with the provider (or recipient), and such a practice is possible only under posttreatment review.[45] Posttreatment review is the least expensive control mechanism to administer over the long term (provided that reimbursement is service-based), and it entails far less direct governmental involvement in medical affairs than, for example, prior authorization or concurrent review.

Unfortunately, in the immediate future it still will be necessary to cope with imprecise standards and the consequent pressure necessary to intervene before treatment is delivered. The choice of which mechanism to employ under national health insurance could be made through a process of elimination. On economic grounds, the least productive control appears to be prior review. To date, prior review mechanisms have been applied only to elective inpatient surgical cases, because of the high reimbursable cost entailed in surgical treatment. But the review itself is expensive. Under the New York union plans, as of July 1, 1978, for example, second surgical consultations by members of a select panel of board-certified surgeons were reimbursed at a rate of forty dollars, exclusive of diagnostic tests, which served to double the cost of review on average. The program appears to be cost-effective because the rate of reversed decisions has been astoundingly high. Of a total of 3,721 second opinions conducted from February 1972 to March 1976, the need for surgery was not confirmed in 1,099 cases.[46] Such figures appear to indicate that the initial recommendations for surgery were made by incompetent or dishonest physicians, but whatever the cause, prior review is an inappropriate remedial action. Problems of incompetence should be handled through qualification requirements for program participation. Fraud or gross abuse can

---

[45] Posttreatment review has not worked well under the current system of utilization control because standards are not precise. Providers have (reasonably) argued that refusal to make payment in all but the most blatant cases of abuse is equivalent to making up the rules of the game after the game has begun. Realizing this, control authorities have been hesitant to deny payment in cases in which any reasonable doubt exists as to medical necessity or appropriateness.

[46] Council on Wage and Price Stability, *Employee Health Care Benefits*, p. 40302.

best be dealt with through civil or criminal penalties. The conditions found in New York City are undoubtedly not typical of the country as a whole, but unless such large discrepancies exist elsewhere as well, second-opinion programs will not prove cost-effective.

The same is probably true of concurrent review. In 1976, the costs of concurrent review performed by state Medicaid agencies ranged from $1.12 per claim to $55.83, with an average cost of $6.83.[47] A cost analysis of the concurrent review activities of eighteen PSROs conducted by the DHEW Office of Planning, Evaluation, and Legislation revealed a mean cost per hospital discharge of $8.81 in 1976.[48] Although on average these rates are considerably lower than the costs of second surgical opinions, the potential unit savings also are correspondingly less—at least when every admission is reviewed, as is now done by a majority of PSROs. The study concluded, in fact, that universal concurrent review costs more than reduced utilization saves. The most recent survey of PSRO cost-effectiveness conducted by the Health Care Financing Administration presents a slightly more optimistic picture. The survey indicated that "PSROs saved some $50 million in Medicare hospitalization costs in 1977 compared with the $45 million cost of the review, for a net saving of $5 million." [49] Both studies argue that selective targeting (focused review) would improve the gross "yield" per review, but such targeting also would increase the cost for each review undertaken.[50] No matter how selective the review process, it will always be expensive to have reviewers stationed at each site where service is delivered.

The last option in this category is prior authorization. Despite its drawbacks (extra time costs imposed on providers

---

[47] DHEW, PHS, HSA, Office of Planning, Evaluation, and Legislation, *PSRO: An Initial Evaluation of Professional Standards Review Organization*, vol. 1, *Executive Summary*, no. 77–12, February 1978, p. 127.

[48] Ibid., pp. 123 24.

[49] Quoted in *American Medical News*, December 1, 1978, p. 1.

[50] Peer review costs would rise because of the high overhead expenses associated with the PSRO program. Although a reduction in the number of reviews might result in a marginal saving in the number of hospital-based nurse coordinators used, this reduction would have little effect on other PSRO office and staff expenses. Spreading these same costs over fewer reviews must, by definition, raise average costs.

and recipients, bureaucratic delays, the increased potential for false positives and false negatives in the review process)[51] this approach has a number of advantages over concurrent review. Prior authorization is considerably cheaper in the aggregate and on a net yield basis.[52] Prior authorization can be applied to ambulatory services and it allows targeting on recipients as well as providers; both practices are impractical under concurrent review. A final advantage of prior authorization is that it can be readily coordinated with exceptions reporting. As a result, the approach offers considerable flexibility in the choice and timing of control targets.

For all these reasons, prior authorization might be considered a legitimate control option during the early years of national health insurance. Although none of the NHI proposals currently under congressional review carries a specific recommendation for prior authorization requirements, the possibility is not excluded either. In fact, present PSRO regulations reflect tacit approval of the approach for elective surgery.[53] However, prior authorization at best can provide a useful bridge until more explicit utilization standards can be developed.[54] When such standards are operationally defined for any treatment procedure or pattern of usage, postdelivery review can provide a more workable and economical approach to utilization control.

ADMINISTRATIVE AND JUDICIAL SANCTIONS

Administrative and judicial sanctions, like posttreatment denial of payments, are appropriate only when standards are clear and explicit, or when there is prima facie case of fraud or gross abuse. The mildest sanction is a simple warning that stronger steps will be taken unless future performance con-

---

[51] See Carl Hopkins et al., "Cost-Sharing and Prior Authorization Effects on Medicaid Services in California: Part II: The Provider's Reaction," *Medical Care* 13 (August 1976):643–47.

[52] See Stuart, "Utilization Controls," pp. 74–76.

[53] 42 U.S.C. § 1320c–4(a)(2) (Supplement II, 1972).

[54] California's experience with prior authorization requirements is particularly revealing in this regard. See Stuart, "Utilization Controls," pp. 65–80.

forms to the relevant standards. Warnings serve three purposes. First, they have a presumed deterrent value (if they are believed). Second, the warnings themselves can be used as evidence in administrative or judicial proceedings if subsequent performance does not improve. Third, warnings can be used to target payment sanctions such as prior authorization or posttreatment denials. In each instance, the control authority must be prepared to actively monitor and pursue the case.

The remaining sanctions (administrative restrictions, cancellation of program affiliation, and civil and/or criminal prosecution) involve long and expensive investigation, hearings, and litigation. Theoretically, there may be some question as to whether the threat of legal action or the potential loss of payment offers the greater incentive for providers or recipients to conform to program standards, but in practice, there is a compelling economic reason for choosing payment sanctions. In the short term, the "fraud squad" approach may return more dollars than the agency incurs in investigation expenses (largely because the agency will begin with a backlog of suspected cases), but in the long term these returns are likely to disappear.[55] The main reason to employ legal sanctions is psychological rather than economic. Legal sanctions may provide a certain degree of deterrence, but their real value probably lies in their punitive implications.

Evaluation

Periodic evaluation is the last, but certainly not the least important, component of a utilization control system. Evaluation serves two functions: It provides an empirical assessment of the effectiveness of the intervention strategy with respect to control objectives, and it provides the basis for directing

---

[55] Some evidence for this argument of diminishing returns may be seen in a comparison of cases closed to recoveries for Medicaid fraud and abuse activities during 1976 and 1977. In 1976, a total of 2,641 cases were closed, resulting in recoveries of $1.6 million or $613 per case. A year later, 4,270 cases were closed and $1.0 million recovered, for a recovery rate of $241 per case. See DHEW, Medicaid Bureau, *Data on the Medicaid Program*, p. 99.

future utilization policy and control activities. Although this is not an appropriate place to review evaluation methodologies,[56] the question of why particular control mechanisms prove to be effective or ineffective is of obvious concern. A control can fail for various reasons, including external influences beyond the reach of the system, design faults in the application of the control itself, and administrative shortcomings.

Serious errors in control design and application under national health insurance might be avoided through proper prospective targeting, but control authorities probably will have inadequate information before the fact to determine how selective a particular control should be. It is a safe bet to suggest that the application of direct utilization controls to all recipients, providers, or categories of service will almost never pay. Experience can provide a guide on where to draw the line, but only if this experience is evaluated in a timely fashion. In California, for example, prior authorization requirements were imposed on drugs and routine physician visits in 1971, but the experience with these controls was not systematically reviewed until 1975, when the controls were found not to be cost-effective.[57] Moreover, it was another year before the regulations were changed. A similarly drawn-out approach to evaluation has characterized the blanket PSRO concurrent review requirements. Even though there are potential dangers associated with evaluation during a program's initial phases of operation, failure to generate timely performance indicators has proved costly.

The same arguments are relevant for control management and administration. Intervention could prove appropriate with respect to target and degree of selectivity but still fail because administrative procedures are lax. Ongoing evaluation is necessary to identify the degree of compliance with existing controls, to assess the productivity of program staff and capital resources, and to analyze the extent and impact of enforcement procedures. When new controls are being considered

---

[56] For a recent treatment of evaluation methodologies see Stephen Shortell and William Richardson, *Health Program Evaluation* (St. Louis: C.V. Mosby Co., 1978).

[57] California Department of Health, "Prior Authorization Study," pp. 21, I 3–4, and L. 5.

for adoption, it is all the more important that the program managers have this information to ensure that adequate planning and administrative preparation are forthcoming. In an undertaking the size of national health insurance, failure to do so may be costly indeed.

Summary and Conclusions

The development of utilization policy for national health insurance is akin to the process of defining the "deliverables" in a government contract Unless the product is precisely delineated, the contractors may provide too little or too much at a cost that is out of line with value received. Failure to delineate exposes the system to possible abusive and fraudulent practices. These issues, repeatedly raised in other areas of government contracting, have yet to be adequately addressed in the field of health financing.

A comprehensive NHI plan could easily exceed $250 billion in annual expenditures within five years. Even a modest program covering just one-third of all personal health expenses could cost $125 billion a year in less than ten years. Utilization controls are a way to rationalize expenditures of this magnitude within the context both of national health needs and other societal goals. Although many of the conclusions reached in the present chapter are tentative, the framework for analysis outlined here should be useful to further conceptual and empirical research.

To summarize briefly, it is recommended that policy options for utilization control be viewed within a systems framework comprising six basic functions: (1) surveillance of current patterns and observable trends in medical utilization and delivery, (2) standard setting to establish desired objectives with regard to utilization and delivery patterns, (3) assessment of current performance vis-à-vis the standards, (4) targeting of priority areas for intervention, (5) implementation of specific control procedures designed to correct identified deficiencies, and (6) evaluation of the control process and the effects of intervention.

For each of these six functions a number of specific considerations have been discussed. Under program surveillance the most obvious need is to develop an accurate and consistent means of profiling patient utilization patterns and provider delivery patterns. Use of a claims-based system modeled on the surveillance and utilization review component of the Medicaid Management Information System offers several advantages over other options such as reliance on hospital abstracting services or independent development of a periodic sample survey. Costs of data acquisition and verification are minimal because claims information must be collected in any event. The system has the capacity to provide routine exceptions reporting necessary for control targeting and monitoring, with a turnaround time impossible under the other two approaches. The system collects data on all reimbursed services and thus permits analysis of changing patterns of service utilization (particularly among potential outpatient substitutes for inpatient care)—analysis which, again, is impossible under more limited approaches.

It is clear that some form of surveillance would be conducted regardless of which NHI plan was enacted. The characteristics of the plan, however, would influence the development of this activity. Several NHI proposals, the CHIP bill being the best example, would be so administratively decentralized and complex that implementation of a nationwide surveillance and utilization review approach might never prove feasible. The more centralized plans such as the Health Security proposal offer better long-range potential for development of integrated surveillance procedures. But in the short term, the most important factor may well be the general emphasis placed on review by Professional Standards Review Organizations. Assuming that PSROs would continue as the primary utilization control mechanism for publicly financed health programs, there would be a marked increase in demand for hospital profile data regardless of information source, scope, or method of data processing. Unless standardized working relationships were systematically developed between PSROs and the claims payment agencies (whether they were fiscal intermediaries or a government administration), the result would be a haphazard surveillance effort that would jeopardize any serious attempt to control the level or pattern of medical service usage.

The same might be said for standard-setting activities. In the short term, utilization control decisions would have to be based on standards related to current norms of practice (the "bottom-up" approach). Only the Health Security bill gives lip service to a "top-down" approach by which explicit utilization standards would be derived from program objectives for cost, distribution of services, and quality of care. All other NHI proposals are caught up in the conundrum created by the PSRO amendment: How can one policy tool be used to meet the conflicting objectives of improving quality while reducing costs? There is no concrete evidence that PSROs have had much impact in either direction, but there is considerable speculation that, at the operational level at least, cost considerations are not top priority. The key to reform is standard setting. PSROs employ explicit length-of-stay norms, but the impact is diluted, or even eliminated, through the subjective process of establishing acceptable ranges about the norms. If this practice were to continue under national health insurance, either utilization control policy would become an empty shell or pressure would develop to try other approaches. The latter appears more likely.

Choosing among alternative controls is the function of assessment and targeting. There have been no systematic studies comparing the relative benefits and costs of different forms of regulatory intervention; nor have regulatory options been systematically compared with incentive approaches to utilization control. A framework for analyzing the various possibilities has been outlined. The methodology is based on an accounting of direct and indirect benefits and costs of feasible control options, tempered by considerations of intangible and probable outcomes. It is not suggested that NHI policy be based on such a methodology alone. The political process leading from program enactment through administrative interpretation, congressional oversight, judicial review, and legislative amendment is far too complex to model. Nonetheless, policy makers learn from experience, and the manner in which the experience is presented does have an effect. As interest in utilization control mounts, one may expect that a fuller accounting of present and past control efforts would influence the direction of future NHI policy decisions.

These control efforts fall under the two broad categories of incentives and regulatory approaches to intervention. The incentive strategies dealt with elsewhere in this volume attempt to influence utilization patterns through manipulation of demand and resource constraints. Regulatory strategies rely on the threat of sanctions to reach utilization objectives. The sanctions include moral suasion, program reimbursement tied to "approved" behavior, and various administrative and judicial procedures. No one approach appears best under all circumstances, but experience does provide some general guidelines for NHI policy development. As noted in the chapter on patient cost sharing, there is danger in influencing utilization through demand deterrents. The only deterrent that can be readily manipulated is the user price, and a price structure high enough to have the desired effect might either conflict with the distributional objectives of national health insurance or be undercut as consumers purchased supplementary private coverage. Resource constraints such as certificate-of-need resource programs and stringent rate review could conceivably be designed to give providers an incentive to reduce the supply of services. However, because most past public policies dealing with health and medical resources have been expansive, there is little empirical evidence on which to base a prediction should an NHI plan constrict resources. It is possible that successful resource constraints would produce results inimical to other NHI objectives for quality of care and distribution of services, in which case the government would be left with the option of direct regulation.

It would appear that if cost-effectiveness is a criterion for control selection, the regulatory options are also limited. Efforts to change delivery patterns through moral suasion and peer pressure are valuable complements to any control procedure, but alone they offer no assurance that utilization objectives will be met, particularly if those objectives call for a reduction in aggregate usage. Administrative and judicial sanctions may prove cost-effective for short periods of time, but in the long term their value is primarily punitive. Tying reimbursement to prior or concurrent review procedures is the most expensive approach to utilization control. There is no evidence that universal targeting of such procedures is cost-effective except under the most unusual circumstances. Even when targeted prior review and concurrent review proved cost-effective, larger savings could be obtained from other regulatory controls such as prior authorization requirements and posttreatment review. Over time, claims review is probably the control mechanism with the highest potential for positive net returns, but to be effective the process must be based on explicit and enforceable medical protocols.

This bleak picture is not meant to suggest that there is no hope of controlling utilization should a national plan be enacted. Many of the conditions affecting the outcome of present and past control activities would change under national health insurance. Expanded eligibility would increase the aggregate costs of control, but unit costs should decline given some reasonable expectation of economies of scale. As a larger percentage of the population (both providers and consumers) was covered, the possibilities of escape from the impact of utilization controls would drop. On another plane, the expansion in benefit coverage implicit in every NHI plan would, by increasing the service choices available at the same low user price, make utilization control activities more important than they now are. The likelihood that providers would continue to be paid on a service-by-service basis under national health insurance also increases the importance of control efforts. In short, if there is one common denominator among all NHI proposals, it is that utilization control options cannot be ignored.

Chapter 10
LONG-TERM CARE

WILLIAM POLLAK

L ONG-TERM care refers to health and social services that are provided inside or outside an institution over an extended period to chronically ill, functionally impaired people, most of whom are elderly. Although long-term care has generally been ignored in deliberations on national health insurance, government on all levels has become overwhelmingly important in its financing. Public spending on nursing home care in fiscal year 1977 totaled $7.2 billion—57 percent of the $12.6 billion total nursing home bill, and 13 percent of public spending on all personal health care. Within Medicaid, nursing home care absorbs almost 40 percent of all expenditures. Thus, it is evident both that government is a major, even dominant, element in the long-term-care system, and that long-term care is a sizable governmental health care responsibility.[1]

Concern is widespread, however, that this public involvement is not producing satisfactory results. Inappropriate emphasis on institutional care, failure to provide the desired continuum of services, and continued financial and patient care scandals are among the most frequent criticisms of current long-term-care policy. With or without changes in the financing of acute care, long-term-care policy should be reevaluated.

In this reevaluation, uncertainty about costs is a paramount concern. Perhaps more than any other benefit, long-term care raises the specter of uncontrollable demand for services and ever-growing public expenditures. To deal with this concern, it is essential to address two critical features of a

---

[1] Figures are based on estimates presented by Robert M. Gibson and Charles R. Fisher, "National Health Expenditures, Fiscal Year 1977," *Social Security Bulletin* 41 (July 1978):7.

long-term-care benefit: the services it incorporates and the mechanisms it employs for organizing and controlling service use. This chapter will review policy options in each of these areas and the possibility each offers for achieving a desirable balance between access to service and expenditure control.

Long-term care comprises a broad range of services: skilled nursing care (such as changing of catheters and dressings, monitoring conditions, administering medications); physical and occupational therapy; personal care services (assistance with bathing, dressing, eating, walking, and toileting); counselling; case management or coordination (selecting, coordinating, and monitoring formal and informal services); homemaker services (light housekeeping, meal preparation, and shopping); and chore services (heavier and less frequent tasks necessary to maintain a house or apartment). It is almost always technically possible to provide the required mix of these services in any of a number of settings—from the client's home, to a "congregate care" facility, to a twenty-four-hour, full-care institution—as well as to provide them to one individual in a combination of settings, for example, home and a day care center.

Even this simple listing makes it apparent that many long-term-care services are neither medically nor technically complex, and that, as a consequence, they often can be provided by untrained family and friends. Numerous studies reveal the importance of such informally provided services. For example, in a study in Cleveland, Ohio, the U.S. General Accounting Office found that 63 percent of the extremely impaired elderly and 92 percent of the greatly impaired elderly live not in institutions, but in the community.[2] Furthermore, the study revealed that most of the care provided to these people is provided by family and friends. The fraction of all care provided informally rises with the severity of impairments, from 57 percent for the slightly impaired, to 80 percent for the extremely impaired.[3] The significance of informal care also is revealed by data that show that, when age and

---

[2] Comptroller General of the United States, *Home Health—The Need for a National Policy to Better Provide for the Elderly* (Washington, D.C.: The General Accounting Office, 1977), p. 20. The terms used to classify people in this study were in order of increasing severity: "unimpaired," "slightly," "mildly," "moderately," "generally," "greatly," and "extremely" impaired.

[3] Ibid., p. 17.

sex are held constant, married people use nursing home care only one-third to one-fourteenth as much as the nonmarried people do. This statistic suggests that spouses, rather than any formal service, are by far the most important "alternative to institutional care."[4]

These characteristics of long-term care raise several policy concerns. First, should a public program subsidize the full range of services, particularly unskilled services like homemaker and chore services? On one hand, it is argued that failure to cover these services will force institutionalization of persons who could otherwise remain in their homes. On the other hand, many persons who are unlikely to seek institutionalization may use covered in-home services to substitute for informal services that would otherwise be provided. Whether and on what terms the government should offer these additional, potentially costly, benefits is a primary policy concern.

A second concern in the design of long-term-care policy relates to its social, as opposed to medical, intensity. Because long-term care is, by definition, for an extended period— usually for the remainder of the recipient's life—the nonmedical or social aspects of care cannot be neglected on the ground that care is an unpleasant but temporary departure from a normal and full life. Selection of roommates, meaningful tasks, recreational activities, personalization of rooms, and environmental cues to time and space are nonmedical dimensions of care that matter to people and to their emotional and physical health whether they are in an institution or at home. Consequently, if long-term institutional care is to be humane and effective, these nonmedical or social dimensions of care must influence the design of care regimens and facilities and must receive attention and resources that can often be more justifiably denied in acute care.

---

[4] The smallest differential was among women over age eighty-five and the largest differential was among men between the ages of sixty-five and seventy-four. William Pollak, "Utilization of Alternative Care Settings by the Elderly" in Powell M. Lawton, Robert V. Newcomer, and Thomas O. Byerts, eds., *Community Planning for an Aging Society* (Stroudsburg: Dowden Hutchinson and Ross, 1976), p. 120. These same data suggest that the widely noted higher utilization of institutions by women than men is, to a significant extent, explained by the fact that at every age, once-married women are more likely than men to have lost their spouses.

A third concern relates both to the social intensity of care and to the multiplicity of services that must be meshed, particularly in the providing of a satisfactory noninstitutional care regimen. Arranging a person's long-term care in consultation with client and family, dealing with and helping relatives to cope with their feelings, and, in the case of noninstitutional care, coordinating the efforts of formal and informal care providers are the foundation, and not the periphery, of long-term care. As Eric Pfeiffer has written, ". . . the most important service offered . . . is not a specific therapeutic intervention but rather the coordination effort of all the services while continuing contact is maintained with the individual."[5] Unless this coordination or case management function is explicitly and appropriately provided for, a program of long-term care is unlikely to meet beneficiaries' needs.

Finally, the role of the physician must be reconsidered in light of the nature of long-term care. Obviously, a physician is required to diagnose chronic conditions and to specify the medical dimensions of the continuing care regimen. Nonetheless, although medical condition and prognosis must be taken into account, many decisions in long-term care are social in character and depend more on the client's functional competence and social supports than on medical diagnosis. Additionally, most of the continuous tasks that constitute long-term care need not be and usually are not under the immediate direction of a physician. Goals in long-term care are usually different from those of acute care, because "cure" is rarely sought in long-term care. Restoration of function should be sought whenever possible, but maintenance of the client's condition and functioning, or minimization of decline, in a humane dignified manner, frequently are appropriate goals. They do not, however, generally attract or satisfy physician interest. In acute care, the physician is, in Fuchs' words, "the captain of the team." The physician's role often is equally controlling in long-term care.[6] The points suggested here, however, indicate the importance of examining the role of the physician, particularly with respect to the coordination func-

[5] Eric Pfeiffer, "Designing a System of Care: The Clinical Perspective," in Eric Pfeiffer, ed. *Alternatives to Institutional Care: Practice and Planning* (Durham, N.C.: Duke University, 1973), p. 17.

[6] Victor R. Fuchs, *Who Shall Live?* (New York: Basic Books, 1974), p. 56.

tion, for physicians probably should be members, rather than captains, of the long-term-care team.

The following sections address the issues involved in defining the long-term-care benefit under national health insurance. Proposed coverage for institutional and noninstitutional service is examined and the mechanisms that could be used to organize and coordinate long-term care while controlling program costs are discussed.

The Nature and Scope of the Long-Term-Care Benefit Under National Health Insurance

Corresponding to the spectrum of needs of long-term-care clients is a continuum of services that generally can be provided in more than one setting: a home or apartment, a residential facility, or a nonresidential place (day care program). Although most services are financed in at least one setting by at least one program, the existing array of programs is notable for its failure to cover several services in specific settings. Thus personal and maintenance care services that will be paid for if provided in residential facilities (nursing homes) will not be paid for when provided in the home or as part of a day care program. In this sense, a continuum of care is not now available. This section discusses the definition of the long-term-care benefit, that is, the services and settings that should be included in a national health insurance program. First, we consider whether a long-term-care program should extend coverage to home care services and to day care programs. Second, we examine problems in present coverage in institutional settings. Specifically, we consider whether institutional benefits should continue to be partitioned into several distinct levels of care, or whether a long-term-care program should encourage provision of service across several levels of care in a single institution.

HOME CARE

The primary issue in defining the long-term-care benefit package is also the central issue of long-term-care policy:

Should personal care and maintenance care services be provided on a long-term basis to persons in the community who need such services even if they do not need medical (or "skilled") services frequently and regularly? It is accepted that skilled home care is and will continue to be provided and that personal and maintenance services will be provided in conjunction with skilled home care to persons who need both. But broad coverage—the independent extension of the provision of those same personal and maintenance services in homes and other noninstitutional settings to impaired persons who have no regular and frequent need for medical attention— is unresolved and problematic.

This topic has not lacked attention. A long series of publications—congressional, other governmental, interest group, and independent—document the now inadequate provision of noninstitutional care and the problems created thereby: the institutionalization of people who otherwise could live at home, inadequate care for impaired people living in the community, excessive burdens on family, and excessive public expenditures. These publications also call attention to a corresponding set of benefits that allegedly would flow from broad coverage. The most important would be the substitution of preferred community care for institutional care and the saving of public resources because community care is assumed to be less expensive than institutional care. Several bills reflecting these beliefs have been submitted in Congress either to broaden home health coverage under existing programs or to create a new program that would incorporate broad coverage.[7]

Publicity has not brought enlightenment, but instead has tended to deflect attention both from lacunae in our knowledge and from difficult policy choices that must be made if we do elect to provide broad coverage. It is critical to note that if broad coverage should be provided, home care (and possibly other forms of community care) would flow to two distinct groups. First, some people now live in institutions either because needed community care services are unavailable or not financed or because, in the absence of such services, their conditions deteriorate to the point at which institutionalization

---

[7] These include H.R. 2268 introduced in 1975 by Rep. Barber Conable, H.R. 9829 introduced in 1975 by Rep. Ed Koch, and H.R. 10738 introduced in 1978 by Rep. Claude Pepper.

is dictated. Some of this first group of people who now are institutionalized would live in the community if home care were available and publicly financed. Second, many impaired persons already live in the community, with most of their care provided informally by a spouse, other relatives, or friends.

If formal care were financed and available, relatives and friends would undoubtedly continue to provide some care, but they also would inevitably substitute some formal for informal care to free themselves, at least partially, from burdensome and frequently unpleasant tasks. Other impaired persons in the community need but do not now receive any care—either from programs or from kin. Presumably, broadened coverage would also be intended to serve these people.

This distinction between persons who under existing arrangements are institutionalized and those who under existing arrangements live in the community has critical implications for the cost of broad coverage. Home care provided to the former would replace institutional care that may be more expensive and that often is publicly financed. The provision of home care to this group thus might reduce public expenditures. New home care provided to persons now in the community, conversely, would either substitute for care now provided informally by family or friends or would add to care now provided. Provision of such care may well be desirable, but it could only increase public expenditures on long-term care.

Discussions of broadened home care often ignore this distinction and focus almost entirely on the former group. Thus home care and other forms of noninstitutional care are often termed "alternatives to institutions" as if their only clientele would be persons who would receive institutional care if home care were not available.

Home Care for Persons Likely to be Institutionalized Under Existing Arrangements

A series of studies sought to identify the fraction of currently institutionalized elderly who should, could, or would be cared for in the community (or in a lower level of institutional care) if adequate home care were available and if placements were more carefully made. Because these studies are based on different institutional populations and use different criteria in making hypothetical "ideal" placements, the estimates of misplacement vary widely. A Congressional Budget Office survey of such studies "conservatively" concluded "that 10 to 20 percent of SNF (skilled nursing facility) patients and 20 to 45 percent of ICF (intermediate care facility) residents are receiving unnecessarily high levels of care." [8] Although these percentages do not translate exactly into latent demand for home care, they do support the notion that provision of adequate home care would enable many people who now become institutionalized to remain in the community.

The study that most carefully assesses the cost-effectiveness of alternative placements was carried out in Minnesota by Jay Greenberg.[9] Although costs are obviously not the sole consideration in making actual placements, this study estimated both the proportion of current residents of skilled nursing facilities who could be cared for at lower cost in the community and the cost savings to Minnesota if care were provided for these people in the community rather than in a nursing home. In making its estimates, this study included the same cost categories when calculating the cost of care in different settings rather than excluding the cost of housing, food, and miscellaneous items from the cost of home care as several studies have done. The Minnesota study also recognized, as some have not, that the relative cost of home care versus institutional care varies with the level of client impairments, and the difference tends to diminish and be eliminated as more severe impairments are dealt with.[10] Greenberg concluded that 9 percent of Minnesota's present skilled nursing facility

---

[8] Congressional Budget Office, *Long-Term Care for the Elderly and Disabled* (Washington, D.C.: U.S. Government Printing Office, 1977), p. 18.

[9] Jay Greenberg, "The Cost of In-Home Services," in *A Planning Study of Services to Non-Institutionalized Older Persons in Minnesota* (St. Paul: The Governor's Citizens Council on Aging, 1974) Part 2.

[10] The confusion prevalent in this area is evident in a General Accounting Office (GAO) report, which recognized the significance of impairment levels, but excluded housing, food, and other costs in calculating the cost of home care. The GAO study also focused on the relative cost of home and institutional care for those now in the community more than on relative costs for those now in institutions who are the more significant targets of such comparisons. *Home Health—The Need for a National Policy to Better Provide for the Elderly.* (Washington, D.C.: U.S. General Accounting Office, 1977).

residents would be cared for at lower cost in the community and that Minnesota could save approximately $400,000 annually by providing care for these people in the lower-cost setting.[11] Similar examinations of an intermediate care facility population, which is less impaired, would probably yield a higher percentage of persons who could be served in the community at lower costs.

Greenberg's figures cannot be extrapolated with any precision to the rest of the country because the size and characteristics of nursing home populations vary significantly across states. Nonetheless the Greenberg study provides the best available evidence on the savings that might be achieved by providing more home care of the elderly. The statistics suggest that for some significant proportion of the institutionalized population, broad coverage would reduce expenditures.

The substitution of noninstitutional for institutional care also is widely thought to benefit the emotional and physical well-being of the impaired. Surprisingly, there is little clear evidence on the harmfulness of institutional care or on the superiority of home care when other variables are controlled.[12] There is evidence that people awaiting or receiving institutional care would prefer community care. In the absence of contrary evidence on the inferiority of community care, it seems reasonable to assume that such care is preferred when it does not cost more than institutional care does. Hence on grounds of preference as well as costs, broadened coverage appears to be desirable when applied to the population that uses institutional care under the policies we now have.

Home Care for Persons Now Living in the Community

If a broad coverage program were implemented, it is unlikely that service could be limited to people who, in the absence of service, would be institutionalized. Many people who under present policy live in the community also would seek publicly funded formal care either to substitute for or add to informal care they now receive. Because many of these people have impairments comparable to those of the

---

[11] Greenberg, "The Cost of In-Home Services," p. 46.

[12] See the excellent survey of such studies in S.V. Kasl, "Physical and Mental Effects of Involuntary Relocation of the Elderly—A Review," in *American Journal of Public Health* 72 (March 1972):377–93.

institutionalized population, no reasonable criteria based on functional or medical condition could include the latter and exclude the former. Thus any reasonable, broad-coverage program would serve some people who now receive no care and some people who now receive informal care from kin and friends.

A number of studies have examined the benefits that flow from the provision of personal and maintenance care to people in the community. William Weissert recently examined several demonstration projects that provided homemaker services.[13] The specific services provided varied slightly among projects but generally corresponded to those referred to here by the expression *broadened coverage:* home management, personal care, supportive activities, and health care management. Medicare financed these services under provisions of Section 222 of PL 92-603 that permit relaxation, within funded demonstrations, of two of Medicare's provisions that most restrict the use of home care: the denial of payment for housekeeping services that would increase significantly the length of a home health visit and the limitation of the home health benefit to service provided in conjunction with skilled nursing care. Although these changes represent a significant expansion of Medicare coverage, it is important to remember that the service focuses basically on acute rather than long-term care.

Data presented in the study indicate that the availability of homemaker service did not reduce the likelihood that recipients would use skilled nursing facilities. Hence, homemaker services are an addition to and not a substitute for existing Medicare benefits. According to this well-designed and well-executed study, recipients benefited only in increased contentment. Social and mental functioning were unaffected. The study did not provide information on an additional benefit that would not have gone directly to service recipients, that is, reduced strain on family members who might otherwise have provided service.

Although broader than the services now covered by Medicare, the study's services were restricted to posthospital care, and presumably the number and duration of visits were

---

[13] William Weissert, Thomas T.H. Wan, and Barbara Liveratos, *Effects and Costs of Day Care and Homemaker Services for the Chronically Ill: A Randomized Experiment,* preliminary report, Department of Health, Education, and Welfare (DHEW), Office of the Assistant Secretary for Health, National Center for Health Services Research, January 1979.

limited. Thus these services do not correspond directly to a long-term benefit independent of prior hospitalization that is the prototype for our discussion. The study nonetheless strongly suggests that broadened home care coverage would not prevent institutionalization and would benefit those who, under existing arrangements, receive no care or receive informal care from kin.

Provision of this new service necessarily increases total program costs. The study found that the average net homemaker program cost $3,432.[14] The study does not incorporate possible reduced use of the Medicaid nursing home benefit, but the study's author implies that this factor would not significantly alter the net increase in costs reported.

Total Program Costs

More carefully than most, the Weissert study documents the benefits provided by a particular broadening of home health benefits. Because of its specific benefit design and its recognized experimental character, the study provides only limited information on the utilization and costs that would arise under a broad-coverage program. Utilization and costs obviously would depend on cost-sharing terms, eligibility criteria, subtle organizational and administrative features of the program, criteria and judgments used in assigning services to clients, and availability of services. Total costs would include the savings associated with community care for people who would otherwise be institutionalized and the additional costs of serving a previously unserved population. The extensive social experiments that would be necessary to measure utilization and costs under different arrangements have not been, and probably will not be, conducted. As a result, total program cost projections are rough estimates of actual costs.

The Congressional Budget Office prepared cost estimates for an open-ended entitlement program that would provide a spectrum of institutional and noninstitutional services to elderly and disabled persons on the basis of their medical condition, and, if they lived with relatives, the capacity of kin to provide care. Both the low and high estimates of expenditures by these authors reflect their view that potential demand for services would far exceed supply, and that home health outlays therefore would depend primarily on the rate

---

[14] We use the term *net* because some other Medicare costs are slightly different for the control group and the service groups.

at which service supplies could be augmented. Low expenditure estimates start at $1.7 billion in 1980 and rise rapidly to $7.6 billion in 1985; high estimates range from $3.2 billion in 1980 to $27.1 billion in 1985. The magnitude of these figures and the range of uncertainty in the estimates led the Congressional Budget Office to conclude "that the cost of such a program is likely to be very large and that much further research is needed before its implications can be assessed accurately." [15]

The European experience, although not yet analyzed in depth, seems consistent with these conclusions. Most West European countries do provide more extensive home health benefits and a broader spectrum of long-term-care services than does the United States. Although these services may add up to better care for the elderly and, as a result, the elderly in those countries may be more competent and contented than are old people in the United States, these services do not appear to reduce sharply the use of institutions. Sweden, for example, has almost one home helper for every 100 people, whereas we provide one helper for about every 6,000 people. Despite these home helpers, financial support for family nursing, and relatively abundant special housing for the aged, elderly people in Sweden are institutionalized at almost the same rate as are our elderly.[16]

Expectations of increased costs may not justify continued neglect of home care, but they do not justify expanded efforts to estimate probable costs and, perhaps more important, to identify program characteristics that may limit expenditures. These characteristics include the organization of a long-term-care program and patient cost sharing, both of which are discussed later in this chapter.

DAY CARE

Coverage of day care poses virtually the same issues as does coverage of home care, and can be dealt with briefly. Adult

---

[15] Congressional Budget Office, *Long-Term Care: Actuarial Estimates* (Washington, D.C.: U.S. Government Printing Office, 1977), pp. 99–100.

[16] Robert L. Kane and Rosalie A. Kane, *Long-Term Care in Six Countries* (Washington, D.C.: John E. Fogarty International Center for Advanced Study in the Health Sciences, DHEW, 1976), pp. 74–78.

day care programs provide a variety of health and social services to groups of people in a setting other than the clients' residences. Weissert usefully distinguishes between "day hospital" programs that have a strong health orientation and seek rehabilitation as a treatment goal, and multipurpose programs that do not provide rehabilitative care but focus instead on "less infirm participants' need for social services, meals, social interaction and activities." [17] Day care programs are often particularly appropriate when kin can provide housing and assistance part of the time, but are unable to provide care during the day or do not have the skill required to provide certain needed services.

Like expanded home care benefits, day care would serve two groups: people who otherwise would use no care or informal care, and people who would use institutional care if day care were not covered.[18] With respect to the former, coverage would involve increased public expenditures that might well be justified by benefits received.

A study by Weissert involving four day care programs provides relevant information on benefits and on cost.[19] As in his evaluation of homemaker demonstrations, Weissert compared these day care services with Medicare-covered services which, we must remember, focus on acute care. On the basis of multivariate analysis involving the use of control groups, Weissert concluded that if day care were a Medicare-covered service, death rates might be slightly reduced. Dependency, contentment, and mental and social functioning would be minimally affected. In contrast to the expected results from provision of homemaker services, the provision of day care benefits was accompanied by reduced use of both skilled nursing facilities and hospitals. But this reduction in institutional service use did not mean lower total cost. The cost of day care services for institutionalized people who thereby reduced their use of institutions and for others who were not in institutions

---

[17] William Weissert, "Rationales for Public Health Insurance Coverage of Geriatric Day Care: Issues, Options, and Impacts," *Journal of Health Politics, Policy and Law* 3 (Winter 1979):555–68.

[18] Day care also would presumably serve some people who now receive formal home care, but because that group is relatively small, it is not discussed here.

[19] Weissert, Wan, and Liveratos, "Effects and Costs of Day Care and Homemaker Services."

but used the day care services more than offset the reduction in institutional service costs. The net per user cost of day care was $2,692—a somewhat smaller amount than the gross cost of $3,235 because users of day care had used hospital and skilled nursing home care somewhat less than did the matched controls.

This study also provides some evidence on limits to demand if noninstitutional service coverage were to be expanded. Weissert found that one-fourth of the patients who were assigned to day care in the experiment failed to use the services. Poor health status (in the extreme, death) accounted for some of the nonuse, but the failure of many in this group to use the services offered without charge remains unexplained.

Another Weissert study, which was not experimental, provides information on day care as long-term care rather than acute care. This study compared the cost and average use of day care services to the cost and use of long-term nursing home care. The findings suggest how public expenditures would be affected if day care were to substitute directly for those nursing home services. Day care costs were somewhat higher per day than were nursing home care costs, but day care cost somewhat less per case because it was provided for only two-and-one-half to four days per week, whereas nursing home care was provided continuously. From the perspective of a health care finance program, Weissert estimates that day care could effect cost savings of between 37 percent and 60 percent of the cost of nursing home care. When the cost concept is broadened to include nonhealth program expenses that day care users incur while living in the community, however, savings were projected at between 12 percent and 35 percent.[20]

There is no reason to consider day care (or home care)

---

[20] William G. Weissert, "Costs of Adult Day Care: A Comparison to Nursing Homes," *Inquiry* 15 (March, 1978) :17. Weissert asserts that the higher range is relevant from the perspective of a health care payer. Whether that assertion is correct, however, depends on the cost-sharing terms that are established. If residents of institutions must share in costs more than users of noninstitutional care (as might well occur), then the 12 percent to 35 percent range might reflect the health program's cost savings more accurately than the 37 percent to 60 percent range. It is the lower range, too, that is relevant from the perspective of the public sector if the patient's normal living costs are paid for from income maintenance benefits that terminate if the individual is institutionalized.

simply as an "alternative" to nursing home care. Day care facilities and nursing homes serve overlapping populations, but each type of facility has characteristics that make it appropriate for some people who would be inappropriately served by the other. Policy makers might attempt to restrict utilization of day care only to those persons who otherwise would use nursing home care. Aside from the great practical difficulty of enforcing such a restriction, the restriction is in fact inconsistent with the view of day care as more than an institutional alternative. Like home care coverage, then, day care coverage would tend to increase costs (and benefits) by serving a population not currently served and would tend to decrease costs (with a likely increase in benefits) by serving the population now using institutional care.

THE NATURE OF THE INSTITUTIONAL BENEFITS

Attention to benefit expansion, although important, should not obscure problems in benefits currently provided. A thorough analysis of nursing home benefits is beyond the scope of this chapter, but one issue deserves attention here— that is, the way in which current arrangements treat the continuum of institutional care.

Because users of long-term institutional care present a variety of needs, institutions must provide a varied range of care. The United States provides this breadth by having a variety of facilities, each specializing in a particular level of care: skilled nursing facilities; one or more levels of intermediate care facilities; and, outside Medicare and Medicaid, domiciliary care homes that also may be regarded as part of the long-term-care system.

Through this approach the system provides a range of care, but individual facilities often do not. This situation is not the product of a grand coherent plan; instead the "policy" simply developed in a series of responses to discrete problems. Thus the Medicaid program initially covered only skilled nursing home care. Because only one level of care was covered, people who needed less intense care than that offered by skilled nursing facilities were nevertheless placed in skilled nursing facilities in order to provide them with at least some form of care. This practice was expensive, of course, because these people could have been served at lower cost in a facility offering less skilled care. Coverage of a second ("intermediate") level of care was therefore added to the Medicaid program, primarily to reduce expenditures but also to permit the continued operation of some homes that could not meet rising federal skilled care standards by reclassifying them as "intermediate" facilities. Subsequent adjustments and additions to the level-of-care system have followed this pattern. They represent ad hoc responses of states to changing federal policies, or federal reactions to restrain or reverse unanticipated and undesired state reactions to prior federal policies. Each response may have improved an existing situation, but it is not clear that the policy structure that has evolved is sensible.

Curiously, observers who comment on the possibly inevitable problems in the operation of level-of-care arrangements often propose correctives without ever comparing the merits of the basic approach with an obvious alternative: a system of general facilities, each capable of providing a wide range of care. After a brief review of the current arrangements, this alternative is explored here.

The Levels-of-Care System in Practice

The most striking characteristic of the present system is the wide variation that exists among states in the way that the several levels of care are defined in practice. This variation is apparent even in gross data on nursing home beds. Thus a state such as Oklahoma that has virtually no skilled nursing facilities must be defining as *intermediate care facilities* homes that serve many patients who in other states would be placed in skilled nursing care facilities.

The significance of such interstate variation in the populations served by identically named facilities depends in part on whether services vary to match the varying needs of residents. One study has looked at these issues in some detail. It confirms our inference drawn from gross data by finding striking differences among patients in intermediate care facilities across states in terms of the quality and nature of patient service needs. But, reassuringly, the study also found "marked differences in the amount of per-patient service time" that were "strongly related" to observed differences in service needs.[21] In other words, states whose intermediate care facilities served unusually impaired populations were likely to be states whose intermediate care facilities provided unusually high levels of care.

Less reassuring are observations which suggest that if services are matched to meet service needs within states, such matching occurs only haphazardly. A Minnesota report states that "when national leaders prescribed the 2 levels of nursing home care . . . they apparently assumed that physicians could and would classify patients consistently according to patients' needs." But their analysis suggests that "patient, relative, and facility satisfaction" probably count more than do patient needs for twenty-four-hour care when the choice is made between skilled nursing facilities and intermediate care units.[22] Similarly, the New York State Moreland Act Commission observed that whether a person was placed in a skilled nursing facility, an intermediate facility, or a domiciliary care home "depends all too much on happenstance."[23] The commission concluded that enforcement of federal staffing and facility regulations "makes little sense if there is no adequate control over the types of patient or resident [obtaining] services in regulated industries."

Even if the differentiation of facilities by level of care has inherent advantages, this brief review suggests that these advantages are probably eroded or eliminated in practice by significant mismatching of patients to facilities, and/or by the particular ways that individual states differentiate their intermediate care facilities from their skilled care facilities. Furthermore, the lack of consensus among the states on how the levels of care should be differentiated at least suggests the possibility that an absence of level-of-care distinctions may be as satisfactory as any particular distinction employed

---

[21] Douglas Holmes et al., *A National Study of Levels of Care in Intermediate Facilities (ICFs)*, prepared by Community Research Applications, Inc., Contract Number HSA 105–74–176 (Washington, D.C.: Health Services Administration, 1976), p. v.

[22] *Quality Assurance and Review Procedure Programs: Summary Report, 1975* (Minneapolis: Minnesota Department of Health, 1976), p. 161.

[23] New York State Moreland Act Commission on Nursing Homes and Residential Facilities, *Assessment and Placement: Anything Goes*, (Albany, New York State Government, 1976), p. 27.

to date. That possibility and the issues it raises are discussed in the next section.

General Facilities as an Alternative

A system of general facilities could improve affairs if individual homes were capable of providing a wide range of care and were more effective at matching internal services to residents than people now making placements are at matching patients to facilities. The greatest advantage of such a system would be its consistency with the needs of nursing home patients. The conditions of nursing home residents, though chronic, often change and require altered care regimens. Whether the care has been altered for medical or for other reasons (e.g., to comply with regulations), the provision of altered care will obviously require more frequent movement of residents in specialized institutions than in general institutions (where several levels of care can be provided in the same building and possibly even in the same room). The movement of geriatric patients required in a system of specialized institutions has been shown to induce morbidity and mortality.

General facilities could reduce the need for movement as patient conditions change. A system of general facilities, however, might impose certain economic and operational costs. First, general facilities must be larger in scale then specialized ones if specialized inputs are to be kept fully employed. Below some threshold facility size, therefore, high-quality care probably can be provided in general facilities only at higher cost than in specialized facilities. Without further empirical research, however, it is not possible to determine whether the cost advantage of specialized homes is significant over the range of scales of American nursing homes. Nor is it possible to identify the scale required to exhaust any cost advantage that specialized homes may have.

Apart from this economic question, a shift to a system of general facilities would require major changes in current approaches to payment and regulations. Existing arrangements for financing and regulating institutions generally relate to entire facilities rather than to the individuals living in them. For example, each skilled nursing facility is typically paid a uniform amount for each of its residents and is required by certification (and licensure) standards to have specified numbers of certain staff and to have specified facilities and physical features on its premises. Thus regulations promote quality by ensuring that the facility has the means to provide adequate care for the residents it serves.

This arrangement is reasonable, given homes that are specialized to provide a particular level of care, but it would be relatively unreasonable if each facility were to provide a continuum of care to a wide variety of residents. Consider uniform per diem reimbursements. If reimbursements were set at a level sufficient to finance care for a resident with great need, a facility would be excessively rewarded at public expense for its care of less needy individuals. If reimbursements were set at a level insufficient to finance care for residents with high needs, homes would tend to refuse admittance to costly patients.[24] Although this problem exists to some degree today when single-level institutions serve a narrow range of residents, the problem obviously would be exacerbated if homes serving a much wider range of residents were reimbursed on the same basis.

Similar problems would be raised by existing types of regulations. Assuming that homes have varying patient mixes, uniform facilitywide standards unrelated to the needs of a home's particular residents would, in most instances, err in one of two ways: by requiring staff and physical facilities that are excessive for the facility's residents and therefore excessively expensive, or by requiring staff and physical facilities that are inadequate for the needs of a particularly impaired population.

In a system of general facilities, reimbursements to a home could no longer be independent of the characteristics of its residents, but would have to be determined by the mix of patients or set individually for each resident on the basis of the needs presented and, possibly, the changes in status that

---

[24] Surprisingly, this phenomenon would exist even if the uniform per diem amount were cost-related. See the discussion in William Pollak, "Long-Term Care Facility Reimbursement," in John Holahan et al., *Altering Medicaid Provider Reimbursement Methods* (Washington, D.C.: The Urban Institute, 1977), pp. 118–19.

have occurred.[25] Regulatory standards similarly would have to be made dependent on the mix of patients in a facility or specific to individual residents and their needs. Input-oriented standards would be based on patient mix, while output-oriented standards could be created to apply to the appropriateness and quality of care received—as revealed in selected care-related aspects of resident condition. Such "output" or "performance" standards have obvious conceptual advantages over input standards that at best can only guarantee the presence of necessary inputs. But output standards may be as problematic in practice as they are attractive in concept. What indicators of patient condition would be examined? How much standardization is possible and how consistently can the indicators be measured? With what confidence can observed problems be attributed to patient care? Finally, what conflicts might there be between the use of such standards and patients' rights? These questions cannot be answered until more detailed performance standards are developed and implemented on at least a demonstration basis. Their evident advantages justify such a trial, but our current ignorance dictates an incremental approach to their use.

In sum, the inherent advantages of general facilities and the disorderly and ineffective way in which the levels-of-care system operates argue for experimentation with and, possibly, implementation of a system that eschews levels-of-care distinctions. Such a system, like the present one, would pose implementation and administrative problems, particularly with respect to enforcement of standards and reimbursement. In prospect, however, these problems seem no more troublesome than those now faced.

The Organization of a Long-Term-Care System

Despite the limits to our information, it seems reasonable to assume that financing an expanded range of long-term-care services is likely to increase utilization and public expen-

---

[25] The entire reimbursement could be split into a component that is specific to individual patients (or patient mix) and a component that is uniform for all patients, the latter corresponding to those facility cost components that are independent of the care needs of residents.

ditures. If expansion has advantages, however, analysts must seek mechanisms to control its potential costs. We propose to consider these mechanisms under the rubric of organization, that is, the structures through which resources are distributed and managed in a long-term-care program.

At present, the complex organizational arrangements for long-term care pose three types of problems. First, financing is highly fragmented. Although the financing of institutional care is dominated by Medicaid, noninstitutional long-term-care services are funded by a multitude of disparate programs with varying financial arrangements, eligibility criteria, and general regulations. A recent survey counted nineteen distinct federal programs, each of which finances at least one "alternative to institutional care" for the elderly.[26]

Second, the form of service financing creates problems. Some services (e.g., home health care under Medicaid) are financed through purchase decisions made by or on behalf of individual clients. Other public and private programs make direct grants to or contracts with service providers (e.g., Title XX in some instances, the nutrition program of The Older Americans Act, and virtually all charitably funded services) who then independently accept or reject requests made for service. The latter approach poses enormous difficulties for the professional seeking long-term care for a client. Unlike the physician engaging in acute care, whose prescription for service virtually assures third-party financing, a long-term-care coordinator must obtain services for a client from agencies whose funding comes from some other source and does not depend on serving this particular client. As a result, the central tasks of "coordination" (selecting services, meshing services with one another and with the needs and capacities of families, and monitoring services to assure that their quality is satisfactory and that they continue to meet changing needs) often are dominated by efforts (1) to locate agencies that will provide service free or on favorable terms and (2) to extract services or financing from private and public agencies with limited resources and varying eligibility requirements and regulations.

---

[26] Joan Shea, "Alternatives to Institutional Care," paper developed for the Task Force on Alternatives to Institutional Care, Chicago, Office of the Regional Director, Region V, DHEW, 1977 (mimeographed).

A third organizational problem is the fragmentation of the coordination task itself. Institutional placement and procurement of noninstitutional services are tasks carried out by hospital social workers, by workers in public welfare departments and in a variety of private social service agencies, by physicians, and by families. Under current arrangements, no unit is assigned formal responsibility for coordinating the care of an individual, and no units are financed to perform this function. Consequently, there is no systematic effort to match needs to a comprehensive array of available services. Rather, services obtained tend to reflect the information, biases, and convenience of the individual taking responsibility for action.

Because most coordinators lack a continuing relationship with the patient, services received may not be monitored for appropriateness or quality. This is a particular problem with respect to noninstitutional services, for which delivery is dispersed and monitoring is time consuming. Critics have observed, however, that even in institutional care decisions, persons making placements often demonstrate ignorance about methods of assessing clients' conditions or show too little consideration for social supports and circumstances. Then, even when assessments are accurately completed, inconsistent criteria may be used to translate them into placement decisions. Finally, persons making placements often do not know about the services and quality of various facilities, or do not share what knowledge they have with patients and their families.[27]

If long-term-care benefits are to be expanded, these organizational attributes of the long-term-care system must be analyzed. First, financing and eligibility options that will offer cost-effective coverage must be identified. Second, patient cost-sharing options that encourage cost-effective choice must be explored. Third, the task of coordination must be addressed directly; alternative techniques must be identified and assessed. These issues are discussed in the following sections.

Unless the financing of all long-term-care services is channeled through a single local agency, integrated delivery of noninstitutional and institutional services is virtually impossible. This discussion therefore assumes that this channeling

---

[27] For a detailed discussion, see the New York State Moreland Act Commission, *Assessment and Placement.*

occurs, and explores methods for allocating resources to each agency and methods for distributing the agency's funds among recipients and services.

FINANCING, ENTITLEMENT, AND RULES GOVERNING ELIGIBILITY AND PRESCRIPTION OF SERVICES

The basis on which the single local agency obtains federal funds critically affects its spending decisions. Financing can be provided either through a fixed budget or on an open-ended basis. With the former, the agency must operate within a budget set in advance. The budget would most likely be determined by the size and, possibly, the problem intensity of the agency's target population (as measured, for example, by its age structure) as well as by the federally mandated, nationwide level of long-term-care expenditures. Under open-ended financing, agency funding is not subject to a fixed maximum and its level is determined by the interaction of (1) requests for service, (2) rules that guide the prescribing or assigning of service to individuals, and (3) the supply responses of providers to program-financed demands.

The attractiveness of fixed-budget funding from a cost control perspective is obvious. Costs can be controlled at any desired level by a tight budget that forces agencies to economize in their service assignment and other decisions. Against the value of this control must be set the risks of a fixed budget that is set too low: worsened care for some individuals and, at a system level, the possibility that the potential benefits of a broadened service package will be obscured, not by the weakness of the program concept, but by the inadequacy of the resources committed to it.

The merit of a fixed-budget approach thus depends on an ability to fix the budget at the right level: below levels that will foster inefficiency, yet above levels that will deprive the needy of care and doom the program's prospects. Our knowledge about utilization and costs facilitates the setting of fixed budgets in acute care and makes it possible, for example, to set appropriate capitation amounts (a form of fixed budget) for health maintenance organizations. Our knowledge about costs and utilization in long-term care is generally weaker. Furthermore, because this knowledge is derived largely from experience under Medicaid, it would be of limited use in setting the fixed budget for a program serving a broader population with an expanded set of services. Uncertainty obviously complicates the setting of an appropriate fixed budget and the possibility of error should be weighed in choosing whether to implement a fixed-budget program.

The choice between a fixed and open-ended budget is, to some degree, determined by whether the program is an entitlement one. Entitlement means that eligible individuals meeting specified conditions have a right to care. Because a fixed-budget approach may provide inadequate funds to deliver that care, such an approach may be inconsistent with entitlement. Choice, therefore, is restricted to an entitlement program that is funded on an open-ended basis or to a nonentitlement program that could be funded on an open-ended or on a fixed-budget basis.

Entitlement becomes more feasible as the predictability of its costs rises, and the appropriateness of entitlement increases with the intensity of the belief that people have a right to service. Present ignorance about costs, consequently, weakens the case for entitlement. With respect to rights, matters are more elusive. Although most Americans probably believe that impaired people have a right to some (affordable) form of long-term care, there probably is less consensus concerning the right of an impaired individual living with an able spouse or sibling to the full array of noninstitutional services provided by a broad long-term-care benefit. Thus it seems likely that attitudes concerning long-term-care entitlement would be influenced by the rules that govern who is entitled and what they are entitled to.

In any discussion of these matters, it should be noted that rules will be used to guide the assigning of services to individuals, whether the program is open-ended and entitlement, or fixed-budget and nonentitlement. Consequently, although this discussion focuses on eligibility and service assignment rules in the context of an entitlement program, similar issues would be faced under a nonentitlement program.

Both age and income may be considered in establishing an individual's eligibility for benefits, as well as the services to which he or she is entitled. The age threshold used to establish eligibility will have an enormous impact on the character of the program, determining whether it will be a program for the aged alone, for all disabled adults, or for all disabled people. Although the issues raised by this choice are very important, they are beyond the scope of this chapter. Income eligibility issues also are important, but they are related to questions concerning patient cost sharing and are discussed in the cost-sharing segment of this chapter. Functional limitations are obviously central. Because they are certain to be considered in determining the services an individual receives, the critical questions concern how such limitations will be translated into service awards. Can the process be made routine so that service assignments are determined by applying a schedule to a person's limitations as established by some objective measures? Or will service assignment be left to professional opinion directed only by unstructured guidelines? The answer probably lies between these extremes, but the breadth and detail of the spectrum between them puts a satisfactory discussion of these issues beyond this chapter's scope.

Finally, there are questions concerning the role that family status should play in determining the services to which people are entitled, given their functional limitations. Because these questions are little discussed, yet peculiarly important in long-term care, they are singled out for particular attention here.

There are good reasons to design a long-term-care program so that it displaces to the smallest extent possible the informal family efforts that now provide the bulk of noninstitutional care. This goal not only is consistent with the preservation of family bonds and supports that may be an independent objective; but such a goal also will permit costs to be controlled to a degree that would be impossible if publicly financed formal care were to substitute for informal care on a large scale.

Thus while it is reasonable to displace as little formal effort as possible, it may be unreasonable to make entitlement depend on family status, for example, by withholding service(s) entitlement from persons who live with a spouse or sibling who can provide care. Such a restriction might prove unreasonable because it would withhold entitlement in the presence of a "responsible relative" even if that relative

irresponsibly refused to provide needed care.[28] Eligibility
criteria based on "outmoded concepts of family responsibility"
therefore are probably socially and politically unacceptable.[29]

If a person's entitlement is not to be eliminated or reduced
because of family status or living situation, what measures
can be used in an entitlement program to control the use of
formal subsidized care by people who have informal alternatives? Cost sharing to place some service costs on users is
one possibility that is considered at length later. Because distributional considerations limit its application for low-income
persons, however, cost sharing, even if used, would have to
be supplemented with some form of administrative rationing.
For example, discussion and negotiation might be used to
encourage families to provide care even though, because the
program is an entitlement one, service would not ultimately
be withheld in order to induce the provision of care by reluctant relatives. Under this arrangement, service allocations
would be intended generally to reflect family status and living
arrangements; but legal entitlement, or rights to service,
would depend only on the condition and needs of the client.
This is a reasonable approach and one that is comparable to
the procedures of many nonprofit social service providers,
which try to involve family but may provide compensatory
service if their efforts fail.

Discussion and negotiation, however, are influenced by their
context. Under a fixed-budget, nonentitlement program, a
client has no legal right to service and the agency has no
legal obligation to provide it. The agency, therefore, can withhold some or all service and can use the threat of limiting
service to encourage families to cooperate. Furthermore, the
fixed budget lends credibility (and often reality) to agency
statements that there is a limit to what the agency can provide.

An open-ended entitlement program would provide a funda-

---

[28] This discussion ignores the additional problems, some of which are
mechanical, that would complicate implementation of such a standard.
For example, how would the capacity of the relatives to provide care
be assessed? Other implementation problems relate to behavioral responses; refusing to provide care to persons living with relatives, for
example, might induce some relatives to desert.

[29] Dorothy P. Rice and Saul Waldman, "Issues in Designing a National
Program of Long-Term Care Benefits," *Medical Care* 14 (Supplement,
May 1976):103.

mentally different context. A client's right to service would be unaffected by the presence of family. The agency could negotiate and discuss in order to encourage family to assist, but ultimately could not restrict service below the level dictated by the needs of the client. As time passes and as people understand and adapt to the character and services of the program, one critical question will assume increasing importance: Will negotiation and discussion limit the substitution of publicly funded formal services for informal ones when it is known that formal services will not ultimately be withheld simply because someone is present who can provide care?

The complexity and interrelatedness of the several issues discussed here justify a brief summary. The basic funding choice is between a fixed-budget, nonentitlement approach and an open-ended, entitlement approach. The former can ensure that costs are predictable and controllable, but carries the risks of inadequate care and program failure. Ignorance complicates the setting of an initial budget level and increases these risks. If, to reduce the risks, budget increases are planned once experience shows the initial budget level to be inadequate, the cost control advantage of the fixed-budget program would be considerably weakened.

An open-ended entitlement approach would further reduce control over costs. It would require central specification of rules to govern entitlements to service. These rules would certainly limit entitlements to persons with functional limitations, but equity considerations would probably prevent further limiting of entitlement to only those among the impaired who live alone. Although administrative procedures (rather than service entitlements) might be used to control service use by those who do live with "competent others," it is not certain that such procedures would be effective in the long run under an entitlement program.

PRODUCER VERSUS CONSUMER SUBSIDIES

Regardless of how benefits were financed, they could be channeled in two ways. The first would be to subsidize consumers, by paying some or all the costs of the care they select. With consumer subsidies, providers would be paid only if their services were selected by consumers or those who choose for them. The alternative would be to subsidize providers, that is, to grant them funds directly, independent of the demands consumers express for their particular outputs.

Several considerations favor consumer subsidies as the primary mode of service financing.[30] Three considerations would flow directly from the financial dependence of providers on consumers when consumers are subsidized. First, this dependence would make it relatively unlikely that producers would reject requests for service. Second, and more important for the evolution of the service system, producers would survive and flourish only insofar as they provided service whose quality and characteristics appealed to clients or their representatives.[31] The purchase decisions of clients would thus become a form of evaluation to which response was compelled by the finance mechanism. Conversely, if producers were subsidized directly, consumer preferences might not be recognized and, even if recognized, they would certainly have less influence on the fortunes of competing providers.

The third advantage of consumer subsidies relates to planning. With financial flows determined by the choices made by or on behalf of individuals, the production of various services would expand and contract in response to those choices. The level and distribution of services would correspond to individual choices, reducing the need for planning agencies, plans, needs surveys, and the like.

With provider subsidies, in contrast, the government would have to allocate funds among types of service and service locations. Individual providers would have to ration their funds—accepting some requests for service and rejecting others. This policy would have two major disadvantages. First, decentralization of rationing would increase the likelihood that persons in similar circumstances will be treated differently, receiving service in some instances and being denied it in others. Moreover, because selection of a service does not

---

[30] Primary reliance on consumer subsidies could be supplemented by producer subsidies to support promising service innovations that are risky or that are, for some other reason, difficult to finance from regular sources of capital.

[31] If financing is deficient, there will be few providers from which to choose and this mechanism will not operate. But deficient financing will impair all quality control mechanisms.

carry payment with it, much of the case manager's time would be absorbed in extracting subsidized services from agencies whose limited resources compel rejection of many requests for service. As a result, the tasks of selecting and monitoring services are likely to get slighted.

PATIENT COST SHARING

Cost-sharing terms determine the level of consumer subsidy, that is, the proportion of costs that users have to pay for nursing home care, home care, and other services. Cost-sharing terms are critical because they determine the distribution of costs between the users and the public program for a given quantity of care, and because they influence both the volume of care and the distribution of that care among different users. In general, cost-sharing terms represent compromises between desires to ration care and to control utilization and costs on one hand, and efforts to foster access and to remove cost burdens on the other.

Patient cost sharing in long-term care has not received the analytical attention that cost sharing in acute care has received. Furthermore, data and insights developed in acute care have only limited applicability to long-term care because of differences between the two types of care. Because these important differentiating characteristics have received so little attention in the context of cost sharing, we present them here.

Presence of Informal Substitutes

Acute-care services have few close substitutes, are technically complex, and can be provided only with highly trained personnel, or specialized equipment. By contrast, long-term-care services tend to be technically simple, and can be and are provided on a significant scale by untrained relatives and friends who "substitute" for formal services that otherwise might be required. The availability of substitutes is likely to make demands for long-term-care services more responsive (elastic) to cost-sharing variations than are demands for acute-care services which have few close substitutes.

The existence of informal substitutes also affects how cost-sharing terms influence the distribution of care burdens. Low cost-sharing terms obviously place dollar costs on the public sector that would be paid by clients and families if cost sharing were higher. However, to the degree that they encourage the substitution of formal for informal care, low cost-sharing terms also shift to the public sector, in monetary form, a burden that would be borne in physical form by informal providers if cost sharing were higher or if care were not covered.

A consensus seems to be emerging that most of the financial burden for acute care should be removed from the user. Cost sharing, therefore, is not advocated as a means to distribute cost burdens equitably. Instead, cost sharing is tolerated as an expedient to control utilization and program costs. A similar consensus might evolve in favor of greatly expanded public assumption of the physical and financial burdens of long-term care that now fall disproportionately on those who, by chance, are relatives of the impaired. But no such consensus is apparent yet. Indeed, expressions of concern over the possibly high cost of expanded home care imply a rejection of the notion that burdens should be shifted, because home care would be a truly expensive program only if there were substantial substitution of formal for informal care.

Nature of the Costs of Institutional Long-Term Care

Acute-care costs generally add significantly to the normal costs of living of families and individuals. Cost-sharing terms, therefore, are constrained from a desire to limit the excess burdens that fall on those who incur significant medical expenses. Many of the institutional long-term-care costs, however, are not illness-induced net additions to the cost of living, but rather are costs that would be borne by the recipient even if care were not required: nutrition, housing, housekeeping, some maintenance and other services.

Because these costs are not additional burdens, it is reasonable for the client to pay for them, as "cost sharing," in an institution, just as the client would pay for them as normal living costs in the community. This conclusion is reinforced when the facts are considered from a slightly different perspective. Medical care cost-sharing terms are constrained, implicitly if not explicitly, at least in part to protect clients' income for alternative targets of expenditure: food, clothing, transportation, recreation, and so forth. Yet some of these items are (or should be) provided by the institution, while the need for others is partially preempted by the nature of the institution and its residents. This reasoning suggests that patients should bear more of the costs of institutional long-term care than of acute care. It also suggests that, within long-term care, higher cost-sharing terms should be applied to institutional than to home care.

Significance of Family Status

Cost sharing on formal care in order to control utilization by encouraging the provision of informal care is reasonable only if informal care is a feasible option—and it is not for a single individual without family. Similarly, the argument that institutional care substantially substitutes for, as well as adds to, normal living costs is accurate for a single individual but relatively inaccurate for a couple, one member of which continues to remain in the community at a cost much larger than one-half of the couple's normal costs of living. Thus, the appropriate cost-sharing policy may depend on the individual's family status.

Assets

Assets rarely enter discussions of health care cost sharing, but accumulated assets can make a low-income person ineligible for Medicaid, and thus are, in a sense, part of that program's implicit cost sharing. Personal assets also might be tapped to pay for institutional care under a universal long-term-care program. Although this practice may seem odious, it should be noted that because people with similar incomes often have very different assets, it may be more equitable to draw on both wealth and income components of economic position than to draw just on income.

The arguments against tapping nonfinancial wealth (primarily homes) are weakest when considering persons who are permanently institutionalized. Indeed, it is their heirs rather than they who will bear most of the cost-sharing burden for their care. Obviously drawing on clients' wealth might help control program costs, particularly with respect to institutional care, for which costs often exceed users' incomes. Only about 18 percent of the nonmarried elderly (who are the primary users of institutional care) had incomes as high as the average charge for nursing home care in 1974; and approximately 50 percent had incomes that were insufficient to cover even half of the charges for such care in that year.

The characteristics of long-term care, then, suggest the following cost-sharing rules: Cost-sharing terms should consider a client's assets as well as income and should vary with that person's economic position defined in terms of either or both. Cost-sharing terms also may have to vary according to the type of care required and differences in family status. When different arrangements are designed, care should be taken that cost-sharing arrangements do not negate the apparent breadth of the program by making persons who are eligible for one benefit (e.g., nursing home care) ineligible for another (e.g., home health care), as in fact occurs under the Medicaid program. In general, policy makers who set cost-sharing terms should be aware of the influence those terms exert on access, on choices between institutional and noninstitutional care and between using formal and informal care, and on program costs. The following cost-sharing options represent an effort to incorporate these objectives.

Separate cost-sharing options are presented for single and married individuals for both institutional and noninstitutional (home) care. The options presented here are not the only possible ones, but they incorporate the features already suggested and promote discussion of cost-sharing issues that are rarely considered. In this discussion, patient cost shares are made to depend on income, but they could be made to depend on assets as well. One such approach would be to define income as the sum of current income (excluding returns on investments) plus the annuitized value of the individual's wealth.

Cost-Sharing Options for a Single Individual

Starting with the single individual, Table 24 shows cost-sharing terms for home care and nursing home services. Looking first at home care, payments would be zero for persons with monthly incomes of $200 or less (the income maintenance or Supplemental Security Income [SSI] minimum assumed for illustrative purposes) and would rise regularly with income. This arrangement would serve to protect low-income persons, while limiting the extent to which the program would subsidize people who could afford to pay. Payments would be moderate for other low-income people who used moderate amounts of home care; payments would rise to only a $60 (15 percent) share for an individual with a $350 monthly income who used $400 worth of home health care a month. This policy reflects a desire to assure coverage to single individuals who often have few or no informal supports.

Table 24

COST-SHARING PAYMENTS FOR HOME CARE AND NURSING HOME CARE AT DIFFERENT LEVELS OF INCOME: SINGLE INDIVIDUALS

| Monthly Income | Total Monthly Cost of Home Care Services | | | | | |
	$100	$200	$300	$400	$500	$600
	Cost-Sharing Payments by Individuals					
$200	0	0	0	0	0	0
250	5	10	15	20	25	30
350	15	30	45	60	75	90
500	30	60	90	120	150	180
700	50	100	150	200	250	300
950	75	150	225	300	375	450
1,250	90*	180*	270*	360*	450*	540*

Figures without asterisks are derived from the formula:

$$P_{hc} = \frac{Y-200}{1,000} \times C_{hc}$$

where P_{hc}, Y, and C_{hc} represent payment for home care, income, and cost of home care respectively. Asterisked figures result from a payment ceiling of $.9 \times C_{hc}$ imposed so that all people are eligible for program benefits.

| Monthly Income | Total Monthly Cost of Nursing Home Care | | | | |
	$500	$600	$700	$800	$900
	Cost-Sharing Payments by Individuals				
$200	165	165	165	165	165
250	193	198	203	208	213
350	248	263	278	293	308
500	330	360	390	420	450
700	440	490	540	590	640
950	450*	540*	630*	720*	810*
1,250	450*	540*	630*	720*	810*

Figures without asterisks are derived from the formula:

$$P_{nh} = 165 + .7(Y - 200) + \frac{Y-200}{1,000}(C_{nh} - C_t)$$

where P_{nh}, Y, C_{nh}, and C_t represent payment for nursing home care, income, cost of nursing home care, and a cost target ($650 in this example), respectively. Asterisked figures result from a payment ceiling of $.9 \times C_{nh}$ that displaces the formula-derived figure when the formula figure exceeds the ceiling.

For persons above the minimum income level, payments would rise with the cost of home care. This arrangement would give beneficiaries an incentive to compare the costs of different home care services and to compare the costs of home care with nursing home care. For higher-income users of larger amounts of care, cost sharing would become quite significant. Users of $600 worth of home health care monthly, for example, would pay $180 monthly if their incomes were $500, and $300 monthly if incomes were $700. Such payments obviously would tax users significantly and might well be unsupportable, particularly because users would be paying not only the cost-sharing amount but also the normal costs of living. This result, however, might be desirable, because when an individual requires $500 or $600 worth of home care, the total cost of home health care and the publicly borne cost of home care are likely to exceed the corresponding total and publicly borne costs of institutional care.[32] More-than-nominal cost shares would provide a financial reason for clients not to remain at home when home care is, both for society and for government, a significantly more expensive setting than care in a residential facility.

Turning to nursing home care, cost-sharing terms are structured differently but directed toward similar objectives. Cost-sharing obligations would be much higher for nursing home care than for home care, because recipients would be expected to contribute to their normal costs of living. Nursing home residents would retain a specified income, beginning at $35 a month, approximately the amount Medicaid now permits low-income nursing home residents to keep for personal needs. Unlike the terms of the Medicaid programs, however, these terms would cause the amount available to the client after payment to rise with income. With $700 nursing home care, this residual rises from the $35 amount protected for the

---

[32] The total costs of care referred to here included care costs and other costs of a person's living in a setting. Thus, the total cost associated with $500 of home health care is $500 plus the cost of housing, food, transportation, and so forth. The publicly borne cost of care are the total cost of care less the amount contributed by the user as a cost share. Thus, the publicly borne cost of institutional care is reduced either by the amount of the resident's contribution or by the reduction in income maintenance that occurs when a welfare recipient moves from the community into an institution.

lowest-income client to the $160 that would be protected for the client with a monthly income of $700. These terms also should encourage beneficiaries to consider and compare costs when choosing a home, since cost sharing rises with the cost of care.[33] As Table 24 shows, a person with a monthly income of $700, for example, could save $100 by choosing a facility costing $600 monthly rather than one costing $800. This situation contrasts with current Medicaid arrangements, under which subsidized users and their families have no reason at all to concern themselves with costs.

Finally, for both home care and nursing homes, Table 24 incorporates a payment ceiling of 90 percent of the cost of care. As a result, all persons would receive at least a 10 percent subsidy and would be to that degree eligible for the program. The ceiling percentage obviously could be raised to control program costs or lowered to make the minimum subsidy more meaningful. It should be noted here that universal eligibility would not ensure universal participation. In the case of long-term care, people (and institutions) might not participate in the program because reimbursement restrictions might constrain quality (and profits), because regulations might prevent patients from supplementing program payments to purchase above-standard care, or for other reasons. The smaller the minimum subsidy, the greater would be the relative weight given to these considerations that would discourage the participation of higher-income people in the program.

Cost-Sharing Options for Married Couples

Under current arrangements, the placement of a spouse in a nursing home is financially devastating for the spouse remaining in the community, who must continue to meet all of the normal costs of living. Many of these costs are nearly as great for one person as for a couple, and they may be difficult to reduce quickly. Yet, if Medicaid pays any of the costs of the nursing home resident's care, the spouse in the community

---

[33] The cost variations described in the table are cost variations for the same level of care. Separate tables would be required for other levels of care, since it is intended only that people have some incentive to prefer low-cost versions of needed care—not that they have an incentive to use less than the required level of care.

will, regardless of income, retain only that income protected by the state, essentially the income maintenance level for a single individual on welfare.

This approach is hard to justify on the basis of distributional or cost control considerations. Only 12 percent of nursing home residents are married.[34] Consequently, moderating payments of these people for nursing home care relative to current levels would not add greatly to public long-term-care expenditures. We therefore propose the policy presented in Table 25. As the table shows, if a couple had a monthly income of $1,000 and one entered a nursing home costing $600 per month, the spouse remaining in the community would retain more than $600.

The cost-sharing terms Table 25 proposes for nursing home care would lessen the burdens now imposed on couples. Just as under the terms proposed for single individuals, couples' nursing home burdens would increase with the cost of the care purchased. Again, this practice is designed to encourage people, as they are not now encouraged, to consider price when selecting care that is at least partly financed by the public sector.

The design of home care cost-sharing terms for married couples raises a policy dilemma. The desire to assure low-income couples access to care dictates low cost-sharing terms here as elsewhere for the poor. Low cost-sharing terms on home care also are desirable to discourage inappropriate use of institutional care. Yet, informal home care is available to many married people. Efforts to discourage substitution of formal for informal care would dictate relatively high cost-sharing terms on formal care, perhaps higher than those for single individuals.

This dilemma is not superficial. A single instrument—cost sharing on home care—cannot simultaneously be moved in one direction to encourage the use of formal home care rather than institutional care, and in another direction to encourage the use of informal care rather than formal care. The severity of the dilemma depends on the responsiveness of

---

[34] Aurora Zappolo, "Characteristics, Social Contacts, and Activities of Nursing Home Residents, United States, 1973–74 National Nursing Home Survey," *Vital and Health Statistics*, series 13, No. 27, DHEW Publication No. HRA 77–1778, Washington, D.C., p. 18.

Table 25

COST-SHARING PAYMENTS FOR NURSING HOME AND HOME CARE AT DIFFERENT LEVELS OF INCOME: MARRIED COUPLES

Monthly Income	Monthly Cost of Nursing Home Care					
	$100	$200	$300	$400	$500	$600
	Cost-Sharing Payments by Married Couples					
$250	0	0	0	0	0	0
300	5	10	15	20	25	30
400	15	30	45	60	75	90
550	30	60	90	120	150	180
750	50	100	150	200	250	300
1,000	75	150	225	300	375	450
1,300	90*	180*	270*	360*	450*	540*

Figures without asterisks are derived from the formula:

$$P_{hc} = \frac{Y-250}{1,000} \times C_{hc}$$

Asterisked figures result from application of a payment ceiling of 90 percent of the cost of care.

Monthly Income	Monthly Cost of Nursing Home Care				
	$500	$600	$700	$800	$900
	Cost-Sharing Payments by Married Couples				
$250	0	0	0	0	0
300	19	23	27	31	35
400	58	69	81	92	104
550	115	138	162	185	208
750	192	231	269	308	346
1,000	288	346	404	462	519
1,300	404	485	565	646	727

All figures are derived from the formula:

$$P_{nh} = (Y-250) \times \frac{C_{nh}}{2 \times C_t}$$

utilization to cost-sharing variations. For example, the problem would not be great if high cost-sharing rates on home care induced a great deal of informal care provision but did little to increase the use of institutional care. We know too little about these responses, however, to count on such a reaction. As a practical matter, administrative mechanisms will undoubtedly have to be employed to foster use of an appropriate mix of services. For this reason, Table 25 shows a cost-sharing structure for married couples that is the same as that presented for single individuals. The only difference is in the amount of protected income, here set at the SSI level for a couple, $250 a month.

COORDINATION OF SERVICES

Successful resolution of financial issues may establish an environment that facilitates and promotes the choice of cost-effective service packages. But the mental impairments of many clients and the complexity of the long-term-care system require that explicit provision be made for the ongoing coordination of services on behalf of individuals. This function, also called case management, has several elements: assessing the client's medical condition, functional competence, and social circumstances; selecting the appropriate setting and services to meet client and family preferences as well as assessed needs; choosing service providers and securing services; and regularly monitoring client and services to assure that services are satisfactory and that they continue to meet the changing needs of client and family.

Earlier it was argued that all financing should be channeled through a single, local, public long-term-care agency. Coordination could be handled directly by that agency or given over to a variety of agents, including existing agencies—area agencies on aging, public welfare offices, family service agencies, health maintenance organizations, homemaker agencies—and new agencies established solely to coordinate services or to provide certain long-term-care services as well.

Coordination of services by a single long-term-care agency would provide central control over the providers, the mix of services, and the service system. But central control also would provide little recourse for clients and families who were dissatisfied with the coordination they received. Moreover, the central agency would be responsible not only for financing services, but also for the assessment and tracking of all of its clients and the selection and monitoring of their services. Although these tasks would obviously be distributed among branch offices, they would constitute a heavy load to impose on a single new entity that served all of the adult or elderly impaired persons in a local area.

If coordination were decentralized, clients and their families could choose among various case-manager organizations. As a result, these organizations might be forced to be more responsive to clients and their preferences than would be the case if coordination were centralized and no choice were possible. Furthermore, the tasks of managing a large number of complex cases might be eased if that job were divided among agencies (some of which may already exist) rather than assigned to a single new agency.

Coordination could be further decentralized by allowing individuals, with their families, to coordinate their own services. Individuals could be assigned a financial grant proportioned to the cost of services necessitated by their impairments (less an amount called for by the program's cost-sharing provisions). Then they would be free to purchase the services they found most appropriate to their needs and to select the providers whose cost and quality mix best met their preferences. Such an arrangement would obviously be inappropriate for persons living alone whose impairments prevented them from effectively coordinating on their own behalf. But for people who are themselves competent to select and shop for needed services (or who live with such persons), an impairment payment program would have definite advantages. It would permit people to use a broad range of commodities and services (restaurants, drugs, taxis, grocery delivery, etc.) rather than restricting them to specifically long-term-care services that sometimes may be more expensive or less effective. More important, it would permit individuals maximum flexibility in fitting services to their preferences and living situations, and would clearly identify them as consumers of service rather than recipients of public benefits.

Some of this flexibility might be opposed on grounds that it might permit recipients to purchase goods and services unrelated to their impairments. In response to this criticism, cash grants could be eschewed in favor of vouchers restricted to goods and services deemed appropriate to long-term care. This practice would, however, increase administrative costs and, if readily enforced, could thwart the flexibility that is the impairment payment scheme's primary virtue.[35]

---

[35] These issues are discussed in greater detail in William Pollak, "Organizational Issues in the Provision of Community Care to the Impaired Elderly" in Joel Bergsman and Howard L. Weiner, eds., *Urban Problems and Public Policy Choices* (New York: Praeger, 1975), pp. 23–43.

Because cash and voucher payments would be inappropriate for many long-term-care clients, an impairment payment program should not exist in isolation. It should instead be considered only as a possible complement to a program that provides case management for people who need it either on a centralized or decentralized basis.

The variety of ways in which coordination might work may be clarified by reviewing some organizational options in detail. The first option would be to rely solely on local long-term-care agencies, as proposed in the Conable bill.[36] Under this organizational structure, a single long-term-care agency in each locality would be the conduit for all public financing flowing to long-term care. Ideally, even if its total budget were fixed and came from several federal sources, the local agency would control how the fixed total was divided among health, social services, housing, and income maintenance. A multidisciplinary team would initially assess client functioning, medical status, and social supports in order to determine major aspects of the client's care, particularly whether institutional care was required or whether some other group residential setting or the client's home was more appropriate to the client's condition and preferences and to the family's preferences and capacities. Responsibility would then shift to an agency coordinator, who would continue to monitor the client, would arrange the specific (nonmedical) services to be provided, and would schedule service provision. In this model, the local agency also would actually produce most noninstitutional services, although institutional care would be purchased from independent agencies.

It is assumed that coordinators would ration resources through their selection of services. Economy would be encouraged in a fiscally pressed agency (or in an agency forced to be economical by its state or federal funders) by administrative orders specifying when particular services should and should not be assigned and by regular administrative reviews of allocations or targeted reviews when a coordinator's allocations seemed out of line.

As already noted, a centralized organizational structure presents serious problems. Simply coordinating care for all

---

[36] The Conable bill is vague on many specifics. It does not indicate which activities would be internal to the agency, does not identify the force that might encourage economy by the local agency, and does not indicate mechanisms through which economy might be exercised.

impaired persons (or the impaired elderly) in a community would be a very large task for a single (new) organization. But this proposed organizational structure compounds this burden by adding to it the actual production of services. Aside from the administrative and technical difficulty of establishing a single organization to produce as well as coordinate so many services for a dispersed population, this arrangement would create a monopolistic production organization. The organization would be protected from quality and price competition and would provide no alternative for dissatisfied clients or their case managers. Moreover, such a program probably could not be implemented because it would be opposed by the strongest natural supporters of broadened coverage: existing providers of noninstitutional care.

The proposed rationing arrangements also present problems. Restrictive administrative guidelines and procedures could undoubtedly force strict service rationing behavior on even liberally inclined coordinators. But the rigidity that would inevitably accompany very restrictive administrative procedures would probably be unfortunate, given the complexity of long-term care. More flexible guidelines that would give individual coordinators more discretion pose a different problem. Individual coordinators would perceive the benefits their clients would derive from services but not their costs. If funds were limited, these costs would be lost services for someone else's clients. Insensitive to the costs, each coordinator would undoubtedly have a tendency to overprescribe.

To remedy these problems, it is useful to consider a second coordination option—one that (1) would retain the single local financing and coordinating agency but not require that agency to produce services and (2) would implement a different rationing mechanism. A team would assess the client, select a care setting, and then establish a level of resources to be granted to finance the client's care if a noninstitutional setting were selected. This level would be proportioned to the particular impairments, income, and social supports of the client, but also would reflect the financial constraints within which the agency operated. The amount would be net of any cost sharing required of the client. Given fixed resources, coordinators then would try to provide the best possible care for each client. Coordinators could not benefit their clients by channeling more resources to them—a strategy that, given scarcity, (unintentionally) must come at the expense of other clients. But coordinators could benefit their clients by judiciously selecting services and service providers and by counseling clients and their families.

Allowing production of service by external suppliers would have several advantages. Coordinators would have a maximum of flexibility in selecting services fitted to the needs and tastes of client and family. Coordinators could use unconventional as well as conventional suppliers to provide services; for example, taxi money could be provided for a neighbor to shop for a client when such a practice proved less expensive than (and as effective as) a special transportation service. The coordinator and the family presumably would choose among competing suppliers of homemaker, home nursing, and other services those suppliers whose cost and quality were most satisfactory. Coordinators could withdraw from unsatisfactory suppliers because alternatives would exist. Coordinators would support beneficiaries and their families in monitoring and evaluating services, and the shopping patterns of all coordinators taken together would exert pressure on providers to supply high-quality service.

This arrangement not only would facilitate quality competition, but also could be used to foster price competition that is lacking under most other financing and organizational schemes. With individuals' care budgets predetermined, it might be possible to avoid setting rates for noninstitutional services and instead to allow service producers to set whatever price they chose. They would be constrained by the economizing behavior of coordinators shopping for optimal service packages within individual fixed budgets.

A third organizational option would encourage competition for coordination services as well. This option would have the single, local long-term-care agency responsible for assessing clients and authorizing resource amounts for individual clients, but would decentralize coordination to a designated set of public and private agencies. Individuals would choose a coordinating agency from the designated set, and this agency, in turn, could purchase services from a variety of service suppliers who were independent of the coordinating agencies. This system resembles existing arrangements, but with several important differences. Responsibility for coordination would be explicit; coordinators would be able to pay directly for services; and individuals and coordinators would have considerable leeway in the types of services and providers they chose to use.

Because this arrangement would continue and expand the functions of existing agencies, it would involve less institution building and less change in social service networks than the more centralized systems described earlier. Consequently, this arrangement might have greater likelihood of enactment. The decentralization of coordination, however, might weaken central control over providers and would make it harder to develop a broad information base for coordinators to draw upon in making service and service-provider selections.

One solution to this problem would be to have coordination agencies provide most of the services they coordinate. Reliance on coordinator-providers, proposed by Robert Morris as "personal care organizations," [37] would reduce competition in the provision of service while enhancing the possibility for nonmarket administrative control of service delivery.

The choice of an organizational arrangement raises an important question not previously addressed, that is, Who should be allowed to provide long-term-care services? Specifically, should a long-term-care program allow the provision of less technical noninstitutional services by untrained or minimally trained self-employed individuals, or should that provision be limited to licensed and regulated formal agencies? Self-employed providers are likely to be more readily available

---

[37] Personal care organizations are discussed in several papers, including one prepared for the Senate Special Committee on Aging by Robert Morris, *Alternative to Nursing Home Care: A Proposal*, U.S. Senate, Special Committee on Aging (Washington, D.C.: U.S. Government Printing Office, 1971). Although Morris refers to capitation financing for such agencies, such financing seems inappropriate to long-term care if it implies a uniform dollar payment for each client for whom the agency is responsible. The needs of clients who are chronically ill vary greatly and are largely apparent at the beginning of a payment period. Under uniform capitation payments, provider agencies would have an incentive to reject or discourage clients with above-average (high-cost) needs and would try to care for relatively unimpaired populations. Those agencies that did accept relatively impaired populations would either have to provide low-cost inferior service or be financially disadvantaged because they served high-cost patients in return for the single (average) capitation payment. Varying payments in response to centrally administered assessments, therefore, appear a more appropriate way to finance a "personal care organization" in long-term care.

and to supply care at lower cost than are professional home-makers and aides employed on a regular basis by an agency. Although it can be argued that licensed agencies are necessary to assure adequate training and supervision of services, the validity of the argument depends on other aspects of the service organization. Thus, continued neglect of coordination as a distinct function strengthens the case for restricting supply to formal agencies. If coordination were effectively provided for within the program, however, coordinators could assist clients in locating, monitoring, hiring, and discharging self-employed helpers and could make this less formal option satisfactory on grounds of quality as well as cost and availability.

Resolution of this issue will significantly affect the cost and character of a long-term-care program. Because the cost savings and quality risks of informal supply within various organizational contexts cannot be assessed a priori, they should be given the empirical study that their importance justifies, either in experimental programs or through analysis of ongoing programs such as Title XX, under which some states use self-employed chore workers on a significant scale.

Because very little is known about the feasibility and effectiveness of the organizational options we have described or of other possible arrangements, a long-term-care program could allow several different types of organizations. Each state could select the organizational form it preferred. Then policy makers could compare the various implementation and administrative problems presented by the various forms, and assess how effectively each form allocated and rationed services and stimulated the supply of high-quality service.

Summary and Conclusions

This chapter has explored three aspects of a long-term-care benefit for national health insurance—the services to be covered, the organizational arrangements to control service delivery, and the terms for patient cost sharing. Evidence on service costs, though limited, indicates that expanding present coverage of noninstitutional services would probably increase public expenditures because services would undoubtedly be used by persons not now receiving formal or "covered" long-term care as well as by persons who now enter institutions.

However, the availability of subsidized noninstitutional services might well improve the living conditions of impaired individuals and justify the cost increases.

With program cost estimates ranging as high as $27 billion in 1985, the need for mechanisms to encourage cost-effective service delivery is obvious. To this end, several organizational options for a long-term-care program were examined. All options are based on the channeling of all financing—long-term maintenance, social support and personal care—through a single local agency. Without such financial channeling, we have argued, integrated delivery of institutional and noninstitutional services becomes virtually impossible. Given channeling, however, considerable leeway still exists in program design.

Local agencies could receive funds in one of two ways—fixed-budget or open-ended financing. The fixed budget is more conducive to cost containment, and, when accompanied by administrative discretion in the distribution of benefits, provides an opportunity to target publicly financed benefits to those without family or other supports. But current ignorance about appropriate long-term-care expenditures makes it difficult to fix a budget with confidence. The alternative is an open-ended entitlement program, in which cost containment depends on the ability to specify and enforce equitable rules for resource allocations. In allocating benefits, a local agency again has two choices—to subsidize consumers who in turn pay providers, or to subsidize providers directly. Analysis suggests that consumer subsidies are preferable, for they enhance the likelihood that providers will respond readily and equitably to beneficiaries' demands for services.

Because of the availability of informal care and of different types of formal care, cost sharing is far more important and acceptable for long-term care than for acute-care benefits. In designing cost-sharing terms, we argue, it is necessary to distinguish between institutional and noninstitutional services (charging more for the former than the latter), and between married and single individuals (assuring the noninstitutional spouse adequate income to remain in the community). In addition, cost sharing should vary inversely with income and directly with the cost of service. We have presented a structure for cost sharing in long-term care based on these and other considerations.

A cost-effective long-term-care program must provide for the coordination of services to each beneficiary. Coordination can be made the responsibility of a single, local long-term-care financing agency, or individuals could be allowed to choose among several agencies offering that service. The former option relies heavily on centralized administration to monitor performance; the latter relies on the market. These control mechanisms may be combined by allowing the central agency to assess client needs and allocate subsidies accordingly, while leaving clients free to use subsidies to choose their own coordinating agencies or, perhaps, to coordinate for themselves. This policy would provide centralized control over expenditures while allowing individuals and coordinators considerable flexibility in the choice of a service package. Without more experience, however, no organizational option can be unequivocally recommended. Experimentation and variation therefore seem in order.

In proposing cost sharing and other policy options, we have not intended to identify the precise mechanisms a long-term-care program should adopt. Rather we have presented an analytic framework for comparing and evaluating a multitude of specific proposals. Using this framework, it becomes possible to design a long-term-care policy that expands access to care without losing control of public expenditures.

Chapter 11
PRESCRIPTION DRUGS

ROBERT T. KUDRLE
KAREN D. LENNOX

T HE purpose of this chapter is to explore ways to deal with both cost and quality issues in providing prescription drug coverage under national health insurance, while increasing access or alleviating the financial burden for persons with high drug expenditures. National health insurance bills have more varied approaches to outpatient drugs than to virtually any other major benefit, partly because of the difference between drugs and most other services considered for coverage. Although costs pose less of a problem in drug coverage than in other service areas, the structure of the drug industry raises particular cost issues that national health insurance must address. Furthermore, the expansion of insurance coverage raises greater quality concerns with respect to drugs than to other benefit areas.

Outpatient prescription expenditures in the United States were estimated to total about $9.6 billion in 1976.[1] For most

---

[1] No method for estimating prescription drug expense is universally accepted. One approach applies a Department of Commerce formula to the government statistical category "Drugs and Drug Sundries"; this approach was used by the Department of Health, Education, and Welfare (DHEW) Task Force on Prescription Drugs, *The Drug Users* (Washington, D.C.: U.S. Government Printing Office, 1968), p. 13. The formula of 0.71 (prescriptions as a fraction of drugs) times 0.85 (drugs as a fraction of drugs and drug sundries) of Drugs and Drugs Sundries is employed. The problem with this approach is that the gross figure does not include sales by hospital outpatient outlets or by dispensing physicians (see Robert M. Gibson and Marjorie Smith Mueller, "National Health Expenditures, Fiscal Year 1976," *Social Security Bulletin*, April 1977, pp. 5–6). A wholly different approach is to use the average price of prescriptions dispensed and to estimate the total number filled in a given year. Thomas Fulda, in *Prescription Drug Data Summary, 1974*

521

people these expenditures do not appear to be a financial burden. In 1970, the last year for which there are detailed data on outlays by spending units, 47 percent of all persons reported no expense at all for prescription drugs, only 8.1 percent reported expenses over $100, and only 0.3 percent had expenses in excess of $500. For the entire population in that year these expenses were estimated to average $27 per person.[2] Some segments of the population, however, had much higher expenditures. Costs for persons ages sixty-five and over were 2.5 times the national average in the 1970 survey,[3] and for the 3.1 percent of the population classified as severely disabled, expenditures were 4.5 times the national average.[4] Even among the elderly, however, only 1.6 percent spent more than $500.[5]

(Washington, D.C.: DHEW, 1976), estimates the growth of hospital out-patient prescriptions for 1970–74 on the basis of linear extrapolation from earlier years when direct estimates were available; he uses a 12 percent figure for annual growth. The number of retail prescriptions filled in the United States actually fell during 1975 and 1976. If we take the conservative position that during this downturn, the share of hospital outpatient prescriptions filled continued to grow only in terms of their share of total prescriptions rather than in terms of their previous growth rate (their share had averaged 4.6 percent during the previous seven years), the 1976 share can be estimated at 14.8 percent. Hence if the average prescription written in 1976 sold at $5.60 (*Pharmacy Times*, April 1977), and, if as one team using IRS data has reported, the number of ordinary retail outlet prescriptions written was 1.46 billion (Milton Silverman and Mia Lydecker, *Drug Coverage Under National Health Insurance: The Policy Options*, National Center for Health Services Research [NCHSR] Report Series [Washington, D.C.: DHEW, 1977], p. 19), 0.85 X = 1.46 billion and X = 1.71 billion. Thus, the total value of prescription drugs sold was almost $9.60 billion ($5.60 × 1.71 billion) or almost 0.86 of the government's "Drugs and Drug Sundries" category.

[2] DHEW, Public Health Service (PHS), Health Resources Administration (HRA), "Personal Out-of-Pocket Health Expenses, United States, 1970," *Vital and Health Statistics*, series 10, no. 91. Although these statistics were cited as "provisional," they have not been subsequently revised and thus remain the source for "personal" as opposed to "family" data. See DHEW, PHS, HRA, "Family Out-of-Pocket Health Expenses, United States, 1970" (Washington, D.C.: U.S. Government Printing Office, 1975), p. 1.

[3] Fulda, *Prescription Drug Data Summary*, p. 6.

[4] DHEW, "Out-of-Pocket Cost and Acquisition of Prescribed Medicines—United States, 1973" (Washington, D.C.: U.S. Government Printing Office, 1977), p. 20.

[5] Fulda, *Prescription Drug Data Summary*, p. 8.

Despite typically modest expenditures, 70.3 percent of the American people had some insurance for drug expenses in 1975 (see Table 26). Among the elderly, however, only 21.8 percent had coverage, and benefits per enrollee were very small. Most coverage, in fact, includes a high deductible, significant coinsurance, or both. As a privately insurable expense, low copayment insurance—even with the usual tax subsidies—has not grown rapidly because of the high administrative cost generated by the large volume of small claims.[6] Furthermore, most coverage is part of group medical insurance; drug insurance alone has faced a formidable self-selection problem (i.e., people who anticipate high drug expenses tend to buy drug insurance).[7] It is not known to what extent high drug users are protected by private insurance, but for most people drug expenditures do not pose the potential financial catastrophe that may result from other medical expenses.

The other cost issue so familiar to NHI discussion, "uncontrollably" rising expenditures, also does not apply to drug expenditures. Outpatient drugs and drug sundries, the only category for which reliable time-series data are available, accounted for 13.7 percent of total health care costs in 1950 but for only 9.3 percent in 1976. Thus, in a quarter-century, the share dropped by 32 percent.[8] The general health care expenditure explosion is, of course, responsible for such a large relative drop. Drug use has expanded continuously over time; per capita prescriptions rose from 5.0 in 1965 to 8.2 in 1974.[9] Nonetheless, while the medical care component of the consumer price index rose from 79 in 1960 to 150 in 1975 and the entire index moved from 89 to 161, the component for prescription drugs actually dropped from 115 to 109.[10]

---

[6] A few more wide-ranging prepayment plans exist, most of them handled through unions; in 1975, this subset held only 2.8 percent of the drug insurance market. Marjorie Smith Mueller, "Private Health Insurance in 1975: Coverage, Enrollment, and Financial Experience," *Social Security Bulletin* 40 (June 1977):6.

[7] Albert I. Wertheimer, *Economic Analysis of Selected Factors in Drug Delivery*, report prepared for the National Center for Health Services Research and Development (HSRD), Office of Scientific and Technical Information, HSRD 73–71, NTIS No. PB 212 038, pp. 6–7.

[8] Gibson and Mueller, "National Health Expenditures," p. 15.

[9] Calculated from Fulda, *Prescription Drug Data Summary*, p. 35.

[10] *Statistical Abstract of the United States*, 1976, p. 440; Fulda, *Prescription Drug Data Summary*, p. 36.

Even when better indices (ones that sample more representatively) are used, drug price increases are relatively modest.[11]

Yet, the structure of the drug industry makes cost an issue in the expansion of drug insurance. Although some data exaggerate industry profitability, there is little doubt that the industry possesses considerable monopoly power.[12] At the other end of the drug provision chain as well—the pharmacy—considerable evidence exists of suboptimal performance to society. In fact, over the years the "drug store" industry has become a classic example of excess capacity production and protectionism in collective politics.[13] The industry is famous in Congress for its promotion of the Robinson-Patman Act and resale price maintenance laws that blunt the competitive thrust of outlets that enjoy economies of scale in purchasing and service provision. At the state level, as recently as 1975, thirty-three states directly forbade (or allowed pharmacy boards to forbid) price advertising. A plethora of less well known but important regulations controlling pharmacy operations also exist.[14]

Political support within states for resale price maintenance has eroded over the years, culminating in 1976 in amendment

---

[11] Fulda, *Prescription Drug Data Summary*, p. 37.

[12] A particularly lucid account of the industrial characteristics that lead to high profit rates can be found in Richard E. Caves, *American Industry: Structure, Conduct, Performance*, 4th ed. (Englewood Cliffs, N.J.: Prentice Hall, Inc., 1977). On drug profits, see Booz, Allen and Hamilton, *The Impact of National Health Insurance on the Pharmaceutical Industry* (Final Report), submitted to the U.S. Department of Commerce, September 2, 1975 (mimeographed), Exhibit V: and Thomas R. Fulda, "Drug Cost Control: The Road to Maximum Allowable Cost," in Kenneth M. Friedman and Stuart H. Rakoff, eds., *Toward a National Health Policy* (Lexington, Mass.: D.C. Heath, 1977), pp. 57–58. For an excellent recent attempt to trace the role of the accounting treatment of promotion and research and development expenditure in exaggerating the industry's profitability, see Kenneth W. Clarkson, *Intangible Capital and Rates of Return: Effects of Research and Promotion on Profitability*, (Washington, D.C.: American Enterprise Institute for Public Policy Research, 1977), especially pp. 59 ff.

[13] For example, see Joe S. Bain, *Industrial Organization*, 2nd ed. (New York: John Wiley and Sons, Inc.), pp. 609–22, and Fredric M. Scherer, *Industrial Market Structure and Economic Performance* (Chicago: Rand McNally and Company, 1970), pp. 512–16.

[14] John F. Cady, *Drugs on the Market* (Lexington, Mass.: D.C. Heath, 1976).

Table 26

PRIVATE OUT-OF-HOSPITAL DRUG
INSURANCE COVERAGE, 1975

Type of Insuring Organization	Number of Persons Enrolled (in thousands)			Benefits Paid in Millions	Benefits per Enrollee
	All Ages	Under Age 65	Ages 65+		
Insurance companies	104,033	101,714	2,319	$327.0	$3.14
Blue Cross— Blue Shield	46,122	43,914	2,208	252.1	5.46
Independent plans	6,437	5,924	513	90.2	14.01
Total	160,592	151,552	5,040	669.3	4.27

Source: Marjorie Smith Mueller, "Private Health Insurance in 1975: Coverage, Enrollment, and Financial Experience," *Social Security Bulletin*, June 1977.

of the Federal Trade Commission Act to effectively forbid "fair trade" restrictions. Another blow to the drug industry that year was the Supreme Court's rejection of bans on price advertising. Thus, market forces promise to increase in the coming years. Nevertheless, organized pharmacists' self-protective ingenuity should not be underestimated. The National Association of Retail Druggists and the American Pharmaceutical Association (a pharmacy group) suggested recently that some categories of over-the-counter drugs—some cold and cough medicines and antacids—should be sold only by pharmacists.[15] The pharmacy industry's efforts to protect itself must be kept in mind in the design of national health insurance.

---

[15] Ibid., p. 130. In recent years pharmacists have contended that they should provide more than just a dispensary for drugs—that they should become more important members of the "health care team." While their arguments should be seriously considered, the preservation of excess capacity in pharmacies appears to be neither a necessary, sufficient, nor efficient solution to any of the current major problems of the drug delivery system. For an evaluation of the arguments, see Robert T. Kudrle, "Outpatient Drug Coverage Under National Health Insurance," prepared for the Robert Wood Johnson Foundation under Grant No. 2505, 1978 (mimeographed), pp. 10–14.

The problem of access to drug care can be considered in conjunction with the expenditures on prescribed drugs by income class, as presented on Table 27. Some readers may be surprised that drug expenditures for the poor are larger than for the rest of the population, and that except for the highest income group, total expenditure figures decline substantially with family income. This phenomenon is explained in part not only by the heavy concentration of old people among the poor but also by the low incomes of persons who are partially or totally disabled, many of whom receive public medical assistance. Coverage of outpatient drugs, not covered by Medicare, is a state option under Medicaid. In the early 1970s, all states except Alaska, Wyoming, and Arizona provided some kind of drug benefit.[16]

Access to prescription drugs is affected not only by the availability of drug insurance but also by insurance for physician visits. The demand for prescription drugs is, by definition, the outcome of consultation with a physician. Estimates of the percentage of doctor visits resulting in medication of some kind vary between 50 percent and 90 percent.[17] But it is indisputable that, if other factors are held constant, an increase in physician visits will result in an increase in prescriptions. Thus drug use will rise with increased medical care under national health insurance even in the absence of drug coverage.

In contrast to the favorable way that observers have viewed the growth in most other medical services, the growth in prescriptions per capita has not been regarded generally as an indication of improved quality of medical treatment. One source maintains that 25 percent of all prescriptions written are either unnecessary or for drugs of unproven efficacy.[18] In a careful investigation of the practices of twenty-four primary-care physicians, a research team determined that prescribing quality was inversely related to the average number of prescriptions per patient visit.[19] Another authority has

---

[16] Office of the Secretary, DHEW, *Maximum Allowable Cost for Drugs*, February 9, 1977 (mimeographed), p. 12.

[17] David L. Robin and Patricia Bush, "Who's Using Medicines?" *Journal of Community Health*, Winter 1975, 115.

[18] Silverman and Lydecker, *Drug Coverage*, p. 5.

[19] P.D. Stolley et al., "The Relationship Between Physician Characteristics and Prescribing Appropriateness," *Medical Care* (1972):17–28.

noted that 3 percent to 5 percent of all admissions to hospitals are for drug reactions and that one-seventh of all hospital days are devoted to the care of persons suffering from drug toxicity.[20] It has been alleged that poor prescribing is the leading cause of iatrogenic (physician-caused) disease.[21] A critical study of the drug industry suggests that drug-caused hospitalization in 1971 cost about $3 billion, by comparison with an estimated $10 billion direct prescription payments.[22]

Concern about inappropriate or excessive use of drugs is closely tied to concern about the drug industry. Despite the impressive—even central—role drugs have played in improving health status,[23] there is much evidence that the drug industry has produced a great number of new drugs that do little but compound the prescribing problem and increase manufacturers' profits. The Mississippi Medicaid program found in 1972 that "among the 10 leading drugs ranked by total amount paid, five drugs are specified as 'not recommended' or as 'irrational mixtures' by the *AMA Drug Evaluations.*" [24] A 1974 report by the Commissioner of the Food and Drug Administration (FDA) concluded that of the hundreds of new agents introduced between 1950 and 1973, 67 percent had "little or no therapeutic merit." [25]

This experience suggests that physicians fail to choose wisely from the myriad of available drugs, a problem partially attributed to the drug industry. Harried physicians typically get most of their information from printed matter or personal presentations by the drug companies. This material discusses virtually all product characteristics except price, and allegedly exaggerates the virtues of the company's product at

---

[20] Kenneth L. Melmon, "Preventable Drug Reactions: Causes and Cures," *New England Journal of Medicine*, June 17, 1971.

[21] This is Silverman and Lydecker's conclusion based on a review of several studies, *Drug Coverage*, p. 2.

[22] Milton Silverman and Phillip R. Lee, *Pills, Profits, and Politics* (Berkeley and Los Angeles: University of California Press, 1974), p. 256.

[23] Victor Fuchs, *Who Shall Live?* (New York: Basic Books, Inc., 1974), pp. 105–106.

[24] Alton B. Cobb, Donnie P. Wilson, and John M. Abide, "Use of Drugs Under the Mississippi Program," *Journal of the Mississippi State Medical Association* 13 (1972):82.

[25] Cited in Booz, Allen and Hamilton, *Impact of National Health Insurance on the Pharmaceutical Industry*, p. 9.

Table 27

INDIVIDUAL EXPENDITURES FOR PRESCRIBED
DRUGS BY SELECTED CHARACTERISTICS, 1973

Source of Payment
(percentage distribution)

Characteristic	Purchased by Family Alone	Private Health Insurance	Public Organization	Free from Physician	Other Source	Percentage of Acquisitions with no Out-of-Pocket Expenditure	Number of Acquisitions per Person per Year	Average Cost per Purchase	Average Annual Expenditure
Total Population	74.1%	7.9%	10.4%	3.4%	4.2%	13.1%	5.8	$4.80	$27.84
Age									
Under age 17	72.8	6.6	12.2	4.4	4.0	16.5	3.1	3.60	11.16
17–24	75.4	5.4	7.2	6.1	6.0	16.9	4.1	4.00	16.40
25–44	73.6	8.9	8.4	4.5	4.6	14.3	5.4	4.60	24.84
45–64	73.6	10.6	9.1	2.2	4.4	11.0	8.2	5.40	44.28
65+	75.7	5.1	14.3	2.0	2.9	10.5	13.0	5.40	70.20
Sex									
Male	73.0	8.9	9.6	3.9	4.6	13.7	4.5	4.90	22.05
Female	74.8	7.2	10.9	3.2	3.9	12.8	7.1	4.70	33.37

Family Income

Less than $3,000	59.5%	1.5%	30.0%	3.9%	5.0%	25.5%	9.5	$4.80	$45.60
$3,000–$4,999	69.9	2.7	19.6	3.1	4.8	19.5	7.8	5.20	40.56
$5,000–$6,999	76.6	6.8	9.9	3.1	3.6	12.0	6.3	4.90	30.87
$7,000–$9,999	79.6	8.3	5.1	2.9	4.2	8.8	5.5	4.60	25.30
$10,000–$14,999	76.8	9.8	5.0	4.1	4.3	10.9	5.0	4.50	22.50
$15,000+	76.7	13.1	2.8	3.6	3.9	8.2	5.1	4.80	24.48

Source: DHEW, "Out-of-Pocket Cost and Acquisition of Prescribed Medicines, United States, 1973," *Vital and Health Statistics*, series 10, no. 108, 1977.

the expense of other manufacturers' products—even when the therapeutic properties of the products in question are similar or, in some cases, virtually identical.[26] Such salesmanship, it is argued, leads both to overprescribing and to identification of medicines by brand names rather than by generic names. Prescribing by brand name can significantly raise drug costs— in a few cases by as much several hundred percent.[27]

It must not be assumed that increased public drug insurance will, by itself, vastly increase drug consumption. In fact, some estimates suggest that when the protection afforded high drug spenders (many of whom now have private insurance) is balanced against the withdrawal of Medicaid, the Kennedy-Mills and Kennedy-Corman bills might not greatly increase coverage. Of the NHI bills which have received most attention in recent years, only the Nixon-Ford Comprehensive Health Insurance Plan (CHIP) would provide substantial extra prescription insurance by comparison with the present situation. Some people expect that the Kennedy-Corman drug benefit would be expanded over time, however, and, in any event, any change in the pattern of coverage would be significant (as, of course, is increased government financing). Furthermore, other features of national health insurance, notably expansion of physician benefits, would expand drug use. Thus, whether national health insurance would avoid or exacerbate the inappropriate use of drugs is a critical question. To the extent that the quality issue is not addressed squarely through innovative policy, inappropriate use is an almost certain outcome.

With these quality, access, and cost issues in mind, the design of a drug benefit for national health insurance can be considered. Specifically, this chapter identifies and explores options in the following areas: types of drugs covered, approaches to payment, patient cost sharing, and administration. In each area, the authors draw on experience in the United States and in other countries to indicate both problems and solutions in providing drug insurance.

---

[26] Walter Measday, "The Pharmaceutical Industry," Chapter 5 in Walter Adams, ed., *The Structure of American Industry* (New York: The Macmillan Company, 1971), pp. 176–78.

[27] Fulda, "Drug Cost Control," p. 57.

Types of Coverage

Drug benefits under national health insurance could be virtually open-ended or restricted in several ways. The more liberal drug benefit proposals cover all prescription drugs. The Nixon-Ford CHIP proposal, for example, would impose no limit on the types of prescription drugs covered and, in fact, would empower the Secretary of the Department of Health, Education, and Welfare (DHEW) to cover nonprescription "life-saving and -sustaining drugs" (e.g., insulin) at his discretion. Prescription drugs constitute about 70 percent of total drug expenditures each year and typically are more expensive than other drugs. Generally, exclusion of over-the-counter drugs is justified in terms of the desire to limit total expenditures, to reduce the administrative burden of a large volume of small claims, and to avoid problems in the control of utilization and quality.

Coverage of prescription drugs promises to increase drug utilization greatly in the absence of other policy measures. To reduce undesirable use and to limit government cost, specific drugs or categories of drugs—such as antiobesity drugs, vitamins, tranquilizers, oral contraceptives, antacids, drugs for refractions, injectibles, and immunization agents—could be excluded.[28] Many of those drugs are not used for treatment of illness, or they are nonspecific and are used for a wide range of situations; they are seen as areas of marginal necessity, potential abuse, and aggregate high cost.[29] Other drugs that may be excluded are those available at no cost from local health agencies—for example, drugs used in the treatment of venereal disease or tuberculosis.[30]

Cost and quality control are improved when drugs or categories of drugs to be included under the program are specified. The benefit package can be structured to meet certain medical needs of the population covered, and individual drugs can be chosen in terms of efficacy and cost. Administrative

---

[28] Charlotte Muller, "Drug Benefits in Health Insurance," *International Journal of Health Services* 4 (Winter 1974):163.

[29] Muller, "Drug Benefits," p. 163.

[30] DHEW Task Force on Prescription Drugs, *Approaches to Drug Insurance Design* (Washington, D.C.: U.S. Government Printing Office, February 1969), p. 5.

burdens can be reduced by limiting the number of drugs covered.

This approach resembles that of the institutional formulary, a list of drugs carried by a hospital or group practice pharmacy. A therapeutic committee composed of physicians and pharmacists chooses the drugs to be included in the formulary and updates the list periodically, thereby monitoring the quality and efficacy of drugs. Both the Kennedy-Mills and the Kennedy-Corman bills would rely on formularies; under the former plan, the formulary would be established by a Formulary Committee, and under the latter plan, by the Health Security Board.[31] In Saskatchewan's health insurance plan, the formulary's exclusion of many kinds of combination drugs significantly altered physicians' prescribing practices.[32]

In addition to controlling cost and quality, a formulary can be used to target benefits to a particular segment of the population. This approach, employed by the United Mine Workers Welfare and Retirement Fund, limits drug coverage to long-term maintenance drugs which are needed on a continuing basis for the treatment of chronic disease. The stated objective of the fund is to cover the relatively expensive long-term drugs and to prevent hospitalization resulting from the lack of proper medication.[33] This approach was recommended as a Medicare drug benefit option designed by the DHEW Task Force on Prescription Drugs (which operated between May

---

[31] The mere existence of a formulary, of course, does not guarantee its effectiveness. Some hospital formularies not only have added to the complexity and rigidity of prescribing, but also have failed to maintain high standards, to provide timely and accurate information, or to achieve efficiency in drug dispensing. T. Donald Rucker and James Visconti, "A Descriptive and Normative Study of Drug Formularies," Ohio State University Research Foundation, Columbus, Ohio, June 1978.

[32] J. A. Bachynsky, "Pharmaceutical Benefit Programs in Canada," presented to the Conference on Drug and Pharmaceutical Reimbursement, sponsored by the National Center for Health Services Research, November 2–5, 1976, Washington, D.C. (mimeographed) p. 6. Part of Bachynsky's paper is reproduced in Albert I. Wertheimer, ed., *Proceedings of the International Conference on Drug and Pharmaceutical Services Reimbursement*, NCHSR Research Proceedings Series, Washington, D.C., 1977.

[33] DHEW Task Force on Prescription Drugs: *Current American and Foreign Programs* (Washington, D.C.: U.S. Government Printing Office, December 1968), p. 127.

of 1967 and February of 1969) and has been proposed in both the Kennedy-Mills and Kennedy-Corman bills.

The task force was established at the directive of the president to study the coverage of prescription drugs under Medicare. It investigated the diagnostic categories for which drug therapy was frequently used in the treatment of the elderly, and then classified the most frequently dispensed drugs. The diagnostic categories were headed by heart disease, high blood pressure, mental and nervous conditions, digestive system conditions, genitourinary conditions, and diabetes (see Table 28). The most widely used drugs paralleled the diagnostic categories. These included cardiovascular preparations (vasodialators, digitalis, hypotensive drugs), tranquilizers, diuretics, sedatives, and antibiotics.[34] Analysis of drug use by dose-days or size of the prescription showed that a sizable proportion of these drugs were long-term maintenance drugs used primarily for the control of chronic disease. About half of all drugs were prescribed for thirty days or more.

From this analysis, the task force concluded that limiting coverage to "those drugs which are important for the treatment of chronic illness among the elderly, and which usually are required on a continuing or recurring basis, would concentrate the protection provided by a drug problem where in most cases it is most clearly needed."[35] For the population as a whole, Silverman has estimated that the prescription drugs for chronic disease represent from 40 percent to 60 percent of total drug expenditure.[36] Furthermore, because average doses for chronic conditions are high, administrative costs would be lower than those for general coverage of other drugs. To assure quality, a drug advisory committee could determine the drugs to be included in the formulary and review drug utilization.

In 1972 the Senate Committee on Finance drafted an amendment to Medicare for coverage of maintenance drugs which

---

[34] DHEW Task Force on Prescription Drugs, *The Drug Users*, Washington, D.C.: U.S. Government Printing Office, October 1968), pp. 73–75, Table 32.

[35] DHEW Task Force on Prescription Drugs, *Third Interim Report*, (Washington, D.C.: U.S. Government Printing Office, December 31, 1968), p. 6.

[36] Silverman and Lydecker, *Drug Coverage*, p. 72.

Table 28

NUMBER OF PRESCRIPTIONS USED IN TREATMENT
OF DIAGNOSED CONDITIONS AMONG THE AGED, 1966

Diagnosed Conditions	Number of Prescriptions
	(thousands)
Heart conditions	46,512
High blood pressure	19,681
Arthritis and rheumatism	17,343
Mental and nervous conditions	11,578
Digestive system conditions	9,147
Genitourinary conditions	9,127
Diabetes	8,085
Colds, coughs, throat conditions, and influenza	7,504
Disorders of circulatory system	4,776
Chronic skin diseases	4,362
Injuries and adverse reactions	4,000
Neoplasm	3,701
Eye conditions	3,683
Emphysema	2,766
Anemia and other blood conditions	2,581
Asthma and hay fever	2,547
Peptic ulcers	2,524
Other respiratory conditions	2,415
Sinus and bronchial conditions	2,138
Ear	2,113
Pneumonia	1,531
Thyroid	1,491
Nephritis, nephrosis, and other kidney conditions	1,248
Epilepsy	672
Varicose veins	617
Avitaminosis	317
Lymphatic hemopoietic	142

Source: DHEW Task Force on Prescription Drugs. *The Drug Users* (Washington. D.C.: U.S. Government Printing Office, October 1968), pp. 76
and 77, Table 33.

followed many of the recommendations of the task force.[37]
The committee decided to limit the benefits, however, to those
drugs that are important in the treatment of certain crippling
and life-threatening chronic diseases of the elderly. Mental
and nervous conditions, chronic skin disease, anemia, and gas-

---

[37] U.S. Congress, Senate, Committee on Finance, *Social Security
Amendments of 1972*, *H.R. 1*, 92nd Congress, 2nd Session, 1972, pp.
270–71.

trointestinal disorders were excluded because several of the drugs used for treatment (tranquilizers, antacids, antispasmodics, antidiarrheals, vitamins, iron, and skin ointments) could also be used by nonbeneficiaries.

In addition to lowering the potential for abuse by nonbeneficiaries, several other advantages were cited for reducing the diagnostic chronic disease categories. Utilization could be more easily and cheaply controlled. A relatively small number of drugs would be involved, and their necessity for use in treatment would be easy to establish. Overall, administration, number of claims, and total drug benefit expenditures would be reduced.[38]

This approach to drug coverage, which was directly incorporated into the Kennedy-Mills bill, raises the problem of translating general criteria for coverage into decisions on specific drugs. This problem is compounded in the Kennedy-Corman bill, which does not provide disease or condition categories and thus leaves selection criteria extremely vague. When benefits are subject to complex restrictions, problems arise in communicating to the beneficiaries, physicians, and pharmacies exactly which drugs would be included under the program. The system could be abused if physicians and beneficiaries were to pressure pharmacies to dispense noncovered drugs and charge the program for a covered item. In addition, if the covered drugs targeted for treatment of chronic illness also can be used for treatment of acute, short-term illness, the program's intent can be subverted. To avoid these results, the Kennedy-Corman bill would authorize the Health Security Board to require physicians to certify that the covered disease is present before drug benefits would be paid.

Using the formulary to restrict coverage to the chronically ill would mean a reduction in current benefits available to the

---

[38] The 1972 Medicare drug amendments suggested the formation of a drug advisory committee, composed of nongovernment experts in the field of pharmacology and consumer groups, to establish a Medicare formulary. Efficacy, quality, safety, cost, and substitutability of specific drugs would be investigated before drugs could be included in the list of reimbursable drugs. Current prescribing habits, existing programs that maintain formularies, and drug manufacturers would serve as sources of information. As new drug therapies were introduced, the formulary would be revised and changed to reflect current expert medical judgment. Ibid., p. 273.

poor under Medicaid. If the experience of the Mississippi
Medicaid program is any guide, reintroducing market prices
would dramatically reduce demand.[39] This result may be a high
price to pay for the sake of administrative tractability and
cost control.

Aside from using the formulary, it is possible to limit benefits by explicitly restricting the quantity of drugs covered.
Quantity limits can set the maximum amount of dose-days
allowed per prescription. For example, the Health Insurance
Plan of New York allows 30 dose-days for regular prescriptions and 100 dose-days for drugs on a maintenance drug list.[40]
Limiting the number of days covered by a prescription encourages contact between physician and patient and thus promotes continued supervision of the drug therapy. Quantity
limits also can be set on the number of refills allowed per
year or on the length of time during which a prescription is
renewable (e.g., a one-year limit). These controls similarly
increase reliance on physician supervision, decrease the potential for habituation, and decrease the probability that drugs
will be passed on to nonbeneficiaries. The problem with the
limits, however, is that they tend to be arbitrary and may
serve to restrict benefits without regard to a patient's clinical
condition. This charge has been leveled at state Medicaid
programs in which limits have been introduced as a means
to control costs.[41]

In sum, it appears that any limitations on drug coverage
are likely to be contested. Some measures seem to be arbitrary
or to exclude some persons with drug expenditures that might
be considered catastrophic. In addition, provider and consumer
responses to restrictions may ultimately subvert the program's
intent. These costs must be weighed against the potential benefits for quality and expenditure control that restrictions offer.

Methods of Payment

A prescription drug program raises several reimbursement
issues. First, who will be reimbursed—the beneficiary or the

---

[39] Charles E. Phelps and Joseph P. Newhouse, *Coinsurance and the
Demand for Medical Services* (Santa Monica: The Rand Corporation,
1974), pp. 28–32.

[40] Muller, "Drug Benefits," p. 166.

[41] DHEW memorandum, "Cutbacks in State Medicaid," January 1976.

drug vendor? Who should be responsible for keeping track of and submitting claims? How much will be reimbursed? Should a distinction be made between coverage of ingredients and of pharmacy services? Should ingredient reimbursement be based on actual prices or subject to explicit limits? How should dispensing fees be calculated?

REIMBURSEMENT OF THE BENEFICIARY VERSUS THE VENDOR

The choice between reimbursement of the beneficiary or the vendor must take into account both economic and administrative considerations. If the beneficiary is to be reimbursed, the individual user must pay for the prescription at the time of dispensing and be responsible for the collection and submission of claims for reimbursement. If the vendor is to be reimbursed, the vendor must be responsible for the collection and submission of claims and for collection of any cost sharing, including the entire prescription charge if no deductible has been reached.[42] Another alternative, implied by the overall payment mechanisms of the Kennedy-Mills and CHIP bills, would be for the patient to "charge" the prescription on a credit card, after which the government would pay the pharmacist and collect cost-sharing payment, if any, from the patient.

A possible problem of beneficiary reimbursement is that people who could not come up with the necessary cash at the point of service (those who could benefit from the program the most) would be excluded. Moreover, claims might be lost or never filed. Administratively, reimbursement of the beneficiary would require processing millions of individual claims and mailing several small checks. It appears easier to reimburse 50,000 drug vendors, allowing them to accumulate drug claims, submit them in larger batches, and receive lump payments.

The Pharmacare drug program of Manitoba, Canada, indicates that the problems of beneficiary reimbursement may be exaggerated. The Manitoba program was started in 1973 to cover 80 percent of the cost of all prescription drugs for the

---

[42] Arguments in favor of beneficiary reimbursement are presented in DHEW Task Force, *Approaches to Drug Insurance Design*, p. 13.

elderly after an initial deductible of $40.[43] This cost sharing was instituted as a cost control device. Pharmacists were allowed to charge the cost of the ingredients plus their dispensing fee up to a maximum of $2.90 and were required to substitute lower-cost drugs if listed in the interchangeable drug formulary developed by the Manitoba Drug Standards and Therapeutics Committee.[44] To aid the elderly in retention and submission of claims, Pharmacare introduced a double prescription label. In typing out the prescription labels for dispensing, the pharmacist includes additional information such as the name of the drug, quantity, and price. One label goes on the prescription while a duplicate label is given to the beneficiary for attachment to a government form which is to be completed and mailed by the beneficiary for reimbursement. The anticipated problems of requiring the elderly to file claims never arose. In fact, the success of the drug program for the elderly led to expansion of the program to cover all residents of the province in 1975 with a $50 deductible.[45] Preliminary estimates indicate that the plan has been both workable and administratively efficient.[46]

Benefit payment to the vendor, however, has been the preferred method for state Medicaid programs, private prescription plans, most foreign programs, and NHI proposals.[47] The pharmacist rather than the beneficiary would extend credit for products dispensed and perform the administrative duties of claims collection and submission. Fewer lost or incomplete claims would probably result. In addition, a more complete data base would be available from vendors to aid utilization review.

A third method, the "credit card," is one with which there is no experience. Patients would "charge" their services with providers, after which the governments would both pay the vendor and bill the patient for all cost sharing. The scheme has been discussed in connection with both the CHIP and the

---

[43] "Manitoba Elderly to Get Drug Refunds," *Geriatrics* 28 (July 1973): 32.

[44] Bachynsky, "Pharmaceutical Benefit Programs in Canada," p. 76.

[45] Information provided by Kenneth Brown, Director of Medical Services, Pharmacare, Manitoba.

[46] Ibid.

[47] DHEW Task Force, *Current American and Foreign Programs.*

Kennedy-Mills bills. If used as part of a general electronically linked drug use system, such a method has promise and is discussed later.

REIMBURSEMENT OF PRODUCT COSTS

Reimbursement policy is an important determinant of total program expenditures, provider participation, and perhaps the quality and appropriateness of care in a drug insurance program.

Testimony by DHEW representatives before the Senate Committee on Human Resources, Subcommittee on Health and the Environment, in July 1977, revealed that similar drugs were sold for widely varying prices and that the range of prices for different drugs varied without an obvious pattern.[48] Two factors appeared to account for those pricing phenomena. First, drug companies' wholesale prices to vendors vary with the cost of dealing, the strength of competition, and the bargaining power of the purchasers. Second, retailers mark up these variously priced products according to their individual predilections. Until recently, restrictions on price advertising have limited the market response to price variations, and many pharmacists remain reluctant to advertise.

Industry drug-pricing practices, research and development, competition, and distribution are important areas for investigation; all have a profound impact on total expenditures for a drug benefit program. These areas are currently being investigated by DHEW, the Federal Trade Commission, and congressional committees. Although allegedly undesirable industry practices and proposed solutions are beyond the scope of this book, they explain some of the concerns involved in choosing a reimbursement mechanism for drug insurance.

Reimbursement of actual acquisition costs would interfere least with current market conditions. At the same time, this approach offers little hope for cost control and would tend to ratify the current size distribution of pharmacies. Payment

---

[48] Vincent Gardner, Chief, Drug Studies Branch, Social Security Administration, DHEW, in hearings before the U.S. Congress, Senate, Committee on Human Resources, Subcommittee on Health and the Environment, July 14, 1977.

would simply reflect existing variations in costs of supplying drugs by different classes of vendors. For example, large discount houses or chain drug stores might be reimbursed at levels different from those of small community pharmacies or dispensing physicians. The result of this practice would be to support current inefficiencies in dispensing. In addition, a cost-based system would require extensive auditing to assure that only costs actually incurred were reimbursed. Finally, unless pharmacies were provided with some other cost control incentive, this approach like other cost-based systems would encourage continual escalation in costs actually incurred.

Control is increased if limits on acquisition costs are set. The Department of Health, Education, and Welfare recently adopted such a method for reimbursement of drugs under federal programs; limits on acquisition costs also were used by several state Medicaid programs prior to the federal regulations.[49] Vendors are reimbursed a "maximum allowable cost" for multiple-source drugs and "estimated acquisition cost" for all others.

Maximum allowable cost represents the lowest unit price at which a multiple-source drug is widely and consistently available from any formulator or labeler. A Pharmaceutical Reimbursement Board made up of five DHEW officials determines these costs. The Food and Drug Administration reviews multiple-source drugs for quality or equivalence problems. An advisory committee (fifteen nongovernmental appointees) then reviews costs and proposes regulations subject to public comment and hearings. Maximum costs are published in final form in the *Federal Register.*[50]

Limiting payment to the lowest-price source for a multiple-source drug implied a significant change from previous prescription practices. Historically, most state regulations made it necessary for pharmacists to fill prescriptions exactly as written. By the late 1960s, pressure began to build against this stricture. Public and private insurers were concerned about cost control and many pharmacists sought recognition

---

[49] Health Care Financing Administration (HCFA), "Limits on Drug Reimbursements to Save Millions," *Record* 1 (June/July 1977):13,

[50] Ibid., pp. 13–14, and National Pharmaceutical Council, "Pharmaceutical Benefits Under State Medical Assistance Programs," National Pharmaceutical Council, Washington, D.C., 1977.

of the social utility of their professional discretion. By mid-
1977, twenty-six states had repealed or modified their anti-
substitution laws.[51] All new laws allow physicians to stipulate
that prescriptions are to be filled as written including brand
designation, but in the absence of such stipulation on prescriptions, pharmacists have complete discretion. These laws do
not require pharmacists to select the lowest-cost substance,
and apparently pharmacists rarely do so. They make a choice
according to their own perceptions of the appropriate quality-
cost trade-off. By limiting payments, maximum-allowable-cost
regulations reduced discretion in these states. At first the
regulations also appeared to conflict with state laws. Discussions at the time when the regulations were introduced suggest
that it was expected that pharmacists would need to get physician permission by telephone to fill prescriptions not written
in such a way as to allow the pharmacist leeway to use the
government-designated limits.

For a program that never claimed to save more than $37
million on all multiple-source drugs available in 1975,[52] the
maximum-allowable-cost regulation generated enormous outcry. In litigation that was ultimately decided in the government's favor in May 1977, the American Medical Association
attacked what was alleged to be interference with the physician's right to prescribe, while the Pharmaceutical Manufacturers' Association (PMA) alleged that DHEW exceeded its
authority. The PMA saw well that although only about 42 of
the top 200 most widely used drugs were then available from
multiple sources, the number would increase rapidly in the
coming years. Of those 200 drugs, 117 will be available by
1984.[53] Furthermore, the Food and Drug Administration is
implementing new regulations that require the manufacturers
of all new drugs and certain others to establish the "bioavailability"—that is, the rate at which an active ingredient in a
drug becomes available at the site of drug action—of their
products.[54] Bioavailability, in turn, is used to establish bio-

---

[51] Silverman and Lydecker, *Drug Coverage*, pp. 15 and 75.

[52] Paul F. Dickens, "The Maximum Allowable Cost Regulations and
Pharmaceutical Research and Development," *Research and Statistics
Note*, Office of Research and Statistics, SSA, DHEW, March 4, 1976.

[53] Booz, Allen and Hamilton, *Impact of National Health Insurance on
the Pharmaceutical Industry*, p. 53.

[54] Ibid., p. 48.

equivalence of products. The lawsuits were grounded in part on the contention that the grounds for bioequivalence for substances to be covered under the maximum-allowable-cost regulation had not been adequately established. How important the bioequivalence issue will be in the future is not clear. A recent FDA report claims that of the thousands of drug products now on the market, only 130 have serious bioequivalence problems.[55]

Although the courts did not accept the industry arguments, the lawsuits had a significant effect on implementation of the maximum-allowable-cost regulation. The first limit (on ampicillin) was not announced until May 27, 1977, almost two years after the program was officially established,[56] but DHEW estimated that maximum cost limits would be set for drugs constituting the bulk of the multiple-source market (approximately 65 high-volume drugs) by mid-1979.[57]

For multiple-source drugs for which no maximum allowable cost is set and for single-source drugs, each state Medicaid program pays estimated acquisition costs. States may conduct their own audits of the actual acquisition costs at which wholesale drugs can be purchased in the state, or they can use DHEW estimates which will "be an approximation of the actual acquisition costs at which most providers can obtain the product in the most frequently purchased package size" for providers of different sizes.[58]

A review of Medicaid reimbursement policies reveals estimated acquisition costs based on several different methods, including published average wholesale prices such as those found in the *Red Book* or *Blue Book*, state-set maximums or fee schedules, negotiated price lists, or reimbursement of actual pharmacy acquisition costs.[59] The clear intent of the new federal activity, however, is to improve upon *Red Book* and *Blue Book* prices, which have been criticized as being higher than actual acquisition costs, thus increasing pharmacy

---

[55] Food and Drug Administration, *Holders of Abbreviated New Drug Applications for Drugs Presenting Actual or Potential Bioequivalence Problems*, FDA Publication No. 56–3009, June 1976.

[56] National Pharmaceutical Council, "Pharmaceutical Benefits," p. 18, and HCFA, "Limits on Drug Reimbursement," p. 13.

[57] Ibid.

[58] DHEW, *Maximum Allowable Cost*, p. 1.

[59] National Pharmaceutical Council, "Pharmaceutical Benefits."

profits. Although most transaction prices are lower than reference published prices, small pharmacies often criticize list prices as being unrealistically low for their size of outlet. Further, small pharmacists sometimes maintain that the price advantages that large outlets obtain result less from efficiency than from market power over the seller, and hence constitute "unfair competition." Most economists view such charges skeptically.[60]

The reimbursement system based on estimated acquisition cost would perpetuate the ability of pharmacies of different sizes to have their differing costs reimbursed because the survey data employed would allow for pharmacy characteristics such as volume. But such reimbursement is superior to reimbursement of individual pharmacies on the basis of their own incurred costs, in that firms with unusually high costs for their class would be under greater economic pressure. Thus industry consolidation would be less hindered than would otherwise be the case.

The Kennedy-Corman plan's proposed limits on drug acquisition cost may have much the same intent as that of the maximum-allowable-cost regulations, but the Kennedy-Corman language is obscure: "Product prices shall be so fixed as to encourage the acquisition of drugs in substantial quantities, and differing product prices for a single drug may be established only to reflect regional differences in cost or other factors not related to the quantity purchased."[61] What this appears to mean is that a high-volume reimbursement rate would apply regardless of the volume at which the provider actually purchased. Taking the retail outlet's total sales volume of a drug as given, however, there is only one cost-minimizing purchasing pattern available to that outlet. Thus there is little that the board could "encourage" in the apparently desired direction of scale economies except an increased volume of business by more efficient retailers. Given Kennedy-Corman's cost-plus focus and other sections of the bill favoring the preservation of existing pharmacy outlets, it is likely that this section would be modified by its sponsors.

---

[60] Such claims provide the rationale for the Robinson-Patman Act. See Bain, *Industrial Organization*, pp. 609–626.

[61] U.S. Congress, House, *A Bill to Create a National System of Health Security*, H.R. 22, 93rd Congress, 1st Session, 1973.

How maximum-allowable-cost limits might be incorporated in national health insurance depends on other features of the drug coverage program. The maximum-allowable-cost arrangement was designed for the Medicaid program, which, like the Kennedy-Corman plan, allows for little or no patient cost sharing. One can only speculate about how such cost control measures might be introduced into an NHI plan with a substantial average deductible, coinsurance, and flexibility in provider charges such as the CHIP plan. An important question might be, How legitimate is the government's interference with the general pattern of drug use when only a part of the total bill will in fact be paid with tax money? One option would be to disallow government credit on the health card (and hence from the contribution toward the deductible and maximum family medical expenses as well as for government reimbursement to the pharmacist) any excess of ingredient charges above maximum allowable costs. This seems to be the most straightforward way of combining maximum allowable costs with CHIP proposals, and appears consonant with the statement of DHEW Secretary Casper Weinberger during the 1974 national health insurance congressional hearings that "CHIP would reimburse providers on the price at which the lowest cost-equivalent product was generally available." [62]

In addition to enforcing maximum-allowable-cost regulations, DHEW is providing information to facilitate price comparisons on different brands of the same drug, a scheme modeled after the Ontario PARCOST Plan.[63] The drug makers claim that any resulting increase in generic drug prescribing will tend to limit further their returns on research and development, and thus reinforce other regulations that have retarded new drug development. Even if the drug makers have a legitimate grievance, however, limiting information is not the way to deal with it. Other measures—perhaps including both a reduction in government-mandated testing costs and an

---

[62] Statement of Secretary Weinberger, Hearings before the Committee on Ways and Means, House of Representatives, 93rd Congress, 2nd Session, on the Subject of National Health Insurance, vol. I (Washington, D.C.: U.S. Government Printing Office, 1974), p. 587.

[63] DHEW, *Maximum Allowable Cost*, p. 3; R. G. Evans and M. F. Williamson, *Extending Canadian Health Insurance: Options for Pharmacare and Denticare* (Toronto: University of Toronto Press), p. 81.

increase in the gross margins on new products during the life of the patents—are far more appropriate.[64]

California developed an alternative to limiting drug ingredient payment that is worth consideration, although the plan was never implemented. California Medicaid officials apparently believed that a simple comparison of declared prices for multiple-source drugs was insufficient to get a drug at the lowest possible cost. Hence in 1975, the California Department of Health devised a pilot scheme, similar to some plans being tried in Canada, to require potential suppliers of the seventy-five most widely used, multiple-source drugs to submit sealed bids for the exclusive right to supply the state's Medi-Cal beneficiaries over a set period of time. Anticipated administrative problems led the state to modify its original plans to acquire the drugs itself, but in 1977 it announced that it planned to institute a new procedure for setting prices. In addition to setting prices for various volumes to be available to wholesalers and pharmacies (and upon which the state's previous acquisition cost controls had been based), the state proposed to invite all manufacturers to submit rebate bids. The manufacturer with the lowest *net* price to the state would then be given the right to supply the program. Pharmacists' cooperation in using the designated product and reporting it to the state was to be encouraged by payment of thirty cents for each such prescription dispensed. The state was to record the volume of business done with each volume-purchase-plan drug and submit invoices for rebates to manufacturers. The Pharmaceutical Manufacturers' Association attacked the scheme in Sacramento Superior Court as an abuse of the authority of the Department of Health, however, and the plan was subsequently disapproved by the California Joint Legislative Committee.[65]

---

[64] The financing burden of the collective good of pharmaceutical research is now more arbitrarily borne than in some alternative arrangements. To the extent that sales of a product (or its profitability) sharply dropped after that product's patent life ran out, and this drop was thought to be adversely affecting innovation, a new patenting system with some longer-lived patents could be developed for the drug industry.

[65] The description of the plan in its original and modified forms is taken from Department of Health, Health and Welfare Agency, *Modified Volume Purchase Project* (Sacramento: California Department of Health, 1977); the demise of the plan was described in a letter from Eloise Barton of the California Department of Health dated December 27, 1977.

The crucial assumptions behind the California scheme were that state monopsony power can significantly reduce profit margins, and that the profit margins of the lowest-price generic suppliers are high. In an industry in which production barriers to entry are low (manufacturing scale economies are modest)[66] and in which international competition is becoming ever more keen, significant margins would be somewhat surprising. Furthermore, maximum-allowable-cost legislation at the national level would probably increase the total demand for generic drugs, which in turn should further increase supplier competition. All these considerations notwithstanding, projects such as the one proposed for California deserve careful study—if they are ever allowed to begin.

Finally, perhaps the most restrictive approach to price limits was incorporated in a 1977 proposal in the Senate for drug coverage for the elderly. The bill, which was not passed, was sponsored by Senators Kennedy and Thurmond. In this proposal, manufacturers would be expected to hold prices charged to the program constant for six-month periods. Within three years, the DHEW secretary was to report to Congress on "an improved method of determining and assuring an appropriate allowable drug product acquisition price, including methods for negotiating such price directly with drug product formulators and labelers."[67] The secretary was (somehow) to relate these recommendations to the impact of the prices of specific products on research and development in the industry, to all of the marketing practices of the industry, and to the profitability of the product in question. On balance, there is little doubt that this bill posed the most dire threat that the industry has yet faced. It would have required the government to sharpen its skills as a purchaser for about 25 percent of all prescription drugs sold in the United States.

REIMBURSEMENT OF DISPENSING COSTS

As the determinant of income to an organized profession, pharmacy, policy toward dispensing fees is a critical and un-

---

[66] A discussion of scale economies in production can be found in David Schwartzman, *Innovation in the Pharmaceutical Industry* (Baltimore: Johns Hopkins University Press, 1976), pp. 308–9.

[67] U.S. Congress, Senate, *A Bill to Establish a Program of Drug Benefits for the Aged*, S. 2144, 95th Congress, 1st Session, 1977, p. 18.

avoidably controversial issue. As with other fees, the payment system must balance concern with cost control against the desire to provide fair compensation. Experience to date indicates that this is not a simple task.

One way to treat dispensing fees in a public insurance program is to leave them to the market—not to cover them. Evans and Williamson have justified differences in treatment of product costs and dispensing costs:

> The consumer can hardly be expected to judge his need for the ingredients (that is why . . . he consults a physician) or to price shop intelligently in the fecund jungle of pharmaceutical preparations. But the dispensing process is much more standardized and susceptible to consumer judgements.[68]

Saskatchewan's drug insurance plan tried to implement this approach, proposing to pay pharmacies only for ingredient costs. Pharmacists then would be allowed to charge up to two dollars for dispensing. Following an enormous outcry from the pharmacists, a compromise was worked out in which most small and medium-size pharmacies got seventy-five cents above ingredient cost from the government and large pharmacies only fifty cents. During the negotiations, persons speaking for organized pharmacists tried to get the maximum dispensing fee made mandatory, but the government claimed that "it could not insist on patients paying $2.00 if some pharmacies wished to charge only $1.00 or $1.50." [69] The pharmacists did, however, wring from the government an agreement to enforce a ban on price advertising. In the 1975-76 Report of the Saskatchewan Prescription Drug Plan,[70] 299 of the 352 pharmacies in the province (85 percent) were reported to be charging the full two dollars.

The implementation of the Saskatchewan plan thus has features that greatly blunt its potentially competitive impact: what amounts to a twenty-five cents differential subsidy for small-scale pharmacy and the prevention of low-cost sellers from advertising their lower costs. Nevertheless, the Saskatchewan experience underlines the point that compensation

---

[68] Evans and Williamson, *Extending Canadian Health Insurance*, p. 81.

[69] Bachynsky, "Pharmaceutical Benefit Programs in Canada," p. 6.

[70] Unless otherwise noted, material in this section is drawn from Saskatchewan Prescription Drug Plan, *Annual Report* 1975-76.

beyond ingredient costs is not an all-or-nothing choice. If policy makers deem the full dispensing fee to be an unwise deterrent to persons facing it, the government can pay whatever portion of dispensing fees it designates as appropriate, while retaining competition among outlets.

Political pressure could require substantial or complete coverage of dispensing fees under national health insurance, thereby posing several options. In the past, pharmacists have often calculated their compensation through a percentage mark-up on the drugs they sell. Because the mark-up encourages dispensation of the most expensive preparations, private third-party payers and the government have substituted a flat fee for pharmacy services. Concern then shifts to determination of the fees. A look at Medicaid suggests some of the reasons for concern. In virtually all states, the dispensing fee first emerged from lobbying by pharmacies, with state officials offering varying degrees of resistance.

In 1974, the fee ranged between $1.90 and $2.50 across the states[71] and appears generally not to have been based on actual cost experience. The Illinois Medicaid Report of 1976 reported that:

> Although dispensing fees account for about one-third of the expenditures for pharmacy products, (the Department) has no clear procedure for insuring that this rate reflects the pharmacist's actual costs. Rather, this fee appears to be set more on the amount of political pressure which pharmacists can bring to bear on (the Department).[72]

In the same survey, the Illinois study reported that pharmacies were making much more money on their Medicaid business than from sales to ordinary customers despite the declared goal (presumably the goal of their programs as well) of not paying more than retail drug prices.[73] (It is not known to what extent excessive fees or inflated ingredient costs produced this result, however.) As part of the maximum-allowable-cost program, DHEW is now requiring the states to

---

[71] Fulda, *Prescription Drug Data Summary*, p. 10.
[72] Illinois Economic and Fiscal Commission, *Medicaid Costs and Controls: An Analysis*, December, 1976 (mimeographed), p. 53.
[73] Ibid., p. 51.

conduct a thorough survey of pharmacy operating costs upon which volume-related dispensing fees are to be based.[74] Total reimbursement is then to be limited to the sum of the estimated acquisition costs plus the estimated fee or the "usual and customary" charge, whichever is lower.

As with professional compensation, NHI plans for dispensing fees propose variations on the "usual and customary" or "fee schedule" approaches. The Kennedy-Mills bill is an example of a plan that endorses the former approach. The bill would require each pharmacy electing to participate in the program to file a statement of its pharmaceutical service charge with the administrative agency. These charges would apply during the first year of the program unless they exceeded 90 percent of the *average* charges "in the same locality." Higher charges would be reduced to the 90 percent level. The 90 percent amount would be adjusted in subsequent years—not to actual changes in fee levels but "to the extent necessary on the basis of appropriate economics index data." What an appropriate index would be is not clear, but the apparent intent is to maintain the real value of the maximum allowed fee.

This proposal aroused a strong reaction from organized pharmacists. Although no explanation was offered (there appears to be nothing like the uncollected bills problems that justified a discount from physician fee schedules in Canada), the implication of the legislation appeared to be that the government would be justified in paying less than the full average dispensing fee. If, as the pharmacists strongly urged in their congressional testimony, the legislation were to be recast as the 90th percentile in the overall distribution, the situation would be more "fair" but still flawed. In both cases, pharmacists would have an incentive to exaggerate their charges. The principal restraining factor would be price sensitivity of their uninsured customers, but only to the extent that pharmacists were actually constrained to charge them the same fee as the one declared. Given the low marginal cost of dispensing, one could not expect low-cost suppliers to exercise collective price restraint. Few high-cost dispensers could be driven out of the program in the short run, thereby leaving more business for those who remained.

---

[74] DHEW, *Maximum Allowable Cost*, p. 3.

In contrast, the Kennedy-Corman bill proposes a fee schedule for pharmacists, which would be designed to "afford reasonable compensation to independent pharmacies after taking into account variations in their cost of operation resulting from regional differences, differences in the volume of drugs dispensed, differences in services provided, and other factors which the Board finds relevant." The schedule would be determined "in consultation with representatives of the pharmaceutical profession." Whether an NHI program would be more successful than state Medicaid programs have been in resisting industry pressure remains to be seen.

Fee schedules have the potential to encourage certain types of pharmacist behavior—notably, quality control. Some drug insurance programs have experimented with using fees to obtain "desirable" pharmacy services. For example, Paid Prescriptions, Inc., a drug insurer, offers pharmacists twenty-five cents extra per prescription if they keep patient medication profiles.[75] In some Canadian provincial schemes, a $1.45 fee was awarded in the mid-1960s to pharmacists who detected a problem with a prescription and therefore did not dispense it.[76] This detection of problems could include excessive use of drugs, interaction effects, multiple prescribing by separate physicians, or use of expensive drugs with less expensive equivalents. Pharmacists are rewarded for saving the cost of an inappropriate prescription as well as for protecting the patient from unnecessary drug use. It should be noted, however, that rewards for documentable contribution to patient health or cost savings can be made in ways other than through a negotiated fee schedule. A pharmacist in another kind of plan could simply file for a government credit or rebate.

When out-of-pocket payments are not employed, the only way to encourage dispensing efficiency in a fee-for-service system is to employ reimbursement that reflects average costs of a specific set of pharmacies and is not tied to the actual costs of each individual outlet. Average costs can be ascertained by grouping pharmacies (e.g., by volume) and reimbursing according to a group norm.

As with other providers, it is also possible to reimburse

---

[75] David Knapp, "Reimbursement Systems," in Wertheimer, *Proceedings*, p. 130.
[76] Ibid.

pharmacists on a capitation basis. Capitation payments could be paid to medical groups or to pharmacies.[77] Payments would be based on the number of patients served. The medical group (such as a prepaid group practice) or the pharmacy would be responsible for providing all necessary drugs to the designated group of recipients. Administratively, the use of capitation rates could be quite complex because capitation rates must be set and enrollment into plans established. Yet, once rates are determined, administrative tasks would decline. Rather than continuous claims processing, yearly reviews would be required to adjust capitation rates and to monitor the quality and costs of services provided. Interim payments could be used to spread the capitation fee across time. Reinsurance against high-risk utilizers would be necessary to prevent high cost burdens for small pharmacy operations. Capitation reimbursement has in fact been used by Paid Prescriptions, Inc., and by the drug programs of Belgium and Sweden.[78] The Kennedy-Corman plan would require health maintenance organizations to provide complete drug coverage.

Patient Cost Sharing

Patient cost sharing is seen as a method to limit the effect of the moral hazard of drug insurance (i.e., for patients to demand more because they are insured) to reduce total program expenditures, control unnecessary utilization, and to provide incentives to shop for the lowest-cost supplier. At the same time, cost sharing might cause certain individuals to forgo necessary purchases. The various cost-sharing mechanisms have different goals, and the effects of each depend on the dollar amount and its size relative to the individual's finances.

OPTIONS FOR COST SHARING

Cost sharing may include deductibles (first "x" dollars of coverage are to be paid by the beneficiary), coinsurance (a

---

[77] DHEW Task Force, *Approaches to Drug Insurance Design*, pp. 30–32.
[78] Ibid., and Silverman and Lydecker, *Drug Coverage*, p. 86.

percentage of each prescription is to be paid), copayment (a set fee is collected from the beneficiary each time), or some form of maximum liability for the insurer. Current drug insurance plans and most NHI proposals rely on one or more of these mechanisms. CHIP, for example, proposes an income-related deductible, set at zero for persons with incomes of $1,750 or less (family incomes of $2,500 or less) and at fifty dollars for individuals with incomes greater than $3,500 (or family incomes greater than $5,000). Similarly, CHIP imposes coinsurance ranging from 10 percent to 25 percent of charges. Kennedy-Mills, in contrast, proposes a deductible of $150 and a fixed copayment of $1 per prescription. (These dollar figures were developed in the early 1970s and would be revised if the plans were considered now.) The Kennedy-Corman bill would impose no cost sharing at all.

The purpose and likely effect of cost sharing vary with the instrument employed. The use of deductibles (payment of the initial expenses before receiving benefits) makes recipients incur some drug expenses, makes them aware of drug costs, offers control of unnecessary utilization, lowers total program cost, and eases the administrative burden of filing several small claims. Furthermore, cost sharing is the only feasible means by which market forces can rationalize the dispensing function. The experience of other countries suggests that when cost-plus reimbursement for such services is employed, the existing, inefficient distribution system is frozen in place.

The effect of the deductible depends on its size relative to total drug expenses, as well as on the income of the beneficiary. If the deductible is large—for example, greater than the median charge—the majority of beneficiaries will not receive benefits under the public program. If the deductible is large relative to income, it may result in underutilization or in unfilled prescriptions. A balance must be achieved between the positive cost control advantages of cost sharing and underutilization resulting from financial constraints.

Once a beneficiary incurs drug expenses and approaches the deductible amount, there are incentives to use higher-cost medicines or to submit additional claims in order to reach the deductible level. Once the deductible has been met, drug use is free unless other means of cost sharing are employed.

Unlike hospital deductibles, which often are met after a patient is admitted, the drug deductible might be met only after many prescriptions had been filled. Thus, because a

beneficiary must maintain several records of bills before submission for reimbursement, the likelihood of lost, incomplete,
or unsubmitted claims is increased. As already noted, however,
experience with Manitoba's Pharmacare drug program indicates that unsubmitted claims may not be a significant problem. Administratively, an out-of-pocket deductible would
eliminate the processing of several small claims for reimbursement,[79] but the task of reviewing those claims to determine if
the deductible requirement has been met would remain.

Coinsurance (a percentage payment) and copayment (a
fixed charge) would have different effects. Coinsurance would
place a heavier burden on people with expensive prescriptions,
but also would provide an incentive to substitute lower-cost
drugs when possible. Coinsurance would curb total program
expenses as prices rose. Payments by beneficiaries would automatically adjust upward with increases in prescription prices.
Copayments would have to be adjusted by the program. Copayments would lower the relative burden on persons with
expensive prescriptions, but copayments would increase an
incentive to provide larger quantities per prescription to avoid
an additional fee for refills.

Cost sharing also could be imposed by setting ceilings on
reimbursement, either per drug or on an annual expenditure
basis; beneficiaries would be responsible for payment of the
remaining drug charges. This cost-sharing method would deter
overprescribing or the use of excessively expensive drugs, but
it would penalize persons requiring costly drugs or persons
suffering from catastrophic illness (i.e., people who could most
benefit from drug coverage). This "shallow" insurance reduces
support just when it is most needed, and most analysts consider it inferior to a "deep" plan of similar cost. No major
NHI plans propose such cost sharing.

All forms of cost sharing could be adjusted upward or downward to reflect desired beneficiary burden or public expenditures, and to respond to price inflation or increased drug
utilization. Cost-sharing amounts also could be adjusted to
reflect individual beneficiary financial status or drug use burdens. Sliding-scale deductibles or copayment amounts related
to incomes or past drug expenditures could be used. Limits
also could be set on the amount of out-of-pocket payments a

---

[79] This would not be true of the credit card systems employed by CHIP
and Kennedy-Mills.

beneficiary would have to absorb by establishing a catastrophic benefit, after which all cost sharing would cease. Administrative problems and costs would increase substantially with the complexity of the program.

Independent of other variations, virtually any scheme of patient cost sharing can be designed to allow out-of-pocket costs to vary with the costs of individual pharmacies. At the very least, cost sharing should be used to encourage efficiency.

EXPERIENCE WITH COST SHARING

Few controlled studies have been undertaken to analyze the effect of cost sharing, and investigators disagree about the way cost sharing affects demand.[80] Some data show that demand rises as little as 25 percent or even less in response to zero out-of-pocket payment; in a comparison of three diverse studies, however, Phelps and Newhouse found a dramatically greater effect.[81] Despite the different characteristics of the

---

[80] Evans and Williamson, *Extending Canadian Health Insurance*, pp. 36–46. There is evidence in many discussions of elasticity that the critical distinctions between "demand response" and "demand elasticity" are not well understood. A demand response of 130 percent from a market price to zero corresponds to an arc elasticity along the associated demand function of $(-).39$. This "arc" elasticity is found by finding the "average" percentage change in quantity over the "average" percentage change in price. The convention for finding the average in each case is to divide the change by the average of the two absolute values involved. For price this would be $(p_2 - p_1)/\dfrac{(p_1 + p_2)}{2}$. In addition there is often a failure to recognize that elasticity ("arc"—as just discussed—or "point") changes continuously over most demand curves. Even some otherwise careful studies fail to pay sufficient attention to the enormous variation in demand elasticity estimates that result from using different segments of the same demand function. For an example of the nominal recognition of the problem with insufficient attention to the difference it makes, see DHEW, PHS, HRA, Bureau of Health Manpower, *The Impact of Comprehensive National Health Insurance on Demand for Health Manpower* (Washington, D.C.: DHEW, 1976), p. 55.

[81] Charles E. Phelps and Joseph P. Newhouse, *Coinsurance and the Demand for Medical Services* (Santa Monica: The Rand Corporation, 1974), pp. 28–32; the results are summarized in terms of their total response implications in Joseph P. Newhouse, *Health Care Cost Sharing and Cost Containment* (Santa Monica: The Rand Corporation, 1976), p. 24.

three populations (the British population using the National Health Service; a relatively small drug insurance plan in Windsor, Ontario; and the recipients of Medicaid in Mississippi), the studies consistently indicated that demand among an insured population will range between 90 percent and 130 percent greater than the demand among an uninsured population, while a 25 percent coinsurance rate will reduce the increase to between 78 percent and 124 percent.

A Medicaid copayment experiment in California employed a one-dollar copayment on the first two physician visits and a fifty-cent copayment charge on prescription drugs.[82] The study controls for some intervening factors by comparing drug utilization of the cost-sharing group with a matched control group, but the findings are confounded by the existence of a copayment charge for physician services. The physician copayment may deter a patient from visiting a physician and receiving a prescription for medicine. The study found drug utilization decreased as physician visits decreased and as prescribing patterns changed. Once patients acquired prescriptions, they were no less likely to have them filled than were Medicaid beneficiaries who are not liable for copayment. This fact suggests that although some physicians may have become more careful in prescribing, physician copayment was the critical factor in decreasing utilization.

A later analysis of the same cost-sharing experiment questioned the wisdom of deterring both medical care access and drug utilization.[83] The researchers concluded that postponement of ambulatory care could result in progression of a disease to a more serious stage requiring more advanced patient care, thus reversing any short-term saving resulting from decreased utilization. It should be noted that the findings of both studies of the California copayment experiment have been subject to much criticism, primarily centering on the use of relatively short follow-up periods and on methodological difficulties related to original experimental design.[84]

---

[82] Earl W. Brian and Stephen F. Biggens, "California's Medi-Cal Copayment Experiment," *Supplement to Medical Care* 12 (December 1974): 1–303.

[83] Milton Roemer et al. "Copayment for Ambulatory Care: Penny-Wise and Pound-Foolish," *Medical Care* 13 (June 1975):457–66.

[84] John Holahan and Bruce Stuart, *Controlling Medicaid Utilization Patterns* (Washington, D.C.: The Urban Institute, June 1977), pp. 10–13.

DHEW funded the most careful study to date specifically addressing the use of deductibles, copayments, and coinsurance on drugs used by a Medicare population.[85] The study compared drug use, program costs, and administrative costs for four elderly groups receiving identical drug benefits. One group had coverage with no cost sharing, a second had coverage with a copayment of one dollar per prescription, a third had coverage with coinsurance of 25 percent, and the last had coverage with 25 percent coinsurance after a fifty-dollar deductible was met. Pharmacists were responsible for collecting cost-sharing payments in the second and third groups. Members of the last group received their drugs without cash payment and were billed by the intermediary for the full amount up to the deductible and the coinsurance amount thereafter (this is the mechanism in CHIP).

The study found that all forms of cost sharing appeared to affect use by reducing the number of eligible beneficiaries receiving drugs. Once services were used (one prescription filled), however, utilization rates were the same. Once again, the possibility that deterrence of care could ultimately lead to higher-cost care must be weighed against program cost savings.

The study revealed other interesting findings. The administrative costs of providing a patient billing system were significantly higher than normal claims processing. A claims review was necessary to determine if deductibles were met and what the subsequent bill to the patient should be. In groups two and three, the deductible was absent and the administrative cost of determining and collecting the coinsurance or copayment amount was passed on to the pharmacy. In all cases, pharmacies tended to charge higher prices to participants in the third-party program than to the general public. Thus the already high administrative costs would have to have been even higher to prevent provider abuse.

In summary, cost sharing can be applied using various dollar levels and combinations of methods. The choice of certain alternatives will reflect the goals of the program, whether they are to control program expenditures, to minimize administrative costs, or to promote proper use of health services. All

---

[85] DHEW, *Ambulatory Prescription Drug Study*, Division of Health Insurance Studies, HCFA, November 1977.

types of cost sharing seem to deter utilization in comparison with utilization by similar groups not subject to copayment. How much of this deterred utilization is desirable is not currently known.

Administration

Regardless of the design of a drug benefit, two administrative issues require critical attention: claims processing and utilization review. Poor performance of either task would undermine beneficiary satisfaction, provider cooperation, and cost and quality control.

CLAIMS PROCESSING

Claims processing includes the following: (1) recording and submission of claims information by the pharmacist or beneficiary; (2) receipt and entry of information for processing by the administrative agency after checking for completeness; (3) verification of beneficiary and vendor eligibility and of the drug claim legitimacy if formularies, dosage limits, refill limits, or other limits are used; (4) determination of benefits payable, product price, professional fee, deductibles, or cost-sharing obligations; and (5) timely reimbursement or payment to the vendor or beneficiary.

The potentially large number of drug claims per year and the low average prescription cost mean that administrative costs are likely to be a large proportion of total program expenditures, and program expenditures excluding administration costs are estimated to be at least several billion dollars.[86] Administrative costs have been estimated at a high of one dollar to two dollars per prescription for manual processing to a low of twenty cents per prescription if an automated claims processing system is used. In Wertheimer's review of administrative costs of drug programs in the early 1970s, costs ranged from forty-four cents per claim under Michigan Blue

---

[86] See Kudrle, "Outpatient Drug Coverage Under National Health Insurance."

Shield (carrier for the United Auto Workers' drug benefits),
to forty cents per claim for Pharmaceutical Card Service and
Paid Prescriptions, Inc. (two private drug reimbursement
companies), and anywhere from thirteen cents to $1.20 per
claim under Medicaid drug programs.[87] Wertheimer has
pointed out that quoted administrative costs may cover very
different types of administrative functions; for example, they
may or may not include utilization review procedures. He also
noted that accurate processing estimates covering a fair share
of overhead, depreciation, and required administrative functions were yet to be determined.

Estimates made for CHIP indicate a wide variation in perspectives on administrative costs. A careful study for the
Social Security Administration directed by Joseph Higgins
estimated that computer equipment could be leased (including
a terminal in every pharmacy), information recorded, and
claims processed for about twenty cents per claim. The study,
conducted in the early 1970s, related to first-dollar coverage
under Medicare, but Higgins believes that costs have not risen
appreciably in the period since the original study was done and
that the same costs would apply to CHIP.[88]

Other observers differ. In an analysis of the costs of national health insurance, Gordon Trapnell has estimated that
gathering statistical data for a drug scheme similar to that
maintained under Medicare would run to 5 percent of "prescription bills paid," while the processing health credit card
bills (used in CHIP and Kennedy-Mills) would add another 5
percent.[89] Trapnell's figures implied a cost of between forty
cents and fifty cents for a prescription in the mid-1970s. T.
Donald Rucker, formerly with the Social Security Administration, has recently put forward an estimate of from thirty to
forty cents without utilization review.[90]

Other authorities are more pessimistic. One government

---

[87] Wertheimer, *Economic Analysis*, pp. 24, 28–30.

[88] All of the information on the Higgins study was provided directly
by Joseph Higgins.

[89] Gordon R. Trapnell Consulting Actuaries, *A Comparison of the Costs
of Major National Health Insurance Proposals*, prepared for the Office
of the Assistant Secretary for Planning and Evaluation, DHEW, January 1976, revised September 1976 (mimeographed), pp. 42–43.

[90] Silverman and Lydecker, *Drug Coverage*, p. 17, citing personal communication with Rucker.

authority compared the administrative shock of the onset of a high deductible scheme for drugs to only one previous event: the inauguration of the entire Medicare system. This person believes it unlikely that such a scheme could be administered for 10 percent of benefits; his cost estimate is 20 percent of benefits paid. Furthermore, this estimate is based on a system in which most claims are handled by patients who would submit accumulated bills. His assumption is that 30 million people would submit at least 250 million claims.[91] When one considers that the number of drug transactions handled under the CHIP health card scheme would run well over a *billion*, most of which would not be involved in any benefit whatever, the alarm over administrative implications is not surprising.

Proponents of the system reply that although there is little doubt that the proposed volume of claims would be unmanageable under current conditions, a computerized system could be devised to handle the job. Several drug insurance carriers already rely on automated claims processing, but no established system is available at this time to handle the large volume of claims that would accompany national health insurance.

Rucker was one of the first to propose an electronic network to link vendors, suppliers, administrative agencies or payers, and subscribers. He foresees a series of regional computer centers linked electronically via telephone lines to terminals located in each of the nation's pharmacies.[92] The major advantages of such a system would be automated drug inventory, immediate status on beneficiary eligibility and deductible payments, reduced time for submitting claims information and receiving reimbursement, and electronic drug profiles of patients.

But there are problems connected with the use of a nationwide drug computer network. Besides cost, the one most often mentioned is that of confidentiality. Rucker has argued, however, that a carefully designed program could reduce abuse of patient records to a minimum. The development of such sys-

---

[91] Memorandum from Anthony Graziano, Project Leader, Administration Task Force, NHI to Peter Fox, Director of Health Analysis, June 18, 1973.

[92] Rucker, cited in Diane Wickware, "Automation is Vital to Prescription Drug Coverage," *American Druggist* 160 (October 6, 1969) :40.

tems obviously depends on the availability of technology and the necessary financial resources to design and install a system of this size.

UTILIZATION REVIEW

Earlier this chapter noted that quality issues should be extremely important in the design of a drug benefit. Effective utilization review provides the only hope that the American people who, in the eyes of many qualified observers, are already vastly "overdrugged" will not become even more so with the inauguration of national health insurance.

Utilization review is intended to improve the quality of care, to minimize program expenditures, and to minimize fraud and abuse. The process involves monitoring and control of drug utilization, assuring that payment for drugs supplied under the plan are legitimate, and promoting proper drug therapy by provision of feedback to pharmacies and drug prescribers.

In a monograph on drug utilization review, Brodie and Benson have described the essential components of a successful program.[93] These elements include collection of drug use data to generate utilization, prescription, and dispensing files; setting of standards or criteria to evaluate utilization; development of a review process to judge the appropriateness of drug utilization; and provision of corrective measures once problems are exposed by the review.

Utilization review is integrally tied to the claims-processing system which would provide the necessary information. Drug use profiles would describe drugs or drug categories ranked by frequency or cost. These drugs could be analyzed to detect the most frequently and least frequently prescribed drugs, the range of drug prices, and dosage sizes. Frequently prescribed drugs could then be analyzed for efficacy, and the availability of lower-cost substitutes could be ascertained. Changes in utilization and costs could be noted and the impact of utilization review procedures or changes in drug program policies analyzed. The drug profile would provide valuable information on

---

[93] Donald Brodie and Roger Benson, *Drug Utilization Review and Drug Usage as a Determinant of the Quality of Health Care*, Health Services Research, DHEW, January 1976.

drug use of particular segments of the population, and help determine patterns of drug use and health status.

Physician profiles would provide information on the types of drugs prescribed, frequency of prescribing, and size of dosage. Such questions as the appropriateness of drug therapy for the ailment diagnosed, the choice of drugs, and the appropriateness of dosage size could be addressed. Overprescribing or misprescribing of drugs could be detected; fraudulent or deceitful practices would be subject to legal discipline or termination of the physician's participation in the program.

Pharmacy profiles would provide information on dispensing volume and costs. High-volume pharmacies offering no apparent customer advantages could be investigated for the possibility of kickbacks to providers. Spot-checking of prescriptions received by beneficiaries against claims submitted would detect areas of fraud and abuse.

Comprehensive beneficiary profiles would be feasible. Drugs prescribed from various sources and dispensed at several locations could be accumulated in a single file which could be reviewed to detect drug incompatibilities, drug overuse, misuse, or abuse. A patient's receipt of multiple prescriptions from separate physicians and excessive use of narcotics or potentially abusive drugs could be detected. If certain drugs were recalled, beneficiary profiles would also provide ready identification of users.

Utilization review would entail identification of abnormalities in utilization, prescribing, or dispensing. To keep utilization review costs from becoming prohibitive, particular drugs, beneficiaries, physicians, or pharmacies could be selected for review. Panels of physicians, clinical pharmacists, and nurses could investigate deviations from normative or statistically derived standards. Alternatively, this investigation could be delegated to area Professional Standards Review Organizations (PSROs), which review appropriateness of medical care for Medicare and Medicaid beneficiaries.

The timing of the review process is important for the functions it can serve. Administrative review, decisions on appropriateness of payment, and detection of fraud and abuse could be performed retrospectively. Retrospective medical reviews could identify areas of potentially high cost or questionable quality. Retrospective review, however, is far from ideal. Denial of payment and legal action as remedies for inappropriate charges, fraud, or abuse might lead to widespread provider dissatisfaction and a decline in participation if they were heavily relied upon. What is more important, although drug utilization patterns could be identified and interpreted after the fact, the drugs would by that time already have been consumed.

Some computerized drug benefits systems promise concurrent or even prospective utilization review provided at low marginal costs above the system's claims-processing functions. The system would require that not just pharmacies but all places of prescribing be linked to the data system. Prospective and concurrent review would provide the mechanism for prevention of potential misuse or abuse—the former through inspection of a patient's drug history prior to, and the latter during the course of, treatment. Provision of patient drug profiles prior to prescribing or dispensing of a drug would alert physicians and pharmacies to drugs currently prescribed for a particular person and to the possibility of drug interactions and adverse reactions. Data files could be prepared as investigators establish drug research and clinical norms that would recommend the use of certain drugs for certain medical conditions and patient characteristics.

In a proper cost-benefit analysis of various forms of utilization review (which may involve determining shared computer costs), the costs of the program must be set against a rather broad range of benefits. Benefits include not only relief from unnecessary pain and suffering and avoidance of the considerable loss of national output now resulting from drug-induced illness, but also savings from the reduction of excessive and unnecessarily expensive prescribing.

Summary and Conclusions

Although drugs pose cost and quality issues that are different from issues posed by other medical expenses, the treatment of drugs under national health insurance raises policy choices common to all benefits: limited versus open-ended coverage, methods and controls on payment, patient cost sharing, and administrative complexity.

Cost issues are important in the consideration of drug coverage under national health insurance. The pharmaceutical industry has a long, well-documented record of excess profits, and many of the 50,000 pharmacies in the United States are too small to be efficient. A well-designed NHI program should address both these issues. The quality issue in drug coverage, however, probably is paramount. Most observers are concerned that in aggregate, Americans already consume excessive amounts of drugs, and this problem would be vastly exacerbated by NHI coverage simply because such coverage would certainly increase physician visits, which in turn would increase the number of prescriptions written. Only new utilization controls on the entire drug care system could avoid even worse drug-induced problems than those we now have.

Concerns about the costs of a drug benefit have led to proposals for limited coverage, notably through the creation of a formulary for the NHI program. The formulary could be used to control the quality and efficacy of drugs covered by the program, and to target benefits to a particular segment of the population—specifically, persons suffering from chronic diseases. In neither case would establishment of a formulary be simple. Difficult decisions would have to be made about the inclusion or exclusion of individual drugs, problems might develop in communicating coverage limits to beneficiaries and providers, and people might resort to manipulation or fraud to obtain coverage. Despite these problems, a formulary might be preferable to other control mechanisms, like quantity limits on benefits, that have been employed by the Medicaid program. The arbitrary nature of these limits might serve to restrict benefits without regard to patients' clinical conditions.

Public drug insurance plans that are founded on the assumption of no patient cost sharing would have to rely on special administrative mechanisms to control costs. One of the most important of these mechanisms—the maximum-allowable-cost regulations, which attempt to control costs of both ingredients and dispensing fees—developed out of dissatisfaction with the apparently excessive costs of drug benefits under Medicaid. Ingredient reimbursement would be set to approximate the actual prices at which outlets of various sizes could expect to obtain drugs. To be fair, reimbursement rates would have to allow for various reimbursement levels to pharmacies in different classes, because pharmacies do experience different wholesale prices. In dispensing fees, too, economies of scale imply that a "fair" rate for one class of pharmacy would not be "fair" for another. How well the regulations would work remains to be seen. Although drug coverage under the original Kennedy-Corman bill calls for administrative arrangements of this type, Senator Kennedy has proposed an alternative: direct negotiation between the government and drug manufacturers to obtain the best ingredient prices possible for materials used in federally paid benefits.

The challenge faced by administrative costs controls would be less formidable in an NHI system that involved cost sharing. With cost sharing, the final purchaser would have a real incentive to seek out the most efficient source of supply, and now that pharmacies may advertise, such seekers might more easily be able to find the most efficient source. One of the simplest cost-sharing schemes proposes to cover drug ingredients only, with the patient paying the dispensing fee. Perhaps a more effective cost-sharing method would be a scheme to cover drugs only after a significant deductible had been met.

Any drug cost-sharing scheme may be criticized on grounds that it deters needed utilization, but the burden of proof appears to lie solidly with people who claim such a problem is serious for other than the poor. The problems of the poor, however, are important enough to suggest reconsideration of the loss of substantial drug benefits that is implied by the planned elimination of Medicaid and by CHIP's cost-sharing requirements, by the cost-sharing and limited benefits of the Kennedy-Mills plan, and by the limited benefits of the Kennedy-Corman bill. In any case, one approach to cost sharing appears inferior to the others—that is, payment that is not allowed to vary by outlet. With such an approach, the competitive potential of patient-shared payment would simply be squandered.

In addition to the formidable administrative issues associated with the flow of funds in a drug insurance system, there is also widespread concern that excessive and uncoordinated drug taking does exist. The needs of both reimbursement and utilization review could be served through use of a computerized system in which a terminal would be located in nearly every pharmacy. There have been several proposals to introduce such a system at the same time that NHI coverage is introduced, but opponents argue excessive costs. Although such a system might not be able to pass a cost-benefit test, it appears that investigation of the matter remains to be done. The benefits of the system would include reduced loss of national output from improper drug use, reduced unnecessary pain and suffering, reduced excessive and costly drug prescribing, and quicker and more efficient processing of claim information.

Significant changes in the pattern of drug use in the United States would powerfully affect the nation's health. Under a national health insurance program, the aggregate use of drugs would certainly rise as a consequence of increased physician visits and increased drug insurance coverage for part of the population. Conversely, the abolition of Medicaid could reduce drug benefits for many persons; the effect of reduced benefits on the health of affected persons is uncertain. Such a major change in coverage without a better understanding of the effects on health, as well as on total and government drug expenditures, appears most unwise. Equally important is the study of a control mechanism to facilitate both utilization review and cost control.

Chapter 12
DENTAL CARE

ROBERT T. KUDRLE

S EVERAL major national health insurance bills include important provisions for dental care.[1] Although such benefits would certainly cost billions of dollars, dental coverage has received little attention from government researchers, academic analysts, or congressional committees.[2] This chapter explores the issues that must be faced in considering dental coverage. First, the present dental care situation is examined; then various questions surrounding the provision of publicly provided benefits are investigated.

Dental health care has many characteristics that differentiate it from medical care in general. Perhaps most important is that while oral health is a well-defined concept, oral disease is seldom debilitating or fatal. This fact goes far to explain the enormously varied habits of individuals and families with respect to dental care. In the most recent survey of Americans concerning their dental habits, taken in 1975, only 50 percent of the population had seen a dentist at all during the year,

---

[1] This chapter is concerned with routine dental care. Dental treatment that requires hospitalization is covered by most national health insurance bills as if it were medical treatment.

[2] There has been some important research on the subject but most of it has not principally concerned U.S. national health insurance. See Paul J. Feldstein, *Financing Dental Care: An Economic Analysis* (Lexington, Mass.: D.C. Heath, 1973) and his *Health Associations and the Demand for Legislation* (Cambridge, Mass.: Ballinger Publishing Company, 1977), Chapter 3; Owen McBride, "Restrictive Licensing of Dental Paraprofessionals," *The Yale Law Journal* 83 (1974):806–26; R.G. Evans and M.F. Williamson, *Extending Canadian Health Insurance: Options for Pharmacare and Denticare* (Toronto: University of Toronto Press, 1978); Willard G. Manning and Charles E. Phelps, *Dental Care Demand: Point Estimates and Implications for National Health Insurance* (Santa Monica: The Rand Corporation, 1978).

more than 14 percent of the population had not seen a dentist for five years or more, and another 10 percent had never seen a dentist. People who visit the dentist regularly may constitute only 25 percent to 30 percent of the population.[3]

Although there is widespread disagreement about the most appropriate set of indices of poor dental health,[4] three measures appear most often in the literature: the extent of untreated dental caries ("cavities"), the extent of periodontal (tissues surrounding the teeth) disease, and the extent of edentulousness (toothlessness) in the population. Oral cancer, which attacks perhaps 24,000 persons annually, is a vastly more serious affliction, but the treatment, as opposed to the detection, of the malady is beyond the scope of dentistry.[5] Dentistry also treats dental malocclusion and various major and minor oral disorders resulting from infection, accidents, or congenital factors.

Dental disease is rampant in the United States. The average sixteen-year-old has 1.9 untreated decayed teeth; the average adult between the ages of thirty-five and forty-four has 8.1 missing teeth. Moreover, in a survey taken in the early 1960s, three-quarters of all adults had periodontal disease, one-quarter of them to an extent professionals deemed "serious." [6]

[3] U.S. Department of Health, Education, and Welfare (DHEW), Public Health Service (PHS), Health Resources Administration (HRA), *Current Estimates from the Health Interview Survey, United States, 1975* (Washington, D.C.: U.S. Government Printing Office, 1976), p. 28; John F. Newman and Odin W. Anderson, *Patterns of Dental Service Utilization in the United States: A Nationwide Survey* (Chicago: Center for Health Services Administration, University of Chicago, 1972).

[4] Children's Dental Health Research Project, *Report to the Minister of Health, British Columbia and the President, The College of Dental Surgeons of British Columbia* (Victoria: Queen's Printer, 1975), Chapter 2, pp. 1–10.

[5] Max H. Schoen, "Dental Care Delivery in the United States," in John I. Ingle and Patricia Blair, eds., *International Dental Care Delivery Systems* (Cambridge, Mass.: Ballinger Publishing Company, 1978), p. 188. Furthermore, it is possible to have nondentists inspect for symptoms of such disease as part of a physical examination.

[6] DHEW, National Center for Health Statistics, *Decayed, Missing, and Filled Teeth Among Youth 12–17 Years, United States*, series 11, no. 144 (Washington, D.C.: U.S. Government Printing Office, 1974), p. 13; DHEW, National Center for Health Statistics, *Decayed, Missing, and Filled Teeth in Adults, United States, 1960–1962*, series 11, no. 23 (Washington, D.C.: U.S. Government Printing Office, 1967), p. 4;

Poor dental health hastens the onset of tooth loss, although the rates of loss differ widely among people of different nations.[7] In 1971, 11.2 percent of all adults in the United States had no natural teeth (down from 13 percent in 1957–58). This figure climbs to about half in the group age sixty-five and older.[8]

Not only are most dental problems not fatal, they also are often virtually undetectable by the patient for a long period of time—sometimes until the problem has become so serious as to be beyond repair. A trip to the dentist takes both time and money. It also evokes the (largely unjustified) fear of pain, a further reason for low utilization relative to medical care even when symptoms of trouble are present.[9] Considering these factors, it is perhaps not surprising that contact rates— the percentage of all persons getting dental care in any one year—show relatively small differences for fully insured and for uninsured populations. In the United States today, contact rates are about 50 percent, while studies of fully insured populations in the United States and elsewhere in North America have seldom found utilization rates that exceeded 70 percent. These use rates contrast with dentists' judgment that everyone should seek professional care at least once a year.[10]

Few people maintain that any "crisis" exists in dentistry: The subsector is too small, and concern about services is of

---

DHEW, National Center for Health Statistics, *Periodontal Disease in Adults, United States, 1960–1962*, series 11, no. 36 (Washington, D.C.: U.S. Government Printing Office, 1965).

[7] Experts are at a loss to understand the variation, which appears only loosely related to the extent of dental disease. See Lois K. Cohen, "Dental Care Delivery in Seven Nations: The International Collaborative Study of Dental Manpower Systems in Relation to Oral Health Status," in Ingle and Blair, eds., *International Dental Care*, p. 213.

[8] Data are shown later in this chapter, Table 29.

[9] Newman and Anderson, *Patterns of Dental Service Utilization*, p. 58; James Hassett, "Why Dentists Are a Pain in the Mind," *Psychology Today* 11 (January 1978):60–64.

[10] A large part of the dental profession advocates more frequent visits, and the slogan "See your dentist twice a year" became well known in the United States during the 1960s. Many analysts in the profession, however, doubt that there are significant gains from checkups at less than yearly intervals. See Evans and Williamson, *Extending Canadian Health Insurance*, p. 150; A. Shieman, "An Evaluation of the Success of Dental Care in the United Kingdom," *British Dental Journal* 135 (September 18, 1973):277.

insufficient intensity to attract much public attention[11] Yet problems exist in dental care. Before examining possible features of NHI dental coverage, it is useful to consider those problems under the rubrics familiar to those examining the difficulties of the medical care system: cost, access, and quality.

The most widely accepted justification for government action in the health care field, catastrophic expense, is certainly a minor problem in dentistry. In 1970, when dental expenditure in the United States was about $22 per capita, only 11.5 percent of families and single adults reported spending more than $250 a year for dental services and only 4.1 percent more than $500.[12] When one considers that these figures include the costs for correction of nondebilitating orthodontic problems—expensive procedures that would not be covered under any proposed public dental insurance—it seems clear that unanticipated dental expenditure is unlikely to be a significant hardship for many families. Because of the discretionary nature of most dental work, high levels of observed expenditures usually do not imply catastrophe. This is true both when there is a vast amount of routine work necessary because of accumulated neglect and when expensive procedures are elected at a certain time.

Private insurance has grown rapidly in recent years but still plays only a minor role in dental coverage. In 1974, only 15.8 percent of the civilian population had some form of dental coverage, and nearly all of it included coinsurance. Dental coverage is dominated by group policies; adverse selection plagues individual coverage. Of the total $10 billion expenditure on dental care in 1977, only 15.5 percent was paid by private insurance and 5.0 percent by the government; the rest was out-of-pocket.[13]

Table 29 shows some important data about the changing dental care sector. Although dental fees and expeditures have risen dramatically in recent decades, the increase has been

[11] American Dental Association (ADA), Task Force on National Health Programs, *Dentistry In National Health Programs* (Chicago: American Dental Association, 1971), pp. 94–96; Burson-Marsteller, *Dental Health and the Power Elite, Survey I*, 1975 (mimeographed).

[12] DHEW, PHS, HRA, "Family Out-of-Pocket Health Expenses—U.S. 1970," *Vital and Health Statistics*, series 10, no. 103, p. 22.

[13] Robert M. Gibson and Charles R. Fisher, "National Health Expenditures, Fiscal Year 1977," *Social Security Bulletin* 41 (April 1978):7.

Table 29

SELECTED CHARACTERISTICS OF THE U.S. DENTAL CARE SYSTEM, VARIOUS YEARS

Year	1 Dental Expenditures per Capita (in current dollars)	2 Dental Expenditures per Capita (in 1967 dollars)	3 Annual Dental Visits per Capita	4 Annual Visits per Dentist	5 Population per Dentist	6 Expenditures per Dentist (in 1967 dollars)	7 Auxiliaries per Dentist
1950	$ 6.12	$ 8.49	1.47	2,604			1.04
1955	8.72	10.87	1.51	2,977	1,977	$21,095	1.18
1960	10.65	12.01	1.56 (1958)		2,017	24,224	
				3,119 (1961)			1.31 (1961)
				3,343 (1964)			1.36 (1964)
1965	13.87	14.68	1.62 (1964)	3,565	2,070	29,947	
1970	21.56	18.54	1.81	3,670	1,967	36,468	1.40
1975	36.06	22.81	1.91		1,907	43,499	1.81

Source: All data except those for 1975 are derived from material appearing in Tables 2.1–2.5, and 3.5 of Paul Feldstein, *Financing Dental Care: An Economic Analysis* (Lexington, Mass.: D.C. Heath, 1973). The 1975 data on dental expenditures are from Robert M. Gibson and Charles R. Fisher, "National Health Expenditures, Fiscal Year 1977," *Social Security Bulletin*, July 1978. Data on dental visits in 1975 are from American Dental Association, *The 1975 Survey of Dental Practice*, Chicago, 1975. Data on dentists and auxiliaries for 1975 were provided by Mr. Jim Ake of Bureau of Health Manpower, Health Resources Administration, Public Health Service, Department of Health, Education, and Welfare.

overshadowed by even more rapidly rising subsectors in medical care. Between 1950 and 1976 dental fees rose by 173 percent, by comparison with 245 percent for medical care as a whole and 139 percent for all goods and services. In 1929, per capita dental care costs of $3.87 amounted to 13 percent of total per capita health expenditure, while the 1977 per capita figure of $45.41 was only 6.2 percent.[14]

Although costs for dental services may not have caused popular alarm, these costs have been a continuing source of concern for policy analysts, who note that there are two candidates for every place in dental school and that the rate of return to dental education (one measure of the "profit rate" from being a dentist) is about 25 percent.[15] The American Dental Association (ADA) effectively controls the number of dentists produced through the stringency of its accreditation standards.[16]

Any NHI plan should aim to promote the more efficient delivery of health care services and to avoid freezing in place any present inefficiencies. This consideration is of utmost importance in the design of a dental care benefit, because there is overwhelming evidence that the present personnel mix in the delivery system is extremely inefficient. There are too many fully trained dentists in relation to auxiliary personnel, and the potential savings from rationalization are much greater than those that would result from reducing the rate of return to dentists.[17]

The issue of auxiliary use is perhaps more sharply posed in the dental profession than in any other health profession. Dentistry is very largely the application of a series of manual techniques of various kinds; for decades observers both inside and outside the profession have questioned whether it is really necessary to employ a completely trained dentist to perform

---

[14] Ibid., p. 15; *Statistical Abstract of the United States* (Washington, D.C.: U.S. Government Printing Office, 1978).

[15] Alex R. Maurizi, *Public Policy and the Dental Care Market* (Washington, D.C.: American Enterprise Institute for Public Policy Research, 1975), p. 7.

[16] Feldstein, *Health Associations and the Demand for Legislation*, p. 93.

[17] DHEW, PHS, HRA, *The Effects of Task Delegation on the Requirements for Selected Health Manpower Categories in 1980, 1985, and 1990* (Washington, D.C.: U.S. Government Printing Office, 1974), pp. 3.1–3.24.

most of the functions for which he or she is formally trained and legally responsible.[18]

Dental auxiliaries include dental technicians, dental hygienists, and dental assistants, as well as secretary receptionists.[19] Of the 2 percent to 3 percent annual increase in the productivity of dental practice between 1955 and 1970, about 1 percent is attributable to technical change, principally higher-speed drilling equipment, while the remainder can be assigned to increased scale and increased use of auxiliaries shown in Table 29.[20] By the late 1960s, more than half of all dentists still employed only one auxiliary or none, despite estimates that practice productivity strongly increases with use of as many as six or seven auxiliaries (with net income rising accordingly).[21]

In an attempt to explain the apparently modest use of auxiliaries, several observers have suggested that the demand for dental services has not been strong enough to permit greater auxiliary use. Such a suggestion, however, involves considerable theorizing about the behavior of the market for dental services. If the market were competitive, dentists would expand their own practices through the use of auxiliary personnel and price competition—essentially forcing the rationalizing of production in the industry. In fact, most members of the dental profession, in common with other health professionals, have maintained that price competition is unethical, and the pro-

---

[18] G.S. Millberry, "Possibilities and Means of Improving Dental Conditions in the United States," *American Journal of Public Health* 29 (April 1939):321–25.

[19] Dentists undergo four years of professional training, but dental technicians, who work in dental laboratories fabricating artificial teeth and dentures, usually have two years of formal training beyond high school. Dental hygienists, who perform prophylaxes (teeth cleaning), expose and process radiographs, apply fluoride solutions, and teach proper toothbrushing and other dental health practices, also are usually trained two years beyond high school. Dental assistants sometimes are formally trained in courses of various lengths but most often are trained on the job. Assistants prepare patients for treatment, keep the operating field clear, mix filling materials, and pass instruments; many assistants also perform clerical functions.

[20] For a discussion of alternative measures of technological progress, see Feldstein, *Financing Dental Care*, pp. 68–73.

[21] Ibid.; DHEW, *Task Delegation*, pp. 3.1–3.24.

fession typically has banned advertising.[22] Fees have been kept at levels that allow for a comfortable net income on the basis of a very "dentist-intensive" practice. There is considerable evidence that many dentists—particularly older dentists with little if any formal training in the use of auxiliaries—have little "taste" for supervision, and the absence of price competition in the industry has permitted dentists practicing with modest assistance to flourish. Thus, while practices employing auxiliaries have grown more rapidly than the others and auxiliary use has grown with the market, there has been no compulsion for the less efficient practitioners to conform.[23]

Turning from cost to access, there is abundant evidence that both level of income and class-related attitudes are powerful determinants of contact with the dental care system. One of the most frequently used measures of contact with the system is the number of persons who make the professionally suggested annual visit. Table 30 shows the change over time for

[22] The Federal Trade Commission recently has moved to bar organized dentistry from disallowing advertising by dentists, but it is unlikely that this action will produce a marked change in the behavior of the industry. Although there are more than 100,000 dentists in the country, professional solidarity will probably prevail in the future as it has in the past in those few states where advertising has been legal. Evans and Williamson (*Extending Canadian Health Insurance*, pp. 165–66) rightly note that the professional office is an effective advertising medium; it is particularly effective for propagandizing patients about the poor care delivered by dentists who do not meet generally accepted canons of behavior.

[23] In addition to the problems of varying tastes and inadequate demand, dentists face uncertain demand and uncertain input markets. Expansion of a practice requires commitment of capital, and when uncertainty about utilization exists, caution is dictated. This caution is reinforced by the fact that all auxiliary personnel work directly under the dentist's supervision, and the entire operation must shut down if the dentist is ill (another factor contributing to the lower use of auxiliaries by older dentists). In sparsely populated areas where there are thin labor markets for the auxiliaries themselves, it may be risky to set up facilities based on the use of auxiliaries. The young women who dominate the market participate in it for unusually short periods of time. (Evans and Williamson, *Extending Canadian Health Insurance*, pp. 171–213.) The experience of medicine suggests another reason for caution about auxiliary use: fear of malpractice suits. Although dentists are responsible for all of the work that goes on in their offices, malpractice is not a serious problem in dentistry, a fact reflected in the low cost of malpractice insurance. Joseph Lipscomb, *Legal Restrictions on Input Substitution for Production: The Case of General Dentistry* (Durham, N.C.: Duke University Institute for Policy Sciences and Public Affairs, 1977) (mimeographed), p. 33.

Table 30

PERCENTAGE OF PERSONS VISITING A DENTIST
DURING SELECTED YEARS, BY SELECTED
CHARACTERISTICS, 1953, 1963, AND 1970

Characteristic	Percentage Seeing a Dentist		
	1953	1963	1970
Sex			
Male	31	36	44
Female	36	40	46
Ages			
1– 5	10	12	21
6–17	44	47	56
18–34	44	46	52
35–54	39	43	46
55–64	25	32	34
65+	13	19	26
Family income			
Under $2,000	17	16	23
$ 2,000–$3,499 }	23	25	23 } 28
3,500– 4,999 }	33		33 }
5,000– 7,999 }	44	40	35 } 40
7,500– 9,999 }			44 }
10,000–12,499 }	56	58	51 }
12,500–14,999 }			50 } 55
15,000–17,499 }			53 }
17,500+ }			67 }
Race			
White	—[a]	43	47
Nonwhite	—	20	24
Education of family head			
8 years or less	—[a]	25	27
9–11 years	—	35	39
12 years	—	48	49
13+ years	—	55	61
Residence			
Standard Metropolitan Statistical Area (SMSA), central city }	—[a]	42	41 }
SMSA, other urban }	—		54 } 47
Urban, non-SMSA }	—		45 }
Rural, nonfarm	—	37	41
Rural, farm	—	27	40
Total	34	38	45

[a] Not available for 1953.

Source: Ronald Andersen, Joanna Lion, and Odin W. Anderson, *Two Decades of Health Services* (Cambridge, Mass.: Ballinger Publishing Company, 1976), p. 61.

the U.S. population according to various characteristics. Females see dentists more regularly than do males, although the gap has narrowed substantially over time; the contact rate by age is higher for adolescents and young adults than for young children or older persons.

Blacks have a much lower contact rate than do whites, persons with higher education have more contact than persons with less education, and the rich have much higher contact than the poor. Despite their greater contact with dentists, higher-income groups have a somewhat higher level of dietary-induced dental disease than do less affluent groups. More than lack of money keeps the poor (and other people) away from dentists. The typical state Medicaid program provides free, routine dental services for children, and persons under age twenty constituted about 60 percent of all of those enjoying some Medicaid dental benefits. Nevertheless, only a fifth of the persons in this group received any dental care at all in 1970.[24] The income difference in untreated disease is clearly shown in Figure 8.

Finally, although rural and urban populations had markedly different levels of contact with the dental care system in earlier years, the rural population's contact has increased greatly in recent years. The most common measures of geographic maldistribution of personnel in medical practice are closely paralleled in dentistry.[25] In a 1970 survey of dentists, the percentage of dentists in small towns who were "too busy to treat all people requesting appointments" was more than four times as large as the percentage in cities of 1 million or more (35.6 percent to 8.3 percent), while nearly twice as high a fraction in the larger places were "not busy enough" (10.3 percent to 19.6 percent).[26]

---

[24] DHEW Advisory Committee on Dental Health to the Secretary, *Report and Recommendations* (Washington, D.C.: U.S. Government Printing Office, 1973), p. 13.

[25] The oft-cited difference between New York and South Dakota, the two states with the greatest and least number, respectively, of non-federally employed physicians (there are 2.79 times as many physicians per capita in New York as in South Dakota) can be compared to the most extreme dentist ratio of 2.75 that is found by comparing New York with Mississippi. The comparison with South Dakota is 1.83. U.S. Congress, *National Health Insurance Sourcebook* (Washington, D.C.: U.S. Government Printing Office, 1976), pp. 118, 201–02.

[26] *Journal of the American Dental Association* 85 (1972):669–72.

Figure 8

AVERAGE NUMBER OF FILLED, DECAYED, AND
MISSING PERMANENT TEETH PER PERSON
AMONG YOUTHS AGES 12–17 IN THE UNITED STATES,
BY FAMILY INCOME, 1966–70

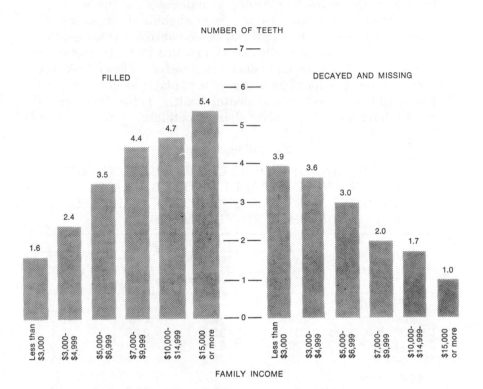

Source: DHEW, National Center for Health Statistics, Decayed, Missing, and
Filled Teeth Among Youth 12-17 Years, United States, series 11,
no. 144 (Washington, D.C.: U.S. Government Printing Office, 1974),
p. 10.

The distribution of dentists in the United States is not wholly a reflection of dentists' practice preferences interacting with demand. Dentists are licensed to practice by the states, and there is evidence that licensing exams have been widely used to bar entry. The failure rate may be controlled at a high level, and certain procedures heavily stressed in dental schools located in the state may figure prominently in the exams.[27] Nevertheless, practitioners are overwhelmingly opposed to general relicensure or recertification to control service quality once a dentist has been allowed to practice in a given state.[28]

The roles of income and education deserve a closer look, for each has independent importance in explaining contact with the dental care system and dental health. Table 31 shows a cross-tabulation of the edentulous (toothless) population of

Table 31

PERCENTAGE OF EDENTULOUS PERSONS AGES
45+ IN THE U.S. POPULATION, BY FAMILY
INCOME, AGE, AND EDUCATIONAL LEVEL
OF THE INDIVIDUAL, 1971

Age and Educational Level	Family Income			
	All Incomes	Less than $5,000	$5,000–$9,999	$10,000+
			Percent	
45–64 Years				
Total [2]	23.3	32.9	27.7	16.3
Less than 9 years	34.3	36.9	34.3	30.1
9–11 years	28.7	33.9	30.4	24.9
12+ years	15.9	25.2	21.4	12.1
65+ Years				
Total [2]	50.7	56.4	46.6	38.9
Less than 9 years	58.0	60.2	56.1	50.1
9–11 years	51.1	54.9	47.0	42.4
12+ years	37.2	46.1	33.9	29.6

[1] Includes unknown income.
[2] Includes unknown education.

Source: DHEW, National Center for Health Statistics, *Edentulous Persons, United States, 1971*, series 10, no. 189 (Washingon, D.C.: U.S. Government Printing Office, 1974), p. 5.

---

[27] L. Benham, A. Maurizi, and M.W. Reder, "Migration, Location and Remuneration of Medical Personnel: Physicians and Dentists," *Review of Economics and Statistics* 50 (August 1968):338.

[28] *Journal of the American Dental Association* 85 (1972):1270.

the United States by education and income. It can be seen that, in percentage terms, education is actually a more powerful determinant of this ultimate measure of dental health than is income. Obviously, people do not study the benefits of dental care in high school or college. What the education variable shows is that personal attitudes about dental care are heavily tied to class-related values, and that volition is a widely varying determinant of the use of the dental care system.

Quality problems also are important in dental care, but they have generated little public outcry. There is a widespread belief, not controverted by objective evidence, that the average quality of dentistry performed in the United States is unsurpassed by that in any other country. But abundant evidence also exists that a substantial amount of inferior work is performed in this country. A study of the dental work done on a group of urban schoolchildren in the Midwest found that in 44.3 percent of the cases, the work was of unacceptable quality.[29] This result is very similar to that of another survey done several years earlier with a completely different population.[30]

Public programs also have experienced quality problems. A commentator on the New York City Medicaid experience reported that some Medicaid spot checks revealed such negative indications of quality as to suggest, "aside from the obvious," that the standards established by Medicaid with the assistance of academicians might not adequately reflect the realities of daily practice. Alternatively, he said, Medicaid examiners might have been too rigidly interpreting these ideal standards in completing their evaluation forms. The dental profession was therefore asked to help revise the standards.[31] The New York experience indicates that quality of care varies considerably and that average care quite possibly falls short of what is considered good dental practice. The monitoring academicians were, after all, teachers of dentistry who, in most cases, were also practicing dentists.

It is important to emphasize two other considerations about

---

[29] R.A. Bagramian, J. Jenny, P.J. Woodbury, and J. Proshek, "Quality Assessment of Restorations in a Population of School Children," *American Journal of Public Health* 65 (April 1975):397–99.

[30] D.L. Moore and J.L. Stewart, "Prevalence of Defective Dental Restorations," *Journal of Prosthetic Dentistry* 17 (1967):372–78.

[31] Morton A. Fisher, "Quality Controls," *The New York State Dental Journal* 37 (1971):26.

dental care before discussing approaches to care under a national health insurance program. The first point is that probably no other part of the health care system better illustrates the difference between professionally defined need and effective demand than does dental care. The most casual discussion with a dental practitioner reveals a deep regret—sometimes angry, usually wistful—that people simply do not care enough about their teeth. Unlike physicians' views of the situation in medicine, members of the dental profession do not regard most people's contact with the dental care system, even by the educated and the affluent, as generally adequate.

The second point also illustrates a current distinction in health policy discussions with respect to the relative effectiveness of personal "preventive" behavior, the impact of professional "prevention," and the treatment of disease. Despite the enormous growth in recent years of preventive procedures in dentistry, the lion's share of effective activity in the U.S. dental care sector is now expended in treatment of disease. There is some evidence that the preventive procedure, plaque removal, can lessen the ravages of periodontal disease, but little that "prevention" can significantly retard the onset of decay. The only widely used preventive measure that has been shown to result in a lower incidence of dental caries is the introduction of fluoride into the mouth. Although fluoride can be applied to the teeth during a visit to the dentist, introducing fluoride into the public water supply is more effective and much cheaper. By the use of fluoridated water or fluoride treatments, caries incidence can be reduced by as much as two-thirds.[32]

This discussion is not intended to suggest that preventive behavior is unimportant; indeed, most people could dramatically increase their dental health at the cost of only a few minutes a day. Still, it is not clear that *any* significant long-range behavior modification for any large group has resulted from the broad range of foreign or domestic programs aimed

[32] Advisory Committee, *Report and Recommendations*, p. 21. Some people argue that preventive action has had meager results because it has been too infrequently employed. A recent Swedish study showed that professional plaque removal at close intervals combined with hygiene instruction and practice produced a dramatic improvement of dental health. The experiment made no distinction between clinical and personal intervention in attribution of the improvement. Jan Erik Ahlberg, "The Effect of Plaque Control in Sweden—A Preventive Experience," in Ingle and Blair, *International Dental Care*, pp. 215–24.

at raising dental health consciousness.[33] The provision of free dental care for children, therefore, should not be based on the assumption that such care will induce long-term improvement in dental health attitudes.

As alternative government dental benefit packages are considered, each proposal must be tested against the criteria of (1) increasing the efficiency of provision and avoiding unnecessary services, (2) improving quality, and (3) increasing access or lightening the financial burden for persons for whom the benefit package is designed. In dental care policy design, moreover, it is vital to consider the extent to which any proposed public plan will equalize access across income and education lines. Having pointed up these considerations, this chapter now turns to the following question:

- Who should receive any new government dental benefits?
- Which benefits should be offered?
- How should the system employ providers?
- Should patient cost sharing have any role in dental benefits?
- What are the central administrative issues for a dental benefit?

Coverage Alternatives

BENEFICIARIES

In a discussion of dental care coverage, it is convenient first to consider alternative population groups for government support. As for any benefit, a number of possible groups present themselves: young people, old people, high chronic users, catastrophic-level spenders, poor people, or the entire population. Special characteristics of dental care, however, have in fact generated only four main types of coverage suggestions: coverage for everyone, coverage for the aged, coverage for the poor, and coverage for children.

Only one major NHI proposal of recent years, the Kennedy-Corman plan, envisages covering the entire population for most dental services. In this plan, half the population—persons below the age of twenty-six—would receive entitlement during the first five years of the plan's operation, while the rest of

---

[33] Cohen, "Dental Care Delivery in Seven Nations," p. 211.

the population would be subsequently enrolled on a timetable to be determined by the governing Health Security Board. If there were no supply constraints, estimates suggest that universal coverage would lead the entire population to consume more than twice as much dental care as is currently being delivered. Such consumption could be expected to greatly reduce dental disease. All other countries that have introduced extensive publicly funded dental services have, as they overcame supply problems, experienced improved dental health (whether measured by a reduction in the extent of untreated disease or by a decline in edentulousness) in subsequent years above what would have been expected on the basis of increasing income and education.[34]

It is not clear, however, that these results justify universal national health insurance coverage of dental care. People already served by the system would probably account for most increased use of dental care. What some people might regard as an "access" problem—the failure of persons with adequate incomes to obtain as frequent or as complete care as the dental profession recommends—raises far more difficult philosophical questions in dentistry than this problem raises in medicine.

Proponents of NHI dental care coverage could argue that inadequate information about the consequences of lack of dental care provides a rationale for government intervention. The overwhelming majority of the population, however, must understand the relationship between lack of dental care and eventual loss of teeth.[35] To the extent that this relationship is now imperfectly understood, the appropriate public policy would be to improve that understanding. Moreover, the loss of natural teeth upsets the public less than it bothers dentists. An international study recently conducted by the World Health Organization and the U.S. Public Health Service revealed that "satisfaction with the condition of one's mouth shows close correlation with the percentages of edentulousness in each

---

[34] Material on the foreign experience is presented in Ingle and Blair, *International Dental Care,* passim. The Manning and Phelps estimates of the income elasticity of demand for dental care range from .55 for adult women to .87 for children while price elasticities are −.65 for adult men, −.78 for adult women, and −1.4 for children. The latter estimates are really only valid in a range close to market prices. (Elasticity is the ratio of percentage change of one variable—quantity—to percentage change in another—income or price.) Manning and Phelps, *The Demand for Dental Care,* pp. 21–22.

[35] Evans and Williamson, *Extending Canadian Health Insurance,* p. 125.

sample area. The more edentulous a population, the more satisfied they appear to be." [36] Furthermore, the maintenance of
functioning natural teeth is on average more expensive than
replacement by dentures,[37] which is the typical but scarcely
universal remedy. It is not clear why the preservation of a
nonpoor person's natural teeth at public expense in the face of
the person's own indifference should be considered sound public
policy.

In addition to violating the presumption of consumers' right
to choose for themselves by weighing benefits and costs, broad
NHI dental coverage could cost more than $20 billion in
taxes.[38] Apparently the public understands at least some of
these arguments, because only a minority of Americans reportedly favor "free" dental coverage.[39]

The feasibility of phasing in universal dental care over
several years, as the Kennedy-Corman bill proposes, also can
be strongly criticized. What might appear to be a prudent
phase-in of beneficiaries actually might increase total demand
by 70 percent over a five-year period; more than half the increase would take place immediately with free care for persons
under age eighteen.[40] Despite rapidly increasing capacity in
recent years, the current delivery system could not possibly
handle such an increase.[41]

---

[36] Cohen, "Dental Care Delivery in Seven Nations," p. 213.

[37] Evans and Williamson, *Extending Canadian Health Insurance*, p. 113.
The issue is treated somewhat more tentatively in Max H. Schoen,
"Dental Care and the Health Maintenance Organization Concept,"
Milbank Memorial Fund Quarterly 53 (Spring 1975):187.

[38] See the material on the Kennedy-Corman bill in the Appendix of
Robert T. Kudrle's "Dental Coverage Under National Health Insur-
ance," a report prepared for the Robert Wood Johnson Foundation under
Grant No. 2505, 1978 (mimeographed).

[39] ADA Task Force, *Dentistry in National Health Programs*, pp. 94–96.

[40] Kudrle, "Dental Coverage Under National Health Insurance,"
Appendix.

[41] The 1963 Health Professions Educational Assistance Act provided
funds for physical improvement and expansion of existing dental schools
and for construction of new schools. Although the ADA proclaimed its
interest in at least maintaining the then-prevailing dentist-population
ratio—which allowed for a very high proportion of dentists with more
patients than they could treat—it soon became apparent that funds were
being used mainly at existing schools and to an unintended extent for
improvements not related to class expansion. Beginning in 1965, Congress, over ADA objections, began mandating expansion of output as a
condition for funding. In the expansion that took place subsequently,
ten new dental schools were constructed to supplement the forty-eight

Moreover, it is difficult to imagine that the future supply of dentists could be expanded with the speed envisaged by the Kennedy-Corman bill, despite the fact that the dentist-population ratio is projected to rise by 19 percent between 1975 and 1990.[42] Hence extensive queuing for service would result, and the poor would be especially disadvantaged. In medicine it is often assumed that—because of the behavior of both physicians and patients—queuing will result in the earliest attention to the most serious medical problems, but the result is less certain in dentistry. Under a scheme like the Kennedy-Corman bill which disallows fee supplementation, uncovered individuals who could pay full market rates could be expected to get the maximum attention of most dental practices. The rest of the dentists' time could be directed to patients most closely linked to the more lucrative part of the practice, that is, young people whose parents were already patients. This bias could be partly overcome if government-paid fees were not controlled, but it is exactly this control that is hailed as an advantage of the NHI plans with central budgets and no charge at the point of service. The problem would moderate when and if supply conditions eased.

Furthermore, if the delivery system were to remain fundamentally unchanged, increased public coverage would generate a significant increase in dentists' incomes—even in the absence of an increase in fee schedules. There would thus be more "room" for dental practice in more desirable areas. How this factor might interact with the increased purchasing power of persons in underserved areas to increase or decrease service availability cannot be estimated with confidence.

Some analysts have tended to favor a rapid expansion in demand precisely in order to inundate the system and in so

---

already in existence. Feldstein, *Health Associations and the Demand for Legislation*, pp. 98–99; DHEW, *The Supply of Health Manpower: 1970 Profiles and Projections to 1990* (Washington, D.C.: U.S. Government Printing Office, 1974), p. 82.

[42] Ibid., p. 84. The ratio, 52.1 in 1975, is projected at 61.8 in 1990. Neither the Kennedy-Corman bill nor any of the other national health insurance bills makes explicit provision for the manpower its entitlements seem to imply. Kennedy-Corman mentions financial support for "the inclusion of dental services in systems of comprehensive health care," but it is silent on the means toward this end. As a practical matter, given the relative intensities of pressures for different services, it seems unlikely that dental services would have a very high priority as the Health Services Board allocated funds under Section F of the act.

doing to stimulate change. These people reason that expanded demand would provide a pretext for removal of present legal strictures on employment of so-called "expanded function dental auxiliaries." How these auxiliaries can be used is already one of the most controversial subjects in dentistry. Although definitions vary, all these auxiliaries are trained to perform many duties, including placing and carving dental restorations, activities that most states stipulate must be handled only by dentists. For example, only six states in 1977 allowed placement of amalgam ("silver") restorations by persons other than dentists. Yet the federal government has made special grants to dental schools to train dentists in the use of auxiliaries. Why does the dental profession resist the legal sanctioning of this new category of manpower?

Although some similarities exist between the productivity-increasing capabilities of the new auxiliaries and the capabilities of the accepted auxiliary categories, there are some critical differences. First, acceptance of the "expanded" functions is a long step toward admission that many traditional dentists' activities, including many in the restorative area, can be effectively delegated. Second, the expanded-function dental auxiliary adds to the capacity of dentistry in its central established role, restoration, rather than offering as the hygienist does a (lamentably) largely noncompeting service, "prevention." In fact, some proponents of the expanded-function auxiliary are interested in allowing the new personnel to do extractions and complete restorations;[43] a tiny minority even advocates unsupervised independent practice.

Third, the economies of scale that the use of the new auxiliaries promise are quite beyond anything experienced hitherto; such economies, up through the use of seven or even more auxiliaries per dentist, imply that if some dentists did want to compete on price, they would not quickly be limited by practice

---

[43] The issue has become a source of controversy in Kentucky, the state with the most liberal auxiliary laws. The state dental society became involved in a quarrel with the University of Kentucky Dental School about teaching hygienists to drill teeth and make extractions. While the university claimed that the dental school's academic freedom was being threatened, the dental society appeared to be supported by a statement of the president of the American Dental Association who urged that the Council on Dental Education, the ADA affiliate which accredits dental schools, be empowered to remove accreditation from a school with a curriculum that is at variance with ADA policies. *Los Angeles Times*, November 3, 1972, p. 8.

capacity. Such potential price cutters include some prepaid dental group practices and all dental services operated by health maintenance organizations.

Finally, much of dentists' recent resistance to use of expanded-function dental auxiliaries is rooted in the expansion of dental schools and the rising dentist-population ratio. Although as late as 1969 an overwhelming proportion of dentists believed a dentist shortage existed, opinion had reversed by 1976.[44] Dentists understandably view with alarm the prospect of yet more dental capacity through the use of expanded-function auxiliaries. Moreover, dentists' ability to "create" demand for their services is generally thought to be lower than physicians' ability to create demand.[45]

Proponents of NHI plans that would rapidly expand demand for dental care through universal coverage are motivated by a desire to weaken and override dentists' resistance to federal moves to limit state control of auxiliaries. It is far from certain, however, that the dental profession's opposition to the use of expanded-function auxiliaries would be overcome without an intervening period of chaos in the delivery of dental care. The possibility of inadequate supply raises serious doubts about the impact of universal coverage on the poor's use of dental care.

Universal dental coverage also can be objected to on grounds that it could tend to redistribute income from lower-income people who would not use the dental services offered to the mid- and higher-income people who would. As mentioned earlier, in contrast to similar demands by various classes when medical care is "free," the use of a "free" dental care system

---

[44] The survey evidence is cited in Lawrence H. Meskin, "Too Many Dentists? If So, What Then?" *Journal of Dental Education* 41 (1977): 602.

[45] Ibid. Some indication that dentists hold views about their ability to "administer" demand that differ from those of physicians is the much greater historical use in the dental profession of state examining procedures specifically designed to bar competition for "scarce patients." See Advisory Council, *Report and Recommendations*, p. 60. For observations that stress the dentist's discretion, however, see Michael H. Lewis, "Dental Care Delivery in Saskatchewan, Canada," in Ingle and Blair, *International Dental Care*, p. 56. Meskin suggests that the "target income" hypothesis about doctors' fees and service levels may hold for dentistry, but he suggests it more as a possible argument to use against the continuing increase in the supply of dentists than as established fact.

by persons of all ages is strongly and directly associated with the social class of the household head. The role of social class in determining the use of dental services has been confirmed in a study done for Group Health of New York in the late 1960s (see Table 32). The differences in demand for dental care by class also have been confirmed by the experience of the British National Health Service, although it employs a copayment for adult dental care.[46] Depending on the mix of taxes used to support the system and assumptions about their incidence, therefore, it is quite possible that dental coverage could redistribute income, especially when supply constraints are important, but even in their absence.

Table 32

AVERAGE ANNUAL DENTAL SERVICE USER RATES
PER 100 EXPOSURE YEARS, BY OCCUPATION CLASS
AND AGE OF SUBSCRIBER UNDER
PREPAID COVERAGE

Occupation Class	*All Ages*	*Age 2 or Under*	*Ages 3–5*	*Ages 6–14*	*Ages 15–54*	*Ages 55+*
Semiskilled or unskilled	27	11	29	40	26	17
Skilled and clerical	46	21	41	59	46	32
Professional, executive, and sales	55	15	49	61	57	54

Source: Helen Hershfield Avnet and Mata Kouvari Nikias, *Insured Dental Care* (New York: Group Health Dental Insurance, Inc., 1967).

Narrow coverage or plans covering particular segments of the population have been considered or employed in public programs. Dental coverage for the elderly, for example, has some political support, although none of the major NHI bills singles out the aged for dental coverage. Representative Claude Pepper of Florida introduced legislation in the 96th Congress to expand Medicare's Part B benefits to all dental services. But political pressure to make Medicare "complete" has never been so strong with respect to dental care as to drugs, and the reason is clear. Half the population have lost their teeth by

---

[46] Sheiham, "An Evaluation of the Success of Dental Care in the United Kingdom," passim.

age sixty-five; so it is not surprising that the elderly's overall rate of dental visits is half the national average and that more than three-quarters of these people have no dental expenses in any given year. Nonetheless, because many elderly people are poor, many may be failing to get dental care principally for financial reasons. Moreover, of the 23 million edentulous persons in the United States in 1971, most of whom were elderly, 2 million either had no replacement dentures or had incomplete dentures.[47] Because most state Medicaid programs do provide coverage for dentures, most of the people who lack some or complete dentures are likely to be the near poor. Dentures (complete with the necessary extractions) can cost several hundred dollars or more, but for most of the elderly such an expense is neither catastrophic nor continuing.

Extension of dental benefits to all elderly people would lighten the financial burden on some individuals, but would probably alleviate acute suffering for only a small number. Further, on the debit side, in addition to the general arguments advanced against adult coverage, the prospect of free dental care at age sixty-five would provide a perverse incentive in dental care. Many people today already appear rather indifferent to dental care. If that care became "free" at age sixty-five, an even greater number might fail to seek care until the state would pick up the bill. The distribution of need and the reaction to alternative schemes should be carefully studied before dental coverage is seriously considered for Medicare.

The Medicaid plans of some states are the chief public programs providing dental benefits to the adult poor today, and no major national health insurance plan proposes dental services focused on the poor. The reasons are not hard to find. In the face of relative client indifference and evidence in many states of considerable provider fraud and abuse, state govern-

---

[47] Information on the elderly and the dental care system can be found in DHEW, *Family Out-of-Pocket Health Expenses*, p. 22; DHEW, PHS, HRA, *Dental Visits, Volume, and Interval Since Last Visit, United States, 1969* (Washington, D.C.: U.S. Government Printing Office, 1972) p. 8; DHEW, PHS, National Center for Health Services Research, *Edentulous Persons, United States, 1971*, series 10, no. 189 (Washington, D.C.: U.S. Government Printing Office, 1974). Available data do not suggest conclusively whether persons who took good care of their teeth prior to age sixty-five could be expected to have less or greater benefit under a dental plan for the elderly than those who did not. Dentures are expensive, but so too is ongoing restorative dental care.

ments have found it relatively easy to cut dental benefits as they attempt to control the cost of medical assistance. Furthermore, the ease with which dental procedures can be shifted in time and the large numbers of persons who move on and off public assistance also create problems. Persons over age twenty constituted only 40 percent of all eligible beneficiaries of state Medicaid dental services in 1970 and the percentage has dropped in the years since.[48]

Dental care for children has been the principal focus of most domestic and foreign public programs, and such care has been incorporated into two major NHI proposals, the Kennedy-Mills bill and the Nixon-Ford CHIP bill. It is probably easier to justify these services than any other dental care. Permanent teeth are provided on a one-set-to-a-customer basis, and many Americans arrive at adulthood with teeth that are already severely damaged because of the poor judgment or inadequate resources of their parents.

Yet the provision of "free" or reduced charge dental care for children has been found to produce only modest gains in utilization. In their investigation of insured and uninsured young people in British Columbia, a Canadian research team estimated that simply "giving it away" would increase the number of persons brought into contact with the dental care system each year only from about 60 percent to about 70 percent. It cannot be known that contact would increase this much with such a system in the United States, assuming available services, although the initial contact rate is similar: 58.8 percent for persons between the ages of five and fifteen in 1969.[49] Data gathered from special programs within British Columbia suggest that an outreach program involving annual mail and telephone reminders at a cost of about thirty-two cents per child in 1974 might bring the utilization rate for a "free," private-practice-based plan up to 80 percent, but the senior author of the report doubted that such an increase was likely.[50]

Not only are overall utilization gains modest, but it appears that the poor may be as heavily represented in those not receiving care after the system is introduced as they were before. While the structure of demand changes resulting from the

---

[48] Advisory Council, *Report and Recommendations*, p. 13.

[49] Children's Dental Health, *Report*, Chapter 3, p. 3; DHEW, *Dental Visits*, p. 2.

[50] Evans and Williamson, *Extending Canadian Health Insurance*, p. 141.

provision of low-cost dental care for U.S. children is not known, Table 32 presented earlier is quite instructive. It shows the substantial difference in utilization rates by social class, even when price and, to a large extent, geographic access are not important problems. Moreover, it is likely that no really poor families are represented in the Group Health data.

A critical consideration in children's coverage is the age at which eligibility would cease. Both the Kennedy-Mills bill and the CHIP bill would limit coverage to children under age thirteen. The British Columbia team considering the coverage of a provincial plan carefully examined the question of the appropriate age limit, and their preference was for coverage to the seventeenth birthday. "Very high rates of decay are observed in the permanent dentition in the early teen years; it is felt that a plan that terminates too early may simply lead to a high rate of deciduous (baby tooth) restorations with no effect observable in the permanent teeth." [51] In other words, if benefits are terminated early, the entire program might be virtually a complete waste of money. The ADA also has recommended that coverage should extend at least until age seventeen.[52]

It is hard to think of any—except cost savings—rationale for ending the program in the early teens, unless program authorities believe that the regular dental care habit will have been instilled by age thirteen and will be regarded as of sufficiently high benefit to remain in the family budget when the cost goes up. A possible reason for picking age thirteen is that this age was for many years the cutoff time for treatment of children in the New Zealand school-based public dental program, which was initiated in the early 1920s and had reached nearly all schoolchildren in that country by the 1960s. But this age limitation was judged to be inappropriate, and in the 1960s three additional years of public insurance for private office visits were introduced.[53]

---

[51] Children's Dental Health, *Report*, Chapter 3, p. 5.

[52] U.S. Congress, House of Representatives, Committee on Ways and Means, *Hearings on National Health Insurance*, 93rd Congress, 2nd Session (Washington, D.C.: U.S. Government Printing Office, 1974), p. 485.

[53] Jay W. Friedman, "The New Zealand School Dental Service: Lesson in Radical Conservatism," *Journal of the American Dental Association* 85 (September 1972):611.

The New Zealand experience also casts very serious doubt on an argument often used in support of children's coverage: that it significantly shifts attitudes about dental care. Just four years after the cessation of public benefits (age sixteen), only 53 percent of New Zealand young people were receiving regular dental care. Furthermore, a recent survey suggests that only a third of adult New Zealanders—all of whom pay out-of-pocket—regularly visit the dentist for other than symptomatic relief.[54]

As already noted, past experience suggests that public insurance would induce a rather modest number of people to visit dentists regularly, but would considerably increase the demand for dental services among people who already visit dentists. As the discussion of universal coverage suggested, any rapid extension of free care, even if only to children, would enormously increase demand. If all young people under age eighteen were covered, demand is projected to increase by over 50 percent. Even if only those under age thirteen were covered, demand would increase 25 percent.[55] Both figures are for permanent new demand and not the flurry of "catch up" demand that would in fact accompany introduction of the plan. Therefore, however much the supply of dental care providers ultimately increased, there would undoubtedly be widespread bottlenecks and queuing in the short term.

As was suggested earlier, any reduction of attention by a dentist to any member of the affluent families that constituted the bulk of the practice would be expected to generate a negative reaction on the part of the entire family. Thus, in the short term, queuing would compound the differential use by class that would exist under an unconstrained "free" program. And the increases in demand that an exclusively children's program would prompt would be less likely to have the system-changing impact anticipated by some Kennedy-Corman supporters. This is especially true of the bills proposed that not only limit coverage to children under age thirteen but also require considerable cost sharing.

---

[54] James M. Dunning, "Deployment and Control of Dental Auxiliaries in New Zealand and Australia," *Journal of the American Dental Association* 85 (September 1972):621; Cohen, "Dental Care Delivery in Seven Nations," p. 213.

[55] See the Appendix of Kudrle, "Dental Coverage Under National Health Insurance."

The long-term effects on those underserved also are similar to those noted earlier. But, as is true of all of the bills, the further into the future a given program is initiated, the less formidable are the supply obstacles because of the expected increased capacity of the system relative to demand.

As the experience of Medicare and Medicaid reveal, an extremely important problem associated with partial-coverage public insurance systems is the control of practitioner fees. Both of the NHI proposals that would cover children's dental care, the Kennedy-Mills bill and CHIP, would allow fee supplementation—that is, they would permit dentists to charge some patients more than the plan's fee schedule. This provision would add to the attractiveness of serving exactly those young patients who now loom largest in most practices and whose family business dentists are most eager to keep. CHIP would complicate the access problem for the poor by disallowing supplementation in the subplan covering low-income families. Furthermore, to the extent that public insurance would raise average dental fees, dentists could aggravate supply problems by working a shorter week. Some evidence in time-series data indicates that this is likely.[56] Uniform disallowance of supplementation appears the best strategy. Despite the risk that lagging fees would cause dentists to redirect their attention to payers of full fees, children comprise such a large share of dentists' practices (about a third of a typical practice now, more with reduced prices for children) that sustained withdrawal from the program would be infeasible for most dentists. Multiple sources of payment would, however, greatly increase practitioners' bargaining power.[57] The result could be sustained pressure to maintain high fees to maximize access for the poor.

A related issue is the nature of the patient-practitioner relationship. In the British National Health Service, a *physician* must agree to treat a patient on an ongoing basis, but a *dentist* can either accept or reject a patient for a "course of treatment" that will bring the patient to "dental fitness." This option sometimes serves to reduce patients' benefit package because the dentist can claim that the government remuneration for

---

[56] Feldstein, *Financing Dental Care*, p. 68.

[57] In Canada, where strikes by medical personnel have occurred, this power includes the ability to "take a strike." See Evans and Williamson, *Extending Canadian Health Insurance*, p. 158.

the necessary treatment would not be enough to reimburse the dentist in full; therefore if the patient wants the work done, he or she must pay as a private patient. Any NHI dental care scheme introduced in this country should oblige dentists to accept patients for ongoing care.[58]

AN ALTERNATIVE DELIVERY SYSTEM

A major controversy in American dentistry concerns the possible adaptation for the United States of a school-based scheme such as the one pioneered in New Zealand which is now in general use or under official experiment in nineteen countries.[59] The scheme employs dental nurses who are specially trained in the relatively simple procedures of children's dentistry—almost exclusively examinations, radiographs, plastic restorations, prophylaxes, and fluoride treatments.[60] The services are performed in permanent facilities located in schools or in mobile facilities, the choice being determined by the number of children to be served in a given area. Dentists supervise the overall program and check all children periodically, but they are not physically present when most of the work takes place.

Supporters of a "dental nurse" program for this country point out that a major need is to get dental services to geographically isolated areas currently short of dentists. They argue that young people could presumably be recruited and trained in perhaps a two-year program to work in such areas— if only for a few years each. They also note that dentists, whose training takes up to six years, are overtrained for most of the dental care schoolchildren require.

In practice, the scheme has proved to increase the rate of contact children have with the dental care system—and of course the principal justification for dental coverage under

---

[58] For a criticism of this aspect of British dental care, see Michael A. Lennon, "Dental Care Delivery in the United Kingdom (England and Wales)," in Ingle and Blair, *International Dental Care*, p. 99.

[59] E.R. Ambrose, A.B. Hord, and W.J. Simpson, *A Quality Evaluation of the Specific Dental Services Provided by the Saskatchewan Dental Plan: Final Report* (Regina: Commercial Printers, 1976), p. 2.

[60] Evans and Williamson, *Extending Canadian Health Insurance*, pp. 145–47.

national health insurance is, by most accounts, to fight the "epidemic" of poor dental health among children in the United States.[61] Moreover, this increased contact has occurred at a cost considerably less than private practice costs. Estimates vary; the only fully operating North American scheme, in Saskatchewan, Canada, is still in a shakedown phase, but the director claims that already children are being treated for only 72 percent of the estimated private practice cost.[62] This figure corresponds well with careful estimates that the per patient cost of such a scheme would be from 66 percent to 71 percent of the cost of treatment in the private sector.[63]

Yet such a system departs fundamentally from current U.S. practice in two ways: the looseness of professional dentists' supervision of work performed by auxiliaries, and the performance by nondentists of "irreversible" operations, most notably the drilling of teeth for fillings. Even the most liberal states do not now permit such procedures.

Comprehensive outreach employing dentists who would directly supervise traditional or expanded-function auxiliaries, however, is impractical. According to computer simulations performed by the British Columbia team, using dentists to directly supervise all work would cost 10 percent more than the dental nurse scheme (ignoring any necessary changes in dental salaries), even when organized so that each dentist would employ eleven auxiliaries (including clerical help).[64] This implies a scale of operation so large that travel time and transportation costs might negate the access advantages of a "school-based" system.

Some leaders of the dental profession in the United States have announced their support for some version of the dental nurse system.[65] In view of the fact that one-third of the typical

---

[61] In addition to the emphasis of most foreign programs and Medicaid, the American Dental Association and the DHEW secretary's advisory council stress the needs of children above all others.

[62] Lewis, "Dental Care Delivery in Saskatchewan," p. 53.

[63] Evans and Williamson, *Extending Canadian Health Insurance*, pp. 149–55.

[64] Ibid., p. 148.

[65] The proponents, represented before the Ways and Means Committee in 1974 by Dr. Jay Friedman, Professor of Dentistry at the University of Southern California, and Dr. James Dunning, Professor of Dentistry Emeritus of Harvard, presented the dental nurse plan as a way to

dental practice is now devoted to the care of persons who would be treated under a school-based program, however, it is not surprising that most dentists have adamantly refused to consider such a policy.

The intensity of opposition first became evident at the 1972 annual meeting of the American Dental Association, when John Ingle, Dean of the University of South California School of Dentistry, proposed training of dental nurse personnel, even though no state law at that time permitted such persons to perform their full functions anywhere in the United States. The association went on record as opposing any auxiliary activity not carried out under the direct supervision of a dentist, and this position was reaffirmed in 1975. In an interview at the 1972 convention, the president of the ADA even opposed feasibility studies with the comment, "I am wondering what parent in this nation would want his children worked on by a second-rate dentist. I am opposed to this type of study because I don't think we need them (*sic*)." [66]

The ADA's opposition on quality grounds is highly suspect. There are now at least a dozen studies showing high patient satisfaction and no quality problems with properly trained dental auxiliaries. Prestigious, independent reviewers of the Saskatchewan program, in fact, found some procedures performed by auxiliaries to be of higher quality than those performed by dentists on students within the same group.[67] A recent editorial in *Operative Dentistry* admits that the quality issue is specious.

> Much of this research, however, was unnecessary because it had already been shown, in the 1920s in New Zealand and in the 1960s in Britain, that within a period of two years young women can be taught to

permit the extension of dental care to youngsters age seventeen for a cost comparable to the cost of an office-based scheme serving only those up to age thirteen. According to the reckoning of Friedman and Dunning, a child could be served for $35 a year under the school-based plan versus $100 under the present system. The source for the cost estimates provided by the two witnesses is not known, and the differences are considerably greater than those of the careful Canadian study. Committee on Ways and Means, *Hearings on National Health Insurance*, pp. 1217–57.

[66] Carl A. Laughlin, D.D.S., quoted in *Los Angeles Times*, November 3, 1972, p. 8.

[67] Ambrose, Hord, and Simpson, *A Quality Evaluation*, pp. 11–13.

give prophylaxes, prepare cavities, place restorations
of amalgam and silicate, extract teeth for children,
and provide education for patients. Moreover, the
quality of the treatment has been shown to compare
favorably with that provided by dentists.[68]

The provision of a dental benefit for children thus presents
policy makers with a dilemma. Coverage for office-delivered
services would probably have a modest impact on those pres-
ently underserved, while a system of proven effectiveness and
lower cost is stridently opposed by nearly all dentists.

BENEFITS

The precise scope of benefits under national health insurance
typically is a complex issue, but in dental coverage, kinds of
benefits to be covered are less controversial. Because most
people are relatively indifferent to dental treatment, offering
only diagnostic benefits would serve little purpose; no NHI
plan proposes such an approach. There is one benefit, however
—orthodontic treatment for nondebilitating conditions—that
is usually excluded from domestic public plans, from all major
NHI proposals, and from public coverage abroad. Except for
extreme cases which might cause the patient psychological
damage or impair physical functioning, orthodontic treatment
has been regarded as a luxury, much like cosmetic surgery.
While many persons of limited means might gain greatly from
such treatment, appropriate criteria of need are difficult to
apply, and cost might be difficult to control.

Some other benefits have been viewed with skepticism, and
many of these involve procedural frequency. An important
example in the preventive area is counseling. Although patients can be told at length how best to care for their own
teeth, there is little evidence that repetition in this area actually accomplishes much. Under an insured fee-for-service system, dentists would tend to exceed effective levels of instruction. Another area of benefit difficulty may be the removal of
baby teeth. Although this procedure sometimes is warranted
to prevent damage to permanent dentition, it has occurred
much more frequently under some unrestricted public pro-

---

[68] The article attempts to argue that the apparent savings from the
use of auxiliaries is illusory, but the cost concepts employed are faulty.
Operative Dentistry 2 (1977):1–2.

grams (as in Canada's provincial schemes for children) than elsewhere. The Quebec scheme, which is an office-based, fee-for-service type, experienced an extraordinarily high rate of deciduous extractions in its early months—more than three times the rate of the salaried dental nurse program in Saskatchewan. In Nova Scotia, also with a private-practice-based, fee-for-service system, it was necessary to restrict the frequency of performance of various preventive measures.[69]

It is recommended that any NHI dental coverage plan employing fee-for-service reimbursement should (1) restrict frequency of performance of some services for reimbursement, as is now done by most private insurance and Medicaid plans, and (2) monitor patient and practitioner profiles, which is now done only ineffectively.

The other category of benefit demanding close attention is that of extremely expensive procedures which involve considerable practitioner discretion. Some procedures involving endodontics (root-canal and pulp-chamber treatment) and prostheses might be subject to prior authorization as they are in most Medicaid plans, in much private insurance, and in many foreign programs. Like the other measures mentioned, prior authorization is not really a benefit limitation, but merely a check on the appropriateness of the service delivered.

Despite the importance of systems control, the fundamental aim of dental coverage is to induce more people to seek dental treatment. As a result, it is hard to rule out any specific benefits except orthodontics with a largely, or exclusively, cosmetic purpose.[70]

Methods of Payment

Most publicly supported dental care in the United States currently takes place using the fee-for-service system. (The principal exception is provided by the salaried dentists who staff various federal government programs.)[71] Under state

---

[69] Evans and Williamson, *Extending Canadian Health Insurance*, pp. 142–43 and 157.

[70] For a similar view, see Schoen, "Dental Care and the Health Maintenance Organization Concept," p. 185; Schoen, however, does not appear to rule out complete orthodontic coverage.

[71] Advisory Committee, *Report and Recommendations*, pp. 7–12.

Medicaid programs, dentists report services provided to the state agency for medical assistance and are reimbursed according to a "usual, customary, and reasonable" (UCR) fee or some variant on their own or fellow practitioners' fees, an ineffective set of constraints familiar to students of Medicaid and Medicare.[72] Determination of appropriate fees is less complex in dentistry than in medicine. There are relatively few procedures, and all are well defined in the "ADA Code of Dental Procedures and Nomenclature." Some reimbursement schemes attempt to trace the rise of a group of "usual, customary, and reasonable" fees over time by actually keeping track of the changing prices of all procedures, while others continuously survey only the basic unit in the relative value scale.[73]

Dental fees appear to vary considerably. According to one source, if a certain procedure had an areawide average of fifteen dollars, 80 percent of the fees would lie within two or three dollars of this amount, but the observed range, nevertheless, would be from as low as five dollars to as high as twenty-five dollars.[74] It is simply not known how much of the difference represents variations in the cost of practice operation, especially the rental of office space, variations in quality, or differential returns accruing to the dentist in a market characterized by highly imperfect information. As is the case with physician services, fee-for-service payment is overwhelmingly preferred by practitioners. Any substantial increase in public activity that failed to employ fee-for-service payment would encounter stiff opposition from established practitioners.[75]

Many of the disadvantages of a fee-for-service system in

---

[72] For a complete discussion of the problem of fee control under public insurance, see Chapter 2 of this volume.

[73] In addition to UCR systems, some private insurance is written with a table of maximum fees that will vary as a proportion of the average fee actually charged, hence implying varying copayment. This approach is particularly useful when total benefits paid must be kept within strict limits.

[74] This estimate was provided by an employee of Delta Dental Plan of Minnesota; the author has received similar information from other sources as well.

[75] Dentists' preferences about the exact mode of reimbursement within fee-for-service, however, vary considerably among the usual and customary approach, fixed fees, and table of allowances. See Robert D.

dentistry also are similar to those of medicine. Dentists have a continuing incentive to push against whatever fee restrictions might be instituted. They can, moreover, be expected to "administer" demand to the maximum extent ethically or legally permissible, and there is considerable latitude with respect to "appropriate" professional practice in both prevention and restoration. This discretion, combined with some conscious abuse, led to the difficulty already noted in the Quebec and Nova Scotia provincial programs for children.

The Saskatchewan dental nurse program's apparent success in controlling procedural frequency and other dimensions suggests that extensive use of salaried personnel in an NHI dental care benefit—at least in one aimed at children—should be seriously considered. It is often assumed that public employees are far outstripped by their private sector counterparts in the performance of similar tasks, but in dentistry, the meager available evidence suggests that the two groups have similar productivity.[76] If the experience of private versus public provision of services in other fields is any guide, however, dental practitioners in the public sector may demonstrate greater resistance to innovation and greater ability to press excessive wage claims than do private personnel. For these reasons, it appears that any study of the use of salaried personnel for the provision of dental services for children should consider the feasibility of contracting for services with competing private firms.[77]

The third major system of payment, capitation, has a scant history in dental care. As has been often noted, the term "capitation" is ambiguous in that it may refer either to the payment method by (or on behalf of) the patient, or to the

Eilers and Robert C. Jones, *The Attitudes and Anticipated Behavior of Dentists Under Various Reimbursement Arrangements* (Homewood, Ill.: Richard D. Irwin, Inc., 1972).

[76] One North American study is reported in Neville Doherty and Iftkhar Hussain, "Costs of Providing Dental Services for Children in Public and Private Practices," *Health Services Research* 10 (Fall 1975): 244–53. Comparable productivity is also reported in Sweden, with the salaried personnel only slightly behind. Jan Erik Ahlberg, "Dental Care Delivery in Sweden," in Ingle and Blair, *International Dental Care*, p. 140.

[77] The author of this chapter believes that all providers of publicly financed dental benefits should be far more carefully monitored than is now the case.

means of payment received by the provider. The dental market has so far produced three main varieties of the former kind of capitation scheme.

In recent years, dental service corporations, the so-called Delta Dental plans, have grown very rapidly in many states. These nonprofit corporations offer prepaid care (with deductibles and coinsurance) and are a professionally sponsored answer to a growing market for group insurance.[78] Although the conservative dental profession originally opposed the Delta plans, the plans have now won the support of those professionals and of state legislatures and are established in almost every state. There is some peer review, but most plans are sponsored by state dental societies and operate on as close to a fee-for-service basis as is possible for a prepaid plan. These plans have little incentive to control costs unless sharp competition is present; in this way they are much like both medical care foundations and Blue Shield plans.

Until recently, health maintenance organization (HMO) coverage for dental services had almost always involved contracts with fee-for-service dentists. Unlike the case in medicine, there is no good statistical comparison of the cost and quality of genuine HMO dentistry versus fee-for-service dentistry. Group Health of Minnesota, one of the nation's largest health maintenance organizations, recently opened a major in-house dental clinic for its subscribers, and its experience should be carefully observed. There is some indication that the hopes of the plan's designers to avoid point-of-service charges may have to be abandoned. The initial premium was set to compete with Delta Dental plans, which employed extensive cost sharing. By early 1979, too little revenue had been produced, but the plan's managers feared that if they raised the premium, enrollments would fall drastically.[79] This situation

---

[78] A cynic might conclude that, although dental care has never been an urgent item on the bargaining agenda between employers and employees, as many other health benefits have been won and as income gains have increased the cost difference between sheltered and unsheltered benefits, the "cheap" dollars of government-subsidized fringe benefits finally generated a demand for dental care. If the rate of growth of dental insurance coverage experienced during the *lowest* growth year of the early 1970s (14.7 percent) had continued, by the beginning of 1985, 63 percent of the population would have been covered. In 1974, however, there was an astonishing 52 percent growth in coverage.

[79] Information was provided by several employees and observers of Group Health Dental Plan in late 1978 and early 1979.

suggests some important lines of inquiry about possible differences between HMO medicine and dentistry. Group Health plan managers fear that, by comparison with the fee-for-service sector, the scope for cost savings through provision of fewer resources in treatment (consonant with good care) is far less in dentistry than in medicine. They also fear that the typical subscriber will not be willing to pay the extra dollars necessary to provide the volume of care the most demanding patients want.

In contrast to nonprofit health maintenance organizations such as Group Health, some for-profit prepaid dental group practices, particularly in California, have been accused of doing an extremely lucrative business by providing minimal care. The perverse temptations that have been regarded as immoral and unlikely in the case of HMO medicine, most notably letting the patient die, have a less dire and therefore perhaps a more relevant analogy in dentistry. It is usually cheaper to remove teeth than to care for them, so in a system with a strong incentive to limit the cost of treatment, standards of professional quality might need especially careful monitoring.

This discussion is particularly germane to the Kennedy-Corman bill, which specifically suggests that dental coverage for persons over age twenty-five may be limited to approved modes of service such as health maintenance organizations or prepaid nonprofit dental plans. (Under a Kennedy-Corman plan, the prepaid nonprofit dental plans could be expected to be quite different from the present nonprofit plans because the capitation fees presumably would be closely controlled.) Dealing with for-profit prepaid plans by simply disallowing them, however, seems inferior to careful monitoring of the quality of the care they give. In any event, such monitoring should take place in a publicly supported dental plan.

Patient Cost Sharing

It is no more technically difficult to employ patient cost sharing in dental care than it is in medical care, and private insurance coverage virtually always employs it. Furthermore, recent estimates of the price elasticity of dental care suggest that coinsurance could have considerable impact on demand.

Manning and Phelps estimate that a typical adult will demand 12 percent to 15 percent less service at 25 percent coinsurance than at zero price and that the comparable figure for children is about 22 percent.[80] Some state Medicaid programs have introduced copayment (Michigan, for example, charged three dollars for an adult visit in the mid-1970s), and although no formal statistical evidence is known to the writer, demand has been cut and some program savings realized. Copayment for children has been more widely resisted.

The practices of commercial insurers and the Delta Dental plans appear to be a poor guide for the use of cost sharing. They typically use a varying cost-sharing scheme in which preventive and diagnostic services and sometimes routine restorative services have minimum cost sharing (25 percent or less), while the most expensive restorative and replacement services require the highest payment (75 percent or more). In addition, there are usually both a deductible and a maximum annual benefit. Thus this schedule could be said to punish "bad behavior" and to reward continuing care. The fact is that most dental care is a budgetable expense. High episodes of expense rarely occur in the absence of sustained causative behavior by the person insured, and in any case, the high expenses can be rather easily spread over time. From another perspective, however, this schedule appears to put certain individuals (those who may be victims of earlier ignorance or family circumstances over which they had little or no control) at greater financial risk than other insured persons under a typical commercial or Delta plan.

The reasons for this coverage are obvious and have little to do with dental health. Changing populations of enrollees, many of whom may be calculating how to get the most out of temporary insurance coverage, could cause enormous cost control problems were cost sharing not handled as it now is. The Swedish national dental insurance scheme takes largely the opposite approach. It has low coinsurance for prophylaxis, but coinsurance for most procedures falls as the patient incurs more expenses in any one period.[81]

---

[80] Calculated from Manning and Phelps, *The Demand for Dental Care*, p. 25.

[81] Ahlberg, "Dental Care Delivery in Sweden," in Ingle and Blair, *International Dental Care*, p. 141.

As noted earlier, unlike the situation in medicine, public provision of benefits in dental care—even free care—does not disproportionately induce poor people to use the system. If, therefore, increasing the equality of access to the health care system for people in various social classes is a declared objective of the more comprehensive NHI plans, any cost sharing by the poor is inappropriate. Despite the earlier discussion that indicated that poor people are more indifferent toward dental care than rich people are, the poor are not insensitive to the prices they pay. No good evidence on their responsiveness exists,[82] but the very poorest children in the country more than doubled their annual contact with the dental care system between 1963 and 1970 when welfare entitlement burgeoned and Medicaid was introduced. This group experienced a much higher percentage increase than any other group in the country.[83] Still, many poor people consume less dental care at zero price than middle-class people consume at the market price. NHI bills have ignored this critical aspect of consumer behavior and have tended to treat dental coverage in much the same way as they treat other benefits. Kennedy-Mills would offer no deductible for special children's services such as dental care, but all beneficiaries would have to pay 25 percent coinsurance. CHIP would charge only 10 percent coinsurance for the very poorest and would offer no deductible for them, but both barriers would rise sharply with income.

A possible role for cost sharing in children's coverage schemes such as CHIP and the Kennedy-Mills plan might be to provide especially favorable prices for poor children when demand exceeds supply. The simplest version of this proposal would be to provide benefits to the poor alone; this solution might be superior to inundating the system with the demand

---

[82] Manning and Phelps have found that the rich are generally more responsive to price in dentistry than are the poor, and their explanation is plausible. The poor seek dental help in response to acute symptoms and thus have less flexibility with respect to price. Unfortunately, Manning and Phelps were unable to estimate the elasticity of demand for poor children satisfactorily. Manning and Phelps, "The Demand for Dental Care," p. 22.

[83] Ronald Andersen, Joanna Lion, and Odin W. Anderson, *Two Decades of Health Services* (Cambridge, Mass.: Ballinger Publishing Company, 1976), p. 61. The relevant category is that for children ages six to seventeen in families with annual incomes of less than $2,000.

that would result from providing free dental care benefits to all children. Nevertheless, if the objective of dental coverage for children is to prevent *both* the poor judgment and the low incomes of their parents from permanently ruining the children's teeth, a public program should not be satisfied with equalizing contact rates for various classes but should bring them all up to an acceptable level. As already noted, many children of even quite affluent parents do not have what professionals regard as an appropriate level of contact with the system.

Administration

In most respects, a dental care benefit is easier to administer than a medical care benefit. Although the variety of distinct dental procedures should not be underestimated, isolating procedures so that meaningful comparisons can be made appears generally easier in dental than in medical care. Furthermore, at least in principle, it is far easier to detect fraud and abuse and to control quality for a much larger amount of the total value of dental treatment than is the case in medicine. As one observer has noted, "Dentistry is unique in that almost all services involve hard tissues and therefore present the opportunity for an X-ray trail." [84] Radiographs supplemented by inspections of actual work done theoretically could hold dental practitioners' quality of performance to a very high standard. Dentists, however, have resisted quality monitoring, and their fear that high standards are not being widely met may be part of the reason.

Monitoring quality in a public dentistry program is closely linked to detection of intentional fraud. In their report on the problems of the New York City Medicaid program, Bellin and Kavaler estimated that between 5 percent and 10 percent of all dental work was of unacceptable quality or involved fraud.[85]

---

[84] Nathan C. Coms, "The Clinical Evaluation of Medicaid's Patients in the State of New York," *Journal of Public Health Dentistry* 33 (1973): 192.

[85] Lowell Eliezer Bellin and Florence Kavaler, "Policing Publicly Funded Health Care for Poor Quality, Overutilization and Fraud— The New York City Medicaid Experience," *American Journal of Public Health* 60 (May 1970):814.

Concern over statistics of this sort is evident in the attempts by private insurers to employ prior authorization for expensive procedures. Dentists have countered such attempts with legal challenges, just as they have sometimes fought prior authorization in Medicaid.

Possibilities for control in the dental area are suggested by the results of some state Medicaid initiatives. When the state of Michigan began requiring postprocedure X-rays for endodontics in order to verify that the work had been properly done, the number of claims dropped by 50 percent. Savings from this measure alone are estimated to be $1 million annually.[86] An ADA spokesman has lamented that between 5 percent and 10 percent of all dental practitioners were probably cheating on Medicaid claims.[87]

A comparison of the costs and benefits of a more careful monitoring of Medicaid dental claims is complicated by (among other things) the difficulty of separating out the dental costs from the other costs of a state's medical assistance program. Nevertheless, all available evidence indicates that monitoring state Medicaid programs for system abuse is below optimal level. Although Medicaid programs typically computer-check statistically deviant dental practices, some checking routines are rather unsophisticated, and often little is done to follow up deviant behavior. In the state of Minnesota, for example, only one dentist has been successfully challenged by the monitoring system in the recent past, and, perhaps significantly, the one success was related to undeniable fraud: the back-dating of a bill in response to a patient's loss of program eligibility.[88]

One spokesman for a state Medicaid program explained inattention to dental monitoring quite simply—"dentistry isn't where the bucks are." Given the relatively small size of dental payments in relation to total Medicaid expenses (an average of only 2.4 percent in 1978),[89] the scarcity of resources avail-

---

[86] Information provided to the writer by Kenneth Tannenbaum, D.D.S., formerly of the Insurance Commission of the State of Michigan.

[87] Gerald Larson, D.D.S., in an informal discussion with dental students, University of Minnesota, March 1, 1977.

[88] Information supplied by the Medical Assistance Program, State of Minnesota.

[89] Gibson and Fisher, "National Health Expenditures," p. 7.

able to most Medicaid monitoring units, and the resistance of
the dental profession to intrusion from outsiders, it is unsur-
prising that the Medicaid programs are not viewed as an ideal
model of administration for a dental benefit. Both Medicaid
and the provincial experience in Canada suggest, however,
that prior authorization for expensive procedures, controls on
the frequency of relatively inexpensive services such as hygiene instruction and prophylaxes, and careful attention to
practitioner profiles would almost certainly be necessary in a
responsibly administered program.

Not only is public experience in controlling a dental benefit
far from encouraging, but there are no specific control provisions in the major NHI bills. The bills typically invoke the
concept of the Professional Standards Review Organization
with no suggestions about how it might be adapted to dentistry. The introduction of NHI dental coverage should not be
seriously considered until much more study has been done of
the appropriate costs and benefits of various methods of system control.

Summary and Conclusions

Dental coverage under national health insurance has received remarkably little attention for a benefit that is—in
terms of present spending and the potential for service expansion with public subsidy—of the same order of magnitude as
prescription drug coverage. The key reason seems to be that
dental care is not only a relatively small part of the total health
care bill but also relatively unimportant to most people's
health. Dentistry tends to be different from medicine in that
patients in most income and educational categories value its
ministrations less than do providers. Thus even people who
have the benefit of prepaid dental care tend to underuse the
system (in terms of initiation of contact). Yet, once under
treatment, the insured patient may receive an excessive
amount of service in the fee-for-service delivery system.

Dental care is far more expensive than it otherwise might
be because the dental profession has restricted the number of
dentists trained and controlled the amount of activity that
can be delegated to auxiliaries. Dentist hostility to more task
delegation to auxiliaries can be traced to a general fear of loss

of prestige and income. The prospect of a significant rise in the dentist-population ratio during the next few years has galvanized that hostility. The dental profession's control of the number and type of dental health personnel has affected access as well as cost. The distribution of dentists in the United States is very similar to the distribution of doctors; dentists in underserved areas are much more likely to be excessively busy than are their colleagues elsewhere. The quality of American dentistry appears to vary substantially, and there has been a large amount of poor treatment under public programs.

The foremost questions of public dental insurance relate to beneficiaries. There is little justification for spending the estimated $20 billion price of a free universal dental care system. Most adults are capable of judging for themselves how much to spend for dental care, and the overwhelming majority can easily afford dental care if they choose. The most persuasive justification for public intervention appears to be to protect the long-term dental health of children from the problems caused by the low income or poor judgment of their parents. But a scheme that would simply reduce the price of fee-for-service dentistry for all children would be most unwise. The capacity to meet the estimated demand is not in place, and it can be expected that services would be provided first to those already enjoying most contact with the system. Because poor people do not perceive dental care to be important, the offer of free care is not expected to significantly increase their relative contact with the dental care system. Free dental care for children (or for the general population) therefore could easily be "welfare for the rich."

The proven way to increase poor children's access to dental care under public insurance is to provide services in a school-based dental nurse program. Not only could school-based provision of care reach the people most in need of treatment, but also it could serve all children far more cheaply than does the present system. (One estimate is from 66 percent to 71 percent of the per capita cost of using the present delivery system.) Both the cost and the quality of care in dental nurse programs abroad appear to confirm the claims of their proponents. But this solution is an anathema to the dental profession because it would preempt one-third of a typical dental practice.

If a traditional approach to insurance is taken instead, it seems counterproductive to ask the poor to make a copayment for dental services. Yet both the CHIP and the Kennedy-Mills bills require part of the cost to be borne by all patients (and CHIP offers no benefits until a substantial deductible has been met). Another potentially crippling feature of proposed children's coverage is the service cutoff age of thirteen. Such a limitation promises that the system would expire for most children just at the time of greatest need for treatment to avoid damage to the permanent teeth.

In contrast to drug coverage and some other benefits, the administration of dental claims appears to be a most neglected area. Such evidence as is available from Medicaid and Canadian provincial programs suggests the importance of special attention to expensive services, services most likely to be repeated unnecessarily frequently, and ones involving considerable professional discretion. Beyond these cautions, assurance of accountability would require a much higher level of inspection for quality than prevails at present in any public program in the United States. It is easier to detect fraud and to control quality in dentistry than in medicine because most dental treatment leaves trails traceable by X-ray on hard tissue.

Federal public policy initiatives to improve the performance of the dental care sector are not limited to national health insurance. The recent attack against dentistry's ban on advertising is a positive step. In addition, the government could urge states to encourage the dental profession to liberalize its position on use of dental auxiliaries. Greater freedom of activity by auxiliaries not only should moderate the prices faced by current consumers of dental services but also would improve access by "stretching" dentists in underserved areas. The government could reduce or eliminate federal subsidies for the training of dentists—a subsidy that increases what would, in any event, be a high rate of return on educational investment —while taking a close look at the role of the American Dental Association in controlling the number of dental school places. The government might insist on greater quality control in federally funded programs such as Medicaid and explore the obstacles to having dentists relicensed at regular intervals. Finally, the government could give all possible support to measures to reduce the incidence of dental disease through fluoridation of public water supplies. Only about half the nation now receives this protection, and in recent years opposition to fluoridation, although apparently lacking in scientific merit, has halted progress in many areas.

It is hard to argue that dental coverage for the population above the poverty line is a national health care priority; a more convincing case can be made for the provision of services for all children. If legislators decide that increased utilization of dental care by the young is an important national goal, they should heed the 1972 recommendation of the Advisory Committee on Dental Health to the Secretary of DHEW:

> Departmental dental efforts should give priority attention to the prevention and control of dental diseases of children at least up through secondary school age. Emphasis should be placed on exploring the achievement of these goals within the framework of school-based programs. Accordingly, the Secretary should appoint a combined government and nongovernmental task force whose charge would include, but not be limited to, the study and evaluation of all aspects of school-based children's dental care programs, and the making of appropriate recommendations thereupon.[90]

A study of the possibilities of a school-based program should be pursued at the same time that the government attempts to learn more about the feasibility of greater public payment for treatment delivered through the fee-for-service system. It should examine alternative monitoring systems for quality control, avoidance of fraud, and provision of unnecessary services; and it should investigate the cost and effects of different patient "reminder" systems that could be used in conjunction with office-based delivery.[91]

Further investigation of these subjects is vital. The inclusion of dental services under the major national health insurance proposals as written would be excessively expensive and would have an unacceptably modest impact on persons not now receiving regular dental care.

---

[90] Advisory Committee, *Report and Recommendations*, pp. 26–27.

[91] To this list might be added additional government research about how to motivate people to care more about their teeth. Unfortunately, while a breakthrough in this area might be very welcome, past experience in other countries does not make one optimistic. For a plea for more attention to motivation, see Cohen, "Dental Care Delivery in Seven Nations," pp. 211–13.

SUMMARY AND
RECOMMENDATIONS

The compatibility of benefit expansion and expenditure control has become the fundamental question in the debate on national health insurance. Unless ways are found to assure that providers will deliver services to program beneficiaries at reasonable prices, the total costs of national health insurance will exceed levels that liberals as well as conservatives can accept. To address this issue, it is necessary to go beyond the intentions of various NHI plans to examine the feasibility of specific mechanisms proposed to control costs.

With this book, we hope to provoke interest and debate on those mechanisms necessary to implement any NHI legislation. Specifically, we have addressed options for the delegation of administrative authority, the payment and training of physicians and other health professionals, the payment and regulation of hospitals, the operation of utilization controls (both through cost sharing and regulation), and the organization of benefits not necessarily included in medical insurance—long-term care, prescription drugs, and dental care. The authors approached each issue by asking what would happen if policy makers were to choose a particular method to pay for or to control service delivery and use. What additional decisions would that initial choice entail? How would administrators, providers, or consumers react to those decisions? What unintended consequences could their reactions produce? And, finally, what options do policy makers have available to mitigate (if not to avoid) undesirable outcomes?

Sometimes the method or policy instrument in question is integral to a particular NHI bill and must be analyzed in that context. As discussed in Chapter 3, the Kennedy-Corman bill raises particular problems with its proposed method for encouraging the development of health maintenance organizations within a fixed budget for medical care. Similarly, Chapter 7 argues that enactment of catastrophic insurance in the

611

absence of payment limitations would place untenable burdens
on health facility regulators. Although this book has dealt with
issues raised by particular bills, it has concentrated particularly on choices likely to arise regardless of a bill's particular
characteristics. Whatever NHI proposal Congress might enact,
decisions would have to be made on terms of physician participation, provider payment, utilization controls, and a host
of other matters.

Some of these decisions may be addressed in an NHI statute.
The law is likely, for example, to outline the delegation of
administrative authority among governments and between
government and private agents. Specifications for provider
payment and regulation also may be included. To the extent
that these issues are incorporated in legislation, we believe
they must receive the same degree of analysis and debate as
does the scope of coverage under national health insurance.
Here as with all legislation, however, Congress will undoubtedly leave a multitude of decisions to administrative discretion.
Our analysis is directed at this administrative process as much
as at legislative decisions. In its emphasis on what are often
regarded as technical matters, this book serves less to guide
choices among alternative NHI bills than to analyze decisions
necessary to improve any bill's operation. No bill will be free
from problems. Although some problems may be so serious as
to make a particular bill unacceptable, others may well be cor-
rectable. This chapter summarizes our authors' views on policy
problems and the measures they recommend to improve the
probability of successful program operations.

Administration

A national health insurance plan must include policies on
eligibility, benefits, provider payment and regulation, quality
and utilization control, and claims administration. In theory,
these policies can be made and implemented by the federal
government, by state governments, or by insurance carriers.
In practice, functions have been and may continue to be distributed among them. Feder and Holahan analyzed the way
in which the distribution of administrative authority is likely
to affect NHI policies and their implementation.

The federal government's usual role in social policy has been to promulgate objectives, to provide funds to support achievement of those objectives, and to delegate responsibility for using those funds to others, primarily state governments. The alternative to this arrangement is to have a nationally administered program, in which the federal government not only makes but implements its policies. The choice between these approaches depends on (1) the strengths and weaknesses of the federal government as administrator and (2) the capacity of state governments to perform as well as or better than a nationally administered program.

National administration, modeled on the Social Security Administration (SSA), has the greatest potential for uniform and in that sense equitable treatment of beneficiaries across the nation. But SSA's own experience in implementing the Supplemental Security Income program reveals that uniformity cannot be assumed to follow automatically from national administration. Rather, to achieve uniformity it appears necessary either to adopt simple, explicit administrative rules (for eligibility, payment, utilization review, or whatever) or, if rules are complex, to rely on comprehensive and systematic monitoring of administrative behavior. Monitoring, however, imposes a cost. As internal review expands, a program's capacity to respond quickly to beneficiaries' claims is likely to contract. Even if a nationally administered program allowed district officials considerable discretion, a balance between uniformity and responsiveness would be difficult to achieve. This balance also would be a problem in coping with varied preferences across geographic areas. The authors concluded that national administration would produce equity only at the expense of some responsiveness to beneficiaries.

Administration by the federal government also appears to imply limited willingness or capacity to adjust to rising costs. A comparison between Medicare (nationally administered) and Medicaid (state administered) indicates that national government has, in fact, demonstrated less flexibility than have state governments in tackling the cost implications of health financing policies. Attributing at least part of the difference in cost containment activity to the greater ease with which the federal government can raise revenues or engage in deficit spending, Feder and Holahan argued that the federal government might be reluctant to limit expenditures even if it were to become the sole payer for medical care.

The limits to national administration led Feder and Holahan to explore the possibility of delegating authority to state governments. The task, as they see it, is to design a national health insurance plan that would prohibit undesirable state performance while facilitating desirable state initiatives. Feder and Holahan's review of the state-run Medicaid program suggests that the risk of undesirable state performance is real but often exaggerated. Most states have implemented national objectives for Medicaid coverage, and several states have been innovative in program design, particularly with respect to controlling provider payment. Yet, some states do continue to provide unacceptably low coverage and to administer programs so poorly as to jeopardize their effectiveness. To ignore these variations and to rely fully on all states would undoubtedly risk program failure in some states.

Feder and Holahan recommended four policy measures to prevent this outcome and encourage innovation. First, to assure adequate insurance coverage throughout the nation, the federal government should establish uniform minimum standards for eligibility and benefits under national health insurance. Second, NHI financing arrangements should increase federal and state governments' sensitivity to the fiscal consequences of their actions. The Medicaid experience reveals cost-consciousness in some states. But open-ended matching of state expenditures, Medicaid's current financing mechanism, is less likely than other mechanisms are to encourage sensitivity to costs. Feder and Holahan therefore recommended that limits be set on the national revenues devoted to health and that they be allocated to states according to more restrictive funding arrangements—budget, block grants, or closed-ended matching. Third, to prevent discrimination, any policies made by state governments should affect not only the poor, but the entire state population. If state payment policies, for example, affect only the poor, as in Medicaid, policy makers cannot simultaneously control costs and maintain access. To remedy this situation it is not necessary to implement a single insurance program for all citizens, but, instead, payment and other policies must be made uniform across all kinds of purchasers. Finally, to protect citizens against program failure in any state, uncritical reliance on all states should be replaced by selective reliance on states that perform well. State performance in such areas as service use, quality, and provider payment could be evaluated against national norms. The federal government would undoubtedly be reluctant to take over administrative responsibilities from a state performing poorly, but a state's voters themselves might seek national action if they were continually dissatisfied.

Decisions on the distribution of responsibilities between the federal and state governments do not preclude a role for private insurance carriers in national health insurance. A public program could use insurers as administrative agents as they do under Medicare, or insurers could continue to underwrite and sell insurance policies according to publicly set rules. Because private industry has more flexibility in management than the public sector has, use of insurance carriers as administrative agents for national health insurance is an attractive possibility. Whether flexibility would be used to the government's advantage, however, would depend on the incentives carriers face to shift overhead costs from their private to their public operations. To discourage these shifts, Feder and Holahan recommended that the public programs pay carriers a fixed amount to cover administrative costs per claim. The amount would be arrived at through competitive bidding. To assure qualified participants, the public program would have to specify the tasks private agents would perform, establish standards for satisfactory performance, and then accept the lowest bidder meeting those qualifications. Performance would be reviewed periodically, on a sample basis, to verify the appropriate disposition of claims. Agents could be rewarded or penalized according to their performance. To encourage competition, the program should avoid large contracts and instead promote involvement of a large number of firms. This approach should encourage efficient administration and claims control. The disadvantage, however, would be the disruption associated with competition.

An NHI plan could make greater use of competition by retaining the private insurance market for some or all of the population. The objective behind such a plan would be to allow individuals a choice of coverage arrangements while assuring everyone, including the poor and the sick, access to adequate insurance protection. Feder and Holahan argued that to achieve this objective, more would be required than nationally determined standards for benefits, enrollment, and premiums.

Access and cost containment also would require the federal or state governments to take responsibility for cost containment activities and the availability of a public—national or state—insurance plan alongside private plans in the marketplace. Taken together, these actions would reduce the likelihood of discrimination against the poor and the sick, while retaining the market's flexibility to respond to consumer preferences on price, comprehensiveness, convenience, and style of medical practice.

Physician Payment and Supply

The choice among methods of paying physicians is one of the most important decisions to be made in formulating national health insurance programs. Payments to physicians currently account for 20 percent of national health expenditures. Moreover, physicians play a critical role in determining the use of many other services. Systems of reimbursement of physicians' services have been just as important in recent years for Medicare, Medicaid, and other third-party carriers; yet, little consensus exists today on appropriate methods of paying physicians.

Fee-for-service—that is, a separate payment for each unit of care provided—is now the dominant form of physician reimbursement in the United States, and, Holahan argued, is likely to be the central method in any NHI plan Congress enacts. Of all possible reimbursement systems, fee-for-service poses the greatest problem for people concerned with the control of health care costs. There are, however, strategies to address this problem. To contain costs in a fee-for-service system, Holahan emphasized, policy makers must confront three distinct policy issues: (1) the mechanism employed to set NHI rates, (2) physicians' freedom to charge patients above those rates, and (3) controls over the total volume (as well as unit price) of physician services.

In a fee-for-service system, there are two ways to control payments. Payment rates can be controlled by fee screens based on average charges for each procedure over a previous period, as is currently done under "usual, customary, and reasonable" charge systems. Alternatively, payment rates can be controlled by fee schedules negotiated between physician organizations and payers. After reviewing the options, Holahan concluded that fee schedules—fixed sets of permissible charges for specific, well-defined procedures—are the most effective mechanism for controlling the absolute level of fees and for pursuing other policy objectives. To control costs, fees could be determined according to the availability of funds or targets for physician incomes. To influence the mix of services delivered, fee schedules could be structured to redistribute income among specialties and between urban and rural physicians, and to quickly change the relative values given different procedures. Although employment of a fee schedule requires considerable administrative attention, Holahan argued that administration of a fee schedule would be less complex and less costly than effective operation of a usual and customary charge system, like that used today by Medicare and private insurers.

The second major issue in using fee-for-service concerns provisions for physicians to charge in excess of the fee schedule. Such a provision is usually considered necessary to assure a high level of physician participation. But, Holahan observed, arrangements that would make it relatively easy for physicians to opt out would severely hamper cost control objectives. The assignment billing system used under Medicare undermines efforts to control costs. Under assignment billing, physicians can choose on a claim-by-claim basis whether to accept the program's approved fee as payment in full. If they do not accept the program's fee, physicians can charge patients whatever they like. Assignment billing therefore permits physicians to shift costs to patients. It also encourages physicians to provide a higher quality and more comprehensive range of services to those able and willing to pay more than the allowed fee. In contrast, systems that would require physicians either to accept the NHI program's fee schedule or forfeit any payment would be most effective in inducing participation and reducing discrimination against low-income persons. But, Holahan argued, adoption of such a stringent system is likely to encounter considerable resistance from physicians and the well-to-do. Efforts to overcome that resistance might produce very generous fees.

Holahan therefore suggested that the most effective NHI physician payment strategy would be one which permitted physicians to bill patients above the government fee, but which also included strong incentives to accept the government fee schedule. Physicians would be required to choose either direct billing of the patient or billing of the government for that patient; billing the government would mean accepting the fee schedule as payment in full. The choice would be binding for all patients and all procedures for that year. The government would guarantee prompt and certain payment if the physician billed the program, but would place full collection responsibility on the physician if he or she billed patients directly. Patients whose physicians chose direct billing would be reimbursed less than the fee schedule, perhaps 60 percent. Such penalties would place indirect pressure on physicians. This arrangement would reduce the likelihood of a two-class system and permit strong control over fees.

Controlling the level of fees is only one element in expenditure control. There are widespread beliefs supported by some empirical evidence that physicians are able to influence patients' decisions to use services and to increase reimbursements through manipulation of the procedure coding terminology. Holahan made several recommendations to limit physicians' discretion. First, fees should be structured so that they reflect the costs of services when produced in an efficient manner. The incentives for "demand creation" are strongest when fees exceed the costs of provision. Although developing precise fee schedules is difficult, much better approximations, particularly in diagnostic procedures and in-hospital services, can be made than now exist.

A second proposal to limit physicians' discretion is to reduce substantially the number of procedures for which a physician can bill. A procedure coding system with a large number of visits and separate codes for a wide range of ancillary services permits physicians broad flexibility in setting rates, and rewards the provision of several ancillary services during the course of a visit. Alternatives include permitting billing for a few widely different types of visits, or carefully defining and reimbursing physician visits by the amount of time involved.

Third, indexing arrangements are attractive because they allow considerable program control over costs. Indexing refers to the tying of fee increases to aggregate changes in physician incomes. A portion of the increase in physician income would come from fee increases, the remainder from changes in service provision. If physicians' incomes should increase faster than the desired rate, fee increases the next years would be reduced. The main problem with such arrangements is that although incomes would be controlled in the aggregate, individual physicians would still have clear incentives to increase incomes by increasing their supply of services. An inequitable distribution of incomes among physicians could result, creating political pressure to change the system. Alternatively, physicians would be forced to monitor carefully patterns of service delivery.

Although fee-for-service reimbursement would undoubtedly dominate under national health insurance, Holahan argued that alternative arrangements would remain feasible for at least some physicians. Salary reimbursement is particularly amenable to control. A serious limitation on the implementation of salaried reimbursement, however, is the need for service delivery organizations responsible for and capable of monitoring performance and adjusting salaries over time. Most of the U.S. medical care delivery system is not now organized in this way. Development of such organizations would occur only if physicians were to become sufficiently disenchanted with fee-for-service reimbursement. This disenchantment might, in fact, occur following experience with controls of fees and incomes.

Short of such a major change in the system, the most promising reform would be the Kennedy-Corman proposal to require compensation by hospitals of professional practitioners, such as pathologists, radiologists, and anesthesiologists who are associated with a hospital and whose services are generally available to patients of the hospital. Coupled with fixed overall budget reimbursement of hospitals, that proposal would force hospital attention to rates of payment and to the level of services provided, thereby further encouraging cost containment. Under these conditions, salaried reimbursement would probably result.

Capitation reimbursement, or lump sum payments to physicians for a specified period regardless of the number of services they provide, is another type of payment that theoretically can be made to physicians in solo as well as group practices. Although capitation payments are employed for solo practitioners in the United Kingdom, Holahan argued that this practice is too unfamiliar and too complex for widespread use in the United States. Capitation is more likely to be used in the context of health maintenance organizations, to which we now turn.

HMOs are a major innovation in medical care delivery that must be considered in the design and implementation of NHI options. The available evidence concerning HMO performance is sufficiently favorable to lead many analysts to argue for HMO promotion under national health insurance. In a review of this evidence, Luft, Feder, Holahan, and Lennox found that total medical care costs are substantially lower for HMO enrollees than for the general population and that these lower costs are attributable to lower hospitalization rates. The reasons for this lower hospitalization are less clear. The major factor is lower admission rates, but admissions do not appear differentially lower for surgical cases or even particular types of surgery often identified as being discretionary. While the lower admission rate for HMO enrollees might imply less care than is medically appropriate, there is little evidence that the quality of care in HMOs is poor or that HMO enrollees have worse health outcomes. A second explanation, that HMOs provide much more preventive care, which leads to less illness, is not supported by the data. Two major alternative explanations remain: (1) that HMOs provide the appropriate level of care, and the conventional system too much; and (2) the utilization differences are attributable to the self-selection of different types of people into HMOs and into the conventional system.

Although the true situation may be represented by a combination of these explanations or some other unexplained mechanism, the potential importance of HMOs led the authors to an investigation of alternative policies towards HMOs. The current federal policies are represented by the Medicare and Federal Employees Health Benefits Program. Medicare emphasizes cost reimbursement for HMOs; for those HMOs wishing to be at risk, complicated formulas are required to compute the capitation payments, and savings must be shared with the Medicare program. The implicit assumption seems to be that HMOs might skimp on services in ways that beneficiaries will not be able to detect or should not be allowed to tolerate. The Medicare program also assumes that cost differences attributable to appropriate differences in services should be largely captured by the government, not retained by the HMO. The FEHBP is somewhat different. It provides a fixed contribution that the consumer can allocate to any of a broad selection of alternative plans. The program attempts to set the rate below the costs of care under all available insurance arrangements. FEHBP's implicit assumption is that consumers can evaluate health insurance and delivery options, and should bear the cost consequences of their needs or preferences for coverage.

The Medicare and the FEHBP models differ primarily with respect to who wins or loses from HMO rates that differ from the costs of care. In the FEHBP model, if the program established a rate too low for the costs of care for a particular individual or group, that individual or group would have to make supplementary payments. In the Medicare model, the government would bear the costs of inaccurate rates. If rates were set too low, HMOs would avoid high-cost enrollees and "cream" or seek out low-cost enrollees. The government's costs for HMO enrollees could then be higher for those people than costs would have been under fee-for-service arrangements.

The Medicare model seems most appropriate if there is a real concern that HMOs will underserve their enrollees, jeopardize their health, and pocket the profits. Conversely, the FEHBP model is most appropriate if one believes that HMOs are responsive to consumer needs and provide reasonable levels of appropriate quality care.

All of the available studies of HMO performance have dealt with relatively isolated programs within the context of a highly diversified health insurance market generally not conducive to HMO development. (For instance, the dual-choice provisions of the 1973 HMO Act are only beginning to be exercised, let alone studied.) Thus, the authors emphasized that any projection of HMO performance under alternative NHI schemes must not only extrapolate from current experience with established HMOs, but also imagine their behavior in the context of a market environment drastically altered by national health insurance. Some of the proposals, such as CHIP, give little attention to HMOs, but establish an environment and incentives that, perhaps inadvertently, may substantially encourage HMO development. In contrast, the Kennedy-Corman proposal includes specific policies to promote HMOs and, in particular, prepaid group practices. Some of the other aspects of the proposal, however, eliminate most of the incentives for consumers to join HMOs, and may inadvertently strengthen the power of the medical profession in resisting government budgetary controls. Failure to consider such unintended consequences would lead to unexpected and undesirable outcomes under national health insurance.

Physician payment mechanisms—inside or outside HMOs—are important for other reasons than their effects on the costs of care. In conjunction with other policies, they also influence both the supply and distribution of health personnel. Hadley addressed national health insurance plans' effects on physician supply and distribution by exploring the likely results from three types of policies: (1) altering financial returns to physicians who practice various specialties or locate in certain types of areas; (2) directly intervening in the delivery system through regulatory/legislative actions for direct provision of services by public authorities; and (3) influencing the medical education system. Hadley's conclusion was that all three methods should be used in efforts to influence total physician supply and specialty and geographic distribution. Specific recommendations reflect the point of view that although the current aggregate supply of physicians and the capacity of the medical education sector are adequate, there are too few physicians (or, more accurately, physicians' services) available to populations in certain rural and low-income urban areas, and the proportion of physicians practicing primary care (general and family practice, general internal medicine, and general pediatrics) is too low.

The belief that the aggregate supply of physicians is adequate stems largely from the observation that recent growth in supply—intended to correct a perceived physician shortage —has had little effect on geographic or specialty distribution. Most of this growth stemmed from two factors: relaxed immigration barriers and federal subsidies to medical schools. In order to stabilize, or perhaps even to reduce, the flow of new physicians into the U.S. medical care system, Hadley recommended the following measures: First, restrict the entry of graduates of foreign medical schools, except for educational or research activities, a measure that is part of the Health Professions Educational Assistance Act of 1976. Second, phase out medical school subsidies that encourage expansion of class sizes and development of new facilities.

Two potential consequences of these actions should be anticipated. First, some hospitals will be disproportionately affected by the reduced flow of foreign medical school graduates.

Therefore, areas served by these hospitals should be given high priority with regard to any compensatory distributional policies. Second, medical schools should be expected to increase tuitions in the face of reduced public subsidies. To the extent that maintaining equity of access to medical careers is also a public objective, a system of loans and scholarships based on financial need should be established to encourage medical school applications from low-income individuals.

To address geographic distribution problems, Hadley recommended that efforts to increase physicians' earnings in shortage areas be coupled with attempts to constrain earnings in sufficiency areas. The reimbursement system is probably the most powerful policy mechanism for influencing physicians' incomes. The current system may be particularly difficult to manipulate, however, because of (1) physicians' discretion in setting fees, (2) the usual-customary-reasonable payment methods used by most insurers, and (3) the multiplicity of payment plans and insurers in most areas. Reimbursement reforms, therefore, would consist of the development of area-wide, negotiated fee schedules applicable to most patients. Negotiations between physician groups and public representatives would provide a forum for setting explicit distribution and income objectives. Finally, data systems should be established to monitor both physician productivity and geographic distribution. The requisite data can be easily generated as byproducts of a fee-for-service reimbursement system.

Another policy option for influencing geographic distribution is the loan forgiveness program, which offers to cancel loans for medical students who agree to practice in physician shortage areas. However, past loan forgiveness programs appear to have had too little financial clout to have any impact on geographic distribution. If average indebtedness and the cost of buying out of service obligations were increased, more physicians could be expected to choose the service obligation. But the indentured service aspect of forgiveness programs makes it unlikely that many physicians would remain to practice in shortage areas. In addition, solo private practice may not be an appropriate institutional mode for providing physicians' services in shortage areas. Heavy patient loads, inadequate backup, lack of collegial contacts, and inability to control hours are frequently cited as reason for leaving or forgoing practices in shortage areas.

Therefore, altering practice arrangements should be encouraged through the reimbursement system and through a program of grants and loans. One class of alternatives consists of multiple-physician arrangements, such as Neighborhood Health Centers, Area Health Education Centers, rural medical clinics, or small group practices or partnerships. Because some areas may be too small or too isolated to support an additional full-time physician, another set of policy options should focus on increasing the productivity of existing physicians' practices. To encourage efficiency in organizing and operating prospective ambulatory care institutions, grants and loans should be provided only for various start-up expenses.

Hadley also recommended specific measures to address specialty maldistribution, that is, the shortage of primary-care physicians. This problem is thought to reflect, in part, the structure of the medical education system, which traditionally has emphasized specialty practice. From a somewhat different perspective, the specialty maldistribution problem may be seen as a maldistribution of types of services (e.g., too many operations and radiological procedures, and not enough preventive or health maintenance visits). Thus, any attempt to alter the distribution of specialists in training should be supplemented with a fee schedule to encourage or discourage certain procedures. Ultimately, policy makers may want to consider limiting access to or ownership of certain types of capital equipment, such as operating rooms, X-ray facilities, and laboratories.

Therefore, potential policies should focus on inducing both medical schools and teaching hospitals to alter their teaching programs. One needed policy change is the gradual elimination of the system of capitation grants to medical schools. These grants have little direct effect on students' specialty choices. Furthermore, the requirement that ties receipt of a grant to the national percentage of residency training positions in primary care is too vague and easily influenced by nominal changes in residency programs. If future reimbursement systems continue to treat inpatient services more generously than ambulatory services, however, some direct support may be necessary to compensate for reimbursement bias. This support could take the form of project or categorical grants for primary-care teaching and residencies, or a modified capitation scheme that would make payments to a medical school for each graduate entering a first-year primary-care residency or to a teaching hospital for each physician completing a primary-care residency. (Completion could be defined as "becoming board eligible.")

A potentially important adjunct to policies directed at physicians is increased reliance on new health personnel like nurse practitioners (NPs) and physicians' assistants (PAs). Reviewing the first decade of experience, Robyn and Hadley concluded that these personnel can provide many primary health care services with considerably less training and education (and therefore at lower expense) than physicians, yet with no loss in quality. Their potential for expanding access to care at relatively low cost is therefore considerable. Realizing this potential, however, depends on NPs' and PAs' deployment to areas with medically underserved populations. If, instead, the primary effect of employing these personnel is to reduce the work effort of physicians in adequately served areas, or to provide complementary services, the public may receive little direct benefit from subsidization of NP/PA training.

The main argument against expanding the number of nurse practitioners and physicians' assistants is the expected increase in the supply of physicians. Some argue that an increase in the number of physicians will mean more employment opportunities for nurse practitioners and physicians' assistants, because physicians will increasingly desire to delegate some of their tasks. This possibility seems unlikely, however, given physicians' apparent reluctance to hire NPs and PAs and the conservative attitudes underlying this reluctance. A more reasonable prediction, and one shared by most NP/PA educators, is that a sizable increase in physician supply bodes ill for NPs and PAs, who function more as substitutes for than complements to physicians. This problem night be particularly acute if the national health insurance program were to reimburse employers for NP/PA services at the same rate as for physician services. The fact that medical care standards are traditionally physician-defined gives physicians considerable power to exclude potential competitors with less training. Consumers' lack of information about and inability to judge the quality of the health care they receive compound this problem.

Hence, Robyn and Hadley cautioned against expecting expansion of these occupations to result in greatly increased access to low-cost care. Over the long term, however, the potential of these health personnel to realign provider roles and enhance efficiency in the delivery of care suggests that a national health insurance program should encourage gradual expansion of the nurse practitioner and physicians' assistant occupations. Ideally, expansion would be targeted to underserved areas.

Reimbursement policy is the vital link between national health insurance and these new health occupations. Providing third-party reimbursement for NP/PA services is essential if these health workers are to be accepted and used more fully. Reimbursement of NPs and PAs at the same rate as physicians are reimbursed also is desirable. Equal reimbursement would provide a needed incentive for physicians to hire NPs and PAs and would avoid problems of a two-class system of medicine implied by fractional reimbursement. To be consistent with cost-saving objectives, however, full reimbursement should be used in conjunction with a fee schedule in which prices reflected whether tasks were routine and delegatable. Only by making it unprofitable for physicians not to delegate routine tasks can long-term realignment of medical care delivery roles be encouraged. Fee schedules also can be used to attract NPs/PAs to underserved areas, by reimbursing for NP/PA services performed in underserved areas at a higher rate than the rate used elsewhere. (This incentive is directed less at NPs and PAs than at potential physician employers.) But because the private market is often unresponsive to the demand for care by the needy, new institutions for delivering care may have to be developed to improve geographic distribution. Neighborhood Health Centers, Area Health Educational Centers, and the National Health Service Corps may serve as appropriate models upon which to build. Using NPs and PAs to deliver a defined set of primary-care services and to serve as a point of entry into the larger medical care system may help avoid the establishment of a two-class delivery system.

Hospital Payment and Regulation

Hospitals account for about 40 percent of medical expenses and have become a target of cost containment efforts independent of national health insurance. These efforts are intended to reverse or compensate for widespread public and private insurance coverage which has substantially reduced market constraints on hospital costs and has assured hospitals virtually open-ended revenues. Although access to care and financial burdens remain important issues, cost control has been the primary political focus in NHI policy toward hospitals. The issue has two parts, which were addressed separately: overall hospital payment mechanisms and regulation of capital expenditures.

To identify problems in hospital payment policy, Feder and Spitz traced the origins of current payment criteria and analyzed the political and technical weaknesses in efforts to change these criteria. From their inception, Medicare and Medicaid agreed to pay hospitals the costs they incurred in delivering services to beneficiaries. Each hospital's costs are determined retroactively according to specified rules. Allowable costs were liberally defined and apportioned to public programs. Administrators justified these policies on grounds that they treated all hospitals equitably and encouraged delivery of "mainstream" or quality care to public beneficiaries. The adoption of "reasonable cost" reimbursement, as it is called, was consistent with the conventional wisdom of the mid-1960s that more revenue meant more and better services, and that hospital growth and development were in the public interest.

Payment policy that treats each hospital's incurred costs as "reasonable," equitable, and supportive of quality care has had two major consequences. First, this policy has provided individual hospitals with considerable financial resources to spend as administrators and medical staff see fit, without regard to whether benefits are worth the costs incurred. Reimbursement policy has thereby encouraged an upward spiral in medical expenditures. Second, reasonable cost reimbursement has established incurred costs as a standard of adequate and appropriate hospital payment that has been technically and politically difficult to challenge. It is technically difficult to define what hospitals should or actually produce and to specify what efficient production should cost. Without these specifications, it is politically difficult to challenge a hospital's claims that its costs are, in fact, "reasonable" and should be paid.

Technical and political difficulties have impeded several
efforts to change payment to put decisions on costs, quality,
and utilization of service in the hands of policy makers rather
than providers. Prospective payment, or payment set in advance, has long been advocated as a means to achieve this
objective. But changing the timing of payment from after to
before services are delivered does not eliminate decisions on
what constitutes appropriate payment. Whether payment is
retrospective or prospective, policy makers must decide what
hospital expenses should be covered from patient revenues,
what payments should be contingent upon planners' approval,
what ceilings on total expenses or revenues are legitimate,
what expenses (labor costs, malpractice insurance) should be
exempt from ceilings, what unit of payment (per day, per
admission) will encourage efficiency, and what adjustments
should be allowed after rates have been fixed. Unless payers
depart from incurred costs in each of these areas, they cannot
control their expenses. But each time they take this route, they
face political and legal challenges from hospitals anxious to
protect their autonomy. As long as payment statutes commit
government to paying "the reasonable costs of quality care,"
providers will continue to dominate payment negotiations. One
set of data will be challenged by another, payers will be forced
to seek a level of precision that is beyond both theoretical and
technical capacity, and decisions to limit funds will be overturned on appeal.

No change in payment policy can control costs without
political conflict, but some changes can enhance the government's capacity to resist hospitals' demands. To improve the
government's bargaining capacity under national health insurance, Feder and Spitz recommended (1) that policy makers
change their payment objectives, (2) that national health
insurance adopt the payment method least subject to provider
manipulation, and (3) that payment be uniform across all
payers in order to consolidate payers' market power. Feder
and Spitz recommended that the current objectives of equity
among hospitals and "mainstream" care be replaced with
objectives of relative equity and satisfactory care. Equity in
payment must go beyond hospitals to equity among hospitals,
patients, taxpayers, and the community. Appropriately defined, equity requires that benefits and costs of hospital care
be considered simultaneously and in relation to alternative use

of funds. As long as consumer payment responsibility is limited, only the government can take these considerations into account. The government therefore must assert its responsibility for resource allocation and establish limits on total expenditures for hospital care. These limits should replace currently open-ended commitments to finance whatever the medical and hospital industry define as the "best" in medical care with a commitment to finance satisfactory care fairly.

Changes in payment objectives must be accompanied by a change in payment methods. Reimbursement that continually reflects autonomous hospital expenditure decisions is clearly inconsistent with expenditure control and efficient resource allocation. Despite the inefficiencies that the "reasonable cost" reimbursement system has produced, political acceptance of a new system requires that national health insurance take current aggregate hospital expenditures as a starting point. The new reimbursement system should concentrate on controlling the rate of increase in expenditures in coming years. Initially, this goal can be achieved most easily if policy makers accept each hospital's current level of revenues, establish a ceiling on the rate of increase in all hospitals' revenues for the coming year, and subject all hospital expenditures to the revenue ceiling. If these ceilings are to limit hospital expenditures, payments to individual hospitals cannot be affected by expenditures hospitals incur after the adoption of a national health insurance program. Ceilings based on average hospital performance are therefore undesirable. Instead, rates of increase should be tied to some independent measure of acceptable expenditure increases (for example, the consumer price index less the medical care component of that index). If all sources of expenditure are to be controlled, publicly established revenue ceilings should apply to all purchasers of hospital care, private as well as public, and revenues earned independent of patient care (from endowments or services like parking lots or gifts shops) should be counted toward the ceilings. To prevent provider manipulation and encourage efficient management, hospitals' total expenditures—on ancillary as well as routine services—cannot be allowed to exceed approved revenues. To minimize hospitals' capacity to avoid ceilings by manipulating their volume of services, payments should be tied to admissions, not days of care. Total revenues should not be increased to finance increases in admissions that exceeded a predetermined range.

These actions would close the loopholes in existing payment systems, and would place extremely tight limits on hospital revenues and expenditures. Because they would freeze the existing distribution of resources, such stringent controls could not be imposed over a long period of time. But their adoption at the beginning of a national health insurance program could shift negotiations between the government and the hospital industry from debates on how much to tighten expenditures to debates on how much to loosen expenditures. Such a shift could enhance the government's bargaining power and give public policy makers, rather than providers, the advantage in negotiations.

Over time, the rigid payment system should be replaced with a payment system that would allow shifts in the existing distribution of resources. Nationally set limits on national expenditures should remain, but the mechanism for allocating expenditures to individual hospitals should change. A national budget for hospital care could be prospectively set, apportioned to the states by the federal government, then apportioned to localities or individual hospitals by the states. To simultaneously establish public control and allow managerial flexibility, it seems most appropriate to fix global budgets for hospitals and allow hospitals to spend within those budgets as they see fit. With this budgeting approach, limits would be set by the level of government that faced the broadest cost-benefit trade-offs, represented the largest range of interests, and wielded the most comprehensive authority. Furthermore, setting budget from the top down would establish fiscal constraints at every level of decision making while allowing those closest to hospital operations to decide where funds should be spent.

Feder and Spitz cautioned that allocation responsibility cannot be totally separated from fiscal responsibility. Unless states and localities bear some costs of hospital care, they may have greater interest in promoting expansion of the federal budget than in operating efficiently and effectively within that budget. A state's ability to gain an exception or special rate of increase would be limited by competition for federal dollars among other states and with other users of federal dollars. But the degree of conflict over these dollars could be reduced by including state and local payment obligations in any financing scheme. If states or local communities wanted to spend more on hospital care than their NHI obligations required, they should be allowed to do so. But they should only do so with the understanding that they were obligated for future operating, as well as capital, costs of any investment they undertook.

Delegating the allocation function to the state would not eliminate the constant necessity for political choice. Apportionment procedures will be one long political bargaining session: Will a hospital's performance be reflected in its budget? What costs will be covered? What ceiling will be imposed? What will be the recourse for adjustments and appeals? And what will happen given imminent bankruptcy of a hospital? These difficult and controversial questions cannot be reduced to technical rules. Nor can budgets be assumed to produce efficient outcomes. Experience with budgets in the United Kingdom reveals that long-standing patterns of resource distribution are difficult to change. Political power of particular communities and hospitals would undoubtedly influence any resource allocation system adopted. Furthermore, it should be recognized that budgeting for hospitals alone would not automatically control total medical costs. To the extent that ambulatory care replaced hospital care, total cost savings would be less than savings in hospital costs. Although substitution of ambulatory care might be entirely appropriate, savings could be eliminated altogether if ambulatory services became excessive and expensive. The fact that budgeting does not assure efficiency, however, should not obscure its advantages over other payment systems. In contrast to other systems—especially "reasonable cost" reimbursement—budgets do not preclude efficient outcomes. Instead, budgets create pressure to face rather than ignore the difficult choices expenditure control requires.

There is, at present, no national system for budgeting total hospital expenditures. It has been proposed, however, that budgets be set for hospitals' capital expenditures. This proposal is intended to strengthen what is now the predominant form of federal and state hospital cost containment policies— that is, capital expenditures regulation through certificate-of-need programs. Total or partial budgets should dramatically alter the current operation and effects of capital expenditure controls. Dunham described and explained the limited impact that facility regulation has had to date. Because state and local planning agencies do not operate under a fixed, or even a limited, capital budget, they are not forced to consider whether there might be a cheaper way of obtaining particular results. They can consider such issues, but they are not required to do so. It is quite possible—and indeed it has happened—that an agency would approve every proposal that came before it. Most projects are "needed" in some absolute sense. Without a budgetary limit, therefore, capital expenditures regulation is unlikely to control costs. If, alternatively, national health insurance were to significantly reduce hospital revenues, government allocation and regulation of capital could become a crucial device to control the size, distribution, and mix of hospital expenditures.

To make budgets stick, Dunham recommended other changes in the current regulatory structure. Ultimately, determining the "need" for medical facilities is not simply a question of gathering the best data and employing the proper planning methodology to arrive impartially at objective standards. Facility control is, and must be, a political question. Resolution of this question in favor of cost control will depend on the structure of regulatory agencies. Many observers have blamed the poor record of past health planning on the "capture" of the planning agencies by the providers. Although the 1974 Planning Act does require a consumer majority on the local Health Systems Agency board, the act also requires at least 40 percent provider participation. Studies have shown that consumers on the boards tend to be less active than providers, so the boards often end up provider-dominated despite a consumer majority. This is particularly true of specialized committees like project review. Moreover, consumer members of HSA boards are often selected as representatives of special interest groups which are more concerned about their particular goals than about controlling costs. The representation problem is related more directly to interests than to numbers. To pursue cost control, the membership or constituencies of regulatory agencies at all levels of government must have a financial stake in limiting growth. Unless responsibilities for regulation parallel responsibilities for NHI financing, payment and regulation are bound to work at cross purposes.

If national health insurance is to rely on the existing regulatory structure for resource allocation, other changes in current policy also are required. To date, planning agencies have been funded at a level too low to meet all their responsibilities. The early Comprehensive Health Planning agencies were often financially dependent on the very providers they were supposed to influence. The National Health Planning Act eliminated that problem by prohibiting provider funding; this act also authorized more federal money to the local agencies. But the appropriations have never equaled authorizations, and the funding is still limited. Indeed, at whatever level planning agencies are funded, they still would not be able to fully accomplish all the tasks current law assigns them. There are too few skilled personel to inventory all the health resources and needs of the area, to provide technical expertise to other groups, to draw up a health plan and an annual implementation plan, to review and make recommendations on all capital expenditure projects, and to review the appropriateness of all the health facilities in the area every five years.

Given limited staff, expertise, and time, planners will obviously emphasize some activities over others. Studies suggest that hospitals have shifted investment from beds to plant, because beds receive more scrutiny. There is also evidence of shifts from regulated settings (hospitals) to unregulated settings (physicians' offices). Dunham outlined the variety of ways in which providers try to sidestep regulatory efforts. Providers would undoubtedly continue these efforts, regardless of the resources devoted to regulation. But more realistic delegation of tasks, more supportive funding levels, and more restrictive hospital reimbursement arrangements would assist public policy makers in influencing hospital behavior in desired directions.

Utilization Controls

Service use presents one of the more perplexing dilemmas in national health insurance policy. An important motive for enacting national health insurance is to improve access to medical care. But with resources limited relative to human wants, some mechanism is necessary to allocate limited services among potential users. There are two ways to allocate services. One is to rely on consumer sensitivity to prices by requiring consumers to pay some share of medical costs. The

other is to rely on regulatory controls on service use and
claims payment.

Patient cost sharing, the direct payment by consumers of
some share of the costs of medical care at the time of use,
has received particular attention as concern about inflation
and skepticism toward regulation have mounted. The primary
argument for cost sharing is that it will make consumers
cost-conscious, willing to weigh the benefits of care against
its costs. As Conrad and Marmor indicated, studies leave little
doubt that cost sharing could dramatically reduce the amount
of care (especially ambulatory care) demanded under national
health insurance. There is, however, considerable doubt that
cost sharing would deter utilization equitably or efficiently.
Uniform deductibles or coinsurance rates impose relatively
greater burdens on low-income families than on high-income
families. Unless cost sharing is linked to income, increasing
access to medical care for persons currently underserved—
one of the major stated aims of national health insurance—
is unlikely.

Rather than taking a position for or against cost sharing in
terms of these consequences, Conrad and Marmor considered
whether cost-sharing proposals can be put into effect as their
designers intend. Reliance on cost sharing to control service
use under national health insurance makes sense only under
two conditions: (1) that cost sharing can be effectively administered and (2) that people do not buy supplementary
private insurance to avoid out-of-pocket expenses at the point
of service. Conrad and Marmor found administration of cost
sharing likely to be complex but feasible, even if national
health insurance should attempt to minimize inequities by
linking cost sharing with income. For income-related cost
sharing, feasibility is contingent upon using the Internal Revenue Service (IRS) to determine cost-sharing obligations for
the population not on welfare. The IRS, or the NHI administration agency using IRS data, could inform individuals of
their cost-sharing obligations for the coming year, based on
their previous year's tax returns. To avoid hardship for
families with fluctuating incomes, an exceptions process could
be introduced, and a credit card could be used to avoid cash
flow problems. Rather than denying credit to defaulters, an
approach likely to impede access to care, the IRS could add
unpaid cost-sharing payments to income tax obligations at
the end of each year.

Although feasible, this system would pose some risks. Even if the IRS were able to collect all debts retroactively, the administrative burden and the credit demanded of the program could be great. Furthermore, extensive use of credit could eliminate the deterrent effects of cost sharing. Perhaps even more important, use of the tax system for other than tax purposes could encourage underreporting of income. If, through insufficient monitoring, the IRS should allow taxpayers to shirk income tax and NHI cost-sharing obligations, compliance with the entire income tax system could be jeopardized. The authors recommended that these risks be weighed against cost savings in appraising income-related cost sharing.

Supplementation poses what may be more serious obstacles than administration to cost sharing's effectiveness. Neither Canadian national health insurance (which has no cost sharing for covered services) nor Medicare (which is limited to the elderly) is directly analogous to NHI plans with considerable cost sharing under consideration in the United States. But a review of experience in Canada and under Medicare suggests that factors other than the benefits of risk spreading or the incentives created by a tax subsidy encourage the purchase of supplementary insurance. These factors include the effect of national health insurance on employers' and employees' income after taxes, on the public's attitude toward risks, on private insurers' market practices, and, perhaps most important in the American context, on collective bargaining. Conrad and Marmor argued that strong pressures on union leadership to maintain the size of health and welfare fringe benefits make supplementation particularly likely. The higher the cost sharing an NHI plan imposes, the greater this likelihood becomes. The authors therefore recommended that policy makers take private supplementation into account before adopting an NHI plan, for failure to do so could vitiate cost sharing as a cost containment device.

They further concluded that NHI plans that allow extensive supplementation are best understood as cost-spreading rather than cost-containing policies. The authors note, however, that some services (such as long-term care, drugs, and dental services) are particularly dependent on patient initiation. For these services, selective cost sharing may well be an appropriate means to ration care and to control program costs.

Stuart analyzed the regulatory approach to utilization control as an alternative or complement to cost sharing. He likened definitions of appropriate and covered care under national health insurance to definitions of "deliverables" in a government contract. Unless the product is precisely delineated, contractors may provide too little or too much at a cost that is inappropriate. Failure to define the product exposes the system to possible abusive and fraudulent practices. These issues, repeatedly raised in other areas of government contracting, have yet to be adequately addressed in the field of health financing.

To remedy this situation, Stuart recommended that policy options for utilization control be viewed within a systems framework comprising six basic functions: (1) surveillance of current patterns and observable trends in medical utilization and delivery, (2) standard setting to establish desired objectives with regard to utilization and delivery patterns, (3) assessment of current performance vis-à-vis the standards, (4) targeting priority areas for intervention, (5) implementation of specific control procedures designed to correct identified deficiencies, and (6) evaluation of the control process and the effects of intervention.

For each of these functions, Stuart recommended that some specific considerations be kept in mind. Under program surveillance, the most obvious need is to develop an accurate and consistent means of profiling patient utilization patterns and provider delivery patterns. Use of claims-based systems modeled on the surveillance and utilization review component of the Medicaid Management Information System offers several advantages over other options such as reliance on hospital abstracting services or independent development of a periodic sample survey. Costs of data acquisition and verification are minimal because claims information must be collected in any event. The system collects data on all reimbursed services and thus permits analysis of changing patterns of service utilization (particularly among potential outpatient substitutes for inpatient care)—analysis which, again, is impossible under more limited approaches.

It is clear that some form of surveillance would be conducted regardless of which NHI plan is enacted. The characteristics of the plan, however, would influence the development of this activity. NHI proposals that involve multiple plans may make implementation of a nationwide surveillance and utilization review approach difficult if not impossible. Emphasis on review by Professional Standards Review Organizations also may jeopardize the surveillance and utilization review approach. Assuming that PSROs would continue as the primary utilization control mechanism for publicly financed health programs, there would be a marked increase in demand for hospital profile data regardless of information source, scope, or method of data processing. Unless standardized working relationships were systematically developed between PSROs and the claims payment agencies (be they fiscal intermediaries or a government administration), the result would be a haphazard surveillance effort that would jeopardize any serious attempt to control the level or pattern of medical service usage.

The same might be said for standard-setting activities. In the short term, utilization control decisions would have to be based on standards related to current norms of practice. Only the Health Security bill derives explicit utilization standards from program objectives for cost, distribution of services, and quality of care. All other NHI proposals are caught up in the conundrum created by the PSRO amendment: How can a single policy tool be used to meet the conflicting objectives of improving quality while reducing costs? There is no concrete evidence that PSROs have had much effect in either direction, but there is considerable speculation that, at the operational level at least, cost considerations are not top priority. The key to reform is standard setting. PSROs employ explicit length-of-stay norms, but the impact is diluted or even eliminated through the subjective process of establishing acceptable ranges about the norms. If this practice were to continue under national health insurance, either utilization control policy would become an empty shell or pressure would develop to try other approaches. The latter appears more likely.

To choose among these approaches, Stuart outlined a framework based on an accounting of direct and indirect benefits and costs. Regulatory approaches to utilization control rely on the threat of sanctions to achieve their objectives. The sanctions include moral suasion, program reimbursement tied to "approved" behavior, and various administrative and judicial procedures. Using cost effectiveness as the criterion for control selection limits choice among these options. Efforts to change delivery patterns through moral suasion and peer pressure are valuable complements to any control procedure, but by themselves they offer no assurance that utilization objectives will be met, particularly if those objectives call for a reduction in aggregate service use. Administrative and judicial sanctions may prove cost-effective for short periods of time, but in the long term their value is primarily punitive. Tying reimbursement to prior or concurrent review procedures is the most expensive approach to utilization control. There is no evidence that universal employment of such procedures is cost-effective except under the most unusual circumstances. Even when targeted prior review and concurrent review proved cost-effective, larger savings could be obtained from other regulatory controls such as prior authorization requirements and posttreatment review. Over time, Stuart concluded, claims review is probably the control mechanism with the highest potential for positive net returns, but to be effective the process must be based on explicit and enforceable medical protocols.

In assessing utilization policy, Stuart emphasized that many of the conditions affecting the outcome of present and past control activities would change under national health insurance. Expanded eligibility would increase the aggregate costs of control, but unit costs would probably decline, given some reasonable expectation of economies of scale. As a larger percentage of the population (both providers and consumers) was covered, the possibilities of escape from the impact of utilization controls would drop. On another plane, the expansion in benefit coverage implicit in every NHI plan would, by increasing the service choices available at the same low user price, make utilization control activities more important than they now are. The likelihood that providers would continue to be paid on a service-by-service basis under national health insurance also increases the importance of control efforts. In short, if there is a common denominator among all NHI proposals, it is that utilization control options cannot be ignored.

Type of Coverage

LONG-TERM CARE

Long-term care refers to health and social services that are provided inside or outside an institution over an extended period to chronically ill, functionally impaired persons, most of whom are elderly. Although long-term care has generally been ignored in deliberations on national health insurance, Pollak observed that government has become heavily involved in financing and regulation of the long-term-care system. In designing national health insurance, it is therefore appropriate to examine ways in which current long-term-care policy can be improved. Because costs are a primary concern in this reevaluation, Pollak addressed three critical features of a long-term-care benefit: the services to be covered, the organizational arrangements to control service delivery, and the terms for patient cost sharing.

The primary issue in defining the long-term-care benefit package is also the central issue of long-term-care policy: Should personal care and maintenance services be provided on an extended basis to persons in the community who need such services even if they do not need medical (or "skilled") services frequently and regularly? Advocates of such extensive coverage argue not only that these are desirable and needed services but also that they are cost-effective substitutes for nursing home care that is largely publicly financed.

Evidence on the costs of such services, though limited, led Pollak to conclude that expanding present coverage of noninstitutional services would probably increase public expenditures because of service use by persons not now receiving publicly financed institutional care. Although a subsidy for noninstitutional services might improve the living conditions for impaired individuals, Pollak cautioned policy makers to regard this subsidy as a probable addition to—rather than substitution for—current publicly financed services. The European experience, though not yet analyzed in depth, seems consistent with these conclusions. Most West European countries provide a broader spectrum of long-term-care services than does the United States. Although these services may add up to better care for the elderly, they do not appear to reduce sharply the use of institutions.

Expectations of increased costs may not justify neglect of noninstitutional care, but they demand exploration of mechanisms that may limit expenditures by encouraging cost-effective service delivery. To this end, Pollak explored several organizational options for a long-term-care program. All options are based on the channeling of all long-term maintenance, social support, and personal care financing through a single local agency. Without such financial channeling, Pollak argued, integrated delivery of institutional and noninstitutional services becomes virtually impossible. Given channeling, however, considerable leeway still exists in program design.

Local agencies could receive funds either through a fixed budget or by open-ended financing. The fixed budget is more conducive to cost containment, and, when accompanied by administrative discretion in the distribution of benefits, provides an opportunity to target publicly financed benefits to people without family or other supports. But current ignorance about appropriate long-term-care expenditures makes it difficult to fix a budget with confidence. The alternative is an open-ended entitlement program, in which cost containment depends on the ability to specify and enforce equitable rules for resource allocation. In allocating benefits, a local agency again has two choices—to subsidize consumers who then pay providers, or to subsidize providers directly. Pollak's analysis suggests that consumer subsidies are preferable, for they enhance the likelihood that providers will respond readily and equitably to beneficiaries' demands for services.

In contrast to acute care, long-term care comprises an array of substitutable services that can be provided by family or friends as well as by employed personnel. Pollak argued that price should play a role in the choice of services or provider and therefore found patient cost sharing an important element of long-term-care policy. In designing cost-sharing terms, Pollak recommended a distinction between institutional and noninstitutional services (charging more for the former than the latter) and between married and single individuals (assuring the noninstitutionalized spouse adequate income to remain in the community). In addition, cost sharing should vary with income and with the cost of service. Based on these and other considerations, Pollak developed a structure for cost sharing in long-term care.

To have a cost-effective long-term-care program, policy makers must decide who is to be responsible for coordination of services to each beneficiary. Coordination can be made the responsibility of the local long-term-care financing agency, or individuals could be allowed to choose among several agencies offering that service. The former option relies heavily on centralized administration to monitor performance; the latter relies on the market. These control mechanisms may be combined by allowing the central agency to assess client needs and to allocate subsidies accordingly, while leaving clients free to use subsidies to choose their own coordinating agencies or, perhaps, to coordinate for themselves. This policy would centralize control over expenditures while allowing individuals and coordinators considerable flexibility in the choice of a service package. Without more experience, however, no organizational option can be unequivocally recommended. Experimentation and variation therefore seem in order.

PRESCRIPTION DRUGS

Concern about the costs and quality of a drug benefit have led to proposals for limited coverage, notably through creation of an approved drug list or formulary for the NHI program. The formulary could be used to control the quality and efficacy of drugs covered by the program, and to target benefits to a particular segment of the population—specifically, persons suffering from chronic diseases. In neither case would establishment of a formulary be simple. Kudrle and Lennox observed that difficult decisions would have to be made about the inclusion or exclusion in the formulary of individual drugs, that problems might develop in communicating coverage limits to beneficiaries and providers, and that people might resort to manipulation or fraud to obtain coverage. Despite these problems, a formulary might be preferable to other control mechanisms, like quantity limits on benefits, that have been employed by the Medicaid program. The arbitrary nature of these limits might serve to restrict benefits without regard to patients' clinical conditions.

Public drug insurance plans that are founded on the assumption of no patient cost sharing would have to rely on special administrative mechanisms to control costs. One of the most important of these mechanisms—the maximum-allowable-cost regulations, which attempt to control costs of both ingredients and dispensing fees—were developed as a result of dissatisfaction with the apparently excessive costs of drug benefits under Medicaid. Ingredient reimbursement would be set to approximate the actual prices at which outlets of various sizes could expect to obtain drugs. To be fair, reimbursement rates would have to allow for various reimbursement levels to pharmacies in different classes, because pharmacies do experience different wholesale prices and operating costs. It is not yet clear how these regulations will work. If an NHI plan employed no patient cost sharing, then alternatives like government-industry negotiation on ingredient prices would merit consideration.

The challenge faced by administrative cost controls would be less formidable in an NHI system that involved cost sharing. With cost sharing, the final purchaser would have a real incentive to seek out the most efficient source of supply, and now that pharmacies may advertise, such seekers might be able to find the most efficient source. One of the simplest cost-sharing schemes proposes to cover drug ingredients only, with the patient paying the dispensing fee. Perhaps a more effective cost-sharing method would be a scheme to cover drugs only after a significant deductible had been met. Any drug cost-sharing scheme may be criticized on grounds that it deters needed utilization, but the burden of proof appears to lie solidly with people who claim such a problem is serious for other than the poor. Kudrle and Lennox believe the problems of the poor important enough to recommend against cost sharing for this segment of the population.

The potentially large number of drug claims per year and the low average prescription cost mean that administrative costs are likely to be a large proportion of an NHI drug program's costs. Claims handling could be simplified with the establishment of a nationwide drug computer network, but the costs and feasibility of such a system remain unknown. A principal benefit of such a network could be vastly improved utilization review.

DENTAL CARE

Dental coverage under national health insurance has received remarkably little attention for a benefit that is, in terms of present spending and the potential for service expansion with public subsidy, of the same order of magnitude as prescription drug coverage. The key reason, according to Kudrle, is that dental care not only is a relatively small part of the total health care bill but also is relatively unimportant to most people's health. Dentistry is different from medicine in that patients in most income and educational categories value its ministrations less than providers do. Thus even people who have the benefit of prepaid dental care tend to underuse the system (in terms of initiation of contact). Yet, once under treatment, the insured patient may receive an excessive amount of service in the fee-for-service delivery system.

Kudrle argued that dental care is far more expensive than it otherwise might be because the dental profession has restricted the number of dentists who are trained and has controlled the amount of activity that can be delegated to auxiliaries. Dentist hostility to more task delegation to auxiliaries can be traced to a general fear of loss of prestige and income. The prospect of a significant rise in the dentist-population ratio during the next few years has galvanized that hostility. The dental profession's control of the number and type of dental health personnel has affected access as well as cost. The distribution of dentists in the United States is very similar to the distribution of doctors; dentists in underserved areas are much more likely to be excessively busy than are their colleagues elsewhere. The quality of American dentistry appears to vary substantially, and there has been a large amount of poor treatment under public programs.

Kudrle believes the foremost questions of public dental insurance are related to beneficiaries. He found little justification for spending the estimated $20 billion price of a free universal dental care system. Most adults are capable of judging for themselves how much to spend for dental care, and the overwhelming majority can easily afford dental care if they choose. The most persuasive justification for public intervention appears to be to protect the long-term dental health of children from the problems caused by the low incomes or poor judgment of their parents. But a scheme that would simply reduce the price for fee-for-service dentistry for all children would be most unwise. The capacity to meet the estimated demand is not in place, and it can be expected that services would be provided first to those already enjoying most contact with the system. Because poor people do not perceive dental care to be important, the offer of free care is not expected to significantly increase their elective contact with the dental care system. Free dental care for children (or for the general population) therefore could easily be "welfare for the rich."

To increase poor children's access to dental care under public insurance, Kudrle recommended that the government consider providing services in a school-based dental nurse program. Not only could school-based provision of care reach the people most in need of treatment, but also it could serve all children far more cheaply than does the present system. (One estimate is from 66 percent to 71 percent of the per capita cost of using the present delivery system.) Both the cost and the quality of care in dental nurse programs abroad appear to confirm the claims of their proponents.

If a traditional approach to insurance were taken instead, Kudrle suggested that it would be counterproductive to ask the poor to make a copayment for dental services; both the CHIP and the Kennedy-Mills bill, however, require part of the cost to be borne by all patients (and CHIP offers no benefits until a substantial deductible has been met). Another potentially crippling feature of proposed children's coverage is the service cutoff age at fourteen. Such a limitation promises that the system would expire for most children just at the time of greatest need for treatment to avoid damage to the permanent teeth.

In contrast to the situation with respect to drug coverage and some other benefits, the administration of dental claims appears to be a most neglected area of investigation. Such evidence as is available from Medicaid and Canadian provincial programs suggests the importance of special attention to expensive services, services most likely to be repeated unnecessarily frequently, and ones involving considerable professional discretion. Beyond these cautions, assurance of accountability would require a much higher level of inspection for quality than that which prevails at present in any public program in the United States. It is easier to detect fraud and to control quality in dentistry than in medicine because most dental treatment leaves trails traceable by X-ray on hard tissue.

Conclusions

Expanding access to medical care while controlling costs is obviously not easy. Throughout this book, the authors have identified policy choices they believe necessary to achieving this task. Policy makers must face these choices even if Congress does not enact national health insurance. If we were to continue our current system of mixed public and private financing in which neither the market nor regulation sufficiently controls the allocation of resources to health, medical care would increasingly absorb resources that could be better spent elsewhere. With or without national health insurance, difficult and controversial choices must be made.

The preceding discussion of parts of national health policy suggests some broad guidelines for the whole. First, broader access and cost containment can coexist only if the government asserts its responsibility for allocating resources to medical care. For this purpose, it is necessary to establish formal mechanisms for deciding how much the government is willing to spend on medical care and for distributing government funds among providers of service. Establishment of these mechanisms would mean replacement of the current payment system in which providers are, for the most part, able to set their own income or revenue targets, with a system in which providers and the government negotiated acceptable levels of payment for services rendered. Our authors argued that limits should be set on total expenditures for physician and hospital care. Physician fee schedules and hospital budgets that determine the distribution of those expenditures would be negotiated in a public forum. Although providers' interests would undoubtedly influence public payment provisions, this forum would allow other considerations—in particular competing demand for public funds—to affect allocation decisions. The result would be a political decision on what medical services are worth in relation to other goods and services.

As policy makers decide how much to spend on medical care, they will also influence how and where medical care is provided. Policies directed toward cost containment will affect resource distribution and vice versa. Our authors' second conclusion, then, was that policies cannot be developed in isolation from each other. For hospitals, capital expenditures regulation and payment policies must operate in concert, not opposition. For physicians, fee negotiations must pay as much attention to relative fees across geographic areas and across medical specialties as to absolute levels of payment to any particular group of physicians.

Limits on total expenditures would encourage consistency among policies, but they would not assure it. Our authors' third conclusion is that policy makers will treat resources as limited only if they or their constituencies bear the costs of policies made. In other words, allocation or regulatory decisions cannot be separated from payment responsibility. Achieving this objective does not require that all financial, policy-making, and administrative responsibilities be concentrated in a single agency or level of government. Authority can be delegated and responsibilities shared among levels of government and among public and private organizations. But whoever makes regulatory decisions—at the federal, state, or local level—must contribute to NHI financing.

Finally, if these decisions are to promote equitable access to care as well as to contain public expenditure, payments, and regulations must be uniform across all purchasers, public and private. Policies that apply to only one segment of the purchasing public encourage providers to discriminate against patients for whom payments are lower or regulation is more burdensome. The results are inequities in access and escape valves from public controls.

These broad rules for the design of national health insurance can apply to a variety of specific plans. They apply to the health benefits this book has discussed, and to health benefits that have not been addressed here. They apply as well to the current financing system as to an expansion in public coverage. It is our hope, then, that whatever legislative action Congress takes, this book will provide a useful guide to policy choices.

SELECTED
BIBLIOGRAPHY

Altman, Drew. "Connections Between Hospital Rate Setting and Planning in Maryland and Rhode Island." Harvard Center for Community Health and Medical Care, Boston, Mass. Report Series R–45–6, June 1976.

————. "The Politics of Health Care Regulation: The Care of the National Health Planning and Resources Development Act." *Journal of Health Politics, Policy, and Law* 12 (Winter 1978): 560–80.

Ambrose, E. R.; A. B. Hord; and W. J. Simpson. *A Quality Evaluation of the Specific Dental Services Provided by the Saskatchewan Dental Plan: Final Report*. Regina: Commercial Printers, 1976.

American Dental Association (ADA), Task Force on National Health Programs. *Dentistry in National Health Programs*. Chicago: American Dental Association, 1971.

American Medical Association, Center for Health Services Research and Development. *Profile of Medical Practice*. 1975–76 ed. Chicago: American Medical Association, 1976.

Andersen, Ronald; Joanna Lion; and Odin W. Anderson. *Two Decades of Health Services*. Cambridge, Mass.: Ballinger Publishing Company, 1976.

Anderson, C. E.; E. A. Nehan; F. I. Ravenscroft; and D. M. Vickery. *A Site-Specific Study of Physician Extender Staffed Primary Care Centers*. McLean, Va.: The MITRE Corporation, February 1977, Publication No. MTR7495.

Anderson, Odin W. *Health Care: Can There Be Equity? The United States, Sweden and England*. New York: John Wiley and Sons, 1972.

Anderson, Odin W., and Paul B. Sheatsley. *Comprehensive Medical Insurance: A Study of Costs, Use, and Attitudes Under Two Plans*. Research Series No. 9. Health Insurance Foundation, 1959.

Andreopolous, Spyros, ed. *National Health Insurance: Can We Learn From Canada?* New York: John Wiley and Sons, 1975.

Annual Report 1974–1975: Hospital Insurance and Diagnostic Services. Health and Welfare, Canada.

"Annual Report of Financial and Statistical Data for Fiscal Year Ended June 30, 1976, for Civil Service Retirement, Federal Employees Group Life Insurance, Federal Employees Health Benefits and Retired Federal Employees Health Benefits." Bureau of Retirement, Insurance, and Occupational Health, U.S. Civil Service Commission (CSC).

Appel, Gary L., and Aaron Lowin. *Physician Extenders: An Evaluation of Policy-Related Research.* Minneapolis: Interstudy, January 1975.

Armstrong, Robert A. "Canada's Health Insurance Programs." Paper presented to the Association of University Programs in Health Administration, Carleton University, Ottawa, Ontario, June 1973.

Arthur Anderson and Co. "Study of Reimbursement and Practice Arrangements of Provider-Based Physicians." Unpublished, 1977.

Bachynsky, J. A. "Pharmaceutical Benefit Programs in Canada." Paper presented to the Conference on Drug and Pharmaceutical Reimbursement, sponsored by the National Center for Health Services Research, Washington, D.C., November 1–5, 1976. Mimeographed.

Badgley, Robin F.; Catherine A. Charles; and George M. Torrance. *The Canadian Experience with Universal Health Insurance* Draft. Toronto: Department of Behavioral Science, University of Toronto, 1975.

Bagramian, R. A.; J. Jenny; P. J. Woodbury; and J. Proshek. "Quality Assessment of Restorations in a Population of School Children." *American Journal of Public Health* 65 (April 1975): 397–99.

Bailey, D. R., and D. C. Riedel. "Recertification and Length of Stay." *Blue Cross Reports* 4 (July 1968).

Bashshur, Richard L., and Charles A. Metzner. "Vulnerability to Risk and Awareness of Dual Choice of Health Insurance Plan." *Health Services Research* (Summer 1970):106–113.

Bauer, Katherine G. "Containing Costs of Health Services Through Incentive Reimbursement: Some Approaches by Third Party Payers." *Cases in Health Services.* Series no. 4. Harvard Center for Community Health and Medical Care, Boston, Mass., December 1973.

————. "Hospital Rate Setting—This Way to Salvation?" *Milbank Memorial Fund Quarterly* 55 (Winter 1977):117–58.

————. "Improving the Information for Hospital Rate Setting." Report Series R–45–15. Harvard Center for Community Health and Medical Care, Boston, Mass., September 1976.

Bauer, Katherine G., and Drew Altman. "Linking Planning and Rate-Setting Control to Contain Hospital Costs." Harvard Center for Community Health and Medical Care, Boston, Mass., October 24, 1975.

Bauer, Katherine G., and Arva Rosenfeld Clark. "New York: The Formula Approach to Prospective Reimbursement." Harvard Center for Community Health and Medical Care, Boston, Mass., March 1974.

Bauer, Katherine G., and Paul M. Densen. "Some Issues in the Incentive Reimbursement Approach to Cost Containment: An Overview." Health Care Policy Discussion Paper No. 7, Harvard Center for Community Health and Medical Care, Program on Health Care Policy, Boston, Mass., May 1973.

Baum, Martin A.; Peter McMenamin; and Mel Rudov. *Program Evaluation Plan: Professional Standards Review Organizations.* Office of the Assistant Secretary for Health; Office of Professional Standards Review; Department of Health, Education, and Welfare, September 1975.

Becker, B., and P. Bonner. *Criteria in Peer Review.* Cambridge, Mass.: Arthur D. Little, 1974.

Bellin, Lowell Eliezer, and Florence Kavaler. "Policing Publicly Funded Health Care for Poor Quality, Overutilization and Fraud—The New York City Medicaid Experience." *American Journal of Public Health* 60 (May 1970) :814.

Benham, Lee; Alex Maurizi; and Melvin V. Reder. "Migration, Location and Remuneration of Medical Personnel: Physicians and Dentists." *Review of Economics and Statistics* 50 (August 1968) :332–47.

Berki, S. E. *Hospital Economics.* Lexington, Mass.: Lexington Books, 1972.

Berki, S. E.; Marie Ashcraft; Roy Penchansky; and Robert S. Fortus. "Enrollment Choice in a Multi-HMO Setting: The Roles of Health Risk, Financial Vulnerability, and Access to Care." *Medical Care* 15 (February 1977) :95–114.

Berry, Charles; J. Alan Brewster; Philip J. Held; Barbara H. Kehrer; Larry M. Manheim; and Uwe Reinhardt. "A Study of the Responses of Canadian Physicians to the Introduction of Universal Medical Care Insurance: The First Five Years in Quebec." Final report. Princeton, N.J.: Mathematica Policy Research, February 28, 1978.

Bible, B. L. "Physicians' Views of Medical Practice in Nonmetropolitan Communities." *Public Health Reports* 85 (January 1970) :11–17.

Bicknell, William J., and Diana C. Walsh. "The Certificate-of-Need: The Massachusetts Experience." *New England Journal of Medicine* 290 (May 15, 1975):1054–1061.

Blagg, Christopher, and Tom Sawyer. "Letters to the Editor." *New England Journal of Medicine* 289 (September 6, 1973):537.

Blair, Roger D., and Ronald J. Vogel. "The Cost of Administering Medicare." *Quarterly Review of Economics and Business* 17 (1977):67–77.

Bliss, Ann A., and Eva D. Cohen, eds. *The New Health Professionals.* Germantown, Md.: Aspen Systems Corporation, 1977.

Blumberg, Mark S. "Rational Provider Prices: An Incentive for Improved Health Delivery." In George K. Chacko, ed. *Health Handbook.* Amsterdam: North Holland Publishing Co., 1978.

Booz, Allen and Hamilton. *The Impact of National Health Insurance on the Pharmaceutical Industry* (Final Report). Submitted to the U.S. Department of Commerce, September 2, 1975. Mimeographed.

Breslow, Lester. "Do HMOs Provide Health Maintenance?" Paper presented to Delta Omega, San Francisco, Calif., November 7, 1973.

Breslow, Lester, and Joseph R. Hochstim. "Sociocultural Aspects of Cervical Cytology in Alameda County, California." *Public Health Reports* 79 (February 1964):107–112.

Brian, E. "Foundation for Medical Care Control of Hospital Utilization: CHAP–A PSRO Prototype." *New England Journal of Medicine* 288 (April 26, 1973).

Brian, Earl W., and Stephen F. Biggens. "California's Medi-Cal Copayment Experiment." *Supplement to Medical Care* 2 (December 1974):1–303.

Brodie, Donald, and Roger Benson. *Drug Utilization Review and Drug Usage as a Determinant of the Quality of Health Care.* Washington, D.C.: U.S. Department of Health, Education, and Welfare, Health Services Research, January 1976.

Broida, Joel H. "Macro and Micro Assessment of an Alternative Delivery System: The HMO: Methodology and Output." Presented at American Public Health Association, Chicago, November 16–20, 1975.

Brook, Robert H. "Critical Issues in the Assessment of Quality of Care and Their Relationship to HMOs." *Journal of Medical Education* 48 (April 1973 part 2):114–34.

————. *Quality of Care Assessment: Comparison of Five Methods of Peer Review.* Washington, D.C.: National Center for Health Services Research and Development, U.S. Government Printing Office, 1973.

_____. "A Skeptic Looks at Peer Review." *Prism* (October 1974) : 29–32.

Brook, Robert, and Kathleen Williams. "Evaluation of the New Mexico Peer Review System 1971 to 1973." *Medical Care* 14 (December 1976), Supplement.

Brown, Murray G. "Analysis of Physician Practice Location Decisions in Nova Scotia." Paper presented at ORSA-TIMS meeting, Las Vegas, November 1975.

Bunker, J. P. "Surgical Manpower, A Comparison of Operations and Surgeons in the United States, England, and Wales." *New England Journal of Medicine* 285 (January 1970) :135–44.

Butler, J. R., and R. Knight. "The Designated Areas Project Study of Medical Practice Areas." Health Services Research Unit, University of Kent at Canterbury, June 1974.

Cady, John F. *Drugs on the Market.* Lexington, Mass.: D.C. Heath and Co., 1976.

California Department of Health, Field Services Section. *Prior Authorization Study Project Final Report.* Sacramento: California Department of Health, March 24, 1975.

California Department of Health, Health and Welfare Agency. *Modified Volume Purchase Project.* Sacramento: California Department of Health, 1977.

California Medical Association, Bureau of Research and Planning. "Physician Dissatisfaction with Medi-Cal." *Socioeconomic Report* 15 (April 1975).

_____. "A Survey of Physician Participation in the Medi-Cal Program." *Socioeconomic Report* 15 (February/March 1975).

Carlson, Rick J. *The End of Medicine.* New York: John Wiley and Sons, 1975.

Cauffman, Joy G.; Milton I. Roemer; and Carl S. Schultz. "The Impact of Health Insurance Coverage on Health Care of School Children." *Public Health Reports* 82 (April 1967) :323–38.

Charney, Evan, and Harriet Kitzman. "The Child-Health Nurse (Pediatric Nurse Practitioner) in Private Practice: A Controlled Trial." *New England Journal of Medicine* 285 (December 1971) :1353–58.

Children's Dental Health Research Project. *Report to the Minister of Health, British Columbia and the President, The College of Dental Surgeons of British Columbia.* Victoria: Queen's Printer, 1975.

"Civil Service Should Audit Kaiser Plans' Premium Rates Under the Federal Employees Health Benefits Program to Protect the Government." U.S. GAO Report HRD 78–42, January 1978.

Clark, Wayne. *Placebo or Cure? State and Local Health Planning Agencies in the South.* Southern Governmental Monitoring Project, Southern Regional Council, 1977.

Clarkson, Kenneth W. *Intangible Capital and Rates of Return: Effects of Research and Promotion on Profitability.* Washington, D.C.: American Enterprise Institute for Public Policy Research, 1977.

Cobb, Alton B., Donnie P. Wilson, and John M. Abide. "Use of Drugs Under the Mississippi Program." *Journal of the Mississippi State Medical Association* 13 (1972):82.

Cochrane, A. L. *Effectiveness and Efficiency: Random Reflections on Health Services.* London: The Nuffield Provincial Hospital Trust, 1972.

Cochrane, A. L., and P. C. Elwood. "Screening: The Case Against It." *Medical Officer* 121 (January 31, 1969):53–57.

Cohen, Eva D.; Linda M. Crootof; Marsha G. Goldfarb; Kathleen Keenan; Mieko M. Korper; and Mary Triffin. *An Evaluation of Policy Related Research on New and Expanded Roles of Health Workers.* Office of Regional Activities and Continuing Education, Yale University School of Medicine, October 1974.

Cohen, Harris S., and Winston J. Dean. "To Practice or Not to Practice: Developing State Law and Policy on Physician's Assistants." *Milbank Memorial Fund Quarterly: Health and Society* (Fall 1974):349–76.

Cohodes, Donald R. "Certificate-of-Need Controls and Hospitals: An Outcome Assessment." n.d. Mimeographed.

Collen, Morris F.; Loring G. Dales; Gary D. Friedman; Charles D. Flagle; Robert Feldman; and A. B. Siegelaub. "Multiphasic Checkup Evaluation Study No. 4, Preliminary Cost Benefit Analysis for Middle-Aged Men." *Preventive Medicine* 2 (June 1973):236–46.

Commerce Clearing House, Inc. *Medicare and Medicaid Guide* (updated biweekly). Three current volumes plus year-by-year "New Development" binders.

Committee for Economic Development. "Revitalizing the Federal Personnel System: A Statement by the Program Committee for Economic Development." February 1978, unpublished paper.

Committee for the Special Research Project in the Health Insurance Plan of Greater New York. *Health and Medical Care in New York City.* Cambridge, Mass.: Harvard University Press, 1967.

The Committee of Relative Value Studies. *1969 California Relative Value Studies.* San Francisco: California Medical Association, 1969.

Comptroller General of the United States. *Comprehensive Health Planning as Carried Out by States and Areawide Agencies in Three States.* Washington, D.C.: U.S. Government Printing Office, 1974.

Comptroller General of the United States. *Home Health—The Need for a National Policy to Better Provide for the Elderly.* Washington, D.C.: The General Accounting Office, 1977.

Comptroller General of the United States. *Report to the Congress: Potential Effects of National Health Insurance Proposals on Medicare Beneficiaries.* Washington, D.C.: U.S. Government Printing Office, February 24, 1977.

Coms, Nathan C. "The Clinical Evaluation of Medicaid's Patients in the State of New York." *Journal of Public Health Dentistry* 33 (1973):192.

Cooper, Michael H. *Rationing Health Care.* New York: John Wiley and Sons, 1975.

Copeman, W. J. "177 of 203 Doctors Stay in Underserved Areas." *Ontario Medical Review* (December 1973):774–77.

Crane, Steven. "The Effect of Formal Control on the Provision and Distribution of Hospital Facilities." Stanford, Calif.: Stanford University, Health Services Research Program, Research Workshop in Health Economics, May 1978.

Crawford, R., and R. L. McCormack. "Reasons Physicians Leave Primary Care Practice." *Journal of Medical Education* 46 (April 1971):263–68.

Cutler, John L.; Savitri Ramcharan; Robert Feldman; A. B. Siegelaub; Barbara Campbell; Gary D. Friedman; Loring G. Dales; and Morris F. Collen. "Multiphasic Checkup Evaluation Study: 1. Methods and Population." *Preventive Medicine* 2 (June 1973):197–206.

Davis, Karen. "Economic Theories of Behavior in Nonprofit, Private Hospitals." *Economic and Business Bulletin* 24 (Winter 1972): 1–13.

————. "Equal Treatment and Unequal Benefits: The Medicare Program." *Milbank Memorial Fund Quarterly: Health and Society* 53 (Fall 1975):449–88.

————. "Hospital Costs and the Medicare Program." *Social Security Bulletin* 36 (August 1973):18–36.

————. *National Health Insurance: Benefits, Costs, and Consequences.* Washington, D.C.: The Brookings Institution, 1975.

Dean, Winston J. "Physician Extender Reimbursement Under Title XVIII of the Social Security Act (Medicare)." Memorandum prepared for DHEW, Health Resources Administration Work Group, February 28, 1977.

————. "State Legislation for Physician's Assistants, A Review and Analysis." *Health Services Reports* 88 (January 1973): 3–12.

Defriese, Gordon H. "On Paying the Fiddler to Change the Tune: Further Evidence from Ontario Regarding the Impact of Universal Health Insurance on the Organization and Patterns of Medical Practice." *Milbank Memorial Fund Quarterly: Health and Society* 53 (Spring 1975):117–48.

Derthick, Martha. *The Influence of Federal Grants: Public Assistance in Massachusetts.* Cambridge, Mass.: Harvard University Press, 1970.

de Vise, Pierre. "Physician Migration from Inland to Coastal States: Antipodal Examples of Illinois and California." *Journal of Medical Education* 48 (February 1973):141–51.

Diehr, P. K.; W. C. Richardson; W. L. Drucker; S. M. Shortell; and J. P. LoGerfo. "The Seattle Prepaid Health Care Project: Comparison of Health Services Delivery." Grant no. R18 HS 00694, DHEW, HRA, National Center for Health Services Research, November 1976.

Dickens, Paul F. "The Maximum Allowable Cost Regulations and Pharmaceutical Research and Development." Research and Statistics Note, Office of Research and Statistics, SSA, DHEW, March 4, 1976.

Directory of Accredited Residencies, 1975–76 and 1977–78. Chicago: American Medical Association, 1976.

Doherty, Neville, and Iftkhar Hussain. "Costs of Providing Dental Services for Children in Public and Private Practices." *Health Services Research* 10 (Fall 1975):244–53.

Donabedian, Avedis. "An Evaluation of Prepaid Group Practice." *Inquiry* 6 (September 1969):3–27.

————. "Evaluating the Quality of Medical Care." *Milbank Memorial Fund Quarterly* 44 (July 1966, part 2):166–203.

————. *A Guide to Medical Care Administration.* Medical Care Appraisal—Quality and Utilization, vol. 2. Washington, D.C.: The American Public Health Association, 1969.

Dowling, William L. "Prospective Reimbursement of Hospitals." *Inquiry* 11 (September 1974):163–80.

Dozier, Dave. "1970–71 Survey of Consumer Experience: Report of the State of California Employees' Medical and Hospital Care Program." Prepared Under the Policy Direction of the Medical Advisory Council to the Board of Administration of the Public Employees' Retirement System, Sacramento, May 1973.

Dumbaugh, Karin A. "Hospital Information Systems in the Province of Quebec." Report Series R–45–2, Harvard Center for

Community Health and Medical Care, Boston, Mass., January 1976.

Duncan, Burris; Ann N. Smith; and Henry K. Silver. "Comparison of the Physical Assessment of Children by Pediatric Nurse Practitioners and Pediatricians." *American Journal of Public Health* 61 (June 1971) :1170–78.

Dunham, Andrew. "The Impact of Certificate-of-Need Regulation." Address to the Center for Health Administration Studies Workshop, University of Chicago, May 18, 1978.

Dunning, James M. "Deployment and Control of Dental Auxiliaries in New Zealand and Australia." *Journal of the American Dental Association* 85 (September 1972) :621.

Dutton, Diana Barbara. "A Causal Model of the Use of Health Services: The Role of the Delivery System." Ph.D. dissertation. Massachusetts Institute of Technology, February 1976.

Earnings of Physicians in Canada. Annual. Health and Welfare Canada, Health Economics and Statistics Directorate, Health Programs Branch.

The Economic Report of the President. Washington, D.C.: U.S. Government Printing Office, 1978.

Egdahl, Richard H. "Foundations for Medical Care." *New England Journal of Medicine* 288 (March 8, 1973) :491–98.

Egdahl, Richard H.; R. H. Taft; J. J. Friedland; and K. Linde. "The Potential of Organizations of Fee-for-Service Physicians for Achieving Significant Decreases in Hospitalization." *Annals of Surgery* 186 (September 1977) :388–99.

Eilers, Robert D., and Robert C. Jones. *The Attitudes and Anticipated Behavior of Dentists Under Various Reimbursement Arrangements.* Homewood, Ill.: Richard D. Irwin, 1972.

Ellwood, Paul M. *The Health Care Alliance.* Excelsior, Minnesota: Interstudy.

"The 11th Report of the Human Renal Transplant Registry." *Journal of the American Medical Association* 226 (December 3, 1973) :1197.

Emery, David; Dan Calvin; and Allen Dobson. "An Analysis of NHSC Economic Performances for Quarter 3 FY 1975." Working paper No. 3. Office of Policy, Evaluation, and Legislation, Health Services Administration, DHEW, February 1976.

Enterline, Philip E.; Vera Slater; Alison D. McDonald; and J. Corbett McDonald. "The Distribution of Medical Services Before and After 'Free' Medical Care—The Quebec Experience." *New England Journal of Medicine* 289 (November 29, 1973): 1174–78.

Enthoven, Alain C. "Consumer-Choice Health Plan." *New England Journal of Medicine* 298 (March 23, 1978):650–58 and (March 30, 1978):709–20.

Ertel, Paul, and M. Gene Aldridge, eds. *Medical Peer Review: Theory and Practice.* St. Louis: C. V. Mosby Co., 1977.

"Evaluation of Blue Cross and Medicaid Prospective Reimbursement Systems in Downstate New York." Final Report, June 1976, HEW–OS–74–248. Principal Investigator: William Dowling, Department of Health Services, School of Public Health and Community Medicine, University of Washington.

Evans, John R. "Health Manpower Problems: The Canadian Experience." In *Manpower For Health Care,* papers of the spring meeting, Institute of Medicine. Washington, D.C.: National Academy of Sciences, May 1974.

————. "Health Manpower: Issues and Goals in Canada." *Pan American Health Organization Bulletin* 8 (1974):309.

Evans, R. G. "Beyond the Medical Market Place: Expenditures, Utilization, and Pricing of Insured Health Care in Canada." In S. Andreopolous, ed. *National Health Insurance: Can We Learn From Canada?* New York: John Wiley and Sons, Inc., 1975.

————. "Does Canada Have Too Many Doctors?—Why Nobody Loves an Immigrant Physician." *Canadian Public Policy* 2 (Spring 1976):147–60.

————. "Supplier-Induced Demand: Some Empirical Evidence and Implications." in Mark Perlman, ed. *The Economics of Health and Medical Care.* New York: Halsted Press (1974):163–64.

Evans, Robert G.; E. M. A. Parish; and Floyd Scully. "Medical Production, Scale Effects, and Demand Generation." *Canadian Journal of Economics* 6 (August 1973):376–93.

Evans, R. G., and M. F. Williamson. *Extending Canadian Health Insurance: Options for Pharmacare and Denticare.* Toronto: University of Toronto Press, 1978.

Evans, Robert G., and Alan D. Wolfsen. "Moving the Target to Hit the Bullet: Generation of Utilization by Physicians in Canada." Paper presented at the National Bureau of Economic Research Conference on the Economics of Physician and Patient Behavior, Stanford, Calif., January 27–28, 1978.

Executive Office of the President, Council on Wage and Price Stability. "The Problem of Rising Health Care Costs." Staff Report. Washington, D.C.: April 1976.

Feder, Judith M. *Medicare: The Politics of Federal Hospital Insurance.* Lexington, Mass.: Lexington Books, 1977.

————. "Private Health Insurance and the Health Care Systems: Problems and Solutions." Report R–359. Washington, D.C.: Government Research Corporation, September 15, 1975.

Feder, Judith, and John Holahan. *Financing Health Care for the Elderly: Medicare, Medicaid, and Private Health Insurance.* Washington, D.C.: The Urban Institute, February 1979.

"Federal Employees Health Benefits Program 1978 Monthly Health Benefits Rates." Bureau of Retirement, Insurance, and Occupational Health, CSC.

Fein, Rashi. *The Doctor Shortage: An Economic Diagnosis.* Washington, D.C.: The Brookings Institution, 1967.

Feldman, Roger, and Richard Scheffler. "The Supply of Medical School Applicants and the Rate of Return to Training." *Quarterly Review of Economics and Business* (Spring 1978):91–98.

Feldman, Roger, and Sunny Yoder. "Financing Graduate Medical Education: An Economic Analysis of Public Policy Options." Unpublished paper, Department of Economics, University of North Carolina, 1978.

Feldstein, Martin S. "Hospital Cost Inflation: A Study of Non-Profit Price Dynamics." *American Economic Review* 61 (December 1971):853–72.

————. "A New Approach to National Health Insurance." *The Public Interest* 23 (Spring 1971).

————. *The Rising Cost of Hospital Care.* Washington, D.C.: Information Resources Press, 1971.

Feldstein, Paul J. *Financing Dental Care: An Economic Analysis.* Lexington, Mass.: D.C. Heath and Co., 1973.

————. *Health Associations and the Demand for Legislation.* Cambridge, Mass.: Ballinger Publishing Company, 1977.

Feldstein, Paul J., and John Goddeeris. "Payment for Hospital Services: Objectives and Alternatives." Ann Arbor: The University of Michigan, Health Manpower Policy Studies Group, School of Public Health, December 1976.

Fisher, Morton A. "Quality Controls." *The New York State Dental Journal* 37 (1971):26.

Fitzmaurice, J. Michael. "An Evaluation of Alternative Systems for Establishing Hospital Reimbursement Limits Under Medicare." Photocopied. Paper presented at the American Public Health Association Annual Meeting, October 1976.

Foster, Richard. "HMO: A Synthesis of the Evidence of Use." Paper presented at the Center for Health Administration Studies Workshop, University of Chicago, April 1977.

Fox, Douglas M. *The Politics of City and State Bureaucracy*. Pacific Palisades, Calif.: Goodyear Publishing Co., Inc., 1974.

Fox, J. Ronald. *Arming America: How the U.S. Buys Weapons*. Cambridge, Mass.: Harvard Business School, 1974.

Freidson, Eliot, ed. *The Hospital in Modern Society*. Glencoe, Ill.: Free Press, 1963.

Friedman, Eli. "Letters to the Editor." *New England Journal of Medicine* 289 (September 6, 1973):537.

Friedman, Jay W. "The New Zealand School Dental Service: Lesson in Radical Conservatism." *Journal of the American Dental Association* 85 (September 1972):1243.

Friedman, Kenneth M., and Stuart H. Rakoff, eds. *Toward a National Health Policy*. Lexington, Mass.: D.C. Heath and Co., 1977.

Fuchs, Victor. *Who Shall Live?* New York: Basic Books, Inc., 1974.

Fuchs, Victor R., and Marcia J. Kramer. *Determinants of Expenditures for Physicians' Services in the United States, 1948–68*. National Center for Health Services Research and Development, DHEW Publication No. (HSM) 73–3013. Washington, D.C.: DHEW, Health Services and Mental Health Administration, December 1972.

Fulda, Thomas. *Prescription Drug Data Summary, 1974*. Washington, D.C.: DHEW, 1976.

Fuller, Norman, and Margaret Patera. *Report on a Study of Medicaid Utilization of Services in a Prepaid Group Practice Health Plan*. Washington, D.C.: DHEW Public Health Service (PHS), Bureau of Medical Services, January 1976.

Gaus, Clifton. In "Hospital Costs, Stay Vary Widely Across U.S." *American Medical News* 19 (March 22, 1976).

————. "Who Enrolls in a Prepaid Group Practice?: The Columbia Experience." *Johns Hopkins Medical Journal* 128 (January 1971):9–14.

Gaus, Clifton, and Barbara Cooper. "Technology and Medicare: Alternatives for Change." Paper presented at the Conference on Health Care Technology and Quality of Care, Boston University Policy Center, Boston, Mass., November 19–20, 1976.

Gaus, Clifton; Barbara Cooper; and Constance Hirschman. "Contrasts in HMO and Fee-for-Service Performance." *Social Security Bulletin* 39 (May 1976):3–14.

Gaus, Clifton R., and Fred J. Hellinger. "Results of Hospital Prospective Reimbursement in the U.S." Paper presented to the International Conference on Policies for the Containment of Health Care Costs and Expenditures. The John E. Fogerty International Center, June 3, 1976.

Gibson, Robert M., and Charles R. Fisher. "National Health Expenditures, Fiscal Year 1977." *Social Security Bulletin* 41 (April 1978).

Gibson, Robert M., and Marjorie Smith Mueller. "National Health Expenditures, Fiscal Year 1976." *Social Security Bulletin* 40 (April 1977) :19–20.

Gibson, Robert M.; Marjorie Smith Mueller; and Charles R. Fisher. "Age Differences in Health Care Spending, Fiscal Year 1976." *Social Security Bulletin* 40 (August 1977) :Table 5.

Ginsburg, Paul B. "Resource Allocation in the Hospital Industry: The Role of Capital Financing." *Social Security Bulletin* 35 (October 1972) :20–30.

Ginzberg, Eli. "Physician Shortage Reconsidered." *New England Journal of Medicine* 275 (July 14, 1966) :85–87.

Glaser, William A. *Health Insurance Bargaining: Foreign Lessons for Americans.* New York: Halsted Press, 1978.

_____. *Paying the Doctor.* Baltimore: The Johns Hopkins Press, 1970.

_____. *Paying the Doctor Under National Health Insurance: Foreign Lessons for U.S.* New York: Columbia University, 1976.

Goldberg, Lawrence G., and Warren Greenberg. "The Health Maintenance Organization and Its Effects on Competition." Staff Report to the Federal Trade Commission, July 1977.

Golloday, Frederick L.; Marianne Miller; and Kenneth R. Smith. "Allied Health Manpower Strategies: Estimates of the Potential Gains from Efficient Task Delegation." *Medical Care* 11 (November/December 1973).

Gordis, Leon. "Effectiveness of Comprehensive Care Programs in Preventing Rheumatic Fever." *New England Journal of Medicine* 189 (August 16, 1973).

Gordon, David W. "Health Maintenance Service: Ambulatory Patient Care in the General Medical Clinic." *Medical Care* 12 (August 1975).

Gornick, Marian. "Medicare Patients: Regional Difference in Length of Stays, 1969–1971." *Social Security Bulletin* 38 (July 1975): 16.

_____. "Medicare Patients: Geographic Differences in Hospital Discharge Rates and Multiple Stays." *Social Security Bulletin* 40 (June 1977).

_____. "Ten Years of Medicare: Impact on the Covered Population." *Social Security Bulletin* 39 (July 1976) :14.

Green, Richard. *Assuring Quality in Medical Care.* Cambridge, Mass.: Ballinger Publishing Company, 1976.

Greenberg, Jay. "The Cost of In-Home Services." In *A Planning Study of Services to Non-Institutional Older Persons in Minnesota.* St. Paul: The Governor's Citizens Council on Aging, 1974.

Groner, Pat N. "Study Shows Changing Pattern of Financing." *Hospitals* 46 (March 1, 1972):135–37.

"Guidelines for Comprehensive Medical Plans Seeking Approval to Participate in the Federal Employees Health Benefits Program." Comprehensive Health Plans Office, Bureau of Retirement, Insurance, and Occupational Health, CSC.

Guptill, Paul B., and Fred E. Graham II. "Continuing Education Activities of Physicians in Solo and Group Practices: Report on a Pilot Study." *Medical Care* 14 (February 1976):173–80.

Hacon, William S. "Health Manpower in Canada." Paper presented at the Northeast Canadian/American Health Seminar, Montreal, Quebec, March 1975.

Hadley, Jack. "Canadian Evidence on the Income Elasticity of Physician Supply." The Urban Institute Working Paper 1225–02. Washington, D.C.: The Urban Institute, October 1978.

————. "A Disaggregated Model of Physicians' Specialty Choices." In Richard M. Scheffler, ed. *Research in Health Economics: An Annual Compilation,* vol. 1. Greenwich, Conn.: JAI Press, forthcoming.

————. "An Econometric Analysis of Physician Participation in the Medicaid Program." Washington, D.C.: The Urban Institute, April 1978.

————. *Models of Physicians' Specialty and Location Decisions.* Technical Paper No. 6. National Center for Health Services Research, DHEW, October 1975.

Hadley, Jack; John Holahan; and William Scanlon. "Can Fee-for-Service Reimbursement Coexist with Demand Creation?" The Urban Institute Working Paper 998–14. Washington, D.C.: The Urban Institute, April 1979.

Hadley, Jack, and Robert Lee. "Physicians' Price and Output Decisions: Theory and Evidence." Washington, D.C.: The Urban Institute, April 1978.

————. "Toward a Physician Payment Policy; Evidence from the Economic Stabilization Program." *Policy Sciences* 10 (1978–1979):105–20.

Hadley, Jack; Frank Sloan; Robert Lee; and Roger Feldman. "Financing Medical Education: Issues and Options." Final Report, The Urban Institute Working Paper 5925–3. Washington, D.C.: The Urban Institute, June 30, 1978.

Hall, Thomas D. "An Economic Model of Medical School Behavior." Ph.D. dissertation. Dept. of Economics, University of California, Los Angeles, 1975.

Hamerstein, Eric J.; W. D. Stanhope; and A. W. Horseley. "The Effects of Physicians' Assistants on Patient Care." Mimeographed. University of Oklahoma Health Sciences Center, 1973.

Harrison, Jeffrey L., and G. Donald Jud. "A Regional Analysis of Physician Availability." Paper presented at Southern Economic Association, Houston, Texas, November 8, 1973.

Hassett, James. "Why Dentists Are A Pain in the Mind." *Psychology Today* 11 (January 1978) :60–64.

Hastings, J. E. F.; F. D. Mott; A. Barclay; and D. Hewitt. "Prepaid Group Practice in Sault Ste. Marie, Ontario, Part I: Analysis of Utilization Records." *Medical Care* 11 (March/April 1973) : 91–103.

Havighurst, Clark, ed. *Regulating Health Facilities Construction*. Washington, D.C.: American Enterprise Institute for Public Policy Research, 1974.

————. "Regulation of Health Facilities and Service by 'Certificate-of-Need.' " *Virginia Law Review* 59 (1973) :1143–1232.

Havighurst, Clark C., and James F. Blumstein. "Coping with Quality Cost Trade-Offs in Medical Care: The Role of PSROs, (Professional Standards Review Organizations). *Northwestern University Law Review* 70 (March–April 1975) :6–68.

Health Care Financing Administration. "Limits on Drug Reimbursements to Save Millions." *Record* 1 (June/July 1977) :13.

Health Care Foundation of Western Massachusetts. *Newsletter* 4 (February 1977) :2.

Heclo, Hugh. *A Government of Strangers: Executive Politics in Washington*. Washington, D.C.: The Brookings Institution, 1977.

Heidenheimer, Arnold J.; Hugh Heclo; and Carolyn Teich Adams. *Comparative Public Policy: The Politics of Social Choice in Europe and America*. New York: St. Martin's Press, 1975.

Held, Philip J., and Uwe E. Reinhardt. "Health Manpower Policy in a Market Context." Paper presented at the annual meeting of the American Economic Association, Dallas, Texas, December 1975.

Hellinger, Fred J. "The Effect of Certificate-of-Need Legislation on Hospital Investment." *Inquiry* (June 1976).

————. "Hospital Charges and Medicare Reimbursement." *Inquiry* 12 (December 1975) :313–19.

Henderson, Sharon R., ed. *Profile of Medical Practice 1977.* Chicago: American Medical Association, 1977.

Henriques, Charles C.; Vincent G. Virgadamo; and Mildred D. Kahane. "Performance of Adult Health Appraisal Examinations Utilizing Nurse Practitioners-Physician Teams and Paramedical Personnel." *American Journal of Public Health* 64 (January 1974) :47–53.

Hetherington, Robert W.; Carl E. Hopkins; and Milton I. Roemer. *Health Insurance Plans: Promise and Performance.* New York: Wiley-Interscience, 1975.

Hiatt, Howard. "Protecting the Medical Commons—Who Has the Responsibility?" *New England Journal of Medicine* 293 (1975): 235–41.

Hirsch, E. O. "A Problem and Objective Oriented Approach to Patient Care Evaluation." *New England Journal of Medicine* 292 (1975).

Hirschfield, Daniel S. *The Lost Reform.* Cambridge, Mass.: Harvard University Press, 1970.

"HMO-GPP Enrollment Totals Through December 1977." Division of Group Health Plan Operations, Health Care Financing Administration.

Holahan, John. *Financing Health Care for the Poor: The Medicaid Experience.* Lexington, Mass.: Lexington Books, 1975.

————. "Physician Availability, Medical Care Reimbursement and the Delivery of Medical Services: Evidence from the Medicaid Program." *Journal of Human Resources* (Summer 1975).

————. *Physician Supply. Peer Review and Use of Health Services in Medicaid.* Washington, D.C.: The Urban Institute, 1976.

Holahan, John; Bruce Spitz; William Pollak, and Judith Feder. *Altering Medicaid Provider Reimbursement Methods.* Washington, D.C.: The Urban Institute, June 1977.

Holahan, John, and William Scanlon. "Medicaid: Current Issues and Potential Reforms." In George Peterson, *Fiscal Choices.* Washington, D.C.: The Urban Institute, forthcoming.

————. *Price Controls, Physician Fees and Physician Incomes.* Washington, D.C.: The Urban Institute, 1978.

Holahan, John; William Scanlon; and Bruce Spitz. *Restructuring Federal Medicaid Controls and Incentives.* Washington, D.C.: The Urban Institute, June 1977.

Holahan, John, and Bruce Stuart. *Controlling Medicaid Utilization Patterns.* Washington, D.C.: The Urban Institute, June 1977.

Hollister, Robert M.; Bernard M. Kramer; and Seymour S. Bellin, eds. *Neighborhood Health Centers.* Lexington, Mass.: D.C. Heath and Co., 1974.

Hood, Christopher. *The Limits of Administration.* New York: John Wiley and Sons, 1976.

Hopkins, Carl; Milton I. Roemer; Donald M. Procter; Foline Gartside; James Lubitz; Gerald Gardner; and Marc Moser. "Cost-Sharing and Prior Authorization Effects on Medicaid Services in California: Part II: The Provider's Reaction." *Medical Care* 13 (August 1975):643–47.

Hughes, Edward F. X. "Residency Distribution: The Need for Partnership." Testimony before the Senate Subcommittee on Health, Hearings on S.989, September 30, 1975.

————. "Surgical Workloads in a Community Practice." *Surgery* 7 (1972).

Hughes, E. F. X., et al. "Utilization of Surgical Manpower in a Prepaid Group Practice." *Surgery* 77 (March 1975):371–83.

Human Resources Research Center. *Determinants of Physician Specialty and Location Choices.* Final report on Grant no. 3330 from the Robert Wood Johnson Foundation, 1978.

————. *Specialty and Location Choices of Physicians.* Final report of Grant no. 359 from the Robert Wood Johnson Foundation, 1975.

Hyman, Herbert H., ed. *Health Regulation.* Germantown, Md.: Aspen Systems Corporation, 1977.

Iglehart, John K. "And Now It's Carter's Turn to Try to Control Costs." *National Journal* 9 (April 9, 1977):556.

————. "Carving Out a Role for the States in Controlling Hospital Costs." *National Journal* 10 (July 1, 1978):1045–49.

————. "The Cost and Regulation of Medical Technology: Future Policy Directions." *Milbank Memorial Fund Quarterly* 55 (Winter 1977):32–33.

————. "Government Searching for a More Cost-Efficient Way to Pay Hospitals." *National Journal* (December 25, 1976):1822–29.

————. "Medical Cost Quandary." *National Journal* 7 (September 20, 1975):1319–28.

————. "Stemming Hospital Growth—The Flip Side of Carter's Cost Control Plan." *National Journal* 9 (June 4, 1977):848–52.

Illinois Economic and Fiscal Commission. *Medicaid Costs and Controls: An Analysis.* Mimeographed. December 1976.

Illych, Ivan, *Medical Nemesis: The Expropriation of Health.* New York: Pantheon Books, 1976.

Ingle, John I., and Patricia Blair, eds. *International Dental Care Delivery Systems.* Cambridge, Mass.: Ballinger Publishing Co., 1978.

Institute of Medicine. *Assessing Quality in Health Care: An Evaluation.* Washington, D.C.: National Academy of Sciences, November 1976.

_____. *Controlling the Supply of Hospital Beds.* Washington, D.C.: National Academy of Sciences, October 1976.

_____. *Medicare-Medicaid Reimbursement Policies.* Final report of Contract no. SSA–PMB–74–250. Social Security Administration, DHEW, March 1976.

_____. *Reliability of Hospital Discharge Abstracts.* Washington, D.C.: National Academy of Sciences, February 1977.

"Instructions for Development of 1878 Federal Rates from Community Rates." Bureau of Retirement, Insurance, and Occupational Health, CSC.

Jacobs, Philip. "A Survey of Economic Models of Hospitals." *Inquiry* 11 (June 1974) :83–97.

Kaufman, Herbert, with the collaboration of Michael Couzens. *Administrative Feedback: Monitoring Subordinates' Behavior.* Washington, D.C.: The Brookings Institution, 1973.

Keeler, Emmett B.; Daniel T. Morrow; and Joseph P. Newhouse. *The Demand for Supplementary Health Insurance, or Do Deductibles Matter?* R–1958–HEW. Santa Monica: Rand Corporation, July 1976.

Kimball, Larry J., and John H. Lorant. "Physician Productivity and Returns to Scale." Paper presented at the Health Economics Research Organization Meeting, New York, December 1973.

_____. "Production Functions for Physicians' Services." Paper presented at the Econometric Society meeting, Toronto, December 1972.

Kingsdale, Jon. "Labor and Management-Sponsored Innovations in Controlling the Cost of Employee Health Care Benefits." Council on Wage and Price Stability. *Federal Register* (September 17, 1976) :40298–40326.

Klarman, Herbert. "Application of Cost-Benefit Analysis to the Health Services and the Special Case of Technological Innovation." *International Journal of Health Services* 4 (1974): 325–52.

_____. "Economic Research in Group Medicine." In *New Horizons in Health Care,* proceedings of the First International Congress on Group Medicine, Winnipeg, Manitoba, April 26–30, 1970.

_____, ed. *Empirical Studies in Health Economics.* Baltimore: Johns Hopkins Press, 1970.

_____. "Reimbursing the Hospital—The Differences the Third-Party Makes." *Journal of Risk and Insurance* (December 1969):563.

Kleinman, Joel C., and Ronald W. Wilson. "Are Medically Underserved Areas Medically Underserved?" *Health Services Research* 12 (Summer 1977): 147–62.

Komaroff, Anthony L.; W. L. Black; Margaret Flatley; Robert H. Knopp; Barney Reiffen; and Herbert Sherman. "Protocols for Physicians' Assistants." *New England Journal of Medicine* 290 (February 7, 1974):307–12.

Korcok, Milan. "Medical Dollars and Data: Collection, Recollection. Part II Medicare Benefits Statisticians." *CMA Journal* 112 (March 22, 1975):773–77.

Krieg, Richard. "Utilization Review." Mimeographed. Chicago: University of Chicago, December 1976.

Kudrle, Robert T. *Dental Coverage Under National Health Insurance*. Report prepared for the Robert Wood Johnson Foundation under Grant No. 2505, 1978.

Lairson, Paul D.; Jane C. Record; and Julia James. "Physician Assistants at Kaiser: Distinctive Patterns of Practice." Paper presented at the annual meeting of the American Public Health Association, November 1972.

Laudicina, Susan S. "Prospective Reimbursement for Hospitals: A Guide for Policymakers." Department of Public Affairs, Community Service Society of New York, October 1976.

Lave, Judith R., and Lester B. Lave. *The Hospital Construction Act*. Washington, D.C.: American Enterprise Institute for Public Policy Research, 1974.

Lave, Judith R.; Lester B. Lave; and Lester P. Silverman. "A Proposal for Incentive Reimbursement for Hospitals." *Medical Care* 11 (March–April 1973):79–90.

Law, Sylvia A. *Blue Cross: What Went Wrong?* New Haven: Yale University Press, 1974.

Leach, Richard H. *American Federalism*. New York: W. W. Norton and Co., 1970.

Lee, M. W., and R. L. Wallace. "Demand, Supply, and the Distribution of Physicians." Report No. 5, Studies in Health Care. Dept. of Community Health and Medical Practice, University of Missouri, 1970.

Lefkowitz, Bonnie. "Health Planning and Certificate-of-Need Regulations in Maryland." Mimeographed. Harvard University, June 1975.

Levit, Edithe J.; Melvin Sabshin; and Barber C. Mueller. "Trends in Graduate Medical Education and Specialty Certification." *New England Journal of Medicine* 290 (March 7, 1974):545–49.

Lewin and Associates, Inc. *Evaluation of the Efficiency and Effectiveness of the Section 1122 Review Process: Part I.* Washington, D.C.: September 1975.

————. *Government Controls on the Health Care System: The Canadian Experience.* Washington, D.C., January 31, 1976.

————. *Government Health Care Systems, the Canadian Experience: Supplementary Health Insurance in Canada.* HRP–0009349. Washington, D.C.: National Technical Information Service, 1976.

————. "Nationwide Survey of State Health Regulations." Contract No. HEW–05–73–212. September 16, 1974.

Lewin, Lawrence; Anne Somers; and Herman Somers. "State Health Cost Regulation: Structure and Administration." *The University of Toledo Law Review* 6 (Spring 1975):670.

Lewis, Michael H. "Dental Care Delivery in Saskatchewan, Canada." In Ingle and Blair, *International Dental Care.*

Light, Judy A.; Mary Jane Crain; and Donald W. Fisher. "Physicians' Assistant: A Profile of the Profession, 1976." *The P.A. Journal: A Journal for New Health Professionals* 7 (Fall 1977):109–123.

Lindsay, Cotton M. "Real Returns to Medical Education." *Journal of Human Resources* 8 (Summer 1973):3331–48.

Lippard, Vernon W., and Elizabeth F. Purcell, eds. *Intermediate-Level Health Practitioners.* New York: The Josiah Macy, Jr., Foundation, 1973.

Lipscomb, Joseph. *Legal Restrictions on Input Substitution for Production: The Case of General Dentistry.* Durham, N.C.: Duke University Institute for Policy Sciences and Public Affairs, 1977.

Long, Elliot. *The Geographic Distribution of Physicians in the United States.* Final report of Grant no. NSF–C814, National Science Foundation. Minneapolis: Interstudy, January 1975.

Long, S., and M. Cooke. "Discussion Paper: Financing National Health Insurance." Prepared for National Health Insurance Advisory Committee, January 6, 1978.

Lorant, John H., and Larry J. Kimball. "Determinants of Output in Group and Solo Medical Practice." *Health Services Research* 11 (Spring 1976):6–20.

Lowenstein, Regina. "Early Effects of Medicare on the Health Care of the Aged." Reprinted from *Social Security Bulletin* (April 1971):3.

Lowi, Theodore J. *The End of Liberalism.* New York: W. W. Norton and Co., 1969.

Luft, Harold. *Health Maintenance Organizations: Dimensions of Performance.* New York: Wiley-Interscience, forthcoming.

————. "How Do Health Maintenance Organizations Achieve Their 'Savings'? Rhetoric and Evidence." *New England Journal of Medicine* 298 (June 15, 1978) :1336–43.

————. "Why Do HMOs Seem to Provide More Health Maintenance Services?" *Milbank Memorial Fund Quarterly: Health and Society* 56 (Spring 1978) :140–68.

McBride, Owen. "Restrictive Licensing of Dental Paraprofessionals." *The Yale Law Journal* 83 (1974) :806–26.

McCarthy, Carol. "Incentive Reimbursement as an Impetus to Cost Containment." *Inquiry* 12 (December 1975) :320–29.

McClure, Walter. "The Medical Care System under National Health Insurance: Four Models." *Journal of Health Politics, Policy and Law* 1 (Spring 1976) :32.

————. *Reducing Excess Hospital Capacity.* Prepared for Bureau of Health Planning and Resources Development. Minneapolis: Interstudy, 1976.

McConnell, Grant. *Private Power and American Democracy.* New York: Alfred A. Knopf, 1966.

Manley, Sallie, and Susan Ashby. "Sources of Funding for Construction." *Hospitals* 46 (June 19, 1977) :59–63.

Manning, Willard G., and Charles E. Phelps. *Dental Care Demand: Point Estimates and Implications for National Health Insurance.* Santa Monica: The Rand Corporation, 1978.

Marine, David E., and John A. Henderson. "Trends in the Financing of Hospital Construction." *Hospitals, Journal of the American Hospital Association* 48 (July 1, 1974) :13.

Marmor, Theodore R. "The Politics of Paying Physicians: U.S., U.K., and Sweden." *International Journal of Health Services* 1 (1972).

————. "Rethinking National Health Insurance." *The Public Interest* (Winter 1977).

Marmor, Theodore R.; A. Bridges; and W. Hoffman. "Health Policies and Comparative Politics: Notes on Costs, Benefits, Limits." In D. Ashford, ed. *New Approaches in Comparative Politics.* Los Angeles: Sage Yearbook in Public Policy, 1978.

Marmor, Theodore R., with Jan S. Marmor. *The Politics of Medicare.* Chicago: Aldine Publishing Co., 1973.

Marmor, Theodore B., and James Marone. "Consumer Representation and Health Planning." *Health Law Library Bulletin* 4 (April 1979) :117–28.

Marmor, Theodore R., and David Thomas. "Doctors, Politics, and Pay Disputes: Pressure Groups Politics Revisited." *British Journal of Political Science* 2, Part 4 (October 1972) :437.

Marmor, Theodore R.; Donald Wittman; and Thomas Heagy: "The Politics of Medical Inflation." *Journal of Health Politics, Policy and Law* 1 (Spring 1976) :81

Martin, Beverly C., ed. *Socioeconomic Issues of Health, 1975–76.* Chicago: American Medical Association, 1976.

Maurizi, Alex R. *Public Policy and the Dental Care Market.* Washington, D.C.: American Enterprise Institute for Public Policy Research, 1975.

Maw Lin Lee. "A Conspicuous Production Theory of Hospital Behavior." *Southern Economic Journal* 38 (July 1971) :48–58.

_____. "Interdependent Behavior and Resource Misallocation in Hospital Care Production." *Review of Social Economics* 30 (March 1971) :84–95.

May, J. Joel. "The Impact of Regulation on the Hospital Industry." Mimeographed. Center for Health Administration Studies, University of Chicago, May 1974.

_____. "Will Third Generation Planning Succeed?" Reprinted from *Hospital Progress* (March 1976).

Maynard, Alan. "Health Care Planning in the United Kingdom." Prepared for a Conference on Policies for the Containment of Health Care Expenditures, Fogarty Center, Department of Health, Education and Welfare, May 1976.

Mechanic, David. *The Growth of Bureaucratic Medicine.* New York: Wiley-Interscience, 1976.

_____. "The Organization of Medical Practice and Practice Orientations Among Physicians in Prepaid and Nonprepaid Primary Care Settings." *Medical Care* 13 (March 1975) :189–204.

"Medicare Regulation Which Prevents Reimbursement Claims for Services Unless a Physician is Physically Present." Memorandum from Director, Bureau of Health Insurance, Social Security Administration, to the Assistant Secretary for Health, U.S. Public Health Service. July 30, 1976.

Meglen, M. C. "Final Report of Cost-Effect-Potential of a New Maternal and Infant Care Health Team." Mimeographed. Jackson: University of Mississippi, 1976.

Melmon, Kenneth L. "Preventable Drug Reactions: Causes and Cures." *New England Journal of Medicine,* June 17, 1971.

Mennemeyer, Stephen T. "Really Great Returns to Medical Education." *Journal of Human Resources* 13 (Winter 1978) :790.

Meskin, Lawrence H. "Too Many Dentists? If So, What Then?" *Journal of Dental Education* 41 (1977) :602.

Millberry, G. S. "Possibilities and Means of Improving Dental Conditions in the United States." *American Journal of Public Health* 29 (April 1939) :321–25.

Minnesota Department of Health. *Quality Assurance and Review Program.* Summary Report 1975. Minneapolis, 1976.

Monsma, George N. "Marginal Revenue and the Demand for Physicians' Services." In Herbert Klarman, ed. *Empirical Studies in Health Economics.* Baltimore: The Johns Hopkins Press, 1976.

Moore, D. L., and J. L. Stewart. *Journal of Prosthetic Dentistry* 17 (1967) :372.

Morris, Robert. *Alternative to Nursing Home Care: A Proposal.* United States Senate, Special Committee on Aging. Washington, D.C.: U.S. Government Printing Office, 1971.

Morris, Stephen B., and David B. Smith. "The Diffusion of Physician Extenders." Mimeographed. Working Paper No. 1, The Physician Extender Reimbursement Study, DHEW, Social Security Administration, Office of Research and Statistics, 1977.

Moustafa, A. Taher; Carl E. Hopkins; and Bonnie Klein. "Determinants of Choice and Change of Health Insurance Plan." *Medical Care* 9 (January/February 1971) :32–41.

Mueller, Marjorie Smith. "Private Health Insurance in 1975: Coverage, Enrollment, and Financial Experience." *Social Security Bulletin* 40 (June 1977) :6.

Mueller, Marjorie Smith, and Paula A. Piro. "Private Health Insurance in 1974: A Review of Coverage, Enrollment, and Financial Experience." *Social Security Bulletin* 39 (March 1976) :18.

Muller, Charlotte. "Drug Benefits in Health Insurance." *International Journal of Health Services* 4 (Winter 1974) :163.

Muller, Charlotte F., and Jonah Otelsberg. "Interim Research Findings on Physician Reimbursement Under Medicare." DHEW Contract No. 600–76–0145. Center for Social Research, City University of New York, 1978.

Murnaghan, J. H., ed. "Ambulatory Care Data: Report on the Conference on Ambulatory Care Records." *Medical Care* 11 (Supplement 1973) :2.

Murphy, Jerome T. *State Education Agencies and Discretionary Funds: Grease the Squeaky Wheel.* Lexington, Mass.: D. C. Heath, Lexington Books, 1974.

————. "Title I of ESEA: The Politics of Implementing Federal Education Reform." *Harvard Educational Review* 41 (February 1971) :35–63.

National Academy of Sciences, Institute of Medicine. "Computed Tomographic Scanning: A Policy Statement." Washington, D.C.: National Academy of Sciences, 1977.

————. "Controlling the Supply of Hospital Beds." Washington, D.C.: National Academy of Sciences, 1976.

National Council of MEDEX Programs. *A Progress Report on MEDEX Programs in the United States.* University of Washington MEDEX Program, 1974.

National Governors' Conference. *Federal Roadblocks to Efficient State Government,* vol. 1. Washington, D.C.: National Governors' Conference, February 1977.

————. "The State of the States 1974: Responsive Government for the Seventies." Washington, D.C.

National Health Council. *1976 National Conference on Health Manpower Distribution.* New York: National Health Council, Inc., June 1976.

"National Health Insurance Administrative Alternatives—Option Papers for the Secretary; Income Determinations." Memorandum from the Commissioner of Social Security to the Assistant Secretary for Planning and Evaluation, DHEW, January 10, 1975.

"National HMO Census Survey, 1977." Washington, D.C.: Group Health Association of America, Inc., 1978.

National Pharmaceutical Council. "Pharmaceutical Benefits Under Medical Assistance Programs." Washington, D.C.: National Pharmaceutical Council, 1977.

Nelson, Eugene C.; Arthur R. Jacobs; and Kenneth G. Johnson. "Patient Acceptance of Physicians' Assistants." Mimeographed. Dartmouth Medical School, 1974.

Newhouse, Joseph P. "The Economics of Group Practice." *Journal of Human Resources* 8 (Winter 1973) :37–56.

————. *Health Care Cost Sharing and Cost Containment.* Santa Monica: The Rand Corporation, 1976.

Newhouse, Joseph P.; Charles E. Phelps; and William B. Schwartz. "Policy Options and the Impact of National Health Insurance." *New England Journal of Medicine* (June 13, 1974) :1345–58.

Newhouse, Joseph P., and V. Taylor. *The Economics of Moral Hazard: Further Comment.* Santa Monica: The Rand Corporation, 1970.

Newman, John F., and Odin W. Anderson. *Patterns of Dental Service Utilization in the United States: A Nationwide Survey.* Chicago: Center for Health Services Administration, University of Chicago, 1972.

New York State Moreland Act Commission on Nursing Homes and Residential Facilities. *Assessment and Placement: Anything Goes.* Albany, 1976.

Noll, Roger. *Reforming Regulation: An Evaluation of the Ash Council Proposals.* Staff paper, Studies in the Regulation of Economic Activity. Washington, D.C.: The Brookings Institution, 1971.

Osborne, C. E., and H. C. Thompson. "Criteria for Evaluation of Ambulatory Child Health Care by Chart Audit: Development and Testing of a Methodology." *Pediatrics* 65 (Part 2, Supplement, 1975) :4.

Parker, R. L., and T. G. Tuxill. "The Attitudes of Physicians Toward Small Community Practice." *Journal of Medical Education* 42 (April 1967) :327–44.

Pauly, Mark. "Efficiency, Incentives and Reimbursement for Health Care." *Inquiry* 7 (March 1970) :114–31.

Payne, B. C., and T. F. Lyons. *Method of Evaluating and Improving Personal Medical Care Quality: Episode of Illness Study and Office Care Study.* Chicago: American Hospital Association, 1973.

Peirce, Neal R. "State-Local Report/Civil Service Systems Experience 'Quiet Revolution.'" *National Journal* (November 29, 1975) :1643–48.

_____. "State-Local Report/Proposed Reforms Spark Civil Service Debate." *National Journal* (December 5, 1975) :1673–78.

_____. "State-Local Report/Public Worker Pay Emerges as a Growing Issue." *National Journal* (August 23, 1975) :1199–1206.

_____. "State-Local Report/Structural Reform of Bureaucracy Grows Rapidly." *National Journal* (April 5, 1975) :502.

Pfeiffer, Eric. "Designing a System of Care—The Clinical Perspective." Presented at the National Conference on Alternatives to Institutional Care for Older Americans, Practice and Planning, Duke University, June 1972.

Phelps, Charles E. "Statement Before the Subcommittee on Public Health and the Environment." In *National Health Insurance Implications.* Hearings before the Subcommittee on Public Health and Environment, House Committee on Interstate and Foreign Commerce, 93rd Cong., sess. 1, 2, 1974.

Phelps, Charles E., and Joseph P. Newhouse. *Coinsurance and the Demand for Medical Services.* Santa Monica: The Rand Corporation, 1974.

Pollak, William. "Organizational Issues in the Provision of Community Care to the Impaired Elderly." In Joel Bergsman, and Howard L. Weiner, eds. *Urban Problems and Public Policy Choices.* New York: Praeger, 1975.

Pondy, Louis R.; Jeffrey M. Jones; and John A. Braun. "Utilization and Productivity of the Duke Physician's Associate." *Socio-Economic Planning Science* (1973) :327–52.

Porter, David O., and Eugene Olsen. "Some Critical Issues in Government Centralization and Decentralization." *Public Administration Review* 36 (January 2, 1976) :72–84.

Powell, Robert S., Jr. *Bureaucratic Malpractice: Hospital Regulation in New Jersey.* Princeton, N.J.: The Center for Analysis of Public Issues, 1974.

Price, Daniel N. "Cash Benefits for Short-Term Sickness, 1948–1972." *Social Security Bulletin* 37 (January 1974) :19–30.

The Profile of Medical Practice. Chicago: American Medical Association, 1976.

Rafferty, John, ed. *Health Manpower and Productivity.* Lexington, Mass.: D. C. Heath, 1974.

Rafferty, John, and Mark Hornbrook. "The Hospital Cost Containment Problem." Division of Intramural Research, National Center for Health Services Research, October 1976.

Ramaswamy, Krishnan, and George Tokuharta. "Determinants of Expenditures for Physicians' Services in Pennsylvania: Differences Across Counties, 1972: An Econometric Analysis." Paper presented at the Joint Statistical meetings of the American Statistical Association, the Biometric Society and the Institute of Mathematical Statistics (Business and Economic Statistics Section) at Atlanta, Ga., August 28, 1975.

Record, Jane C., and Joan E. O'Bannon. *Cost Effectiveness of Physicians' Assistants.* Washington, D.C.: DHEW, Bureau of Health Manpower, and Portland, Ore.: Kaiser Foundation Health Services Research Center, 1976.

Redisch, Michael A. "Cost Containment and Physician Involvement in Hospital Decision-Making." Photocopied. Social Security Administration, Office of Research and Statistics.

Regan, Michael D. *The New Federalism,* New York: Oxford University Press, 1972.

Reider, Alan; John R. Mason; and Leonard Glantz. "Certificate-of-Need: The Massachusetts Experience." *American Journal of Law and Medicine* 1 (March 1975) :13–40.

Reinhardt, Uwe. "Alternative Methods of Reimbursing Non-Institutional Providers of Health Services." Paper presented to the

Institute of Medicine Conference on Regulation in the Health Industry, January 7–9, 1974.

————. "Health Manpower Policy in the United States." Paper presented at the Bicentennial Conference on Health Policy, University of Pennsylvania, November 1976.

————. *Physician Productivity and the Demand for Health Manpower.* Cambridge, Mass.: Ballinger Publishing Co., 1976.

————. *Physician Productivity and Health Manpower Policy.* Cambridge, Mass.: Ballinger Publishing Co., 1975.

————. "A Production Function for Physician Services." *Review of Economics and Statistics* 54 (February 1972):55–66.

————. "Proposed Changes in the Organization of Health Care Delivery: An Overview and Critique." *Milbank Memorial Fund Quarterly* (Fall 1973).

————. "Reimbursement for Ambulatory Physicians' Services in the Federal Republic of Germany." Paper presented at Fogarty International Center Conference on Policies for the Containment of Health Care Costs and Expenditures, June 2–4, 1976.

Reitemeier, Richard J.; J. A. Spittell, Jr.; R. E. Week; G. W. Daugherty; F. T. Nobrega; and R. W. Fleming. "Participation by Internists in Primary Care." *Archives of Internal Medicine* 135 (February 1975):255–57.

Reynolds, Roger. "Improving Access to Health Care Among the Poor—The Neighborhood Health Center Experience." *Milbank Memorial Fund Quarterly* (Winter 1976).

Rice, Dorothy P., and Saul Waldman. "Issues in Designing a National Program of Long-Term Care Benefits." *Medical Care* 14 (Supplement, May 1976):103.

Robin, David L., and Patricia Bush. "Who's Using Medicines?" *Journal of Community Health* (Winter 1975):115.

Roemer, Milton I. "Bed Supply and Hospital Utilization: A Natural Experiment." *Hospitals* 35 (November 1, 1961):36–42.

Roemer, Milton; Carl E. Hopkins; Lockwood Carr; and Foline Gartside. "Copayment for Ambulatory Care: Penny-Wise and Pound-Foolish." *Medical Care* 13 (June 1975):457–66.

Roemer, Milton, and William Shonick. "HMO Performance: The Recent Evidence." *Milbank Memorial Fund Quarterly/Health and Society* 51 (Summer 1973).

Roghmann, Klaus J. "Who Chooses Prepaid Medical Care?: Survey Results from Two Marketings of Three New Prepayment Plans." *Public Health Reports* 90 (November/December 1975): 516–27.

Roos, Noralou P.; Michael Gaumont; and John M. Horne. "The Impact of the Physician Surplus on the Distribution of Physicians Across Canada." *Canadian Public Policy* 2 (Spring 1976):178.

Roos, N.; P. Henteleff; and L. Roos. "A New Audit Procedure Applied to an Old Question: Is the Frequency of T&A Justified?" *Medical Care* 15 (January 1977) :1–18.

Rosenberg, Charlotte L. "How Much General Practice by Specialists?" *Medical Economics* (September 15, 1975) :131–35.

Rosenthal, Gerald. "Setting the Floor: A Missing Ingredient in an Effective Health Policy." *Journal of Health Politics, Policy and Law* 1 (Spring 1976) :2–3.

Rosett, Richard N., ed. *The Role of Health Insurance in Health Services Sector.* New York: National Bureau of Economic Research, 1976.

Rothenberg, Eleanore. *Regulation and Expansion of Health Facilities: The C/N Experience in New York State.* New York: Praeger, 1976.

Rowland, Diane. "Data Rich and Information Poor: Medicare's Resources for Prospective Rate Setting." Report Series R–45–12, Harvard Center for Community Health and Medical Care, Boston, Mass., July 1976.

Roy, William R., ed. "Effects of the Payment Mechanism on the Health Care Delivery System." Proceedings of a Conference Held at Skyland Lodge, Shenandoah National Park, Virginia, November 7–8, 1977, DHEW, PHS, National Center for Health Services Research, DHEW Publication No. (PHS) 78–3227.

Rucker, T. Donald, and James Visconti. "A Descriptive and Normative Study of Drug Formularies." Columbus: Ohio State University Research Foundation, June 1978.

Russell, Louise B. "The Diffusion of New Hospital Technologies in the United States." *International Journal of Health Services Research* 6 (1976) :557–80.

Sagel, Stuart S.; Ronald G. Evans; John V. Forrest; and Robert T. Bramson. "Efficacy of Routine Screening and Lateral Chest Radiographs in a Hospital-Based Population." *New England Journal of Medicine* 291 (November 1974) :1001–04.

Salkever, David S., and Thomas W. Bice. *Hospital Certificate-of-Need Controls, Impact on Investments, Costs, and Use.* Washington, D.C.: American Enterprise Institute for Public Policy Research, 1979.

Sanford, Terry. *Storm Over the States.* New York: McGraw-Hill Book Co., 1967.

Saskatchewan Prescription Drug Plan. *Annual Report 1975–76.*

Savas, E. S., and Sigmund G. Ginsburg. "The Civil Service: A Meritless System?" *Public Interest* 32 (Summer 1973) :30–85.

Scanlon, William. "A Theory of the Nursing Home Market." *Inquiry,* forthcoming.

Schattscheider, E. E. *The Semisovereign People: A Realist's View of Democracy in America.* New York: Holt, Rinehart and Winston, Inc., 1960.

Scheffler, Richard M. "Characteristics of Physicians' Assistants: A Focus on Specialty." *The P.A. Journal: A Journal for New Health Practitioners* 5 (Spring 1975) :30–41.

_____. *Factors Affecting the Employment of Physician Assistants and MEDEX: Preliminary Report No. 1.* Chapel Hill: University of North Carolina at Chapel Hill, January 1977.

_____. "The Supply of and Demand for New Health Professionals: Physician's Assistants and MEDEX." Executive Summary of Contract No. 1–44184, DHEW, Bureau of Health Manpower, 1977.

Scherer, Frederic M. *Industrial Market Structure and Economic Performance.* Chicago: Rand McNally and Company, 1970.

Schultze, Charles L. *The Politics and Economics of Public Spending.* Washington, D.C.: The Brookings Institution, 1968.

Schwartzman, David. *Innovation in the Pharmaceutical Industry.* Baltimore: Johns Hopkins University Press, 1976.

Schweitzer, Stuart O., and Jane C. Record. "Third-Party Reimbursement for New Health Professionals in Primary-Care: An Alternative to Fractional Reimbursement." Paper presented to a conference sponsored by the National Rural Center on "Nurse Practitioners/Physician Assistants: A Research Agenda," Airlie, Va., June 21–22, 1977.

Seidman, Harold. *Politics, Position and Power: The Dynamics of Federal Organization.* New York: Oxford University Press, 1970.

Shanas, Ethel; Peter Townsend; Dorothy Wedderburn; Henring Friis; Paul Milhöji; and Jan Stehouwer. *Old Age in Three Industrial Societies.* London: Routledge, 1968.

Shapiro, Sam; Louis Weiner; and Paul Densen. "Comparison of Prematurity and Perinatal Mortality in a General Population and in the Population of a Prepaid Group Practice Medical Care Plan." *American Journal of Public Health* 48 (February 1958): 170–85.

_____. "Further Observations on Prematurity and Perinatal Mortality in a General Population and in the Population of a Prepaid Group Practice Medical Care Plan." *American Journal of Public Health* 50 (September 1960): 1304–17.

_____. "Patterns of Medical Use by the Indigent Aged Under Two Systems of Medical Care." *American Journal of Public Health* 57 (May 1967) :784–90.

Sharkansky, Ira. *The Maligned States: Policy Accomplishments, Problems, and Opportunities.* New York: McGraw-Hill Book Co., 1972.

Shea, Joan. *"Alternatives to Institutional Care."* Paper developed for the Task Force on Alternatives to Institutional Care, Chicago, Office of the Regional Director, Region V, Department of Health, Education and Welfare (DHEW), 1977. Mimeographed.

Shieman, A. "An Evaluation of the Success of Dental Care in the United Kingdom." *British Dental Journal* 13 (September 18, 1973):277.

Shortell, Stephen, and William Richardson. *Health Program Evaluation.* St. Louis: C. V. Mosby Co., 1978.

Silverman, Milton, and Phillip R. Lee. *Pills, Profits, and Politics.* Berkeley and Los Angeles: University of California Press, 1974.

Silverman, Milton, and Mia Lydecker. *Drug Coverage Under National Health Insurance: The Policy Options.* National Center for Health Services Research Report Series. Washington, D.C.: DHEW, 1977.

Sindler, Allen P., ed. *Policy and Politics in America.* Boston: Little, Brown, 1973.

Slesinger, Doris P.; Richard C. Tessler; and David Mechanic. "The Effects of Social Characteristics on the Utilization of Preventive Medical Services in Contrasting Health Care Programs." *Medical Care* 14 (May 1976):392–404.

Sloan, Frank A. "The Demand for Higher Education: The Case of Medical School Applicants." *Journal of Human Resources* 6 (Fall 1971):466–89.

————. "Economic Models of Physician Supply." Ph.D. dissertation, Harvard University, Department of Economics, 1968.

————. "Lifetime Earnings and Physicians' Choice of Specialty." *Industrial and Labor Relations Review* 24 (October 1970):47–56.

————. "A Microanalysis of Physicians' Hours of Work Decisions." In Mark Perlman, ed., *The Economics of Health and Medical Care.* New York: John Wiley and Sons, 1975.

————. "Physician Supply Behavior in the Short Run." *Industrial and Labor Relations Review* 28 (July 1975):549–69.

Sloan, Frank A.; Jerry Cromwell; and Janet B. Mitchell. *Private Physicians and Public Programs.* Lexington, Mass.: D. C. Heath, Lexington Books.

Sloan, Frank A., and Roger Feldman. "Monopolistic Elements in the Market for Physician Services." Paper presented at the Federal Trade Commission Conference, June 1, 1977.

Sloan, Frank A., and Cotton M. Lindsay. "Real Returns to Medical Education: Comment and Reply." *Journal of Human Resources* 11 (Winter 1976) :118–30.

Sloan, Frank A., and Bruce Steinwald. "The Role of Health Insurance in the Physician's Services Market." *Inquiry* 12 (December 1975).

Smith, Randall F. "Living with Civil Service: The Massachusetts Experience." Report Series R–45–4. Harvard University Center for Community Health and Medical Care, March 1976.

Sobaski, W. I. "Effects of the 1969 California Relative Value Studies on Costs of Physicians' Services Under SMI." *Health Insurance Statistics* 69. SSA, Office of Research and Statistics, June 20, 1975.

Somers, Anne R. *State Regulations of Hospitals and Health Care: The New Jersey Story.* Research Series No. 11. Chicago: Blue Cross Reports, July 1973.

Somers, Anne R., ed. *The Kaiser-Permanente Medical Care Program: A Symposium.* New York: The Commonwealth Fund, 1971.

Somers, Herman M., and Anne R. Somers. *Medicare and the Hospitals.* Washington, D.C.: The Brookings Institution, 1967.

Sparer, G., and A. Anderson. "Cost of Services at Neighborhood Health Centers—A Comparative Analysis." In R. Holister, ed. *Neighborhood Health Centers.*

Spaulding, W. B., and N. U. Spitzer. "Implications of Medical Manpower Trends In Ontario, 1961–71." *Ontario Medical Review* (September 1972) :527–33.

Spitzer, Walter O.; David L. Sackett; John C. Sibley, Robin S. Roberts; Michael Gent; Dorothy J. Kergin; Brenda C. Hackett; and Anthony Olynich. "The Burlington Randomized Trial of the Nurse Practitioner." *New England Journal of Medicine* 290 (January 31, 1974) :251–56.

Stanfield, Rochelle. "The Suburban Counties are Flexing Their Muscles." *National Journal* (May 7, 1977) :704–09.

Starr, Paul. "Too Many Doctors?" *The Washington Post.* 13 March 1977, p. 63.

Statistical Abstract of the United States. Washington, D.C.: U.S. Government Printing Office, 1978.

Steiner, Gilbert Y. *Social Insecurity: The Politics of Welfare.* Chicago: Rand McNally and Co., 1966.

Stevens, Robert and Rosemary Stevens. *Welfare Medicine in America: A Case Study of Medicaid.* New York: The Free Press, 1974.

Stolley, Paul D.; Marshall H. Becker; Louis Lasagna; Joseph D. Mc-
Evilla; and Lois M. Sloane. "The Relationship Between Physi-
cian Characteristics and Prescribing Appropriateness." *Medical
Care* (1972):17–28.

Stuehler, G. "Certificate-of-Need: A Systems Analysis of Maryland's
Experience and Plans." *American Journal of Public Health* 63
(November 1973).

Sundquist, James L., with David W. Davis. *Making Federalism
Work*. Washington, D.C.: The Brookings Institution, 1969.

Teh-Wei Hu, ed. *International Health Costs and Expenditures*.
DHEW Publication No. (NIH) 76–1067. Washington, D.C.:
Department of Health, Education and Welfare, Public Health
Service, National Institutes of Health, 1976.

Tessler, Richard, and David Mechanic. "Factors Affecting the Choice
Between Prepaid Group Practice and Alternative Insurance
Programs." *Milbank Memorial Fund Quarterly: Health and So-
ciety* 53 (Spring 1975):149–72.

Theodore, Chris N., and James N. Hang. *Selected Characteristics of
the Physician Population, 1963 and 1967*. Chicago: American
Medical Association, 1968.

Touche Ross and Co. "Study of State Agency Performance Under
Medicaid." Report to the Department of Health, Education, and
Welfare, June 21, 1973.

Gordon R. Trapnell Consulting Actuaries. *A Comparison of the Costs
of Major National Health Insurance Proposals*. Prepared for
the Office of the Assistant Secretary for Planning and Evaluation. Mimeographed. DHEW, January 1976 (revised September
1976).

Tuohy, Carolyn J. "Medical Politics After Medicare: The Ontario
Case." *Canadian Public Policy* 2 (Spring 1976):198.

U.S., Congress. *The Health Professions Educational Assistance Act
of 1976*. Public Law 94–484, 94th Cong., 2d sess., 90 Stat. 2243.

U.S., Congress, Congressional Budget Office. "Catastrophic Health
Insurance." Washington, D.C.: U.S. Government Printing Office,
1977.

————. *Long-Term Care: Actuarial Estimates*. Washington, D.C.:
U.S. Government Printing Office, 1977.

————. *Long-Term Care for the Elderly and Disabled*. Washington, D.C.: U.S. Government Printing Office, 1977.

————. *Expenditures for Health Care: Federal Programs and
Their Effects*. Washington, D.C.: U.S. Government Printing
Office, August 1977.

U.S., Congress, House of Representatives. *Health Professions Educational Assistance Act of 1976.* House Report 94–266 to accompany H.R. 5546, 94th Cong., 2d sess., 1976.

U.S., Congress, House of Representatives, Committee on Interstate and Foreign Commerce. *National Health Policy, Planning and Resources Development Act of 1974.* 93rd Cong., 2d sess., H. Rept. 93–1382. September 26, 1974.

U.S., Congress, House of Representatives, Committee on Interstate and Foreign Commerce, Subcommittee on Public Health and Environment. *National Health Insurance Implications.* 93d Cong., 1st and 2d sess., 1974.

U.S., Congress, House of Representatives, Committee on Oversight and Investigations. *Getting Ready for National Health Insurance: Unnecessary Surgery.* 94th Cong., 1st sess., 1975.

U.S., Congress, House of Representatives, Committee on Ways and Means. *Hearings on National Health Insurance.* 93rd Cong., 2d sess. Washington, D.C.: U.S. Government Printing Office, 1974.

_____. *Report of the Committee on Ways and Means on H.R.L.: Social Security Amendments of 1971.* 92nd Cong., 1st sess., House Report No. 92–231. May 26, 1971.

U.S., Congress, House of Representatives, Committee on Ways and Means, Subcommittee on Health. "Medicare Reimbursement for Physician Extenders Practicing in Rural Health Clinics." 95th Cong., 1st sess., February 28, 1977.

U.S., Congress, House of Representatives, Committee on Ways and Means, Committee on Interstate and Foreign Commerce and the Subcommittee on Health and the Environment. Statement by Joseph A. Califano, Jr., Secretary of Health, Education, and Welfare, May 11, 1977.

U.S., Congress, Senate. "Health Manpower Legislation 1975." Report on S.989, Part 1. Washington, D.C.: U.S. Government Printing Office, July 31, 1975.

_____. "Health Professions Educational Assistance Act of 1974." Report of S.3585. Washington, D.C.: U.S. Government Printing Office, September 3, 1974.

U.S., Congress, Senate, Committee on the Budget. *Hearings on the First Concurrent Resolution of the Budget, Fiscal Year 1978.* Vol. 3. 95th Cong., 1st sess. 1977.

U.S., Congress, Senate, Committee on Finance. *Medicare and Medicaid: Problems, Issues and Alternatives.* Report of the Staff. 91st Cong., 1st sess., February 9, 1970.

_____. *Social Security Amendments of 1972.* 92nd Cong., 2d sess., 1972, H. Rept. 1.

————. *The Supplemental Security Income Program.* Report of the Staff to the Committee on Finance. 95th Cong., 1st sess., April 1977.

U.S., Congress, Senate, Committee on Human Resources, Subcommittee on Health and Scientific Research. "The Hospital Cost Containment Act of 1977: An Analysis of the Administration's Proposal." Prepared by the Congressional Budget Office. 95th Cong., 1st sess. Washington, D.C.: U.S. Government Printing Office, June 1977.

U.S., Congress, Senate, Special Committee on Aging, Subcommittee on Long-Term Care. *Nursing Home Care in the United States: A Failure of Public Policy.* 93d Cong., 2d sess., December 1974.

U.S., Department of Health, Education, and Welfare. *Ambulatory Prescription Drug Study.* Division of Health Insurance Studies, Health Care Financing Administration, November 1977.

————. *Edentulous Persons, United States, 1971.* Series 10, no. 189. Washington, D.C.: U.S. Government Printing Office, 1974.

————. *Out-of-Pocket Cost and Acquisition of Prescribed Medicines United States, 1973.* Washington, D.C.: U.S. Government Printing Office, 1977.

————. *The Supply of Health Manpower: 1970 Profiles and Projections to 1990.* Washington, D.C.: U.S. Government Printing Office, 1974.

————, Advisory Committee on Dental Health to the Secretary. *Report and Recommendations.* Washington, D.C.: U.S. Government Printing Office, 1973.

————, Division of Health Maintenance Organizations. *Health Maintenance Organizations Third Annual Report to the Congress.* DHEW Publication No. (PHS) 78–13058. Washington, D.C.: U.S. Government Printing Office, September 1977.

————, Health Resources Administration, Bureau of Health Resources Development. *Factors Influencing Practice Location of Professional Health Manpower: A Review of the Literature.* Publication No. (HRA) 75–3, July 1974.

————, Health Resources Administration, National Center for Health Services Research. "Nurse Practitioners and Physicians' Assistants Training and Deployment Study." September 30, 1976.

————. "Persons Hospitalized by Number of Episodes and Days Hospitalized in a Year—United States—1972." *Vital and Health Statistics,* series 10, no. 116. DHEW Publication No. (HRA) 77–1544. Washington, D.C.: U.S. Government Printing Office.

————, Health Services Administration. "National Health Service Corps, First Annual Report to Congress, 1977." Washington, D.C.: The Blue Sheet, November 1, 1978.

————, National Center for Health Services Research. "Medical Care Appraisal and Quality Assurance in the Office Practice of Internal Medicine." R. C. Hare and S. Barnoon. Publication No. (HSM) 110–70–420, July 1973.

————, National Center for Health Statistics. *Decayed, Missing and Filled Teeth Among Youth 12–17 Years, United States.* Series 11, no. 144. Washington, D.C.: U.S. Government Printing Office, 1974.

————. *Decayed, Missing, and Filled Teeth in Adults, United States, 1960–1962.* Series 11, no. 23. Washington, D.C.: U.S. Government Printing Office, 1967.

————. *Periodontal Disease in Adults, United States, 1960–1962.* Series 11, no. 36. Washington, D.C.: U.S. Government Printing Office, 1965.

————, Office of the Secretary. *Maximum Allowable Cost for Drugs.* Mimeographed. February 9, 1977.

————, Public Health Service. "Levels of Support for National Health Service Corps (NHSC) and NHSC Scholarship Programs." Memorandum to the Assistant Secretary for Health, March 1978.

————, Public Health Service. *Personal Out-of-Pocket Health Expenses, United States, 1970. Vital and Health Statistics*, series 10, no. 91.

————, Public Health Services, Health Resources Administration. *Current Estimates from the Health Interview Survey, United States, 1975.* Washington, D.C.: U.S. Government Printing Office, 1976.

————. *Dental Visits, Volume and Interval Since Last Visit, United States, 1969.* Washington, D.C.: U.S. Government Printing Office, 1972.

————. *The Effects of Task Delegation of the Requirements for Selected Health Manpower Categories in 1980, 1985, and 1990.* Washington, D.C.: U.S. Government Printing Office, 1974.

————. *Uniform Hospital Abstract: Minimum Basic Data Set.* Vital and Health Statistics, series 4: Documents.

————. *Family Out-of-Pocket Health Expenses, United States— 1970.* Washington, D.C.: U.S. Government Printing Office, 1975.

————. "Health, United States 1976–1977." DHEW Publication No. (HRA) 77–1232.

_____, Public Health Service, Health Resources Administration, Bureau of Health Manpower. *The Impact of Comprehensive National Health Insurance on Demand for Health Manpower.* Washington, D.C.: DHEW, 1976.

_____. "Supply and Distribution of Physicians and Physician Extenders." Graduate Medical Education National Advisory Committee Staff Paper, Publication No. (HRA) 78–11, 1978.

_____, Public Health Service, Health Resources Administration, National Committee on Vital and Health Statistics. "Ambulatory Medical Care Records: Uniform Minimum Data Set." *Vital and Health Statistics*, series 4, no. 16. Publication No. (HRA) 75–1453, 1974.

_____, Public Health Service, Health Resources Administration, Office of Health Resources Opportunity. "Project Summary: Board and Staff of Health Planning Agencies." DHEW Pub. No. (HRA) 78–609.

_____, Social Security Administration, Office of Research and Statistics. *National Health Insurance Proposals: Provisions of Bills Introduced in the 94th Congress as of February 1976.* By Saul Waldman. Publication No. (SSA) 76–11920.

_____, Task Force on Prescription Drugs. *Approaches to Drug Insurance Design.* Washington, D.C.: U.S. Government Printing Office, February 1969.

_____, Task Force on Prescription Drugs. *Current American and Foreign Programs.* Washington, D.C.: U.S. Government Printing Office, December 1968.

_____, Task Force on Prescription Drugs. *The Drug Users.* Washington, D.C.: U.S. Government Printing Office, October 1968).

_____, Task Force on Prescription Drugs. *Third Interim Report.* Washington, D.C.: U.S. Government Printing Office, December 31, 1968.

U.S., Executive Office of the President, Council on Wage and Price Stability. "The Problem of Rising Health Care Costs." Staff Report. April 1976.

U.S., Food and Drug Administration. *Holders of Abbreviated New Drug Applications for Drugs Presenting Actual or Potential Bioequivalence Problems.* FDA Publication No. 56–3009, June 1976.

U.S., General Accounting Office. "Home Health Benefits Under Medicare and Medicaid." B–146031, July 9, 1974.

_____. *Home Health—The Need for a National Policy to Better Provide for the Elderly.* Washington, D.C.: U.S. General Accounting Office, 1977.

Vahovich, Stephen G. "Physicians' Supply Decisions by Specialty: 2SLS Model." *Industrial Relations* 16 (February):51–60.

Vayda, Eugene. "Prepaid Group Practice Under Universal Health Insurance in Canada." *Medical Care* 15 (May 1977):382–90.

Vayda, Eugene, and G. D. Anderson. "Comparison of Provincial Surgical Rates in 1968." *The Canadian Journal of Surgery* 18 (January 1975):18–26.

Vickrey, William. "Comment: Group Health Insurance as a Local Public Good." In Richard N. Rosett, ed. *The Role of Health Insurance in Health Services Sector.* New York: National Bureau of Economic Research, 1976.

Warner, J., and D. Aherne. *1974 Profile of Medical Practice.* Chicago: American Medical Association, 1974.

Weissert, William G. "Costs of Adult Day Care: A Comparison to Nursing Homes." *Inquiry* 15:1.

————. "Rationales for Public Health Insurance Coverage of Geriatric Day Care: Issues, Options, and Impacts." *Journal of Health Politics, Policy and Law.* Forthcoming.

Wells, Sandra M., and Klaus J. Roghmann. "GM Inpatient Utilization Before and After Offering Prepayment Plans." Paper presented at 105th Annual Meeting of the American Public Health Association, Washington, D.C., October 1977.

Wersinger, Richard P. *The Analysis of Three Prepaid Health Care Plans in Monroe County, New York, Part III: Inpatient Utilization Statistics, January 1, 1974–December 31, 1974.* Rochester, N.Y.: University of Rochester School of Medicine and Dentistry, Department of Preventive Medicine and Community Health, October 1975.

Wertheimer, Albert I. *Economic Analysis of Selected Factors in Drug Delivery.* Report prepared for the National Center for Health Services Research and Development (HSRD), Office of Scientific and Technical Information, HSRD 73–71; NTIS No. PB 212 038.

————, ed. *Proceedings of the International Conference on Drug and Pharmaceutical Services Reimbursement.* NCHSR Research Proceedings Series. Washington, D.C., 1977.

Wickware, Diane. "Automation is Vital to Prescription Drug Coverage." *American Druggist* 160 (October 6, 1969):40.

Wolkstein, Irwin. "The Legislative History of Hospital Cost Reimbursement." In DHEW, SSA, Office of Research and Statistics, *Reimbursement Incentives for Hospital and Medical Care: Objectives and Alternatives.* Research Report No. 26, 1968.

Wood, Jack, ed. *Topics in Health Care Financing* 2 (Winter 1975), Appendix C, p. 93.

Wright, George E., Jr. "The Efficiency of Federal Subsidies to Medical Education." *Health Manpower Policy Discussion Paper Series.* Ann Arbor: University of Michigan, April 1974.

Yedidia, Avram. "Dual Choice Programs." *American Journal of Public Health* 49 (November 1959) :1475–80.

Yett, Donald E. "An Evaluation of Alternative Methods of Estimating Physicians' Expenses Relative to Output." *Inquiry* 4 (March 1967) :3–27.

Yohalem, Martha Remy. "Employee-Benefit Plans, 1975." *Social Security Bulletin* 40 (November 1977) :19–28.

Ziegler, Harmon. *Internal Groups in American Society.* Englewood Cliffs, N.J.: Prentice Hall, Inc., 1964.

Zubkoff, Michael, ed. *Health: A Victim or Cause of Inflation?* New York: Prodist, for the Milbank Memorial Fund, 1976.

Zubkoff, Michael; Ira E. Raskin; and Ruth S. Hanft, eds. *Hospital Cost Containment.* New York: Prodist, for Milbank Memorial Fund, 1978.

APPENDIX

Carter National Health Plan (Phase I)

Introduced September 25, 1979, as S.1812

Subject	Provisions	
General Concept and Approach	The program will encompass two components:	
	Healthcare—a public plan providing comprehensive coverage to the aged, the disabled, and the poor and the near poor and offering catastrophic coverage to those individuals and firms unable to obtain such insurance in the private sector; and	
	Employer Guaranteed Coverage—a program requiring employers to provide all full-time employees, their spouses, and dependent children with health benefits meeting uniform federal standards. Employers must pay at least 75 percent of the premium for health insurance.	
	Healthcare	**Employer Guaranteed Coverage**
Coverage of Population	All those now eligible for Medicare plus any person over age 65 whose income is less than 55 percent of the federal poverty standard.	All full-time employees, their spouses, and dependent children.
	All persons currently eligible for cash assistance and others whose income is less than 55 percent of the federal poverty standard.	
	Any person whose medical expenses cause a "spend down" to 55 percent of the federal poverty standard.	
	Any other person or group who pays a specified premium (coverage subject to $2,500 deductible).	
	(Eligibility levels are intended to rise to the full poverty standard in a later phase of the plan.)	

Subject	Provisions
Benefit Structure	Institutional Services: Hospitals Skilled Nursing Facilities: 100 days per year Mental Hospitals: 20 days per year Personal Services: Physicians Diagnostic Services Home Health Services (200 visits per year) Outpatient Mental Health Care: $1,000 a year Medical Equipment Laboratory and X-ray Other Services and Supplies: Prenatal care, delivery, and preventive and acute child health care in the first year of life Family planning Immunizations (Drug benefits, child care up to age 6, and preventive care for all persons are proposed as future additions to the Phase I plan.) Cost Sharing No cost sharing for people with income below 55 percent of the federal poverty standard. Aged and disabled: Cost sharing similar to Medicare's but subject to a ceiling of $1,250 per year in out-of-pocket costs. Other eligibles: Deductible of $2,500 in Healthcare. Maximum deductible of $2,500 in employer plans; after deductible has been met, plans must offer all benefits available under Healthcare and may offer broader coverage. No cost sharing on prenatal services, delivery, and prevention and acute care in child's first year of life. (Deductibles to be replaced with coinsurance and out-of-pocket limits to be lowered in a later phase of the plan)

Carter National Health Plan (Phase I)

Introduced September 25, 1979, as S.1812 (continued)

Subject	Provisions
Administration	The federal government will administer Healthcare through fiscal agents, as it does Medicare, and it will regulate private plans.
	Private insurers will market and underwrite qualified insurance plans for most current beneficiaries and add new beneficiaries through employer guaranteed coverage.
Relationship to Other Government Programs	Medicare and Medicaid will be consolidated under Healthcare with standardized eligibility benefits and reimbursement policies. Medicaid will continue for noncovered services.
Financing	Hospital insurance portion of the Social Security tax, premiums paid by nonpoor aged and disabled enrollees equivalent to Medicare Part B premiums, state government revenues, and federal general revenues.
	Premiums by individuals and employers will finance insurance plans (at least 75 percent by employers; up to 25 percent by employees).
Standards for Providers of Services	Similar to Medicare.
Reimbursement of Providers of Services	Under Healthcare, hospital services will be reimbursed as they are under Medicare, but in both Healthcare and private plans payment will be limited according to hospital cost containment legislation, separately introduced.
	Physicians and other providers of ambulatory services to Healthcare patients will be reimbursed under fee schedule. All physicians who accept Healthcare claims must accept fee schedule amount as payment in full. After first year of implementation, alterations in schedule will be developed by negotiation between Healthcare and physician representatives.

Subject	Provisions
Reimbursement of Providers of Services (continued)	Under private plans these fee schedules may or may not be used, but plans will furnish enrollees with lists of physicians in states who accept a particular plan's reimbursement as full compensation for their services.
Delivery and Resources	Dollar limit on changes in hospital capital expenditures a state can approve through certificate of need.
	Proposes to encourage HMOs in Healthcare through adoption of advance capitation approach and, in the employer plans, by requiring multiple choice with equal employer contributions to all offered plans.
	Expansion of PSRO activities.

Consumer Choice Health Plan
Developed by Alain Enthoven for Secretary of Health, Education, and
Welfare Joseph A. Califano, Jr., September 1977

Subject	Provisions
General Concept and Approach	Program would provide tax credits based on income and actuarial risk categories for a proportion of premiums paid for private health insurance plans. Low-income persons would receive vouchers for premium payments. Modeled on the Federal Employees Health Benefits Plan.
Coverage of Population	**Private Plans** All legal U.S. residents, except those eligible for Medicare.	**Medicare** All legal U.S. residents ages 65+, plus others (disabled, renal disease victims) now covered.
Benefit Structure	Not specified in detail. To qualify for tax credits or vouchers, private insurance plans would have to provide a basic, minimum-benefit package (oriented toward protection against catastrophic costs) and to specify a maximum on individual (or family) out-of-pocket outlays in a 1- or 2-year period. The dollar amount of the maximum and benefits beyond the minimum would be set by the individual plans. Participating plans would include HMOs and traditional insurance plans. All plans would be required to set community rates, participate in a periodic government-run open enrollment, and offer a "low option" plan limited to the basic benefits defined in the law.	Benefits would be expanded to conform to benefits for the rest of the population. The 150-day limit on hospital days would be removed, and an annual limit on out-of-pocket expenses would be established.
Administration	Program could be administered by federal government or jointly by the federal government and the states under federal standards. Tax credits would be administered through the IRS. Vouchers would be administered through a reformed cash assistance system which would be almost entirely federal. Supervision of enrollment and plan qualifications could be handled by federal or state governments.

Subject	Provisions
Relationship to Other Government Programs	Medicare: Would continue but with expanded benefits. There would be a change in the law to include a "freedom of choice provision" that would permit any beneficiary to direct that the Adjusted Average Per Capita Cost for beneficiaries in his or her actuarial category be paid to any qualified plan as a fixed, prospective periodic payment.
	Medicaid: Replaced by voucher system, paying up to 100 percent actuarial costs of basic benefits for low-income persons.
	Persons eligible for CHAMPUS, veterans, or other government programs that provide care directly would be required to choose either to continue to receive care in the government system or to use the credit/voucher approach.
Financing	Primarily federal general revenues, with perhaps some contribution from the states, plus premiums for costs of insurance that exceed tax credits.
Standards for Providers of Services	Not specified.
Reimbursement of Providers of Services	Not specified; could be left to discretion of insurance plans, or subject to regulation.
Delivery and Resources	Program aims to promote the development of cost-effective delivery systems by encouraging consumer sensitivity to premium levels and by discouraging insurers from competing through favorable risk selection. Regulation would be designed to enhance competition through minimum qualifications and disclosure requirements, rather than to prescribe all aspects of insurer behavior.
	HMOs: Would be one of several types of competing systems offering care, but would not be subsidized in this program. HMOs and similarly organized plans would be exempted from planning controls to encourage this type of cost-effective system.
	HSAs: Would continue current responsibilities and would also compile a standardized total per capita cost for its area to be compared with costs in other areas and national and statewide averages.
	Relocation and conversion assistance programs would be established to encourage physicians and hospitals to adjust their practices to changes in demand.

Kennedy-Corman Bill: Health Security Act
S.3, 94th Congress, February 1976

Subject	Provisions
General Concept and Approach	A program administered by federal government and financed by special taxes on earned and unearned income and by federal general revenues. Supported by Committee for National Health Insurance and AFL-CIO.
Coverage of Population	All U.S. residents.

Benefit Structure	Benefits with no limitations, except as noted. No cost sharing by patient.
	Institutional services:
	  Hospital.
	  Skilled nursing facility: 120 days.
	
	Personal services:
	  Physicians.
	  Dentists: For children under age 15; scheduled extension to age 25; eventually to entire population.
	  Home health services.
	  Other health professionals.
	  Laboratory and X-ray.
	
	Other services and supplies:
	  Medical appliances and ambulance services:
	  Eyeglasses and hearing aids.
	  Prescription drugs needed for chronic illness and other specified diseases.

Administration	Federal Government: Special board in DHEW, with regional and local offices to operate program.
Relationship to Other Government Programs	Medicare: Abolished. Medicaid and other assistance programs: Would not pay for covered services. Other programs: Most not affected.

Subject	Provisions
Financing	Special taxes: On payroll (1.0 percent for employees and 2.5 percent for employers), self-employment income (2.5 percent) and unearned income (2.5 percent).
	Income subject to tax: Amount equal to 150 percent of earning base under Social Security (i.e., $22,950 in 1976).
	Employment subject to tax: Workers under Social Security and federal, state, and local government employment.
	Federal general revenues: Equal to amount received from special taxes.
Standards for Providers of Services	Same as Medicare but with additional requirements: Hospitals cannot refuse staff privileges to qualified physicians. Skilled nursing facilities must be affiliated with hospital which would take responsibility for quality of medical services in home. Physicians must meet national standards; major surgery performed only by qualified specialists.
	All providers: Records subject to review by regional office. Can be directed to add or reduce services and to provide services in a new location.
Reimbursement of Providers of Services	National health budget established and funds allocated, by type of medical services, to regions and local areas.
	Hospitals and nursing homes: Annual predetermined budget, based on reasonable cost.
	Physicians, dentists,, and other professionals: Methods available are fee-for-service based on fee schedule, per capita payment for persons enrolled, and (by agreement) full- or part-time salary. Payments for fee-for-service may be reduced if payments exceed allocation.
	Health maintenance organizations: Per capita payment for all services (or budget for institutional services). Can retain all or part of savings.
Delivery and Resources	Health planning: DHEW responsible for health planning, in cooperation with state planning agencies. Priority to be given to development of comprehensive care on ambulatory basis.
	Health resources development fund: Will receive, ultimately, 5 percent of total income of program, to be used for improving delivery of health care and increasing health resources.
	Health maintenance organizations: Grants for development, loans for construction, and payments to offset operating deficits.

Kennedy-Corman Bill: Health Security Act
S.3, 94th Congress, February 1976 (continued)

Subject	Provisions
Delivery and Resources (continued)	Manpower training: Grants to schools and allowances to students for training of physicians for general practice and shortage specialties, other health occupations, and development of new kinds of health personnel.
	Personal care services: Demonstration projects to provide personal care in the home, including home-maker, laundry, meals-on-wheels, transportation, and shopping services.

Source: U.S. Department of Health, Education, and Welfare, Social Security Administration, Office of Research and Statistics, National Health Insurance Proposals, Provisions of Bills introduced in the 94th Congress as of February 1976, compiled by Saul Waldman.

Kennedy-Mills Bill: Comprehensive National Health Insurance Act
H.R. 13870, 93rd Congress, April 1974

Subject	Provisions
General Concept and Approach	Program provides comprehensive benefits on a social insurance basis to all Americans except those covered under Medicare. Administered by an independent Social Security Administration with the use of private health insurers as administrative agents.
Coverage of the Population	All U.S. residents (not eligible under Medicare) covered through contributions to the system. Includes all persons fully or currently insured for purposes of Social Security, persons not eligible under Medicare but receiving Social Security cash benefits, plus dependents of all such persons. Special provisions for persons who first begin to contribute.

Benefit Structure	No limits on amount of benefits listed below, except where indicated:
	Institutional services:
	  Hospital inpatient and outpatient
	  Posthospital extended care (100 days per year)
	
	Personal services:
	  Physicians
	  Laboratory and X-ray
	  Home health services (100 visits per year)
	  Medical supplies and appliances, ambulance
	  Prescription drugs: for specified chronic conditions
	
	Preventive care services:
	  Dental care: for children under age 13
	  Eyeglasses and hearing aids (and eye and ear exams): for children under age 13.
	  Well-child care to age 6
	  Prenatal care and family planning services
	
	Deductible of $150 per person on all services except those listed as preventive care. All services except drugs subject to 25 percent coinsurance. $1 copayment per prescription drug. Total cost sharing (except for drugs) limited to $1,000 annually. Special provision for reduced cost-sharing amounts for persons with lower incomes, with no cost sharing for lowest-income families, financed out of general revenues.

Kennedy-Mills Bill: Comprehensive National Health Insurance Act
H.R. 13870, 93rd Congress, April 1974 (continued)

Subject	Provisions
Administration	Administered by a new, independent Social Security Administration with the use of intermediaries for institutional services in a way similar to Medicare. For physicians' and other noninstitutional services, carriers selected by large employers would administer the program on behalf of employees of that employer. For persons not covered by large employers, SSA would award 2-year competitive carrier contracts in each geographic area of the country.
Relationship to Other Government Programs	Medicare: Program continues as federal plan for the aged but is amended to cover prescription drugs (with $1 copayment) and voluntary long-term-care program. Catastrophic element in basic plan would also apply to Medicare. Current day limitation on inpatient hospital care would be removed, as would the so-called blood deductible. Medicaid: Abolished. Other Programs: Most not affected directly.
Financing	Tax on payroll, self-employed, and unearned income and federal general revenues. Tax rates: (a) 1 percent on employee wages, (b) 3 percent for employers, (c) 2.5 percent for self-employed, (d) 2.5 percent on unearned income (except on certain welfare payments, where tax would be 1 percent on recipient and 3 percent on the state or federal government). Income subject to tax: First $20,000 annually for individuals and employers. Reduced cost-sharing provision for persons with lower incomes to be financed through federal general revenues with contributions from states related to 1973 Medicaid expenditures.
Standards for Providers of Services	Similar to Medicare. Only recognized specialists would be paid for certain physicians' services; surgery only after referral; requirement for consultation with additional specialists for certain surgical and other major procedures. All covered services subject to review by PSROs.
Reimbursement of Providers of Services	Institutional providers: In lieu of present "reasonable cost" system used under Medicare, would be paid on basis of prospective payment systems with financial incentives for efficient performance. Physicians, dentists, certain other practitioners: Payment based on fee schedules established by professions subject to total figure in base year. Participating physicians would be paid the full fee schedule amount; nonparticipating physicians would bill the patient, who would be reimbursed by the program for the fee schedule amount less deductibles and coinsurance.

Subject	Provisions
Delivery and Resources	Establishes Health Resources Board charged with assuring nationwide availability of services covered under the program, with a certain percentage of total income to the program to be set aside for these purposes.
Encouragement of Improved Insurance	Provisions for a voluntary system of approval for private health insurance supplementing benefits under national health insurance program.

Source: U.S., Congress, House of Representatives, Committee on Ways and Means, **National Health Insurance Resource Book**, April 11, 1974. Bill summaries were based on materials prepared by Saul Waldman.

Kennedy-Waxman Bill: Health Care for All Americans Act
H.R. 5191, 96th Congress, Introduced September 6, 1979

Subject	Provisions
General Concept and Approach	Provides comprehensive health care benefits by mandating enrollment in a private health insurance plan, either through an employer or on an individual basis. Premiums would vary with income, with government paying in full for the poor. Premiums and payments to providers would be negotiated within a predetermined NHI budget.
Coverage of Population	All U.S. citizens, permanent resident aliens, legal nonpermanent aliens employed by a foreign embassy or international organization, and foreign visitors whose governments make agreements with the U.S. government.

Benefit Structure	Benefits with no limitations, except as noted:
	Institutional Services:
	  Hospital inpatient and outpatient services (with limits on services for mental illness).
	  Skilled Nursing Facilities: 100 days following a hospitalization of three days or more.
	Personal Services:
	  Physician services (with limits on services for mental conditions).
	  Home health services: 100 visits per year.
	  Preventive services including basic immunizations, pre- and postnatal maternal care and well-child care (up to age 18).
	Other Services and Supplies:
	  Medical and other health services, includes X-ray and laboratory, medical equipment, prosthetic devices, etc.
	  Outpatient drugs only for Medicare eligibles and only for chronic illness.
	  Outpatient physical, speech, and occupational therapy.
	  Mental health day care services: 2 days a year for each day of allowed inpatient psychiatric benefits.
	  Audiological exams and hearing aid coverage: 1 exam per year; 1 hearing aid every 3 years.

Administration	Federal Government: National Health Board, newly established by this program, would be responsible for establishing national policy guidelines and overseeing the program's implementation, computing national and state NHI budgets, and setting rules for paying for services within the budgets.

Subject	Provisions
Administration (continued)	State: State governments would nominate members of newly created State Health Boards, which, under contract with the National Board, would be responsible for negotiating prospective budgets and fee schedules for payment of providers, overseeing insurance enrollment, and guaranteeing provider payment. State governments would administer residual Medicaid program and certificate-of-need.
	Private Insurers and HMOs: Establish national consortia that collect and distribute premiums and participate in provider payment negotiations. Individual plans enroll members and pay providers.
Relationship to Other Government Programs	Medicare: The bill would— Make payroll tax applicable to all employment. Remove limitations on days of hospital coverage. Remove deductible and coinsurance requirements for inpatient hospital services and post-hospital extended care services. Extend automatic eligibility to all persons ages 65+. Delete Part B deductible and 20 percent coinsurance requirements (except for treatment for mental conditions). Mandate Part B enrollment. Add drug benefits to list of covered services.
	Medicaid: Federal government would pay 90 percent of administrative costs of residual Medicaid programs if state programs meet federal standards.
Financing	Program financing would be from 7 primary sources: Premiums on wage income and premiums on substantial amounts of nonwage income (premiums calculated as a percentage of income); state payments on behalf of AFDC and state institutional populations; federal payments on behalf of SSI beneficiaries and federal institutional populations; voluntary payments on behalf of U.S. residents who are employees of foreign governments or of international organizations; Medicare taxes and premiums; and general revenues.
Standards for Providers of Services	Similar to Medicare's, with authority to apply more stringent conditions for coverage of specified high-risk, high-cost, elective, or overutilized services.
Reimbursement of Providers of Services	Hospitals, Home Health Agencies, Neighborhood Health and other Health Centers, and Skilled Nursing Facilities: Would be reimbursed based on prospective rates consistent with approved budgets.

Kennedy-Waxman Bill: Health Care for All Americans Act
H.R. 5191, 96th Congress, Introduced September 6, 1979 (continued)

Subject	Provisions
Reimbursement of Providers of Services (continued)	Physicians: Fee schedules subject to overall budget limits. HMOs: Capitation payments.
Delivery and Resources	Health Planning: National Health Board would establish national health care improvement and planning objectives. The board would prepare and annually update a 5-year plan describing national health care needs. The national plan would be based on state 5-year plans, prepared and annually updated by governors at the national board's request. PSRO: Would review all covered services. Health Resources Distribution: Under this plan, $500 million would be authorized for the first year of benefits (rising in each successive year) to be used by the national and state boards for a variety of purposes, including conversion or closure of underutilized facilities, provision of services in shortage areas, stimulation and support of HMOs and other cost-effective delivery systems, start-up programs of continuing educational and professional development through PSROs or other private agencies, and other purposes appropriate to achieving quality, accessibility, and other objectives for health care under the program. Health Education: State boards would carry out program to educate all residents on health, self-care, effective use of health care system, and rights and privileges under the NHI program. Personal Care Services: National Health Board would be required to carry out a demonstration program in the organization, delivery, and financing of personal care services. The board would make grants to assist in the development of community programs which seek to maintain people in their homes who, without personal care services, would require institutionalization.

Long-Ribicoff-Waggonner Bill: Catastrophic Health Insurance and Medical Reform Act
S.2470, 94th Congress, February 1976

Subject	Provisions			
General Concept and Approach	Proposal includes (1) a catastrophic illness insurance program for the general population provided through a federally administered plan or alternatively under approved private plans and (2) a federal medical assistance program for the poor and medically indigent. Also includes provisions for federal certification of qualified private basic health insurance.			
	Catastrophic Insurance			**Medical Assistance Plan**
	Government plan		Private plans	
Coverage of the Population	All U.S. residents, except persons under private plans.		Employees (and their families) of employers who voluntarily elect private plan. Self-employed who voluntarily elect.	Without regard to age or employment, low-income families and families qualifying under "spend-down" provisions.
Benefit Structure	After person spends 60 days in the hospital, following benefits become available: Additional hospital days, skilled nursing facility (100-day limit), and home health services. After family spends $2,000 on medical expenses, following benefits become available to all members of family: Physicians' services, laboratory and X-ray, home health services, medical supplies and appliances. No limit on amount of services (except skilled nursing facilities) and no cost sharing.			No limits on services and no cost sharing except as indicated: Institutional services: Hospital (60 days), skilled nursing and intermediate care facilities. Personal services: Physicians ($3 per visit for first 10 visits), laboratory and X-ray, family planning, maternity, and exams for children. Other: Medical supplies and appliances.

Long-Ribicoff-Waggonner Bill: Catastrophic Health Insurance and Medical Reform Act

S.2470, 94th Congress, February 1976 (continued)

Subject	Provisions		
Administration	Similar to Medicare program.	Employers and self-employed purchase approved private insurance from approved carriers. DHEW supervises program.	Similar to Medicare program.
Relationship to Other Government Programs	Catastrophic benefits payable without regard to coverage under other government programs or private plans. Medical assistance benefits secondary to all other programs and plans. Medicare program continues and Medicaid abolished.		
Financing	Payroll tax of 1 percent on employers, including federal, state, and local governments; employers allowed a credit against their federal income tax of 50 percent of the tax. Similar provisions for self-employed.	Employers are subject to regular 1 percent payroll tax, but this tax is reduced by the actuarial value of their private coverage; also receive the 50 percent tax credit. Similar provisions for self-employed.	Financed by federal and state general revenues. State share is fixed annual amount based on state cost under Medicaid for types of services under new program, with some additions and subtractions.
Standards for Providers of Services	Same as Medicare.		
Reimbursement of Providers of Services	Same as Medicare.	Determined by carrier.	Same as Medicare, but physicians must accept plan's payment as payment in full.
Delivery and Resources	Government catastrophic program and medical assistance plan incorporate HMO and PSRO provisions now applicable to Medicare.		
Encouragement of Basic Insurance	Under provisions designed to encourage improved basic health insurance, DHEW would certify private policies meeting specified standards (including coverage of 60 hospital days and first $2,000 in medical services). States would arrange marketing of this insurance through pools and reinsurance arrangements. DHEW would offer certified insurance in states where not available.		

Source: U.S. Department of Health, Education, and Welfare, Social Security Administration, Office of Research and Statistics, **National Health Insurance Proposals**, Provisions of Bills introduced in the 94th Congress of February 1976, compiled by Saul Waldman.

Nixon-Ford Administration Bill: Comprehensive Health Insurance Act
H.R. 12684, 93rd Congress, February 1974

Subject	Provisions		
General Concept and Approach	A 3-part program including (1) a plan requiring employers to provide private health insurance for employees, (2) an assisted plan for the low-income and high-medical-risk populations, and (3) an improved federal Medicare program for the aged. The states would supervise providers of health service and insurance carriers, under federal guidelines. Supported by the administration in the 93rd Congress.		
	Employee plan	**Assisted plan**	**Plan for aged**
Coverage of the Population	Full-time employees, including employees of state and local governments.	Low-income families, employed or nonemployed. Also, families and employment groups who are high medical risks.	Aged persons insured under Social Security.
Benefit Structure	No limits on amount of benefits listed below, except where indicated: Institutional services: Hospital inpatient and outpatient. Skilled nursing facility: 100 days per year. Personal services: Physicians. Dentists: For children under age 13. Laboratory and X-ray. Home health services: 100 visits per year. Family planning, maternity care, and well-child care (under age 6). Other services and supplies: Prescription drugs. Medical supplies and appliances. Eyeglasses and hearing aids (and eye and ear exams): For children under age 13.		
	Deductible of $150 per person and 25 percent coinsurance, but total cost sharing limited to $1,500 annually per family ($1,050 for individuals).	Maximum cost-sharing provisions are same as employee plan, but reduced according to individual or family income.	Deductible of $100 per person and 20 percent coinsurance, but total cost sharing limited to $750 per person annually. Reduced cost sharing according to individual income for low-income aged.

Nixon-Ford Administration Bill: Comprehensive Health Insurance Act
H.R. 12684, 93rd Congress, February 1974 (continued)

Subject	Provisions		
Administration	Insurance through private carriers (or self-insured arrangements) supervised by states, under federal regulations.	Administered by states, using private carriers to administer benefits, under federal regulations.	Administered by federal government in way similar to present Medicare program.
Relationship to Other Government Programs	Medicare: Program continues as the federal plan for the aged. Medicaid: No federal matching funds for covered benefits (or for premiums or cost sharing) under new program, but funds continue for specified noncovered services (such as intermediate-care facilities).		Continuation of present Medicare payroll taxes and premium payments by aged (but no premiums for low-income aged). Federal and state general revenues used to finance reduced cost sharing and premiums for low-income aged.
Financing	Employer-employee premium payments, with employer paying 75 percent of premiums (65 percent for first 3 years). Temporary federal subsidies for employers with unusually high increases in payroll costs. Special provisions to assure coverage for small employers.	Premium payments from enrollees according to family income (none for lowest income groups). Balance of costs from federal and state general revenues, with state share varied according to state per capita income.	
Standards for Providers of Services	Similar to Medicare, with additional standards for participation of physician extenders.		
Reimbursement of Providers of Services	Reimbursement rates established by states, according to federal procedures and criteria. Providers of service who elect as "full participating" would be paid the state-established rates, including the cost sharing, as full payment of their charges. Providers who elect as "associate participating" could charge more than the state rate for employee plan patients, but must collect the extra charges and cost sharing from the patients. However, all hospitals and skilled nursing facilities must be fully participating providers.		
Delivery and Resources	Prepaid practice plans: Under all plans, option available to enroll in approved prepaid group or individual practice plans (which meet special standards).		

Subject	Provisions
Delivery and Resources (continued)	Regulation of insurance carriers: By state, including approval of premium rates, enforcement of disclosure requirements, annual CPA audit, and protection against insolvency of carriers.
	Regulation of providers: By state, including standards for participation in program, approval of proposed capital expenditures, and enforcement of disclosure requirements.
	Professional Standards Review Organization (PSRO): Applies to all services under program.

Source: U.S. Congress, House of Representatives, Committee on Ways and Means, **National Health Insurance Resource Book**, April 11, 1974. Bill summaries were based largely on materials prepared by Saul Waldman.

INDEX